Automobile Manufacturers Worldwide Registry

Automobile Manufacturers Worldwide Registry

MARIÁN ŠUMAN-HREBLAY

McFarland & Company, Inc., Publishers
Jefferson, North Carolina, and London

Library of Congress Cataloguing-in-Publication Data

Šuman-Hreblay, Marián.
Automobile manufacturers worldwide registry / Marián
Šuman-Hreblay.
p.   cm.
Includes bibliographical references.
ISBN 0-7864-0972-X (softcover : 50# alkaline paper) ∞
1. Automobiles — Registers.   2. Automobile industry and trade —
Directories.   3. Automobiles — History.   I. Title.
TL12.S85   2000
338.4'76292'025 — dc21   00-42719

British Library cataloguing data are available

Cover image © 2000 Digital Vision

©2000 Marián Šuman-Hreblay. All rights reserved

No part of this book may be reproduced or transmitted in any form
or by any means, electronic or mechanical, including photocopying
or recording, or by any information storage and retrieval system,
without permission in writing from the publisher.

Manufactured in the United States of America

 McFarland & Company, Inc., Publishers
Box 611, Jefferson, North Carolina 28640
www.mcfarlandpub.com

To the memory of
Michael C. Sedgwick (1926–1983),
who stimulated my interest
in motoring history

Contents

Acknowledgments ix

Preface and User's Guide 1

Inclusion Criteria 1
Structure of the Entries 2
Abbreviations 2
Anglo-American Terminology 3
Glossary of Vehicle Types 4

THE MANUFACTURERS 7

Bibliography 315

Acknowledgments

In the compilation of this work, over a period of many years, the number of people who have assisted is considerable. During about three decades, I came in contact with many persons who helped me with literature, correspondence, corrections or advice. I am indebted to numerous libraries, musems, clubs and associations for their help in searching out basic material during my preparation of this list. I wish to thank the following for their generous assistance in the compilation of my own files and this registry.

In Austria: Wolfgang M. Buchta, Hans Seper

In Australia: Pedr Davis, John Wien-Smith

In Belgium: Jacques Kupelian, Ghislain Mahy

In Brazil: Jose Geraldo, Lizandro de Castro Tramonte

In Canada: Stan Passfield, R. Perry Zavitz

In Czechoslovakia, Czech Republic, Slovak Republic: Karel Černý, Pavol Ďurčo, Karel Jičinský, Petr Kožíšek, Jaroslav Krajčír, Jan Králik, Adolf Kuba, Ladislav Mergl, Miroslav Mráz, Václav Petřík, Emil Příhoda, Karel Rosenkranz, Mojmír Stojan, Jan Tulis, Václav Zapadlík, Rudolf Zerbs. My special thanks go to all members of my family who helped and encouraged me.

In Denmark: Erik Ebsen Petersen

In Estonia: Margus H. Kuuse

In Finland: Jussi Juurikkala

In France: C. Basset, Jean-Francois Blattner, Alain Boutet, Paul Bracq, Jean Fondin, Christian Huet, Jean Lorfray, Maurice Louche, Jan P. Norbye, Serge Pozzoli, Claude Reynaud, Edouard Seidler, Jacques Wolgensinger

In Germany: Georg Amtmann, Béla Barényi, Lothar Boschen, Hans-Rudiger Etzold, Hans-Heinrich von Fersen, Olaf von Fersen, Dieter Günther, Thomas Günther, Wiebke Hillers, Peter Kirchberg, Hans Joachim Klersy, Dieter Korp, Jurgen Lewandowski, Harald H. Linz, Hartmut Loges, Hans-Ulrich von Mende, Hans-Otto Neubauer, Harry Niemann, Werner Oswald, Max Geritt von Pein, Max Rauck, Klaus-Josef Rossfeldt, Lore Sautter, Friedrich Schildberger, Hans-Jürgen Schneider, Halwart Schrader, Martin Schröder, Hans C. Graf von Seherr-Thoss, Jerry Sloniger, Klaus Vollmar, Otto Walenta, Michael Graf Wolff Metternich, Walter R.J. Zeichner

In Hungary: Szabolcs Gimesi, Pál Négyesi

In Ireland: J.A. Barrow

In Italy: G. Molineri, Giorgio Nada, Gian Beppe Panicco

In Japan: Joe Honda, Shotaro Kobayashi, Shizuo Takashima

In the Netherlands: Geert de Kleijn, Erik van Ingen-Schenau, Kees Smit

In Norway: Asbjörn Rolseth

In Romania: G.L. Hartner

In Russia: Lev Shugurov

In Spain: Miguel Cabre Llistosella, Manuel Lage Marco

In Sweden: Claes Aberg, Gert Ekström, Sixten Pettersson

In Switzerland: Rodney Abensur, Adolf Babuška, Hanspeter Bröhl, Pierre-Marcel Favre, Roger Gloor, Pierre Le Grand, Sigvard Heringa, Jean-Rodolphe Piccard, Max J.B. Rauck, Rob de la Rive Box, Ernest Schmid

In the United Kingdom: Ian Bond, Nick G. Georgano, Edwin & Jean Hammond, Anthony Harding, David Hodges, Mike Lawrence, Ivan Margolius, Cyril Posthumous, Peter Roberts, Michael C. Sedgwick, Michael E. Ware, Michael Worthington-Williams, Eoin Young

In the USA: David Ash, Scott Bailey, Dean Batchelor, June Baxter, Charles Betts, William E. Bomgardner, Thomas E. Bonsall, James J. Bradley, Brooks T. Brierley, Grace R. Brigham, Don Butler, Henry Austin Clark, Jr., Ed Chandler, John A. Conde, Quentin Craft, George H. Dammann, Robert R. Ebert, Bill Emery, Fred K. Fox, Patrick R. Foster, William R. Franson, Jules M. Heumann, Beverly Rae Kimes, Chester L. Krause, James C. Leake, David L. Lewis, Karl E. Ludvigsen, Robert L. Lyon, G. Marshall Naul, James F. Petrik, Henry Rasmussen, Arthur

G. Rippey, Matthew C. Sonfield, William E. Swigart, Jr., Lester C. Thomas, Jr., Alec E. Ulmann, Z. Taylor Vinson, Angelo Wallace

I apologize if I have omitted any individual deserving of special mention and would like to place on record my thanks to everybody who has helped me in whatever way.

Preface and User's Guide

Welcome to the *Automobile Manufacturers Worldwide Registry*. This volume is not an encyclopedia but instead a very complete cataloging of manufacturers listing basic facts about each. It is not intended to provide a full accounting of any individual manufacturer, but rather to serve as a ready reference and a starting point for researchers. In this book can be found essential data on cars and their builders from 1770 to date — nearly 11,000 manufacturers in all. The information contained herein should be valuable to people with a general interest in historic and contemporary automobiles as well as to historians, journalists and librarians. For detailed marque histories, readers are encouraged to consult more narrowly focused sources.

I began to assemble this listing more than 30 years ago in an effort to better understand the companies listed herein and their interrelationships. None of these cars was created in a vacuum, and it is not possible to fully understand the history of a single marque or car without studying the people who created it, related cars, regional influences and the time period in which the company produced cars.

The information in this registry has come from a wide variety of sources (the most important of which are listed in the Bibliography). I did my research both in my native Czechoslovakia and abroad, studying hundreds of books and thousands of periodicals and trade catalogs published in all over the world. The project began in 1968 (I was then 18) when the Yugoslavian magazine *Moto Revija* (it was possible to subscribe only to journals from socialist countries in my homeland at that time) started to publish a listing of automobile manufacturers. About 150 marques were shortly described, and I have tried continuously since then to learn more by studying all literature available in the libraries and in my increasing private collection as well.

Inclusion Criteria

Types of Vehicles Included

- All kinds of passenger carrying vehicles on at least 2 but no more than 8 wheels (touring cars, sports cars, fully-bodied two-wheeled cars, tricycles with steering wheel, three-wheelers and others) of any design, either manufactured for sale to the public or built as one-off specials, experimental cars or prototypes. Kit cars are included regardless of whether fully assembled models were not available from the manufacturer.
- Vehicles powered by internal combustion, steam and electric engines.
- Pioneer cars by such inventors as Lenoir or Marcus. Our starting date is 1770 when Nicolas Joseph Cugnot tested in Paris his steam carriage — inefficient, slow and cumbersome, but a first.
- Tuning companies which built cars with modified bodies and mechanical parts.
- Coachbuilders whose cars were marketed under their names.

Excluded Vehicles

- Racing cars and vehicles built solely for land speed record attempts.
- Commercial vehicles and buses.
- Mobile caravans built on goods vehicle chassis.
- Motorcycles and scooters.
- Tricycles with handlebars.
- Coachbuilders whose cars were not marketed under their names.
- Muscle and or wind powered carriages.
- Designs of vehicles that have never been built in at least one example; companies which planned but did not build an actual car.

Structure of the Entries

All entries contain these elements:

I. (a) name of a car or a company, (b) country of origin, (c) production year(s),

II. (d) full name of a producing company or a builder, (e) factory location,

III. (f) brief description and or remarks.

Only those marques for which at least (a), (b), (c), and (f) could be determined are included. Parts (d) and (e) are in the language of the country of origin except in the case of manufacturers from China and Japan where English translation is used. Part (f) is absent when no more data were found or when it was a thoroughly conventional car of a certain period, or when the name of a car or of a building firm indicates its type (e.g., Acme Motor Buggy Mfg. Co., American Voiturette Co. etc.) A question mark, as in "1965-?," indicates that the compiler has not been able to determine the missing datum. When "c" (circa) is shown, it is not possible to determine the precise date company activity began or was terminated.

Quotation marks around a vehicle name indicate that the name is listed separately within the registry.

The nationality of a car is indicated by internationally recognized abbreviations, a list of which is provided, and refers to the country where the parent firm was situated. Production under license in other countries is mentioned only when such a car bears another name. When a car made under license is of different country of origin from the parent company, the descriptive line of the entry indicates its nationality; for example, Trojan GB .... "Heinkel" (D) license. Dual nationality may arise in these ways:

1. Cars were issued from factories in two or more countries at the same time, or used engines from one country and chassis from another; for example, Belgian/Italian Hermes or H.I.S.A., indicated by (B/I).

2. Change of nationality for political reasons. For example, the provinces of the Austro-Hungarian Empire after 1918 became Czechoslovakia, and the provinces of Alsace and Lorraine were German to 1918 and French thereafter; these are indicated by (A;CS), or (D;F). Similar is the case of cars built in the Union of Soviet Socialist Republics from 1917 to 1992 and later in Russia, Latvia, and Ukraine (SU;RUS), and in some Balkan states created from the former Yugoslavia (YU;BIH, YU;SLO).

The marques are listed in alphabetical order, with extensive cross-referencing. Identical names are listed in chronological order and or alphabetical order according their nationality. The following points should be also noted:

- Makes having full personal names as part of their corporate names are alphabetized by the first name; e.g., Georges Irat, not Irat, Georges.
- Makes beginning with "Mc" are alphabetized as spelled, not as if spelled "Mac."
- Makes beginning with "De" are placed under the letter D. Thus De Lavaud is found in D, not L.
- Makes beginning with "Le" or "La" are alphabetized under the letter L. Thus La Salle is found in L, not S.
- Alphabetization is letter by letter, without regard to word breaks. Makes using initial letters joined by "and," such as S. and M. Simplex, or S. and S., or S & S, are alphabetized as if they were spelled "Sand..."
- Names with modified letters (ü, ö, ẞ, etc.) are treated alphabetically as if they had unmodified letters.
- Chinese characters are romanized using both Pinyin and Wade-Giles systems.

Much care has been taken in compiling this book to ensure a high degree of accuracy. Nevertheless, additional research may yield data or conclusions other than those presented here. Both the publisher and the compiler welcome additions and suggestions.

Abbreviations

International Registration Letters

The country of manufacture is indicated in the text by the International Registration Letters used by the United Nations.

Abbr.	Full Name	Number of Entries
A	Austria	95
AUS	Australia	78
B	Belgium	139
BG	Bulgaria	5
BIH	Bosnia and Herzegovina	1
BR	Brazil	45
CDN	Canada	140
CH	Switzerland	122
CO	Colombia	1
CS	Czechoslovakia	115

Abbr.	Full Name	Number of Entries
CY	Cyprus	1
CZ	Czech Republic	7
D	Germany	805
DDR	German Democratic Republic	10
DK	Denmark	45
E	Spain	103
EC	Ecuador	1
EST	Estonia	1
ET	United Arab Republic (Egypt)	2
F	France	1,161
FIN	Finland	3
FL	Liechtenstein	3
GB	Great Britain and Northern Ireland	1,346
GBM	Isle of Man	1
GR	Greece	6
H	Hungary	34
HR	Croatia	1
I	Italy	575
IL	Israel	2
IND	India	12
IR	Iran	8
IRL	Ireland	3
J	Japan	61
LT	Latvia	2
MAL	Malaysia	1
MC	Monaco	1
MEX	Mexico	3
N	Norway	8
NL	Netherlands	61
NZ	New Zealand	2
P	Portugal	9
PAK	Pakistan	1
PI	Philippines	6
PL	Poland	34
PRC	People's Republic of China	34
RA	Argentina	27
RC	Republic of China (Taiwan)	4
RCH	Chile	1
RI	Indonesia	3
RM	Malagasy Republic (Madagascar)	1
RO	Romania	9
ROK	Republic of Korea	5
RSM	San Marino	1
RUS	Russia	13
S	Sweden	38
SK	Slovakia (from 1993)	2
SLO	Slovenia	2
SO	Slovakia (1939–1945)	1
SU	Soviet Union (pre–1917 Russia also)	60
T	Thailand	1
TR	Turkey	8
U	Uruguay	4
UA	Ukraine	3
USA	United States of America	5,394
VN	Vietnam	2
WAN	Nigeria	1
YU	Yugoslavia	8
ZA	South Africa	11
Total		**10,693**

European Corporate Designations

The following abbreviations have been used in the names of European companies:

AB	Aktiebolaget (S): joint-stock company
AG	Aktiengesellschaft (D): joint-stock company
Akc. spol.	Akciová společnost (CS): joint-stock company
AS	Aksjeselskapet (N), Aktieselskabet (DK): joint-stock company
Cia	Compagnia (I), compania (E): company
Cie	Compagnie (F): company
GmbH	Gesellschaft mit beschränkter Haftung (D): limited-liability company
KG	Kommanditgesellschaft (D): partnership with limited liability
n.p.	Národní podnik (CS): national corporation
NV	Naamloze vennootschap (NL): limited-liability company
SA	Societa anonima (I), Société anonyme (F), Sociedad anonyma (E): limited-liability co.
SpA	Societa per azioni (I): joint-stock company
Spa	Société per actions (F): joint-stock company
Srl	Société à responsabilité limité (F): partnership with limited liability
Sta	Societa (I): company
Sté.	Société (F): company
Vorm.	Vormalig (D): former(ly)

Anglo-American Terminology

A short list of the more frequently used terms:

British	*American*
bonnet	hood
capacity (of engine)	displacement

British	American
coupe de ville	town car
dickey	rumble seat
estate car	station wagon
gearbox	transmission
hood	top
paraffin	kerosene
petrol	gasoline
saloon	sedan
sedanca de ville	town car
shooting-brake	station wagon
two-stroke	two-cycle
windscreen	windshield
wing	fender

Glossary of Vehicle Types

The following is a brief guide to the terms used more frequently herein. The definitions of body styles are very general. No attempt has been made to give a complete glossary of the motorcar. (All terms were chosen from the *Complete Encyclopedia of Motorcars 1885 to the Present*, edited by G. N. Georgano [1973]).

Buckboard *see* Cyclecar.
Buggy *see* Cyclecar.
Cabriolet *see* Drophead coupe.
City car. Small gasoline or electric car used primarily for driving in a town.
Convertible. Any car with folding roof and wind-up windows; the term is largely found in American usage, and dates only from the early 1930s.
Cyclecar. A simple light car whose design was derived from motorcycles, of which a large variety were made from 1912 until about 1922. The typical cyclecar had an engine of fewer than four cylinders, often air-cooled, with final drive by belts or chains. Cyclecars flourished in England, France and the United States, but disappeared with the coming of mass-produced light cars such as the Austin Seven and Citroën 5 CV.
Dos-a-dos. A four-seat car in which the passengers sat back to back. Seldom seen after about 1900.
Dune buggy. Light open recreational vehicle with plastic body and (usually) Volkswagen chassis and engine.
Estate car *see* Shooting brake.
Highwheeler. A simple car with the appearance of a motorized buggy which enjoyed a brief period of popularity in the United States and Canada between 1907 and 1912.
Light car. In general, a scaled-down version of larger cars, with four-cylinder engines of capacities of between 1000 cc and 1500 cc, although some designs of this kind had capacities under 1000 cc.
Limousine. A closed car with glass division between driver and the passenger compartment.
Minicar. A large variety of small cars, from the smallest runabouts for one or two persons having simple two-stroke engines of from only 50 cc capacity to the largest light cars having two- or four-cylinder engines up to 750 cc capacity and capable of carrying four passengers and luggage. Very popular in the 1950s and the 1960s.
Monocar. Single-seat cyclecars of the 1912 to 1915 period.
Motor buggy *see* Highwheeler.
Phaeton. An early word for an open car, especially used in the term double phaeton which was a four- or five-seat tourer.
Roadster. A two-seat open car of sporting appearance.
Runabout. A general term for a light two-seat car of the early 1900s, especially those made in America.
Saloon (US: **Sedan**). A closed car for four or more passengers, with either two or four doors.
Shooting brake, brake, estate car, station wagon. The original brake or shooting brake was similar to the waggonette, and was used in large estates for carrying members of shooting parties. Station wagons were made by American manufacturers in the 1930s, and the fashion spread to Europe, where the name estate car was more often used, after World War II.
Spyder. A light two-seat car, sometimes with a precarious looking third seat behind, used in the early years of the 20th century. Beginning in the 1950s the word was revived by some Italian manufacturers for an open two-seat sports car.
Surrey. An open four-seat car, often with a fringed top.
Tonneau. A four-seat car in which access to the rear seats was by a door at the rear of the body. This layout was used up to about 1904.
Torpedo (or **torpedo tourer**). An open touring car with an unbroken line from bonnet to windscreen, and from windscreen right through to the back of the car, the seats being flush with the body sides. Bodies of this design began to appear in about 1910, and after 1920 the name torpedo was usually dropped in favour of tourer.
Tourer. An open car with seats for four or more passengers. Early tourers had no weather protection at the sides, later ones being provided with detachable sidescreens and curtains. After about 1930 the mass-produced closed car replaced the tourer as the most popular type.
Vis-à-vis. A four-seat car in which two passengers sat facing each other, flanking the driver.

Voiturette. A French term for the light car, applied to any small car. The voiturette class has had various definitions: up to 1905, a weight limit of 400 kg, 1906–1910 a limited bore varying with the number of cylinders; 1921–1925, a capacity limit of 1500 cc. After 1925 the term was used only loosely for small racing cars, and not for production cars at all.

Waggonette. A large car usually for six or more passengers, in which the rear seats faced each other. Entrance was at the rear, and the vehicles were usually open.

THE MANUFACTURERS

A

A.A.A.
D 1919–1922
A.G. für Akkumulatoren- und Automobilbau, Berlin. Electric cars, vans and lorries. For petrol cars see "Alfi."

A.A.A.
F 1920
Ateliers d'Automobile et d'Aviation, Paris. Electric saloons.

AACHENER
D 1908–1926
Aachener Stahlwarenfabrik AG, Aachen.
See "Fafnir."

A.A.G.
D 1900–1901
Allegemeine Automobil-Gesellschaft Berlin GmbH, Berlin. Voiturettes with one-cylinder engines.

A&M
USA 1901
Believed to be initials of Automobile & Machine Power Co., Camden, New Jersey. Builder of "New Era" cars.

AARTS
NL 1899
Neerlandia, Ant. Aarts, Dongen.

ABADAL
E 1912–1914; 1930
F.S. Abadal y Cia, Barcelona. Sporting tourers.

ABAG
D c. 1900
Allgemeine Betriebs-Aktiengesellschaft für Motorfahrzeuge, Köln. Electric car.

A.B.A.M.
F
See "Krieger."

ABARTH
I 1950–1971
Abarth & Co., Torino. "Fiat" based sports cars.

ABBEY
GB 1922
Abbey Auto Engineering Co. Ltd., London. Two-seat car with 4-cylinder Coventry engine and friction drive.

ABBOTT
USA 1917–1918
The Abbott Corp., Cleveland, Ohio. Succeeded Consolidated Car Co. Detroit, Michigan. Formerly "Abbott-Detroit." Touring cars.

ABBOTT-CLEVELAND
USA 1917–1918
See "Abbott."

ABBOTT-DETROIT
USA 1909–1916
Abbott Motor Co. (1909–1914). Abbott Motor Car Co. (1915–1916). Consolidated Car Corp. (1915–1916), Detroit, Michigan. 4 and 6-cylinder models used Continental motors, 8-cylinder used Herschell-Spillman motors. Became "Abbott."

ABC
D 1983–c. 1990
ABC-Exclusive Tuning Company, Bonn. Tuning.

A.B.C.
GB 1920–1929
A.B.C. Motors Ltd., Hersham, Surrey. Light cars.

A.B.C.
USA 1900
American Bicycle Co. Steam and electric cars.

A.B.C.
USA 1905–1911
A.B. Cole (1905). Auto Buggy Mfg. Co. (1906–1909). ABC Motor Vehicle Mfg. Co., St. Louis, Missouri. Highwheelers.

A.B.C.
USA 1922
Arthur Boynton Corp., Albany, N.Y. Built for export.

ABEILLE
F 1906–1915
See "A.M."

ABEL
USA 1901
Abel Bros. Machine Shop, Fond du Lac, Wisconsin. One car produced May 1901.

ABENAQUE
USA 1900
Abenaque Machine Works, Westminster Station, Vermont. Experimental gasoline automobiles. Main products were traction engines.

ABERCOMBIE
USA 1969
Glassic Industries Inc., Palm Beach, Florida.
See "Glassic."

ABERDONIA
GB 1911–1915
Aberdonia Cars Ltd., London. 4-cylinder 3.2 litre cars.

ABF
GB 1918–1922
All British Ford, Kenilworth. Sports car.

ABINGDON
GB 1902–1903
John Child Meredith Ltd., Birmingham. Voiturette.

ABINGDON
GB 1922–1923
Abingdon Works Ltd., Tyseley, Birmingham. Light cars.

ABLE
F 1920–1925
Paul Toulouse, Orgon/Bouches-du-Rhone. Paul Toulouse, Avignon, Vaucluse. Light cars.

ABLE EIGHT
USA 1915–1920
Vernon Automobile Co., Mt. Vernon, N.Y.

See "Vernon." Both names apply to same vehicle.

ABOLEIRO
E   c. 1985
Aboleiro S.A., Madrid
Replicars.

ABRESCH
USA   1899–1909
Charles Abresch Co., Milwaukee, Wisconsin. 7-passenger cars.

ABT
D   1982–present
Auto-Abt, Kempten. Tuning.

A.C.
GB   1908–present
Autocars and Accessories Ltd., London (1908–1911). Autocarriers Ltd., Thames Ditton, Surrey (1911–1922). A.C. Cars Ltd., Thames Ditton, Surrey (1922–present). High performance sports cars. Minicars in the 1950s.

A.C.
USA   1914
Autocycle Company, New Orleans, Louisiana. Cyclecar prototypes.

A-C
USA   1915–1917
Alter Motor Car Co., Plymouth, Michigan.
   See "Alter."

ACA
CH
   See "Sbarro."

ACADEMY
GB   1906–1908
E.J. West & Co. Ltd., Coventry, Warwickshire. Cars fitted with duplicate clutch and brake controls.

ACADIA
USA   1903–1904
Ernest R. Kelly, Wilmington, Delaware. Runabouts.

ACADIAN
CDN   1961–1971
General Motors Corp. of Canada, Oshawa, Ontario. Hybrid based on "Chevrolet" and "Pontiac" (USA).

ACB
F   1982–1984
Ateliers Construction Carrosserie Broual, Briare. "Delage" replicars.

ACCARY
F   1913–1914
   See "Hedea."

ACCESSIBLE
USA   1908–1910
   See "Hobbie Accessible."

ACCLESS-TURRELL
GB   1900–1902
Accless-Turrell Autocars Ltd., Birmingham (1900–1901). Pollock Engineering Co. Ltd., Ashton-under-Lyne, Lancs. (1901–1903). Tonneau.

ACCUMULATOR INDUSTRIES
GB   1902–1903
Accumulator Industries Ltd., Woking, Surrey. Electric car.

ACE
AUS   1904
Holding & Overall, Drummoyne, N.S.W. Light cars.

ACE
GB   1912–1914
Salmon Motor Co. Ltd., Burton-on-Trent, Staffs. Light cars.

ACE
USA   1919–1922
Apex Motor Corp., Ypsilanti, Michigan. Rotary disc valve motor by Fred Gay and O.W. Heine. Touring cars.

ACE CLASSIC
USA   c. 1990
Ace Auto Services (USA) Ltd., Reseda, California. Replicars.

ACE SIX
USA   1933
Continental Automobile Co., Grand Rapids, Michigan.
   See "Continental."

ACETYLENE
USA   1899
   See "Auto-Acetylene."

ACHENBACH
D
   See "Hexe."

ACHILLE PHILION
USA   1892
Achille Philion, Akron, Ohio. Steam cars.

ACHILLES
GB   1903–1908
B. Thompson and Co. Ltd., Frome, Sommerset. 6 to 12 hp 2-cylinder cars.

ACHILLI
I   c. 1975
Achilli Motors SaS, Milano. Replicars.
   See "Leontina."

ACKERMAN
USA   1897–1899
W.K. Ackerman, Detroit, Michigan. Experimental cars. Became "Reliance."

ACL
F   1970–1975
Atelier de Construction du Libradois, Arlanc. Sté. des Ets Teilhol, Courpiere. Terrain-vehicle on "Renault" 4 and 6 chassis.

ACM
I   1988–c. 1994
Ali Ciemme SpA, Gissi. 4 × 4 vehicle.

ACM
USA   1913
Mason Motor Co., Flint, Michigan. Kerosene-powered car.

A.C.M.A.
F   1957–1961
A.C.M.A., Fourchambault, Nievre. Minicar "Vespa."

ACMAT
F   c. 1983
Acmat, Saint-Nazarre. 4 × 4 vehicle.

ACME
CDN   1910–1911
Acme Motor Carriage & Machine Co., Goderich, Ontario. Canadian bodies with U.S. mechanical components.

ACME
USA   1902–1903
Reber Mfg. Co., Reading, Pennsylvania.
   See "Reber." Became "Acme" 1904.

ACME
USA   1904–1910
Acme Motor Co., Reading, Pennsylvania. Succeeds Reber Mfg. Co. 1902–1903. Became SGV Co.
See "Reber" and "SGV."

ACME
USA   1907
Acme Engine Co., Spokane, Washington. Prototypes.

ACME
USA   1908–1909

Acme Motor Buggy Mfg. Co., Minneapolis, Minnesota. Highwheelers. Became "MB" 1910.

ACME
USA 1912
Acme Motor Car Co., Worcester, Massachusetts.

ACME
USA 1914
Acme Cyclecar Co., Xenia, Ohio. Cyclecars. Became Hawkins Cyclecar Co. 1914.
See "Xenia."

ACOMA
F 1976–1977
ACOMA S.A., Angers. Three-wheeled minicars.

ACORN
USA 1910–1912
Acorn Motor Car Co., Cincinnati, Ohio. Highwheelers.

AC SCHNITZER
D
See "Schnitzer."

ACURA
J/USA 1985–present
Acura Automobile Division, American Honda Motor Co., Gardena, California. "Honda" (J) luxury division for the USA.

ADAMI
I 1901–1906
Adami & C., Firenze.

ADAMS
GB 1903–1906
Adams & Co., Tunbridge Wells, Kent. Small cars.

ADAMS
GB 1905–1914
Adams Manufacturing Co. Ltd., Bedford.

ADAMS
USA 1906–1907
Adams Automobile Co., Hiawatha, Kansas.
See "Average Man's Runabout."

ADAMS
USA 1911–1912
Adams Bros. Co., Findlay, Ohio. Trucks and some passenger cars.

ADAMS-FARWELL
USA 1898–1913
Adams Co., Dubuque, Iowa. Experimantal 1898–1904. First shown at Chicago Automobile Show, 1905. Revolving rotary engine of 3 or 5 cylinders.

ADAMSON
GB 1912–1924
R. Barton Adamson & Co. Ltd., Enfield, Middlesex. Cyclecars.

ADAMS PROBE
GB
See "Probe."

ADDAX
F 1975–1977
Société d'Études et de Construction Automobiles et Motocycles, Chambly. Three-wheeled minicars.

ADELPHIA
USA 1920
Winfield-Barnes Co., Philadelphia, Pennsylvania. Built for export only. Plant sold by receivers June 1922. Built by Piedmont Co.

ADER
F 1900–1907
Sté. Industrielle des Téléphones-Voitures Automobiles. Systéme Ader, Levallois-Perret/Seine (1904–1907). Sté. Ader, Levallois-Perret/Seine (1904–1907). V-2 and V-4 cars.

ADI
D 1950
Artur Diebler, Berlin. Three-wheelers.

A.D.K.
B 1924–1931
SA des Automobiles de Kuypers, Bruxelles. 2-litre cars.

ADLER
D 1900–1939
Adler Fahrradwerke vorm. Heinrich Kleyer AG (1900–1906). Adlerwerke vorm. Heinrich Kleyer AG, Frankfurt/Main (1906–1939). Passenger and sports cars.

ADLER
D 1920
E. Adler, Pirna. Propeller-powered three-wheeler.

ADRIA
USA 1921–1922
Adria Motor Car Co., Batavia, N.Y. Touring cars.

ADRIAN
USA 1902–1903
Adrian Motor Works. Church Manufacturing Co., Adrian, Michigan.
See "Murray."

ADVANCE
USA 1899
Advance Mfg. Co., Hamilton, Ohio. One experimental car built.
See "Ritchie."

ADVANCE
USA 1908
Advance Company, Chicago, Illinois. Dual purpose wagon.

ADVANCE
USA 1911
Advance Motor Vehicle Co., Miamisburg, Ohio. "Advance " is company name of Advance Motor Vehicle Co., Miamisburg, Ohio, not name of vehicle. Company built "Kaufman."

ADVANCED
USA 1982
Advanced Vehicle Systems, Inc., Troy, Michigan. Sports cars.

ADVIS
USA 1913–1914
Davis Cyclecar Co., Detroit, Michigan Cyclecars. Believed to be "Davis" misspelled.

A.E.C.
USA 1915–1916
Anger Engineering Co., Milwaukee, Wisconsin. Custom-built cars only.
See "Anger."

AEG
D
See "NAG."

A.E.M.
F 1926–1927
Electric city cars with front-wheel drive. Electric cyclecar "Electrocyclette."

AEOLUS
D
See "Passat."

A.E.R.
F
See "B.N.C."

AERIC
F
See "Corre."

AERMACCHI
I 1946–1963
Aermacchi & Cie., Varese. Light cars.

AERO
CS 1929–1947
Aero, továrna letadel, Praha. Small and sports cars powered by 2-stroke 1-, 2- and 4-cylinder engines.

AERO
USA 1923–1924
Victor W. Pagé Motors Co., Stamford, Connecticut. "Aero" and "Pagé" are the same car. No production is known for either car, but at least 3 prototypes were built.
See "Pagé."

AERO AUTO-BOB
USA 1914
Jack Hickman, East Pittsburgh, Pennsylvania.
See "Auto Bob."

AEROCAR
D 1968
Wagner Helicoptertechnik, Friedrichshafen. Combination of a car and a helicopter.

AERO CAR
GB 1919–1920
Aero Car Engineering Co., London.

AEROCAR
USA 1905–1908
The Aerocar Co., Detroit, Michigan. Some motors built by Reeves Pulley Co., Columbus, Ohio. Touring cars. First "Hudson" cars built in this factory.

AERO-CAR
USA 1921
See "Reese."

AEROCAR
USA 1948–1969
Aerocar Inc., Longview, Washington. Detachable wings, flew like an airplane.

AEROCARÉNE
F 1947
Courbevoie/ Seine. Three-wheelers.

AEROFORD
GB 1920–1925
Aeroford Cars, London.

AEROCOUPE
USA 1936
Richard Crossley, East Haven, Connecticut. Three-wheeled speedster.

AEROLITHE
F
See "Coadou-Fleury."

AERO-MINOR
CS 1947–1952
Letecké závody, n.p., Praha. Front-wheel drive small cars derived from the "Jawa" Minor.

AEROMOBILE
USA 1959–1961
Bertelsen Mfg. Co., Peoria, Illinois.

AERO TYPE
USA 1921–1924
See "Pagé" and "Aero."

AERO WILLYS
USA 1952–1954
Willys Overland Motors, Inc., Toledo, Ohio (1951–1953). Willys Motors Inc., Toledo, Ohio (1954–1955). 1955 model was basically the same as previous models, but no designated "Aero."
See "Willys."

AESCULAP
A c. 1900
Erste Automobil-Gesellschaft für Österreich, Wien. Voiturette.

AETNA
USA 1910
Aetna Investment Company, Detroit, Michigan. Prototype.

A.F.
A
See "Austro-Fiat."

A.F.
GB 1969–1980
Alexander Fraser, Lincolnshire. Three- and four-wheeled vehicles with wooden chassis and body.

AFA
D 1893; 1918–1936
Aktiengesellschaft für Akkumulatoren- und Autobau, Berlin. Electric cars.

A.F.A.
E 1943
5 hp electric cabriolet.

AFM
D 1949–1951
Alexander von Falkenhausen, München. Sports cars.

A.F.N.
GB
See "Frazer-Nash."

A.G.
I 1925–1927
Istituto Feltrinelli. Alfieri Giuseppe, Milano. Small sports cars.

A.G.
P 1992–1996
A.G. Engineering, Lisboa. Convertible replicars.

AGA
D 1919–1928
AG für Automobilbau (1919–1926). Aga-Fahrzeugwerke, Berlin-Lichtenberg (1926–1928). Sports cars. Also built under license in Sweden by "Thulin."

AGEA
CH 1954–1955
Atelier Genevois d'Etudes Automobiles, Geneve. Sports car prototype.

AGÉRON
F 1908–1910
Construction d' Automobiles Agéron et Cie., Lyon. Chain-driven cars.

AGNOLETTO
I 1911–1915
Parma.

AGONTZ
USA 1916
Agontz Motor Car Co., Sandusky, Ohio.
See "Ogontz."

A.G.R.
GB 1911–1912
Ariel & General Repairs Ltd., London Open four-seater.

AGUZZOLI
I 1962–1964
Sergio Aguzzoli & Luigi Bertocco, Parma.

AHK-BUGATTI
D 1977–c. 1996
Autohaus R. Kühn KG, Hamburg. "Bugatti" replica.

AHRENS-FOX
USA 1913

Ahrens-Fox Fire Engine Company, Cincinnati, Ohio. About 6 cars were sold.

AIGLON
F
See "Alliance."

AIKEN
USA c. 1850
University of Maryland, Baltimore, Maryland. One built by Dr. William A.E. Aiken (professor of chemistry) 1838–1888.

AILEEN
CS 1961
Jiří Bulíček, Praha. 1100 cc sports car.

AILLOUD; AILLOUD & DUMOND
F 1897–1904
Automobiles Ailloud, Lyon (1897–1900). Automobiles Ailloud et Dumond, Lyon (1900–1904). 5 hp 2-cylinder vertical engines.

AILSA
GB
See "Kennedy."

AILSA CRAIG
GB
Putney Motor Co., London.
See "Craig-Dörwald."

AIRCAR
USA 1970–1973
Advanced Vehicle Engineers, Van Nuys, California. Car/plane conversion.

AIREDALE
GB 1919–1924
Nanson, Barker & Co., Esholt, Yorkshire (1919–1922). Airedale Cars Ltd., Esholt, Yorkshire (1922–1924). Cyclecars and tourers.

AIREX
GB
See "Rex."

AIRMOBILE
USA 1916–1919
Rotary Products Co., Los Angeles, California. Four wheel air drive car.

AIROMOBILE
USA 1937
Lewis American Airways, Inc., Rochester, N.Y.; Denver, Colorado. Streamlined coupe prototype.

AIRPHIBIAN
USA 1946–1952
Continental Incorporated, Danbury, Connecticut. Prototypes only. First Civil Aeronautic Authority licensed flying automobile.

AIRSCOOT
USA 1947
Aircraft Products Co., Wichita, Kansas Foldable light cars.

AIRWAY
USA 1948–1950
T.P. Hall, Airway Engineering Co., San Diego, California. 2 air-cooled cars built.

AISA
E 1955
Actividades Industriales SA, Barcelona. 197 cc three-wheeler prototype.

AIXAM
F 1984–1994
Aixam Automobiles, Aix-en-Provence. Aix-les-Bains. Electric city cars.

AJAMS
F 1919–1920
Cyclecars. Patents sold to "Sizaire-Naudin" in 1920.

AJAX
CH 1906–1910
Dr. G. Aigner Automobilfabrik (1906–1907). Ajax AG, Zürich (1907–1910). Touring and sports cars.

AJAX
F 1913–1914
Briscoe Fréres, Neuilly/Seine. Cyclecars.

AJAX
USA 1901–1903
Ajax Motor Vehicle Co., New York, N.Y. Electric cars.

AJAX
USA 1914
Brisco Motor Co., New York, N.Y. Cyclecars.

AJAX
USA 1914–1915
Ajax Motors Co., Seattle, Washington. Used sleeve or piston valve engine.

AJAX
USA 1920–1921
Ajax Motors Corp., Hyde Park, Massachusetts. 6-cylinder touring cars.

AJAX
USA 1925–1926
Ajax Motors Corp., Racine, Wisconsin. Touring cars.

A.J.S.
GB 1930–1933
A.J. Stevens Ltd., Wolverhampton, Staffs (1930–1931). Willys-Overland-Crossley Ltd., Stockport, Cheshire (1931–1933). Light cars.

AJT ATWOOD
USA 1912
Weston, Massachusetts.

AK
D c. 1993
AK Spezialfahrzeuge, Neuweiler. Tuning.

A-K
USA 1907–1909
New York Car and Truck Co. Allen-Kingston Motor Car Co., Kingston, N.Y. "A-K" name used at start of production.
See "Allen-Kingston."

AKA
CS 1925
Alfred Kunze, stavba automobilu a opravna, Ružodol. Light car.

AK ELLAS
GR c. 1968–1984
Agelopulos & Karkanis, Athenai. Three-wheelers.

AKRON
USA 1899–1901
Akron Machine Co., Akron, Ohio. Single-cylinder gasoline stanhope.

AKRON
USA 1905
Akron Two Cycle Automobile Co., Akron, Ohio. Four touring cars built.

AKSAI
SU 1911
Zavod Aksai, Nakhitchevan. Very few made; coachbuilders.

AL
GB 1971
Crompton Leyland. Electric city car prototype.

ALAMAGNY
F 1948
13 hp minicar with rhomboid wheel placement.

ALAMOBILE
USA 1902
Alamo Mfg. Co., Hillsdale, Michigan. Stationary engine manufacturer.

ALAN
D 1923–1925
J. Mayer, Bamberg. Small cars.

ALAND
USA 1916–1917
Aland Motor Car Co., Detroit, Michigan. A 16-valve 4-cylinder motor designed by R.C. Aland, "Pilgrim" designer.

ALATAC
B 1913–1914
Automobiles Catala, Braine-le-Comte.

ALBA
A 1906–1908
Automobilwerke Alba AG, Trieste. 25 and 45 hp models.

ALBA
F 1913–1928
Construction Metallurgiquess, Suresnes/Seine. Light cars.

ALBANESI
I 1968
Stab. Albanesi, Brescia. Replica of "Fiat" Balilla Coppa d'Oro.

ALBANI
AUS 1921–1922
Albani Motor Construction Pty Ltd., Melbourne, Victoria. Touring cars.

ALBANUS
USA 1899–1900
Roach & Albanus, Ft. Wayne, Indiana.
   See "Roach & Albanus."

ALBANY
GB 1903–1905
Albany Manufacturing Co. Ltd., London. Gasoline and steam cars.

ALBANY
GB 1971–c. 1995
Albany Motor Carriage Co., Christchurch, Hampshire. Replica.

ALBANY
USA 1906–1908
Albany Automobile Co., Albany, Indiana. Highwheelers. Announced assets would be sold September 1908. 850 cars built.

ALBAR
CH 1991–1993
Alois Barmettler Fahrzeug AG, Bouchs. Sports cars.

ALBA REGIA
H 1956
Minicar prototype.

ALBATROS
F 1912
Henri Billouin, Paris. Light cars.

ALBATROS
GB 1923–1924
Albatros Motors Ltd., Coventry, Warwickshire. Light cars.

ALBATROSS
USA 1939
Brewster Aeronautics, Long Island, N.Y. Sports convertible prototype.

ALBAUGH
USA 1910
Albaugh-Dover Co., Chicago, Illinois. Company name, not name of vehicle. Company built "Aldo."

ALBERT
GB 1920–1924
Adam Grimaldi & Co. Ltd., London (1920). Gwynne's Engineering Co. Ltd., London (1920–1924). 12 and 14 hp light cars.

ALBERTI
I 1906
Giuseppe Alberti, Firenze. One car was built.

ALBION
GB 1900–1913
Albion Motor Car Co. Ltd., Glasgow. Touring cars.

ALBRECHT
USA 1900
Charles Albrecht & Co., Milwaukee, Wisconsin. Advance announcement of car production February 1900. This was simply a typographical error.
   See "Abresch."

ALBRUNA
GB 1908–1912
Brown Bros. Ltd., London. Light cars.

ALCA
I 1947
Anonima Lombarda Cabotaggio Aereo, Milano.
   See "Volpe."

ALCO
NL 1951
"Alco" Wielen Constructie- en Wagenfabriek, Jutphaas.

ALCO
USA 1909–1913
American Locomotive Automobile Company, Providence, Rhode Island. Succeeded "American Berliet" 1905–1908. Also called "Locomotive Car," 1909. Touring cars.

ALCYON
F 1906–1928
Edmond Gentil, Neuilly/Seine (1906–1912). Edmond Gentil, Courbevoie/Seine (1912–1914). Automobiles Alcyon, Courbevoie/Seine (1914–1928). Voiturettes and sports cars.

ALDA
F 1912–1922
Fernand Charron, Courbevoie/Seine (1912–1920). Automobiles Farman, Billancourt/Seine (1920–1922). Touring cars.

ALDEN
USA
   See "Bennett."

ALDEN SAMPSON
USA 1904
Alden Samson Mfg. Co., Pittsfield, Massachusetts. Touring cars.

ALDO
USA 1910
Albaugh-Dover Co., Chicago, Illinois. Buggy-type.

ALDRICH
USA 1897–1898
Robert Aldrich, Milville, Massachusetts; C.H. Thurston, Worcester, Massachusetts, announced plans to produce the car 1898. Auto-buggy.

ALEKO
RUS 1994–present
Successor of "Moskvich."

ALENA
USA 1922
Alena Steam Prod. Co., Indianapolis, Indiana. Steam cars.

ALES
J 1921
Hakuyosha Ironworks Ltd., Tokyo. Water- and air-cooled prototypes.
   See "Otomo."

ALESBURY
GB 1907–1908
Alesbury Bros., Edenderry, King's County, Northern Ireland. Light cars.

ALEX
GB 1908
Alexander & Co., Edinburgh. One light car was made.

ALEXANDRIA
GB 1905–1906
Phoenix Carriage Co., Birmingham. Electric car.

ALF
I 1950
Torino. 750 cc Sport/Corsa built by Sandro Fiorio, father of Cesare Fiorio, director of Fiat's racing program ("Abarth").

ALFA
I 1907–1908
Anonima Lombarda Fabbricazione Automobile, Novara. Steam cars.

A.L.F.A.
I 1910–1918
Anonima Lombarda Fabbrica Automobili, Milano.
See "Alfa Romeo."

ALFA-LEGIA
B c. 1919
M. Klinkenhammers, Liege. "Austro-Daimler" (A) assembled cars.

ALFANG
DK 1912–1914
Silkeborg.

ALFA ROMEO
I 1910–present
A.L.F.A. (Anonima Lombard Fabbrica Automobili), Milano (1910–1914). SA Italiana Ing. Nicola Romeo & C., Milano (1914–1930). SA Alfa Romeo, Milano (1930–1942). Alfa Romeo SpA, Milano (1942–present). Passenger and sports cars.

ALFI
D 1922–1924
Aktiengesellschaft für Akkumulatoren- und Automobilbau, Berlin. Electric and gasoline cars.
See "AAA."

ALFI
D 1927–1928
"Alfi"-Automobile GmbH, Berlin. Small cars.

ALGER
USA 1902
R.A. and F.M. Alger, Jr., Detroit, Michigan. Gasoline automobile. Joined "Packard" 1902.

ALGOL
I
See "Caprera."

ALKEN
USA 1958
Venice, California. Kit cars.

ALLAMAGNY
F 1948
M. Allamagny. Rhomboid wheel placement.

ALLARD
CDN 1983–c.1986
Allard Motor Company Ltd., Mississauga, Ontario. Replicars.

ALLARD
GB 1899–1902
Allard Cycle Co. Ltd., Coventry, Warwickshire. Voiturettes.

ALLARD
GB 1937–1960
Adlards Motors Ltd., London (1937–1945). Allard Motor Co. Ltd., London (1946–1960). Sports cars.

ALLARD-LATOUR
F 1899–1902
E. Allard-Latour, Lyon. Belt- or chain-driven cars.

ALL-BRITISH
GB 1906–1908
All-British Car Co., Glasgow. Large 8-cylinder cars.

ALL CARS
I 1972; 1979–1985
All Cars Autozodiaco, Pianoro (Bologna). VW based buggy by Tom Tjaarda.

ALLDAYS
GB 1898–1918
Alldays and Onions Pneumatic Engineering Co. Ltd., Birmingham. 4- and 6-cylinder cars.

ALLEGHENY
USA 1905
Allegheny Automobile Co., Allegheny, Pennsylvania. Both steam and gasoline cars.

ALLEN
USA 1896
C.F. Allen, Hueneme, California. Auto-buggy.

ALLEN
USA 1895–1900
G.Edgar Allen, New York, N.Y. Gasoline runabouts.

ALLEN
USA 1902
George C. Allen, New Bedford, Massachusetts. Gasoline cars.

ALLEN
USA 1913–1922
Allen Motor Car Co., Fostoria, Ohio (1913–1920); Columbus, Ohio (1920–1922). Became part of Willys-Overland Corp. 1921. Touring cars.

ALLEN
USA 1913–1914
Allen Iron & Steel Co., Philadelphia, Pennsylvania. Cyclecars.

ALLEN & CLARK
USA 1908–1909
Allen & Clark Co., Toledo, Ohio. Electric cars.
See "Clark Electric."

ALLEN-KINGSTON
USA 1907–1910
New York Car & Truck Co. (1907–1908). Allen-Kingston Motor Car Co., Kingston, N.Y. (1908–1910). First production cars called "A-K." Built by Bristol Engineering Corp., Bristol, Connecticut. Touring cars.

ALLGEMEINE BETRIEBS-AG FÜR MOTORFAHRZEUGE
D
See "ABAG."

ALLIANCE
D 1904–1905
Automobil- und Motorenwerke Alliance Fischer & Abele, Berlin. 2- and 4-cylinder cars.

ALLIANCE
F 1905–1908
Alliance Automobiles B. Baud, Paris. 2- and 4-cylinder cars. In 1905 known as "Aiglon."

ALLIANCE
USA 1895
Alliance Carriage Co., Cincinnati, Ohio.
See "MacLeod."

ALLIANCE
USA 1910
Alliance Motor Co., Garfield, Ohio. Runabouts.

ALLIED
USA 1932–1935
Allied Cab Manufacturing Company, Elkhart, Indiana. Taxicabs and passenger cars.

ALLITH
USA 1909
Allen & Clark Co., Toledo, Ohio. There never was an "Allith" car; this was an error made in a listing compiled in the 1960s. The only car was the "Clark" Electric.

ALLRIGHT
D 1908–1911
Köln-Lindenthaler Metallwerke AG, Köln. For export under "Vindec."

ALLSTATE
USA 1952–1953
Sears-Roebuck & Co., Chicago, Illinois. Built by Kaiser-Frazer on "Henry J" chassis, with engine and major body stampings identical to those of "Henry J." 2,363 cars were built.

ALL STEEL
USA 1915–1917
All Steel Motor Car Co., St. Louis, Missouri; Macon, Missouri (1916). Became "Macon."
 See "Alstel."

ALLWYN
GB 1920
Allwin Cyclecars, Bournemouth, Hampshire.

ALLYNE-ZEDER
USA
 See "Rollin."

ALMA
F 1926–1929
Établissements Alma, Courbevoie/Seine. 6-cylinder 1.6 litre small cars.

ALMA
I 1907–1909
Accomandita Lombarda per Motori e Automobili di. G. Monaco & Co., Busto Arsizio.

ALMA
USA 1938
Alma Steam Motors, Newton, Massachusett. Steam cars.

ALMERAS
F 1994
Almeras Freres, Saint-Jean-de-Vedas. "Porsche" (D) tuning.

A.L.P.
B 1919–1921
SA des Automobiles Lerous-Pisart, Bruxelles. Light cars.

ALPENA
USA 1910–1914
Alpena Motor Car Co., Alpena, Michigan. Absorbed Wolverine Motor Car Co., Mt. Clemens, Michigan 1910. Touring cars.

ALPHA
USA 1903
R.E. Jarrige, New York, N.Y. Runabout.

ALPHI
F 1929–1931
Sté. Alphi, Paris. 4 cars were made.

ALPINA
D 1977–present
Alpina Burkard Bovensiepen KG, Buchloe. "BMW" Tuning.

ALPINE
BR 1961–c. 1967
Willys Overland do Brasil, São Paulo. "Alpine Interlagos" made under "Renault Alpine" (F) license.

ALPINE
F 1955–present
Sté. des Automobiles Alpine, Dieppe; Epinay-sur-Seine. Sports cars. To "Renault" belongs from 1973.

ALSACE
USA 1919–1921
Automotive Products Corp., New York, N.Y.; Philadelphia, Pennsylvania. Built by Piedmont Motor Co., Lynchburg, Virginia, and Simms Motor Car Co., Atlanta, Georgia, for export only. Passenger cars.

ALSTEL
USA 1915–1916
All Steel Motor Car Co., St. Louis, Missouri.
 See "All Steel."

ALTA
GB 1931–1954
Alta Car and Engineering Co., Kingston-upon-Thames, Surrey. Sports cars.

ALTA
GR 1968–1970
Alta Inc., Athenai. Three-wheelers similar to "Fuldamobil" (D).

ALTENA
NL 1904–1907
NV Haarlemsche Automobiel- en Motorrijvielfabriek, voorheer. A. van Altena, Haarlem. About 40 cars were made.

ALTENBERG
USA 1906
George P. Altenberg, Cincinnati, Ohio. One prototype.

ALTER
USA 1914–1916
Alter Motor Car Co., Plymouth, Michigan. Became Hamilton Motor Corp. January 1917. 4- and 6-cylinder cars.

ALTHA
USA 1901–1905
Alta Auto.and Power Co., Dover, Delaware. Electric cars.

ALTHAM
USA 1896–1901
George J. Altham, Fall River, Massachusetts (1896). Altham International Motor Co., Boston, Massachusetts (1897–1899). Altham Auto and Motor Co., Fall River, Massachusetts (1900–1901). Auto-buggy.

ALTMAN
USA 1901
Henry J. Altman, Mesopotamia (Cleveland), Ohio. One car produced.

ALTMANN
D 1905–1907
Kraftfahrzeugwerke GmbH, Brandenburg/Havel. Steam cars.

ALUMINIUM
USA 1897
Aluminium Motor Vehicle Co., Chicago, Illinois. Electric car. Forerunner of "Wood" electric.

ALUMINIUM
USA 1922
Aluminium Manufacturers Inc., Cleveland, Ohio. About 6 built.
 See "Pomeroy."

ALVA
F 1913–1923
Automobiles Alva, Courbevoie/Seine. 1.5 and 2.5-litre ohc engines.

ALVECHURCH
GB 1911
Alvechurch Light Car Co., Alvechurch, Birmingham. Air-cooled engines.

ALVIS
GB 1920–1967
T.G. John Ltd., (1919–1921). Alvis Car & Engineering Co. Ltd., (1921–1937). Alvis Ltd., (1931–1967), Coventry, Warwickshire. Sports and touring cars.

AM
CS 1948
Anton Majer, Volyně. 250 cc two-seater minicar prototype.

A.M.
F 1906–1915
Ateliers Veuve A. de Mesmay, St. Quenti/Aisne. 2- and 4-cylinder cars.

AM
GB 1990s
AM Sportscars Ltd., Redditch, Worcestershire. Sports kit cars.

A.M.
I 1921–1924
Armino Mezzo, Torino. Cyclecar.

AMA
B 1913
American Motor Car Agency, Bruxelles U.S. chassis with Belgian body.

AMALGAMATED
USA 1905, 1917–1919
Amalgamated Machinery Co., Chicago, Illinois. Machine builders who built "Doble" steam cars.

AMANTE GT
USA 1969–c.1973
Voegele Industries Inc., Santa Clara, California. Kit car. Began March 1969 using fiberglass body and "Chevrolet" Corvair or "Volkswagen" (D) chassis.

AMAZON
GB 1921–1923
Amazon Cars Ltd., London. Light cars.

AMBASSADOR
USA 1921–1926
Yellow Cab Mfg. Co., Chicago, Illinois. Company also built some "Hertz" cars.

AMBASSADOR
USA
See "American Motors" Corp., Detroit, Michigan.

AMBLER
USA 1914
King Cyclecar Co., Cleveland, Ohio. Cyclecar.

A.M.C.
USA 1919
A.M.C. Truck Company, Chicago, Illinois. Touring cars.

AMC
USA 1966–1987
American Motors Corporation, Detroit, Michigan. An independent passenger car marque.

AMCO
USA 1917–1922
American Motors, Inc., New York, N.Y. A specially built car designed by D.M. Eller for export only.

AME
D 1987–1995
AME Chopper GmbH, Schauenburg. Sports car replicas.

AMÉDÉE BOLLÉE
F 1885–1922
Amédée Bollée fils, Le Mans/Sarthe. Sports, touring and racing cars. Steam cars from 1873 onwards, designed by A. Bollée Father.

AMERICA
E 1917–1922
America Autos SA, Barcelona. Light cars.

AMERICA
USA 1911
Motor Car Co. of America, New York, N.Y. Absorbed by W.H. McIntyre Co. Became "McIntyre Special."

AMERICAN
USA 1896–1902
American Electric Vehicle Co., Chicago, Illinois (1896–1900); Hoboken, New Jersey (1900–1902). Electric cars.

AMERICAN
USA 1897
American Motor Wagon Co., Boston, Massachusetts. Electric cars.

AMERICAN
USA 1896–1898
American Motor Co., New York, N.Y.

AMERICAN
USA 1898–1900
Automobile Company of America, East Orange, New Jersey.

AMERICAN
USA 1899
American Automobile Co., New York, N.Y. Car designed by J. Frank Duryea. Three-cylinder hydro-carbon engine.

AMERICAN
USA 1902–1905
American Motor Carriage Co., Cleveland, Ohio. Became American Automobile Co.

AMERICAN
USA 1903
American Motor Car Co., St. Louis, Missouri.

AMERICAN
USA 1903–1904
American Touring Car Co., Brooklyn, New York.

AMERICAN
USA 1904
American Mfg. Co., Alexandria, Virginia.

AMERICAN
USA 1904
American Automobile Co., Huron, South Dakota.

AMERICAN
USA 1905–1906
American Motor Co., Brockton, Massachusetts. Also called "Marsh."

AMERICAN
USA 1906–1911
American Motor Car Co., Indianapolis, Indiana. Became "American Motors Co."
See "American Underslung."

AMERICAN
USA 1907
American Metal Wheel & Auto Co., Toledo, Ohio.

AMERICAN
USA 1907
American Automobile Vehicle Co., Detroit, Michigan.

AMERICAN
USA 1911–1912
Believed to be company name of American Automobile Mfg. Co., Kansas City, Missouri, not a name of

car. Company affiliated with "Jonz" of Beatrice, Nebraska, and continued production of "Jonz" at New Albany, Indiana. Re-organized as Ohio Falls Motor Co. to manufacture light commercial cars.

AMERICAN
USA 1913–1914
American Cyclecar Co., Seattle, Washington. Cyclecars.

AMERICAN
USA 1914
American Mfg. Co., Chicago, Illinois. Cyclecars.

AMERICAN
USA 1916–1920
American Motor Vehicle Co., Lafayette, Indiana.

AMERICAN
USA 1916–1924
American Motors Corp., Plainfield, New Jersey. Designed by Louis Chevrolet. 1923 became Bessemer-American Motors Corp. 1924 joined "Winther" and "Northway" truck in Amalgamated Motors Corp.

AMERICAN AUSTIN
USA 1930–1941
American Austin Car Co. Inc. (1929–1934). American Bantam Car Co. (1935–1941).
See "American Bantam," "Bantam" (1938–1941) and "Austin Bantam."

AMERICAN AUTOMOBILE
USA 1899
American Automobile Co., New York, N.Y.
See "American." Both names apply to same vehicle.

AMERICAN BALANCED SIX
USA 1916–1924
American Motors Corp., Painfield, New Jersey.
See "American."

AMERICAN BANTAM
USA 1937–1941
American Bantam Car Co., Butler, Pennsylvania. Succeeded "American Austin." See "Bantam." Became first Army "Jeep."

AMERICAN BEAUTY
USA 1916
American Motors Corp., Plainfield, New Jersey.
See "American."

AMERICAN BEAUTY
USA 1915–1916
American Beauty Car Co., Adrian, Michigan. Colonial Car Co., Jonesville, Michigan. Electric car.

AMERICAN BEAUTY
USA 1920
Pan American Motors Corp., Decatur, Illinois. *Automobile* trade journal of February 1920 lists car as a make.

AMERICAN BENHAM
USA 1914
Benham Mfg. Co., Detroit, Michigan. Abount 19 cars built.
See "Benham."

AMERICAN BERLIET
USA 1905–1908
American Locomotive Automobile Co., Providence, Rhode Island.
See "Berliet" (USA).

AMERICAN BORLAND
USA 1914
American Electric Car Co., Saginaw, Michigan. Electric car. Succeeded "Borland" electric.

AMERICAN BRASS
USA 1907–1908
American Brass Co., Waterbury, Connecticut

AMERICAN BROC
USA 1914–1916
American Electric Car Co., Saginaw, Michigan. Electric car. Succeeded "Broc" electric.

AMERICAN BUCKBOARD
USA 1955
American Buckboard Corp., Los Angeles, California. Tiny roadster powered by rear-mounted 2-cylinder air-cooled motocycle engine that drove a fifth wheel.

AMERICAN CARBONIC ACID
USA 1900
American Automobile Motor & Power Co., Brooklyn, New York.

AMERICAN CARRIAGE
USA 1896–1897
American Carriage Motor Co., New York, N.Y.

AMERICAN C.G.V.
USA 1903
Smith & Mabley, New York, N.Y. Built at Rome Locomotive Works, Rome, N.Y.
See "C.G.V."

AMERICAN CHOCOLATE
USA 1903–1906
American Chocolate Machinery Co., New York, N.Y.

AMERICAN DE DION
USA 1900–1901
De Dion-Bouton Motorette Company, Brooklyn, N.Y. Small motorettes.

AMERICAN EAGLE
USA 1909
Eagle Automobile Co., St. Louis, Missouri.
See "Eagle."

AMERICAN EAGLE
USA 1911–1912
American Eagle Motor Car Co.

AMERICAN ELECTRIC
USA 1899–1902
American Electric Vehicle Co., Chicago, Illinois.
See "American" electric.

AMERICAN ELECTRO-MOBILE
USA 1906–1907
American Electro-Mobile Co., Detroit, Michigan. Electric cars.

AMERICAN FIAT
USA 1910–1918
Fiat Company, Poughkeepsie, N.Y.
See "Fiat" (USA).

AMERICAN GAS
USA 1895
American Motor Carriage Co., Cleveland, Ohio. Company is only listed as in business 1902–1905. Runabouts.

AMERICAN JUVENILE ELECTRIC
USA 1907
American Metal Wheel Co., Toledo, Ohio.
See "American."

AMERICAN-LA FRANCE
USA 1907–1914
American-La France Fire Engine Co., Elmira, N.Y. Roadsters.

AMERICAN LIQUID AIR
USA c. 1900

American Liquid Air Co., New York, N.Y.
See "Liquid Air."

AMERICAN LOCOMOTIVE
USA 1907
American Locomotive Automobile Co., Providence, Rhode Island. From 1905 to 1906 vehicle was known as "Berliet" or "American Berliet." In 1908 they returned to the Berliet name and then to "Alco" in 1909.

AMERICAN LOCOMOTOR
USA 1901
Baldwin Automobile Co., Connelsville, Pennsylvania. Steam car. Company name, not name of vehicle. Company changed name to American Locomotor Mfg. Co. January 1901.
See "Baldwin."

AMERICAN MATHIS
USA 1930
American Mathis Inc., Dover, Delaware; Lansing, Michigan.
See "Mathis."

AMERICAN MERCEDES
USA 1904–1907
Daimler Mfg. Co., Long Island City, N.Y. Exact copy of German "Mercedes." Plant destroyed by fire December 13, 1907.

AMERICAN MORS
USA 1906–1909
St. Louis Car Co., St. Louis, Missouri. Absorbed "Kobusch." Successor to Kobusch Automobile Co. Became Standard Automobile Co. of America.
See "Standard Six."

AMERICAN MOTOR
USA 1900
American Motor & Vehicle Co., New York, N.Y.

AMERICAN MOTORETTE
USA 1913
American Motorette Co., Detroit, Michigan. Cyclecars. Name changed to Lincoln Motor Car Co. December 1913.

AMERICAN NAPIER
USA 1906–1912
Napier Motor Car Co. of America, Boston, Massachusetts; Jamaica Plain, Massachusetts.

AMERICAN PNEUMATIC
USA 1900
American Vehicle Co., West Virginia.

AMERICAN POPULAIRE
USA 1904
American Automobile & Power Co., Lawrence, Massachusetts; Sanford, Maine. Light cars.

AMERICAN POWER CARRIAGE
USA 1899–1900
American Power Carriage Co., Boston, Massachusetts.

AMERICAN ROTARY
USA 1900
American Rotary Engine Co., Boston, Massachusetts.

AMERICAN SIMPLEX
USA 1905–1910
Simplex Motor Car Co., Mishawaka, Indiana. Company organized 1904. First car put on the road July 1905. Name changed to "Amplex" 1910. Passenger and sports cars.

AMERICAN SIX
USA 1921
American Motors Corp., Plainfield, New Jersey.
See "American" 1916–1924. Name used in advertising "American."

AMERICAN STANDARD
USA 1914
American Standard Automobile Co., Edwardsville, Missouri.

AMERICAN STANDARD
USA 1914
American Standard Motor Co., Indianapolis, Indiana.

AMERICAN STEAM
USA 1903–1904
American Steam Motor Co., Milwaukee, Wisconsin.

AMERICAN STEAM BUGGY
USA 1898–1899
American Waltham Mfg. Co., Waltham, Massachusetts.
See "American Waltham" steam.

AMERICAN STEAM
USA 1926–1942
American Steam Automobile Co, West Newton, Massachusetts. Built with "Hudson" components.

AMERICAN STEAMER
USA 1860
American Steamer Carriage Co., J.K. Fisher, New York, N.Y.

AMERICAN STEAMER
USA 1922–1924
American Steam Truck Co., Elgin (Chicago), Illinois. Very limited production of passenger cars.

AMERICAN-TEXAS
USA c. 1984
American-Texas International Limited, Dallas, Texas. Stretched limousines.

AMERICAN TRICAR
USA 1912
Tricar Company of America, Denver, Colorado. Runabout.

AMERICAN UNDERSLUNG
USA 1911–1914
American Underslung Company, Indianapolis, Indiana. Previously called "American" (1906–1911).

AMERICAN VOITURETTE
USA 1899–1900
Automobile Co. of America, Marion, New Jersey.

AMERICAN WALTHAM
USA 1898–1899
American Waltham Mfg. Co., Waltham, Massachusetts. Steam cars.

AMES
USA 1895–1898
Owatonna Mfg. Co., Owatonna, Wisconsin. Gasoline vehicles.

AMES
USA 1896
A.C. Ames, Chicago, Illinois. Steam car.

AMES
USA 1910–1917
Carriage Woodstock Co., Owensboro, Kentucky. Became Ames Motor Car Co. Touring cars.

AMESBURY
USA 1899
Amesbury Automobile Co., Amesbury, Massachusetts. Electric car.

AMESBURY
USA 1902
Boston-Amesbury Mfg. Co., Amesbury, Massachusetts.
See "Boston Amesbury."

AMESBURY
USA 1915
Amesbury Auto Co., Amesbury, Massachusetts.

AMES-DEAN
USA 1909–1910
Ames-Dean Carriage Co., Jackson, Michigan.

AMG
D 1979–1995
AMG Motorenbau GmbH, Affalterbach. Tuning.

A.M.G.
S 1903
AB Motorfabriken, Göteborg. Only nine cars were made.

AMHERST 40
CDN 1911–1912
Two In One Co., Amherstburg, Ontario. Seven-passenger touring car that converted to a pickup truck. No more than 6 made.

AMIGO
A 1972
Fa. Custako, Gerhard Höller, Kraubath. Dune buggy.

AMILCAR
F 1921–1939
Sté. Nouvelle pour l'Automobile Amilcar, St. Denis (1921–1937). Sté. Financiére pour l'Automobile, Boulogne-sur-Seine (1937–1939). Touring and sports cars.

AMILCAR ITALIANA
I 1925–1929
Societa Italiana Licenza Veronese Amilcar (SILVA), Roma. Compagnia Generale Automobili, Roma.

AMIOT-PENEAU
F 1898–1902
L'Avant-Train Amiot et Peneau, Asniéres/Seine. Gasoline and electric cars.

AMO
SU 1927–1931
Závod Avtomobilnovo Moskovskovo Obshchestva, Moscow. Passenger cars.
See "ZIL."

AMOR
D 1924–1925
Amor Automobilbau GmbH, Köln. Small cars.

AMORE
USA 1982
Amore Cars Ltd., Milwaukee, Wisconsin. Sports car.
See "Cimbria."

AMP
I 1948
Alfa Maserati Prete, Roma.

AMPÉRE
F 1906–1909
Sté. des Établissements Ampére, Billancourt/Seine. 4-cylinder 10/16 hp cars.

AMPHICAR
D 1961–1968
Deutsche Industrie-Werke, Lübeck (1961–1962). Deutsche Waggon- und Maschinenfabriken GmbH, Berlin (1962–1968). Amphibian vehicle, about 3,500 produced.
See "Trippel."

AMPHI CAT
USA 1967–?
Mobility Unlimited Inc., Auburn Heights, Michigan. Off road amphibian vehicle.

AMPHI RANGER
D 1983–1993
Gerhard Faulhaber, Rheinische Maschinenfabrik, Kehl am Rhein. Amphibian.
See "RMA."

AMPLEX
USA 1910–1915
American Simplex Co. (1910–1912). Amplex Motor Co. (1912–1913). Amplex Mfg. Co. (1914–1915), Mishawaka, Indiana. Succeeded "American Simplex" 1905–1910. Bought by Gillette Motors Co. 1916 (King C. Gillette).

A.M.S.
I 1969–1980
Attrezzature Meccaniche Speciali, Bologna. Sports cars.

AMS-STERLING
USA 1917–1918
Sterling Motor Co., Amston, Connecticut.
See "Sterling," Paterson, New Jersey.

AMSTUTZ-OSBORN
USA 1900–1902
Amstutz-Osborn Co., Cleveland, Ohio.

A.N.
F 1921–1923
Allain et Niguet, Kremlin-Bicetre/Seine. Cyclecars.

ANADOL
TR 1966–present
Otosan Otomobil Sanayii AS, Istanbul Passenger cars.

ANADOLU
TR 1970s–1986 ?
Anadolu Otomotiv, Istanbul. "Škoda" (CS) 1202 license.

ANASAGASTI
RA 1911–1915
Horacio Anasagasti & Cia, Buenos Aires. 30 cars with French components were made.

ANCHOR
USA 1910–1911
Anchor Buggy Co. (1910). Anchor Motor Car Co. (1911), Cincinnati, Ohio.

ANDERHEGGEN
NL 1901–1902
Ferdinand Anderheggen, Amsterdam. Light vis-à-vis four-seater.

ANDERSON
USA 1899
Albert Anderson, South Boston, Massachusetts. Steam carriage to have been built under Whitney patents.

ANDERSON
USA 1906
Anderson Machine Co., Bedford, Indiana. Highwheelers. Succeeded by "Postal" 1907.

ANDERSON
USA 1907–1919
Anderson Electric Car Co., Detroit, Michigan. Company name, not name of vehicle. Company built "Detroit Electric."

ANDERSON
USA 1908
N.M. Anderson, Los Angeles, California.

ANDERSON
USA 1909–1910
Anderson Carriage Mfg. Co., Anderson, Indiana. Also called "Anderson Motor Carriage."

ANDERSON
USA 1916–1926
Anderson Motor Co., Rock Hill, South Carolina. Subsidiary of Rock Hill Buggy Co.
See "Rock Hill" (1910–1915).

ANDERSON STEAM
USA 1902
Anderson Steam Carriage Co., Anderson, Indiana.

ANDERSON STEAMER
USA 1873
Leonard Anderson, Painesville, Ohio. One steam carriage produced.

ANDERSON-WHITNEY
USA 1899–1900
Albert Anderson (1899). Anderson Mfg. Co. (1900), South Boston, Massachusetts.
See "Anderson" steam carriage.

ANDINO
RA 1967–1973
Automotores 9 de Julio SA, Buenos Aires. Rear-engined GT coupe.

ANDOVER
USA 1914–1916
Andover Motor Vehicle Co. Joly & Lambert Electric Co. (1916), Andover, Massachusetts. Electric cars. Also built commercial vehicles.

ANDRÉ
GB 1933–1934
T.B. André, London. Light sports cars.

ANDREAS
D 1900–1902
Sächsische Accumulatoren-Werke AG, Dresden. Electric cars.

ANDRÉ PY
F 1899
Cie des Automobiles du Sud Ouest. Light three-wheelers.

ANDREWS
USA 1895
A.B. Andrews, Center Point, Iowa. Listed entry for Chicago Times-Herlad Race.

ANGEL CITY
USA 1916
Ernest Clyde Low, Los Angeles, California. Roadster.

ANGELES
USA 1913
Los Angeles Cyclecar Co., Los Angeles, California. Cyclecars. Pacific Model for 1913.
See "Los Angeles."

ANGELI
F 1926–1927
Automobiles Angeli, Neuilly-Plaisance, Seine. Small saloon prototype.

ANGER
USA 1914–1917
Anger Engineering Co., Milwaukee, Wisconsin.
See "A.E.C."

ANGLADA
E 1904–1907
Anglada y Cía, Puerto de Santa Maria, Cadiz. 6 to 36 hp cars.

ANGLADA
USA 1914
Joseph Anglada, New York, N.Y. Cyclecar. Anglada was name of "Liberty" designer.
See "Liberty."

ANGLIN
USA 1899
M.I. Anglin, La Porte, Indiana.

ANGLO-AMERICAN
USA 1900
Anglo-American Rapid Vehicle Co., New York, N.Y.
See "Pennington."

ANGLO-DANE
DK 1902–1917
H.C. Fredericksen, Copenhagen. Friction-driven vehicles.

ANGLO-FRENCH
F
See "Roger."

ANGLO-SPHINX
F
See "Sphinx."

ANGUS
USA 1908–1909
Angus Automobile Co., Angus, Nebraska. Company name, not name of vehicle. Company built "Fuller."

ANGUS-SANDERSON
GB 1919–1927
Sir William Angus, Sanderson & Co., Birtley, Co Durham (1919–1921). Angus-Sanderson (1921) Ltd., Hendon, Middlesex (1921–1927). Medium-sized cars.

ANHEUSER
USA 1905
Mathias Anheuser, Green Bay, Wisconsin. Experimental car.

ANHEUSER-BUSCH
USA 1917–1925
Anheuser-Busch Brewing Association, St. Louis, Missouri. Promotion car.

ANHUT
CDN 1909–1910
Onathan, Ontario.

ANHUT
USA 1910–1911
Anhut Motor Car Co., Detroit, Michigan. Became Barnes Motor Car Co. Roadsters.

ANKER
D 1918–1920
Anker Automobilfabrik Paul Griebert, Berlin.

ANNA
USA 1912
Anna Motor Car Co., Anna, Illinois Had kerosene engine.

ANN ARBOR
USA 1903–1904
Ann Arbor Autobile Co., Ann Arbor, Michigan.

ANN ARBOR
USA 1911–1912
Huron River Mfg. Co., Ann Arbor, Michigan. Touring cars.

ANNESLEY
USA 1899; 1914
C.G. Annesley, Detroit, Michigan. Electric and gasoline carriages.

ANNONAY
F 1948
Annonay Cie., Ardeche, Lyon. Minicar.

ANSALDI
I
See "Fiat Ansaldi."

ANSALDO
I 1919–1936
SA Ansaldo Automobili (1919–1932). CEVA — Costruzioni e Vendita Automobili Ansaldo (1932–1934). Ansaldo-Ceva SA, Torino (1934–1936). 4-, 6- and 8-cylinder touring and sports cars.

ANSBACH
D 1910
Fahrzeugfabrik Ansbach GmbH, Ansbach. Small cars called "Kauz."

ANSERMIER
CH 1906
Geneve.

ANSTED
USA 1921
Lexington Motor Car Co., Connersville, Indiana.

ANSTED
USA 1926–1927
Ansted Motors, Connersville, Indiana. *See* "Lexington." Passenger cars.

ANTHONY
USA 1897
Earl C. Anthony, Los Angeles, California. One electric car produced.

ANTHONY
USA 1900–1902
W.O. Anthony Motor & Mfg. Co., Colorado Springs, Colorado. Three or four gasoline cars built.

ANTIQUE & CLASSIC
USA 1975–1986
Antique & Classic Automotive, Inc., Buffalo, N.Y. "Bugatti" and "Jaguar" SS 100 replicar.

ANTOINE
B 1900–1902
Antonie Fils et Cie, Liege. Voiturettes.

ANTOINETTE
F 1906
Sté. Antoinette, Puteaux/Seine. V-8 engines.

ANTONIETTI & UGOLINI
I 1905–1906
Torino.
See "Fert."

ANZANI
I 1923–1924
Motocicli e Motori Anzani, Milano. Cyclecars.

APACHE
USA 1966–?
Interco Development Corp., New York, N.Y. Similar to European economy cars.

A.P.A.L.
B 1961–c. 1992
A.P.A.L. S.a.r.l., Liege. Automobiles Apal S.A., Blegny. Sports cars and replicars.

APER
D 1983–1985
Aper Automobile & Design, Mainz. Replicars.

APEX
USA 1901
Apex Wheel Co., Rochester, N.Y.

APOLLO
D 1910–1926
Ruppe & Sohn AG (1910–1912). Apollo-Werke AG, Apolda (1912–1926). Sports cars.

APOLLO
USA 1906–1907
Chicago Recording Scale Co., Waukegan, Illinois. Announced entry into automobile manufacturing May 1904. No known production until 1906.

APOLLO
USA 1962–1964
International Motor Cars Inc., Oakland, California (1962). Apollo International Corp., Pasadena, California (1963–1964). 88 high-performance sports cars were made. *See* "Vetta Ventura."

APOLLO
USA 1982–1983
Apollo Motor Cars, Berkeley, California. "Verona" roadster, replicar of Jaguar XJ.

APOLLO MOPS
USA 1962–1964
See "Appolo." Both names apply to same vehicle.

APPERSON
USA 1902–1926
Apperson Bros. Automobile Co. (1902–1924). Apperson Automobile Co. (1924–1926), Kokomo, Indiana. Reincorporated 1924. Also petitioned to change name to "Pioneer Automobile Co." Touring cars.

APPERSON-TOLEDO
USA 1909
Toledo Motor Co., Toledo, Ohio.
See "Toledo."

APPLE
USA 1915–1916
W.A. Motor Car Co. Apple Automobile Co., Dayton, Ohio. Incorporation announced September 1915. 8-cylinder cars.

APPLETON
USA 1921–1922
Appleton Mfg. Co., Batavia, N.Y.

AQUILA
B 1901–1902
Société Générale de Constructions Mécaniques, Bruxelles.

AQUILA
F
See "Mailard."

AQUILA
I 1898–1906
See "Majocchi."

AQUILA ITALIANA
I 1905–1917
Aquila (1905–1906). Aquila Italiana (1906–1908). Aquila Italiana di L. Marsaglia (1909–1917), Torino. Large touring and sports cars.

ARAB
GB 1926–1928
Arab Motors, Letchworth, Herts. Sports cars.

ARABIAN
USA 1915–1917
The William Galloway Co., Waterloo, Iowa. Touring cars.

ARATRICE
I 1915
La Moto di Ing. Pavesi & Tolotti, Milano.

ARBEE
GB 1904
Rogers Bros., London. Light cars.

ARBEL
F 1957
Automobiles Francois Arbel, Paris. Fiberglass body.
See "Symetric."

ARBENZ
USA 1911–1918
Scioto Auto Car Co. Arbenz Motor Car Co., Chillicothe, Ohio. Formerly "Scioto" 1910–1911. Taken over by National United Service Co. of New York March 18, 1916.

ARCADIA
USA 1903
Believed to be "Acadia" misspelled.

ARCHER
GB 1920
2-seater 8/10 hp cyclecar.

ARCHER
USA 1910
W.L. Archer, Rutland, Vermont. Prototype.

ARCHIMEDE
I 1905
Ugo Pettini, Roma.

ARDEN
D 1981–present
Arden Jaguar Automobilbau, Kleve. Tuning.

ARDEN
GB 1912–1916
Arden Motor Co. Ltd., Coventry, Warwickshire. Cyclecars.

ARDENT
F 1900–1901
Caron et Cie., Paris. Vis-à-vis light cars.

ARDIE
D 1926–1929
Ardie Werke GmbH, Nürnberg. Three-wheelers.

ARDIE
D 1930
Josef Ganz, Nürnberg. Light car prototype.
See "Standard."

ARDITA
I 1918
Costruzioni Automobili Ing. A. Gallanzi, Milano and 1.3-litre cars.

ARDSLEY
USA 1905–1906
Ardsley Motor Car Co., Yonkers, N.Y. Designed by W.S. Howard.
See "Howard," 1903.

ARENDT
D c. 1987
Arendt GmbH, Landsweiler-Reden. Tuning.

ARGEO
D 1925
Argeo Fahrzeugwerk Georg Kulitzky, Berlin. Three-wheelers.

ARGO
USA 1910–1916
Argo Electric Vehicle Co., Saginaw, Michigan. Electric cars. Became American Electric Car Co. with "Borland" and "Broc."

ARGO
USA 1914–1916
Argo Motor Co., Jackson, Michigan Light cars. Called "Ajax" in France. Name changed to "Hackett" 1916.

ARGON
GB 1908
Grannaway Engineering Co. Ltd., London. Large touring cars.

ARGONAUT
USA 1877
J.W. Wilkins, San Francisco, California. Steam carriage.

ARGONAUT
USA 1959–1963
Argonaut Motor Machine Co., Cleveland, Ohio. Aluminium-bodied luxury cars.

ARGONNE
USA 1919–1920
Argonne Motor Car Co., Jersey City, New Jersey. Custom-built roadsters only.

ARGUS
D 1902–1910
Internationale Automobilzentrale KG Jeannin & Co. (1902–1904). Argus Motoren-Gesellschaft Jeannin & Co. KG, Berlin (1904–1910). 2-, 4- and 6-cylinder cars.

ARGYLL
GB 1899–1932
Hozier Engineering Co. Ltd., Glasgow (1899–1905). Argyll Motors Ltd., Glasgow (1905–1906; 1914–1932). Argyll Motors Ltd., Alexandria by Glasgow (1906–1914). Touring cars.

ARGYLL
GB 1976–c. 1984
Minnow Fish Carburetters, Lochgilphead, Argyll. Sports cars.

ARIANE
F 1907
Automobiles Ariane, Suresnes/Seine. Small friction-drive two-seater.

ARIEL
GB 1898–1915; 1922–1925
Ariel Motor Co. Ltd., Birmingham (1898–1906). Ariel Motors Ltd., Birmingham (1906–1915). Ordnance Works Ltd., Coventry, Warwickshire (1922–1925). Quadricycles and tricycles; large tourers; three-seater small cars.

ARIEL
USA 1905–1907
Ariel Motor Car Co., Boston, Massachusetts (1905–1906). Sinclair-Scott Co., Baltimore, Maryland. Touring cars. Name changed to "Maryland" 1907.

ARIES
F 1903–1938
SA Aries, Courbevoie/Seine. Touring cars.

ARIMOFA
D 1921–1922
ARI-Motorfahrzeugbau GmbH, Plauen. Small two-seater.

ARISTA
F 1912–1915
Établissements Ruffier, Paris. 6–12 hp cars.

ARISTA
F 1956–1963
Automobiles Arista, Paris. Sports coupe.

ARISTON
USA 1906
D. Sheppard, Chicago, Illinois.

ARISTOS
USA 1912–1913
Aristos Company, New York, N.Y. Company built Mondex-Magic engines, but may have built a car as well in 1914.

ARIZONA
USA 1998–to present
Arizona Prototype Co., Phoenix, Arizona. Sports kit cars.

ARKANSAS
USA 1912
L. Fodrea Co., Arkadelphia, Arkansas.

ARKLEY
GB 1970–1988
Arkley Engineering, John Britten Garages, Arkley, Hertfordshire. "MG" Midget replicars.

ARKLEY
USA 1982
North American Arkley, Portland, Oregon. Kit cars.

ARMAC
USA 1905–1906
Armac Motor Co., Chicago, Illinois.

ARMADALE
GB 1906–1907
Armadale Motors Ltd. (1906). Northwood Motor & Engineering Works, Northwood, Middlesex. Three-wheelers.

ARMARETTA
USA 1986
Lerini Coach Corporation, North Hollywood, California. "Cord" 810 replicars.

ARMINO MEZZO
I
See "A.M."

ARMOR
F 1925–1928
98 cc 1-cylinder or 496 cc 2-cylinder cyclecars.

ARMSTRONG
GB 1913–1914
Armstrong Motor Co., Birmingham. Cyclecars.

ARMSTRONG
USA 1896–1897
Armstrong Mfg. Co., Bridgeport, Connecticut.

ARMSTRONG
USA 1903–1904
Armstrong & Co., New Haven, Connecticut. Electric cars.

ARMSTRONG SIDDELEY
GB 1919–1960
Armstrong Siddeley Motors Ltd., Coventry, Warwickshire. Passenger cars. Complicated inter-relationship between "Armstrong," "Siddeley," "Deasy" and "Wolseley."

ARMSTRONG-WHITWORTH
GB 1906–1915
Sir W.G. Armstrong, Whitworth & Co. Ltd., Newcastle-upon-Tyne. Large limousines and tourers.

ARNA
I 1983
Arna Srl., Pomigliano d'Arco. "Alfa Romeo" Alfasud mechanic parts and "Datsun" (J) Cherry body.

ARNAULT
F 1967–1970
Carrossier Arnault, Garches. City cars.

ARNO
GB 1908
Arno Motor Co., Coventry, Warwickshire. 35 hp 4-cylinder cars.

ARNOLD
GB 1896–1898
Arnold Motor Carriage Co., East Peckham, Kent. About 12 cars of "Benz" (D) design were made.

ARNOLD
USA 1895
B.J. Arnold, Chicago, Illinois. Electric cars.

ARNOLT-BRISTOL
USA 1953–1964
S.H. Arnolt Inc., Chicago, Illinois. Sports cars with bodywork by Nuccio Bertone of Italy.

ARNOTT
GB 1951–1957
Arnott's Garages (Harlesden) Ltd., London. Sports cars.

ARNTZ
USA 1974
Sports car.

ARO
RO 1968–present
Interprinderea Mecanica Muscel, Pitesti; Cimpulung. 4 × 4 vehicles.

AROLA
F 1976–1984
Arola, Corbas. Three-wheeler minicars.

ARROL-ASTER
GB
See "Arrol-Johnston."

ARROL-JOHNSTON
GB 1897–1931
The Mo-Car Syndicate Ltd., Glasgow (1897–1906). The New Arrol-Johnston Car Co. Ltd., Paisley, Renfrewshire (1906–1913). Arrol-Johnston Ltd., Dumfries (1913–1927). Arrol-Johnston & Aster Eng. Co. Ltd., Dumfries (1927–1931). "Dogcart"; large saloons.

ARROS
F 1906
F. Couuillens et Fils, Plaisance du Gers Voiturette.

ARROW
USA 1903
George N. Pierce Co., Buffalo, N.Y.

ARROW
USA 1912–1913
Arrow Motor Car Co., Long Island City, N.Y.

ARROW
USA 1914
Arrow Cyclecar Co., Minneapolis, Minnesota. Cyclecars.

ARROW
USA 1914
M.C. Whitmore Co., Dayton, Ohio. Cyclecars.

ARROW
USA 1922
Arrow Motors, Sandusky, Ohio. Company formed to take over assets of "Maibohm." Car sold as "Courier" (1923–1924) not "Arrow."

ARROWBILE
USA 1937–1958
Waterman Arrowplane Corp., Santa Monica, California. Early serious attempt to produce a flying car for commercial sale in U.S. About 8 vehicles produced.

ARROWHEAD
USA 1936
Advanced Auto Body Works, Inc., Los Angeles, California. Three-wheelers.

ARROW LOCOMOTOR
USA 1896
Adolph Moesch Co., Buffalo, N.Y. Auto-buggy.

ARROW MOTOR BUGGY
USA 1907
Arrow Motor Buggy Co., St. Louis, Missouri.

ARROW PLANE
USA 1932
Hill Auto Body Metall Co., Cincinnati Rear-engined teardrop of a car.

ARTES
E 1967
Jose Artes de Marcos, Barcelona. Sports cars.

ARTESI
I 1948
Antonio Artesi, Palermo.
See "Pulcino."

ARTON
D c. 1994
Arton Automobile, Stansdorf. Electric cars.

ARTZ
D 1982–c. 1993
Artz Automobile GmbH, Hannover. Tuning.

ARTZBERGER
USA 1904
Artzberger Automobile Co., Allegheny,

Pennsylvania. Built both steam and gasoline cars.
See "Foster" steam.

ARUANDA
BR 1965
Minicar bodied by Fissore, Italy.

ARZAC
F 1927
Front-wheel drive cyclecars.

ARZENS
F 1942
Electromobile.

AS
D 1982–1999
Automobilbau Saier, Sonnenbuhl-Willmandigen. Sports car.
See "Saier."

A.S.
F 1924–1928
Voiturettes Automobiles AS, Courbevoie, Seine (1924–1926). La Garenne-Colombes, Seine (1926–1928). Sporting light cars.

A.S.
PL 1927–1930
Tow. Budowy Samochodow, Warszawa Touring cars and taxicabs.

A.S.A.
I 1962–1969
Autocostruzioni S.p.A., Milano.

ASA
I 1981–?
ASA, Advanced Security Agency, Milano. Armored cars.

ASAHI
J 1937–1939
Miyata Works Ltd., Tokyo. Light cars.

ASAP
CS 1930–1945
Akciová společnost pro automobilový prumysl, Mladá Boleslav. Company name.
See "Škoda."

ASARDO
USA 1959
American Special Automotive Research & Design Org., North Bergen, New Jersey. GT cars by Helmut Schlosser using Alfa Romeo Giulietta components.

ASB
D c. 1985
ASB-Tuning, Gelsenkirchen. Tuning.

ASC
USA c. 1991
ASC Incorporated, Southgate, Michigan. Sports car.

ASCARI
D 1998–present
Ascari Automobilmanufaktur, Röttingen. Tuning.

ASCORT
AUS 1959–1969
Continental Coachwork Co., Sydney, N.S.W. GT coupe.

ASCOT
F 1914–1915
Société Buchet, Levallois-Perret/Seine. Light cars.

ASCOT
GB 1928–1930
Ascot Motor & Manufacturing Co., Letchworth, Herts. 4- and 6-cylinder cars.

ASCOT
USA 1955
Glasspar Co., Santa Ana, California. Fiberglass roadsters.

ASDOMOBIL
E 1913
Alfred Schwefringhaus, Düsseldorf. Three-wheelers.

ASHBY
GB
Ashby Motors Ltd., Manchester.
See "Short-Ashby."

ASHEVILLE
USA 1914–1915
Asheville Light Car Co., Asheville, North Carolina. Runabouts.

ASHLEY
GB 1958–1961
Ashley Laminates Ltd., Loughton, Essex; Harlow, Essex. Sports cars.

ASHTON-EVANS
GB 1919–1928
Ashton-Evans Motors Ltd., Birmingham. Light cars with tubular chassis.

ASIA
ROK 1990–present
Asia Motors, Youngdeungpo-Gu, Seoul. 4 × 4 vehicles.

ASPA
CS 1925–1927
Příbramská strojírna a slévárna, Příbram. Light cars.
See "Stelka."

ASPINWALL
USA 1892
L.M. Aspinwall, Washington, D.C. Experimental three-wheel electric car.

ASPROOTH-LEONI
USA 1926–1927
A.M. Leoni, Philadelphia, Pennsylvania. Gas-electric car.

ASQUITH
GB 1901–1902
William Asquith Ltd., Halifax, Yorks. 1-cylinder tonneau.

ASQUITH
GB 1987–present
Asquith Motor Carriage Co. Ltd., Great Yeldham, Essex. Replicars.

ASQUITH
USA 1901
S.A. Asquith Runabout Co., Waterloo, Iowa. Light car.

A.S.S.
F 1919–1920
Automobiles Sans Soupapes, Lyon. 2-cylinder 2-stroke cars.

ASSO
I 1921–1925
Andreotti e Spada, Roma.

ASTATIC
F 1920–1922
Automobiles Astatic, St. Ouen/Seine. Light cars.

ASTER
F 1900–1910
Ateliers de Construction Mécanique l'Aster, Saint-Denis/Seine. Voiturettes.

ASTER
GB 1922–1930
Aster Engineering Co. Ltd., Wembley, Middlesex (1922–1927). Arrol-Johnston Ltd., and Aster Engineering Co., Heathall, Dumfries, Scotland (1927–1930). Finely constructed 2.6 and 3.5-litre cars.

ASTER
I 1906–1908
Societa Italiana Motori, Milano.
See "SIMA."

ASTER
USA 1906

Aster & Co., New York, N.Y. Also built Aster-Tricar 1906–1907.

ASTON
USA 1908–1909
Aston Motor Car Co., Bridgeport, Connecticut. 25- and 45-hp cars.

ASTON MARTIN
GB 1922–present
Bamford and Martin Ltd., London (1922–1925). Aston Martin Motors Ltd., Feltham, Middlesex (1926–1929). Aston Martin Ltd., Feltham, Middlesex (1929–1957). Aston Martin Lagonda Ltd., Newport Pagnell, Bucks. (1958–present). High-performance sports cars.

ASTON MARTIN TICKFORD
GB 1985–?
Aston Martin Tickford, Milton Keynes Sports cars.

ASTOR
USA 1925–1927
M.P. Moller Motor Co., Hagerstown, Maryland. Taxicabs mainly.

ASTRA
B 1930
Automobiles Astra, Liege. Almost exact copy of the "Tracta" (F).

ASTRA
F 1922
D.Pasquet, Paris. Cyclecars.

ASTRA
GB 1956–1959
Astra Car Co. Ltd., Hampton Hill, Middlesex. Small cars.

ASTRA
RO 1922–1924
Prima Fabrica Romana de Vagoarne si Motoare, Arad. Cars built in the former "Marta" factory.

ASTRA
USA 1920
Astra Motors Corp., St. Louis, Missouri. Built by Dorris. Astra existed November 1919 – June 1920. Touring cars.

ASTRA
USA 1962
Astra Automotve Division, Sacramento, California. Kit car.

ASTRA-GNOME
USA 1956
Richard Arbib Co., Inc., New York, N.Y.

ASTRAL
GB 1923–1924
Hertford Engineering Co. Ltd., Barking, Essex. Advanced cars with 4-wheel brakes.

A.T.A.
B 1914
Ateliers de Construction d'Automobiles Texeira, Trooz.

ATALANTA
GB
  See "Owen."

ATALANTA
GB 1916–1917
Atalanta Light Cars Ltd., London. Light cars.

ATALANTA
GB 1937–1939
Atalanta Motors Ltd., Staines, Middlesex. Sports cars.

ATHMAC
GB 1913
Athmac Motor Co., Leyton, Essex. Cyclecars.

ATHOLL
GB 1907–1908
Angus Murray & Sons, Glasgow. Touring cars.

ATKINS
USA 1899–1900
Hughes & Atkin, Providence, Rhode Island.
  See "Hughes" steam and "Rhode Island" (1899–1900). 80 cars were built.

ATKINSON & PHILIPSON
GB 1896
Atkinson & Philipson, Northumberland Coach Factory, Newcastle-on-Tyne. Steam carriage.

ATLA
F 1958
Jacques Durand, Paris. Small fiberglass coupe with gull-wing doors.

ATLANTA
CS 1929
Front-wheel drive car with 500 cc JAP engine.

ATLANTA
USA 1910–1911
Atlanta Motor Car Co., Atlanta, Georgia.

ATLANTIC
E 1921–1923
Atlantic AG für Automobilbau, Berlin. Two-wheel cars.

ATLANTIC
USA 1899–1900
Company name for Atlantic Automobile Manufacturing Company which succeeded. Marsh Motor Carriage Company, Brockton, Massachusetts.
  See "Marsh" steam.

ATLANTIC
USA 1912–1914
Atlantic Vehicle Co., Newark, New Jersey. Electric cars.

ATLANTIS
GB 1983–1988
Atlantis Co., Thetford, Norfolk. Atlantis Motor Company, Attleborough, Norfolk. Replicars.

ATLAS
F 1951
Sté. Industrielle de Livry, Paris. Minicars.

ATLAS
USA 1902
Atlas Automobile Co., Newark, New Jersey.

ATLAS
USA 1906–1907
Atlas Automobile Co., Pittsburgh, Pennsylvania. Runabouts.

ATLAS
USA 1907–1912
Atlas Motor Car Co., Springfield, Massachusetts. Runabouts and touring cars.

ATLAS
F 1949–1952
Sté. Industrielle de Livry, Paris. Three-wheelers.

ATLAS-DETROIT
USA 1916
Atlas-Detroit Motor Co., Detroit, Michigan.

ATLAS-KNIGHT
USA 1912–1913
Atlas Motor Car Co., Springfield, Massachusetts. Became Lyons-Atlas Co., Indianapolis, Indiana, along with Atlas Engine Works.

ATLAS MOTOR BUGGY
USA 1909

Atlas Engine Works, Indianapolis, Indiana. Built two-cylinder Auto Buggy. Became part of Lyons-Atlas Co.

ATOMETTE
GB 1922
Allan Thomas Ltd., Wolverhampton, Staffs. Three-wheelers.

ATOMO
I 1947–1948
S.A.M.C.A., Parma. Three-wheeled minicars.

A.T.S.
I 1962–1969
Scuderia Serenissima, Modena (1962). Automobili Turismo e Sport, Bologna (1963–1969).
   See "Serenissima."

A.T.S. EVOLUTION
F 1995
A.T.S. Evolution, Arcueil. "Shelby" (USA) Daytona Cobra replicars.

ATSUTA
J 1933–1934
Japan Wheel Co. Ltd., Tokyo. 8-cylinder cars.

ATTERBURY
USA 1911
Atterbury Motor Car Co., Buffalo, N.Y. 10-passenger touring car.

ATTICA
GR 1960s–1970s
Vioplastic Co. Ltd., Dimitriadi, Pireus. Three-wheelers.
   See "Fuldamobil" (D) and "Sabra" (IL).

ATTILA
D 1900–1901
Attila Fahrradwerke AG vorm. Kretzschmar & Co., Dresden. Three-wheelers.

ATVIDABERG
S 1910
Atvidabergs Vagnfabrik, Atvidaberg. Motor buggy.

ATW
D 1983–1993
AutoTechnik Walther GmbH, Bad Rappenau. Electric cars.

AUBREY
USA 1900
L.J. Aubrey Carriage Co., New Haven, Connecticut.

AUBURN
USA 1900–1936
Auburn Automobile Co., Auburn, Indiana. Formerly Eckhart Carriage Works. Became part of Cord Corp. with "Duesenberg" 1929. 4-, 6-, 8- and 12-cylinder luxury and sports cars.

AUBURN
USA 1912–1915
Auburn Motor Chassis Co., Auburn, Indiana. Highwheelers, some trucks.

AUBURN
USA 1967–1982
Auburn-Cord-Duesenberg Co., Tulsa, Oklahoma. Produced replicars of 1935 "Auburn" Speedster.

AUBURN-CUMMINS
USA 1935
Auburn Automobile Co., Cummins Diesel Co., Columbus, Indiana. Four-cylinder diesel engine in Auburn car.

AUBURN MOORE
USA 1906
A.S. Moore, Cleveland, Ohio. One car produced.
   See "Moore" (1902–1903).

AUBURN MOTOR BUGGY
USA 1911–1914
Highwheeler built by Auburn Motor Chassis Company at Auburn, Indiana.
   See "Auburn" (1911–1915).

AUDAX
F 1914
Lenefait et Cie., Rouen. Light cars.

AUDAX
F 1997–present
Audax Ingenierie, Gallargues. Sports cars.

AUDAX
I 1907
Automobili e Motori Audax, Palermo.

AUDI
D 1910–1939; 1965–present
Audi Automobilwerke GmbH, Zwickau/Sachsen (1910–1939). Auto Union GmbH, Ingolstadt (1965–1969). Audi NSU Auto Union GmbH (1969–1984). Audi AG, Ingolstadt (1985–present). Passenger and sports cars.

AUDIBERT-LAVIROTTE
F 1894–1901
Sté. Anon. Des Anciens Établissements Audibert et Lavirotte, Lyon. 2- and 4-cylinder cars.

AUDINEAU
F 1897
Paul Audineau, Paris. Voiturette.

AUGÉ
F 1898–1901
Daniel Augé et Cie., Levallois-Perret/Seine. 5, 7 and 8 hp voiturettes.

AULTMAN
USA 1898; 1901–1902
Henry J. Aultman, Cleveland, Ohio (1898). The Aultman Company, Canton, Ohio (1901–1902). Steam cars.

AUREA
I 1920–1933
Societa Italiana Ferrotaie, Torino (1920–1922). Fabbrica Anonima Torinese Automobili (F.A.T.A.), Torino (1922–1933). Touring cars.

AURORA
I
   See "Fusi-Ferro."

AURORA
USA 1905–1909
Aurora Automobile Co. (1905). Aurora Motor Works Emancipator Automobile Co. (1909), Aurora, Illinois. Touring cars and runabouts.

AURORA
USA 1958
Fater Alfred Juliano, Bradford, Connecticut. Experimental safety car.

AURORA
USA 1982
Aurora Cobra East, Saratoga Springs, N.Y. "Cobra" replicars.

AURORE
H
   See "Hora-Aurore."

AUSCA
AUS 1956
135 hp sports car kit.

AUSFOD
GB 1947–1948
Ausfod Motor Engineering Co. Ltd., Manchester. Sports cars.

AUSONIA
I 1903–1906
Camona Giussani Turrinelli e Cia., Milano. Electric cars.

AUSTEN
USA 1863
William Austen, Lowell, Massachusetts

This car is a "Roper." W. Austen was S. Roper's agent.
See "Roper."

AUSTENIUS
USA 1864
Possibly an error for "Roper."

AUSTIN
GB 1906–1988
Austin Motor Co. Ltd., Birmingham (1906–1970). Austin-Morris Division, British Leyland Motor Corporation Ltd., Birmingham (1970–1988). British Leyland UK Ltd., Austin-Morris Group, Longbridge, Birmingham. 1988 owned by British Aerospace.
See "Mini," "Rover." Passenger and sports cars.

AUSTIN
USA 1903–1921
Austin Automobile Co., Grand Rapids, Michigan. Touring cars.

AUSTIN-BANTAM
USA 1930–1937
American Austin Car Co., Butler, Pennsylvania. Became American Bantam Car Co.
See "American Bantam."

AUSTIN-HEALEY
GB 1953–1971
Austin Motor Co. Ltd., Birmingham (1953–1970). Austin-Morris Division, British Leyland Motor Corporation Ltd., Abingdon, Berks. (1970–1971). Sports cars.

AUSTIN-LYMAN
USA 1909
Austin-Lyman Co., Buffalo, N.Y.

AUSTRALIAN SIX
AUS 1919–1924
F.H. Gordon & Co., Rushcutters Bay, N.S.W. (1919). Australian Motors Ltd., Ashfield, N.S.W. (1920–1924). Harkness & Hillier, Sydney, N.S.W. (1924) Mass-produced assembled cars.

AUSTRALIS
AUS 1901–1906
Australis Motors, Leichardt, N.S.W. DeDion powered light cars.

AUSTRO
A/CS 1913–1914
Fritz Hückel, Nový Jičín. Cyclecars.

AUSTRO-DAIMLER
A 1899–1936
Österreichische Daimler-Motoren AG, Wiener Neustadt (1899–1934). Steyr-Daimler-Puch AG, Wiener Neustadt (1934–1936). Touring and sports cars.

AUSTRO-FIAT
A 1921–1936
Österreichische Fiat-Werke AG, Wien Touring cars. Associated with "Austro-Daimler" and "Puch" from 1925.

AUSTRO-GRADE
A 1923–1926
Austro-Grade AG, Klosterneuburg. Cyclecars.

AUSTRO-TATRA
A 1937–1939
Austro-Tatra Werke AG, Wien. "Tatra" (CS) Type 57A license. 515 cars were made.

AUTHI
E 1965–1975
Pamplona. "Mini" (GB) license.

AUTO-ACETYLENE
USA 1899–1900
Auto-Acetylene Co., New York, N.Y. Three models (runabouts) described and illustrated 1899.

AUTOAR
RA 1950–1962
Automotores Argentinos, Buenos Aires Passenger cars. Also "NSU" (D) Prinz license.

AUTO AVIO COSTRUZIONI
I 1939–1940
Modena.

AUTOBIANCHI
I 1899–1938; 1957–1981
Lancia Autobianchi, Fiat Auto SpA, Torino.
See "Bianchi." "Fiat" sold "Autobianchi" under the name "Lancia" from 1981.

AUTOBLEU
F 1955–1958
Automobiles Autobleu, Paris. Small cars.

AUTO-BOB
USA 1914–1915
Jack Hickman, East Pittsburgh, Pennsylvania. Juvenile cars.

AUTO-BUG
USA 1909–1910
Auto-Bug Co., Norwalk, Ohio. Autobuggy. Became "Norwalk."

AUTO BUGGY
USA 1906–1907
Auto Buggy Mfg. Co., St. Louis, Missouri. Highwheelers.
See "A.B.C."

AUTO BUGGY
USA 1906–1907
Success Auto Buggy Co., St. Louis, Missouri. Became "Success."

AUTOCAR
USA 1901–1911
The Autocar Co., Pittsburgh, Pennsylvania; Ardmore, Pennsylvania. Runabouts. Succeeded Pittsburgh Motor Vehicle Co.

AUTOCAR
USA 1900
Autocar Company, Hartford, Connecticut. Compressed air car.

AUTO-CAR
USA 1904–1910
Auto-Car Equipment Co. (1904–1909). Auto-Car Mfg. Co. (1909–1910), Buffalo, N.Y. Trucks and 8–12 passenger limousines. Became "Atterbury."

AUTOCARETTE
USA 1900–1901
American Autocarette Co., Washington, D.C. Automobile Mfg. Co., Baltimore, Maryland.

AUTO-CARIAGE
USA 1905
Johnson Service Co., Milwaukee, Wisconsin.
See "Johnson."

AUTO CARS
I 1907–1911
Societa Italiana Auto Cars (SIAC), Alessandria.

AUTOCOPTER
A 1949
U.Köpruner & H. Rauch, Bregenz. Flying car.

AUTOCRAFT
BR 1966–c. 1985
L'Automobile Ltda., São Paulo. Replicars.

AUTOCRAT
GB 1913–1926
Autocrat Light Car Co., Birmingham. Light cars.

AUTOCRAT
USA 1899
The Autocrat Manufacturing Co., Hartford, Connecticut. Compressed air carriage was announced but actual production is unknown.

AUTO CUB
USA 1956
Randall Products, Hampton, New Hampshire. Single-passenger, tiller-steered runabout. Companion to "Daytona."

AUTOCYCLE
USA 1900
Keystone Motor Co., Philadelphia, Pennsylvania. Became "Keystone."

AUTOCYCLE
USA 1906–1907
Vandergrift Automobile Co., Philadelphia, Pennsylvania. Rhomboid wheel placement.
See "Vandergrift."

AUTOCYCLE
USA 1913
Toledo Autocycle Car Co., Toledo, Ohio. Cyclecars.

AUTOCYCLE
USA 1983
Rhomboid wheel arrangement.

AUTO-CYCLECAR
USA 1913
Automobile Cyclecar Co., Detroit, Michigan. Cyclecars.

AUTOCYKL
CS 1948
Rastislav Dýma, Raška. 500 cc BSA motorcycle engine powered light car prototype.

AUTO DESIGN
USA 1982
Auto Design, San Jose, California. "Jaguar" (GB) XK 120 replicars.

AUTO-DYNAMIC
USA 1900–1905
Auto-Dynamic Co., New York, N.Y. Electric cars.

AUTODYNAMICS
USA 1964–1975 ?
Autodynamics, Inc., Marblehead, Massachusetts. Sports cars.

AUTOETTE
USA 1912–1914
Manistee Motor Car Co., Manistee, Michigan (1912–1913). Autoette Co., Christman, Illinois (1914). Cyclecars.

AUTOETTE
USA 1952–1957
Autoette Electric Car Co., Long Beach, California. Small electric shopping three-wheelers.

AUTOFIORETTI
I 1980–c. 1984
Roma. Three-wheelers.

AUTOFIX
D 1950–1951
Mertiny KG, Berlin. Three-wheelers.

AUTO FORE CARRIAGE
USA 1900–1901
Automobile Fore Carriage Co., New York, N.Y.
See "Automobile Fore Carriage."

AUTOGEAR
GB 1922
Foster Engineering Co. Ltd., Letchworth, Herts. Light cars.

AUTOGEAR
GB 1922–1923
Autogears, Leeds, Yorks. Three-wheeler.

AUTOGEN
D 1921
Amphibious three-wheeler.

AUTOGNOM
D 1907
Deutsche Motorfahrzeugfabrik GmbH, Berlin.

AUTO KING
USA 1900
New England Auto King Co., Portland, Maine.

AUTOKIT
USA c. 1975
Autokit Industries. Kit car.

AUTO LÉGER
F 1904–1907
Autos Léger V. Crepet, Lyon. Shaft- and chain-driven cars.

AUTOLET
USA 1904
Holson Motor Patents Co., Inc., Grand Rapids, Michigan. Electric cars.
See "Holson."

AUTOLETTE
NL 1905–1906
S. Bingham & Co., Rotterdam. Three-wheelers.

AUTOLUX
I 1937; 1943–1944
Milano. Electric three-wheelers.

AUTOMATIC ELECTRIC
USA 1921–1922
Automatic Electric Transmission Co, Buffalo, N.Y. Small electric two-seaters.

AUTOMATIC STURTEVANT
USA 1904–1907
Sturtevant Mill Co., Boston, Massachusetts.
See "Sturtevant."

AUTOMIRAGE
I 1974–1982
Automirage Srl, Rastignano (Bologna) Dune buggy and minicars. 318 cars built in 1974.

AUTO-MIXTE
B 1906–1912
Société Anonyme L'Auto-Mixte, Herstal. Gasoline-electric cars.
See "Pescatore."

AUTOMOBILE AIR CARRIAGE
USA 1898–1900
Automobile Air Carriage Co., Albany, N.Y.

AUTOMOBILE FORE CARRIAGE
USA 1900–1901
Automobile Fore Carriage Co., New York, N.Y. Converted carriages to motor-powered vehicles.

AUTOMOBILETTE
F 1911–1914; 1920–1924
Sté. Cognet & Ducruzel, Billancourt/Seine. Tandem cyclecars; light cars.

AUTOMOBILE VOITURETTE
USA 1899–1900
Automobile Company of America, Marion, New Jersey.
See "American Voiturette." Became "Gasmobile," 1900.

AUTOMOBILI INTERMECCANICA
USA 1982
Automobili Intermeccanica, Fountain Valley, California. Replicar.

AUTOMOTE
USA 1900
Schaap Cycle Co., Brooklyn, N.Y.

AUTOMOTETTE
F 1898–1899
Paris. Light three-wheelers.

AUTOMOTO
F 1901–1907
Chavanet, Gros, Pichard & Cie., St. Etienne. 4-cylinder cars.

AUTOMOTOR
USA 1901–1905
Automotor Co., Springfield, Massachusetts. Body and sheet metal by Springfield Body Co. Formerly Springfield. Cornice Works, 1900–1901. Runabouts.

AUTOMOTOR
USA 1902
Lowell Model Co., Lowell, Massachusetts.

AUTO-MOTOR
USA 1912
Bryn Mawr, Pennsylvania.

AUTOMOTORETTE
USA 1900–1902
L. Dyke, St. Louis, Missouri.
  See "Dyke."

AUTONACIONAL
E 1953–1960
Autonacional SA, Barcelona. "Biscuter" minicars.

AUTONOVA
D 1965
Sports car prototype.

AUTO-PALACE
NL 1908
Auto-Palace, Den Haag.

AUTO PARTS
USA 1909–1911
Auto Parts Company, Chicago, Illinois A $600 air or water-cooled car sold in kit form.

AUTO-PHAETON
D
  See "Roeder."

AUTOPLAN
F 1973
Flying car.

AUTO PLANE
USA 1932?
  See "Moore Autoplane."

AUTO PRATIQUE
F 1912–1913
Sté. l'Auto Pratique, Paris. Cyclecars.

AUTO-QUAD
USA 1901
C.R. Thomas Motor Co., Buffalo, N.Y.

AUTO-QUADRICYCLE
USA 1903
Auto-Cycle Carriage Co., Chicago, Illinois.

AUTO RED BUG
USA 1916–1923
American Motor Vehicle Co., Lafayette, Indiana (1916–1920). Automotive Electric Service Corp., North Bergen, New Jersey bought rights to Briggs & Stratton (Smith) Flyer electric and gasoline bucboards.

AUTORÉPLICA
E 1985
Autoréplica S.A., Madrid. Replicars.

AUTO SANDAL
J 1954
Japan Auto Sandal Motors, Tokyo. Two-seater minicars.

AUTO SUPPLY
USA 1901
Auto Supply Co., New York, N.Y. Runabouts.

AUTOTRI
USA 1900–1901
E.R. Thomas Motor Co., Buffalo, N.Y.

AUTO TRICAR
USA 1914
A.E. Osborn, New York, N.Y. Light cars.

AUTOTRIX
GB 1913
Edmunds & Wadden, Weybridge, Surrey. Three-wheelers.

AUTOTUNE
GB 1989–present
Autotune Ltd., Blackburn, Lancs. Sports cars and replicars.

AUTO-TWO
USA 1900
Buffalo Auto and Auto-Bi Co., Buffalo, N.Y.
  See "Buffalo."

AUTO UNION
D 1932–1945; 1958–1962
Auto Union, Zschopau (1932–1936); Chemnitz (1936–1945); Ingolstadt (1958–1962). Auto Union (1932–1935) was created by "Audi," DKW," "Horch" and "Wanderer." The AU 1000 S/SP cars (1958–1962) were marketed also under "Auto Union" name.

AUTO-VEHICLE
USA 1902–1905
The Auto-Vehicle Co., Los Angeles, California.
  See "Tourist" (1903–1909).

AUTOVIA
GB 1937–1938
Autovia Cars Ltd., Coventry, Warwickshire. Luxury cars.

AUTO WAGON
USA 1909
International Harvester Co. of America, Chicago, Illinois.
  See "International."

AUTOZODIACO
I 1971–c. 1975
All Cars Srl, Pianoro (Bologna). Sports cars and three-wheelers.

AUTRAM
F 1924
4-cylinder 2,951 cc cars with front-wheel brakes.

AUVERLAND
F 1986–present
Constructeurs Francais de Vehicules 4 × 4 Auverland S.A., Saint Germain-Laval 4 × 4 cars.

A.V.
GB 1919–1926
Ward & Avey Ltd. (1919–1923). A.V. Motors Ltd., Teddington, Middlesex (1923–1926). Cyclecars.

AVA
CS 1947
Autoslužby Praga, Praha. Sports car.

AVALLONE
BR c. 1976–c. 1993
ACIEI Avallone Commercial, Exportadora e Importadora Ltda., Interlagos, São Paulo. "MG" (GB) replicars.

AVANTE
GB 1982–1984 ?
Avante Cars, Clewlows Motors, Stoke-on-Trent. Sports car.

AVANTI
USA 1962–1990
Avanti Motor Corp., South Bend, Indiana. Model of "Studebaker," built by Avanti Motors.

AVELING
GB 1867
Aveling & Porter, Rochester. Steam car.

AVE MIZAR
USA 1972
Flying car.

AVERAGE MAN'S RUNABOUT
USA 1906–1907
Adams Automobile Co., Hiawatha, Kansas. Cars with air-cooled engines.
See "Adams."

AVERIES
GB 1911–1915
Averies-Ponette Ltd., Englefield Green, Surrey. Light cars.

AVERLY
F 1899
E. Averly, Lyon. Light electric cars.

AVERY
USA 1905
Avery Co., Worcester, Massachusetts.

AVERY
USA 1914
Avery Stalnaker, Chicago, Illinois. Cyclecars.

AVIA
CS 1956–1958
Továrna na výrobu automobilu a letadel, Praha. 350 cc Jawa motorcycle engine powered minicar prototypes.

AVIA
GB 1961
Armat Ltd., Sevenoaks, Kent. 2+2 fiberglass coupe.

AVIETTE
GB 1914–1916
Hurlin & Co. Ltd., London. Very light cyclecars.

AVIONETTE
F
See "Gauthier."

AVIOR
B 1947
4-cylinder 1930 cc engine sports car prototype.

AVIS
A 1922–1925
Avis-Werke, Wien. 2-cylinder small cars.

AVOLETTE
F 1956–1957
Air Tourist, Paris. Three-wheelers.

AVON
GB 1903–1912
Avon Motor Manufacturing Co., Keynsham, Bristol. Three-wheeler.

AVRO
GB 1919–1920
A.V. Roe Co. Ltd., Manchester. Light cars.

A.W.
PL 1939
Antoni Wieckowski, Zaklady Blacharske "Bielany," Warszawa. 32 hp 4-cylinder car prototype.

AWE
DDR 1953–1956
Sports cars.
See "EMW."

AWS
D 1949–1951
Autowerke Salzgitter, Salzgitter. Station wagons made from "Jeep" (USA) components.

AWS
D 1971–1974
AWS Autoteile GmbH, Oberbessingen (1971–1973); Berlin (1973–1974). Small cars.

AWZ
D
See "Zwickau."

AYMESA
EC 1983
Sports cars.

AYRES
USA 1900–1902
Ayres Gasoline Engine & Automobile Co., Saginaw, Michigan.

AYRTON & PERRY
GB 1882
Electric three-wheeler.

AZ
F 1979
See "Minicat."

AZLK
SU 1969–1991
Avtomobilnii Zavod Imeni Leninskogo Komsomola, Moscow.
See "MZMA," "Moskvitch."

AZNP
CS 1945–1990
Automobilové závody, národní podnik, Mladá Boleslav. Company name.
See "Škoda."

AZTEC
USA 1965
FiberFab, Sunnyvale, California Kit car for "Corvair" or "Volkswagen" chassis.

B

BAARS BUGGY
ZA c. 1970
Dune buggy with "Chevrolet" (USA) Corvair engine.

BABCOCK
USA 1906–1912
Babcock Electric Carriage Co., Buffalo, N.Y. Electric cars. Merged into Buffalo Electric Vehicle Co. 1912.

BABCOCK
USA 1909–1913
H. Babcock Co., Watertown, N.Y. Highwheelers.

BABOULIN
F 1971–c.1977
Sté. Baboulin, Grenoble. Dune buggy.

BABY
F
See "Fournier."

BABY BLAKE
GB 1922
E.G. Blake, Croydon, Surrey. Friction-driven cyclecars.

BABY BROUSSE
IR 1971
Small car.

BABY LA SABRE
USA 1952
Los Angeles, California.

BABY MOOSE
USA 1914
Bull Moose-Cutting Automobile Co., St. Paul, Minnesota. Cyclecars. Formerly "Continental" cyclecar.

B.A.C.
GB 1921–1923
British Automotive Co. Ltd., London. Light cars.

BACHELLE
USA 1901–1902
Bachelle Automobile Co., Chicago, Illinois. Electric cars.

BACI
USA 1995–1996
Besasie Automobile Company, Milwaukee, Wisconsin. Sports car replicas.

BACK BAY
USA c. 1900
Back Bay Cycle & Motor Co., Boston, Massachusetts.

BACKUS
USA 1903
Backus Water Motor Co., Newark, New Jersey. Runabout.

BACON
USA 1901
Frank W. Bacon, Omaha, Nebraska. Seven cars built.

BACON
USA 1920–1921
Bacon Motors Corp., Newcastle, Pennsylvania; Philadelphia, Pennsylvania.

BADAL
IND c. 1979–1986
Sunrise Auto Industries Ltd., Bangalore. 350cc three-wheelers.

BADEN
USA 1916–1919
Baden Co., Baden, Missouri. About 30–50 cars were built.

BADENIA
D 1925
Badenia Automobilwerke AG, Hamburg; Ladenburg am Neckar. Six-cylinder cars.

BADGER
USA 1861
Louis Badger, Quinci, Massachusetts. Steam car.

BADGER
USA 1901
Badger Brass Manufacturing Co., Kenosha, Wisconsin. Experimental steam car.

BADGER
USA 1909–1911
The Four Wheel Drive Auto Co., Clintonville, Wisconsin. F.W.D. cars.

BADGER
USA 1910–1911
Badger Motor Car Co., Columbus, Wisconsin.

BADMINTON
F/GB 1907–1908
Badminton Motors Ltd., London. Teste & Lassen, London. Chassis were built in (F), and bodies in (GB).

BADSEY
USA 1984
Badsey Bullet USA Inc., Anaheim, California. Three-wheelers.

BAER
D 1921–1926
Paul Bauer Motorenfabrik GmbH, Berlin. 2-cylinder 2-stroke small cars.

BAFAG
D 1924
Bafag GmbH, Aschern i. B. Light car.

BAFFREY
A/CS 1886
Louis Baffrey, Textilfabrik Cosmanos, Josefuv Dul. Steam car.

BAG
D 1906
Berliner Automobilette-Gesellschaft, Berlin. Three-wheelers.

BAGHIRA
CS 1971
Václav Král, Praha. Dune buggy.

BAGNULO
I 1922
Bagnulo Motori, Torino.

BAGULEY
GB 1911–1921
Baguley Cars Ltd., Burton-upon-Trent, Staffs. 88 conventional cars were made.

BAILEY
USA 1907–1910
Bailey-Perkins Auto Co. (1906–1908). Bailey Automobile Co. (1908–1910), Springfield, Massachusetts. Four-cylinder two-cycle revolving air-cooled engine.

BAILEY
USA 1907–1916
S.R. Bailey & Co., Amesbury, Massachusetts. Electric cars.

BAILEY
USA 1912
E.D. Bailey Mfg. Co., Detroit, Michigan.

BAILEY & LAMBERT
GB 1903–1905
Bailey & Lambert Ltd., London. Light cars.

BAILEY ELECTRIC
USA 1902
E.G. Bailey & Co., Manheim, Pennsylvania.

BAILEY-KLAPP
USA 1915
Elwood Iron Works Co., Elwood, Indiana.
    See "Elco."

BAILLEAU
F 1901–1914
A. Bailleau, Longjumeau/Seine-et-Oise. Voiturette.

BAILLE-LEMAIRE
F 1898–1902
Constructeurs Baille-Lemaire, Crosnes/Seine-et-Oise. Belt-driven 8 hp cars.

BAILLEREAU
F 1908
Shaft-drive voiturette.

BAILLEUL
F 1904–1905
Louis Bailleul, Levallois-Perret/Seine. Medium-sized cars.

BAINES
GB 1900
Baines Ltd., Gainsborough, Lincs. Cyclecars.

BAJA
A 1920–1924
Baja Cyclecar Co., Wien. Cyclecars.

BAJA
F 1982

Car Systeme 12, Redon. Offroad version of the "Renault" cars.

BAJA
GB c.1972–1978
The Rodding Scene, Chichester. Dune buggy.

BAJAJ TEMPO
IND 1950s–1980s
Chinchwad, Poona. Three-wheelers.

BAKER
USA 1896–1897
Herbert C. Baker, Manchester, Connecticut. Electric cars, to have been built in plant of Mather Electric Company.

BAKER
USA 1899
Baker Mfg. Co., Tarentum, Pennsylvania.

BAKER
USA 1899
National Machine Co., Hartford, Connecticut. Founder and inventor, Herbert C. Baker, Manchester, Connecticut.

BAKER
USA 1899–1916
Baker Motor Vehicle Co., Cleveland, Ohio (1899–1914). Merged with Rauch & Lang 1914 into Backer, Rauch & Lang Co. Merged with Owen-Magnetic 1915 (Baker Raulang Co.). Industrial truck division started 1922, continued as division of Otis Elevator 1968.

BAKER
USA c. 1900
Robert Baker, Marcellus, N.Y. Motor buggy and runabout.

BAKER
USA 1917–1924
Baker Steam Motor Car & Mfg. Co. (1917–1919). Steam Automotive Works (1920). Baker Motors Inc. (1921), Denver and Pueblo, Colorado. Steam cars.

BAKER-BELL
USA 1913
Baker-Bell Motor Car Co., Philadelphia, Pennsylvania. Also built "Princess" commercial cars for "Metz."
    See "Humming-Bird."

BAKER & DALE
GB 1913
Baker & Dale Ltd., Southbourne, Hampshire. Cyclecars.

BAKER-ELBERG
USA 1894–1895
Dr. H.C. Baker & J.R. Elberg, Kansas City, Missouri. Electric cars.

BAKER-RAULANG
USA 1915–1916
Baker Motor Vehicle Co., Cleveland, Ohio. The 1915–1916 name for the Baker car.
    See "Baker" electric.

BALATON
H 1956
Székesfehérvári Motorjavitó Vállalat, Székesfehérvár. 250 cc minicar prototype.

BALBO
I 1953
Carrozzeria Balbo, Torino. 398 cc minicar prototype.

BALBOA
USA 1924–1925
Balbola Motor Corp., Fullerton, California.

BALDELLI
I 1971
Fratelli Baldelli, Capo d'Orlando, Sicilia. 2-seater coupe prototype.

BALDI
I 1970–1976
Baldi Team, GAMC Sas, San Remo. City cars.

BALDNER
USA 1901–1904
Baldner Motor Vehicle Co., Xenia, Ohio. Auto-buggy.

BALDWIN
USA 1896–1901
Baldwin Automobile Co. (1899–1900). Baldwin Motor Wagon Co. (1901), Providence, Rhode Island. Steam cars.

BALDWIN
USA 1899–1902
Baldwin Automobile Mfg. Co., Connellsville, Pennsylvania. Sold to J.C. Kurtz at trustees' sale April 19, 1902 and moved to Morgantown, West Virginia. Steam cars.

BALIÉR-SCHÄFFER
D c. 1973
Prototype.

BALKAN
BG 1966–c. 1986
Balkan, Lovech. "Fiat" (I) 850 and 124, and "Moskvich" (SU) 408 and 412 license.

BALL
USA 1868
Charles A. Ball, Paterson, New Jersey. One steam experimental car built.

BALL
USA 1901–1902
Charles A. Ball, Miami Cycle & Mfg. Co., Middletown, Ohio; Paterson, New Jersey. Steam cars.
    See "Ramapaugh" steam.

BALL
USA 1902
New York Gear Works, New York, N.Y. Designed by Frederick A. Ball.

BALLARD
USA 1894–1895
E.C. Ballard and Son Co., Oshkosh, Wisconsin. 2-seater buggy.

BALLOT
F 1919–1932
Établissements Ballot, Paris. Sports and touring cars.

BALTIJAS
LT 1997
Baltijas Dzips Ltd., Riga, Latvia. 4 × 4 vehicle.
    See "Tantor."

BALTIMORE
USA 1899
Baltimore Automobile and Mfg. Co., Baltimore, Maryland. Prototype only.

BALTON
USA 1915
Charles A. Balton Engineering Corp., Buffalo, N.Y. Roadster prototype.

BALZER
USA 1894–1899
Stephen M. Balzer, New York, N.Y. (1894–1898). Became Balzer Motor Carriage Co. 1898–1900. Three-cylinder revolving gasoline engine. Balzer's first car, only one known to exist, is in Smithsonian collection.

BALZER
USA 1917
Gus Balzer Co., New York, N.Y. Juvenile cars.

BAMBI
E 1952
Manufacturas Mecanicas Aleu SA, Barcelona. Very light three-wheelers.

BAMBI
RCH
See "Fuldamobil" (D).

BAMBINO
NL 1955–1957
NV Alweco, Veghel. Three-wheelers, as "Fuldamobil" (D).

BAMBY
GB 1983
Bamby Cars Ltd., Hull, Humberside. Three-wheeled minicars.

BANCROFT
D 1993
Bancroft Motorsport, Satzvey. Limited series of 300 sports cars in the 1930s style.

B&B THREE WHEEL
USA 1947
B&B Specialty Co., Rossmoyne, Ohio. Thirty units built.

B&H
USA 1904–1905
Brew & Hatcher Co., Cleveland, Ohio. See "Brew-Hatcher."

BANDIDO
E 1995–present
ARS Jose Franqueira, Madrid. Three-wheeler "Morgan" (GB) replica.

BANDINI
I 1947–1956
Autocostruzione Bandini, Forli. Sports and racing cars.

BANDINO
USA 1969–1972
Sullivan Volkswagen Co., Detroit, Michigan. Dune buggy kit car.

BANFIELD
USA c. 1905
Frdderick E. Banfield, Jr., Newton Centre, Massachusetts. 7hp car.

BANGERT
USA 1956
Bangert Enterprises, Hollywood, California.

BANGS & BUTLER
USA 1908
Calvin Bangs & William Butler, Everett, Massachusetts. Steam car.

BANHAM
GB 1990s
Paul Banham Conversions, Rochester, Kent. Kit cards.

BANKER
USA 1905
C. Banker, Chicago, Illinois. Shaft-drive car.

BANKER BROTHERS
USA 1896
Banker Brothers Co., Pittsburgh, Pennsylvania. Electric car.

BANKER ELECTRIC
USA 1905
Banker Bros., Pittsburgh, Pennsylvania. Juvenile electric car.

BANKS
USA 1900
Robert Banks, Stanton, Delaware. Steam car.

BANNER
USA 1910–1911; 1915
Banner Automobile Co., St. Louis, Missouri. Division of Banner Buggy Co.

BANNER BOY BUCKBOARD
USA 1958–1959
Banner Welder Inc., Milwaukee, Wisconsin.

BANTAM
GB 1913
Slack & Harrison Ltd., Keyworth, Leics. Cyclecars.

BANTAM
USA 1914
Bantam Motor Co., Boston, Massachusetts. Cyclecars.

BARADAT-ESTEVE
E 1922
Cortina Baradat y Esteve, Barcelona. 12 cars with four piston Torus engines were made.

BARAUF
USA 1920
Barauf Motor Co., Port Jefferson, N.Y. For export.

BARBARINO
USA 1923–1925
Barbarino Motors Co., Advance Motors Corp., Stamford, Connecticut. Touring cars.

BARBER
USA 1899
George Barber, Danbury, Connecticut.

BARBOUR
USA 1916
Barbour Buggy Co., South Boston, Virginia. Two cars were made.

BARCAR
GB 1904–1906
Phoenix Motor Co., Southport, Lancs. 3-cylinder 10 hp cars.

BARCLAY
GB 1933
Barclay Motors Ltd., Birmingham. Saloon.

BARCUS
USA 1895
Nemo Barcus, Columbus, Ohio.

BARDON
F 1899–1903
Automobiles Bardon, Puteaux/Seine. Tonneau.

BARDONE
I 1938–1939
Three-wheelers.

BARDWELL
USA 1901
E.H. Bardwell, Flint, Michigan.

BARÉNY
E 1935; 1938
Béla Barény, Stuttgart. Prototype.

BAR HARBOR
USA 1901
Boston Automobile Co., Boston, Massachusetts. Steam car.

BARHOFF
USA 1900
Hartford Accumulator Co., Hartford, Connecticut. Electric car built to test batteries.

BARISON
I 1922–1925
Fabbrica Automobili Barison e Cia., Livorno. 25 cars made.
See "Siva."

BARLEY
USA 1922–1924
Barley Motor Car Co., Roamer Motor Car Co., Kalamazoo, Michigan. Touring cars. Also made taxicabs (Pennant).

BARLOW
USA 1917–1922

Barlow Steam Car Co., Detroit, Michigan. Steam cars.

BARLOW
USA 1924
Barlow Motors Corp., Philadelphia, Pennsylvania.

BARMETTLER
CH 1975–c. 1981
A. Barmettler, Buggy- und Sportwagen-Vertrieb, Buochs/NW. Sports cars.

BARNARD
GB 1921–1922
A.Ward, St. Mark's Engineering Co., London. Sports cars.

BARNARD
GB 1966–c. 1974
Barnard Racing Ltd., Sittingbourne, Kent (1966–1071). Berry, Ede & White Ltd., Rochester, Kent (1971–c.1974). Sports cars and replicars.

BARNARD-BRIGGS
USA 1907
Barnard-Briggs Motor Car Mfg. Co., Boston, Massachusetts. Company offered prize for best name.

BARNES
GB 1904–1906
George A. Barnes, London. Three-wheelers.

BARNES
USA 1899
Barnes Cycle Co , Syracuse, N.Y. Electric car.
See "Van Wagoner" (Century Vehicle Co. in 1900).

BARNES
USA 1908–1912
Barnes Mfg. Co., Sandusky, Ohio. Formerly "Servitor."

BARNES
USA 1910
Barnes Motor Co., Detroit, Michigan. Purchased "Anhut" assets summer, 1910. Company reported sold to Frank Howard January 1911.

BARNHART
USA 1905
Warren Automobile Co., Warren, Pennsylvania. Experimental cars built from 1895–1905. Publicly shown 1905.

BARNHART & BETTS
USA 1899
H.E. Barnhart & C.E. Betts, Warren, Pennsylvania.

BARONTA
USA 1982
See "Tafco." Sports car.

BAROSSO
I 1923–1924
Officine Barosso, Novara. Cyclecar.

BARRÉ
F 1900–1930
G. Barré et Cie. (1900–1923). Barré et Lamberthon (1923–1927). SA des Automobiles Barré (1927–1930), Niort, Sevres. Ballot, DeDion and Aster engines.

BARREIROS
E 1967–c. 1969
Barreiros Diesel SA, Madrid. "Simca" (F) and "Dodge" (USA) license.

BARRETT
USA 1900
S.H. Barrett. M.J. Dunn & Co. Springfield Motor Vehicle Co., Springfield, Massachusetts. Steam car.
See "Springfield."

BARRET & PERRÉT
USA 1896
C.A. Barrett & F. Perrét, New York, N.Y. Electric dos-a-dos.

BARRIE
CDN 1919–1920
Barrie Carriage Co., Ltd., Barrie, Ontario.

BARRINGTON
GB 1932–1936
Barrington Motors Ltd., Sheffield, Yorks. Light two-seater.

BARRIQUAND ET SCHMITT
F 1905
Barriquand et Schmitt, Neuilly/Seine. Large 4-litre cars.

BARRON-VIALLE
F 1923–1929
Fabrique Alsaciene de Moteurs et Automobiles, Strasbourg (1923). Barron, Viale et Cie., Lyon (1924–1929). 2.1 and 3.2-litre cars.

BARROWS
USA 1895–1899
Charles H. Barrows, Willimantic, Connecticut (1896); New York, N.Y. (1897–1899). Built a tri-cycle and one wheel "mechanical horse."

BARSALEAUX
USA 1897
Joseph Barsaleaux, Sandy Hill, N.Y. Built in shape of a horse. Known also as "Motor Horse."

BART & KÖHLER
A 1920–1921
Cyclecar.

BARTHEL
USA 1903
Barthel Motor Co., Detroi, Michigan. One car built.

BARTHOLOMEW
USA 1901–1903
The Bartholomew Co., Peoria, Illinois. Runabout. Became "Glide."

BARTLETT
CDN 1914–1917
Canadian Bartlett Automobile Co. Ltd., Toronto, Ontario.

BARTLETT
USA 1921
National Brick Co., Chicago, Illinois.

BARTLETT ELECTRIC
USA 1915
F.C. Bartlett Co., Philadelphia, Pennsylvania.

BARTON
USA 1903
Barton Bolier Co., Chicago, Illinois. Two "special steam tonneau cars" built to order.

BARTOŠ
CS 1954
Ing. F. Bartoš, Ratočno pri Handlovej 250 cc Jawa motorcycle engine powered 2-wheeled car.

BARY
USA 1878
James B. Bary, Waverly, N.Y. One car produced.

BASCHIERI
I
Carlo Baschieri, Modena. A cycle fendered sports car with "Alfa Romeo" 6C 2500 engine.

BASF BUGGY
D 1969–1971

Badische Anilin-Soda Fabrik AG, Ludwigshafen. Dune buggy.

BASSE
D 1953
Karlheinz Basse, Koln. Minicar kit.

BASSETT
GB 1899–1901
Bassett Motor Syndicate, London. Light cars.

BASSON'S STAR
USA 1956
Basson's Industries Corp., Bronx, N.Y. Three-wheeled minicars with two-cycle, single cylinder engine.

BASTIN
B 1908–1909
Ateliers Bastin, Liege. Shaft-driven small cars.

BAT
GB 1904–1909
Bat Motor Manufacturing Co. Ltd., Penge, Surrey. Three-wheelers.

BATCHELDER & WRITNER
USA 1868
James S. Batchelder & William H. Writner, Manchester, New Hampshire. Steam car.

BATCHELOR
USA 1925
J.H. Batchelor, Savannah, Georgia.

BATEMAN
USA 1917
Bateman Mfg. Co., Grenlock, New Jersey. Company also produced "Frontmobile."

BATES
USA 1897
John W. Bates, Chicago, Illinois. Gasoline runabout.

BATES
USA 1903–1905
Bates & Edmunds Motor Co. Bates Automobile Co., Lansing, Michigan.

BATEUP
AUS 1939
The Australian Car Syndicate, Adelaide, S.A.

BATKAY
H c. 1903
Ernö Batkay, Miskolc. Light car.

BATTEN
USA 1911

Batten-Dayton Motor Co., Chicago, Illinois. Electric car.

BATTEN
GB 1935–1938
Beckenham Motor Co. Ltd., Beckenham, Kent.

BATTEY & CRICKLER
USA 1900
Battey & Crickler, Springfield, Massachusetts.

BATTIN
USA 1856
Joseph Battin. Steam car.

BATTLE
USA 1812
Mellen Battle, Herkimer, N.Y. Steam carriage.

BATTLESHIP
USA 1908
Zachow & Besserdich Automobile Co., Clintonville, Wisconsin. Became "FWD."

BAUCHET
F 1901–1903
SA des Moteurs H. Bauchet, Rethel/Ardennes. Light cars.

BAUDIER
F 1900–1901
G. Baudier, Paris. Voiturette.

BAUDOUIN
B
See "Dechamps."

BAUDUIN-RADIA
F
See "L'Automotrice."

BAUER
D c. 1928
Herman Bauer sen., Braunschweig. Three-wheeler.

BAUER
USA 1914
Bauer Machine Works, Kansas City, Missouri. Cyclecars. Succeeded "Gleason." Built standard cars 1915–1916.

BAUER STEAM
USA 1901
E.H. Bauer, Beaver Falls, Pennsylvania. Built steam cars with one lever control.

BAUGHAN
GB 1920–1929

Baughan Motors, Harrow, Middlesex (1920–1921); Stroud, Gloucestershire (1921–1929). Cyclecars.

BAUMAN
USA c. 1908
J.A. Bauman, Dillsburg, Pennsylvania. 5-passenger touring.

BAUR
D 1936–present
Karosserie Baur GmbH, Stuttgart. Convertibles for "BMW," "DKW," "Bitter," "Auto Union." Coachbuilders since 1910.

BAUROTH
USA 1899
Believed to be misspelling of "Blaurock."

B.A.W.
D 1923–1924
Bayrische Automobilwerk Act.-Ges., München.
See "Schuricht."

BAYARD, BAYARD-CLÉMENT
F
See "Clément-Bayard."

BAYER
USA 1905
Bayer Bros., Leavenworth, Kansas.

BAYERSDORFER
USA 1899
Otto Bayersdorfer, Omaha, Nebraska
See "Ottomobile." Both names apply to same vehicle.

BAYLEY
GB 1903–1904
See "Ailsa-Craig."

BAYLEY
GB
English Motor Car Co. Ltd., London.
See "Lipscomb."

BAYLIFF
USA 1982
Bayliff Coach Corp., Lima, Ohio. "Packard" replica.

BAYLISS-THOMAS
GB 1922–1929
Excelsior Motor Co. Ltd., Birmingham. Assembled light cars.

BAYMONT
USA 1955
Baymont Co., Redwood City, California. Electric 2-passenger small cars.

BAY STATE
USA 1896
Believed to be company name of Bay State Motive Power Co., Springfield, Massachusetts, not name of vehicle.
See "Walkins."

BAY STATE
USA 1900
Bay State Automobile & Engine Co., Boston, Massachusetts.

BAY STATE
USA 1906–1908
Bay State Automobile Co., Boston, Massachusetts. First car put on road January 1906. First car shown March 1907. Touring cars.

BAY STATE
USA 1922–1926
R.H. Long Motors Corp., Framingham, Massachusetts. Became Bay State Cars Inc. Creditors petitioned bankruptcy December 1923. 1,588 cars were made.

BAZ
CS 1982–1991
Bratislavské automobilové závody, Bratislava. Developmemts for "Škoda" and "Tatra." "Volkswagen" (D) assembling from 1991.

BBC
I 1948–1949
Pesaro.

BB BUCHMANN
D
See "Buchmann."

BBR
GB 1991–1993 ?
Brodie Britain Racing Ltd., Brackley, Northamptonshire. "Mazda" (J) based sports car.

B.C.K.
USA 1910–1911
B.C.K. Motor Co., Bath, N.Y. and York, Pennsylvania.
See "Kline Kar."

B.D.A.C.
USA 1904
Company name (Black Diamond Automobile Co.), not name of vehicle. Cars were produced under "Buckmobile" name.
See "Buckmobile"

BEACH
AUS 1914
Cyclecar.

BEACH
USA 1900
Beach Motor Vehicle Co., Everett, Massachusetts.

BEACHAM
GB 1996
Southward Garage, Retford. "Jaguar" Mk. II replicars.

BEACON
GB 1912–1914
Beacon Hill Motor Works (1912). Beacon Engineering Co., Hindhead, Surrey (1912–1913). Beacon Motors Ltd., Liphook, Surrey (1913–1914). Cyclecars.

BEACON
USA 1917
Morgan Potter Motor Co., Beacon, N.Y. Two built.

BEAMER
USA 1923
F.C. Beamer, Oakland, California. One car built for himself.

BEAN
GB 1919–1929
A.Harper, Sons & Bean Ltd. (1919–1926). Bean Cars Ltd., Tipton Dudley, Staffs. (1926–1929). Light cars and saloons.

BEAN
USA 1901
A.E. Bean Automobile Co., Boston, Massachusetts.

BEAN-CHAMBERLAIN
USA 1901–1902
See "Hudson Steamer."

BEARCAT
USA 1984
Sports car.
See "Blakely."

BEARDMORE
GB 1920–1928
W. Beardmore Motors Ltd., Glasgow. Touring cars.

BEARDSLEY
USA 1901–1902
Beardsley & Hubbs Mfg. Co., Shelby, Ohio. Company name, not name of a vehicle. Company produced "Darling."
See "Darling."

BEARDSLEY
USA 1914–1917
Beardsley Electric Co., Los Angeles, California (1914–1915); Culver City, California (1915–1917). Absorbed by Moreland Truck Co. Electric cars.

BEATRIX
F 1907
E. Tisserand, Paris. 6-cylinder monobloc engine.

BEAU BRUMMEL
USA 1917
Universal Car Equipment Co., Detroit, Michigan.

BEAU-CHAMBERLAIN
USA
See "Hudson."

BEAUFORD
GB 1986–1996 ?
Beauford Cars Ltd., Wigam, Lancs. Replicars.

BEAUFORT
D 1901–1906
Beaufort Motorenwerke, Baden. 1-, 2- and 4-cylinder cars.

BEAUMONT
F 1913
Beaumont & Cie., Paris. 1.7 and 2.7-litre engines.

BEAUMONT
CDN
See "Acadian."

BEAUVAIS
F 1922
F. Beauvais, Cambeuvelle. Prototype.

BEAVER
USA 1912–1920
Beaver State Motor Co., Portland, Oregon (1912–1915); Gresham, Oregon (1916–1920). Touring cars.

B.E.B.
D 1922–1923
Busse Elektromobilbau KG, Magdeburg. Electric cyclecar.

BECCARIA
I 1911–1916
Officine Meccaniche Beccaria, Torino.
See "Florio."

BÉCHEREAU
F 1924–1925
Louis Béchereau, Paris. Light cars.

BECK
F 1920–1922
Automobiles Beck, Lyon. Light cars.

BECK
USA 1895
W. Beck, Chicago, Illinois. Chicago Times-Herald Race entry.

BECK
USA 1991?
Beck Development, Upland, California. Sports car replica.

BECK & CLAUSEL
USA 1908
Beck & Clausel, Memphis, Tennessee Advance announcement February 1908.

BECKMANN
D 1900–1926
Otto Beckmann & Cie., Erste Schlesische Velociped- und Automobil-Fabrik, Breslau. Voiturettes and limousines.

BÉDÉLIA
F 1910–1925
Bourbeau et Devaux, Paris (1910–1915). Mahieux et Cie., Levallois-Perret (1920–1925). Cyclecars.

BEDFORD
GB 1904
Wilson Bros., Bedford. Three car types were built.

BEEBE
USA 1906–1907
Western Motor Truck & Vehicle Works, Chicago, Illinois. Offered both highwheel runabouts and conventional touring cars.

BEECH PLAINSMAN
USA 1948
Beech Aircraft Co., Wichita, Kansas. One-off prototype with air-cooled engine that drove an electric generator which powered electric motors placed in each wheel.

BEEDE
USA c. 1905
W.H. Beede, Lynn, Massachusetts. One car built for himself.

BEELEY
USA c. 1905
Henry A. Beeley, Ballardville, Massachusetts. 8-hp car built for himself.

BEEMAN
USA 1900
Ora Beeman, Valley City, North Dakota. 4-hp car.

BEESTON
GB 1899
Beeston Motor Cycle Co., Coventry, Warwickshire. Light cars.

BEETLE FLYER
USA 1909
Fodrea-Malott Mfg. Co., Noblesville, Indiana. Buggy-type built to order.

BEETTLE
USA 1968–1973
Beettle Auto Haus, Vancouver, Washington. Dune buggy kit car.

B.E.F.
D 1907–1913
Berliner Electromobil-Fabrik GmbH, Berlin. Electric three-wheelers.

BEGGS
USA 1918–1923
Beggs Motor Car Co., Kansas City, Missouri. Touring cars.

BÉGOT ET CAIL
F
See "Bégot et Mazurié."

BÉGOT ET MAZURIÉ
F 1900–1902
Bégot et Mazurié, Reims. Voiturettes.

BEHR
D 1907
Alfred Behr, Köthen. Three-wheeler.

BEISEL
USA 1914
Beisel Motorette Co., Monroe, Michigan. Cyclecars.

BEI-JING
PRC 1964–present
Dong Fang Hong Works, Peking. Beijing Jeep Corp. Ltd., Men Wai, Beijing (Peking).
See "Peking."

BEKKA
F 1907
Barclay et Knudsen, Paris. Chain-drive 12/16 and 18/24 hp cars.

B.E.L.
USA 1921–1922
Consolidated Motor Car Co. Inc., Middlefield, Connecticut; New London, Connecticut (1922).
See "Sterling" (1922–1923).

BELCAR
CH
See "Brütsch" (D).

BELCOURT
CDN 1866
Rev. G. Belcourt, Rustico, P.E.I. Steam car.

BELDEN
USA 1907–1911
Belden Automobile Co. (1907). Belden Motor Car C. (1908–1911), Pittsburgh, Pennsylvania. Company started in 1907. No production to 1909. Touring cars.

BELGA
B 1920–1921
Automobiles Belga, Marchienne-Zone. Light cars.

BELGA RISE
B 1929–1931
Sté. Belge des Automobiles Sizaire, Anvers.
See "Sizaire Fréres" (F/B).

BELGER & BOWKER
USA 1900
James E. Belger & Samuel Bowker, Natick, Massachusetts. Steam car to have been built in Francis Bigelow Factory.

BELGICA
B 1902–1909
Sté. des Automobiles Belgica, Saventem; Bruxelles. 1-, 4- and 6-cylinder cars.

BELKNAP
USA 1899
Believed to be company name of Belknap Motor Company, Portland, Maine, not name of a car.
See "Chapman" electric.

BELKNAP
USA 1907
Belknap Motor Co., Detroit, Michigan. Steam car. Changed to Michigan Steam Motor Co., Pontiac, Michigan 1907.

BELL
CDN 1917–1918
Barrie Carriage Co. Ltd., Barrie, Ontario. Assembled from U.S. parts.

BELL
F 1924–1925
Cyclecars Bell, Choisy-le-Roy/Seine. Three-wheelers.

BELL
GB 1905–1914
Bell Brothers, Ravensthorpe, Yorks. Solidly-built cars and taxicabs.

BELL
GB 1920
W.G. Bell, Rochester, Kent. Three-wheeler.

BELL
USA 1901
Carl Bell, Greencastle, Indiana.

BELL
USA 1907
Believed to be company name of W.L. Bell, Kansas City, Missouri. Not name of car.
  See "Croesus Jr."

BELL
USA 1916–1922
Bell Motor Car Co. Inc., York, Pennsylvania. Formerly "Sphinx."

BELLANGER
F 1912–1925
Sté. des Automobiles Bellanger Freres, Neuilly-sur-Seine. 2-, 2.6-, 3- and 6.3 litre cars.

BELLE
CH/GB 1901–1903
E.J. Coles & Co., London. Tonneau.

BELLEFONTAINE
USA 1900
Bellefontaine Carriage Body Co., Columbus, Ohio.

BELLEFONTAINE
USA 1908–1917
Bellefontaine Automobile Co., Bellefontaine, Ohio. 4-cylinder 32-hp cars.

BELLEFONTAINE-TIFFIN
USA 1916
Bellefontaine, Ohio. Believed to be "Bellefontaine."

BELLEFONTE
USA 1913
Bellefonte Automobile Mfg. Co., Bellefonte, Pennsylvania.

BELLIER
F 1976–1993 ?
Automobiles Bellier, Talmont-Saint-Hilaire. Minicars.

BELMOBILE
USA 1912
Bell Motor Car Co., Detroit, Michigan. 20 hp two-passenger roadster shown at 1912 Detroit Auto Show.

BELMONDO
I 1938
Vittorio Belmondo, Torino. Series of modifications to Fiat cars resulting in the Super Sport 1500.

BELMONT
USA 1909–1910
Belmont Automobile Co., New Rochelle, N.Y. (May 1909); Castleton, N.Y. (June 1909). Belmont Automobile Mfg. Co., New Haven, Connecticut (1910). Company organized May 1909. No records have been found after May 1910. Touring cars.

BELMONT
USA 1916
Belmont Electric Automobile Co., Wyandotte, Michigan Announcement March 1916 of gas-electric car.

BELMONT
USA 1917
Belmont Motor Car Co., Toledo, Ohio Advertised March 1917. 6-cylinder cars.

BELMONT
USA 1919–1922
Belmont Motor Co., Lewiston, Pennsylvania.

BEL-MOTORS
F 1976–1983
Minicars.
  See "Minoto," "Veloto."

BELSIZE
GB 1897–1925
Marshall & Co. (1897–1902). Belsize Motor & Engineering Co. Ltd. (1902–1906). Belsize Motors Ltd., Manchester (1906–1925). Touring cars.

BELT
USA 1904–1909
P.P. Belt, Fredonia, Kansas. One car built.

BELTRAME
I 1914
Casa Enrico Beltrame, Novara.

BELVIDERE
USA 1903–1906
National Sewing Machine Co., Belvidere, Illinois.
  See "Eldredge."

BEMIS
USA c. 1905
Robert Bemis, Chicopee, Massachusetts. 6 hp automobile.

BENDER & MARTINI
I 1899–1903
Torino. Cyclecars "Perfecta."

BENDER SPECIAL
USA 1919
Ahlberg Bearing Co., Chicago, Illinois. Sports roadster.

BENDIX
USA 1907–1910
Bendix Company, Chicago, Illinois. Company succeeded Triumph Motor Car Co. and built a line of air-cooled four-cylinder long wheelbase high-wheelers.

BENDIX
USA 1934
Bendix Automotive Development Center, Benton Harbor, Michigan. Streamlined sedan.

BENEDETTI
I 1900
Virginio Benedetti, Brescia.

BENELLI
I 1949–1952
Benelli SpA, Pesaro. Light car prototypes.

BENHAM
USA 1914
Benham Mfg. Co., Detroit, Michigan. Announced April 1914. Goodrich & Ditzler petitioned bankruptcy Fall 1914. Company dissolved March 1915. Formerly "S&M." Roadster.

BEN-HUR
USA 1917–1918
Ben-Hur Motor Co., Willoughby, Ohio. 35–40 cars produced.

BENJAMIN
F 1921–1931
Maurice Jeanson, Asnieres/Seine. Light cars.
  See "Benova."

BENNER
USA 1908–1909
Benner Motor Car Co., New York, N.Y. Company incorporated May 1908. First car finished October 1908. 150–200 units built.

BENNETT
CDN 1905
Essex, Ontario.

BENNETT
USA 1982
Bennett Motor Cars, Inc., Lakeland, Florida. Sports cars.
See "Alden."

BENNETT-BIRD
USA 1905
Bennett-Bird Co., Chicago, Illinois. Runabout.

BENNY-S
D c. 1985
Benny-S Design Team GmbH, Solingen. Tuning.

BENOIS ET DAMAS
F 1903–1904
Benois et Damas, Neuilly/Seine. Shaft-driven light cars.

BENOIT
USA 1902
J.B.A. Benoit, Benson, Minnesota. Motor buggy.

BENOVA
F
See "Benjamin."

BENSON
USA 1901
Andrew & John B. Benson, Chicago, Illinois. Runabout.

BENSON
USA 1901
Benson Automobile Co., Cleveland, Ohio. Steam car. Formerly Eastman Auto Co.

BENTALL
GB 1906–1913
E.H. Bentall & Co. Ltd., Maldon, Essex. About 100 touring cars were made.

BENTEL
USA 1901
Theo. F. Bentel Co., Pittsburgh, Pennsylvania.

BENTEL
USA 1916–1919
Geo. R. Bentel Co., Los Angeles, California.

BENTLEY
GB 1920–present
Bentley Motors Ltd., London (1920–1931). Bentley Motors (1931) Ltd., Derby (1933–1945). Rolls-Royce Motors Ltd., Bentley Motors Ltd., Crewe, Cheshire (1946–present). Luxury and sports cars.

BENTON
USA c. 1905
Samuel Benton, Salem, Massachusetts. 7 hp automobile.

BENTON
USA 1913
Benton Motor Car Co., Benton, Illinois.

BENTON HARBOR
USA 1895–1896
Baushke & Bros. (1895). Benton Harbor Motor Carriage Co. (1896), Benton Harbor, Michigan. Experimented with gasoline and electric vehicles.

BENTON-WINTON
USA 1920
The Benton Co., Los Angeles, California.

BENZ
D 1885–1926
Benz & Co., Rheinische Gasmotorenfabrik (1885–1899). Benz & Cie., Rheinische Gasmotorenfabrik AG (1899–1911). Benz & Cie., Rheinische Automobil- und Motorenfabrik AG, Mannheim (1911–1926). First workable motor car driven by an internal combustion engine. Touring and sports cars.

BENZ SÖHNE
D 1906–1926
C.Benz Söhne, Ladenburg/Neckar. 2.6- and 3.6-litre cars were most popular.

BENZ SPIRIT
USA 1900
The Columbus Automobile Co., Columbus, Ohio. A version of the German "Benz."

BÉRARD
F 1900–1901
Bérard et Cie., Marseilles. About 20 cars with 2-cylinder engines were made.

BERG
USA 1902–1906
Berg Automobile Co., Cleveland, Ohio (1902–1904). Became Worthington Automobile Co., New York, N.Y. Was an exact copy of "Panhard" (F). First car built for Berg by Cleveland Machine Screw Co.

BERG
USA 1920–1921
Berg Electric Car Company, New York, N.Y. Electric cars.

BERGANTIN
RA 1960–1962
Industrias Kaiser Argentina, Santa Isabel. Combination of the "Alfa Romeo" (I) sedan body and a "Willys" (USA) Jeep engine.

BERGDOLL
USA 1908–1914
Bergdoll Motor Car Co. (1908–1910). Louis J. Bergdoll Motor Co., Philadelphia, Pennsylvania (1911–1914). Bergdoll Automobile Co., Trenton, New Jersey (September 1914). 4-cylinder 30 and 40 hp cars.

BERGÉ
F 1923
G.Caillat, Pré St. Gervais/Seine. Light cars.

BERGER
CH 1970
Sports car prototype.

BERGER
D 1901–1902
Chemnitzer Motorwagenfabrik Bruno Berger & Co., Chemnitz. Cars built on Benz principles.

BERGER
USA 1899; 1909
Berger Mfg. Co., Canton, Ohio.

BERGERMOBILE
USA 1948
Berger Air-Turbine Car Co., Mount Vernon, N.Y. Converted "Chevrolet" with air tank and compressed-air turbine. Engine.

BERGHOLT
USA 1932
Fred Bergholt, Minneapolis, Minnesota. Elegant car used to publicize Bergholt's cosmetic business.

BERGMANN
D 1907–1922
Bergmann-Elektrizitäts-Werke AG, Berlin. Electric and gasoline cars.

BERGMANN
D 1894–1910
Bergmanns Industriewerke, Gaggenau.
See "SAF," "Liliput."

BERGMANN-MÉTALLURGIQUE
D
See "Bergmann."

BERGO
D 1924
Fahrzeug-Werk H. Ahlers & Berg, Kiel. Light cars.

BERGSTROM
USA c. 1901
Oscar Bergstrom, Minneapolis, Minnesota. Runabout.

BERKELEY
GB 1913
Light car.

BERKELEY
GB 1956–1961
Berkeley Cars Ltd., Biggleswade, Beds. Small sports cars.

BERKELEY
USA 1903–1904
J.H. Neustadt Co., St. Louis, Missouri.
See "Neustadt."

BERKSHIRE
USA 1904–1907; 1909–1913
Berkshire Motor Co. (1904). Berkshire Automobile Co. (1905–1907). Berkshire Motor Car Co. (1907). Berkshire Auto Car Co. (1909–1912). Berkshire Motors Co. (1912), Pittsfield, Massachusetts. Berkshire Motors Co. (1912). Belcher Engineering Co. (1912–1913), Cambridge, Massachusetts. Effects reported sold at auction May 1908. Reorganized early 1910. In financial trouble again November 1911. Touring cars.

BERLIET
F 1895–1939
Automobiles M. Berliet, Lyon. Touring and sports cars.

BERLIET
USA 1906–1908
American Locomotive Automobile Co., Providence, Rhode Island. Known only as "American Berliet." Succeeded 1909 by "Alco."

BERLINER MOTORWAGEN-FABRIK
D
See "BMF."

BERLO
USA 1900
Peter Berlo, Boston, Massachusetts. Two gasoline automobiles were built.

BERMAN
I 1998–to present
Stabilimenti Berman, San Benedetto Po. Tuning.

BERNA
CH 1902–1907
Joseph Wyss, Bern (1902–1904). J. Wyss, Schweizer Automobilfabrik Berna (1904–1906). Motorwerke Berna AG, Olten (1906–1907). Very few 1- and 4-cylinders cars were made. Berna concentrated on commercial vehicles.

BERNARDET
F 1946–1950
Automobiles Bernardet, Chatillon-sous-Bagneux/Seine. Light cars.

BERNARDI
I 1896–1901
Societa Italiana Bernardi, Padova. Light 3- and 4-wheelers.

BERNARDI
USA 1982
Sports car.
See "Blakely."

BERRENBERG
USA 1897
Motor mounted on wheel.

BERRET
F 1899–1903
Sté. Cannoise d'Automobiles, Cannes. Eight cars with 3-cylinder engines were made.

BERSEY
GB 1895–1899
W.C. Bersey, London. Electric cars.

BERTA
RA 1967–1972
Oreste Berta SA, Alta Gracia, Cordoba. Sports cars.

BERTELSON AEROMOBILE
USA 1959–1961
William R. Bertelson Mfg. Co., Neponset, Illinois.

BERTHIER
F
See "La Buire."

BERTOLDO
I 1908
Fratelli Bertoldo, Forno Rivara.
See "Marca Tre Spade."

BERTOLET
USA 1908–1912
Dr. J.M. Bertolet (1908). Bertolet Motor Car Co. (1909–1910), Reading, Pennsylvania. Model "X" sold with interchangeable 2- or 5-passenger convertible body.

BERTOLINI
I 1948–1950
Parma.

BERTONE
I 1950–present
Carrozzeria Bertone SpA, Grugliasco (Torino). Primarily a coachbuilder (since 1912), but built some cars in partnership with other producers.

BERTONI
I 1948
Lodi. Minicar, similar to "Volpe."
See "ALCA."

BERTRAND
F 1901–1902
Bertrand et Cie., Paris. Voiturettes.

BERTZCHY
USA 1909
A.J.P. Bertzchy, Council Bluffs, Iowa.

BERWICK
USA 1903
O.F. Ferris & Co., Elizabeth, New Jersey. One car completed.

BERWICK
USA 1904
Berwick Auto Car Co., Grand Rapids, Michigan. Electric cars.

BERWICK
USA 1917
Berwick Car Works, Mahanoy City, Pennsylvania.

BESKID
PL 1983–1987
Fabryka Samochodow Malolitrazowych, Bielsko-Biala. Small car prototypes with 594 cc, 703 cc and 1116 cc engines.

BESPOKE
GB 1968–1972
The Bespoke Buggy Co. Ltd., London. Dune buggy and sports cars.

BESSERDICH & ZACHOW
USA 1910
See "Zachow & Besserdich" 1908, Clintonville, Wisconsin. Both names apply to same company which built "Battleship."

BESST
AUS 1926–1927
May's Motor Works, Adelaide, S.A.

BEST
USA 1898–1900
Daniel Best Mfg. Co., San Leandro, California. Highwheeler. Only one built.

BEST
USA 1910
Best Motor Car Co., Indianapolis, Indiana.

BETHEL
USA c. 1918
Carlos O. Spaulding, Bethel, Vermont. 15 hp automobile for himself.

BETHLEHEM
USA 1907–1908
Bethlehem Automobile Co., South Bethlehem, Pennsylvania. First car announced November 1907.

BETHLEHEM
USA 1920
Bethlehem Motor Truck Corp., Allentown, Pennsylvania. Built for export.

BETTERIDGE
USA 1933
Billy Betteridge, Los Angeles, California. Sports cars.

BETTINA
BR 1967
Ten sports cars were built.

BETZ
USA 1902
Frank S. Betz & Co., Chicago, Illinois.

BEUTLER
CH 1983–1987
Carrosserie + Spritzwerk Beutler, Thun Sports car. Coachbuilders since 1948.

BEVERLEY-BARNES
GB 1924–1931
Lenaerts & Dolphens, London (1924–1928). Beverly Works Ltd., London (1928–1931). Expensive 4-litre cars were made.

BEVERLY
USA 1904–1905
Upton Machine Co., New York, N.Y. (1904). The Motor & Mfg. Works Co., Ithaca, N.Y. (1905). Tonneau.

BEYER
USA 1900
Beyer Brothers, Leavenworth, Kansas. Three-wheeler.

BEYSTER-DETROIT
USA 1910–1911
Beyster-Detroit Motor Car Co., Detroit, Michigan. Formerly Beyster-Thorpe Motor Co.

B.F.
D 1922–1926
Bolle-Fiedler Automobilwerk GmbH, Berlin. Light sports cars.

B.F.G.
USA 1946
F. Goodrich Co., Akron, Ohio. Composite test vehicle.

B.G.S.
F 1899–1906
Sté. de la Voiture Bouquet, Garcin et Schivre, Neuilly/Seine. Electric cars.

BIANCHI
I 1899–1939; 1957–1981
Edoardo Bianchi (1899–1905). Fabbrica Automobili e Velocipedi Edoardo Bianchi (1905–1939). Autobianchi SpA (1957–1968). Fiat SpA, Sezione Autobianchi, Milano (1968–1981). Passenger and sports cars.

BIASCHI
I 1949
Pistoia.

BI-AUTOGO
USA 1908–1912
James Scripps Booth, Detroit, Michigan. Two-wheel experimental car with V-8 engine. Took 4 years to build.

BIBBS
USA 1904
Bibbs Engineering Co., New York, N.Y.
See "Gibbs."

BIBLEX
D 1925
Three-wheeler.

BI-CAR
USA 1912
Detroit Bi-Car Co., Detroit, Michigan.

BI-CAR
USA 1914
W.H. Fauber, Elgin, Illinois.
See "Fauber Bi-Car."

BIDDLE
USA 1902
Biddle Manufacturing Co., Knoxville, Tennessee. One prototype built.

BIDDLE
USA 1915–1922
Biddle Motor Car Co., Philadelphia, Pennsylvania. Moved to New York 1919. Became Biddle-Crane Motor Co. 1921.

BIDDLE-CRANE
USA 1921–1923
Biddle-Crane Motor Car Co., New York, N.Y. Limited production by November 1921. Chassis built in New York, then shipped to Baker-Rauch and Lang, Cleveland, Ohio for bodies.

BIEBER
D 1981–1993
Buggy-Center Bieber KG, Borken, Wuppertal. Dune buggy and replica.

BIELKA
SU 1956
IMZ-NAMI, Irbitskii Motocikletnii Zavod, Sverdlovsk. Minicar prototypes.

BIENE
D 1923
Automobilfabrik Curt Zimmermann, Berlin. Cyclecar.

BIFORT
GB 1914–1915
Bifort Motor Co., Fareham, Hampshire. Light cars.

BIG BROWN LUVERNE
USA 1909
Luverne Automobile Co., Luverne, Minnesota.
See "Luverne."

BIGNAN
F 1918–1930
Automobiles Bignan, Courbevoie/Seine. Touring and sports cars.

BIJOU
GB 1901–1904
Protector Lamp & Lighting Co. Ltd., Manchester. 5 hp light cars.

BIJ'T VUUR
NL 1902–1905
C. Bij't Vuur, Arnhem. 4-seater tonneau.

BILLARD
F 1922–1925
E. Billard, Villeneuve-le-Guyard/Yonne. Cyclecars.

BILLIKEN
USA 1914

Billiken Cyclecar Co., Green Bay, Wisconsin. Cyclecars.

BILLINGS
GB 1900
E.D. Billings, Coventry, Warwickshire Voiturette.

BILLINGS STEAMER
USA 1900; 1905
Billings & Spencer Co., Hartford, Connecticut. Experimental steam car. Patents sold to American Bicycle Co., Toledo, Ohio. Believed to be the basis of "Toledo Steamer."

BILLY FOUR
USA 1909–1910
McNabb Iron Works, Atlanta, Georgia. Roadsters.

BIMBO
I
See "Volugrafo."

BIMEL
USA 1916–1917
Bimel Buggy Co., Sydney, Ohio. Formerly "Elco."

BIMOBILE-PIAF
F 1950–1952
Sté. Industrielle de Livry, Paris. Small car.
See "Atlas" and "Kover."

BINATE
USA 1902
Engines built by Coffee & Sons and sold by C.E. Miller, New York, N.Y. Did not built vehicles.
See "Coffee."

BINGHAM
NL 1908
S. Bingham & Co., Rotterdam.
See "Autolette."

BINGHAMTON
USA c. 1900
Binghamton Gas Engine Co., Binghamton, N.Y.

BINGMAN
USA 1912
G.Bingman & Son, Detroit, Michigan.

BINNEY & BURNHAM
USA 1902
Binney & Burnham, Boston, Massachusetts. Cars built to customer's special order.

BIOTA
GB 1968–1976
Houghton Coldwell Ltd., Thurcroft, Yorks. (1968–1970). Biota Products Ltd., Dinnington, Yorks. (1970–1976). "Mini" based sports cars. About 30 were built.

BIRCH
USA 1899
James H. Birch, Burlington, New Jersey. Few cars were produced.

BIRCH
USA 1917–1922
Birch Motor Corp. Birch Motor Cars Inc. (1921–1922). Birch Motor Cars, Chicago, Illinois. Mail order touring cars.

BIRD
USA 1895–1897
Henry R. Bird, Buffalo, N.Y. A friction drive, kerosene-fueled Chicago Times-Herald Race entry, 1895. Four cars were built.

BIRD
USA 1911
Bird Automobile Co., New York, N.Y.

BIRMINGHAM
USA 1903
Birmingham Electric & Mfg. Co., Birmingham, Alabama. Electric car.

BIRMINGHAM
USA 1921–1922
Birmingham No-Axle Motor Co., Jamestown, N.Y. Affiliated with Parker Motor Car Mfg. Co., Montreal, Quebec, Canada. Fraud charged 1922. Continental-engined six-cylinder cars.

BIRMINGHAM FLEXIBLE
CDN 1922
Birmingham Motors Corp., Peterborough, Ontario.

BISCUTER
E 1951–1958
Autonacional SA, Barcelona. Small cars.

BISHOP
GB 1925
Bishop's Garages Ltd., Brighton, Sussex. Sports cars.

BISHOP
USA 1910
Charles Bishop, Fargo, North Dakota. Highwheeler.

BISON
USA 1904
Bison Motor Co., Buffalo, N.Y. Prototype only.

BISSELL
USA 1909
Bissell Electric Co., Toledo, Ohio. Electric cars.

BITTER
D 1971–present
Erich Bitter, Schwelm/Westfalen. Bitter Automobile GmbH & Co. KG, Gevelsberg; Altweilnau. Luxury sports cars.

BIZZARINI
I 1962–1969
Societa Autostar Motori (1962–1964). Societa Prototipi Bizzarini (1964–1966). Bizzarini SpA, Livorno (1966–1969). High-performance sports cars.

BIZZARINI
USA 1994–1997
Watkins Racing, Tustin, California. Sports cars designed by Giotto Bizzarini (I).

BJELLA
USA 1905–1906
McIntosh Iron & Wood Works, McIntosh, Minnesota. One car produced.

BJERING
N 1918–1920
H.C. Bjering, Gjövik. A/S Raufoss Ammunisjonfabrikker, Raufoss. 2 cars with aluminium body and rear-placed engine were built.

BLACK
USA 1897–1900
H. Black Mfg. Co., Indianapolis, Indiana. Runabouts. Some references claim one car built 1893.

BLACK
USA 1902
Seth C. Black, W. Chester, Pennsylvania. Steam car.

BLACK
USA 1906–1909
Black Manufacturing Co., Chicago, Illinois. Highwheelers. Two models (10 and 14 hp) succeeded by "Black Crow."

BLACK BARON
E 1994–1997
Systema Espana Black Baron, Altea, Alicante. Replicars.

BLACKBURN
GB 1919–1925
Blackburn Aeroplane & Motor Co. Ltd., Leeds, Yorks. 3.2-litre conservative cars.

BLACKBURN
USA 1920–1921
Blackburn Automotive Company, Houston, Texas. An attempt to make a better Model T "Ford."

BLACK CROW
USA 1910–1911
Black Manufacturing Co., Chicago, Illinois (1910). Crow Motor Car Co., Elkhart, Indiana (1911). Built 5 models of conventional cars and 2 highwheel models. Succeeded by "Crow."

BLACK DIAMOND
USA 1904–1905
Company name of Black Diamond Automobile Co., Utica, N.Y., not name of automobile.
See "Buckmobile."

BLACKHAWK
USA 1903
Clark Mfg. Co., Moline, Illinois. Runabout.

BLACK HAWK
USA 1929–1930
Stutz Motor Car Co. of America, Blackhawk Division, Indianapolis, Indiana. A lower-priced companion to "Stutz." 1590 cars were made.
See "Stutz."

BLACKISTON
USA 1912
G.P. Blackiston, Canton, Ohio. Experimental runabout.

BLACK MOTOR BUGGY
USA 1909
Black Mfg. Co., Chicago, Illinois. Highwheeler.
See "Black" highwheeler.

BLACK PRINCE
GB 1920
Black Prince Motors Ltd., Barnard Castle, Co. Durham. Very light cyclecars.

BLACKSTONE
USA 1916
Blackstone Motor Co., Momence, Illinois.

BLAIR
USA 1906
Blair Light Co., Northboro, Massachusetts. Steam car. Claimed to be entirely automatic in operation, no fuel or air pumps needed.

BLAISDELL
USA 1903
P. Blaisdell & Co., Brooklyn, N.Y. Steam cars.

BLAKE
GB 1900–1903
F.C. Blake & Co., London (1900–1901); Kew, Surrey (1901–1903). Vis-à-vis and tonneau with 2- and 4-cylinder engines.

BLAKE
USA 1901
James E. Blake, Attleboro, Massachusetts. One gasoline automobile was made.

BLAKELY
USA 1902
Edward B. Blakely, Newport, Rhode Island. Electric car.

BLAKELY
USA 1975–1984 ?
Blakely Automotive Works, Inc., Davis Junction, Illinois; Princeton, Wisconsin. Replica.
See "Bernardi," "Bearcat," "Bantam."

BLAKESLEE
USA 1906–1907
Blakeslee Electric Vehicle Co., Cleveland, Ohio.
See "De Mars."

BLANC & TREZZA
I 1922–1924
Milano.

BLANCHARD
USA 1826
Thomas Blanchard, Springfield, Massachusetts. Steam car.

BLANCHARD
USA c. 1905
Clarence B. Blanchard, Usbridge, Massachusetts. 5 hp automobile for himself.

BLANK & SCHREIBER
USA 1914
R.H. Blank & G. Schreiber, Walcott, Iowa. Cyclecar.

BLATTA
I 1953
Modified Fiat 750 Special.

BLAUROCK
USA 1899–1900
& F.W. Blaurock, Blaurock Carriage Co., New York, N.Y.

BLEICHERT
D 1936–1939
Bleichert Transportanlagen GmbH, Leipzig. Electric cars.

BLÉRIOT
F 1921–1922
Blériot Aéronautique, Suresnes, Seine. Cyclecars.

BLERIOT-WHIPPET
GB 1920–1927
Air Navigation & Engineering Co. Ltd., Addlestone, Surrey. Two-seaters.

BLEVNEY
USA 1901
John C. Blevney, Newar, New Jersey. One steamer built.

BLIMLINE
USA 1898–1899
Sebastian Blimline, Sinking Springs, Pennsylvania. Gasoline carriage.

BLISS
USA 1901–1902
H. Bliss & Son, Bliss Chainless Automobile Co., North Attleboro, Massachusetts. Steam car.

BLISS
USA 1906
W. Bliss & Co., Bliss Engineering Co., Brooklyn, N.Y.

B.L.M.
USA 1906–1907
B.L.M. Motor Car & Equipment Co. B.L.M. Motor Car Co., Brrooklyn, N.Y. (Breese, Lawrence and Moulton). Some assets to be sold announced April 1908. Sports cars.

BLOCK BROS.
USA 1905
Believed to be misspelling of "Blood Bros."

BLODGETT
USA 1921
Blodgett Engineering & Tool Co., Detroit, Michigan. Touring cars.

BLOMSTROM
USA 1897; 1899; 1902–1903
H. Blomstrom, Detroit, Michigan. One car in 1897, one in 1899, 25 cars 1902–1903. Became "Queen."

BLOMSTROM
USA 1907–1909
Charles Blomstrom Co., Adrian, Michigan. Later C.H. Blomstrom joined "Frontmobile."
See "Gyroscope."

BLOMSTROM QUEEN
USA 1902–1907
H. Blomstrom Motor Co., Detroit, Michigan. Known only as "Queen."

BLOOD
USA 1900
Blood & Co., Minneapolis, Minnesota.

BLOOD
USA 1901–1915
Kalamazoo Cycle Co. (1901–1902). Blood Brothers (1902–1905). Blood Brothers Auto & Machine Co. (1905), Kalamazoo, Michigan. Also known as "Kalamazoo" 1901–1902.

BLOOD
USA 1913
Blood Bros. Machine Co., Kalamazoo, Michigan. Cyclecars. Also built "Cornelian."

BLOOM
USA 1914
A.J. Bloom, Detroit, Michigan. Cyclecar prototype.

BLOVSKÝ
CS 1920
J. Blovský, Praha. Light car.

BLUE
USA 1910
True Blue Motor Co., Detroit, Michigan.
See "True Blue."

BLUE & GOLD
USA 1910–1913
Automobile Co., Sacramento, California. 4- and 6-cylinder models.

BLUEBIRD
USA 1910
Bluebird Motor Cab Company, New Rochelle, N.Y.

BLUFF CLIMBER
USA 1901–1902
Neustadt-Perry Co., St. Louis, Missouri. Steam cars.

BLUMBERG
USA 1915–1922
Blumberg Co., San Antonio and Orange, Texas. Touring cars.

BMA
I 1972–1985
BMA SpA, Ravenna. Three-wheeled minicars.

B.M.A. HAZELCAR
GB 1952–1957
Battery Manufacturing Associates, Hove, Sussex (1952). B.M.A. & Electrical Equipment Co., Hove, in conjunction with Hazeldine Motors, Telscombe Cliffs, Sussex (1952–1953) Gates & Pearson Ltd., Hove, Sussex (1952–1953). Electric Motors (Hove) Ltd., Hove, Sussex (1954–1957). Electric cars.

BMC
CH c. 1986
BMC AG, Zürich. Luxury 4 × 4 cars.

B.M.C.
USA 1952
British Motor Car Co., San Francisco, California. English "Singer" chassis with U.S. built body.

B.M.F.
D 1904–1907
Berliner Motorwagen-Fabrik GmbH, vorm. Gottschalk & Co., Berlin. Passenger cars and taxicabs.

BMW
D 1928–present
Bayerische Motoren-Werke, Eisenach, München (1928–1939). Bayerische Motore-Werke AG, München (1952–to date). Passenger and sports cars.

B.M.W.
USA 1949–1966
Boulevard Machine Works, Los Angeles, California. Electric cars.

B.N.
I 1924–1925
Bianchi e Negro, Torino. Cyclecar.

B.N.C.
F 1923–1931
Bollack, Netter et Cie., Levallois-Perret/Seine. Sports cars.

BOA
USA 1978
Boa Marketing Corporation, Ventura, California. Sports cars.

BOB
E 1920–1925
Bob Automobil-Gesellschaft Carpzow & Wachsmann, Berlin (1920–1921). Bob Automobil-GmbH, Berlin (1921–1922). Bob Automobil AG, Berlin (1922–1925). Light sports cars.

BOBBI-KAR
USA 1945–1947
Bobbi Motor Car Corp., San Diego, California. Purchased 1946 by Dixie Motor Car Co., Birmingham, Alabama. Two-passenger roadsters. Became Keller Motors Corp., 1947.
See "Keller."

BOBBY-ALBA
F 1920–1924
Lucien Bollack, Paris. Light cars.

BOB CAT
USA 1922–1925
MacDonald Steam Automobile Corp., Garfield, Ohio. Steam car.
See "MacDonald" steam. Name for "MacDonald" roadster.

BOBSY
USA 1962–1974?
W. Smith Engineering Co., Medina, Ohio. Small sports and racing cars.

BOCAR
USA 1958–1960
Bocar Racing Car Co., Denver, Colorado. About 100 sports cars were made.

BOCHARDING
D 1925
Bocharding GmbH, Berlin. Three-wheeler.

BOCK & HOLLENDER
A 1899–1910
Bock & Hollender, Wien. Voiturettes.

BOES
D 1903–1906
Jacob Boes & Co., Berlin. Taxicabs and sports cars.

BOESSENKOOL
NL 1910
Boessenkool, Almelo.

BOHANNA STABLES
GB 1972–?
R. Stables, Cadmore End, High

Wycombe, Bucks. Fiberglass bodied sports cars.

BÖHLER
D 1947
Ing. Böhler, Riedlingen. Minicar prototype.

BÖHM + KELLENERS
D c. 1985
Böhm + Kelleners GmbH, Dinslaken. Tuning.

BOHNET
USA 1901
George J. Bohnet, Bohnet Motor Car Co., Lansing, Michigan. Two steam cars produced.

BOHSE
D 1988–1993
Bohse Automobilbau GmbH, Dörpen/Ems. "Lada" (SU) based convertible.

BOISSAYE
F 1904
Automobiles Boyssaie, Paris. Shaft-driven light cars.

BOISSELOT
USA 1901
Boisselot Automobile & Special Gasoline Motor Co., Jersey City, New Jersey. Built one three-wheeler for show purposes.

BOITEL
F 1938–1949
Automobiles Boitel, Paris. Minicars.

BOLD CITY
USA 1990s
Bold City Motors, Jacksonville, Florida. Kit cars.

BOLENDER
USA 1914
F.P. Bolender, Dayton, Ohio. Cyclecars.

BOLER
GB 1971–?
Boler Engineering Ltd., Oldham, Lancs. Fun cars using "Ford" components.

BOLIDE
B 1900–1902
Bolide et Cie., Verviers.

BOLIDE
F 1899–1907
Léon Lefebvre et Cie., Paris (1899–1905). Sté. l'Auto-Réparation, Paris (1905–1907). 12-litre horizontal engine.

BOLIDE
USA 1970
Bolide Motor Car Corp., Huntington, N.Y. Two prototype cars: A Can-Am type street car with "Ford" power and a two-passenger electric shopper.

BOLLÉE
F 1872; 1878; 1880–1881
Amedée Bollée, Le Mans. Steam cars named "Obeissante," "Mancelle," "La Nouvelle" and "Rapide."

BOLLEE
USA 1904
Bollee is the wrong name for the "Worthington" Bollee by Worthington Automobile Company, New York, N.Y.
See "Berg" and "Meteor."

BOLLE & FIEDLER
D 1924–1926
Bolle & Fiedler Motorenfabrik, Berlin. Sports cars.

BOLSOVER
GB 1907–1909
Bolsover Bros., Eaglescliffe, Co. Durham. Steam cars.

BOLTE
USA 1900
Thomas H. Bolte, Kearney, Nebraska. Gasoline runabout.

BOLWELL
AUS 1963–1985
Bolwell Cars Pty Ltd., Mordillac, Victoria.
See "Ikara."

BOMBARDIER
USA 1996–present
Bombardier Co., Peachtree City, Georgia. Electric cars.

BONACINI
I 1898
Ciro Bonacini, Modena.
See "Neri & Bonacini."

BON-CAR
GB 1905–1907
Edinburgh & Leith Engineering Co., Leith. Steam cars.

BOND
GB 1922–1928
F.W. Bond & Co., Brighouse, Yorks. Touring cars.

BOND
GB 1948; 1961
Bond Aircraft & Engineering Co. (Blackpool) Ltd., Longridge, Lancs. Front-wheel drive small sports cars.

BOND
GB 1949–1974
Sharps Commercials Ltd., Preston, Lancs. (1949–1964). Bond Cars Ltd., Preston, Lancs. (1965–1970). Reliant Motor Co. Ltd., Tamworth, Staffs. (1971–1974). Three-wheelers and sports cars.

BONESCHI
I 1958–c. 1987
Carrozzeria Boneschi, Cambiago (Milano). "Fiat" Panda based sports cars.

BONIQUET
E
See "J.B.R."

BONNER
USA 1908
C.E. Bonner Mfg. Co., Chrisman, Illinois.

BONNEVILLE
F 1897–1900
L. Bonneville, Toulouse. Voiturettes.

BOON DOCKER
USA 1968–c. 1973
Boon Docker Buggies, Bellflower, California. Dune buggy.

BOOTH-CROUCH
USA 1896
Pierce & Crouch Engine Co., New Brighton, Pennsylvania. One one-cylinder vehicle was built for Dr. Carlos C. Booth.

BORBEIN
USA 1904–1910
H.F. Borbein Co. (1904–1907). Borbein Automobile Co. (1907–1910), St. Louis, Missouri. Complete cars were offered less engine. Borbein succeeded "Brecht." Runabout.

BORBET
D 1991
Borbet Leichtmetallräder, Hallenberg-Hesborn. Sports car prototype.

BORCHARDING
D 1925
Borcharding & Co. GmbH, Berlin. Three-wheeler.

BORDEREL-CAIL
F 1905–1908
Sté. Cail, Denain/Nord. 6-wheel cars.

BORDINO
I 1854
Virginio Bordino, Firenze.

BORGWARD
D 1939–1961
Carl F.W. Borgward Automobil- und Motoren-Werke (1939–1949). Carl F.W. Borgward GmbH (1949–1961). Borgward-Werke AG, Bremen (1961). Passenger and sports cars.

BORGWARD
D c. 1983
Müller-Buchhof, München. "Borgward" (D) Isabella replica.

BORGWARD
MEX 1967–c. 1973
Fabrica Nacional de Automóviles S.A., Monterrey. Made cars under German license.

BORITTIER
F 1899
Mayet, Sarthe. Voiturette.

BORLAND
USA 1910–1914
Ideal Electric Vehicle Co. Borland-Grannis Co. (1912–1913), Chicago, Illinois. American Electric Car Co. (1914), Saginaw, Michigan. Electric cars.

BORLAND
USA 1913
H.W. Borland, Dunseith, North Dakota. Highwheelers.

BORNTRAEGER
USA 1931–1933
Edward A. Borntraeger, Chicago, Illinois. Sports cars.

BOROUGH & BLOOD
USA 1908
Borough & Blood Buggy Company, Marshall, Michigan. Highwheelers.

BORY
H c. 1904
József Bory, Székesfehérvár. Experimental car.

BOSCHERT
D 1990–present
Boschert Automobile GmbH, Emmendingen. Tuning.

BOSCHETTI
F 1991
Michel Boschetti, Gorbio. Replica.

BOSS
USA 1897–1909
Boss Knitting Machine Works, Reading, Pennsylvania. Steam car.

BOSS
USA 1904–1905
Long Crawford Automobile Co., Massilon, Ohio.

B.O.S.S.
USA 1911
B.O.S.S. Company, Detroit, Michigan. Touring cars.

BOSTON
USA 1899
Boston Automobile Mfg. Co., Boston, Massachusetts.

BOSTON
USA 1900
Boston Automobile Co., Bar Harbor, Maine. Steam car.

BOSTON-AMESBURY
USA 1902–1903
Boston-Amesbury Mfg. Co., Amesbury, Massachusetts.

BOSTON ELECTRIC
USA 1907
Concord Motor Car Co., Concord, Massachusetts.

BOSTON HAYNES-APPERSON
USA 1898
Boston Haynes-Apperson Co., Boston, Massachusetts.

BOSTON HIGH WHEEL
USA 1908
Bost Highwheel Auto Mfg. Co., Boston, Massachusetts.

BOSWORTH
USA 1903–1904
Frank C. Bosworth, Saugus, Massachusetts. Steam surrey.

BOTTEGA
I 1950
Giovanni Bottega. Sports cars.

BOTTO
I 1836
Giuseppe Dominico Botto, Torino. Electric car.

BOUHEY
F 1898–1902
Sté. des Usines Bouhey, Paris. Electric cars.

BOULET
F 1902–1903
Boulet et Cie, Paris. Light quadricycle.

BOUND
GB 1920
Bound Brothers, Southampton, Hampshire. Small monocars.

BOURASSA
CDN 1899–1926
H.E. Bourassa, Montreal, Quebec. Runabouts and 6-cylinder tourers.

BOUR-DAVIS
USA 1915–1922
Bour-Davis Motor Car Co., Detroit, Michigan. 1917 absorbed with "Frankfort" into Shadbourne Bros., Frankfort, Indiana. Bour-Davis reorganized as Louisiana Motor Car Co., Shreveport, Louisiana, 1919. 1509 cars made. 1923 became "Ponder."

BOURGEOIS-MAGNIN
F 1920
Bourgeois et Magnin, Macon/Saone-et-Loire. 6-passenger cars.

BOURGUIGNONNE
F 1899–1901
Chesnay, de Falletans et Cie., Dijon. Voiturette.

BOURNONVILLE
USA 1914
Bournonville Motors Co., Hoboken, New Jersey.

BOURNONVILLE
USA 1922–1923
The Bournonville Rotary Valve Motor Co., Hoboken, New Jersey.
See "Rotary" 1922–1923. Both names apply to same vehicle.

BOURSAUD
F 1897–1899
Usines Boursaud, Baignes/Charente. Small rear-engined cars.

BOUTON
USA 1902–1903
Bouton Automobile Company, Rumford Falls, Maine. Simple motorized buggy.

BOVY
B 1908–1914
Ateliers de Construction Albert Bovy, Bruxelles. 2-cylinder landaulets.

BOWEN
GB 1905–1906
J. Bowen, Didsbury, Manchester. Light 2-seater.

BOWEN
GB 1906–1908
Bowen & Co., London. Light 2-seater.

BOWEN
USA 1901
George B. Bowen, Buffalo, N.Y. Gasoline carriage.

BOWKER
USA 1900
Bowker Automobile & Machine Co., Portland, Maine.
See "Belger & Bowker."

BOWLING GREEN
USA 1911–1915
Bowling Green Motor Car Co., Bowling Green, Ohio.

BOWMAN
USA 1895
E.W. Bowman, Evanston, Illinois.

BOWMAN
USA 1900
John & Paul Bowman, Bellefontaine, Ohio. Advance announcement. 2 cars built.

BOWMAN
USA 1902
Bowman Automobile Co., New York, N.Y. Roadster.

BOWMAN
USA 1921–1922
Bowman Motor Car Co., Covington, Kentucky. 27 hp cars.

BOWSER
GB 1922–1923
G. Bowser, Leeds, Yorks. Light cars.

BOW-V-CAR
GB 1922–1923
The Plycar Co. Ltd., London (1922); Luton, Beds. (1922–1923). Chain-driven two-seater.

BOYD
USA 1915
Neustadt Auto & Supply Co., St. Louis, Missouri. Three four-wheel-drive cars built for H.M. Boyd.

BOYDEN
USA 1908
Charles Boyden, Grand Haven, Michigan. 30 hp car prototype.

BOYER
F 1898–1906
Boyer et Cie., Suresnes/Seine; Puteaux/Seine. Voiturette and 12 hp phaeton.

BOYNTON
USA 1922
Arthur Boynton Corp., Albany, N.Y.
See "A.B.C." Both names apply to same vehicle.

BOŽEK
A/CS 1815–1817
Josef Božek, Praha. First steam car in Central Europe.

BOZIER
F 1906–1920
Voiturettes Bozier, Puteaux/Seine.

B.P.D.
GB 1913
Brown, Paine and Dowland Ltd., Shoreham, Sussex. Belt-driven cyclecars.

BP QUIET ACHIEVER
AUS 1983
Experimental solarmobile.

BRA
GB 1978–present
B.R.A. Motor Works, Flint, Flintshire. Three-wheeled kit cars.

BRA
GB 1984–c. 1986
Beriba Replica Automobiles Ltd., Castle Dinnington, Derby. Replicars.

BRABUS
D 1984–present
Brabus Autosport GmbH, Bottrop. Tuning

BRADBURY
GB 1901–1902
Bradbury Bros., Croydon, Surrey. Voiturettes.

BRADDON
USA 1919
Braddon Motors Co., Downers Grove, Illinois. Listed in 1919 Standard Automobile Electric Manual.

BRADFIELD
USA 1929–1930
Bradfield Motors, Inc., Chicago, Illinois. Taxicabs.

BRADFORD
GB 1946–1954
Jowett Cars Ltd., Bradford, Yorkshire.

BRADFORD
USA 1901
William H. Bradford, Lenox, Massachusetts.

BRADFORD
USA 1904–1905
Bradford Motor Works, Bradford, Pennsylvania. An unassembled car for $277.50. Used leftover "Holley" parts.

BRADFORD
USA 1919–1920
Consolidated Motor Car Co., Bradford, Connecticut. Bradford Motor Car Co., Haverhill, Massachusetts.

BRADFORD
USA 1982
Bradford Coach Works, Ft. Lauderdale, Florida. Sports cars.

BRADFORD CYCLECAR
USA 1914
Cyclecar Co. of Delaware, Wilmington, Delaware.

BRADLEY
USA 1895
Wheeler & Co., Kansas City, Missouri.

BRADLEY
USA 1900
Hiram T. Bradley, Oakland, California.

BRADLEY
USA 1920–1924
Bradley Motor Car Co., Cicero, Illinois.

BRADLEY
USA 1971–1978
Bradley Automotive, Minneapolis, Minnesota. Sports car. About 2000 cars built in 1974.

BRADWELL
GB 1914
Bradwell & Co., Folkestone, Kent. Single-seater cyclecars.

BRAGER
USA 1902
Albert Brager, Aneta, North Dakota.

BRAMHAM
GB
See "Stanhope."

BRAMWELL
USA 1900; 1902–1905
Bramwell Motor Co., Boston, Massachusetts. One carriage built 1900 to test engine. Succeeded 1904 by Springfield Automobile Co., Springfield, Massachusetts.

BRAMWELL
USA 1904–1905
Springfield Automobile Co., Springfield, Ohio. Formerly "Springfield." Runabouts.

BRAMWELL-ROBINSON
USA 1899–1902
Bramwell-Robinson Co., Hyde Park, Massachusetts. Three-wheelers.

BRANCA
I 1953–1972
Aquilino Branca, Buscate. Sports and racing cars.

BRANDOLI
I 1950–1953
Marino Brandoli. Sports and racing cars.

BRANDON
USA 1911–1912
Commercial Motor Car Co., Houston, Texas. Report made September 1911 of a front wheel drive car being manufactured.

BRANDT
F 1948
Paris. 4-cylinder engine with opposite pistons.

BRANICK
USA 1908
Earl Branick, Fargo, North Dakota. Sports car.

BRASIE
USA 1914–1916
Brasie Motor Truck Co., Brasie Motor Car Co., Minneapolis, Minnesota. Became Packett Motor Truck Co. March 1916. 4-cylinder 12 hp roadsters.

BRASIER
F 1897–1930
Incl. Georges Richard (1897–1903); Richard-Brasier (1903–1904); Chaigneau-Brasier (1927–1930). Société des Anciens Établissements Georges Richard (1897–1905). Société des Automobiles Brasier (1905–1926). Société Chaigneau-Brasier, Ivry-Port (1926–1930). Touring and sports cars.

BRASINCA
BR
See "Uirapuru."

BRAUKS
USA 1898–1927
George S. Brauks, St. Louis, Missouri Seven cars built 1898–1927.

BRAUN
A 1899–1910
August Braun, Erste Osterreichische Motorfahrzeugfabrik, Wien (1899–1901). August Braun & Co., Wien (1901–1910). Voiturettes and touring cars.

BRAUN
D 1910–1912
Justus Christian Braun, Premier-Werke, Nürnberg.

BRAVO
F 1900
N.H. Bravo, Clichy/Seine. Six-seater waggonette.

BRAVO
D 1921
Union-Kleinauto-Werke, Mannheim. Small cars.
See "Rabag."

BRAY
USA 1897
James B. Bray, Waverly, N.Y. One unit built for builder's own use.

BRAYTON
USA 1856
George B. Brayton, East Greenwich, Rhode Island. Steam car.

BRAZIER
USA 1902–1903
H. Bartol Brazier, Philadelphia, Pennsylvania. Cars built to special order only.

BRECHT
USA 1901–1903
Brecht Automobile Co., St. Louis, Missouri. Retired from automobile business. Business taken over by H.F. Borbein & Co. Steam and electric runabouts.

BREER
USA 1902
Carl Breer, Los Angeles, California. Runabout.

BREESE
F 1911
Robert Breese, Paris. Light sporting cars.

BREESE & LAWRENCE
USA 1905
Breese & Lawrence, Southampton, Long Island, N.Y. Became B.L.M., 1906.

BREEZE
USA 1910
Jewel Carriage Co., Cincinnati, Ohio. Auto-buggy.

BRÉGUET
F 1907; 1942
Ateliers Bréguet, Paris (1907). Sté. des Ateliers d'Aviation Louis Bréguet, Paris; Anglet, Toulouse (1942). Few 6-cylinder cars built in 1907. About 200 electric cars produced in 1942.

BREIDING
USA 1900
A.H. Breiding, Sterling, Illinois. High-wheeler.

BRELSFORD
USA 1900
C.W. Brelsford, Villisca, Iowa. Runabout.

BREMAC
USA 1932
Bremac Motor Corp., Detroit, Michigan. To have been shown at N.Y. Auto Show 1933.

BREMEN
USA 1982
Bremen Motor Corp., Bremen, Indiana. Sports car.

BREMS
DK 1900–1907
A.L. Brems, Viborg. Small vis-à-vis cars.

BRENENSTUL & CARPENTER
USA 1900
Brenenstul & Carpenter, Wakeman, Ohio. Runabout.

BRENNABOR
D 1908–1934
Gebr. Reichstein Brennabor-Werke, Brandenburg. Touring cars.

BRENNAN
USA 1905–1908
Brennan Motor Co., Syracuse, N.Y. Runabout.

BRENNING
USA 1900–1901

Brenning Brothers, Springfield, Ohio. Designed by C.W. Russel.
See "Russel-Springfield."

BRESCIANA
I 1902–1910
Societa Meccanica Bresciana, Brescia.
See "S.M.B."

BREVETTI FIAT
I 1905–1908
S.A. Brevetti FIAT, Torino.

BREWER
USA 1903
W.H. Brewer, Raleigh, North Carolina.

BREWER
USA 1908
Dan Brewer, Berlin, Wisconsin.

BREW-HATCHER
USA 1904–1905
The Brew & Hatcher Co., Cleveland, Ohio. Touring cars.

BREWSTER
USA 1915–1925
Brewster & Co., Long Island City, N.Y.
See "Brewster-Knight." Both names apply to same vehicle.

BREWSTER
USA 1934–1936
Springfield Mfg. Co., Springfield, Massachusetts. Used "Ford" and other chassis. About 300 cars were made. Formerly body building division of "Rolls-Royce" (USA).

BREWSTER-KNIGHT
USA 1915–1925
Brewster & Co., Long Island City, N.Y. Carriage building firm 1819, importer of Delaunay-Belleville 1909. Used 4-cylinder Knight engine. Taken over by Rolls-Royce (USA) 1922. Also called "Brewster."

BRICE
USA 1912
Brice Motor Car Co., Warrensville, Ohio.

BRICKLIN
USA 1974–1975
General Vehicle Inc., Phoenix, Arizona. Bricklin Vehicle Corporation, Scottsdale, Arizona. Sports car. 2897 cars built.

BRIDGEPORT
USA 1901
Bridgeport Boiler Works, Bridgeport, Connecticut. Steam car.

BRIDGES
USA 1900–1901
C.Miller Bridges, Carlisle, Pennsylvania. Single-cylinder gasoline runabot.

BRIDGES
USA 1918
Bridges Motor Car & Rubber Co., Fort Worth, Texas.

BRIDGES
USA 1936
Dr. Calvin B. Bridges, Pasadena, California. Three-wheeler prototype built only.

BRIDGWATER
GB 1904–1906
Bridgwater Motor Co., Bridgwater, Somerset.

BRIERRE
F 1900–1901
E.J. Brierre, Paris. Light voiturette.

BRIEST-ARMAND
F 1897–1898
Eugene Briest et Freres, Nantes. Steam tricycle; 2-, 4- and-seater gasoline cars.

BRIETZKE
USA 1900
Charles F. Brietzke, Racine, Wisconsin. Gasoline automobile.

BRIGGS
USA 1933–1934
Briggs Manufacturing Co., Detroit, Michigan. Custom cars.

BRIGGS & STRATTON
USA 1919–1923
Briggs & Stratton Mfg. Co., Milwaukee, Wisconsin. Formerly "Smith Flyer."

BRIGGS & STRATTON
USA 1980–1983
Electric cars.

BRIGGS-DETROITER
USA 1911–1916
Briggs-Detroiter Co., Detroit, Michigan.
See "Detroiter."

BRIGHTON
USA 1896
Pierce-Crouch Engine Co., New Brighton, Pennsylvania.
See "Crouch."

BRIGHTWOOD
USA 1912–1914
Brightwood Motor Mfg. Co., Springfield, Massachusetts. Company built "Orson."

BRIHAM
GB 1966–1968
Briham Ltd., London. Sports cars.

BRILL
USA 1909
Edward Brill, Appleton, Wisconsin.

BRILLANTE
USA 1989–c. 1991
Classic International Automotive Styling Center, Fountain Valley, California. Sports cars.

BRILLIÉ
F 1904–1907
Société des Automobiles Eugene Brillié, Le Creusot; Le Havre. Cab-over-engine layout.

BRINER
USA 1902
Fred E. Briner, St. Louis, Missouri. Steam car.

BRINKMEYER
D c. 1985
Brinkmeyer GmbH & Co. Kunststoffe KG, Porta Westfalica. Tuning.

BRINTNELL
CDN 1912
Brintnell Motor Car Co., Ltd. Toronto, Ontario. Comany also built "Guy" and "Gray-Dort."

BRISCOE
CDN 1916
The Canadian Briscoe Motors Ltd., Brockville, Ontario.

BRISCOE
USA 1914–1922
Briscoe Motor Corp., Jackson, Michigan. Touring cars.
See "Earl."

BRISCOE FRERES
USA 1914–1915
Argo Motor Co., Inc., Jackson, Michigan. Cyclecars.
See "Argo."

BRISSONNET
F 1953
Ets. Brissonnet, Neuilly sur Seine. 200 cc three-wheeler prototype.

BRISTOL
GB 1902–1908
Bristol Motor Co. Ltd., Bristol, Somerset. 24 cars were built.

BRISTOL
GB 1947–present
Bristol Aeroplane Co. Ltd. (1947–1960). Bristol Cars Ltd., Fulton, Bristol (1960–present). Luxury touring and sports cars.

BRISTOL
USA 1896
H.S. Bristol, Chicago, Illinois.

BRISTOL
USA 1903–1904
Bristol Motor Car Co., Bristol, Connecticut. Absorbed by Corbin Motor Vehicle Co. Runabout.

BRIT
GB 1902–1905
Hunt's Steam Sawmills and Carriage Accessories. E.A. Chard & Co., Bridport, Dorset. Modified "Daimler."

BRITANNIA
GB 1896–1908
Britannia Electric Carriage Syndicate Ltd., (1896–1899). Britannia Engineering Co. Ltd., Colchester, Essex (1906–1908). Electric and gasoline cars.

BRITANNIA
GB 1913–1914
Britannia Engineering Co. Ltd., Nottingham. Cyclecars.

BRITANNIA
GB 1957–1961
Britannia Cars Ltd., Ashwell, Herts. Tojeiro Automotive Developments Ltd., Royston, Herts. 6 sports cars were built.

BRITISH
GB 1905–1907
British Motor & Engineering Co. Ltd., London; Caversham, Reading, Berks. Light cars.

BRITISH COACH WORKS
USA 1982
British Coach Works, Ltd., Arnold, Pennsylvania. Sports car kit.

BRITISH EAGLE
GB
See "Hodgson."

BRITISH ENSIGN
GB 1913–1923
Ensign Motors Ltd., London. Touring cars.

BRITISH IDEAL
GB 1901
Montague Hawnt & Co., Birmingham.

BRITISH IMPERIA
GB 1927
GWK Ltd., Maidenhead, Berkshire.

BRITISH LION
GB 1903–1904
British Lion Co., Leicester. This company supplied all mechanical parts, except engines.

BRITISH SALMSON
GB 1934–1939
Aero Engines Ltd., London. Sports cars.

BRITON
GB 1908–1928
Star Cycle Co. Ltd. (1908–1909). British Motor Co. Ltd., Wolverhampton, Staffs. (1909–1928). Low-priced light cars.

BRITTAIN
USA c. 1905
Samuel Brittain, Boston, Massachusetts. 5 hp car.

BRIXIA-ZÜST
I
See "Züst."

BRIXNER
D 1983–c. 1990
Kurt Brixner, Stuttgart-Kunststoff-Rennkarosserien, Stuttgart. Fiberglass bodied "Porsche" replicars.

BROADSPEED
GB c. 1970
Broadspeed Ltd., Southam, Warwickshire. Sports car and tuning.

BROADWAY
GB 1913
Broadway Cyclecar Co., Coventry, Warwickshire. Cyclecars.

BROC
USA 1909–1916
Broc Carriage & Wagon Co. The Broc Electric Co., Cleveland, Ohio. Electric cars. Became American Electric Car Co., Saginaw, Michigan, 1914.

BROCKLEBANK
GB 1927–1929
Brocklebank & Richards Ltd., Birmingham. 2-litre 6-cylinder saloon.

BROCKSHIRE & ROBINSON
USA 1911
Brockshire & Robinson Company, Saint Paris, Ohio. Prototype.

BROCK SIX
CDN 1921
Brock Motors Ltd., Amhurstburg, Ontario.

BROCKVILLE-ATLAS
CDN 1911–1915
Brockville Atlas Auto Co. Ltd., Brockville, Ontario.

BROGAN
USA 1946–1952
B. & B. Specialty Co., Rossmoyne, Ohio. Three-wheelers.

BROMLEI
SU 1907
Fabrika Avtomobilei Bromlei, Sankt Peterburg.

BRONS
NL 1899
NV Appingedammer Bronsmotorenfabriek, Appingedam.

BRONTO
RUS 1998–present
OAO PSA Bronto, Togliatti. Stretched "Lada" Niva.

BROOK
USA 1909
Brook Motor Car Co., Brook, Indiana.

BROOK
USA 1920–1921
Spacke Machine & Tool Co., Indianapolis, Indiana.
See "Spacke" cyclecar.

BROOKE
GB 1901–1913
J.W. Brooke & Co. Ltd., Lowestoft, Suffolk. Light cars and 6-cylinder tourer.

BROOK-LATTA
USA 1911
Brook-Latta Co., St. Louis, Missouri.

BROOKS
CDN 1923–1931
Brooks Steam Motors Ltd., Stratford, Ontario.

BROOKS
GB 1902
Brooks Motor Co. Ltd., Coventry, Warwickshire. Light cars.

BROOKS
USA 1905–1907
Brooks Automobile Co., Detroit, Michigan.

BROOKS
USA 1911–1912
Brooks Motor Wagon Co., Saginaw, Michigan.

BROOKS
CDN 1923–1926
Brooks Steam Motors Inc., Stratford, Ontario. Steam cars.

BROOKS & WOOLLAN
GB 1907–1910
Brooks & Woollan, Reading, Berks. Built to customers' order.

BROOMELL
USA 1903
Six-wheeler. Designed by A.P. Bromell, York, Pennsylvania. Correct name for vehicle is "Pullman."

BROSE
D 1994–1995
Brose Trend-a-Car, Bonn. "Mazda" (J) based sports cars.

BROSTROM & LANG
USA c. 1904
Brostrom & Lang, Eagle Bend, Minnesota.

BROTHERHOOD
GB 1904–1907
Brotherhood-Crocker Motors Ltd., London (1904–1906); Sheffield, Yorks. (1906–1907). 20 and 40 hp models.

BROTHERTON
USA 1910
N.T. Brotherton, Detroit, Michigan.

BROTZ
USA 1904
Anton F. Brotz, Kohler, Wisconsin. Motor-buggy.

BROUGH
GB 1899–1908; 1913
W.E. Brough, Basford, Nottingham. Belt-drive cars; cyclecars.

BROUGH SUPERIOR
GB 1935–1939
Brough Superior Cars Ltd., Nottingham. Touring and sports cars with American "Lincoln" engines.

BROUHOT
F 1898–1910
Brouhot et Cie., Vierzon/Cher. Light two-seaters.

BROWER
USA 1884
Fred G. Brower, Syracuse, N.Y. Built one runabout for his daughter.

BROWN
GB 1823
Samuel Brown, London. Atmospheric gas motor powered vehicle.

BROWN
GB 1901–1911
Brown Bros. Ltd., London. Touring cars.

BROWN
USA 1884–1891
Edwin F. Brown, Chicago, Illinois. Steam car.
See "Brown's Touring Cart."

BROWN
USA 1899
George D. Brown, Fargo, North Dakota.

BROWN
USA 1905
Brown Brothers, Hutchinson, Kansas. Steam car.

BROWN
USA 1909–1910
Brown Cotton Gin Co., New London, Connecticut.

BROWN
USA 1914
Great Western Automobile Co., Kalamazoo, Michigan.

BROWN
USA 1914
Brown Cyclecar Co., Asbury Park, New Jersey. Air-cooled cyclecar. Announced November 1913.

BROWN
USA 1916
Brown Carriage Co., Cincinnati, Ohio.

BROWN-BURTT
USA 1904
Burt Mfg. Co., Kalamazoo, Michigan. Company name, not name of vehicle. 1904 company built "Cannon."

BROWNE
USA 1903
F.O. Browne, Denver, Colorado.

BROWNELL
USA c. 1905
John P. Brownell, Warren, Rhode Island. 4 hp automobile.

BROWNELL
USA 1910
F.A. Brownell Motor Co., Rochester, N.Y. Three cars built.

BROWNIE
USA 1916
J.O. Carter., Carter Mfg. Co., Hannibal, Missouri.

BROWNIEKAR
USA 1908–1911
Omar Motor Co., Newark, N.Y. Juvenile car designed by W.H. Birdsall, chief engineer of the Mora Motor Car Co.
See "Mora."

BROWN'S TOURING CART
USA 1898
Edwin F. Brown, Evanston, Illinois. Built by George W. Lewis.

BRT
CH 1966–1967
Robert Brliat, Köniz. Sports car prototype.

BRUBAKER
USA c. 1972
The Brubaker Industries, Los Angeles, California. "Safety car."

BRÜCK
D c. 1987
Brück-Design, Schmelz. Tuning.

BRUENING
USA 1901
Bruening Brothers, Ackley, Iowa. Gasoline automobile.

BRULÉ-PONSARD
F 1900–1901
F.Brulé et Cie., Paris. "Avant-train" attachement.

BRUNAU-WEIDMANN
CH 1905–1909
Brunau, Weidmann & Co., Zürich. Limousines and coupe de ville.

BRUNN
USA 1906–1911
Brunn's Carriage Mfg. Co., Buffalo, N.Y. Electric cars.

BRUNNER
USA 1910
Brunner Motor Car Co., Buffalo, N.Y.

BRUNNSCHMID
A 1983
AMD Auto-Motorrad-Design, St. Johann/Tirol. Tuning.

BRUNSWICK
USA 1917
Brunswick Motor Car Co., Newark, New Jersey. Formation of company announced January 1917. Touring.

BRUSH
GB 1902–1904
Brush Electrical Engineering Co. Ltd., London (1902–1904); Loughborough, Leics. (1904). Light tonneau.

BRUSH
USA 1886
Brush Electric Company, Cleveland, Ohio. Electric car.

BRUSH
USA 1907–1912
Brush Runabout Co., Detroit, Michigan. Absorbed by U.S. Motor Co. 1910. Runabouts.

BRÜTSCH
D 1951–1957
Egon Brütsch Fahrzeugbau, Stuttgart. 3- and 4-wheeled minicars.

BRYAN
USA 1918–1923
Bryan Automobile Mfg. Co. Bryan Steam Corp. Bryan Boiler Co., Peru, Indiana. Six steam cars built. 1913 car built by George A. Bryan while he was Atcheson Topeka & Santa Fe R.R. engineer.

B.S.A.
GB 1907–1926; 1933–1936
Birmingham Small Arms Co. Ltd., Birmingham; Coventry. Light cars.

B.S.A.
GB 1929–1940
B.S.A. Cycles Ltd., Birmingham. Touring and sports cars.

BSH
F 1966–1971
Société Marland, Issy-les-Moulineaux. Sports kit cars.

BTAZ
SU 1922–1923
Pervoi Brone-Tanko-Avtoremontnii Zavod, Fila. "Russo-Balt" assembled, only 5 cars built.
See "Prombron."

BUAT
F 1901–1906
Automobiles Léon Buat, Senlis/Oise. Light cars.

BUBBLE CAR
I c. 1987
Bubble Car, Corsico (Milano). Minicars.

BUC
F
See "Bucciali."

BUCCANEER
GB c. 1971
Sports car.
See "Dial."

BUCCIALI
F 1923–1933
Bucciali Freres, Courbevoie/Seine. 151 cars were made, of which 38 were front-wheel-drive models.

BUCHET
F 1911–1929
Société Buchet, Levallois-Perret/Seine (1911–1918). Gaston Sailly, Moteurs et Automobiles Buchet, Billancourt/Seine (1919–1929). Light tourers.

BUCHMANN
D 1982–present
b & b Auto Exklusiv Service KG, Frankfurt am Main. Sports cars and tuning.

BUCK & GRY
DK 1904
Buck & Gry, Horve, Sjaelland.

BUCKAROO
USA 1957
Cleveland, Ohio. Very small $400 cars.

BUCKBOARD
USA 1904
S. Moore, Cleveland, Ohio.

BUCKBOARD
USA 1956
Don Bruce, Bronx, N.Y. Wooden-bodied cyclecars.

BUCKBOARD
USA 1960
McDonough Power Equipment Inc., McDonough, Georgia. Juvenile cars. Replica of "Red Bug."

BUCKEYE
USA 1895
J.W. Lambert, Buckeye Mfg. Co., Anderson, Indiana.

BUCKEYE
USA 1901
Peoples Automobile Mfg. Co., Cleveland, Ohio.

BUCKEYE
USA 1902
Motor Storage & Mfg. Co., Chillicothe, Ohio. 12 hp surrey vehicle.

BUCKEYE
USA 1905–1909
Buckeye Mfg. Co., Anderson, Indiana Company name, not name of vehicle. Company produced "Lambert."

BUCKEYE
USA 1909–1910
Buckeye National Motor Car Co., Columbus, Ohio.

BUCKEYE
USA 1914
Buckeye Cyclecar Co., Columbus, Ohio. Cyclecars.

BUCKEYE MOTOR WAGON
USA 1911
Buckeye Wagon & Motor Car Co., Dayton, Ohio.

BUCKINGHAM
AUS 1933–1934
Buckingham Ward Motors (Australia) Ltd., Footscray, Victoria. Touring cars in limited production.

BUCKINGHAM
GB 1913–1923
Buckingham Engine Works (1913–1915). Buckingham Engineering Co. Ltd., Coventry, Warwickshire (1922–1923). Light cars.

BUCKLE
AUS 1957–1960
Buckle Motors, Sydney, N.S.W. Fiberglass coupe.

BUCKLER
GB 1947–1962
Bucklers, Reading, Berks. (1947–1954). Buckler Cars Ltd., Reading, Berks. (1954–1958). Buckler Cars, Reading, Berks.; Crowthorne, Berks. (1958–1961). Buckler Engineering Ltd., Crowthorne, Berks. (1961–1962). Sports cars.

BUCKLES
USA 1914
T.E. Buckles, Manchester, Oklahoma. Cyclecars.

BUCKMOBILE
USA 1903–1905
Buckmobile Co. (1903–1904). Black Diamond Automobile Co. (1904–1905), Utica, N.Y. Runabouts.

BUEHRIG
USA 1982
Buehrig Motor Car Co., Detroit, Michigan. Sports car.

BUEL
USA 1897–1903
James Frederick Buel, Woburn, Massachusetts. Steam cars.

BUFAG
D 1922–1923
Butenuth-Fahrzeugwerke AG, Hannover. Three-wheelers.

BUFFALO
F c. 1970–1971
SARAP, Strasbourg. Dune buggy.

BUFFALO
USA 1899
Buffalo Cycle Supply Co., Buffalo, N.Y.

BUFFALO
USA 1899–1910
AutoCar & Equipment Co., Buffalo, N.Y. Became "Atterbury" (truck).

BUFFALO
USA 1900–1903
Buffalo Gasoline Motor Works. Buffalo Auto & Auto-Bi Co., Buffalo, N.Y. Became E.R. Thomas Motor Co.

BUFFALO
USA 1900
Buffalo Gasoline Engine Co., Buffalo, N.Y. Complete except for body, gasoline and water tanks.

BUFFALO
USA 1912–1915
Buffalo Electric Vehicle Co., Buffalo, N.Y. Electric car. Succeeded Babcock & Van Wagoner.
See "Babcock."

BUFFALO
USA 1913–1914
Buffalo Co-Operative Motor Co., Buffalo, N.Y.

BUFFALO ELECTRIC
USA 1900–1906
Buffalo Electric Carriage Co., Buffalo, N.Y. Became Babcock Electric Car Co.

BUFFALOMOBILE
USA 1902
Auto-Bi Co., Buffalo, N.Y.
See "Buffalo" 1900–1903.

BUFFALO-ROCHESTER
USA 1900
Buffalo-Rochester Electric Power and Automobile Co., Buffalo, N.Y. Electric cars.

BUFFAUD
F 1900–1902
Buffaud et Robatel, Lyon. Steam cars.

BUFFUM
USA 1900–1907
H.H. Buffum Co., Abington, Massachusetts. Experiments in 1895. First company to offer 8-cylinder car for sale 1904.

BUFFUM
USA 1914
H.H. Buffum, Laconia, New Hampshire.
See "Laconia" cyclecar.

BUFORI
AUS 1994–present
Bufori Motor Car Co., Sydney, N.S.W. Sports cars replica.

BUG
D 1969–1978
Autohaus R. Kühn, Hamburg. Dune buggy and replicars.

BUG
USA 1959–1960
Crofton Marine Engine Co., San Diego, California.
See "Crofton Bug."

BUGATTI
D/F 1909–1918; 1918–1956
Automobiles E. Bugatti, Molsheim, Bas-Rhin. Famous sports and racing cars.

BUGATTI
I 1990–present
Bugatti Automobili SpA, Campogalliano (Modena). High-performance sports cars.

BUGATTI-GULINELLI
I 1901–1903
Officine Gulinelli, Ferrara. Only one sports car was built.

BUGETTA
USA c. 1968
Jerry Eisert Enterprises, Costa Mesa, California. Dune buggy.

BUGGYABOUT
USA 1906–1908
See "Hatfield."

BUGGYAUT
USA 1908–1910
Charles S. Duryea, Reading, Pennsylvania.
See "Duryea."

BUGGYCAR
USA 1908–1909
Buggycar Company, Cincinnati, Ohio Air-cooled highwheelers. Succeeded Postal Automobile & Engine Co., Bedford, Indiana.

BUGGYMOBILE
USA 1907–1909
See "Columbus."

BUGLE
GB 1970–1979
Chris Watson, Knaresborough, North Yorkshire. Dune buggy kit cars.

BUGMOBILE
USA 1908–1909
Bugmobile Co. of America, Chicago, Illinois. Highwheelers.

BUGRE
BR 1984–c. 1993
Industria de Carrocerias Bugre Ltda., Bonsucesso, Rio de Janeiro. Dune buggy and light Jeep-type car.

BUICK
USA 1903–present
Buick Motor Car Co., Detroit, Michigan (1903). Buick Motor Car Co., Flint, Michigan (1904–present). Buick Motor Car Co. succeeded Buick Auto Vim and Power Co. Absorbed Pope-Robinson 1904 and was the first division of General Motors Corp. First Buick started May 20, 1904 and was put on road July 1, 1904. Car was sold to Dr. Hills of Flint, Michigan July 27, 1904. Passenger cars.

BULGARRENAULT
BG 1967–c. 1975
Avtoprom, Plovdiv. "Renault" R8, R10 and Renault-Alpine license.

BULLARD
USA 1885–1887
James H. Bullard, Springfield, Massachusetts. Steam car.

BULLARD
USA 1904
G.A. Bullard, Marshall, Michigan. A car for his own use.

BULL MOOSE
USA 1914
Bull Moose Cutting Automobile Co., St. Paul, Minnesota. Cyclecars.

BULLOCK
USA 1901
Bullock Cycle Works, Adelaide, S.A.

BULLY
D 1933
Bully-Fahrzeugbau AG, Berlin. Three-wheeler.

BUNDY
USA 1895
W.L. Bundy Co., Binghamton, N.Y. One steam car produced.

BUNGER
DK 1947–1949
Borge Bunger, De Forende Automobilfabrikker, Odense. 600 cc three-wheeler prototype.

BURCH
USA 1906
Theodore A. Cook, Calicoon, N.Y. Three autosleighs built for use by Burch Brothers for proposed trip to South Pole.

BURDICK
USA 1909
Burdick Motor Car Co., Eau Claire, Wisconsin. Touring cars.

BURDON
USA c. 1905
Gaylord H. Burdon, Waterbury, Connecticut. One car made.

BURG
USA 1902
Burg Wagon Company, Burlington, Iowa.

BURG
USA 1910–1913
Burg Carriage Co., Dallas City, Illinois. 4- and 6-cylinder touring cars.

BURGERS
NL 1898–1900; 1951
Eerste Nederlandsche Rijwielenfabriek, Deventer. Three-wheeler; minicar prototype.

BURGETT & WEST
USA 1899
Edwards Burgett & William S. West, Middleburgh, N.Y. Steam car.

BURGFALKE
D 1959–1960
Burgfalke-Werke, Burglengenfeld. Minicars built formerly by "Victoria."

BURKE
GB 1906–1907
Burke Engineering Co. Ltd., Clonmel, Tipperary. Chain-driven cars.

BURLAT
F 1904–1905
Burlat Frères Constructions de Moteurs Rotatifs et Chassis Automobiles, Lyon. Cars powered by horizontal rotary engines.

BURLINGAME
USA 1896
A. Burlingame & Co., Worcester, Massachusetts.

BURMAN
USA 1914
L.C. Erbes Co., St. Paul, Minnesota.

BURNEY
GB 1930–1933
Streamline Cars Ltd., Maidenhead, Berks. Streamlined saloon.

BURNS
GB
    See "Billings."

BURNS
USA 1903
Burns Typewriter Company, Buffalo, N.Y. Gasoline automobile.

BURNS
USA 1908–1912
Burns Bros., Havre de Grace, Maryland. Highwheelers.

BURR
USA 1896
Burr & Co., New York City, N.Y.

BURR
USA 1906
E.M. Burr Co., Champaign, Illinois. Touring cars.

BURRINGTON
USA 1902
B.G. Burrington, Holyoke, Massachusetts. Runabout.

BURRO
USA 1968–c. 1974
Burro Co., Santa Ana, California. Dune buggy.

BURROWES
USA 1904–1908
Burrowes Motor Car Co., Portland, Maine. Runabout.

BURROWS
USA 1914–1915
Burrows Cyclecar Co., Ripley, N.Y. Cyclecars.

BURSTALL & HILL
GB 1827
Timothy Burstall & John Hill, Leith; Edinburgh; London. Steam car.

BURTT
USA 1903–1906
Burtt Mfg. Co., Kalamazoo, Michigan. Believed to be company name, not name of vehicle.
    See "Cannon."

BURWELL
USA 1899
George A. Burwell, Toledo, Ohio. Three-wheeled gasoline carriage.

BURY
USA 1927
Charles W. Bury, New York, N.Y. Light roadster.

BUSER
CH 1911
Zürich. Small car.

BUSH
USA 1916–1925
Bush Motor Co., Chicago, Illinois. Mail order sales. Built by Piedmont, Crow-Elkhart and possibily others. Touring cars.

BUSHMASTER
USA c. 1968
Bushmaster Co., Austin, Texas. Dune buggy.

BUSHNELL
USA 1912
Bushnell Press Company, Thompsonville, Connecticut. A car marketed as "Maxim Tri-Car."

BUSHWHACKER
USA c. 1968

Fiber-Motive, North Hollywood, California. Dune buggy.

BUSSE
USA 1903
H.F. Busse, St. Louis, Missouri.

BUSSON
F 1907–1908
Voiturettes Busson, Paris.

BUTCHER & GAGE
USA 1903
Butcher & Gage, Jackson, Michigan. Two cars produced.

BUTLER
USA 1901
Butler Co., Butler, Pennsylvania. Experimental car.

BUTLER
USA c. 1905
Paul Butler, Lowell, Massachusetts.

BUTLER
USA 1908
Butler Co., Butler, Indiana. Highwheeler.

BUTLER
USA c.1991
Butler Racing Inc., Goleta, California. Sports car.

BUTTERFIELD
GB 1961–1963
Butterfield Engineering Co., Nazeing, Essex. "Mini" based kit cars.

BUTTEROSI
F 1919–1924
Sté. Nouvelle des Automobiles Butterosi, Boulogne-sur-Seine. Light cars.

BUTTERWORTH
USA c. 1901
G.Butterworth, Somerville, Massachusetts. Three vehicles built.

BUTZ
D 1934
Bungartz & Co., München. Small two-seater.

BUURRASSA
USA 1902
J.H.E. Buurrassa, Attleboro, Massachusetts. Single automobile built for T.I. Smith & Co., North Attleboro.

B.V.R.T.
GB 1970
British Vita Racing & Tuning Co., Ltd., Littleborough, Lancs. Sports cars.

BYAM
USA c. 1905
C.C. and F.A. Byam, Waltham, Massachusetts. 4 hp vehicle.

BYRIDER
USA 1905–1909
Byrider Electric Co., Cleveland, Ohio. Electric cars.

B.Z.
D 1923–1924
Bootswerft Zeppelinhafen GmbH, Potsdam. Aluminum bodied light car.

B.Z.T.
USA 1914–1915
B.Z.T. Cyclecar Co., Owego, N.Y. Cyclecars.

CA
USA
See "Consulier."

CAB
F 1972
Le Cab, Marseille. Electric three-wheelers.

CABAN
F 1926–1932
Yves Giraud-Cabantous, Boulogne-sur-Seine. 28 cars were made.

CABELL LIGHT VAN
J c.1970
Yuasa Battery Co. Electric car.

CABI-CATTANEO
I 1949
Milano.

CABRIONI
NL c. 1991
Cabrioni Cabrio Design, Huissen. Convertibles.

C-A-C
USA 1914–1915
C.A. Coey, Chicago, Illinois. Cyclecars.

CAD
USA 1991–c. 1994
Corbett Automotive Design, Lompoc, California. Sports cars.

CADET
USA 1925
General Motors Corp., Flint, Michigan. GM's try at a new car for export market. Two prototypes were built.

CADILLAC
USA 1903–present
Cadillac Automobile Co., Detroit, Michigan. Formerly Detroit Automobile Co. and Henry Ford Co. Became Cadillac Motor Car Co. Purchased 1909 by General Motors. Became General Motors Division 1917. Luxury cars and limousines.

CADIX
F 1920–1923
Automobiles Jean Jannel, Cadix-Martinville/Vosges. 2.3-litre cars.

CADY
USA 1899
Frank E. Cady, Auburn, N.Y.

CAESAR
I 1911
Chivasso.
See "Scacchi" and "Storero."

CAESAR
USA 1914
A.R. Marsh, Anderson, Indiana. Cyclecar.

CAETANO
P 1988–1995
Salvado Caetano, Vila Nova De Gaia. "Toyota" (J) assembled.

CAFFORT
F 1920–1922

Sté. des Anciens Établissements Caffort, Paris. Light cars with 1-litre engine mounted over the front wheels.

CAFFREY
USA 1895
Charles F. Cafrey Co., Camden, New Jersey. Steam carriage.

CAFFREY
USA 1897
W.G. Caffrey, Reno, Nevada. Electric highwheeler.

CAIL-BORDEREL
F
See "Borderel-Cail."

CAILLE
USA 1904
Caille Bros. Co., Detroit, Michigan.
See "Dubrie-Caile."

CALCOTT
GB 1913–1926
Calcott Bros. Ltd., Coventry, Warwickshire. About 2,500 cars were made.

CALDWELL
USA c. 1905
W.M. Caldwell, Waltham, Massachusetts. 15 hp automobile.

CALDWELL
USA 1908
Caldwell, Waterloo, Iowa. Automotive fore-carriage.

CALDWELL VALE
AUS 1913
Caldwell Vale Truck & Bus Co., Auburn, N.S.W.

CALEDONIAN
GB 1899–1906
Caledonian Motor Car & Cycle Co., Aberdeen. Voiturettes and touring cars.

CALIFORNIA
USA 1899
Dr. George M. Calmus, San Diego, California. Vehicle with rotary engine.

CALIFORNIA
USA 1900–1902
California Automobile Co., San Francisco, California. Steam and gasoline cars.
See "Calimobile" gasoline.

CALIFORNIA
USA 1901–1905
California Motor Company, San Francisco, California.

CALIFORNIA
USA 1908
Kinsey-McAlvay Company, Los Angeles.

CALIFORNIA
USA 1910
Auto Vehicle Co., Los Angeles, California. Succeeded "Tourist."

CALIFORNIA
USA 1914
California Cyclecar Co., Los Angeles, California. Two-cylinder cyclecar designed by L.E. French, later "Los Angeles" designer.

CALIFORNIA
USA 1920–1921
California Motor Car Corp., Los Angeles, California.

CALIFORNIA CUSTOM COACH
USA 1974–c. 1982
California Custom Coach, Inc., Pasadena, California. Replica and sports car.

CALIFORNIA MIDGET
USA 1908
Brice Cowan, Los Angeles, California.
See "Cowan."

CALIFORNIAN
USA 1912
Californian Motor Car Co., San Francisco, California.

CALIFORNIAN
USA 1945–1946
Warner Mfg. Co., Glendale, California.

CALIFORNIAN
USA 1946
Californian Motor Car Co., Los Angeles, California. Three-wheelers.

CALIFORNIA SPEEDSTER
USA 1982
California Speedster, San Diego, California. Sports cars.

CALIMOBILE
USA 1902–1903
California Automobile Co., San Francisco, California. Steam cars.
See "California" 1900–1901.

CALL
USA 1911
Call Motor Car Co., New York, N.Y.

CALLAWAY
USA 1986–present
Callaway Engineering Corp., Old Lyme, Connecticut. Sports cars.

CALLIHAN
USA 1883–1905
D. Scott Callihan, Woonsocket, South Dakota. Steam three-wheelers.

CALLISTA
F 1948–1953
Sports cars.

CALORIC
USA 1903–1904
Chicago Motor-Cycle Co. Chicago Caloric Engine Co., Chicago, Illinois. Three-cylinder hydro-carbon car. Could be run as hot-air engine or with gasoline or kerosene as fuel. Designed by John Wikström (FIN).

CALTHORPE
GB 1904–1932
Calthorpe Motor Co. Ltd., Birmingham. Touring and sports cars.

CALVERT
USA 1927
Calvert Motor Associates, Baltimore, Maryland. 2 prototypes were built.

CAMAT
P 1987–1995
Camat Espana, Vigo. "MG" replica.

CAMBER
GB 1966–1969
Checkpoint Engineering Ltd. (1966–1967). W. West (Engineering) Ltd., Rye, Sussex (1967–1969). Sports cars.

CAMBIER
B 1898–1900
Cambier Cie., Malines.

CAMBIER
F 1897–1905
Établissements Cambier, Lille/Nord. 1-, 2-, 3- and 4-cylinder cars.

CAMBRO
GB 1920
Central Aircraft Co. Ltd., Northolt, Middlesex. 192 cc single-seater.

CAMELOT
USA 1982
Camelot Motors Corp., Goshin, Indiana. "Ford" Thunderbird replicars.

CAMEN
I 1922

Costruzione Automobili Motori Esposito Napoli, Napoli.

CAMERON
USA 1902–1919
United Motors Corp. (1902–1904). James Brown Mach. Co. (1904–1905), Pawtucket, Rhode Island. Cameron Car Co. (1907–1908), Brockton, Massachusetts. Cameron Car Co. (1908–1912), Beverly, Massachusetts. Six-cylinder models at New London, Connecticut from 1909. Cameron Motor Co. (1912–1913), West Haven, Connecticut. Cameron Motor Co. (1914–1916), New Haven, Connecticut. Cameron Motors Co. (1917–1918), Norwalk, Connecticut. Cameron Motors Co. (1919), Stamford, Connecticut. Runabouts and light touring cars.

CAMERON
USA 1922
F.F. Cameron in plant of F.H. Bultman Co., Cleveland, Ohio. Air-cooled experimental car.

CAMERON STEAMER
USA 1899
E.S. Cameron, Brockton, Massachusetts. Experimental steam car with three-cylinder radial engine.

CAMONA
I 1903–1906
Camona Giussani Turrinelli & C., Milano.
See "SIVE," "Turrinelli," "Ausonia," "Officine di Sesto San Giovanni."

CAMPBELL
AUS 1901
A.M. Campbell, Hobart, Tasmania. Steam car.

CAMPBELL
USA 1897
Campbell Machine Company, Providence, Rhode Island. Electric car.

CAMPBELL
USA 1918–1919
Campbell Motor Car Co., Kingston, N.Y. Formerly "Emerson" (1916–1917).

CAMPBELL-CORWIN
USA 1907
Campbell-Corwin Company, Brooklyn, N.Y. Prototypes only.

CAMPION
GB 1913–1914
Campion Cycle Co. Ltd., Nottingham. Cyclecars.

CANADA
CDN 1911
Canadian Motors Ltd,, Galt, Ontario.

CANADA BABY CAR
CDN 1914
Canadian Baby Car Co., Montreal, Quebec. Cyclecar.

CANADA CARS
CDN
See "Galt."

CANADIAN
CDN 1921
Colonial Motor Ltd., Windsor, Ontario.

CANADIAN BRISCOE
CDN 1916
Canadian Briscoe Co., Montreal, Quebec.

CANADIAN MOTORS
CDN 1900–1902
Canadian Motors Ltd., Toronto, Ontario.

CANADIAN MOTOR SYNDICATE
CDN 1895–1899
Canadian Motor Syndicate, Toronto, Ontario. Electric and gasoline cars.

CANADIAN QUEEN
CDN 1909
Canadian Queen Cycle & Motor Works, Toronto, Ontario.

CANADIAN STANDARD
CDN 1912–1913
Canadian Standard Auto & Tractor Co., Moose Jaw, Saskatchewan.

CANDA
USA 1900–1902
Canda Mfg. Co., New York, N.Y. Carteret, New Jersey. Auto-quadricycle. Remaining cars sold August 1902 by George W. Condon, Newark, New Jersey.

C. & H.
GB 1913
Corfield & Hurle Ltd., London. Cyclecars.

CANDY APPLE
USA 1990s
Candy Apple Cars Ltd., Barrington, Illinois. Sports kits cars.

CANELLO
F c. 1908
Sté. Canello, Courbevoie/Seine. "Dürkopp" (D) assembled.

CANLUBANG
PI 1980s
Canlubang Automotive Resources Corp., Manila. "Mitsubishi" (J) license.

CANNON
GB 1953–1974
M.R.B. Cannon, Tonbridge, Kent. 2- and 4-cylinder tonneau.

CANNON
USA 1901–1904
George C. Cannon, Cambridge, Massachusetts. Steam cars.

CANNON
USA 1902–1906
Burtt Mfg. Co., Kalamazoo, Michigan. 1-, 2- and 4-cylinder cars.

CANNON
USA 1912
Cannon Motor Car Co., Des Moines, Iowa.

CANNON
USA 1955
Cannon Engineering Co., North Hollywood, California.

CANNONBALL
USA 1918–1921
Cannonball Motor Car Co., Texico, New Mexico. Touring cars.

CANSTELL
AUS c. 1971
Specialized Fibreglass Mouldings Pty Ltd., Taren Point, N.S.W.

CANTERBURY
GB 1903–1906
Canterbury Motor Co., Canterbury, Kent. Light cars.

CANTON
USA 1909–1910
Canton Buggy Company, Canton, Ohio. Motor-buggy.

CANTONO
I 1904–1913
Cantono Avantreni (1904–1905). FRAM Fabbricazione Rotabili Avantreni Motori (1905–1906). SALR Societa Anonima Ligure-Romana Vetture (1906–1913), Roma.
See "FRAM," "SALR," "Societa Romana."

CANTONO
I/USA 1900–1911
E. Cantono, Roma (1900–1905). Cantono Electric Tractor Co., Canton, Ohio (1904–1907). Societa Anonima F.R.A.M., Roma (1905–1906); Genoa (1906–1911).

CANTONO
USA 1903–1907
Cantono Electric Tractor Co., Marion, New Jersey. New York, N.Y. Electric cars.

CANZOL
USA 1931
Canzol Co., Cleveland, Ohio. Promotional midget.

CAPEL
GB 1900–1901
Creek Street Engineering Co. Ltd., London. Light cars.

CAPITOL
USA c. 1889
Capitol Automobile Co., Washington, D.C. Steam car.

CAPITOL
USA 1911–1912
Washington Motor Vehicle Co., Washington, D.C. Electric cars. Also built "Washington" truck.

CAPITOL
USA 1914
Denver, Colorado.

CAPITOL
USA 1919–1920
Capitol Motors Corp., Fall River, Massachusetts.

CAPRONI
I 1947
Caponi Elettro Meccanica SA.
See "Cemsa."

CAPS
USA 1902–1905
Caps Brothers Manufacturing Co., Kansas City, Missouri.
See "Kansas City."

CAPUTO
F 1935
Light car prototype.

C.A.R.
GB
See "Cosmos."

C.A.R.
GB 1983–1984
Classic Automotive Reproductions, Bridlington, East Yorkshire. Sports car replica.

C.A.R.
I 1905–1906
Cantieri Automobilistici Riuniti, Palermo. Light and touring cars.

C.A.R.
I 1927–1929
Costruzioni Automobili Riunite, Milano. Cyclecar.

A CAR WITHOUT A NAME
USA 1909
Department C, Chicago, Illinois. Buyer supplied his own name.

CARAMAGNA
I 1898–1900
Officina Elettrotecniche Ing. Caramagna & C., Torino.

CARBAGGIO
CH 1913
Ets. Carbaggio, Sierre. Propeller powered vehicle.

CARBODIES
GB 1958–present
LTI Carbodies Ltd. London Taxis International, Coventry, Warwickshire. Hire cars.

CARCANO
I 1898–1901
Anzano (Milano). Voiturette.

CAR DELUXE
USA 1906–1909
Deluxe Motor Car Co., Detroit, Michigan (1906), Toledo, Ohio (1906–1909). 4–7-passenger touring cars.
See "Deluxe."

CARDEN
GB 1913–1925
Carden Engineering Co. Ltd., Teddington, Middlesex (1913–1920). Ascot, Berks. (1920–1922). Arnott & Harrison Ltd., London (1923–1925). Cyclecars; two/four-seater tourers.

CARDINET
F 1900–1906
Compagnie Francaise des Voitures Electromobiles, Paris. Electric cars.

CARDON
USA 1929–1930
Jeffery Carqueville & Duncan MacDonald, Chicago, Illinois. Conversion of a 1930 "Nash" into a steam car.

CARDWAY
USA 1923–1925
Fred Cardway, New York, N.Y. Six built.

CARENA
I 1911
Auto Costruzioni di Vittorio Carena e Mazza, Torino.
See "Prince."

CAREY
USA 1906
Carey Motor Co., New York, N.Y. Five-cylinder Balzer rotary engine.

CARGY
USA 1904–1905
Cargy Mfg. Co. (1904). Cargy Motor Car Co. (1905), Fairmont, Indiana.

CARHART
USA 1871
Dr. J.W. Carhart & H.S. Carhart, Racine, Wisconsin. Steam car.

CARHARTT
USA 1910–1912
Carhartt Automobile Corp., Detroit, Michigan. Roadster.

CARL ELECTRIC
USA 1913–1914
Carl Electric Vehicle Co., Toledo, Ohio. Formerly Chicago Electric Car Co.

CARLETTE
GB 1913
Holsteing Garage, Weybridge, Surrey. Cyclecars.

CARLEY
USA 1900–1902
Carley Iron Works, Colfax, Washington.

CARLINE
CH 1997–present
Carline, St. Gallen. Tuning.

CARLISLE
USA 1899–1900
Carlisle Mfg. Co., Chicago, Illinois. Electric car.

CARLSON
USA 1904
Carlson Motor Vehicle Company, Brooklyn, N.Y. 40 hp cars. Trucks to 1910.

CARLSON-WENSTROM
USA 1914

Carlson-Wenstrom Manufacturing Company, Philadelphia, Pennsylvania. Cyclecar.

CARLSSON
D 1985–present
Carlsson Motorsport Autotechnik GmbH, Beckingen; Rehlingen. Tuning.

CARLTON
GB 1901–1902
Carlton Motor Co., Coventry, Warwickshire. Light cars.

CARLTON
GB c. 1991
Carlton Automotive, Barnsley, South Yorks. Sports car.

CARLTON
NZ 1928
Carlton Car Co., Gisborne, North Island. Small 4-cylinder cars.

CAR-NATION
USA 1912–1915
American Voiturette Co., Detroit, Michigan. Succeeded Keeton Motor Co. Became Car-Nation Motor Car Co. 1914. Cyclecars and roadsters.

CARNEGIE
USA 1915–1916
Carnegie Engineering Corp., Kalamazoo, Michigan.

CARNEVALLI
I 1947–1951
Sergio Carnevalli, Como.

CAROLETTE
D 1924–1925
Märkische Kraftfahrzeugfabrik Carl Knöllner, Ravensbruck b. Fürstenberg i.M.
    See "Knöllner."

CAROLUS
D
    See "Knöllner."

CARON
F 1900–1901
Caron et Cie., Paris. Voiturette.

CARPENTER
USA 1895
H.H. Carpenter, Denver, Colorado. Electric auto-buggy.

CARPENTER
USA 1910
Carpenter Motor Vehicle Co., Brooklyn, N.Y.

CARPEVIAM
GB 1903–1905
Charles Peacock & Co. Ltd., London. Three-wheeler.

CARQUEVILLE-MCDONALD
USA 1930
Steam car.
    See "Cardon."

CARR CYCLECAR
USA 1914
W.G. Carr, Tacoma, Washington.

CARRIAGE MOBILE
USA 1907
Summit Carriage Mobile Co., Waterloo, Iowa.
    See "Summit" and "Farmer Mobile."

CARRICO
USA 1909
Carrico Motor Car Co., Cincinnati, Ohio. A few buggy-type chassis utilizing a two-cylinder air-cooled engine were built. Company did not built bodies.

CARRICO-DE TAMBLE
USA 1896
Speed Changing Pulley Co., Indianapolis, Indiana.

CARROL
USA 1909
Compressed Air Power Co., East Boston, Massachusetts.
    See "Compressed Air."

CARROLL
USA 1908
John Carrol, Philadelphia, Pennsylvania.

CARROLL
USA 1911–1912
Carroll Motor Car Company, Strasburg, Pennsylvania.

CARROLL SIX
USA 1921–1922
Carroll Automobile Co., Lorrain, Ohio. Touring cars.

CARROW
GB 1919–1923
Whitley Bay Motor Co., Newcastle-on-Tyne (1919–1921). Carrow Cars Ltd., Harwell, Middlesex (1921–1923). Light cars.

CARTER
GB 1913
S. Carter, Birmingham. Cyclecars.

CARTER
USA 1899–1902
Byron J. Carter Motor Car Co., Jackson, Michigan. Gasoline vehicles.

CARTER
USA 1901
Michigan Automobile Co., Grand Rapids, Michigan. Steam runabout.

CARTER
USA 1907–1909
Carter Motor Car Corp., Washington, D.C.

CARTER
USA 1907–1908
Carter Motor Car Corp., Hyattsville, Maryland. Two-engined cars.

CARTER
USA 1919–1920
Richard Carter Co., Gulfport, Mississippi. Steam cars.

CARTERCAR
USA 1906–1925
Motorcar Company (1906–1908), Detroit, Michigan. Cartercar Company (1908–1925), Pontiac, Michigan. Touring cars. Absorbed by General Motors.

CARTER COASTER
GB c. 1956
Electric minicar.

CARTERET
F 1922
Automobiles Carteret, Courbevoie/Seine/904 cc light cars.

CARTERMOBILE
USA 1915
Carter Motor & Manufacturing Co., Hannibal, Missouri. Touring cars.

CARTERMOBILE
USA 1921–1922
Carter Motor Car Co., Hyattsville, Maryland. Prototypes.

CARTERS
GB 1923
Carters, London. Electric car.

CARTERS
USA 1991
Carters Conversions Ltd., Imlay City, Michigan. Sports car.

CARTHAGE
USA 1914–1915
Carthage Motor Car Co., Carthage, Ohio.

CARTUNE
GB c. 1970
Cartune (Teeside) Ltd., Middlesbrough, Teeside. Kit cars.

CARUNA
CH 1974–1990
Erwin Schill, Karosserie Caruna AG, Spretenbach. Sports cars and convertibles.

CARVER
USA 1901
A.F. Carver, New York, N.Y. Three-wheelers.

CARVILLE
CH c. 1992
VESSA, Clarens. Electric city cars.

ČAS
CS 1921
Česká automobilová společnost pro obchod a montáž. motorových vozidel, Praha. Cyclecars.

CASADAY
USA 1904–1905
W.L. Casaday Mfg. Co., South Bend, Indiana.
See "Williams."

CASALINI
I 1971–1989
Casalini Costr. Mec., Piacenza. City cars.

CASE
CDN 1906–1909
Howard Case & Co., Lethbridge, Alberta.

CASE
USA 1911–1927
J.I. Case Threshing Machine Co., Racine, Wisconsin. Touring cars. Formerly "Pierce-Racine."
See "Jay Eye See."

CASEY
USA 1901; 1914
F.A. Casey Co., Billerica, Massachusetts.

CASLER
USA 1901
B.G. Casler, Chicago, Illinois. Electric runabout.

CASSEL
GB 1900–1903
Central Motor Co., Glasgow. 2- or 4-cylinder assembled cars.

CASTAGNERI
I 1900–1902
Sebastiani Castagneri, Alessandria.
See "Folgore."

CASTELFUSANO
I 1958
Ing. Luigi Crispolti, Roma.
See "Crispolti."

CASTLE THREE
GB 1919–1922
Castle Motor Co. Ltd., Kidderminster, Worcestershire. Three-wheelers.

CASTRO
E 1901–1904
J. Castro Sociedad en Comandita (1901–1904). Fabrica La Hispano-Suiza de Automoviles, Barcelona (1904). Tonneau.

CASWELL STEAM
USA 1901; 1905
M.J. Caswell, Sandusky, Ohio.

C.A.T.
F 1911
Construction Automobiles Tarnaise, Rabastens/Tarn. Light two-seater.

CATARACT
USA 1904
Cataract Machine & Automobile Co., Niagara Falls, N.Y.

CATERHAM
GB 1957–present
Caterham Cars Ltd., Caterham Hill, Surrey. Sports cars.

CATO
USA 1910; 1912
J.L. Cato, San Francisco, California. Six-cylinder air-cooled model built 1910 and four-cylinder water-cooled car reportedly built in 1912.

CATORI
D c. 1987
Catori Automobile, Hochdahl. Tuning.

CATROW
USA 1899
Herbert Catrow, Miamisburg, Ohio.

CATTANEO
I 1947
Guido Cattaneo. Sports car.

CAUSAN
F 1923–1924
Automobiles Causan, Levallois-Perret/Seine. Cyclecars.

CAVAC
USA 1910–1911
Small Motor Car Co., Plymouth, Michigan. Roadsters.

CAVALIER
USA 1926
Cavalier Motor Association, Mt. Vermont, N.Y. Roadsters.

CAVALIER CENTAUR
GB c. 1979
Magraw Engineering Ltd., Bromley, Kent. Sports car.

CAWLEY
USA 1917
C.A. Cawley, Salt Lake, Utah.

C.B.
USA 1917–1918
Carter Bros. Motor Co., Hyattsville, Maryland. 4-, 8- and 12-cylinder models.

CBT
BR 1991–1993
Companhia Brasileira de Tratores, Sao Carlos, São Paulo. 4 × 4 vehicle.

C.C.C.
GB 1906–1907
Chassis Construction Co. Ltd., Taunton, Somerset. 4,942 cc chain-driven model.

CD
D c.1985
CD Car Design Automobilveredelungsges. mbH, Pforzheim. Tuning.

CD
D c. 1986
CD Design, Haan. Tuning.

C. DE L.
USA 1913
C. de L. Engineering Works, Nutley, New Jersey. Passenger car and truck chassis.

CECIL
USA 1901
Rueben E. Cecil, Lincoln, Nebraska. Runabout.

CECO
USA 1914–1915
Continental Engineering Co., Minneapolis, Minnesota (1914). Chicago, Illinois (1914–1915). Cyclecars.

CEDERHOLM
S 1890–1892
Cederholm Bros. Steam car.

CEDRE
F 1977–1984
Cedre, Montesquieu-Volvestre, Toulouse. Electric three-wheelers.

CEGGA
CH 1960–1969
Gebruder Gachnang, Fa. Cega, Aigle. Sports cars.

CEIRANO
I 1898–1899
G.B. Ceirano & C., Torino.

CEIRANO
I 1901–1904
Fratelli Ceirano (1901–1903). G.G. Fratelli Ceirano (1903–1904). Ceirano & Cia., Torino (1904). Voiturette.

CEIRANO
I 1919–1931
Giovanni Ceirano Fabbrica Automobili (1919–1924). Societa Ceirano Automobili Torino, Torino (1924–1931). Touring and sports cars.

CEIRANO ANSALDI
I
See "SPA."

CELER
GB 1904
The Celer Motor Car Co., Nottingham. 8 hp light cars.

CELERITAS
A 1901–1903
Automobilfabrik Celeritas, Wien. Voiturette.

CELFOR
USA 1916
Buchanan, Michigan.

CELTIC
F 1908–1913
Marcel Caplet, Le Havre/Seine-Inferieure. Conventional shaft-drive machines of 12 hp.

CELTIC
F 1927–1929
Compagnie Générale des Voitures a Paris, Paris. 700 and 1,086 cc engines.

CELTIC
GB 1904–1908
Bradford Motor Car Co. (1904–1907). Thornton Engineering Co., Bradford, Yorks. (1907–1908). Eight cars were made.

CEMSA
I 1946–1948
Caproni Elettromeccanica Saronno S.A., Sarono. Front-wheel-drive cars.

CENTAUR
GB 1900–1901
Centaur Cycle Co. Ltd., Coventry, Warwickshire. Four-seater dos-a-dos.

CENTAUR
USA 1902–1903
Centaur Motor Vehicle Co. (1902). Centaur Motor Co. (1903), Buffalo, N.Y. Became Towanda Motor Vehicle Co. Gasoline and electric vehicles.

CENTAURUS
BR 1957
Comercio e Industria INDUCA SA, Rio de Janeiro. Three-wheeler prototype.

CENTRAL
USA 1903
Central Motor Car Co., Indianapolis, Indiana. Gasoline car prototype.

CENTRAL
USA 1904
Central Machine & Engineering Co., Detroit, Michigan. Prototype.

CENTRAL
USA 1905
Central Manufacturing Company, Connersville, Indiana. Steam car.

CENTRAL
USA 1905
Central Automobile Co., Pittsfield, Massachusetts. Rotary steam engine.

CENTRAL
USA 1905–1906
Central Automobile Co., Providence, Rhode Island.

CENTRAL
USA 1953
St. Louis, Missouri.

CENTRAL-AUTO
A
See "Wimmer."

CENTRAL GREYHOUND
USA 1905
H.F. Buffum Co., Abington, Massachusetts. 8-cylinder sports car.
See "Buffum."

CENTRON
GB 1970–?
G.P. Speed Shop Ltd., Feltham, Middlesex. Sports cars.

CENTURY
GB 1899–1907
Century Engineering & Motor Co. Ltd., Altrincham, Cheshire (1899–1901); London (1901–1904). Century Engineering Co. Ltd., London (1904–1907). Three-wheelers and light cars.

CENTURY
GB 1928–1929
Century Cars Ltd., London. Light cars.

CENTURY
USA 1901
Century Mfg. Co., St. Louis, Missouri.

CENTURY
USA 1900–1904
Century Motor Vehicle Co., Syracuse, N.Y. Electric car. Formerly "Barnes" electric (1899). Also built gasoline and steam cars. Bankrupt June 1904 and sold out.

CENTURY
USA 1911–1915
Century Electric Vehicle Co., Detroit, Michigan (1913–1915). Also known as Century Electric Motor Car Co. (1911–1913). Reported bankrupt June 1915.

CENTURY STEAMER
USA 1906
Century Auto Power Co., East Orange, New Jersy. Built to order.

CENTURY TOURIST
USA 1901
Ward-Leonard Electric Co., Bronxville, N.Y. Runabout. Also built "Knickerbocker" 1901–1903.

CENTURY TOURIST
USA 1903
Century Motor Vehicle Co., Syracuse, N.Y.
See "Century" electric.

CERTUS
D 1928–1929
Dierks & Wroblewski, Certus Automobil-Werk, Offenburg. 32, 45, 60 and 80 hp cars.

CERTUS
GB 1908
Certus Gearless Co. Ltd., London. Friction transmission.

CESAR
F 1906
David, Boudene & Cie., Paris.

CEVA
I
Costruzioni e Vendita Automobili Ansaldo.
See "Ansaldo."

C.E.Y.C.
E 1922–1926
Centro Electrotecnico y Communicaciones, Ministero de la. Guerra, Madrid. 792 cc light cars.

C-F
USA 1990s
C-F Enterprises, Ltd., Long Beach, California. Kit cars.

C.F.
USA 1907–1909
Cornish-Friedberg Motor Car Co., Chicago, Illinois. Runabout. Sometimes listed as "Cornish-Friedberg."

C.F.B.
GB 1920–1921
C.F.B. Car Syndicate Ltd., London. Light cars.

C.F.L.
GB 1913
F. Clayton & Co., London. Cyclecars.

C.G.
F 1967–c. 1975
Carrosserie Chappe Freres et Gessalin, Brie-Comte-Robert/Seine-et-Marne. Sports cars.

C.G.E.
F 1941 1946
Compangnie Generale Electrique, Paris. Electric cars.

C.G.P.
USA 1915
Dr. Chas. G. Percival, New York, N.Y. One car produced.

C.G.V. (CHARRON)
F 1901–1930
Charron, Girardot et Voigt (1901–1906). Automobiles Charron, Puteaux/Seine (1906–1930). Touring cars.

C.G.V. (AMERICAN)
USA 1902–1903
Charron, Girardot & Voigt, Rome, N.Y. French car built by Rome Locomotive Works in Rome, N.Y. Sold by Smith & Mabley, New York, N.Y. Seven cars built.

CHABOCHE
F 1901–1906
E. Chaboche, Paris. Steam cars.

CHADWICK
USA 1904–1916
Fairmont Engineering Co. (1904–1905). Fairmont Engineering Works (1905–1907). Chadwick Engineering Works (1907–1908), Philadelphia, Pennsylvania. Chadwick Engineering Works (1908–1916), Pottstown, Pennsylvania. Touring cars.

CHADWICK
USA 1960
Chadwick Engineering Works, Pottstown, Pennsylvania. Convertibles.

CHAIGNEAU-BRASIER
F 1929
Light car.

CHAINLESS
F 1900–1903
SA des Voitures Legeres "Chainless," Paris. Voiturette.

CHALFANT
USA 1905–1912
Chalfant Gasoline Motor Car Co., Lenover, Pennsylvania. Touring cars.

CHALLENGE
GB
See "Marcus."

CHALMERS
USA 1910–1924
Chalmers-Detroit Motor Co. Chalmers Motor Co., Detroit, Michigan. Formerly "Chalmers-Detroit." Merged with Maxwell Motor Co. 1919. Became "Chrysler." Touring cars.

CHALMERS-DETROIT
USA 1908–1910
E.R. Thomas-Detroit Co., Detroit, Michigan. Became Chalmers-Detroit Motor Co. July 1908. Became "Chalmers" 1910.

CHAMBERS
GB 1904–1925
Chambers Motors Ltd., Belfast, Northern Ireland. Touring cars.

CHAMBON
F 1912–1914
Auguste Chambon, Lyon. Touring cars.

CHAMEROY
F 1907–1911
Automobiles Chameroy, Le Vesinet/Seine-et-Oise. Voiturettes.

CHAMONIX
BR 1985–present
Chamonix Ind. e Com. Ltda., São Paulo. "Porsche" (D) replicas.

CHAMPION
D 1947–1954
Hermann Holbein, Herrlingen (1947–1950). Champion Automobil GmbH, Paderborn (1950–1952). Rheinische Automobilfabrik Hennhofer & Co. (1952–1954). Rheinische Automobilwerke Thorndal & Co., Ludwigshafen (1954). Small two-seater cars with 250 cc and 400 cc engines.

CHAMPION
USA c. 1902
Champion Wagon Company, Owego, N.Y. Prototype.

CHAMPION
USA 1909–1910
Famous Mfg. Co., East Chicago, Indiana. Air-cooled car.

CHAMPION
USA 1909–1911
Champion Motor Car Co., Milwaukee, Wisconsin (1909–1910).

CHAMPION
USA 1912–1913
Champion Electric Vehicle Co., New York, N.Y. Electric cars.

CHAMPION
USA 1913
Champion Motor Car Co., Minneapolis, Minnesota

CHAMPION
USA 1916–1917
Champion Auto Equipment Co., Wabash, Indiana. Small 4-cylinder cars. Tyres inflatable while in motion.

CHAMPION
USA 1919–1925
Direct Drive Motor Co. Champion Motors Corp., Pottstown, Pennsylvania.

CHAMPION
USA 1920
Champion Motor Car Co., Cleveland, Ohio. 4-cylinder touring car.

CHAMPROBERT
F 1902–1905
De Champrobert & Cie., Levallois-Perret/Seine. Electric cars.

CHANDLER
USA c. 1905
H.N. Chandler, Boston, Massachusetts. 7 hp car.

CHANDLER
USA 1914–1929
Chandler Motor Car Co., Cleveland, Ohio. 1919 Cleveland Automobile Co. was subsidiary. Company name changed to Chandler-Cleveland Motors Corp. 1925. Sale of plant to "Hupmobile" announced November 30, 1928. Touring cars.

CHANG'AN
PRC 1997–present
Chang'an-Suzuki Automobile Corp., Chongquing, Sechuan. "Suzuki" (J) under license.

CHANNON
GB 1903–1907
Channon & Sons, Dorchester, Dorset. Light cars.

CHAPARRAL
D 1986–1990
Walter Scheuer, CEP Classic Cars GmbH, Frankfurt am Main. Sports cars.

CHAPARRAL
USA 1910
Harry Eugene Luck, Cleburne, Texas.
  See "Luck Utility."

CHAPEAUX
F 1940–1941
Voitures E. Chapeaux, Lyon. Two-seater electric car.

CHAPIN
USA c. 1905
Mrs. A.H. Chapin, Bridgeport, Connecticut.

CHAPMAN
USA 1891–1905
Edward D. Chapman & Sons. Mfg. Co., Stoughton, Massachusetts. Electric cars.

CHAPMAN
USA 1899–1901
William H. Chapman, Portland, Maine. Main production was electric car chassis components. Became Belnap Motor Co., 1900.

CHAPMAN
USA 1905
Odell M. Chapman, Stonington, Connecticut. Steam auto-buggy.

CHAPUIS-DORNIER
F 1919; 1921
4-cylinder 3-litre car prototypes by famous engine maker.

CHARENTAISE
F 1899
Pougnaud et Brothier, Ruffec, Charente. Voiturette.

CHARGER
GB 1977–1983
Embeesa Kit Cars., High Wycombe, Bucks. Sports car kit.

CHARLES DIETZ
F 1834
Steam car.

CHARLES RICHARD
F 1901–1902
Sté. des Moteurs et Autos Charles Richard, Troyes/Aube. Belt-driven light cars.

CHARLES TOWN-ABOUT
USA 1958–1959
Stinson Aircraft Tool & Engineering Corp., San Diego, California. Electric cars.

CHARLON
F 1905–1906
Sté. des Automobiles Charlon, Argenteuil/Seine-et-Oise. Belt- and chain-driven light cars.

CHARRON
F
  See "C.G.V."

CHARRON, GIRARDOT & VOIGT
USA 1902
Charron, Girardot & Voigt, Rome, N.Y. American-built with Quimby body. Seven cars built.
  See "C.G.V."

CHARRON-LAYCOCK
GB 1920–1926
W.S. Laycock Ltd., Sheffield, Yorks. Touring cars.

CHARTER
USA 1903–1904
James A. Charter, Chicago, Illinois. Gas & water vapor engined tonneau.

CHARTER OAK
USA 1917
Eastern Motors Inc., Hartford, Connecticut. One car built with USD 30,000 authorized by Allen Shelden.

Fred A. Law, chief engineer. Company in receivership August 1917.

CHASE
USA 1902
F.W. Chase, Worcester, Massachusetts. Steam car.

CHASE
USA 1907–1912
Chase Motor Trucks Co., Syracuse, N.Y. Passenger cars 1907–1912, trucks to 1917.

CHASE
USA 1909
A.F. Chase, Minneapolis, Minnesota. Highwheeler.

CHATEL-JEANNIN
E 1902–1903
Cie de Construction d'Automobiles Chatel-Jeannin, Mulhouse, Alsace. 6 and 12 hp cars.

CHATER-LEA
GB 1907; 1913–1922
Chater-Lea Ltd., London. Light cars.

CHATHAM
CDN 1907–1908
Chatham Motor Car Co. Ltd., Chatham, Ontario.

CHAUSSON
F 1948
Small car prototype.
  See "C.H.S."

CHAUTAUQUA
USA 1913–1914
Chautauqua Cyclecar Co., Jamestown, N.Y. Cyclecar.

CHAUTAUQUA ELECTRIC
USA 1919–1920
Chautauqua Electric Mfg. Co., Falconer, N.Y.

CHAUTAUQUA STEAMER
USA 1911
Chautauqua Motor Co., Dunkirk, N.Y.

CHAVANET
F
  See "Automoto."

CHECKER
USA 1922–1982
Checker Taxicab Mfg. Co. (later Check Motors Corp.). Produced taxicabs only from 1922.

CHELIK
TR 1970s
"Skoda" (CS) assembled cars.

CHELMSFORD
GB
See "Clarkson."

CHELSEA
GB 1922
Wandsworth Engineering Works, London. Electric car.

CHELSEA
USA 1901–1904
Chelsea Mfg. Co., Chelsea, Michigan. Company name of "Welch" manufacturer, not name of vehicle.

CHELSEA
USA 1914
Chelsea Mfg. Co., Newark, New Jersey. Cyclecars.

CHEMNITZER MOTORWAGENFABRIK
D 1901
Chemnitzer Motorwagenfabrik Bruno Berger & Co., Chemnitz.

CHENARD-WALCKER
F 1901–1946
Chenard, Walcker et Cie, Asnieres/Seine (1901–1907). SA des Anciens Établissements Chenard et Walcker, Gennevilliers/Seine (1907–1946). Touring cars.

CHENHALL
GB 1902–1906
Chenhalls Motor Car Ltd. (1902). St. Andrews Cycle and Electrical Co., Plymouth, Devon (1903–1906).

CHENU
F 1903–1907
Automobiles Chenu, Paris. Shaft- and chain-driven cars.

CHESIL
GB 1990s
Chesil Motor Company, Bridport, Dorset. Sports kit cars.

CHESWOLD
GB 1911–1915
E.W. Jackson & Son Ltd., Doncaster, Yorks. 16 hp cars.

CHEVROLET
BR 1964–present
G.M. do Brasil S.A., Sao Caetano do Sul.

CHEVROLET
RA 1962–present
G.M. Argentina S.A., Buenos Aires.

CHEVROLET
USA 1913–present
Chevrolet Motor Co., Detroit, Michigan. First car introduced 1913 at New York Auto Show. Absorbed Little Motor Car Co. 1913. Also Republic Motor Car Co., Detroit, Michigan. Absorbed into General Motors 1918. Passenger and sports cars.

CHEVRON
GB 1961–present
A.D. Bennett and Co., Salford, Lancs. Sports cars.

CHIC
AUS 1923–1929
Chic Cars Ltd., Adelaide, S.A. 50 cars were made.

CHICAGO
USA 1899
Chicago Electric Vehicle and Transportation Co., Chicago, Illinois. Electric car.

CHICAGO
USA 1899–1901
Chicago Electric Vehicle Co., Faribault, Minnesota; Chicago, Illinois. Electric cars.

CHICAGO
USA 1905–1906
Chicago Automobile Mfg. Co., Chicago, Illinois. Steam cars. Company was in business from 1904 to 1907 but only built a 1906 model.

CHICAGO
USA 1906
Chicago Pneumatic Tool Co., Chicago, Illinois. Built 50 highwheelers.
See "C.P.T."

CHICAGO
USA 1905–1907
Company name of Chicago Recording Scale Co., Chicago, Illinois not name of vehicle.
See "Appolo."

CHICAGO
USA 1907
Chicago Coach & Carriage Co., Chicago, Illinois. Company name of "Duer" manufacturer.

CHICAGO
USA 1912–1916
Chicago Electric Motor Car Co. Walker Electric Vehicle Co. (1915–1916), Chicago, Illinois. Electric cars. Frederick J. Newman, designer. Bought by Anderson Electric Car Co. 1916.

CHICAGO
USA 1914
Chicago Cyclecar Co., Chicago, Illinois. Cyclecars.

CHICAGO
USA c. 1990s
Chicago Armor & Limousine Mfg. Co., Lake Zurich, Illinois. Bullet-proof limousines.

CHICAGOAN
USA 1952–1954
Triplex Industries Inc., Blue Island, Illinois. 15 sports cars were built, using "Willys" engine. Name changed to (see) "Triplex" in 1954.

CHICAGO LIGHT 6
USA 1917
Pan American Motors Corp., Chicago, Illinois. Became "Pan American."

CHICAGO MOTOR BUGGY
USA 1908
Chicago Motor Buggy Co., Chicago, Illinois. Highwheelers.

CHIEF
USA 1908
Chief Mfg. Co., Buffalo, N.Y.

CHIEF
USA 1911
Chief Motor Car Co., Detroit, Michigan. Touring car.

CHIHUAHUA
I 1974
G.O.M., Salermo. City car prototype.

CHILTERN
GB 1919–1920
Vulcan Motor & Engineering Co. Ltd., Dunstable, Beds. Sports cars.

CHILTERN
GB 1919–1920
Woodman & Fitch, London.

CHINGKANSHAN
PRC c. 1958
Prototype.

CHIRIBIRI
I 1913–1927

Autocostruzioni Meccaniche Chiribiri & Co., Torino. Passenger cars. Also rhomboid wheel placement prototype. Designed by (see) "Fuscaldo."

CHIVILLE CYCLECAR
USA 1914
Gerard D. Chiville, Chicago, Illinois.

CHIYODA
J 1932–1935
Tokyo Gas and Electric Engineering Co., Tokyo. 4- and 6-wheel 6-7-seaters.

CHOATE
USA 1896
Parker C. Choate, Portland, Maine.

CHOTA
GB
See "Buckingham."

CHRISTCHURCH-CAMPBELL
GB 1922
Campbell Ltd., Christchurch, Hampshire. Six cars were made.

CHRISTENSEN
USA 1908
N.A. Christensen, Milwaukee, Wisconsin.

CHRISTIAEN
B 1900
Emile Christiaen, Plassendaele.

CHRISTIANE HUIT
F 1928–1929
A. Andrieux, Rennes/Ille-et-Vilaine. Sports cars.

CHRISTIE
USA 1904–1910
Christie Iron Works, New York, N.Y. (1904–1905). 1906 became Christie Direct Action Motor Car Co., New York, N.Y. Became Front Drive Motor Co, Hoboken, New Jersey, 1907. Touring cars and taxicabs.

CHRISTMAN
USA 1901–1907
Chas. G. Christman, Los Gatos, California (1901–1905). Christman Automobile Co., San Jose, California (1907). Became Golden State Automobile Co. 1902. Christman continued with mufflers.

CHRISTOPHER
USA 1908–1910
Christopher Bros., Chicago, Illinois. Company name, not name of vehicle. Company built "Triumph."

CHRITON
GB 1904
Chriton Automobile Co., Saltburn-by-the-Sea, Yorks. Shaft-driven light cars.

CHRYSLER
AUS 1928–present
Chrysler Australia Ltd., Adelaide, S.A.

CHRYSLER
F 1970–1983
Chrysler France S.A., Poissy, Seine-et-Oise.

CHRYSLER
USA 1924–present
Chrysler Motor Corp., Detroit, Michigan. Absorbed Maxwell Motor Corp. 1925, Dodge Bros. Motor Car Co. 1928.
See "DeSoto," "Dodge" and "Plymouth." Passenger cars.

C.H.S.
F 1948
SA des Usines Chausson, Asnieres/Seine. Light cars.

CHUBU
J c. 1956
Light car prototype.

CHURCH
USA 1901
Church Automobile Co., Pittsburgh, Pennsylvania.

CHURCH
USA 1913–1914
Church Motor Car Co., Chicago, Illinois. A simple pneumatic car without clutch or valves.

CHURCH-FIELD
USA 1912–1913
Church-Field Motor Co., Sibley, Michigan. Electric cars.

CHURCHILL
GB
See "Hallamshire."

CHURCHILL
USA 1913
D.D. Churchill, Spokane, Washington. 20 hp prototype.

CIA
USA c. 1984
Cia Industries. 62 cars built in 1984.

CICALINA
I 1972
Small car.

CICO
F 1979–1985
City car.

C.I.D.
F 1912–1914
Constructions Industrielles Dijonaises, Dijon. Light cars.

C.I.E.M.
CH 1904–1906
Compagnie d'Industrie Électrique et Mécanique, Geneve. Gasoline-electric cars.

CIMBRIA
USA 1982
See "Amore."

CIMEM
I
See "Girino."

CIMOS
YU 1972–c. 1991
Tovarna Automobilov Cimos, Nova Gorica; Koper. "Citroën" (F) license.

CINCINNATI
USA 1903–1904
Cincinnati Automobile Co., Cincinnati, Ohio. Steam runabout.

CINGOLANI
I 1952
Ezio Cingolani. Three-wheeler "Recanti."

CINO
USA 1900–1913
Haberer & Co., Gest & Summer Sts., Cincinnati, Ohio. Touring and sports cars.

C.I.P.
I 1922–1924
Cyclecar Italiana Petromilli, Torino.

CIRCLEVILLE
USA 1914
Circleville Automobile Company, Circleville, Ohio. Cyclecars.

CIRRUS
GB 1972
Institute of British Carriage & Automobile Manufacturers, London. Sports car prototype.

CISITALIA
I 1946–1964
La Compania Industriale Sportiva Italia (C.I.S.Italia). Cisitalia SpA, Torino. Sports cars.

CISSEL
USA 1938
Humphrey Cissel, Rockville, Maryland. Little midget single-seater.

CITERIA
NL 1958
L.J. van Beekum, Den Haag. Sports car prototype.

CITICAR
USA 1974
Sebring Vanguard Corp., Sebring, Florida. Electric city car. About 3,000 were made.

CITO
E 1905–1909
Cito Fahrradwerke AG (1905–1907). Cito-Werke AG, Köln (1907–1909). Light cars.

CITROËN
F 1919–present
SA Andre Citroën (1919–1968). Citroën SA, Paris (1968–present). Passenger cars.

CITROËN
CB 1960–1964
Citroën Cars Limited, Slough. Light cars based on the "Citroën" (F) 2CV.

CITROËN ITALIANA
I 1924–1925
Societa Anonima Italiana Automobili Citroën, Milano.

CITY
H 1988
Tamás Venéczi, Zsolt Varga, Budapest. Three-wheeled city car prototype.

CITY & SUBURBAN
GB 1901–1905
City & Suburban Electric Carriage Co. Ltd., London. Electric car.

CITYBOY
D 1982–1989
Minimobil-Wagen Fries GmbH, Wielenbach bei Weilheim. Minicar.

CITYCAR
F 1959
Bouffort, Paris. City car prototype.

CITYCAR
GB c. 1970
Mike Forrest. City car prototype.

CITYCOM
DK 1993–1996
CityCom Elektromobilfabrik A/S, Randers. Electric minicars.

CITY WHEELS
GB 1986
London. Electric city car.

CIUDADANO
RA 1956
Buyatti Automotriz SA. Small car prototype.

CIVELLI DE BOSCH
F 1907–1909
Civelli de Bosch & Cie., Paris. Shaft-driven 10–50 hp cars.

CIZETA
I 1988–1995
Cizeta Automobili Srl, Modena. Sports cars.

CLAEYS-FLANDRIA
B 1954
Ateliers Claeys, Zedelgem. Minicar prototype.

CLA-HOLME
USA 1922
Cla-Holme Motor Car Sales Co., Denver, Colorado. One car produced.

CLAN
GB 1971–1974; 1984–1986
Clan Motor Co. Ltd., Washington, Co. Durham. Sports cars. 315 and 40 cars built.
See "Kaisis" (CY).

CLAPP
USA 1898–1900
Henry W. Clapp, New Haven, Connecticut (1898–1899). Clapp Motor Vehicle Co., Jersey City, New Jersey (1900). Auto-buggy.

CLARENDON
GB 1902–1903
Clarendon Motor Car & Bicycle Co. Ltd., Coventry, Warwickshire. Voiturette.

CLARIN MUSTAD
N/F 1916–1917; 1935
Mustad & Son, Oslo, Norway (1916–1917; 1935). Clarin Mustad, Duclair/Seine-Inferieure, France (1917). 6-wheeler cars.

CLARK
GB 1901
Charles Clark & Sons, Retford, Notts. Voiturette.

CLARK
USA 1899–1909
Edward S. Clark, Boston, Massachusetts. Steam car. Steam Boiler Company founded 1895. Gasoline commercial vehicles 1911.

CLARK
USA 1903
A.F. Clark & company, Philadelphia, Pennsylvania. Electric car. Became Electric Vehicle Equipment Co.

CLARK
USA 1901–1903
Clark Manufacturing Co., Moline, Illinois.

CLARK
USA 1905–1906
Clark Motor Car Co., Jackson, Michigan.

CLARK
USA 1908
Allen & Clark Co., Toledo, Ohio. Electric car.

CLARK
USA 1910–1912
Clark Motor Car Co., Shelbyville, Indiana; Andreson, Indiana. Absorbed by "Meteor."

CLARK
USA 1910–1912
Clark & Co., Lansing, Michigan. Highwheeler.

CLARK
USA 1911–1912
Clark Motor Car Co., Louisville, Kentucky.

CLARK-CARTER
USA 1909–1911
Clark-Carter Automobile Co., Jackson, Michigan. Believed to be company name, not name of vehicle. Company built "Cutting."

CLARKE
USA 1907
Clarke Automobile & Launch Co., Jacksonville, Florida.

CLARK-HATFIELD
USA 1908–1909

Clark-Hatfield Automobile Co., Oshkosh, Wisconsin. Highwheelers.

CLARKMOBILE
USA 1903–1906
Clarkmobile Company, Lansing, Michigan. Succeeded by Deere-Clark Automobile Co. January 1906.

CLARKSON
GB 1899–1902
Clarkson & Capel Steam Car Syndicate Ltd., London (1899–1902). Clarkson Ltd., Chelmsford, Essex (1902). Steam cars.

CLARK STEAM
USA 1900–1901
Clark & co., Cleveland, Ohio.

CLARK STEAM
USA 1901–1905
William G. Clark, Cambridge, Massachusetts.

CLASSIC
F 1925–1929
Cie Générale des Voitures a Paris, Paris. 2.2-litre cars.

CLASSIC
USA 1916–1917
Classic Motor Car Corp., Chicago, Illinois. Touring cars.

CLASSIC
USA 1920–1921
Classic Motor Car Co., Lake Geneva, Wisconsin. Reincorporation of 1916–1917 "Classic."

CLASSIC-CAR
D 1979–1983
Classic-Car Janssen, Lüdenscheid. "Jaguar" and "Bugatti" replica.

CLASSIC-CAR
D c. 1979
Classic-Car Wittek GmbH, Langenfeld. Replicars.

CLASSIC CARS OF LONDON
CDN 1982
Classic Cars of London, London, Ontario. "Auburn" replicars.

CLASSIC-CAR-OLDTIMERBAU
D 1977–c. 1989
Classic-Car-Oldtimerbau, Frankfurt am Main. Replicars.

CLASSIC MOTOR CARRIAGES
USA 1982–c. 1988
Classic Motor Carriages, Inc., Miami, Florida. Replicars, kits.
See "CMC."

CLASSIC REPLICARS
GB 1990s
Classic Replicars Ltd., Bournemouth. Kit cars and replicars.

CLASSIC REPRODUCTIONS
USA 1982
Classic Reproductions, Ltd., Costa Mesa, California. "Jaguar" replicars.

CLASSIC ROADSTERS
USA 1982–1993
Classic Roadsters, Fargo, New Dakota. Replicars.

CLAUDE DELAGE
F 1926
Claude Delage, Clichy/Seine. Touring cars.

CLAUSEN
USA 1913
Jake Clausen, Los Angeles, California.

CLAUSET
F 1959–1960
Sté. Clauset, Paris. "Citroën" 2CV based sports cars.

CLAVEAU
F 1926–1934; 1946–1950
Automobiles Claveau, Paris. Mostly experimental cars.

CLAWSEN
USA 1903
Smith Clawsen, Lansing, Michigan. Runabout.

CLAXES
B c. 1955
Small car prototype.

CLAYTON
GB 1867
Clayton & Shuttleworth. Steam car.

C.L.C.
F 1911–1913
Cockborne, Lehucher et da Costa, Paris. Small cars.

CLEARMONT
USA 1922
Clearmont Steamer Inc., New York, N.Y. Steam car. Same as "Coats Steamer."

CLEAVER
USA 1903
Cleaver Motor Vehicle Co., Fond du Lac, Wisconsin. 12 hp passenger car.

CLEBURNE
USA 1913
Cleburne Motor Car Mfg. Co., Cleburne, Texas.
See "Luck Utility."

CLECO
GB 1936–1940
Cleco Electric Industries Ltd., Manchester. Electric car.

CLEGG STEAMER
USA 1884–1886
John and Thomas Clegg, Memphis, Michigan. Steam car.

CLEM
F 1912–1914
Cie Lyonnaise d'Études Mécaniques (1912–1914). Sté. des Voiturettes Clem, G. Gineste-Lacaze et Cie., Lyon (1914). Light cars.

CLÉMENT; CLÉMENT-BAYARD
F 1899–1922
Clément et Cie., Levallois-Perret/Seine (1899–1903). SA des Ets. Clément-Bayard, Levallois-Perret/Seine; Mézieres (1903–1922). Touring cars.

CLEMENT
GB 1908–1914
Clement Motor Co. Ltd., Coventry, Warwickshire. Touring cars.

CLEMENT
USA 1903
A. Clement Cycle Motor & Light Carriage Co., Hartford, Connecticut. Builder's father was the famous French automotive pioneer.

CLÉMENT-PANHARD
F 1899–1903
Société Clément, Paris.

CLÉMENT-ROCHELLE
F 1927–1930
Clément et Rochelle, Clamart/Seine. Light cars.

CLEMENT-TALBOT
GB
See "Talbot."

CLÉNET
USA 1975–1987
Clénet Coachworks, Inc., Goleta, California. Replicars.

CLERMONT
USA c. 1922
George A. Coats, Columbus, Ohio.
See "Coats."

CLESSE
F 1907–1908
Clesse et Cie., Levallois-Perret/Seine. Friction-driven voiturette.

CLETRAC
USA
See "Rollin" 1923–1925.

CLEVELAND
USA 1900
American Bicycle Co., Westfield, Massachusetts. Three-wheelers.

CLEVELAND
USA 1900
Cleveland Machine Screw Co., Cleveland, Ohio. Electric cars.

CLEVELAND
USA 1902
Hansen Automobile Co., Cleveland, Ohio. Became General Automobile & Manufacturing Co. 1902.

CLEVELAND
USA 1903–1904
Cleveland Automobile Co., Cleveland, Ohio.

CLEVELAND
USA 1905–1909
Cleveland Motor Car Co., Cleveland, Ohio (1905–1908); New York, N.Y. (1908–1909). Not connected with "Cleveland" 1903–1904.

CLEVELAND
USA 1904–1909
Cleveland Motor Carriage Co., Cleveland, Ohio. Merchant & Evans Co., Philadelphia, Pennsylvania. Used "Garford" chassis.

CLEVELAND
USA 1909
Cleveland Electric Vehicle Co., Cleveland, Ohio. Electric cars. Former Cuyahoga Motor Car Co.

CLEVELAND
USA 1914
Cleveland Cyclecar Co., Cleveland, Ohio. Cyclecars. Discontinued January 1915.

CLEVELAND
USA 1919–1926
Cleveland Automobile Co., Cleveland, Ohio. Subsidiary of Chandler Motor Car Co. Succeeded by Chandler-Cleveland Motors Corp., December 1925. Touring cars.

CLIDEN
GB
Sports car.
See "Halseylec."

CLIFT
GB
See "Sinclair."

CLIMAX
GB 1905–1907
Climax Motor Co., Coventry, Warwickshire. Assembled cars.

CLIMAX
USA 1906–1911
Climax Electric Works, New Salem, Massachusetts. Air-cooled cars. Became T. & F. Cyclecar Co.

CLIMBER
USA 1919–1924
Climber Motor Corp., Detroit, Michigan; Little Rock, Arkansas. Company started at Poteau, Oklahoma. 1924 became New Climber Co. Touring cars.

CLINTON
CDN 1914
Clinton Motor Car Co., Clinton, Ontario. Cyclecars. Later advertised as "American" cyclecar.

CLINTON
USA 1902
Clinton Machine & Dusting Works, Clinton, Massachusetts. Steam car.

CLINTON E. WOODS
USA 1897–1901
Clinton E. Woods Co., Chicago, Illinois. Electric cars. Became Woods-Waring & Co. 1901 and Woods Motor Vehicle Co. 1902.

CLIPPER
USA 1902
Clipper Autocar Co., Grand Rapids, Michigan. Steam car.

CLODHOPPER
USA c.1968
Fiber Fab, Santa Clara, California. Dune buggy.

CLOSE
USA 1902–1907
Close Cycle Co., Olean, N.Y.

CLOUGH
USA 1869
Enos M. Cough, Lakeport, New Hampshire. One car produced. Also called "Faerie Queen."

CLOUGHLEY
USA 1896–1903
Robert H. Cloughley, Cloughley Motor Vehicle Co. (1901), Parsons, Kansas. Early steam and gasoline cars. First patents 1891. Production began 1902, ended 1903. Plans announced to resume 1904.

CLOUMOBIL
D 1906–1908
Automobilbauerei "Clou" Alfred Karfunkel, Berlin. Voiturette.

CLOVER
USA 1901
H.K. Clover, Salt Lake City, Utah. Steam car.
See "Royalmobile."

CLOYD
USA 1911
Cloyd Auto Co., Nashville, Tennessee. 7-passenger touring.

CLUA
E 1955–1959
Construcciones Metalicas Clua SL, Barcelona. Small sports car.

CLUB
D 1922–1924
Club-Automobilfabrik GmbH, Berlin. Small assembled cars.

CLUB
F
See "Brouhot."

CLUB CAR
USA 1910–1911
Club Car Co. of America, New York, N.Y. Merchant & Evans Co., Philadelphia, Pennsylvania. 40 hp cars. Shareholders got 25% discount toward purchase of the car.

CLULEY
GB 1922–1928
Clarke, Cluley & Co., Coventry, Warwickshire. Light cars.

CLUTS
USA 1903
Oliver Cluts, Cuba, Illinois. Prototype.

CLYDE
GB 1901–1930
Clyde Cycle & Motor Car Co. Ltd. (1901–1904). G.H. Wait (1905–1907) G.H. Wait & Co. Ltd., Leicester (1908–1909). Light cars.

CLYMER
USA 1908
Durable Motor Car Co., St. Louis, Missouri. Roadster.

CLYNO
GB 1922–1930
Clyno Engineering Co. (1922) Ltd., Wolverhampton, Staffs. (1922–1929). R.H. Collier & Co. Ltd., Birmingham (1929–1930). Touring cars.

C.M.
F 1924–1930
Charles Mochet, Saint-Ouen/Seine. Cyclecars and light cars.

CMC
USA 1986–c. 1993
Classic Motor Carriages, Miami, Florida. Replica.

C.M.N.
I 1919–1923
Costruzioni Meccaniche Nazionali SA, Milano (1919–1920). Officine Meccaniche Toscana, Pontendora (1920–1923). Chassis built around an "Isotta-Fraschini" engine.

C.M.V.
E 1944–1946
Construcciones Moviles de Valencia, Valencia. Small electric cars.

COADOU-FLEURY
F 1921–1935
Marcel Coadou, Trebeurden/C.-du-N. Cyclecars.

COASTER
GB c. 1970
Carter Engineering Co. Electric car.

COAST TO COAST
USA 1989–c. 1993
Coast to Coast Auto Styling Inc., Campo Hill, Pennsylvania. Sports car.

COATES-GOSHEN
USA 1909–1910
Coates-Goshen Automobile Co., Goshen, N.Y. Joseph S. Coates built experimental 4-cylinder car 1903. Showed "Mercedes" type car at 1909 New York Auto Show. Reported bankrupt October 1911. Less than 20 cars were built.

COATS
USA 1921–1923
Coats Machine Co., Indianapolis, Indiana. Coats Steam Car Co., Columbus, Ohio. Steam cars.

COBRA
D 1989
Motorsport-Center Mohr, Straubenhardt-Feldrennach. Sports car.

COBRA
USA 1962–1969
Shelby-American Inc., Venice, California. High-performance sports cars based on "Ford."
See "Shelby."

COBURN
USA 1911
Coburn Motor Car Co., Norfolk, Virginia.

COCCINELLE
F 1949
Small car prototype.
See "Atlas."

COCHOT
F 1899–1901
Cochot, Paris. Voiturette.

COCK
NL 1950–1974
Cock b.v., Assen. Gasoline and electric town car.

COCKMOBIL
D 1923–1925
Cockerell-Fahrzeug- und Motorenwerke AG, München. Three-wheelers.

COE
USA 1883
Adelbert Brown Coe, Lima, Ohio. Steam automobile.

COEUR DE BELLE
F 1967
Murasson. Sports car prototype.

COEY
USA 1900–1902
C.A. Coey & Co., Chicago, Illinois. Electric car.

COEY BEAR
USA 1914
Coey Motor Co., Chicago, Illinois. Stripped racing cyclecar offered in quantity sale.

COEY FLYER
USA 1913–1917
Coey-Mitchell Automobile Co. Coey Motor Co., Chicago, Illinois.

COFFEE
USA 1902
R.W. Coffee & Sons, Richmond, Virginia. Built gas car for Charles E. Miller. Transmission gear builders 1903.

COFFIN STEAMER
USA 1901
Howard E. Coffin, Ann Arbor, Michigan. One car built.

COGGINS
USA 1907
Clifford E. Coggins, Berkeley, California. 2-cylinder gasoline automobile.

COGGSWELL
USA 1910–1911
Coggswell Motor Car Co., Grand Rapids, Michigan. 35 hp touring cars.

COGNET DE SEYNES
F 1912–1926
Automobiles Cognet de Seynes, Lyon. 4-cylinder light cars.

COHENDET
F 1898–1914
Cohendet et Cie., Paris. Small and touring cars.

COLANI
D 1964–1980
Lutz (Luigi) Colani, Berlin. Canadur GmbH & Co. KG, Hessisch-Lichtenau. Officine Luigi Colani, Schloss Harkotten, Sassenberg. Sports car prototypes.

COLBURN
USA 1906–1911
Colburn Automobile Co., Denver, Colorado. Touring cars.

COLBY
USA 1911–1914
Colby Motor Co., Mason City, Iowa. Absorbed by Standard Motor Co., Minneapolis, Minnesota with Nevada Mfg. Co. Formerly "Midland." Touring cars.

COLDA
F 1921–1922
Automobiles Colda, Paris. Medium-sized cars.

COLDWELL
GB 1967–c. 1974
Coldwell Engineering and Racing Ltd., Sheffield, Yorks. Sports cars.

COLE
USA 1903
Cole & Son, Rockford, Illinois. Gasoline touring car prototype.

COLE
USA 1909–1925
Cole Motor Car Co., Indianapolis, Indiana. Succeeded Cole Carriage Co. Passenger cars.

COLE & LANG
USA 1900
James E. Cole & Andrew Lang, Topeka, Kansas.

COLE & WOOP ELECTRIC
USA 1902
Cole & Woop, New York, N.Y. One miniature electric car built for Jay Gould, Jr.

COLEMAN
USA 1933–1935
Coleman Motors Corp., Littleton, Colorado. Front wheel drive.

COLEMAN ELECTRIC
USA 1892
Clyde J. Coleman, Chiacgo, Illinois. Electric vehicle.

COLEMAN MILNE
GB 1975–present
Coleman Milne Ltd., Bolton. Stretched limousines.

COLE MOTOR BUGGY
USA 1909
Cole Carriage Co., Indianapolis, Indiana. Highwheeler. Became Cole Motor Car Co. Formerly Gates-Osborne Carriage Co.

COLENTA
D c. 1991
Colenta Elektromobile, Dreisbach. Electric car.

COLE-WIEDEMAN
GB 1905–1906
William Cole & Co. Ltd., London. Touring cars.

COLIBRI
D 1908–1911
Norddeutsche Automobilwerke GmbH, Hameln/Weser.
  See "Sperber."

COLIBRI-GUZZI
I
  See "Stanguellini."

COLIN
F 1934
Automobiles Colin, Gennevilliers/Seine. 500 cc minicars.

COLLI
I 1963–1964
Carrozzeria Colli, Milano. Modified Älfa Romeo'Giuilia TI.

COLLIDAY-CHARIOT
GB 1969
R.G. Collier. Three-wheeler prototype.

COLLIER
USA 1916–1920
Paynesville, Ohio.

COLLINET
USA 1922
Collinet Motor Co., Garden City, N.Y.

COLLINGS
USA 1913–1915
Collings Carriage Co., Camden, New Jersey.

COLLINS
USA 1900
Collins Electric Vehicle Co., Scranton, Pennsylvania. Electric car.

COLLINS
USA 1902
Hartford Motor Machine Co., Hartford, Connecticut. Steam car.

COLLINS
USA 1920
Collins Motor Inc., Huntington, Long Island, N.Y.

COLLINS SIX
USA 1921–1923
Collins Motor Car Co., Detroit, Michigan.

COLLIOT
F 1900–1901
Deliry et Fils, Soissons/Aisne. Light cars.

COLLMAN
USA 1928
Denver, Colorado. Believed to be misspelling of "Coleman," Littleton, Colorado 1933.

COLMORE FRAZER-NASH
GB 1939
Chain-driven sports car.

COLOMBE
F 1920–1925
Automobiles Colombe, Colombes/Seine. Assembled tourers and three-wheelers.

COLOMBO
I 1922–1924
Officine Meccaniche Colombo, Milano. Three-wheelers.

COLONIAL
USA 1899–1900
Colonial Automobile Co., Boston, Massachusetts.
  See "Kent's Pacemaker."

COLONIAL
USA 1911–1912
Colonial Electric Car Co., Detroit, Michigan. Electric cars.

COLONIAL
USA 1916–1917
Colonial Car Co., Detroit, Michigan. Colonial Automobile Co., Indianapolis, Indiana. Touring cars.

COLONIAL
USA 1920
Mechanical Development Corp., San Francisco, California. Straight 8 engine. One car produced.

COLONIAL
USA 1920–1921
Walden W. Shaw Livery Co., Chicago, Illinois. Became "Shaw," "Ambassador," later "Hertz."

COLONIAL
USA 1921–1923
Colonial Motors Corp., Woburn and Boston, Massachusetts.

COLONIAL ELECTRIC
USA 1902
Colonial Carriage Co., Cleveland, Ohio.

COLONIAL 6
USA/CDN 1922
Colonial Motors, Detroit, Michigan; Windsor, Ontario.

COLORNI
I 1915
Mantova.

COLT
USA 1907
Colt Runabout Co., Yonkers, N.Y. Incorporated June 1907. Bankrupt December 1907. Runabout.

COLT
USA 1958
Colt Mfg. Co., Milwaukee, Wisconsin. Fiberglass-bodied two-passenger air-cooled cars.

COLTMAN
GB 1907–1913
I.Coltman & Sons., Loughborough, Leics. 20 hp 4-cylinder cars.

COLUMBIA
USA 1892–1896
Columbia Perambulator Co., Chicago, Illinois. Electric cars.

COLUMBIA
USA 1897–1913
Pope Manufacturing Co. (1897–1899). Columbia Automobile Co. (1899). Columbia & Electric Vehicle Co. (1899). Electric Vehicle Co. (1899–1909). Columbia Motor Car Co. (1909–1913), Hartford, Connecticut. Gasoline and electric vehicles to 1910.

COLUMBIA
USA 1900
Columbia Motor & Mfg. Co., Washington, D.C.; Baltimore, Maryland. Steam car.

COLUMBIA
USA 1900–1907
Believed to be company name of Columbia Electric Co. Not name of vehicle.
See "Leader."

COLUMBIA
USA 1906
Columbia Electric Co., Indianapolis, Indiana. Electric car.

COLUMBIA
USA 1914
American Cyclecar Co., Seattle, Washington. Cyclecar.

COLUMBIA
USA 1916–1924
Columbia Motor Car Co., Detroit, Michigan.

COLUMBIA ELECTRIC
USA 1914
Columbia Electric Vehicle Co., Detroit, Michigan.

COLUMBIA HIWHEEL
USA 1909
Columbia Carriage Co., Hamilton, Ohio.

COLUMBIA KNIGHT
USA 1911–1912
Columbia Motor Car Co., Hartford, Connecticut.

COLUMBIA MAGNETIC
USA 1907–1908
Electric Vehicle Co., Hartford, Connecticut.

COLUMBIAN
USA 1914–1915
Columbian Electric Vehicle Co., Detroit, Michigan. Electric car.

COLUMBUS
USA 1903–1904
Columbus Carriage & Harness Co., Columbus, Ohio.

COLUMBUS ELECTRIC
USA 1903–1915
Columbus Buggy Co., Columbus, Ohio. Electric cars.
See "Firestone-Columbus." Also built gasoline cars.

COMET
CDN 1907–1909
Comet Motor Co. Ltd., Montreal, Quebec.

COMET
GB 1921
Preston Autocar Co. Ltd., London. Light sporting cars.

COMET
GB 1935–1937
Comet Car & Engineering Co. Ltd., Croydon, Surrey. High performance light cars.

COMET
USA 1906–1913
Hall Auto Repair Co., San Francisco; San Jose; Berkeley, California. Runabouts.

COMET
USA 1913–1914
Comet Cyclecar Co., Indianapolis, Indiana. Cyclecars.

COMET
USA 1917–1922
Comet Automobile Co., Rockfort, Illinois; Racine, Wisconsin; Decatur, Illinois. Shown at Chicago, Illinois January 1917. Received large foreign order. June 1920. Touring cars.

COMET
USA 1948
General Developing Co., Ridgewood, Long Island, N.Y. Three-wheelers weighed 175 pounds.

COMET
USA 1951–1955
Comet Mfg. Co., Sacramento, California. Two-seat roadsters.

COMETA
USA 1958
Eakin, Ohio. Three-wheeler prototype.

COMIRATO
I 1948
Sports car.

COMMANDER
USA 1921–1922
Commander Motors Corp., Milwaukee, Wisconsin; New York, N.Y. Designed by Otto Ogren. Successor to Hugo W. Ogren Motors Corp., Chicago, Illinois. 6-cylinder sedan.

COMMERCE
USA 1907–1908
Commerce Motor Car Co., Detroit, Michigan. Model 20 Deluxe Sedan with 4-cylinder engine offered by this truck company.

COMMERCE
USA 1922
Commerce Motor Car Company, Detroit, Michigan. Ten-passenger touring.

COMMERCIAL
USA 1903–1905
Commercial Motor Vehicle Co., Detroit, Michigan. Electric cars. Company also built the "Quadray" truck.

COMMERCIAL STEAM
USA 1904–1909
Commercial Motor Vehicle Co., Jersey City, New Jersey.

COMMINICATION
D 1996
Comminication Elektrofahrzeuge, Ibach. Electric cars.

COMMODORE
USA 1921–1922
Commodore Motors Corp., New York, N.Y. 4- and 6-cylinder 60 hp cars.

COMMONWEALTH
USA 1903–1904
Coburn & Company, Boston, Massachusetts. Runabout.

COMMONWEALTH
USA 1917–1922
Commonwealth Motors Co., Joliet,

Illinois. Succeeded "Partin-Palmer." Roadsters and touring cars.

COMMUTER
USA 1983
Electric car.

COMPANIA COLUMBIANA
CO 1980s
Compania Columbiana Automotriz, Bogota. "Fiat" (I) license.

COMPOUND
USA 1904–1908
Eisenhuth Horseless Vehicle Co., Middletown, Connecticut. From autobuggy to touring cars.

COMTESSE
F 1981
City car.

CONCEPT
GB 1970–1979
Concept car Ltd., Middleton, Leics. Sports car. 15 cars built in 1974.

CONCEPT
USA 1989–c. 1993
Concept Automobiles, Las Vegas, Nevada. Sports car.

CONCORD
USA 1896
Concord Motor Coach Company, Concord, New Hampshire. Steam car.

CONCORD
USA 1907
Believed to be company name of Concord Motor Car Co., Boston, Massachusetts.
See "Boston Electric."

CONCORD
USA 1914
Connersville, Indiana.

CONDON
USA c. 1905
George W. Condon, New Britain, Connecticut. 2.75 hp automobile.

CONDOR
CH 1922
Condor SA, Courfaivre. 5 vehicles were made.

CONDOR
D 1957–1958
Weidner OHG, Schwäbisch Hall. Sports car, about 200 were built.
See "Weidner."

CONDOR
GB 1960
Condor Motorcar Co. Ltd., Guildford, Surrey. Sports cars.

CONDOR AGUZZOLI
I 1964
Sergio Aguzzoli & Luigi Bertocco, Parma.

CONDOR ARH
E 1973
Sports car prototype.

CONE
GB 1914
Cone Car Co. Ltd., Leyton, Essex. Cyclecars.

CON-FERR COUGAR
USA 1964–c. 1971
Noc-Ferr Mfg. Co., Burbank, California. Dune buggy.

CONGER
USA 1902–1903
Conger Mfg. Co., Groton, N.Y. Touring cars.

CONKLIN
USA 1895
Oliver F. Conklin, Dayton, Ohio. Electric tricycle.

CONLEY
USA 1914
G.F. Conley, Chicago, Illinois. Cyclecars.

CONNAUGHT
GB 1949–1957
Continental Cars Ltd. (1949–1951). Connaught Engineering Ltd., Send, Surrey (1951–1957). 17 sports cars built.

CONNECTICUT
USA 1908
Believed to be company name of Connecticut Automobile Works, New Haven, Connecticut.
See "Fulton."

CONNERSVILLE
USA 1914
Connersville Buggy Company, Connersville, Indiana. Cyclecar.

CONNOLY
USA 1901
C.J. Connoly, Rochester, N.Y. Steam runabout.

CONOVER
USA 1907–1910
Conover Motor Car Co., Paterson, New Jersey. Built by Watson Machine Co., Paterson. Touring cars.

CONRAD
USA 1900–1903
Conrad Motor Carriage Co., Buffalo, N.Y. Gasoline and steam cars.

CONRERO
I 1953–1960
Virgilio Conrero, Torino.
See "SIVA."

CONSOLIDATED
USA 1904–1906
Consolidated Motor Co., New York, N.Y.
See "Moyea."

CONSOLIDATED
USA 1934
Consolidated Motors, Los Angeles, California.

CONSTANTINE
USA 1908
See "Crescent."

CONSTANTINESCO
F 1926–1928
I. Constantinesco, Paris. Light tourers.

CONSULIER
USA 1988–1995
Consulier Autoindustries Inc., Riviera Beach, Florida. Sports car.
See "CA." From 1996 see "Mosler."

CONTE
D 1986
Fa. Herzog, Hofheim/Taunus. Amphibian

CONTEMPORARY CLASSIC
USA 1990s
Contemporary Classic, Mamaroneck, N.Y. Kit cars.

CONTESSA
GB c. 1975
Oyler Co. "Mini" based small car.

CONTESSA
J
See "Hino."

CONTINENTAL
GB 1903
The Continental Automobile Co., London.

CONTINENTAL
USA 1907–1908
University Automobile Co. Continental Automobile Mfg. Co., New Haven, Connecticut. Touring cars.

CONTINENTAL
USA 1910–1914
Indiana Motor & Mfg. Co. Martindale & Millikin Co., Franklin, Indiana. Continental Automobile Co., Knightstown, Indiana. Touring cars.

CONTINENTAL
USA 1913–1914
Continental Motor Co., Buffalo, N.Y.

CONTINENTAL
USA 1914
Continental Engine Mfg. Co., Minneapolis, Minnesota; Chicago, Illinois. Cyclecars.

CONTINENTAL
USA 1933–1934
Continental Automobile Co., Grand Rapids, Michigan. 4–and 6–cylinder cars.
  See "De Vaux."

CONTINENTAL
USA 1940–1948; 1956–1958
Lincoln Motor Division, Ford Motor Co., Detroit, Michigan. Also Continental Motor Division, Dearborn, Michigan.
  See "Lincoln."

CONTINENTAL ROADSTER
USA 1907
Continental Motor Car Co., Chicago, Illinois. Little 90–inch roadster.

CONVAIR
GB 1958–1959
Convair Developments, London. Sports cars.

CONVAIRCAR
USA 1941–1948
Consolidated Aviation Co., San Diego, California. Flying auto. Prototype built only.

CONVERSE
USA c. 1905
A.D. Converse, Winchendon, Massachusetts. 10 hp car.

CONY
J 1952–1967
Aichi Machine Industry Co. Ltd., Nagoya. Three-wheelers and small 354 cc cars.

COOK
I 1900
Officine Pastore e Racca, Torino.
  See "Racca."

COOK
USA c. 1880s
Peregrine Cook, Samson County, North Carolina. Steam carriage.

COOK
USA 1896
James M. Cook, Mt. Gilead, Michigan. Built by Thurman & Silvius, Indianapolis, Indiana. Gasoline carriage.

COOK
USA 1897
Frank P. Cook, Salem, Massachusetts. Steam vehicle.

COOK
USA 1900
C.E. Cook, Delaware, Ohio.

COOK
USA 1906
Three vehicles were built by Theodore A. Cook, Calicoon, N.Y. These are believed to be the same as "Burch" autosleigh.

COOK
USA 1908–1909
Cook Motor Vehicle Co., St. Louis, Missouri. Company name, not name of vehicle. Company built "Simplo" highwheelers.

COOK & GOWDEY
USA 1895
Cook & Gowdey Co., Chicago, Illinois.

COOK-SIMPLE
USA 1908
Error in spelling.
  See "Cook" (1908–1909) and "Simplo" highwheeler.

COOLEY
USA 1900
R.L. Cooley, Batavia, N.Y. Gasoline buggy.

COOLEY
USA 1903
Cooley Cycloidal Engine Co., Allston, Massachusetts. Built to demonstrate Cooley Instantaneously Reversible Rotary Steam Engine.

COONEY
USA 1906–1907
Cooney Carriage Co., Toledo, Ohio. Electric cars.

COOPER
GB 1909–1911
Cooper Steam Digger Co. Ltd., Kings Lynn, Norfolk. 2-stroke engines.

COOPER
GB 1919–1923
Cooper Car Co., Bedford (1919–1920). Cooper Car Co. Ltd., Coventry, Warwickshire (1922–1923). 3-cylinder air-cooled engines.

COOPER
GB 1948–1969
John Cooper Car Co. Ltd., Surbiton, Surrey (1948–1969); Byfleet, Surrey (1966–1969). Sports cars.

COOPER
USA 1921
Cooper Motor Company, Kansas City, Missouri. 5-passenger sedan on wooden artillery wheels.

COOT
USA 1964–c. 1972
Carl Enos Jr. & Rober Mauser, San Francisco, California. Jeep-type off road vehicle. Became Rand Tron, San Francisco, California December 1968.

COPELAND
USA 1881–1890
Northrup Manufacturing Company, Phoenix, Arizona; Camden, New Jersey. Steam three-wheelers. Designed by Lucius D. Copeland who built steam bicycle about 1884.

COPELAND & BROWN
USA 1887
Philadelphia, Pennsylvania.
  See "Copeland," Camden, New Jersey.

COPPER
USA 1970–1972
Copper Development Assn. Inc., New York, N.Y. Electric car prototype.

COPPOCK
USA 1906–1910
Coppock Motor Car Co., Marion, Indiana; Decatur, Indiana.
  See "Decatur."

COQ
F 1920

Robert de Coquereamont, Rouen, Seine-Inferieure. Cyclecars.

COQUELIN
D c. 1929
Coquelin, Kraftfahrzeugbau, Ratingen (Rhld.). Three-wheelers.

CORAT
I 1946
Domenico Cosso, Torino.

CORBIN
USA 1905–1912
Corbin Motor Vehicle Co., New Britain, Connecticut. Division of American Hardware Co. Retired from business early 1912. Touring cars and runabouts.

CORBIN
USA 1998–present
Corbin Motors, Hollister, California. Gasoline and electric three-wheelers.

CORBITT
USA 1907–1914
Corbitt Automobile Co., Henderson, North Carolina. Highwheelers and touring cars.

CORD
USA 1929–1932; 1936–1937
Auburn Automobile Co., Auburn, Indiana. Front wheel drive. Division of Cord Corp.

CORD
USA 1964–1970
Cord Automobile Co., Tulsa, Oklahoma (1964–1967). Effman Motors Inc., Philadelphia, Pennsylvania (1968). S.A.M. Co. Inc., Manford, Oklahoma (1969–1970). 1936–1937 "Cord" replicars.

CORIASCO
I 1971–c. 1975
Coriasco Sas, Torino. "Fiat" based cars. 1650 cars built in 1974.

CORINTHIAN
USA 1922–1923
Corinthian Motors Inc., Philadelphia, Pennsylvania. Company formed by Charles B. Lewis, formerly with Lewis Motor Truck Co., San Francisco, California. 4-cylinder 35 hp and 65 hp cars.

CORLISS
USA 1909–1910

Corliss Motor Co., Corliss, Wisconsin.
See "Owen-Thomas."

CORMÉRY
F 1901
Corméry, Billancourt/Seine. Rhomboid wheel placement.

CORNELIAN
USA 1914–1915
Cornelian Co. Blood Bros. Machine Co., Kalamazoo, Michigan; Allegan, Michigan. Cyclecars. Discontinued after building 100 cars.

CORNIANI
I 1948–1950
Officine Corniani, Torino. Sports cars.

CORNILLEAU
F 1912–1914
Automobiles Cornilleau, Asnieres/Seine. Shaft-driven cars.

CORNILLEAU STÉ. BEUVE
F 1904–1909
Cornilleau et Sté. Beuve, Paris. 14/18 and 20/30 hp cars. Also known as "C.S.B."

CORNISH-FRIEDBERG
USA 1907–1909
Cornish-Friedberg Motor Car Co., Chicago, Illinois.
See "C.F."

CORNU
F 1906–1908
Paul Cornu, Lisieux, Calvados. Voiturette.

CORONA
D 1904–1909
Corona Fahrradwerke und Metallindustrie AG, Brandenburg/Havel. Voiturettes.

CORONA
F 1920
Automobiles Corona, Paris. Large 7.2-litre V-12 engine.

CORONA
GB 1920–1923
Meteor Manufacturing Co. Ltd., London. Light cars.

CORONA
USA 1922
Buckboard. Manufacturer unknown.

CORONA VAN
J c. 1970

Chubu Electric Power Co., Tokyo. Electric car prototype.

CORONET
GB 1904–1906
Coronet Motor Co. Ltd., Coventry, Warwickshire. Light cars.

CORONET
GB 1957–1960
Coronet Cars Ltd., Denham, Bucks. Three-wheeler.
See "Excelsior-Talisman."

CORP
USA 1905
Corp Brothers, Providence, Rhode Island.

CORPORATE CONCEPTS
USA 1987–c. 1993
Corporate Concepts Ltd., Capac, Michigan. Sports car.

CORRE; LA LICORNE
F 1901–1950
Sté. Francaise des Automobiles Corre, Courbevoie/Seine. Light touring cars.

CORRE
F 1908–1914
J. Corre et Cie., Rueil/Seine-et-Oise. 8, 10 ad 12 hp cars.

CORREJA
USA 1908–1914
Vandewater & Co., Ilion, New Jersey. Correja Automobile Co., Elizabeth, New Jersey. Correja Motor Car Co., New York, N.Y. Runabouts and touring cars.

CORRICK
USA 1914
J.B. Corrick, Detroit, Michigan. Cyclecar.

CORSON
USA 1993–present
Corson Motorcar Company, Phoenix, Arizona. Sports kit cars.

CORTEZ
USA 1947–1949
North American Motors Inc., Dallas, Texas. Full-size cars intended for volume sale at $1000.

CORTLAND
USA 1916–1924
See "Hatfield."

CORWEG
USA 1905

Corweg Shuttle Valve Motor Co., Atlantic City, New Jersey.

CORWIN
USA 1905–1907
Believed to be company name of Corwin Manufacturing Co., Peabody, Massachusetts, not name of vehicle.
See "Gas-Au-Lec."

CORY
USA 1907
Albany-Cory Automobile Co., Albany, Indiana.

C.O.S.
D 1907
Carl Oskar Schlobach, Breslau. 4- and 6-cylinder models.

COSHOCTON
USA 1913
Coshocton Motor Car Co., Coshocton, Ohio.

COSMOBILE
D/USA 1899
"Wartburg" (D) cars for the USA.

COSMOPOLIT
HR 1995
See "Zlatko."

COSMOPOLITAN
USA 1907–1910
D.W. Haydock Auto Mfg. Co., St. Louis, Missouri. Highwheelers and front-drive cars.
See "Haydock."

COSMOS; C.A.R.
GB 1919–1920
Cosmos Engineering Co. Ltd., Bristol.

COSTIN
GB 1971–1972
Costin Automotive Racing Products Ltd., Little Staughton, Beds. Sports cars.

COSTIN-NATHAN
GB
See "Nathan."

COSWIGA
D 1901
See "Nacke."

COTAY
USA 1920–1921
Coffyn-Taylor Motors Co., New York, N.Y. Roadster.

COTE
F 1900; 1908–1913
Sté. des Automobiles et Moteurs Cote, Saint Dizier/Haute-Marne (1900); Pantin/Seine (1908–1913). Voiturettes and cyclecars.

COTTA
USA 1901–1903
Cotta Automobile Co., Lanark, Illinois (1901–1902); Rockford, Illinois (1902–1903). Four-wheel drive steam vehicles.

COTTEREAU
F 1898–1910
Cottereau et Cie., Dijon. Air-cooled V-twin.

COTTIN-DESGOUTTES
F 1905–1933
Cottin et Desgouttes, Lyon. Tourers.

COTTON
GB 1911
Rennie & Prosser Ltd., Glasgow. About 12 cars were made.

COTTON
USA 1901
I.F. Cotton, Topeka, Kansas.

COUDERT
F
See "Lurquin-Coudert."

COUNE
B 1962–1966
Carrosserie Jacques Coune, Bruxelles. Sports cars based on the "MG" (GB), "BMW" (D) and "Mercedes-Benz" (D).

COUNTRY CLUB
USA 1903–1904
Country Club Car Co., Boston, Massachusetts. Tonneau.

COUNTY
GB 1907
Halifax Motor Car Co., Halifax, Yorks. Medium-sized 4-cylinder cars.

COURIER
F/GB 1906–1908
Euston Motor Co. Ltd., London. Assembled from French components.

COURIER
USA 1904–1905
Sandusky Automobile Co., Sandusky, Ohio. Runabout.

COURIER
USA 1909–1912
Courier Car Co., Dayton, Ohio. Taken with "Stoddard-Dayton" into U.S. Motors Co. 1910.

COURIER
USA 1923–1924
Courier Motors Co., Sandusky, Ohio. Formerly named "Maibohm" taken over by Arrow Motors.

COURNIL
F 1957–c. 1988
Bernard Cournil, Aurillac, Cantal. Four-wheel drive cars.

COUVERCHEL
F
See "C.V.R."

COVEL
USA 1916
Benton Harbor, Michigan.

COVENTRY CLASSICS
USA 1982
Coventry Classics, Santa Ana, California. "Jaguar" (GB) replicars.

COVENTRY-DAIMLER
GB 1900
See "Daimler" (GB).

COVENTRY-MOTETTE
GB
Cars built under "Leon Bollee" license.
See "Leon Bollee" (F).

COVENTRY-PREMIER
GB 1919–1923
Coventry-Premier Ltd., Coventry, Warwickshire. Small touring and sports cars.

COVENTRY-VICTOR
GB 1926–1938
Coventry-Victor Motor Co. Ltd., Coventry, Warwickshire. Three-wheelers.

COVERT
USA 1902–1907
B.V. Covert & Co. Covert Motor Vehicle Co. (1904), Lockport, N.Y. Later built transmissions. Steam cars also 1901.

COVINI
I 1978–1982
Ferruccio Covini, Castel S. Giovanni. Mid-engined sports cars.

COWAN
GB 1861
T.W. Cowan. Steam car.

COWAN
USA 1908

Brice Cowan, Los Angeles, California. Boy's home-built car.

COWEY
GB 1913–1915
Cowey Engineering Co. Ltd., Kew Gardens, Surrey. Light cars, pneumatic suspension.

COWLES McDOWELL
USA 1915
Cowles McDowell Pneumobile Co., Chicago, Illinois. Company built "Pneumobile."

COX
GB
See "G.T.M."

COX
USA 1906
Jas. I. Cox, ? Little roadster.

COX
USA 1914
Claude E. Cox, Detroit, Michigan. Cyclecar and motor buggy.

COYOTE
USA 1908–1909
Redondo Beach Car Works, Redondo Beach, California. Roadster.

COYOTE
USA 1909
Union Automobile Company, Albany, Indiana. Runabout.

C.P. AUTOKRAFT
GB 1983
Sports car replica.

C.P.T.
USA 1906
Chicago Pneumatic Tool Co., Chicago, Illinois. Runabouts.
See "Chicago."

CRAGAR
USA 1933–1934
Cragar Corporation, Los Angeles, California. Cars made to custom order.

CRAIG-DÖRWALD
GB 1902–1912
Putney Motor Co., London. Built to special order.

CRAIG-HUNT
USA 1920
Craig-Hunt Motor Co., Indianapolis, Indiana. City prevented erection of plant November 1920. In receivership for US $125.50 debt. One prototype built.

CRAIGIEVAR EXPRESS
GB c. 1894
Steam car.

CRAIG-TOLEDO
USA 1906–1907
Craig-Toledo Motor Co., Toledo, Ohio. Roadsters.

CRAMPIN-SCOTT
GB 1900–1901
Crampin, Scott & Co., London. 6 hp engine, 12 mph.

CRANDALL
USA 1902
Crandall Machine Co., Groton, N.Y.

CRANE
USA 1912–1915
Crane Motor Car Co., Bayonne, New Jersey.

CRANE & BREED
USA 1902; 1912
Crane & Breed Mfg. Co., Cincinnati, Ohio. Electric car. 6-cylinder 8-passenger cars.

CRANE & WHITMAN
USA 1907–1908
Crane & Whitman Automobile Works, Bayonne, New Jersey.

CRANE-SIMPLEX
USA 1915–1924
Simplex Automobile Co., New Brunswick, New Jersey. Formerly "Simplex" absorbed Crane Motor Car Co. Purchased 1919 by Mercer Automobile Co. Marketed with "Locomobile" and "Mercer" by Hare's Motors Inc.

CRAVERO
I c. 1914–1915
Torino.
See "Zambon" and "Z."

CRAWFORD
USA 1901
J.B. Crawford, Sioux City, Iowa.

CRAWFORD
USA 1905–1924
Crawford Automobile Co., Hagerstown, Maryland. Founded by Robert S. Crawford. Company bought by M.P. Moller 1922. Became M.P. Moller Motor Car Co. 1923.
See "Dagmar."

CRAWSHAY-WILLIAMS
GB 1904–1906
Crawshay-Williams Ltd., Ashtead, Surrey.

CRAYFORD
GB 1962–c. 1993
Crayford Automotive Development Ltd., Westerham, Kent. Convertibles.

CRÉANCHE
F 1899–1906
Sté. L. Créanche, Courbevoie/Seine. Voiturette.

CREATIVE COACH
USA 1990s
Creative Coach, Ontario, California. Kit cars.

CREATIVE INDUSTRIES
USA 1975
Electric Fuel Propulsion Co. Electric car.

CREMORNE
GB 1903–1904
Cremorne Motor Manufacturing Co. Ltd., London. Steam car.

CRESCENT
GB 1911–1915
Crescent Motors Ltd., Walsall, Staffs. (1911–1913); Birmingham (1913–1915). Cyclecars.

CRESCENT
USA 1900
Crescent Automobile Mfg. Co., Wilmington, Delaware.

CRESCENT
USA 1900
Western Wheel Works, Chicago, Illinois. Tricycle.

CRESCENT
USA 1900
Crescent Automobile Co., New York, N.Y. Runabout.

CRESCENT
USA 1905
Crescent Automobile & Supply Co., St. Louis, Missouri. Simple 2-cylinder cars.

CRESCENT
USA 1907–1908
Crescent Motor Car Co. Meldrum & Champlain Sts, Detroit, Michigan. Increased capital US $75,000 to produce touring car "Reliance" and runabout "Marvel." Reportedly bought plant in Goshen, Indiana 1908.

CRESCENT
USA 1914–1915
Crescent Motor Co., Carthago, Ohio. Formerly "Ohio" 1909–1913. Liquidated 1915 by Ralph E. Northway.

CRESPELLE
F 1906–1923
F. Crespelle, Paris. Sports cars.

CRESPI
RA 1972–1992
Tulio Crespi Srl, Carrocerias de Competicion, Buenos Aires. Sports cars.

CRESSON
USA 1915
Cresson-Morris Co., Philadelphia, Pennsylvania. Former "Crowther Cyclecar."

CREST
USA 1901
Crest Mfg. Co., Cambridge, Massachusetts. Early name for "Crestmobile." Runabout.

CREST
USA 1907
Hub Automobile Exchange, Boston, Massachusetts.

CRESTMOBILE
USA 1902–1905
Crest Mfg. Co., Cambridge, Massachusetts (1901–1904); Dorchester, Massachusetts (1905). Formerly made parts. Absorbed with "Moyer" into Alden-Sampson Mfg. Co.

CREWFORD
GB 1920–1921
Crewford Garage, London. Two- or four-seater polished aluminum bodies.

C.R.G.
USA 1908
Charles R. Greuter, Wilkes-Barre, Pennsylvania. Formerly chief engineer for Matheson.

C.R.G. SPECIAL
USA 1920
Green Engineering Co., Dayton, Ohio. Cars built to special order.

CRICKET
USA 1914
Cricket Cyclecar Co., Detroit, Michigan. Cyclecars. Reported absorbed by Motor Products Co., 1914.

CRICKET
USA 1930s
Samuel Eliot, Boston & Holliston, Massachusetts. Rear-engined sedan.

CRIPPS
GB 1913
Cripps Cycle Co., London. Cyclecars.

CRIST
USA 1907
Los Angeles, California. Roadster.

CRITCHLEY-NORRIS
GB 1906–1908
Critchley-Norris Motor Co. Ltd., Bamber Bridge, Lancs. 40 hp cars.

CRITERION
USA 1911–1912
Criterion Motor Co., Pittsburgh, Pennsylvania; Kent, Ohio.
See "Kitto."

CRM
I
Costruzioni e Revisioni Motori.
See "Isotta-Fraschini."

CROCKETT
USA 1917
J.B. Crockett Co., New York, N.Y. For export only.

CROESUS
USA 1906–1907
Croesus Motor Car Co. (1906). W.L. Bell (1907), Kansas City, Missouri. Company charged with fraud after two cars built.

CROFT
USA 1922
William Edgar Croft, Zion City, Illinois. Three-wheeler.

CROFTON
USA 1959–1961
Crofton Marine Engineering Co., San Diego, California. About 200 Jeep-style cars sold. Retained mfg. rights to "Crosley" engine.

CROISSANT
F 1920–1922
SA des Anciens Établissements V. Couverchel, H. Croissant et Cie., Paris. Cyclecars.

CROMPTON
GB 1914
Crompton Engineering Co., Hendon, Middlesex. Cyclecars.

CROMPTON
USA 1902–1905
Crompton Motor Carriage Works, Worcester, Massachusetts. Steam cars.

CRONHOLM & STENWALL
USA 1895
Cronholm & Stenwall Co., Chicago, Illinois.

CRONK
USA 1914
Cronk, White Plains, N.Y. Gasoline car.

CROSLEY
USA 1939–1952
Crosley Motor Inc., Cincinnati, Ohio; Marion, Indiana. Affiliated with Crosley Radio Corp. 2- and 4-cylinder light cars.

CROSMOBILE
USA 1948–1953
Crosley Motors Inc., Marion, Indiana. For export only (export model of "Crosley").

CROSS
USA 1895
E.D. Cross, Chicago, Illinois.

CROSS
USA 1897
A.T. Cross, Providence, Rhode Island. Steam car.

CROSS
USA 1924
Harry Cross, Indianapolis, Indiana. Four experimental cars built.

CROSSLAND
USA 1923
Crossland Steam Motive Corp., Chicago, Illinois. Steam cars.

CROSSLEY
GB 1904–1937
Crossley Brothers Ltd., Manchester (1904–1910). Crossley Motors Ltd., Manchester (1910–1937). Touring cars.

CROSSLEY
USA 1913–1914
Albert D. Crossley, Hartford, Connecticut. Crossley formerly with "Pope." No connection with English cars of same name.

CROSVILLE
GB 1906–1908
Crosville Motor Co. Ltd., Chester. Five cars were made.

CROUAN
F 1897–1904
Sté. des Automobiles Crouan, Paris. 2-cylinder cars.

CROUCH
GB 1912–1928
Crouch Cars, Coventry, Warwickshire. Three-wheelers.

CROUCH
USA 1897–1900
W.B. Lee Crouch, New Brighton, Pennsylvania. Crouch Automobile Mfg. & Transport Company, Baltimore, Maryland. Steam cars.

CROUCH
USA 1905–1906
A. Stilman Crouch, Stoneham, Massachusetts. 3- and 4-wheeled gasoline vehicles.

CROW
CDN 1915–1918
Canadian Crow Motor Co. Ltd., Mt. Bridges, Ontario.

CROW
USA 1911
Crow Motor Car Co., Elkhart, Indiana. Became "Crow-Elkhart."

CROWDEN
GB 1898–1901
Charles T. Crowden, Leamington Spa. Steam and gasoline experimental cars.

CROWDUS
USA 1899–1902
Crowdus Automobile Co., Chicago, Illinois. Electric cars.

CROWDY
GB 1909–1912
Crowdy Ltd., London (1909–1911); Birmingham (1911–1912). 4- and 6-cylinder cars.

CROWE 30
USA 1911
W.A. Crowe, Detroit, Michigan. Crowe Motor Car Co., Grand Rapids, Michigan.

CROW-ELKHART
USA 1911–1923
Crow Motor Car Co. Crow-Elkhart Motor Co., Elkhart, Indiana. Became Century Motor Corp. 1923. Touring cars.

CROWN
GB 1903
Crown Car Co. Ltd., London. Three-wheelers.

CROWN
USA 1905–1907
Detroit Auto Vehicle Co., Detroit & Romeo, Michigan. Organized August 1904. First car put on road April 1905. Runabouts.

CROWN
USA 1908–1910
Crown Motor Vehicle Co., Amesbury, Massachusetts; Boston, Massachusetts. Highwheelers.
See "Graves & Congdon."

CROWN
USA 1913–1914
Buckeye Mfg. Co., Anderson, Indiana. Crown Motor Car Co., Louisville, Kentucky; New Albany, Indiana. Formerly "Jonz," became "Hercules."
See "Dixie-Flyer." Roadsters.

CROWN
USA 1915
Crown Automobile Mfg. Co., Kalamazoo, Michigan.

CROWN ENSIGN
GB
See "British Ensign."

CROWN MAGNETIC
GB
See "British Ensign."

CROWN-MAGNETIC
USA 1921–1922
Owen-Magnetic Motor Car Co., Wilkes-Barre, Pennsylvania.

CROWTHER
USA 1915
Crowther Motor Car Co., Rochester, N.Y. Became "Crowther-Duryea."

CROWTHER
USA 1914
Cresson-Morris Co., Philadelphia, Pennsylvania. Cyclecars.

CROWTHER-DURYEA
USA 1916–1917
Crowther-Duryea Motor Co., Rochester, N.Y.; Greece, N.Y. In hands of receiver early 1917. Plant reported sold July 1918. Touring cars.

CROXTED
GB 1904–1905
Croxted Motor & Engineering Co. Ltd., London. 2- and 4-cylinder cars.

CROXTON
USA 1911–1915
Croxton Motors Co., Cleveland, Ohio; Washington, Pennsylvania. Formerly Croxton-Keeton Motor Co. Became Universal Motor Car Co.

CROXTON-KEETON
USA 1909–1910
Croxton-Keeton Motor Co., Massillon, Ohio. Succeeded Jewel Motor Car Co. Became Croxton Motors Co. 1911.
See "Keeton" and "Croxton." Touring cars and roadsters.

C.R.S.
GB 1960–1961
C.R.S. Auto Enginering Ltd., Footscray, Kent. Sports cars.

CRUICKSHANK
USA 1896–1898
Cruickshank Steam Engine Works, Providence, Rhode Island. Steam car.

CRUISER
USA 1917–1919
Cruiser Motor Co., Madison, Wisconsin; Joliet, Illinois. Convertible touring-camping car.

CRUSADER
USA 1914–1915
Crusader Motor Car Co., Joliet, Illinois.

CRUSADER
USA 1923
Crusader Motors Corp., York, Pennsylvania.

C.R.V.
USA 1964
Borg-Warner Corp., Washington, West Virginia. Experimental car.

CRYPTO
GB 1904–1905
Crypto Engineering Co., London. 2-cylinder assembled cars.

CRYSTAL CITY
USA 1914
Charles Troll and Charles Manning, Corning, N.Y. Cyclecars.

CRYSTIC CAR
GB 1970
Scott Bader Sturge. Vintage car replica.

CS 2
GB 1971–1979
Mini Motors., Rochdale, Lancs. Dune buggy kit car.

CSC
GB 1953–1955
Gainsborough Engineering Co. Ltd., Middleton, Lancs. Wrigley Motors Ltd., Middleton, Manchester. Sports cars.

CSONKA
H 1906–1912
Csonka János Autógyár, Budapest. About 150 small and medium cars were made.

CTA
I 1950
Centro Tecnico dell'Automobile. Sports car "Arsenal."

CUB
GB 1990s
Reef Engineering, Lichfield. Three-wheelers.

CUB
USA 1914
Szekely Cyclecar Co., Richmond, Virginia. Cyclecar.

CUBITT
GB 1920–1925
Cubitt's Engineering Co. Ltd., Aylesbury, Bucks. Simple tourers.

CUBSTER
USA 1949
Osborn Wheel Co., Doylestown, Pennsylvania. Home-assembled 6.6 hp car. Available as chassis only.

CUCCOTTI
I 1903
Fabbrica Automobili a Vapore, Torino. Steam car.

CUDELL
D 1898–1908
Cudell & Co. Motor- und Motorfahrzeugfabrik (1898–1900). AG fur Motor- und Fahrzeugbau vorm. Cudell (1900–1902). Cudell Motor-Compagnie mbH, Aachen (1902–1905). Cudell Motoren-Gesellschaft mbH, Berlin (1905–1908). Voiturette and limousines.

CUGNOT
F 1769–1771
Nicolas Joseph Cugnot, Paris. He built the first real steam vehicle.

CULL
USA 1901
A.B. Cull, St. Louis, Missouri. Gasoline touring.

CULLMAN
USA 1902
Cullman Wheel Works, Chicago, Illinois. Steam car.

CULVER
USA 1905
Culver Practical Automobile Co. (1905). Practical Automobile Co. (1906), Aurora, Illinois. Highwheelers.

CULVER
USA 1917
Culver Mfg. Co., Culver City, California. One-cylinder juvenile car.

CUMBERFORD
USA 1982
Cumberford Corp., Stamford, Connecticut. Sports car replica.

CUMBRIA
GB 1913–1914
Cumbria Motors Ltd., Cockermouth, Cumberland. Single-seater cyclecars.

CUMMIKAR
F
See "Ronteix."

CUMMINGS
USA 1894
G.K. Cummings, Chicago, Illinois. Electric car.

CUMMINGS
USA 1908
Clarence Cummings, Carrington, North Dakota. One-passenger jitney.

CUMMINGS-MONITOR
USA 1916
Cummings-Monitor Co., Columbus, Ohio. Company name, not name of vehicle.
See "Monitor."

CUMMINS
USA 1929–1952
Clessie L. Cummins, Columbus, Indiana. Sports and racing cars.

CUNDALL
GB 1902
R. Cundall & Sons Ltd., Shipley, Yorks. 2-cylinder 7 hp horizontal engines.

CUNNINGHAM
USA 1908–1936
James Cunningham and Sons Co., Rochester, N.Y. Luxury cars. Returned to coachbuilding after 1933.

CUNNINGHAM
USA 1951–1955
Briggs Cunningham, Palm Beach, California. 33 GT production cars were built.

CUNNINGHAM STEAM
USA 1900–1907
Cunningham Engineering Co. Massachusetts Steam Wagon Co., Boston, Massachusetts.

CUPELLE
GB
See "Jackson."

CURRAN
USA 1922–1925
Curran Steam Commercial Vehicle Co., New York, N.Y. Steam car and 3-cylinder touring cars.

CURRIER
USA c. 1905
A.L. Currier, Sommerville, Massachusetts. 7 hp automobile.

CURSOR
GB 1985
Replicar Ltd. Three-wheelers.

CURSY
D c. 1930s
Cursy — Fahrzeugwerk Curt Szymanski, Sommerfeld, Frankfurt/O. Three-wheeler.

CURTIN
USA 1905–1906
Curtin-Williams Automobile Co., Columbus, Ohio.

CURTIS
USA 1867
Frank Curtis, Newburyport, Massachusetts. Built a steam carriage and sold it on the installment plan. Had to repossess it.

CURTIS
USA 1912–1913
Pittsburgh Machine Tool Co., Braddock, Pennsylvania.

CURTIS
USA 1920–1921
Curtis Motor Car Co., Little Rock, Arkansas. 30 cars built.

CURTISS
USA 1920–1921
Curtiss Motor Car Co., Hammondsport, N.Y.

CURTISS AUTOPLANE
USA 1917
See "Curtiss," Hammondsport, N.Y.

CURTISS-WRIGHT
USA 1948
Curtiss-Wright Industries, El Monte, California. The Curtiss-Wright who also operated an aircraft school.

CURTISS-WRIGHT AIR CAR
USA 1959–1960
Curtiss-Wright, South Bend, Indiana. Wheelless vehicle travelled 6–12 inches above land or water on a cushion of low-pressure air.

CUSHMAN
USA 1903–1907; 1948–1980
Cushman Motor Works Inc., Lincoln, Nebraska. Runabouts. Shopper cars.

CUSTEAD
USA 1907
Los Angeles, California. Runabout prototype.

CUSTER
USA 1920–1946
The Custer Specialty Company, Dayton, Ohio. Experimental electric car 1898. Gasoline, electric, handicapped & amusement park cars.

CUSTER
USA 1959–1960
Custer Specialty Co., Dayton, Ohio. Two-passenger electric or gasoline vehicles.

CUSTOCA
A 1971–present
Custoca Kunststoffkarosserien, Leoben. Custoca Fiberglass Austria, Gerhard Höller, Kraubath. Sports cars.

CUSTOM CLASSICS
USA 1982
Custom Classics, Harper Woods, Michigan. Sports car replica.

CUSTOM COACH
USA 1974–1979
Custom Coach Builders, Inc., Forest Park, Illinois. Sports car.

CUSTOM GLASSFIBRE
GB 1971–1979
Custom Glassfibre, Devon Moulding Co. Ltd., Okehampton, Devon. Street rod bodied car.

CUTCHEON
USA c. 1905
James C. Cutcheon, Swampscott, Massachusetts. 5 hp car.

CUTTING
USA 1909–1913
Cutting Motor Co. C.V.I. Motor Car Co., Jackson, Michigan. Formerly "C.V.I." Absorbed by Clark-Carter Automobile Co. 1909. Absorbed by Cutting Motor Car Co. 1912. Touring cars and roadsters.

CUYAHOGA
USA 1909
Cyuahoga Motor Car Co., Cleveland, Ohio. Electric car.
See "Cleveland Electric."

C.V.I.
USA 1907–1908
C.V.I. Motor Car Co., Jackson, Michigan. Became "Cutting." Touring cars.

C.V.R.
F 1906–1907
Automobiles C.V.R., Boulogne-sur-Seine/Seine. 6 models with 4- and 6-cylinder engines.

C.W.B.
USA 1927–1930
C.W.B. Sports Automobiles, New Haven, Connecticut. Sports cars.

C.W.S.
PL 1922–1929
Centralne Warsztaty Samochodowe, Warszawa. The first car built completely in Poland. 1.5- and 3-litre 4-cylinder cars, one 3-litre 8-cylinder car in prototype stage.

CYCAR
D c. 1970
Essen. City car prototype.

CYCAR
GB 1901
Two models have been made.

CYCLAUTO
F 1919–1923
Sté. Francaise du Cyclauto, Suresnes/Seine. Three-wheelers.

CYCLECAR
USA 1914
Cycle Car Co., Wilmington, Delaware.

CYCLEPLANE
USA 1914–1915
Cycleplane Co., Westerly, Rhode Island. Cyclecars.

CYCLOMOBILE
USA 1920–1921
Cyclomobile Mfg. Co., Toledo, Ohio. Runabouts.

CYCLONE
USA 1921–1922
Cyclone Motors Corp., Greenville, South Carolina.

CYCLONE ROAD RUNNER
USA 1968–c. 1973
Road Runner Division, Burbank, California. Dune buggy.

CYCLOP
USA 1910
L. Porter Smith & Bros., Indianapolis, Indiana. About 50 runabouts were made.

CYCLOPS
USA 1914
Cyclops Cyclecar Co., Indianapolis, Indiana. Cyclecar.

CYCO LECTRIC
USA 1914–1916
Cyco Lectric Car Company, New York, N.Y. Electric light cars.

CYKLON; CYKLONETTE
D 1902–1929
Cyklon Maschinenfabrik GmbH, Berlin (1902–1912). Cyklon Automobilwerke AG, Berlin; Mylau (1922–1929). Three-wheelers and small 2-seaters.

CZECH
A/CS 1907
Gabriel Czech, Moravská Ostrava. Voiturette.

D.A.C.
USA 1922–1923
Detroit Air-Cooled Car Co., Detroit, Michigan. Designed by W.J. Doughty. Touring cars.

DAC
USA 1969–1971
Dearborn Automobile Company, Dearborn, Michigan. Dune buggy.

DACIA
RO 1968–c. 1994
Uzina de Autoturisme, Pitesti. Automobile Dacia S.A., Colibasi, Pitesti. "Renault" (F) made under license.

DACON
BR 1982–1984
City cars.

DAEWOO
ROK 1967–present
Daewoo Motor Co. Ltd., Chung-Gu, Seoul. Passenger cars.

DAF
NL 1958–1975
Van Doornes Automobielfanriek NV, Eindhoven. Passenger cars with Variomatic transmission.

DAGMAR
USA 1922–1927
Crawford Automobile Co., Hagerstown, Maryland. Sporting companion cars to the "Crawford."

DAGSA
E 1951–1952
Defensa Antigas SA, Segovia. About 50 light cars were built.

DAIHATSU
J 1954–present
Daihatsu Kogyo Co. Ltd., Ikeda Shi, Osaka Pref. Passenger cars.

DAIMLER
D 1886–1902
Gottlieg Daimler (1886–1890). Daimler Motoren-Gesellschaft, Bad Canstatt (1890–1902). 2- and 4-seater cars. Front engine in 1897, 4-cylinder engine in 1899.

DAIMLER
GB 1896–present
Daimler Motor Syndicate Ltd. (1896–1904). Daimler Motor Co. (1904) Ltd. (1904–1910). Daimler Co. Ltd. Coventry, Warwickshire (1910–present). Luxury touring and sports cars.

DAIMLER
USA 1895–1902
Daimler Mfg. Co., Long Island City, N.Y. Most lists carry this make to 1907. Name changed to "Mercedes" 1902.

DAINO
I 1923–1924
Fabbrica Automobili Daino, Cremona. Light cars.

DAINOTTI
I 1922–1923
Fabbrica Automobili Dainotti, Pavia. 8-cylinder engines.

DAISY
I 1914
Daisy Cyclecar Co., Los Angeles, California. Cyclecars.

DAKAR
GB 1990s
Dakar Cars Ltd., Dartford, Kent. Sports kit cars.

DAKOTA
USA 1910
More Brothers, Wimbledon, North Dakota. High-wheel touring.

DAKOTA
D 1997
Gorgus Engineering, location unknown. Sports cars in two sizes: M and XL.

DALAT
VN 1970–1976
Saigon. Light car based on "Citroën" (F) 2CV.

DALEY
USA 1895–1898
M.H. Daley, Charles City, Iowa. Entered Chicago Times-Herald Race.

DALEY
USA 1900
W.A. Lane Mfg. Co., Barre, Vermont. Steam car.
See "Lane & Daley."

DALGLEISH-GULLANE
GB 1907–1908
Haddington Motor Engineering Co., Haddington, East Lothian. Light cars.

DALHOUSIE
GB 1906–1910
The Anderson-Grice Co. Ltd., Carnoustie, Forfar. Tourers.

DALILA
F 1922–1923
Bouquet et Cie. Light cars.

DALLARA
I 1973–1978
Gianpaolo Dallara Srl, Parma. Sports and racing cars.

DALLAS
F 1981–present
Société des Automobiles Grandin, Montreuil; Cergy Pontoise. Small Jeep-type 4 × 4 cars.

DALLERY
F 1780
Charles Dallery, Amiens. Steam car.

DALLISON
GB 1913
Dallison Gearing and Motor Co. Ltd., Birmingham. Cyclecars.

DALL' OGLIO
I 1913
Milano.

DÁLNÍK
CS 1947
Jan Anderle, Praha. Prototype of two-wheeled experimental car.

DALTON
USA 1911–1912
Dalton Motor Car Co., Flint, Michigan. Formerly "Dalton-Whiting." Only three made.

DAMATI
B 1937
Four-wheel drive.

DANA
DK 1908–1914

Hakon Olsen, Maskinfabriken Dana, Copenhagen. Cyclecars.

DANCE
GB 1831
Sir Charles Dance, Gloucester. Steam car.

D. & H.
GB c. 1971–1981
& H. Fibreglass Techniques Ltd., Greenfield, Oldham. Sports cars.
See "Midas" and "Mini-Marcos."

D & R
USA 1990s
D & R Replicars, Kintnersville, Pennsylvania. Kit cars and replicars

D'ANDREA
USA 1956
Gilbert D'Andrea, New York, N.Y.

DANDURAN & JENNINGS
CDN 1895
J.H. Danduran and William Jennings (and Father), Montreal, Quebec.

D & V
USA 1903
De Vigne & Van Sickle, Paterson, New Jersey.

D & W
D c. 1985
D & W Auto, Sport + Zubehör GmbH, Bochum. Tuning.

DANDY
GB 1922–1925
James Summer & Sons, Southport, Lancs.

DANGEL
F 1969–1973; 1980–present
Henri Dangel, Mulhouse, Haut-Rhin Automobiles Dangel SA, Sentheim. 4 × 4 vehicles.

D'ANGELO
I 1905
Palermo.

DANIELS
USA 1912
Daniels Motor Car Co., East St. Louis, Missouri.

DANIELS
USA 1916–1924
Daniels Motor Car Co., Reading, Pennsylvania. Daniels bought by Levene Motor Co.; planned move to Philadelphia 1924. Touring cars.

DANILO
DK c. 1955
Jens Nilson. Two-seater minicar prototype with fiberglass body.

DANKAR
BR 1981–?
Rio de Janeiro. Luxury version based on "Volkswagen" Passat.

DANNEELS
B c. 1901
Danneels, Gand. Cars made under French license.

DAN PATCH
USA 1910–1912
M.W. Savage Co., Minneapolis, Minnesota. Mail order car. Became "Savage."

DANSK
DK 1901–1908
Dansk Automobil & Cyclefabrik (1901–1903). Dansk Automobilfabrik, Copenhagen (1903–1908). Three-wheelers; four-seater vis-à-vis.

D'AOUST
B 1912–1927
Automobiles J. D'Aoust, Anderlecht. Touring and sports cars.

DARBY
USA 1909–1910
Darby Motor Car Co., St. Louis, Missouri. Roadster.

DARDO
BR 1979–1983
Diadema Ltda. "Fiat" (I) X1/9 based sports cars.

DARE
GB 1998–present
Dare (UK) Ltd., Colchester, Essex. Sports cars.

DARK HORSE
USA 1923
L.H. Damann Motor Co., Rock Island, Illinois.

DARLING
USA 1901–1902
Beardsley & Hubbs Mfg. Co., Massilon, Ohio; Shelby, Ohio. 1902 became Shelby Motor Car Co. Three cars at Chicago Show 1902.

DARLING
USA c. 1905
C.E. Darling, Waltham, Massachusetts. 5 hp automobile.

DARLING
USA 1917
Darling Motor Car Co., Dayton, Ohio. Touring cars.

DARLING STEAM
USA 1899
F.A. Darling, Franklin, Massachusetts.

DARL'MAT
F 1933–1938
Emile Darl'mat, Paris. "Peugeot" based sports car.

DARMONT
F 1922–1936
G. Darmont, Courbevoie/Seine. "Morgan" (GB) three-wheelers made under license.

DARNVAL
F 1972–1974 ?
Sté. Darnval, Le Havre/Seine-Maritine. Sports cars.

DARRACQ
F 1896–1959
Société A. Darracq (1896–1905). A. Darracq & Co. (1905) Ltd. (1905–1920). Automobiles Talbot, Suresnes (1920–1959). Touring and sports cars.
See "Talbot" (F).

DARRACQ ITALIANA
I 1906–1910
Darracq Italiana S.A., Napoli.
See "Alfa Romeo," "SAID," "SIAD."

DARRELL
USA c. 1905
E.W. Darrell, Newton, Massachusetts. 8 hp car.

DARRIN
USA 1946
Howard A. Darrin Automotive Design, Los Angeles, California. Five-passenger convertible. One prototype only.

DARRIN
USA 1953–1954
Kaiser-Frazer Corporation, Willow Run, Michigan. Sliding door roadster. Built or commissioned building of 62 1953 prototypes. Kaiser-Willys Corp., Toledo, Ohio (1954). Built 435 production vehicles at Jackson, Michigan.
See "Kaiser." Several 1954 models customized by Darrin Studios with hard tops and/or V-8 engines up to 1958.

DARROW
USA 1903
Stuart Darrow, Decker & Hinckley Co., Owego, N.Y.

DART
CDN 1914
Dart Cyclecar Co., Toronto, Ontario. Cyclecar.

DART
USA 1909–1911
Dart Engineering Co., New York, N.Y.

DART
USA 1914–1915
Automatic Registering Co., Jamestown, N.Y. Roadsters.

DART
ZA 1958–1963
Glassport Motor Co. Pty. Ltd., Bellville. Sports cars. From 1997 built as replicars.
See "Hayden Dart."

DARTMOBILE
USA 1922
Dart Mfg. Co., Waterloo, Iowa. Lone passenger car effort by succesful truck company.

DASSE
B 1894–1924
Automobiles Gérard Dasse, Verviers. Three-wheelers; touring cars.

DAT; DATSON; DATSUN
J 1912–present
Kwaishinsha Motor Car Works (1912–1918). Kwaishinsha Motor Car Co. (1918–1925). DAT Motor Car Co., Tokyo (1925–1926). DAT Automobile Manufacturing Co., Osaka (1926–1930). DATSON 1931 (becomes a division of the Tobata Imono Co.)

DATSUN
1932–present
DAT Automobile Manufacturing Co., Osaka (1932). Jidosha Seizo Co. Ltd. (1933–1934). Nissan Motor Co. Ltd. (1934–1944). Nissan Heavy Industries Corp. (1947–1949). Nissan Motor Co. Ltd., Yokohama (1949–present). Passenger and sports cars.

DAUER
D 1997
Dauer Racing GmbH, Nürnberg. 730 hp and 402 km/h sports cars. Limited series of 50 cars.

D'AUX
F 1924
Sté. D'Aux, Reims. Cyclecars.

DAVENPORT
USA 1902–1903
Davenport Cycle Works, Davenport, Iowa. Plant reported closed October 1902 under landlord's attachment.

DAVENPORT STEAM
USA 1902–1903
Davenport Mfg. Co., Minneapolis, Minnesota.

DAVID
E 1913–1922; 1936–1939; 1950–1956
David SA, Barcelona. Cyclecars; electric cars; three-wheelers.

DAVIDL
D c. 1923
See "Lesch."

DAVIDSON
USA 1900
William T. Davidson, Mayville, North Dakota.

DA VINCI
USA 1922–1925
James Scripps-Booth, Indianapolis, Indiana.
See "Scripps-Booth."

DAVIS
CDN 1924
Davis Dry Dock Co. Ltd., Kingston, Ontario. Luxury cars.

DAVIS
USA 1895
Davis Gasoline Engine Co., Waterloo, Iowa.

DAVIS
USA 1901
G.H. Davis, Portland, Maine. "Acetylene vehicle."

DAVIS
USA 1908–1929
George Davis Motor Car Co., Richmond, Indiana; Baltimore, Maryland. Touring cars.

DAVIS
USA 1913–1915
Davis Cyclecar Co., Detroit, Michigan. Cyclecars. Used Spacke engine.

DAVIS (TOTEM)
USA 1922
Davis Car Co., Seattle, Washington.

DAVIS
USA 1947–1949
Davis Motor Car Co., Van Nuys, California. Three-wheelers. 17 prototypes built.

DAVIS & WEBSTER
USA c. 1905
W.J. Davis & Webster, Bridgeport, Connecticut.

DAVIS STEAM
USA 1921
Davis Steam Motors, Inc., Detroit, Michigan. Steam touring car.

DAVRIAN
GB 1967–1985
Davrian Developments Ltd., London (1967–1978). Davrian Components, Pontrhydfendigaid, Ystrad Meurig, Dyfed, Wales (1978–1985). About 350 sports cars built.

DAVY
GB 1909–1911
Davy Engineering Ltd., Hulme, Manchester. Hewitt piston valve engine.

DAWB
GB 1967
David Woods, Northern Ireland. Sports car.

DAWSON
GB 1897–1900
The Dawson Gas Engines Syndicate Ltd., London (1897–1900). H.T. Dawson & Son, Canterbury, Kent (1900). 1-, 2- and 3-cylinder light cars.

DAWSON
GB 1919–1921
Dawson Car Co. Ltd., Coventry, Warwickshire. Quality light cars.

DAWSON
USA 1899–1901
Dawson Manufacturing Co., Basic City, Pennsylvania. Steam car.

DAWSON
USA 1904
J.H. Dawson Machinery Mfg. Co., Chicago, Illinois. Light touring cars.

DAX
GB 1979–present
DJ Sportscars International, Harlow, Essex. Sports cars replica.

DAY-LEEDS
GB 1913–1924

Job Day & Sons Ltd., Leeds, Yorks. Cyclecars and light cars.

DAY STEAM
USA 1901–1902
Day Automobile Co., St. Louis, Missouri.

DAYTON
GB 1922
Charles Day Manufacturing Co. Ltd., London. Simple 4 hp cyclecar.

DAYTON
USA 1900–1901
Dayton Motor Vehicle Co., Dayton, Ohio. Steam car. Succeeded Warner Mfg. Co. Steam boilers, pumps, engines and running gear manufacturers.

DAYTON
USA 1904–1909
Dayton Motor Car Company, Dayton, Ohio.

DAYTON
USA 1909
W.O. Dayton Automobile Co., Chicago, Illinois.
See "Reliable–Dayton." Both names apply to same vehicle.

DAYTON
USA 1911–1916
Dayton Electric Car Co., Dayton, Ohio. Electric car. In receivers' hands December 1914.

DAYTON
USA 1913–1914
William Dayton Cyclecar Co., Joliet, Illinois. Cyclecars. Company formed by William O. Dayton of "Reliable-Dayton."

DAYTON
USA 1915
Dayton Motor Car Co., Joliet, Illinois. Formerly "Dayton" cyclecar.

DAYTONA
USA 1956
Randall Products, Hampton, New Hampshire. Two-passenger runabouts.

DAYTONA
USA 1975–1984
Daytona Automotive Fiberglass, Inc., Holly Hill, Florida. "MG" replicars.

DAY UTILITY
USA 1911–1913
Day Automobile Co., Detroit, Michigan. Touring cars.

D.B.
F 1938–1965
Automobiles D.B. Société Bonnet & Cie., Champigny-sur-Marne/Seine (1962–1965). Sports cars.
See "Deutsch & Bonnet." Sold to "Matra" in 1965.

DCA
E 1995–1997
DCA, Madrid. Sports car replica.

DEAL
USA 1905–1911
Deal Buggy Co. Deal Motor Vehicle Co., Jonesville, Michigan. Became Deal Motor Car Co. 1911. Runabouts.

DEARBORN
USA 1910–1911
J & M Motor Car Co., Lawrenceburg, Indiana.
See "James."

DEASY
GB 1906–1911
Deasy Motor Car Manufacturing Co. Ltd., Coventry, Warwickshire. Passenger cars. Complicated inter-relationship between "Deasy," "Armstrong," "Siddeley" and "Wolseley."

DE BAZELAIRE
F 1907–1928
de Bazelaire SA, Paris. Sports and racing cars.

DE BENEDETTI
I
See "FOD."

DE BOISSE
F 1900–1904
J. de Boisse, Paris. Three-wheelers and light cars.

DEBONNAIRE
USA 1955
Replac Corp., Euclid, Ohio. Fiberglass bodied cars.

DE BRUYNE
GB 1968
De Bruyne Motor Car Co. Ltd., Newmarket, Suffolk. Sports cars.

DE CARLO
RA 1967
Small cars.

DECATUR
USA 1896
Decatur Gasoline Engine Co., Decatur, Illinois.

DECATUR
USA 1909–1911
Decatur Motor Car Co., Decatur, Indiana.

DECATUR
USA 1914–1915
Parcel Post Equipment Co., Grand Rapids, Michigan. Runabout.

DECAUVILLE
F 1898–1910
Sté. Decauville, Corbeil/Seine-et-Oise. Voiturette and tourers.

DE CÉZAC
F 1925–1927
Automobiles de Cézac, Perigueux/Dordogne and 1.7-litre cars built to order.

DECHAMPS
B 1899–1906
Ateliers H. Dechamps, Bruxelles. Light cars. From 1904 to 1906 sold under the name "Baudouin."

DECKER
USA 1902–1903
Decker Automatic Telephone Exchange Co. Decker Automobile Co, Oswego, N.Y. Three runabouts built.

DECKERT
F 1901–1906
Deckert, Paris. 1-, 2- and 4-cylinder cars.

DECOLON
F 1957
200 cc three-wheelers.

DE CONINCK
B 1907–1910
Ateliers De Coninck, Bruxelles.
See "Excelsior."

DE COSMO
B 1903–1908
De Cosmo et Cie., Liege. 30 and 55 hp 6-cylinder cars.

DECOSTER
B 1898
I. et H. Decoster, Thielt. Voiturette and three-wheeler.

DE COURVILLE
USA 1983
Replicars.

DECROSS
USA 1914–1915

Decross Cyclecar Co., Cincinnati, Ohio. Cyclecars.

DEDICS
H 1900–1914
Dedics Ferenc, Budapest. Light cars.

DE DIETRICH
D 1897–1904
De Dietrich et Cie., Niederbronn, Alsace.

DE DIETRICH
F 1897–1934
De Dietrich et Cie., Lunéville/Lorraine (1897–1905). Société Lorraine des Anciens Établissements de Dietrich et Cie., Lunéville/Lorraine; Argenteuil/Seine-et-Oise (1905–1934). Touring cars.
See "Lorraine," "Lorraine-Dietrich."

DE DIETRICH-BUGATTI
D 1897–1904
De Dietrich et Cie., Niederbronn/Alsace. 5.4- and 7.3 litre chain-driven cars designed by Ettore Bugatti.

DE DION-BOUTON
F 1883–1932
De Dion, Bouton et Trepardoux (1883–1894). De Dion, Bouton et Cie., Paris (1894–1897); Puteaux, Seine (1897–1932). Steam and gasoline cars.

DE DION-BOUTON
USA 1900–1904
De Dion Motorette Co., Brooklyn, N.Y.
See "American De Dion."

DEEMSTER
GB 1914–1924
Ogston Motor Co. Ltd., London. Sports cars.

DEEMSTER
USA 1923
Deemster Cor. Of America, Hazleton, Pennsylvania. Touring cars.

DEEP SANDERSON
GB 1960–1969
Lawrencetune Engines. Chris Lawrence Racing, London. Sports cars.

DEERE
USA 1906–1907
Deere-Clark Motor Car Co., Moline, Illinois. Started as John Deere Plow Works. Formerly "Deere-Clark."

DEERE-CLARK
USA 1906
Deere-Clark Motor Car Co., Moline, Illinois. Reorganized as Midland Motor Car Co. 1908. Became "Deere." Absorbed Clarkmobile Co.
See "Midland" and "Clarkmobile."

DEERING
USA 1902
R.S. Deering, Chicago, Illinois.

DEERING MAGNETIC
USA 1918–1919
Magnetic Motors Corp., Chicago, Illinois. 7-passenger touring cars.

DEETYPE
GB 1974–c. 1980
Deetype Replicas Ltd., Chelmsford, Essex. "Jaguar" D-Type replica.

DEFENDER
USA 1914
See "Flyer."

DEFIANCE
USA 1909
Miller Machine Co., Defiance, Ohio.

DEFRANCE
F 1922
Cyclecar.

DE FREET
USA 1895
T.M. DeFreet, Indianapolis, Indiana.

DEGALLIER
USA 1902
E.P. DeGallier, Cleveland, Ohio.

DE GROOT
USA 1901
George F. De Groot, Morristown, New Jersey.

DEGUINGAND
F 1927–1930
Sté. des Nouveaux Ateliers A. Deguingand, Puteaux/Seine. 735 cc light cars.

DE HAVEN
USA 1904
De Haven Brothers, Chicago, Illinois.

DEHN
D 1924
Fahrzeug- und Maschinenfabrik H.C. Dehn, Hamburg. Light cars.

DEIBLER
USA 1908
See "Russel-Deibler."

DE KALB
USA 1915
De Kalb Motor Car Co., St. Louis, Missouri.

DEKALB
USA 1915
DeKalb Mfg. Co., Ft. Wayne, Indiana.

DE LA CHAPELLE
F 1978–present
Automobiles De La Chapelle, Brignais/Lyon. Replicars.

DELACOUR
F 1914–1920
Sté. des Automobiles Delacour, Paris. Light cars.

DELAGE
F 1905–1954
Automobiles Delage, Courbevoie/Seine (1905–1935); Paris (1935–1954). Touring and sports cars.

DELAHAYE
F 1894–1954
Emile Delahaye, Tours; Paris (1894–1898). L. Desmarais et Morane, Tours; Paris (1899–1906). Automobiles Delahaye, Paris (1906–1954). Touring and sports cars.

DELAMARE-DEBOUTTEVILLE
F 1884
Edouard Delamare-Deboutteville, Fontaine-Le-Bourg. Gasoline car prototype.

DE LAMINNE-DUCHENE
B 1907
Sports car.

DE LA MYRE-MORY
F 1911–1914
Ets. G. De la Myre-Mory, Neuilly/Seine. 4- and 6-cylinder cars.

DELANOY
USA 1897
Frederick W. Delanoy, Alameda, California.

DE LANSALUT
F 1899
Ateliers De Lansalut, Paris. Voiturette.

DELAUGERE
F 1901–1926
SA des Établissements Delaugere, Clayette, Frères et Cie., Orleans/Loiret. Three-wheelers, runabouts and touring cars.

DELAUNAY-BELLEVILLE
F 1904–1948
SA des Automobiles Delaunay-Belleville, St. Denis/Seine. High quality tourers and limousines.

DELAUNE
F
See "Le Roll."

DE LAVAUD
F 1927–1928
E. Sensaud de Lavaud, Paris. 2.3 litre 6-cylinder cars with automatic transmission.

DE LA VERGNE
USA 1895
De La Vergne Refrigerating Machine Co., New York, N.Y. Hincks & Johnson Co., Bridgeport, Connecticut. Auto-buggy.

DELCAR
USA 1947–1949
American Motors Inc., Troy, N.Y. Small delivery cars. At least one station wagon, possibly more built.

DELECROIX
B 1897–1899
Voiturette.

DE LEON
USA 1905–1906
Archer & Co., New York, N.Y. Exhibited at 1905 New York Auto Show.

DELFOSSE
F 1922–1926
Delfosse et Cie., Cambrai/Nord. Small sports cars.

DELIA
USA 1916
Michael de Cosmo, San Francisco, California. Amphibian.

DELIN
B 1899–1901
Usines Delin, Louvain. Voiturette.

DELISLE & LANDRY
USA c. 1905
Delisle & Landry, New Bedford, Massachusetts. 10 hp vehicle.

DELLA FERRERA
I 1924
Fratelli Della Ferrera, Torino. One cyclecar built.

DELLING
USA 1923–1927
Delling Steam Motor Co., West Collingswood, New Jersey. 92 steam cars were built.

DELLOW
GB 1949–1959
Dellow Motors Ltd. (1949–1956). Dellow Engineering Ltd., Birmingham (1956–1959). About 250 sports cars were made.

DEL MAR
USA 1949
Del Mar Motors Inc., San Diego, California. About 10 subcompact prototypes only.

DELMORE
USA 1923
Delmore Motors Corp., New York, N.Y. Three-wheelers.

DE LONG
USA 1902–1903
Industrial Machine Co., New York, N.Y. DeLong Motor Car Co., Pittsburgh, Pennsylvania. Runabouts.

DELONG
USA 1902
Willis DeLong, Syracuse, Nebraska.

DE LOREAN
USA/GB 1976–1982
De Lorean Motor Co., Bloomfield Hills, Michigan. De Lorean Motor Cars Ltd., Dunmurry, Co. Antrim, Northern Ireland. Sports cars.

DE LOURA
USA 1902–1903
H.G. DeLoura, Ft. Madison, Iowa.

DELPEUCH
F 1922–1925
Automobile Delpeuch, Neuilly/Seine. Touring cars.

DELSAUX
F 1980–c. 1984
Sté. Delsaux. 50cc citycars.

DELTA
D 1954; 1968; 1972
Dornier AG, München. Light car and electric car prototypes.

DELTA
D 1954
Deltawerk Lindner GmbH, München. Three-wheeler. 7 cars were built.

DELTA
D c. 1970
Metzeler AG, Erbach. Sports car kit.

DELTA
D c. 1986
Elastogran GmbH, Lemförde. Citycar.

DELTA
DK 1918
Mammen & Drescher, Jyderup. 4-cylinder 9 hp cars.

DELTA
F 1905–1915
I.de Colange, Puteaux/Seine. Light cars.

DELTA
PI c. 1983
Delta Motor Corporation, Makati, Metro, Manila. 4 × 4 car.

DELTA
USA 1923–1925
Delling and Moulta, Brooklyn, N.Y. Sports cars.

DELTAL
USA 1913–1914
Eric H. Delling, Brooklyn, N.Y. 1923–1925 continued as "Delta."

DELTAMOBIL
D 1954–1955
Deltawerk Lindner GmbH, München. Three-wheelers.

DELTA YETI
I 1968
Four-wheel drive and steering.

DE LUCA DAIMLER
I 1906–1910
SA Fabbrica Automobili de Luca, Napoli. Italian-built "Daimler" (GB) cars.

DELUXE
USA 1906–1909
Deluxe Motor Car Co., Detroit, Michigan.

DELUXE
USA 1910
Deluxe Motor Car Co., Cleveland, Ohio. Organized to manufacture a two-wheel automobile.

DE MARCAY
F 1920–1921
De Marcay et Cie., Paris. Cyclecars.

DE MARS
USA 1902; 1905–1910
De Mars Electric Vehicle Co., Cleveland, Ohio. Electric cars.
See "Blakeslee," "Williams" and "Byrider" Electric.

DEMARS
USA 1907
R.A. Demars, St. Thomas, North Dakota. 4-passenger assembled car.

DEMASSEZ
B 1900
Demassez Freres.

DEMATI
B 1937–1939
Defay, Matthys et Timberman, Bruxelles. Front-wheel-driving and rear-wheel steering.

DEMEESTER
F 1906–1914
Automobiles H. Demeester, Courbevoie/Seine. Light cars.

DEMISSINE
B 1901–1903
E. de Ruyter Demissine, Bruxelles. Electric cars.

DEMOCRATA
BR 1963–1967
Industria Brasileira de Auto, São Paulo. Only fiberglass coupe was built.

DE MONT
USA 1910
Believed to be "De Mot" (DeMotcar).

DE MOOY
USA 1900–1904
De Mooy Bros., Cleveland, Ohio.

DEMOTCAR
1900 1909–1911
DeMotcar Company, Detroit, Michigan. Runabouts.

DE MOTTE
USA 1904
De Motte Motor Car Co., Philadelphia & Valley Forge, Pennsylvania. 2- and 4-cylinder cars.

DEN HELD
NL 1913–1914
A. den Held Azn., Rotterdam.

DENISON
USA 1898–1902
Denison Motor Carriage Co. (1898). Denison Motor Wagon Co. (1899). Denison Electrical Engineering Co. (1900–1902). Julian F. Denison, New Haven, Connecticut. Associated with Tinkham Cycle Co.
See "Tinkham." Electric and steam vehicles.

DENNERT
D 1993–1998
Dennert-Tuning, Duisburg. Tuning.

DENNIS
GB 1899–1915
Dennis Bros. Ltd., Guildford, Surrey. Large touring cars and landaulette.

DENNIS
GB 1911
John Dennis & Co., Harrow, Middlesex. Cyclecars.

DENTIE
USA 1983
Gino Dentie, Beverly Hills, California. Stretched "Cadillac" limousine (40 feet long).

DENZEL
A 1957–1960
Wolfgang Denzel, Wien. Sports cars with "Volkswagen" (D) chassis, "Porsche" (D) engines and own bodies.
See "WD."

DE P
GB 1914–1916
The Depford Co., London. Light cars.

DE PALMA
USA 905–1911; 1916
Ralph De Palma, New York, N.Y.; Detroit, Michigan. Special order cars only.

DE PONTAC
F 1957–1960
De Pontac, Paris. Sports cars.

DEPPE
USA 1917–1920
Deppe Motors Corp., New York, N.Y. New York Air Brake Co., Watertown, N.Y.

DEPUYLT
B 1921–1923
Roulers.

DERAIN
USA 1908–1911
Derain Motor Co. (1908). Simplex Mfg. Co. (1909). Derain Motor Co. (1910–1911), Cleveland, Ohio. 7-passenger touring cars.

DERBAB
USA c. 1905
Y.Q. Derbab, Lynn, Massachusetts. 4 hp automobile.

DERBY
CDN 1924–1926
Derby Motor Cars Ltd., Saskatoon, Saskatchewan. Copy of the U.S. "Davis."

DERBY
CS c. 1928
See "V_chet." Light cars.

DERBY
F 1921–1936
B. Montet, Courbevoie/Seine; Saint-Denis/Seine. Voiturette and light cars.

DERBY
I 1923
Officine Troubetzkoy, Milano. Cyclecar.

DER DESSAUER
D 1912–1913
Anhaltische Automobil- und Motorenfabrik AG, Dessau. Sports cars.

DEREK
GB 1925–1926
Derek Motors Ltd., London.

DE RIANCEY
F 1899–1901
Sté. des Automobiles de Riancey, Levallois-Perret/Seine. Very light tiller-steered cars.

DERIGHT
USA 1905
Deright Automobile Co., Omaha, Nebraska.

DERR
USA 1926–1939
American Steam Auto Co., West Newton, Massachusetts. Steam cars.
See "American Steam Car."

DE SALVERT
F 1904–1906
Perrier et Cie., Paris. 24/30 hp engine.

DE SANCTIS
I 1958–1966
Automobili de Sanctis, Roma. Sports cars.

DESANDE
GB 1980–1983
JBS Associates Ltd., London. "Bentley" replicars.

DESBERON
USA 1901–1904
Desberon Motor Car Co., New Rochelle, N.Y. Runabouts.

DESCHAMPS
F 1913
Deschamps et Cie., Paris. Cyclecars.

DE SCHAUM
USA 1908–1909
De Schaum Motor Syndicates Co., Buffalo, N.Y. Highwheelers and runabouts.
See "Seven Little Buffalos."

DE SCHAUM-HORNELL
USA 1909–1910
De Schaum-Hornell Automobile Co. Hornell Motor Car Co., Hornell, N.Y.; Wyandotte, Michigan.
See "De Schaum."

DESERTER
USA 1968–c. 1971
Dearborn Automobile Co., Marblehead, Michigan. Dune buggy.

DESERT-FLYER
USA 1906
Nevada Motor Car Co., Reno, Nevada. Company was never incorporated nor was a car built. Promoted car was 1906 "Pope Toledo." Also a 1906 "Stearns."

DESGOUTTES
F
See "Cottin et Desgouttes."

DESHAIS
F 1950–1951
Automobiles Deshais, Paris. Front-wheel-drive minicars.

DE SHAW
USA 1907–1909
Charles De Shaw, Brooklyn, N.Y. De Shaw Motor Co. (1907–1910), Evergreen, Long Island, N.Y. Touring cars.

DESIGN PERFORMANCE
F 1987–1996
Design Performance S.A., Rambouillet. Sports cars.

DESMARAIS
USA 1904
P. Desmarais & Sons Motor Co., Holyoke, Massachusetts.

DESMOINES
USA 1902
Desmoines Automobile Co., Des Moines, Iowa. Motorette.

DESMOINES DAZZLER
USA 1906
Motor Components Mfg. Co., Des Moines, Iowa.

DESMOND
USA 1906
Desmond Automobile Co., Chicago, Illinois. Factory to have been built at Oklahoma City, Oklahoma.

DESMOULINS
F 1920–1923
B. Desmoulins, Paris. Used two separate engines.

DE SOTO
CDN 1931–1961
De Soto Motor Corp. of Canada Ltd., Windsor, Ontario.

DE SOTO
USA 1913–1914
De Soto Motor Car Co., Auburn, Indiana; Fort Wayne, Indiana. Built "DeSoto Motorette" 1914–1915. Passenger cars.

DE SOTO
USA 1929–1961
De Soto Motor Corp. and De Soto Division, Chrysler Motor Corp., Detroit, Michigan. Passenger and (later) streamlined cars.

DE SOTO MOTORETTE
USA 1914–1915
De Soto Motor Car Co., Ft. Wayne, Indiana.

DESPERADO
USA 1998
Desperado Motor Racing. One "MTX" (CS/CZ) Tatra V8 assembled in the U.S.

DESSAVIA
D 1907–1910
Anhaltische Fahrzeugfabrik Robert Krause, Dessau. Cyclecar.

DE TAMBLE
USA 1908–1914
Speed Changing Pulley Co., Anderson, Indiana (1908–1909). De Tamble Motors Co., Anderson, Indiana (1910–1914). Roadsters.

D. ET B.
F 1896–1902
Cie des Automobiles David et Bourgeois, Paris. Large vehicles with artillery wheels.

DE TOMASO
I 1959–present
De Tomaso Automobili SpA, Modena. Sports cars.

DETROIT
USA 1899–1902
Detroit Automobile Co., Detroit, Michigan.

DETROIT
USA 1904
Wheeler Mfg. Co., Detroit, Michigan.

DETROIT
USA 1904–1907
Detroit Auto Vehicle Co., Detroit, Michigan.

DETROIT
USA 1905
Detroit Automobile Mfg. Co., Detroit, Michigan. Became "La Petite."

DETROIT
USA 1914
Detroit Cycle Car Co., Detroit, Michigan. Cyclecar. Moved to Saginaw, changed name to "Saginaw."

DETROIT
USA 1916
Detroit Chassis Co., Detroit, Michigan. After 1916 made chassis for "Gem."

DETROIT AIR COOLED
USA 1922–1923
Detroit Air Cooled Car Co., Detroit, Michigan.
See "D.A.C."

DETROIT-CHATHAM
CDN 1911–1912
Chatham Mfg. Co., Chatham, Ontario.

DETROIT-DEARBORN
USA 1909–1910
Detroit-Dearborn Motor Car Co., Dearborn, Michigan.

DETROIT ELECTRIC
USA 1907–1939
Anderson Carriage Co. Became Detroit Electric Car Co. 1919. Absorbed Elwell-Parker Co. Purchased "Chicago Electric" (1899–1916) from Walker Vehicle Co.

DETROITER
USA 1911–1919
Briggs-Detroiter Co. Briggs-Detroiter Motor Car Co. (1911–1915). Detroiter Motor Car Co. (1915–1917). Detroiter Motors Co. (1917–1919), Detroit, Michigan.

DETROITER
USA 1953
Detroit Accessories Co., St. Clair

Shores, Michigan. Fiberglass-bodied convertible with V-8 engine.

DETROIT-OXFORD
USA 1906
Detroit-Oxford Mfg. Co., Oxford, Michigan.
  See "Oxford."

DETROIT SPEEDSTER
USA 1914
Detroit Cyclecar Co., Detroit, Michigan.
  See "Detroit" cyclecar.

DETROIT STEAM
USA 1905
Detroit Steam Engine Co., Detroit, Michigan.

DETROIT STEAM CAR
USA 1924
Detroit Steam Motors Corp., Detroit, Michigan.
  See "Trask-Detroit" steam.

DETROIT TAXICAB
USA 1914–1915
Detroit Taxicab & Transfer Co., Detroit, Michigan. 47 taxicabs were made.

DEUTSCH & BONNET
F
  See "DB."

DEUTSCHLAND
D 1904–1905
Motorfahrzeugfabrik Deutschland GmbH, Berlin. Steam car.

DEUTZ
D 1907–1911
Gasmotorenfabrik Deutz AG, Köln. 4-cylinder cars designed by Ettore Bugatti.

DEVAC
USA 1907
Devac Automobile Co., Newark, New Jersey. Name meant: D-double, E-explosion, V-valveless, A-air, C-cooled.

DEVAUX
USA 1931–1932
Devaux-Hall Motors Co., Oakland, California. 5554 passenger cars built. Absorbed Durant Motor Co. of California, moved to Grand Rapids, Michigan. Absorbed by Continental-Devaux Corp. 1932.

DE VECCHI
I 1905–1917

De Vecchi, Strada & Cia. (1905–1908). De Vecchi & Cia., Milano (1908–1917). Conventional, well-built machines.

DEVEY
USA 1900
John Devey, Lehi, Utah. Motor buggy.

DEVIN
D c. 1968–1970
Souren GmbH, Aachen. Sports kitcars.

DEVIN
USA 1958–1964
Devin Motors, Inc., El Monte, California. High-performance sports cars.

DE-VO
USA 1936–1937
De-Vo Motor Car Co., Dover, Delaware.

DEW
D 1927
Zschopauer Motorenwerke J.S. Rasmussen AG, Berlin. Electric car.

DEWABOUT
USA 1899–1901
Thomas B. Dewhurst, Blue Grass Cycle Co., Lexington, Kentucky. Runabouts.

DEWALD
F 1902–1926
Charles Dewald, Boulogne-sur-Seine. 2.1-, 3.6- and 5.3-litre cars.

DE WANDRE
B 1922–1925
Ets. F. De Wandre, Bruxelles. Based on the Model T "Ford" (USA).

DEWCAR
GB 1913–1914
D.E.W. Engineering Co. Ltd., Eynsford, Kent. Cyclecars.

DE WEESE
USA 1909
Chauncy De Weese. Steam car.

DE WITT
USA 1909–1910
De Witt Automobile Co. De Witt Motor Vehicle Co., North Manchester, Indiana. Motor buggy.

DEXTER
F 1906–1909
Construction d'Automobiles Dexter, Lyon. Large 4- and 6-cylinder 60, 72 and 100 hp chain-driven cars.

DEY
USA 1915–1917; 1919–1925
Dey Electric Vehicle Syndicate. Dey Electric Corp., New York, N.Y. Harry E. Dey Inc., Jersey City, New Jersey. Experimental electric cars.

DEY-GRISWOLD
USA 1895–1898
Harry E. Dey, New York, N.Y. Dey-Griswold Co., New York, N.Y. Electric cars. Became U.S. Motor Vehicle Co.

D.F.P.
F 1906–1926
Doriot, Flandrin et Parant, Courbevoie/Seine. Tourers.

D.F.R.
F 1924
Désert et de Font-Réault, Neuilly/Seine. Cyclecars.

D.H.K.
USA 1909
D.H.K. Motor Car Co., Detroit, Michigan.

DHUMBERT
F 1920–1930
Automobiles Dhumbert, Voiron/Isere. 4-, 6- and 8-cylinder cars.

DIABLE
F 1921–1924
Paris. Three-wheelers.

DIABLO
GB
Bohanna Stables, High Wycombe, Buckinghamshire.
  See "Bohanna Stables."

DIABOLO
D 1922–1927
Diabolo Kleinauto GmbH, Stuttgart. Deutsche Eisenbahnsignalwerke AG, Bruchsal. Three-wheeler.

DIAL
GB c. 1971
Dial Plastics, Grays, Essex. Sports car.

DIAMANT
D 1905–1908
Diamant-Werke Gebr. Nevoigt, Reichenbrand/Sachsen.
  See "Elite," "Elite-Diamant."

DIAMANT
F 1901–1906
Hammond Moteur et Cie., Paris. Sté. La Francaise, Paris

DIAMOND
USA 1904–1905
Diamond Motor Co., New Haven, Connecticut; Meriden, Connecticut.

DIAMOND
USA 1910
Diamond Automobile Co., South Bend, Indiana. 1911–1912 known as "R.A.C." Formerly "Ricketts."

DIAMOND
USA 1914
Cyclecar Co. of Wilmington, Wilmington, Delaware. Cyclecar.

DIAMOND ARROW
CDN 1909–1912
Diamond-Arrow Motor Car Co., Ottawa, Ontario.

DIAMOND T
USA 1907–1911
Diamond T Motor Car Co., Chicago, Illinois. Touring cars.

DIANA
D 1922–1923
Diana Automobilwerk GmbH, München. Three-wheelers.

DIANA
USA 1925–1928
Moon Motor Car Co., St. Louis, Missouri. Passenger cars.
 See "Moon."

DIATTO
I 1905–1927
Diatto, A. Clément Vetture Marca Torino (1905–1909). Societa Officine Fondiere Fréjus Vetture Diatto (1909–1918). Fonderie Officine Fréjus Automobili Diatto (1918–1919). Automobili Diatto (1919–1923). Autocostruzioni Diatto, Torino (1924–1927). Touring and sports cars.

DIAVOLINO
CH 1982–1985
Diavolino AG, Automobile, Zürich. Small Jeep-type cars designed by Marcel Oswald, ZBR Automobile.

DIAVOLINO
I 1982–1983
Torino. Later produced in (CH).

DIAZ Y GRILLO
E 1917–1922
Diaz y Grillo SL, Barcelona. Sporting light cars.

DIBA
CH 1970–1971
Carosserie Werner Dietrich AG, Basel. Sports car prototype.

DICK
D 1932
Carl Dick, Frankfurt am Main. Three-wheeler.

DICKINSON MORETTE
GB 1903–1905
B.E. Dickinson & Co., Birmingham. Three-wheeler.

DICKSON
CDN 1893
Dickson's Carriage Works, Toronto, Ontario. Electric car designed by Frederick Barnard Fetherstonhaugh.

DIEBEL
USA 1900–1901
J.H. Diebel, W. Unity, Ohio. Diebel-Eppler Mfg. Co. Diebel Cox Mfg. Co., Philadelphia, Pennsylvania. Runabout.

DIEBLER & RUSSELL
USA 1908
Diebler & Russell Co., Berlin, Wisconsin. Only three cars were built.

DIEBOLD
USA 1901
Henry C. Diebold, Belleville, Illinois.

DIEDERICHS
F 1912–1914
Société des Automobiles Diederichs, Charpennes/Rhone. About 60 tourers were made.

DIEHL
USA 1935
G.A. Diehl, Portland, Oregon. Rear-engined streamliner.

DIEHLMOBILE
USA 1962–1964
H.L. Diehl Co., South Willington, Connecticut. Folding three-wheelers.

DIE VALKYRIE
USA 1952
Brooks Stevens Design Assoc., Milwaukee, Wisconsin. And Karosserie Spohn, Ravensburg (D). Special-order car on Contemporary "Cadillac" chassis. One made.

DILE
USA 1914–1916
Dile Motor Car Co., Reading, Pennsylvania. Cyclecar. Introduced August 1914. In receivers' hands August 1916.

DIM
GR 1977; 1981–c. 1986
DIM Motor George E. Dimitriadis, Athenai. Air-cooled small cars based on "Fiat" (I) 126 with fiberglass body.

DINARG
RA 1959–1969
Dinamica Industrial Argentina SA (1959–1966). Stad Srl, Cordoba (1966–1969). 1-cylinder small cars.

DINGES
E 1908
Three-wheeler.

DINGFELDER
USA 1902–1903
Dingfelder Motor Co., Detroit, Michigan.

DINGO
D 1969
Adolf Rinne, Viersbach. Sports car kit.

DININ
F 1904
Alfred Dinin et Cie., Puteaux/Seine. Small two-seater electric cars.

DINO
I 1965–1974
Ferrari SpA, Modena. Sports cars.
 See "Ferrari."

DINOS
D 1921–1926
Dinos Automobilwerke AG, Berlin.
 See "Luc."

DIORT
F c. 1905
Diort Cycles et Automobiles.

DIOSS
CZ 1996–present
Dioss s.r.o., Klatovy. Sports cars.

DIRECT
B 1904–1905
Sté. des Constructions Mecaniques et d'Automobiles, Bruxelles. Very flexible 50 hp 4-cylinder engine, no gearbox.

DIRECT DRIVE
USA 1917–1918
Direct Drive Motor Company, Philadelphia, Pennsylvania.

See "Champion." Champion Motors Corp., Philadelphia, Pennsylvania.

DISBROW
USA 1917–1918
Disbrow Motor Co., Cleveland, Ohio. Sports roadsters.

DISPATCH
USA 1910–1922
Dispatch Motor Car Co., Minneapolis, Minnesota. Only single car was built in 1910.

DISK
CS 1924
Československá zbrojovka, akc. spol., Brno. Two-stroke light cars.
See "Z."

DI TELLA
RA 1959–1966
Sociedfad Industrial Americana de Maquinas (SIAM) di Tella. Automotores SA, Buenos Aires. "Austin"/ "Morris" (GB) based cars.

DITTLINGER
USA 1898
Emil V. Dittlinger, St. Louis, Missouri. Auto buggy.

DITWILER CYCLECAR
USA 1914
Ditwiler Mfg. Co., Galion, Ohio.

DIVA
GB 1962–1968
Tunex Conversions Ltd. (1962–1965). Diva Cars Ltd. (1966–1967). Skodek Enginering, London (1967–1968). 65 sports cars were made.

DIXI
D 1904–1928
Fahrzeugfabrik Eisenach (1904–1920) Dixi-Werke AG, Eisenach (1920–1928). Tourers. "Austin" (GB) Seven under license, acquired by "BMW."

DIXIE
USA 1908–1910
Southern Motor Car Factory. Southern Motor Car Co., Houston, Texas. Four-cylinder conventional roadster and "Dixie Jr." highwheelers.

DIXIE
USA 1910–1912
Dixie Motor Co., Frederick, Oklahoma. Also listed as Dixie Motor Car Co., Oklahoma City, Oklahoma.

DIXIE
USA 1915
Dixie Mfg. Co., Vincennes, Indiana. Dixie Motor Car Co., Louisville, Kentucky. Became "Dixie Flyer."

DIXIE FLYER
USA 1916–1923
Dixie Motor Car Co., Louisville, Kentucky. 1919 merged with Kentucky Wagon Works (founded 1859). Joined "National" (1900–1924) and "Jackson" (1903–1923) in Associated Motors Corp. Later became National Motors Corp.

DIXIE TOURIST
USA 1908–1909
Southern Motor Car Factory, Houston, Texas.
See "Dixie." Both names apply to same vehicle.

DIXON
USA c. 1830
Joseph Dixon, Lynn, Massachusetts. Steam car.

DJ
GB c. 1984–1995
DJ Sportscars Limited, Harlow, Essex. Replicars.

D.K.R.
DK 1953–1954
DK Plasticbilen, Kobenhavn. Autofabriken D.K.R. AS, Roskilde. Plastic-bodied motor cars.

DKW
D 1928–1966
Zschopauer Motoren-Werke J.S. Rasmussen, Zschopau; Berlin (1928–1939). Auto Union GmbH, Düsseldorf; Ingolstadt (1950–1966). Passenger and sports cars with 2-stroke engines.

DKW-MALZONI
BR 1964–1966
Gennaro Malzoni, Matao. "DKW" (D) based sports coupe.

D.L.
GB 1913–1920
W. Guthrie & Co. D.L. Motor Mfg. Co. Ltd., Motherwell, Lanarks. Light cars.

D.L.G.
USA 1907
D.L.G. Motor Car Co., St. Louis, Missouri. Runabout.

D.L.M.
GB 1915–1920
D.L.M. Motor Manufacturing Co., Motherwell, Scotland. Light cars.

D.M.C.
GB 1913–1914
Dukeries Motor Co. Ltd., Worksop, Notts. Three-wheeler.

DOBELLI
I 1903–1904
Spartaco Dobelli, Roma.

DOBI
E 1919–1920
Autociclos Dobi, Madrid. Cyclecar.

DOBLE
USA 1913–1917; 1920–1932
Abner Doble, Waltham, Massachusetts (1913). Doble Motor Vehicle Co., Waltham, Massachusetts (1914). General Engineering Co., Detroit, Michigan (1916). Doble-Detroit Steam Motors Co. (1917–1918). Steam cars. Merged with Amalgamated Machinery Co., Chicago, Illinois 1919. Doble Motors Inc., San Francisco, California 1921. Reorganized as Doble Steam Motor Car Corp. 1922.
See "Trask-Detroit."

DOBLE-DETROIT
USA 1918–1919
Doble-Detroit Steam Motors Co., Detroit, Michigan. Steam car.
See "Doble."

DOBLE-SIMPLEX
USA 1923
Doble Steam Motors Corp., San Francisco, California. Steam car. Built on "Jordan" Big Six chassis.

DOBLER INTER
D c. 1955
Three-wheeled minicar.

DOCTORESSE
F 1899–1902
Sté. Francaise d'Automobiles (Systéme Gaillardet), Paris. 6 and 12 hp light cars. "Gaillardet" was a 5 hp three-wheeler.

DODDSMOBILE
CDN 1947
One prototype only.

DODGE
USA 1914

Dodge Motor Car Co., Detroit, Michigan. Light friction drive car by Alvan M. Dodge, formerly with Wahl Motor Car Co.

DODGE
USA 1914–present
Dodge Bros. Motor Car Co. (1914–1930). Dodge Division, Chrysler Motors Corp. (1930 to date), Detroit, Michigan. First car built May 1914. 1915 model car announced December 1914. Passenger and sports cars.

DODGE BROTHERS
USA 1906
Dodge Brothers Mfg. Co., Detroit, Michigan.

DODGESON
USA 1926
John Duval Dodge, Dodgeson Motors, Detroit, Michigan. Rotary valve straight-eight. Built by son of J.F. Dodge. Prototypes only.

DODO
USA 1912
Auto Parts Mfg. Co., Detroit, Michigan. Cyclecars.

DODSON
GB 1910–1914
Dodson Motors Ltd. (David Brown & Son Ltd.), Huddersfield, Yorks. 12/16 and 20/30 hp cars, identical to the equivalent "Renault" (F).

DOE-WAH-JACK
USA 1908–1909
Tulsa Auto Mfg. Co., Dowagiac, Michigan.
See "Lindsley."

DOHERTY
CDN 1897
Thomas Doherty, Sarnia, Ontario.

DOHERTY
USA 1905
Barney F. Doherty, New Britain, Connecticut.

DOLAN
USA 1900
Clarence W. Dolan, Philadelphia, Pennsylvania. Electric car.

DOLBEY
USA c. 1905
Mr. Dolbey, Olneyville, Rhode Island.

DOLLWET
USA 1903

John Dollwet, San Francisco, California. Runabout.

DOLLY
GB 1920
Light cars.

DOLLY MADISON
USA 1915
See "Madison."

DOLO
F 1947–1948
Établissements B.D.G., Pierrefitte/Seine. 571cc and 1,142 cc light cars.

DOLORES
F 1906
Dolores et Cie., Paris. 10, 16, 24 and 50 hp models.

DOLPHIN
GB 1906–1909
The Two-Stroke Engine Co. Ltd., Shoreham, Sussex. Twelve cars with 2-stroke 28 hp engines were made.

DOLPHIN
USA 1990–1996
See "Vortex."

DOLSON
USA 1904–1907
John L. Dolson Automobile Co., Charlotte, Michigan. Plant closing reported November 1907. Receiver permitted 25 more cars to be finished. Spring 1908 plant was sold. Times Square Auto Co. bought stock. Touring cars.

DOMAN
USA 1899–1900
H.C. Doman, Oshkosh, Wisconsin.

DOMAN-MARKS
USA
See "Airomobile."

DOME
J 1978
Sports car prototype.

DOMINION
CDN 1910–1911
Dominion Motors Ltd., Walkerville, Ontario.

DOMINION
CDN 1911
New Dominion Motor Co., Windsor, Ontario.

DOMINION
CDN 1914

Dominion Motor Car Co., Coldbrook, New Brunswick.

DOMMARTIN
F 1949–1950
Compagnie des Moteurs Dommartin, Dommartin/Somme. 800 cc rear-engined 2-cylinder cars.

DONEAUX
B 1970
Jean Doneaux, D'Ougrée. City car prototype.

DONG-FENG
PRC 1958–present
No. 1 Automobile Plant, Changchun, Kirin, Manchuria.

DONINVEST
RUS 1995–present
Doninvest, Rostov na Donu. "Daewoo" (ROK) and "Citroën" (F) license.

DONKERVOORT
NL 1983–present
Joop Donkervoort, Nieuw Loosdrecht. Sports car replica.

DON-MERKUR
D 1929
U. Donath, Coburg. Three-wheeler.

DONNERSTAG
D 1963
Donnerstag GmbH, Frankfurt am Main. "Volkswagen" based convertibles.

DONNET; DONNET-ZÉDEL
F 1924–1934
SA des Automobiles Donnet, Nanterre/Seine; Neuilly/Seine; Pontarlier/Doubs. Light cars.

DONOSTI
E 1922–1923
Garaje Internacional, San Sebastian. 3-litre 6-cylinder twin ohc sports cars.

DORA
I 1899–1909
S.A. Industrale Automobili Elettrici, Alpignano. Electric vehicles.

DORAN
USA 1984–1993
Doran Motor Company, Reno, Nevada. Three-wheelers.

DORAY
USA 1950
Doray, Inc., Miami Springs, Califor-

nia. Roadster prototype on "Willys" Jeepster chassis.

DORCHESTER
USA 1906
Dorchester Motor Car Co., Dorchester, Massachusetts. Hub Automobile Co., Boston, Massachusetts. Succeeded "Crestmobile." Runabout.

DORÉ
F 1900
Sté. G. Doré, Levallois-Perret/Seine. Electric vehicles.

DOREY
F 1906–1907; 1912–1913
W.H. Dorey, Paris. Voiturette and cyclecars.

DORIOT-FLANDRIN-PARANT
F
See "D.F.P."

DORMANDY
USA 1903–1905
United Shirt Collar Co., Troy, N.Y. Four cars were built.

DORN
USA 1910
Dorn Motor Car Co., St. Louis, Missouri. Believed to be error for "Dorris."

DORNER
D 1927
Dorner Ölmotoren AG, Hannover. Diesel-powered light car.

DÖRNHOEFER
D 1930
Wolf Dörnhoefer, Zwickau. Three-wheeler.

DORNIER
D 1948–1958; 1968–1972
Dornier AG, München. Minicars.
See "Zündapp," "Delta."

DORRIS
USA 1897
George Preston Dorris, Nashville, Tennessee. One gasoline buggy built.

DORRIS
USA 1905–1926
St. Louis Motor Carriage Co. (1905–1906). Dorris Motor Car Co., St. Louis, Missouri. Absorbed Astra Motors Corp.
See "Astra." 3,100 cars built.

DORT
USA 1915–1924
Dort Motor Car Co., Flint, Michigan. Canadian version built by Wm. Gray.
See "Gray-Dort." Touring cars.

DOUGHERTY
USA 1955–1956
Frazer Dougherty, Sierra Madre, California.

DOUGILL
GB 1896–1899
A.W. Dougill & Co. Ltd., Leeds, Yorks. Experimental cars with horizontal engines.

DOUGLAS
GB 1913–1922
Douglas Bros. Ltd., Kingswood, Bristol. Cyclecars.

DOUGLAS
USA 1905
W.H. Douglas, Healey & Co., Belleville, New Jersey. Electric coupe.

DOUGLAS
USA 1918–1919
Douglas Motor Corp., Omaha, Nebraska. 334 passenger cars were built.

DOVAL
USA 1983
Don Hart, New Haven, Connecticut. Replicars.

DOVE
GB 1963
L.F. Dove. Sports cars with "Triumph" TR3 components.

DOVETAIL
USA 1900
Dovetail Carriage Co., Crawfordsville, Indiana. Gasoline motor carriage.

DOW
USA 1900
A.L. Dow, Longmont, California.

DOW
USA 1905
A.M. Dow, Braintree, Massachusetts.

DOW
USA c. 1905
Dow Portable Electric Co., Boston, Massachusetts. 5 hp automobile.

DOW
USA 1910
Alec Dow, Appleton, Maine. Gasoline vehicle.

DOWAGIAC
USA 1909–1911
Dowagiac Motor Car Co., Dowagiac, Michigan.
See "Lindsey." Dowagiac Motor Car Co. finished building the last 15 "Lindsey" cars. These are sometimes called "Dowagiac" as well.

DOW ELECTRIC
USA 1960
Dow Testing Laboratory, Inc., Detroit, Michigan. Electric two-passenger, 47-inch wheelbase minicar.

DOWNING
USA 1901
C.J. Downing, New York, N.Y.

DOWNING
USA 1914
Downing Cyclecar Co., Detroit, Michigan. Cyclecars.

DOWNING-DETROIT
USA 1913–1914
Downing Motor Car Co., Detroit, Michigan; Cleveland, Ohio. Cyclecars and touring cars.

DOYLE
USA 1900
Joseph Doyle, West Homestead, Pennsylvania.

DP
D 1985–1994
DP Motorsportm Ekkehard Zimmermann, Overath. Tuning.

D.P.L.
GB 1907–1910
Dawfield, Philips Ltd., West Ealing, Middlesex. Taxicabs.

DRAG
GB
See "Hancock."

DRAGON
F 1913
P. Milhuet, Sancerre/Cher. Light cars.

DRAGON
USA 1906–1908
Dragon Automobile Co., Philadelphia, Pennsylvania. Reorganized as Dragon Motor Co. Touring cars and runabouts.

DRAGON
USA 1920–1921
Dragon Automobile Works, Chicago, Illinois. February 1921 stock sale banned in Illinois. September 1921 Blue Sky

Law violation investigated. Touring cars.

DRAGSPORT
GB 1971–1975 ?
Dragsport Autos, Upper Batley, Yorks. Sports catrs.

DRAKE
USA 1921–1922
Drake Motor & Tire Mfg. Co., Knoxville, Tennessee. Touring cars.

DRAPER
USA 1904
Draper Corp., Hopedale, Massachusetts.

DRB
I 1966
Nicolo Dona delle Rose & Cesare Bossaglia, Torino. Sports car prototype.

DREADNOUGHT
USA 1911–1913
See "Moline."

DREWS
D 1948–1951
Karosserie Drews, Wuppertal-Oberbarmen. About 150 sports cars based on "Volkswagen" were made.

DREXEL
USA 1916–1917
Drexel Motor Car Corp., Chicago, Illinois. Succeeded "Farmack." Car built in "Staver" plant owned by Studebaker.

DREYHAUPT
D 1905
Richard Dreyhaupt, Leipzig. 10 hp small cars.

DRIGGS
USA 1921–1923
Driggs Ordnance & Mfg. Co., New Haven, Connecticut; New York, N.Y. Car advertised in 1921 and 1922. Taxicabs built 1923–1924.

DRIGGS-SEABURY
USA 1915–1916
Driggs-Seabury Ordnance & Engineering Co., Sharon, Pennsylvania.
See "Ritz," "Sharon" and "Twombly."

DRINGOS
D 1925
Berlin. Propeller-powered vehicle.

DRI SLEEVE
GB 1971–1972
Dri Sleeve Car Co., Warminster, Wilts. Bugatti Type 35 replica.

DRIVER TRAINER CAR
USA 1961
Midget Motors Corp., Athens, Ohio.

DROLETTE
CH c. 1969
Andre Thaon. Electric three-wheeler.

DRUMMOND
GB 1905–1909
North British Manufacturing Co. Ltd., Dumfries, Scotland. Assembled 4-cylinder cars.

DRUMMOND
USA 1915–1917
Drummond Motor Car Co., Omaha, Nebraska. 300 cars were built.

DS
B 1934
Dewaet et Stoewer, Bruxelles.

D.S.
D
See "Stoewer."

DSL
GB 1978–c.1980
DS Ltd., Worthing, Sussex. Kit car.

DS MALTERRE
F 1955
Ets Malterre Freres, Paris. Three-wheeler minicar.

D.S.P.L.
F 1910–1914
Comte Pierre d'Hespel, Peranchies/Nord. Sports cars.

D.S.R.
F 1908–1909
Sté. d'Étude Dannadieu, Saussard et Robert, Paris. Light cars.

D.U.
A 1914
Dietrich & Urban, Graz. 4-cylinder cars.

DUAL
USA 1922–1924
T.E. Felt Motor Car Co., Los Angeles & Midway City, California; Pomona, California.

DUAL E TURCONI
I 1899–1901
Dual e Turconi, Milano.

DUAL-GHIA
USA 1955–1958; 1961–1963
Carrozzeria Ghia, Torino (I). Dual Motors Corp., Detroit, Michigan. Italo-American GT cars. Used "Chrysler" components. 117 + 26 cars were produced.

DUBE
USA c. 1905
A.J. Dube, Worcester, Massachusetts. 5 hp automobile.

DUBONNET
F 1933–1936
Andre Dubonnet, Courbevoie/Seine. Sports cars powered by a 6-cylinder "Hispano-Suiza" engine.

DU BRIE-CAILLE
USA 1904
Du Brie Motor Co., Detroit, Michigan. Touring cars.

DUCHATELET
B 1982–?
Carrosserie Duchatelet, Liege. Luxury cars based on "Mercedes-Benz" (D) 500SEL/SEC.

DUCK
USA
Jackson Automobile Co., Jackson, Michigan. Also known as "Jackson" Back Seat Steer.

DUCKHAM
GB c. 1972
Sports car.

DUCOMMUN
D 1903–1904
Werkstätte für Maschinenbau vorm. Ducommun, Mulhouse, Alsace.

DUCROISET
F 1897–1900
Ducroiset et Fils, Grenoble. Large 8 hp cars.

DUDGEON
USA 1857; 1866
Richard Dudgeon, New York, N.Y. Steam car. First car destroyed 1857 in New York Crystal Palace fire. Car No. 2 is in private collection now.

DUDLEY
USA 1915
Electric car.

DUDLY BUG
USA 1913–1914
Dudly Tool Co., Menominee, Michigan. Cyclecars. Reported June 1914

plant taken by Menominee Electric Co. to build electric pleasure car.

DUER
USA 1907–1910
Chicago Coach & Carriage Co., Chicago, Illinois. Highwheelers.

DUESENBERG
USA 1914–1915
Maytag-Mason Auto Co. (1914), Waterloo, Iowa. Duesenberg Brothers (1915), Minneapolis, Minnesota.

DUESENBERG
USA 1920–1937
Duesenberg Automobile & Motors Co. Inc. Duesenberg Automobile Co., Elizabeth, New Jersey. Duesenberg Motors Co., Indianapolis, Indiana. First eight cars built in Elizabeth, New Jersey plant. Company bought by E.L. Cord 1926. Duesenberg Inc. became part of Cord Corp. 1929. Large 6.9-litre cars.

DUESENBERG
USA 1966
Duesenberg Corp. (Fritz Duesenberg), Indianapolis, Indiana. One car produced.

DUESENBERG
USA 1970–1975
Duesenberg Co., Gardena and Inglewood, California. $24,500 replicars.

DUESENBERG
USA 1979
Duesenberg Brothers Co. (Harlan & Kenneth Duesenberg. And Robert Peterson), Mundelein and Evanston, Illinois. One prototype made.

DUFAUX
CH 1904–1907
C.H. Dufaux et Cie., Geneve. Touring and sports cars. A 4-cylinder 26,401 cc car in 1905.

DUGATTO
D c. 1984
Dugatto-Design, Essen. "Jaguar" (GB) XK 120/140 replica.

DUHANOT
F 1907–1908
Sté. des Automobiles Duhanot, Paris. Touring cars and taxicabs.

DULON
GB 1967–1972 ?
Maxperenco Products Ltd., Kidlington, Oxon. (1967–1969). Dulon Cars, Didcot, Berks. (1969–1972 ?). Sports cars.

D. ULTRA
GB 1914–1916
D.U. Manufacturing Co. Ltd., London. Light cars.

DUM
USA 1902
Ed and Harley Dum, Lancaster, Ohio.

DUMAS
F 1902–1903
M.A. Dumas Fils, Champigny-sur-Marne/Seine. Three-wheelers.

DUMONT
F 1912–1913
Automobiles Dumont, Asnieres/Seine. Light cars.

DUMONT
USA 1904
Columbus Motor Vehicle Co., Columbus, Ohio.
See "Santos-Dumont."

DUMONTANT
F 1974–1975
Jacques du Montant. Replicars.

DUMORE
USA 1918
American Motor Vehicle Co., Lafayette, Indiana.
See "American Junior."

DUNA
H 1966
Jusztin Capra, Budapest. Small car prototype.

DUNALISTAIR
GB 1925–1926
Dunailstair Cars Ltd., Nottingham. Only 4 four-seater tourers were made.

DUNAMIS
B 1922–1924
Automobiles Dunamis, Anvers. Large luxury 8-cylinder cars.

DUNBAR
USA 1904
Dunbar & Co., Chicago, Illinois.

DUNBAR
USA 1923
David Dunbar Buick Corp., Walden, N.Y. Roadsters.

DUNE BUGGY
CDN 1968–c. 1973
Bob Irwin Mfg. Co., Weston, Ontario.

DUNE MASTER
USA 1968–c. 1974
Haddock Sand Buggy Const. Co., Santa Ana, California. Dune buggy.

DUNKLE
USA 1908
W.R. Dunkle, Pana, Illinois.

DUNKLE
USA 1910
Ralph W. Dunkle, Greenville, Ohio. Runabout.

DUNKLEY
GB 1896–1924
Dunkley Car Co., Birmingham. Three-wheelers.

DUNN
USA 1916–1918
Dunn Motor Works, Ogdensburg, N.Y. Air-cooled cyclecars.

DUNTON
USA 1896
Frederick W. Dunton, Jamaica, N.Y. Electric tricycle.

DUNTOV
USA 1982
See "American Custom Industries."

DUO
GB 1912–1914
Duocars Ltd. (1912–1913); Duo Cyclecars Ltd., London (1913–1914).

DUO POWER
USA 1984–1993
Duo Power, Inc., Santa Fe Spring, California. Sports cars.

DUPLEX
CDN 1923
United Iron Works Co., Montreal, Quebec. 4-cylinder engine with 2 pistons per cylinder.

DUPLEX
GB 1906–1909
Duplex Motor Engine Co., London. 4-cylinder 2-stroke 30 hp engine.

DUPLEX
GB 1919–1921
British Commercial Lorry & Engineering Co. Ltd., Manchester. Light cars.

DUPLEX
USA 1907–1909

Duplex Automobile Works (1907). Duplex Motor Car Co. (1908–1909), Chicago, Illinois. Stanhope.

DUPONT
USA 1915
Dupont Motor Car Co., Reading, Pennsylvania.

DUPONT
USA 1919–1933
Dupont Motors Inc., Wilmington, Delaware. Assembled in Moore, Pennsylvania. Combined with Indiana. Motorcycle Co., Springfield, Massachusetts (1929). Less than 100 cars with 140 hp engine were made.

DUPORT
F 1977–c. 1993
Sté. Duport, Annecy. Duport Automobiles, St. Ferreol/Faverges. Diesel engine powered city cars.

DUPRESSOIR
F 1900–1914
Paul Dupressoir, Maubeuge/Nord. Voiturettes and conventional cars.

DUQUESNE
USA 1903–1906
Duquesne Motor Car Co., Buffalo, N.Y. 1904 became Duquesne Construction Co., Jamestown, N.Y.

DUQUESNE
USA 1912–1913
Pittsburgh Garage & Supply Co. Duquesne Motor Car Co., Pittsburgh, Pennsylvania. Touring cars.

DURABILE
USA 1902
Amstutz-Osborn Co., Cleveland, Ohio.

DURAND
F c. 1973
Carrossier Jacques Durand, Chatillon-sur-Thouet. Sports cars.

DURANT
CDN 1922–1932
Durant Motors, Leaside, Toronto, Ontario.

DURANT
USA 1921–1932
Durant Motors Inc., Flint, Michigan; Lansing, Michigan; Elizabeth, New Jersey; Muncie, Indiana.
See "Star," "Flint" (1924–1927), "Locomobile" and "Princeton." 153,993 4- and 6-cylinder cars were made.

DURENSEN
USA 1921
Andrew Durensen, Minneapolis, Minnesota.

DUREY-SOHY
F 1899–103
Automobiles Durey-Sohy, Paris. Voiturette.

DURIEZ
F c. 1950s
Small car prototype.

DÜRKOPP
E 1898–1927
Bielefelder Maschinenfabrik vorm. Dürkopp & Co. (1898–1913). Dürkoppwerke AG, Bielefeld (1913–1927). 2-, 3-, 4- and 6-cylinder models up to 7.2-litre capacity.

DURO-CAR
USA 1907–1911
Duro-Car Mfg. Co., Los Angeles, California. Became Amalgamated Motors Corp., Alhambra, California 1911. Touring cars and runabouts.

DURSLEY-PEDERSEN
GB 1912
Dursley-Pedersen Cycle Co., Dursley, Gloucestershire. Cyclecars.

DURYEA
USA 1895–1913
Duruea Motor Wagon Co. (1895–1898). J. Frank Duryea (1899), Springfield, Massachusetts. Duryea Motor Mfg. Co. (1898–1900), Peoria, Illinois. Duryea Power Co. (1900–1907), Reading, Pennsylvania. Western Duryea Mfg. Co. (1901), Los Angeles, California. Charles E. Duryea (1908–1913), Reading, Pennsylvania. 731 cars with 2- and 3-cylinder engines were made.

DURYEA
USA 1914
Cresson Morris Co., Philadelphia, Pennsylvania. Cyclecars (C.E. Duryea). Became "Crowther-Duryea."

DURYEA ELECTA
USA 1911–1912
B.E. Duryea Auto Co., Saginaw, Michigan.

DURYEA GEM
USA 1916–1917
Duryea Tricycle Co., Reading, Pennsylvania. Duryea Motors Inc., Wilkes-Barre, Pennsylvania. Roadsters.

DURYEA TRAP
USA 1898–1900
National Motor Carriage Co. Continental Auto Co., Stamford, Connecticut.

DUSSAULT
USA 1904
Albert Dusseau, Lockport, N.Y. Automobiles to special order.

DUSSEAU
USA 1910–1912
Dusseau Motor Car Co. Dusseau Fore & Rear Drive Auto Co., Toledo, Ohio Four-wheel drive.

DUTTON
GB 1969–present
Dutton Sports Ltd., Fontwell, Sussex; Worthing, Sussex. Sports cars.

DUX
D 1909–1926
Polyphon-Werke AG (1909–1916). Dux-Automobilwerke AG, Wahren bei Leipzig (1916–1926). Light and large cars.
See "Polymobil," "Helios."

DUX
SU c. 1899–1903
"Benz" (D) based carriages.

D-WAGEN
D 1924–1927
Deutsche Werke AG (1924–1925). Deutsche Kraftfahrzeugwerke AG, Berlin (1925–1927). 1.3-litre 4-cylinder cars.

DWBS
GB 1973
David Wood, Belfast Tool and Gauge Co., Belfast. Sports car prototype.

DYKE
USA 1900–1907
A.L. Dyke (1900–1903). A.L. Dyke Automobile Supply Co. (1903–1907), St. Louis, Missouri. Sold unassembled.

DYKE-BRITTON
USA 1902–1904
A.L. Dyke Automobile Supply Co., St. Louis, Missouri.
See "Dyke."

DYLE ET BACALAN
B 1906–1907
Sté. Metallurgique Dyle et Bacalan, Louvain.

DYMAXION
USA 1933–1934
Buckminster Fuller, Bridgeport, Connecticut. Four egg-shaped three-wheelers built in old "Locomobile" factory.

DYNAMIC
CS 1954
Jan Tenora, Brno. Sports car.

DYNAMOBIL
D 1906
E.H. Geist Elektrizitäts-AG, Köln. Gasoline-electric cars.

DYNA-VERITAS
D
See "Veritas."

D'YRSAN
F 1923–1930
Raymond Syran, Cyclecars d'Yrsan, Asnieres, Seine. Three-wheeled cyclecars.

E

EAGLE
GB 1901–1908
Eagle Engineering & Motor Co. Ltd., Altrincham, Cheshire (1901–1907). St. George's Motor Car Co. Ltd., Leeds, Yorks. (1907–1908). Tandem tricar; 2- and 4-cylinder light cars.

EAGLE
GB 1912–1924
Eagle Motor Manufacturing Co. Ltd., London. Light cars.

EAGLE
GB 1981–1993
Eagle Cars Ltd., Storrington, West Sussex. Sports cars.

EAGLE
USA 1904–1905
Eagle Automobile Co., Buffalo, N.Y.

EAGLE
USA 1905–1907
Eagle Automobile Co., Rahway, New Jersey. Air-cooled cars. Company incorporated 1906 with USD 60,000 capitalization by F.C. & E. Van Dernater, A.G. Spencer, G.W. Loft and H.S. Griffin.

EAGLE
USA 1906–1907
Eagle Motor Car Co., Middletown, Connecticut. Air-cooled car.

EAGLE
USA 1908
Eagle Motor Carriage Co., Elmira, N.Y. Highwheeler.

EAGLE
USA 1909
Eagle Automobile Co., St. Louis, Missouri. Roadster.

EAGLE
USA 1914–1915
Eagle Cyclecar Co., Chicago, Illinois. Cyclecars. Became "Eagle Macomber."

EAGLE
USA 1917–1918
Eagle Macomber Motor Co., Sandusky, Ohio. Rotary engine.

EAGLE
USA 1923–1924
Durant Motors, Inc., Flint, Michigan. 6-cylinder touring cars.

EAGLE
USA 1988–1998
Eagle Division, Chrysler Corporation, Southfield, Michigan. Passenger cars.

EAGLE ELECTRIC
USA 1915–1916
Eagle Electric Automobile Co., Detroit. Electric cars.

EAGLE MACOMBER
USA 1915–1917
Eagle Macomber Motor Car Co., Chicago, Illinois; Sandusky, Ohio. 35 cars were made.

EAGLET
GB 1948
Silent Transport Ltd., Woking, Surrey. Electric car.

EAGLET
USA 1914–1915
Eagle Motors Co., Los Angeles, California. Cyclecars. Reported building factory September 1914.

EAM
D c. 1993
Edelsbrunner Automobile München, München. Sports cars.
See "Nuvolari."

EARL
USA 1907–1908
Earl Motor Car Co., Kenosha, Wisconsin. Became "Petrel," Petrel Motor Car Co., Kenosha, Wisconsin (1908). Roadsters.

EARL
USA 1922–1923
Earl Motors Inc. Earl Motors Mfg. Co., Jackson, Michigan. Succeeded "Briscoe." Clarence R. Earl took control of Briscoe Motor Corp. March 1921. 1880 cars were made.

EARLY
USA 1911
Early Motor Car Co., Columbus, Ohio.

EAS
A/CS 1907
Elektrotechnická akciová společnost, dříve Kolben a spol., Praha. Gasoline car. Electric vehicle built in 1900.
See "Kolben NW."

EASTBOURNE
GB 1905–1906
Eastbourne Motor Works, Eastbourne, Sussex. Assembled 2-cylinder cars.

EASTERN
USA 1896–1897
Eastern Motor Carriage Co., New Haven, Connecticut.

EASTERN
USA 1910–1911
Eastern Motor Car Co., Brockton, Massachusetts.

EASTERN
USA 1916
Eastern Motors Inc., Hartford, Connecticut. Eastern Motors Syndicate, New Britain, Connecticut. Became "Charter Oak."

EASTERN ELECTRIC
USA 1921
South Boston, Massachusetts.

EAST GLOWS
PRC 1964–1973 ?
Car Factory No. 1, Peking.

EASTMAN
USA 1899–1900
H.F. Eastman Automobile Co., Cleveland, Ohio. Electric and steam car.

EASTMEAD-BIGGS
GB 1901–1904
Eastmead & Biggs., Frome, Somerset. Three cars were built.

EASTON
USA 1907
Believed to be company name of Easton Machine Co., So. Easton, Massachusetts, not name of automobile.
See "Morse."

EAST WIND
PRC
See "Dong Feng."

EATON
USA 1896
W.S. Eaton, S. Hampton, New Hampshire.

EATON
USA 1898–1900
Eaton Electric Motor Carriage Co., Boston, Massachusetts. Electric cars. First car designed and built in 6 weeks.

EBM
D 1912
EBM Maschinenfabrik. 4-cylinder 3.8 litre cars.

EBRO
E 1959–c. 1976
Viasa, Vehículos Industriales y Agricolas S.A., Barcelona. "Jeep" (USA) under license.

EBS
D 1924–1928
Ernst Bauermeister & Söhne, Berlin. Three-wheelers.

ECHARRI
E 1996–present
Echarri Motor International, Lardero, La Rioja. 1905 styled replicars.

ECK
USA 1899; 1902–1903
Boss Knitting Machine Works, Reading, Pennsylvania. Eckhardt & Souter Automobile Co., Buffalo, N.Y.
See "Boss" steam car.

ECKHART
USA 1903
Eckhart Brothers, Auburn, Indiana.
See "Auburn."

ECKMAN
USA c. 1905
Emil C. Eckman, Wellesley, Massachusetts. 6 hp automobile.

ÉCLAIR
F 1907–1908
SA des Constructions d'Automobiles l'Éclair, Paris. Gasoline and electric cars.

ÉCLAIR
F 1920–1923
Lebeau-Cordier, Courbevoie/Seine. Cyclecars.

ECLIPSE
B 1922
Sté. Eclipse, Keumiée.

ECLIPSE
GB 1901–1904
Eclipse Engineering & Motor Co., London. Light cars.

ECLIPSE
USA 1896; 1904
Eclipse Bicycle Co. Eclipse Mfg. Co., Elmira, N.Y. 20 hp air-cooled touring car (1904).

ECLIPSE
USA 1900–1903
Eclipse Automobile Co., Boston, Massachusetts; Easton, Massachusetts. Steam cars.

ECLIPSE
USA 1902
Eclipse Buggy Co., Ft. Wayne, Indiana. Buyer supplied own engine.

ECLIPSE
USA 1903–1904
Eclipse Machine Co., Columbus, Ohio. Custom built only.

ECLIPSE
USA 1905–1906
Krueger Mfg. Co., Milwauke, Wisconsin. Touring cars.

ECLIPSE
USA 1916
Eclipse Motor Car Co., Detroit, Michigan. 4- and 8-cylinder cars.

ECO
AUS 1923
Eco Motors Co. Ltd., Melbourne, Victoria. Assembled cars powered by a Lycoming engine.

ECO
USA 1921–1922
K. Hamilton-Grapes, Detroit, Michigan. For export to Australia.

ECONOM
D 1950
Econom-Werk Hellmuth Butenuth, Berlin. Small car "Teddy."

ECONOMIC
GB 1921–1922
Economic Motors, London. Three-wheeler.

ECONOMIC
USA 1902
Economic Mfg. Co., East Orange, New Jersey. Steam car.

ECONOMY
USA 1908–1911
Economy Motor Buggy Co., Fort Wayne, Indiana; Kankakee, Illinois; Joliet, Illinois. Highwheelers.

ECONOMY
USA 1917–1922
Economy Motor Car Co., Tiffin, Ohio. Consolidated with Bellefontaine Automobile Co. January 1917 and moved to Bellefontaine, Ohio. 630 cars were made.

ECONOMYCAR
USA 1913–1914
Economycar Co., Indianapolis, Indiana. Also listed as International Cyclecar Co., Providence, Rhode Island. Two-passenger tandem car.

ECONOMY-VOGUE
USA 1920–1921
Vogue Motor Car Co., Tiffin, Ohio.

ECONOOM
NL 1912–1914
Hautekeet & Van Asselt, Amsterdam. 85 cars were built.

ECORRA
CZ 1997–present
Ecorra s.r.o., Kopřivnice. "Tatra" 700 based sports coupe.

ECOSSE
GB 1988–1990
Ecosse Car Co. plc, Knebworth, Hertfordshire. Sports cars.

EDAG
D 2000
EDAG, Fulda. Passenger car prototype.

EDDY
USA 1898–1902
Eddy Manufacturing Co., Windsor, Connecticut. Electric car.

EDDY
USA 1914–1915
Eddy Automobile Co., Cincinnati, Ohio.

EDFORD
P 1930–1938
Ferreirinha et Irmao, Oporto. Sports cars based on "Ford" (GB) components.

EDIE MAC
USA 1900
Edie Mac Automobile Co., Reading, Pennsylvania.

EDIS
E 1919–1922
Carlos Jaumandreu Martorell, Barcelona. 2- and 4-cylinder cars.

EDISMITH
GB 1905
Edwin Smith, Blackburn, Lancs. Small car.

EDISON
USA 1903–1904
Thomas A. Edison, West Orange, N.Y. Edison Automobile Co., Camden, New Jersey. One only for testing electrical devices.

EDISON ELECTRIC
USA 1927
Edison Electric Co., New York, N.Y.

EDISON-FORD
USA 1914
T.A. Edison & A. Ford, Detroit, Michigan. Electric car.

EDIT
I 1924
Armino Mezzo, Torino.
See "AM" Cyclecar di Armino Mezzo.

EDITH
AUS 1953
Gray & Harper Pty., Melbourne. Minicar.

EDMOND
GB 1920–1921
Shand Motor & Engineering Co. Ltd., London. Cyclecars.

EDMOND
USA 1899–1901
E.J. Edmond Cycle Mfg. Co., Mattaewan, N.Y. Tricycle.

EDMUND
GB 1920
C. Edmund & Co. Ltd., Chester. Cyclecars.

EDSEL
USA 1958–1960
Ford Motor Company, Dearborn, Michigan. 5.9 and 6.7-litre V-8 cars.

EDWARDS
USA 1913
Cyclecar.

EDWARDS
USA 1912
Edwards Motor Car Co., Louisville, Kentucky.
See "Longest."

EDWARDS
USA 1949–1955
Edwards Sport Car, Culver City, California. Sports, street or track cars.

EDWARDS
USA 1953–1955
Edwards Engineering Co. (Sterling H. Edwards), South San Francisco, California. 6 convertibles built.

EDWARDS-KNIGHT
USA 1912–1913
Edwards Motor Car Co., Long Island City, N.Y. Absorbed 1913 by Willys-Overland Co. Became "Willys-Knight."

E.E.C.C.
GB 1952–1954
Electrical Engineering Construction Co. Ltd., Totnes, Devon. Three-wheeler.

EFFYH
S/DK 1950–1953
Thorkil Grue, Copenhagen. Sports cars designed by Hakansson brothers from Sweden.

EGAN
AUS 1935–1936
U. Egan, Geelong, Victoria. 80 hp 6-cylinder cars.

EGG
CH 1896–1900
Automobilfabrik Egg & Egli, Zürich. 3- and 4-wheelers.

EGGER-LOHNER
A 1899
Bela Egger & Co., Wien. Electric cars based on "Lohner."

EGLI
CH 1993–1996
Fritz W. Egli, Bettwill. Replica.

EGO
D 1921–1926
Mercur Flugzeugbau GmbH, Berlin (1921–1925). Hiller Automobilfabrik AG, Berlin (1925–1926). Light cars.
See "Hiller."

E.H.P.
F 1921–1929
Ets. H. Precloux, Courbevoie/Seine; La Garenne-Colombes/Seine. Voiturette; sports cars.

EHRENTRAUT
USA 1911
Carl P. Ehrentraut, Pittsburgh, Pennsylvania. Custom built only.

EHRHARDT
D 1904–1922
Heinrich Ehrhardt, Düsseldorf; Zella St. Blasii/Thüringen. Touring cars.

EHRLICH
USA 1918
Lambert & Mann Co., Chicago, Illinois. Electric car.

E.H.V.
USA 1903–1906
See "Compound."

EIA
I 1928
Societa Lombarda Economica Industriale Automobili. Prototype only.

EIBACH
D 1924–1926
Eichler & Bachmann GmbH, Berlin. Three-wheeler.

EICHSTAEDT
USA 1902
Roman Eichstaedt, Michigan City, Indiana. Built to order.

E.I.M.
USA 1915–1916
Eastern Indiana Motor Car Co., Richmond, Indiana. Touring cars.

EINAUDI
F 1926–1927
Cyclecars Einaudi, Bois-Colombes/Seine. 3hp cyclecars.

EINDHOVEN
NL 1983
Eindhoven University, Eindhoven. Electric car.

EINIG
USA 1896
John Einig, Jacksonville, Florida. Steam car.

EISENACH
D 1898–1903
Fahrzeugfabrik Eisenach, Eisenach. Electric and gasoline cars.

EISENHUTH
USA 1896–1900
J.W. Eisenhuth, San Francisco, California; Newark, New Jersey. Eisenhuth Horseless Vehicle Co., Middletown, Connecticut. Called "Graham Fox" 1904. After 1904 "Compound."

EISENHUTH-COMPOUND
USA 1904
Should be "Graham Fox." Later "Compound."
See "Compound," "E.H.V."

EJA
I 1924
Senechal, Milano.

EKAMOBIL
D 1909–1914
Ing. Erhard Brandis, Berlin. Three-wheelers.

ELA
USA c. 1905
E.W. Ela, Waltham, Massachusetts. 5 hp automobile.

ELAN
F 1899–1900
Sté. des Automobiles Elan, Paris. Light voiturette.

ELBERT
USA 1914–1916
Elbert Motor Car Co., Seattle, Washington. Elbert Motor Car Co. of California, San Francisco, California. Cyclecars. Acquired plant at Sunnyvale, California.

ELBIL
N 1972
Electric car prototype.

ELBRIDGE
USA 1908
See "De Long."

ELBURN-RUBY
F
See "Ruby."

ELCAR
USA 1916–1931
Elkhart Carriage & Motor Car Co., Elkhart, Indiana. Succeeded "Pratt" (1911–1915). 18,043 cars were made.

ELCAR-LEVER
USA 1930
Elcar-Lever Motor Co., Elkhart, Indiana. An "Elcar" with Lever engine.
See "Elcar."

ELCO
USA 1915–1916
Elwood Iron Works, Elwood, Indiana. Bimel Buggy Co., Sidney, Ohio. 1916 re-named "Bimel." 1917 plant sold to American Motors Parts.

ELDEN
GB 1969–c. 1975
Elden Motor Company Ltd., London. Sports cars.

EL.DI.CAR
D 1992–present
El.Di.Car GmbH, Ramsloh. Electro-Diesel car. About 20 were built.

ELDIN ET LAGIER
F 1898–1901
Eldin et Lagier, Lyon. Voiturette; large cars.

ELDON
GB 1990s
Eldon House Automotive Ltd., Edenbridge, Kent. Kit cars.

ELDREDGE
USA 1903–1906
National Sewing Machine Co., Belvidere, Illinois. Succeeded Friedman Road Wagon Co. Runabouts.

ELECTRA
D 1899–1900
A. Krüger, Berlin. Electric three-wheeler.

ELECTRA
USA 1913
Storage Battery Power Co., Chicago, Illinois. Electric cars.

ELECTRA
USA 1914–1915
Electra Mfg. Co., Los Angeles, California. Electric roadsters.

ELECTRA
USA 1974–1976
Die Mech Corp., Pelham, N.Y. "Fiat" (I) Sport Spyder converted to electric operation.

ELECTRA KING
USA 1961–1981
& Z. Electric Car Co., Long Beach, California. Electric cars.

ELECTRA SPIDER
USA 1970s
Die Mesh Corp. Electric cars.

ELECTRIC
T 1996
Electric Car Company Ltd., Pathumthani. Electric cars.

ELECTRICAL
USA 1906
Electrical Construction Co., Los Angeles, California.

ELECTRICAR
F 1920–1924
Couaillet, St. Ouen/Seine. Electric three-wheelers.

ELECTRICAR
USA 1950–1966
Boulevard Machine Works, North Hollywood, California. Small electric runabouts.

ELECTRICAR
USA 1972
Electric Fuel Propulsion Corp. Electric car prototype.

ELECTRIC CARRIAGE
USA 1896–1897
Electric Carriage & Wagon Co., New York, N.Y. Electric auto-buggy.

ELECTRIC FUEL PROPULSION
USA 1977
Electric Fuel Propulsion, Inc., Troy, Michigan. Electric car.

ELECTRICIT
NL 1899–1900
Nederlandsche Metaalwarenfabriek, Amsterdam. Electric cars.
See "Scholte."

ELECTRIC MOTORCYCLE
USA 1895
Sturges Motorcycle Co., Chicago, Illinois. Built for Times-Herald race.

ELECTRICSHAW
USA c. 1974
Dr. Peter Quandt, Edmonton, Alabama. Electric car prototype.

ELECTRIC SHOPPER
USA 1956–1962
Electric Car Co., Long Beach, California. Electric three-wheelers.

ELECTRIC VEHICLE
USA 1897
Electric Carriage & Wagon Co., New York, N.Y.; Philadelphia, Pennsylvania. Succeeded Morris & Salom.

ELECTRIC VEHICLE
USA 1897–1901
Electric Vehicle Co., New York, N.Y.

ELECTRIC WAGON
USA 1897
Electric Carriage & Wagon Co., New York, N.Y.; Philadelphia, Pennsylvania.
See "Electric Vehicle."

ELECTRIQUETTE
USA 1915
Osborn Electriquette Mfg. Co., Los Angeles, California. Small 2-passenger electric vehicle with all-wicker body.

ELECTRO
USA c. 1905
Electro Motor & Vehicle Co., Springfield, Massachusetts. 2.5 hp electric car.

ELECTROBAT
USA 1895–1897
Morris & Salom, Philadelphia, Pennsylvania. Electric car. Original car built by Crawford Wheel & Gear Co., with body by Chas. S. Caffrey Co., for Chicago Times-Herald Race. Completed August 1894. The Times-Herald car, called Electrobat II, won the Gold Medal in that event.
See "Electric Vehicle."

ELECTROBILE
USA 1902
National Vehicle Co., Indianapolis, Indiana.
See "National Electric."

ELECTROBILE
USA 1951
Chicago. Electric three-wheelers.

ELECTROCAR
USA 1922
Electrocar Corp., New Brunswick, New Jersey. Electric taxicabs.

ELECTROCICLO
E 1945–1946
Electrociclo SA, Bario Chonta, Eibar, Guipuzcoa. Small two-seater electric cars.

ELECTROCYCLETTE
F
See "A.E.M."

ELECTRODYNE
USA 1972
City car.

ELECTROGÉNIA
F
See "Champrobert."

ELECTROLETTE
F 1941–1943
P.A. André, Nice. Very light electric cars.

ELECTROMASTER
USA 1962–1964
Nepa Manufacturing Co., Div. of Parker-Pattern & Foundry Co. Distributed by Auto Electric Car Co., Passadena, California. Small electric shopping cars.

ELECTROMOBILE
GB 1901–1902
British Electromobile Co. Ltd., London. Electric car.

ELECTROMOBILE
USA 1899–1902
Belknap Motor Co., Portland, Maine.
See "Chapman Electric."

ELECTROMOBILE
USA 1905–1907
American Electromobile Co., Detroit, Michigan. One electric car was built.

ELECTROMOTION
F 1900–1909
Sté. l'Électromotion, Paris. Electric town cars.

ELECTRONIC
USA 1955
Electronic Motor Corp., Salk Lake City, Utah. A hybrid-power car.

ELECTRONOMIC
USA 1900–1901
Simplex Motor Vehicle Co., Danvers, Massachusetts. Steam car.
See "Hood" steam.

ELECTRO-RENARD
F 1943–1946
Lyon. Electric two-seater minicars.

ELECTROSPORT
USA c. 1972
Electric Fuel Propulsion Inc., Ferndale, Michigan.

ELECTROVAIR
USA 1966
General Motors Corp., Detroit, Michigan. Experimental electric car with "Chevrolet" Corvair body.

ELEGANT
USA 1971–c. 1994
Elegant Motors, Inc., Indianapolis, Indiana. "Auburn," "Cord" and "Cobra" replica.
See "Le Grande."

ELEKTIAR
GB 1984
Elektiar Ltd., London. Stretched Range "Rover."

ELEKTRIC
D 1922–1924
Automobil- und Akkumulatoren-Bau GmbH, Berlin; Driesen-Vordamm.
See "Alfi."

ELEKTRON
D 1933–1934
Elektron-Fahrzeugbau, Duisburg.

EL-FAY
USA 1931–1935
Elcar Motor Co., Elkhart, Indiana. Taxicabs for Larry Fay.

ELFE
F 1919–1922
Ateliers Defrance Freres, Vierzon/Cher. Cyclecar.

ELFIN
AUS c. 1956–1977?
Elfin Sports Cars, Edwardstown, S.A.

ELGÉ
B 1912–1914
Lambin et Gendebien, Houffalise. 2.3-litre 4-cylinder monobloc engine.

ELGIN
USA 1899–1901
Elgin Automobile Co., Chicago, Illinois.
See "Winner."

ELGIN
USA 1916–1924
Elgin Motor Car Corp., Chicago, Illinois. Elgin Motors Inc., Indianapolis, Indiana. Absorbed "New Era" (new Era Motor Car Co. 1916). Receiver discontinued production July 1924. 16,784 cars were made.

ELGIN ELECTRIC
USA 1899
Elgin Sewing Machine & Bicycle Co., Elgin, Illinois. 5 electric cars were built.

ELGIN LIGHT CAR
USA 1914
Elgin Light Car Co., Fenton, Michigan.

ELIA
D 1993–present
Elia Motorsport, Hiltmannsdorf. Tuning.

ELIESON
GB 1897–1898
Elieson Lamina Accumulator Syndicate Ltd., London. Electric car.

ELIETTE
SU c. 1975
Name for in Western Europe sold "Zaporozhets."

ELIJAH WARE
USA 1871
Elijah Ware, San Francisco, California. Steam car.
See "Ware."

ELITE
D 1920–1928
Elite Motorenwerke AG (1920–1922). Elitewerke AG (1922–1927). Elite-Diamant-Werke AG, Brand-Erbisdorf (1927–1928). Sports tourers.
See "Elite-Diamant."

ELITE
USA 1901–1902
D.B. Smith & Co., Utica, N.Y. Steam car.
See "Saratoga Tourist."

ELITE
USA 1907
Hughson & Burchett Motor Co., Newark, New Jersey. Runabout for children.

ELITE
USA 1909–1910
Johnson Service Co., Milwaukee, Wisconsin.
See "Johnson."

ELITE
USA 1973–c. 1977
Elite Enterprises, Inc., St. Dakota, Minn. Sports car and replica. 75 cars built in 1974.
See "Laser."

ELITE-DIAMANT
D 1927–1928
See "Elite."

ELITE HERITAGE
USA c. 1982
Elite Heritage Motors Corp., Elroy, Wisconsin. "Duesenberg" replica.

ELITEWAGEN
D 1917–1923
Elitewagen AG, Berlin. Electric three-wheeler.

ELITEWAGEN
D 1921–1923
Elitewagen AG, Berlin. Richard & Hering AG, Ronneburg. "Rex Simplex" was continued under this name.

ELIZALDE
E 1914–1928
Biada, Elizalde y Cia., Barcelona. Fabrica Espanola de Automoviles Elizalde, Barcelona. Large 8-litre sports cars and limousines.

ELKA
I 1912–1914
"Laurin & Klement" (A/CS) assembled in Italy.

ELKHART
USA 1908–1911
Elkhart Carriage & Mfg. Co. (1908). Elkhart Motor Car Co. (1908–1909), Elkhart, Indiana.

ELKHART
USA 1910–1916
Elkhart Carriage & Harness Mfg. Co., Elkhart, Indiana.
See "Pratt" and "Pratt-Elkhart."

ELKHART
USA 1922–1925
Crow-Elkhart Motor Corp., Elkhart, Indiana.
See "Crow-Elkhart."

ELLEMOBIL
DK 1909–1911
J.C. Ellehammer, Copenhagen. Cyclecars.

ELLENA
I 1962–1964
Carrozzeria Ellena, Torino. Sports cars.

ELLER
D c. 1984
Firma Philipp Eller, Ober-Ramstadt. Tuning.

ELLI
A 1976
Bewag, Eisenstadt. Electric car prototype.

ELLICOTT
USA 1906–1907
Buffalo, N.Y.

ELLINGEN & PARKS
USA 1896
W. Ellingen & W.J. Parks, LaSalle, Illinois.

ELLIOTT
USA 1897–1899
W.L. Elliott Motor Carriage Co., Oakland, California. Gasoline carriage.

ELLIOT
USA 1925
H.E. Elliot & C.W. Lang, Dayton, Ohio.

ELLIPSIS
F 1992
Philippe Charbonneaux, Reims. Rhomboid wheel placement, prototype.

ELLIS
USA
See "Triumph."

ELLIS
USA c. 1892
George H. Ellis, Minneapolis, Minnesota. Motor buggy.

ELLIS ELECTRIC
USA 1901
Triumph Motor Vehicle Co., Chicago, Illinois.

ELLIS & TURNER
USA 1901
Ellis & Turner Co., Peoria, Illinois. One car was built.

ELLSWORTH
USA 1907–1908
J.H. Ellsworth, New York, N.Y.

ELMER
USA 1898–c.1906
Elmer F. Johnson, Kalkaska, Michigan. Gasoline and steam light cars.

ELMER SIX
USA 1911
Elmer Co., Elkhart, Indiana. Touring cars.

ELMO
BG 1970
NIPKIDA, Sofia. Electric car prototype.

ELMORE
USA 1899–1912
Becker Bros. Elmore Bicycle Co., Clyde, Ohio. Ten cars built. Resumed production 1902–1912. Elmore Mfg. Co., Clyde, Ohio. Touring cars.

EL MOROCCO
USA 1956–1957
Almquist Engineering Co., Milford, Pennsylvania. Rueben Allenden, Detroit, Michigan. About 30 styling conversions of the "Cadillac."

EL NASR
ET 1958–c.1973
El-Nasr Automotive Manufacturing Co., Wadi Hof, Helwan. "Fiat" (I) license.

ELPO
CS 1948
Ladislav Požárek, Praha. 125 cc minicar prototype.

ELRICK
USA 1896
George Elrick, Joliet, Illinois.

ELSTON
USA 1895
R.W. Elston, Charlevoix, Michigan. Chicago Times-Herald race entry.

ELSWICK
GB 1903–1907
Elswick Motor Co., Newcastle-upon-Tyne.

EL-TRANS
DK 1990–c.1993
El-Trans A/S, Randers. Electric car.

ELVA
F 1907
Voitures Elva, Paris. 8 hp 2-cylinder two-seater and 14 hp 4-cylinder phaeton.

ELVA
GB 1955–1968
Elva Engineering Co., Bexhill and Hastings, Sussex (1955–1966). Elva Cars (1961) Ltd., Rye, Sussex (1961–1966); Croydon, Surrey (1966–1968). Elva Cars Ltd., Shenley, Herts (1967). About 670 sports cars were built.

ELWELL-PARKER
USA 1896; 1905–1908
Elwell-Parker Electric Co., Cleveland, Ohio. Electric cars.

ELWOOD
USA 1915
Elwood Iron Works, Elwood, Indiana. See "Elco."

ELYSÉE
F 1921–1925
Automobiles Elysée, Paris. Light cars.

EMA
CS 1969–1970
Výzkumný ústav stroju točivých, Brno. Electric car prototypes.

EMANCIPATOR
USA 1909
Emancipator Automobile Co., Aurora, Illinois.
See "Aurora" (1905–1909).

EMANUEL
I 1899–1904
A. Roselli, Torino.

EMBEESEA
GB 1974–1983
Embeesea Kit Cars, High Wycombe, Bucks. Sports and kit cars.

EMBREE
USA 1910
McLean Carriage Co. Embree-McLean Carriage Co., St. Louis, Missouri. 30 and 35 hp cars.

EME
SLO c.1991
EME Engineering d.o.o., Slovenska Bistrica. Stretched limousines based on "Citroën" (F) XM.

EMELBA
E 1980s
Emelba S.A., Barcelona. Special bodied "Seat."

EMERALD
GB 1903–1904
Douglas S. Cox & Co., London. Very light two-seater voiturette.

EMERALD
USA c.1905
George W. Emerald, Cambridge, Massachusetts. 3 hp automobile.

EMERAUDE
F 1913–1914
Constructions Industrielles Dijonaises (C.I.D.), Dijon. Cyclecars.

EMERSON
USA 1900–1901
Emerson-Fisher Co. (1900). B.L. Emerson (1901), Cincinnati, Ohio.

EMERSON
USA 1916–1917
Emerson Motors Co., New York, N.Y.
See "Campbell" (1917–1920). Touring cars.

EMERSON-FISHER
USA 1896
Emerson & Fisher Co., Cincinnati, Ohio. Motor wagon.

EMERY
GB 1964
Paul Emery Cars Ltd., London. Sports cars.

EMERYSON
GB 1949–1952; 1960–1961
Emeryson Cars Ltd., Twickenham, Middlesex (1949–1952). Connaught Cars Ltd., Send, Surrey (1960–1961).

E.M.F.
USA 1908–1913
Everett-Metzger-Flanders, Detroit, Michigan. Absorbed "Northern," "Wayne" (1904–1908). Absorbed by Studebaker Corp. 1910. 25,967 cars were built.

EMMEL
B 1924–1925
Carrosserie Emmel, Bruxelles.

EMMS
GB 1922–1923
Emms Motor Co., Coventry, Warwickshire. Light car.

E.M.P.
GB 1897–1900
Electric Motive Power Co., London. Electric carriages.

EMPHE
USA 1920
Tsacomas Demos, New York, N.Y. At least two cars were built for export to Greece.

EMPI-IMP
USA 1968–1973
Motor Products Inc., Riverside, California. Dune buggy built on cut down VW chassis.

EMPIRE
USA 1896
Empire Motor Co., Pittsburgh, Pennsylvania.

EMPIRE
USA 1909–1918
Empire Motor Car Co., Indianapolis, Indiana (1909–1918); Greenville, Pennsylvania (1912–1914). Reorganized 1912 as Empire Auto Co. Touring cars and roadsters.

EMPIRE STATE
USA 1898
Empire State Motor Co., Catskill, N.Y.

EMPIRE STATE
USA 1900–1901
Empire State Automobile Co., Rochester, N.Y. Runabout.

EMPIRE STEAMER
USA 1901–1902
Empire Mfg. Co. Inc., Sterling, Illinois.

EMPIRE STEAMER
USA 1904–1905
Wm. H. Terwilliger & Co., Amsterdam, N.Y.

EMPRESS
GB 1907–1910
Empress Motor Co. Ltd., Manchester. 4- and 6-cylinder cars.

EMPRESS
USA 1908–1910
Johnson Service Co., Milwaukee, Wisconsin. Gasoline car; firm also built steam.
  See "Johnson" (1905–1912).

EMSCOTE
GB 1920–1921
Emscote Motor Co. Ltd., Warwick. Light cars.

E.M.W.
D 1926–1929
E.M.W. Motor-Transportwagen-Werk, H. Schivelbusch, Leipzig. Three-wheelers.

EMW
D/DDR 1945–1955
Eisenacher Motoren-Werke, Eisenach. Passenger cars based on pre-War "BMW" (D).

ENBERG
USA c. 1905
A.E. Enberg, Worcester, Massachusetts. 4.5 hp automobile.

ENDURANCE
GB 1899–1901
Endurance Motor Co. Ltd., Coventry, Warwickshire. Cars based on "Benz" (D) designs.

ENDURANCE
USA 1924
Endurance Steam Car Co., Los Angeles, California. Steam cars.

ENFIELD
GB 1906–1915
Enfield Autocar Co. Ltd., Redditch, Worcs (1906–1908); Birmingham (1908–1915). Touring cars.

ENFIELD
GB 1969–c. 1976
Enfield Automotive, London. Electric cars.

ENFIELD-ALLDAY
GB 1919–1925
New Allday & Onions Ltd., Birmingham. Air-cooled 5-cylinder radial engine; mid-sized saloons.

ENGELHARDT
D 1900–1902
Hermann Engelhardt Motoren- und Automobilfabrik, Berlin. 6 hp small cars.

ENGER
USA 1909–1917
Frank J. Emger, Cincinnati, Ohio. Enger Motor Car Co., 1910. Plant sold at auction May 1917. 4514 cars were built.

ENGESA
BR 1985–c. 1993
Engesa Engenheiros Especializados SA, Barueri, São Paulo. 4 × 4 vehicle.

ENGLAND
USA 1901
Arthur England, Amesbury, Massachusetts.

ENGLEHART
USA 1901
A.J. Englehart, Northampton, Massachusetts. Gasoline carriage.

ENGLER
USA 1913–1914
William B. Engler, Pontiac & Detroit, Michigan. Cyclecars.

ENGLISH
GB c. 1982
D. English Ltd., Coachwork Division, Poole, Dorset. Convertibles.

ENGLISH MECHANIC
GB 1900–1905
This was never a make or company, only detailed instructions how to build a car, published by "The English Mechanic and World of Science and Art" in a series of articles.

ENGSTRÖM
S 1900
C.A. Engström Vagnfabrik, Eskilstuna 3-hp gasoline car with chain drive.

ENIAK
RA c. 1990
Eniak S.A., Buenos Aires. Replicars.

ENKA
CS 1925–1929
F. Kolanda a spol., továrna kvalitních lidových vozu, Praha. 2-stroke engined light cars.
  Later development see "Aero."

ENNEZATA
I 1974–1978
Milano. Took over from "Iso" Rivolta.

ENSIGN
GB
  See "British Ensign."

ENSLOW
USA 1910
Frank Enslow, Huntington, West Virginia.

ENTERPRISE
USA 1913

Enterprise Machinery Co., Chicago, Illinois. Cyclecars.

ENTROP
NL 1909
De s'Gravenmoersche Rijwielen- en Motorrijwielenfabriek, s'Gravenmoer. Only 4 three-wheelers were made.

ENTYRE
USA 1910–1911
Believed to be "Etnyre" misspelled.

ENTZ
USA 1914
Entz Motor Car Corp., New York, N.Y. 6-cylinder touring cars.

E.N.V.
F 1908
E.N.V. Motors Ltd., Courbevoie/Seine. 40 ho V-8 engine.

ENVEMO
BR 1966–c. 1993
Engenharia de Veiculos e Motores Ltda., Marginal Pinheiros, São Paulo. Replicars, 4 × 4 and sports cars.

ENVOY
GB 1960
Sewell and King Ltd., Chelmsford, Essex. Sports cars.

ENZMANN
CH 1957–1970
Garage Enzmann, Schüpfheim. Sports cars.

EOLE
F 1899–1901
J.B. Clement et Cie., Paris. Voiturette.

EOLIA
F
See "Traction Aerienne."

EOS
A 1919–1920
Eos-Automobil-Ges.m.b.H., Wien. Cyclecars.

EOS
D 1922–1923
Rossineck & Co., Automobilfabrik, Berlin.
See "Erco."

ÉPALLE
F 1910–1914
Épalle et Cie., St. Etienne/Loire. Shaft-driven conventional cars.

EPOCAR
RSM 1986–1993
Epocar S.A. Fabbrica di Automobili Classiche, Galazzano. Replicars.

EPPS
USA 1902
Sold by Mead Cycle Co., Chicago, Illinois. One car produced.

EQUIPOISE
USA 1911
E.L. Tunis, Baltimore, Maryland. 2-wheeler with side balancing wheels.

E. & R.
D 1905
Eugen & Richard Benz, Benz Söhne, Ladenburg.
See "Benz Söhne."

E.R.A.
GB 1934–1952
English Racing Automobiles Ltd., Bourne, Lincs. (1934–1945); Dunstable, Beds. (1946–1952). Sports and racing cars.

E.R.A.
USA 1982–present
E.R.A. Replica Automobiles, New Britain, Connecticut. Kit cars and replicas.

ERAD
F 1981–present
Erad S.A., Aniche. Electric city cars, replicas.

ERCO
D 1921–1922
Rossineck & Co., Berlin. Small car with 2-stroke 3-cylinder engine.
See "Eos."

ERDMANN
D 1904–1908
Friedrich Erdmann, Gera. Friction-drive design.

ERIC
GB 1911–1914
E.and C. Syndicate Ltd., Northampton. Three-wheelers.

ERIC-CAMPBELL
GB 1919–1926
Eric, Campbell & Co. Ltd., London (1919–1922). Vulcan Iron & Metal Works Ltd., Southall, Middlesex (1922–1926). Light sports cars.

ERIC-LONGDEN
GB 1922–1927
Air Navigation & Engineering Co. Ltd., Addlestone, Surrey. Sports cars or saloons.

ERIDANO
I 1911–1914
Ditta Sclavo, Torino. Light cars.
See "Sclavo."

ERIE
USA 1899–1902
Erie Cycle & Motor Carriage Co., Anderson, Indiana.

ERIE
USA 1916–1919
Erie Motors Co., Painesville, Ohio. Roadsters.

ERIE & STURGIS
USA 1897
Erie & Sturgis, Los Angeles, California. J. Phillip Erie, inventor (Sturgis Iron Works). Large rear and small front wheels. Four one-cylinder connected engines.

ERIKSSON
S 1896–1897
Gustaf Eriksson.

ERK
D 1991
ERK Solartechnik, Kassel-Waldau. Electric car.

ERLA
DK c. 1950
Kobenhavn. Front-wheel drive prototype, license "Wendax" (D).

ERMINI
I c. 1950–1960
Pasquino Ermini, Firenze. Sports car.

ERNOULT
F 1910
Francois Ernoult. Streamlined car.

ERNST
CH 1905–1908
Ateliers Gustave Ernst, Geneve. Small number of assembled cars.

ERNST
USA 1895–1896
Ernst Power Vehicle Co., New York, N.Y. Steam vehicle.

ERPI
SU c. 1971
Electric car prototype.

ERSKINE
USA 1927–1930
Studebaker Corp., South Bend, Indiana.

See "Studebaker." Cars initially built in Detroit; relocated in early 1929. 95,104 cars were made.

ERWIN
USA 1913–1914
Erwin Motor & Machine Co., Philadelphia, Pennsylvania.

ESA
A 1917–1926
Egon Seilnacht, Wien. Cyclecars.

ESAP
I 1968
Gianfranco Padoan, Mirano. "Minimach" sports car.

ESCOL
B 1923–1929
Ets. Escol, Chatelet, Charleroi.

ESCULAPE
F 1899
Automobile Union, Paris. Voiturette.

ESCULAPIUS
GB
See "Knight of the Road."

ESHELMAN
USA 1955–1960
The Eshelman Co., Baltimore, Maryland.

ESOX
CS 1974
Pavel Mikšík, Bratislava. Sports car prototype.

ESPANA
E 1917–1927
Automoviles Espana, Barcelona. Touring and sports cars.

ESPENLAUB
D 1953
Sports car prototype.

ESPERIA
I 1905–1909
Societa Automobili Lombarda, Bergamo.
See "SAL."

ESS EFF
USA 1912
Ess Eff Silent Motor Co., Buffalo, N.Y. Runabouts.

ESSEX
USA 1901–1902
Essex Automobile & Supply Co., Haverhill, Massachusetts (1901). Essex Automobile Co., Lynn, Massachusetts (1902).

ESSEX
USA 1906
Essex Motor Car Co., Boston, Massachusetts. Steam car.

ESSEX
USA 1918–1933
Essex Motors, Detroit, Michigan. Subsidiary of Hudson Motor Car Co. Absorbed by "Hudson" 1922. Became "Essex Terraplane" 1932, and "Terraplane" 1933.

E.S.W.
D 1993–1996
E.S.W. Automobile GmbH, Aschaffenburg. Replicars.
See "Verona."

ETNYRE
USA 1910–1911
Etnyre Motor Car Co., Oregon, Illinois. Touring cars and roadsters.

ÉTOILE
B c. 1984
Ronny Coachbuilding Company L'Étoile, Roksem. Stretched limousine.

EUCLID
USA 1903–1904
Berg Automobile Co., Cleveland, Ohio.

EUCLID
USA 1907–1908
Euclid Motor Car Co., Cleveland, Ohio. Company formed May 1907 to build a three-cylinder, two-cycle air-cooled car.

EUCLID
USA 1909–1910
Euclid Motor Car Co., Trenton, New Jersey.

EUCLID
USA 1914
Euclid Motor Car Co., New York, N.Y. Cyclecars. By E.S. Cameron. Built at West Haven, Connecticut.

EUCORT
E 1946–1951
Automoviles Eugenio Cortes SA, Barcelona. 2-stroke 2-cylinder 765 cc and 3-cylinder 990 cc "DKW" (D) based cars with own designed body.

EUDELIN
F 1905–1908
M.A. Eudelin, Paris. 8hp engine with opposed pistons.

EUREKA
AUS 1974
Sports car.
See "Purvis."

EUREKA
F
See "Parisienne."

EUREKA
F 1906–1908
Automobiles Mainetty, La Garenne-Colombes/Seine. Voiturette.

EUREKA
USA 1899–1900
Eureka Automobile & Transportation Co., San Francisco, California. Gasoline carriage.

EUREKA
USA 1902
Eureka Automobile Agency, New York, N.Y. 4.5 hp gasoline carriage.

EUREKA
USA 1907–1909
Eureka Motor Buggy Co., Beavertown, Pennsylvania. Name changed to "Kearns" 1908. Kearns Motor Buggy Co.

EUREKA
USA 1907–1910
Eureka Motor Buggy Mfg. Co., St. Louis, Missouri. Highwheelers. Charles Zimmerman, designer.

EUREKA
USA 1909
Eureka Motor Car Manufacturing Co. Inc., St. Louis, Missouri. Highwheeler.

EUREKA
USA 1909
Eureka Co., Rock Fall, Illinois. Highwheelers.

EURICAR
GB 1930
J.V. & E.G. Eurich, Manchester. Three-wheeler.

EUROCCO
GB 1978–c.1980
Embeesea Kit Cars, High Wycombe, Bucks. Kit cars.

EUROPÉENNE
F 1899–1903
Sté. Européenne d'Automobiles, Paris. Light steam cars.

EURO-STAR
D 1988
Bohse Automobilbau GmbH, Dörpen. Pick-up on "Lada" base.

EUROSTYLE
I 1968–1970
Costruzione Carrozzerie e Automobili Eurostyle, Torino. Sports coupe.

EUSKALDUNA
E 1928
Compania Euskalduna de Construccion y Reparacion de Buques SA, Madrid. Light cars.

EUSTON
GB c. 1920
Cyclecar.

EVAN
CDN 1990s
EVAN Auto Styling, Brantford, Ontario. Kit cars.

EVANS
USA 1804
Oliver Evans, Philadelphia, Pennsylvania. Steam amphibian.

EVANS
USA 1903–1905
F.S. Evans Co., Detroit, Michigan. Electric car.

EVANS
USA 1910–1911
Automobile Mfg. & Engineering Co., Detroit, Michigan.

EVANS
USA 1914
Evans Motor Car Co., Nashville, Tennessee.

EVANSVILLE
USA 1907–1909
Evansville Automobile Co., Evansville, Indiana. Highwheeler. Became "Simplicity."

EVANTE
GB 1979–1993
Evante Cars Ltd., Spalding, Lincolnshire. Evante Sportscars Ltd., Newark, Nottinghamshire. Sports cars.

EVELYN
GB 1913–1914
Carrette Company, London. Light cars.

EVERETT
USA 1898–1899
Everett Motor Carriage Co., Everett, Massachusetts. Steam car. Built under Whitney licence.

EVERETT-MORRISON
USA 1990s
Everett-Morrison Motorcars, Tampa, Florida. Kit cars.

EVERITT
USA 1909–1912
Metzger Motor Car Co., Detroit, Michigan. Absorbed Hewitt Motor Co. 1911. Absorbed with Flanders Motor Co. into Maxwell Motor Co. 1913. Touring cars and runabouts.

EVERITT
USA 1915
Barney Everitt, Detroit, Michigan.

EVERLING
D 1934
Prof. Dr. Ing. E. Everling, Technische Hochschule, Berlin. Streamlined car prototype.

EVERYBODY'S
USA 1907–1909
Everybody's Motor Car Mfg. Co., Alton, Illinois. Runabout.

EVERY-DAY
CDN 1912
Woodstock Automobile Mfg. Co. Ltd., Woodstock, Ontario.

EVEX
D 1978–c. 1989
Evex Kunststoffbau GmbH, Solingen. Sports car and tuning.

EVI
USA 1970s
EVI Inc., Sterling, Michigan. Three-wheeled electric car prototypes.

EVR
GB 1977
Elec Traction Ltd., Maldon, Essex. Electric city car prototype.

EWBANK ELECTRIC
USA 1916–1918
Ewbank Electric Transmission Co., Portland, Oregon.

EWING
USA 1908–1911
Ewing Co., Geneva, Ohio. Town car.

EXAR
USA 1978
Amectran Company, Dallas, Texas. Electric car.

EXAU
F 1922–1924
Cyclecars Exau, Paris.

EXCALIBUR
USA 1952–1953
Beassie Engineering Company, Milwaukee, Wisconsin. Three prototypes built using re-worked "Henry J" chassis.

EXCALIBUR
USA 1961–1993
Excalibur Automobile Corporation, Milwaukee, Wisconsin. Replicars of SSK "Mercedes-Benz." Power and suspension same as "Chevrolet" Corvette.

EXCEL
USA 1914
Excel Distributing Co., Detroit, Michigan. Cyclecars.

EXCELLENT SIX
USA 1907–1909
Rider-Lewis Motor Car Co., Muncie, Indiana. Trade name for six-cylinder car by "Rider-Lewis."

EXCELSIOR
A 1900
Theyer, Rothmund & Co., Wien. Electric cars.

EXCELSIOR
B 1903–1932
Compagnie National Excelsior, Bruxelles (1903–1907). De Coninck et Cie., Bruxelles; Liege (1907–1911). SA des Automobiles Excelsior, Saventem (1911–1929). SA des Automobiles Imperia-Excelsior, Saventhem; Nessonvaux-les-Liege (1929–1932). Touring and sports cars.

EXCELSIOR
CH 1905–1907
Motorwagenfabrik Excelsior, Wollishofen. Light cars.

EXCELSIOR
D
See "Exor."

EXCELSIOR
USA 1899
Excelsior Machine Co., Buffalo, N.Y.

EXCELSIOR
USA 1904
Augusta, Maine. Steam car.

EXCELSIOR-MASCOT
D 1910–1922

Excelsior Werk, Fabrik für Feinmechanik GmbH, Köln. Small cars with 2- and 4-cylinder engines.

EXCELSIOR-TALISMAN
GB 1960
Coronet Cars Ltd., Denham, Bucks. Three-wheeler.
See "Coronet."

EXEL
F c. 1993
Distribution High Tech Service, Alby-sur-Cheran. Electric city cars.

EXOR
D 1923
Excelsior Maschinen-GmbH, Berlin. 5/16 hp small cars.
See "Excelsior" (Berlin).

EXPLORER
USA 1967
Rohm & Haas Co., Philadelphia, Pennsylvania. Sports car prototype.

EXPRESS
D 1901–1910
Express-Fahrradwerke AG, Neumarkt. Gasoline and electric car.

EXPRESS
D 1928
Express-Fahrzeugfabrik, Ansbach.

EXXON
GB 1978
Exxon Enterprises, Inc., Florham Park, New Jersey. Electric cars.

E.Y.M.E.
GB 1913
Cyclecar.

EYRE
USA 1936
Los Angeles, California.

EYSINK
NL 1899–1920
M. & A. Eysink, Amersfoort. Light cars.

FA
D 1928–1930; 1949–1950
Friedrich Albrecht Fahrzeugbau, Berlin. Three-wheelers.

F.A.B.
B 1912–1914
Fabrique Automobile Belge, Bruxelles. 2- and 3.5-litre cars.

FAB
CH 1997–present
FAB-Design AG, Mellingen. Tuning.

FACCIOLI
I 1902–1908
Ing. A. Faccioli & C. (1902–1905). Soc. Ing. Aristide Faccioli (1905–1906). Societa Faccioli Ferro Rampone (1906–1908), Torino. Light cars.

FACEL VEGA
F 1954–1964
Facel SA, Pont-à-Mousson. Luxury high-performance cars.

FACTOR
USA 1915
Bloomfield, New Jersey. New York, N.Y.

FACTORY FIVE RACING
USA 1990s
Factory Five Racing, Wareham, Massachusetts. Kit cars.

FADAG
D 1921–1925
Fahrzeugfabrik Düsseldorf AG, Düsseldorf. 4- and 6-cylinder cars.

FADELEY-HILL
USA 1910
Fadeley-Hill Co., Washington, D.C.

FADIN
I 1924–1926
Fabbrica Automobili Officine Troubetzkoy, Milano. "Derby" (F) license.

FAF
I 1900–1901
Fabbrica Automobili Furfanelli, Novara.

FAFAG
D 1921–1924
Fahrzeugfabrik AG, Darmstadt. Small cars.

FAFNIR
D 1908–1926
Aachener Stahlwarenfabrik, Fafnir-Werke AG, Aachen. Touring and sports cars. Fafnir engines were used by firms in many countries.
See "Aachener," "Cito," "Corna," "Erdmann," "Express," "Falke," "Feldmann," "Omnimobil," "VCS," "Westfalia."

FAGEOL
USA 1917–1918
Fageol Motors Inc., Oakland, California. Used Hall-Scott aviation engines. 13.5 litre luxury car, $17,000.

F.A.I.F.
I
"Isotta Fraschini."

FAIRBANKS-GRANT
USA 1905
Fairbanks-Grant Mfg. Co., Ithaca, N.Y. Experimental cars.

FAIRBANKS-MORSE
USA 1908
Fairbanks-Morse Co., Chicago, Illinois.

FAIRBURY
USA 1909
Fairbury Motor Car Works, Fairbury, Illinois. Highwheeler.

FAIRCHILD-HILLER
USA 1972
"Safety car."

FAIRCLOUGH MINI
GB 1983
Fairclough Electric Vehicles Ltd., Fairclough. Electric cars based on the "Austin" Mini.

FAIRFAX
GB 1906

Jas. Fairley & Sons Ltd., Sheffield, Yorks. Light tourer.

FAIRFIELD
USA 1895–1896
C.S. Fairfield, Portland, Oregon. Steam cars.

FAIRFIELD
USA 1926
Automotive Development Corp., Stamford, Connecticut.

FAIRTHORPE
GB 1954–1976
Fairthorpe Ltd., Chalfont St. Peter, Bucks (1954–1961). Gerrards Cross, Bucks (1961–1964). Denham, Bucks (1964–1976). 550 sports cars were made.

F.A.I.T.
I 1903–1904
Fabbrica Automobili Italiana Tozzi, Bologna.

FAIVRE
CH 1901
Sté. Faivre, Geneve. Light car.

F.A.L.
USA 1909–1915
F.A.L. Motor Co., Chicago, Illinois (1909–1913). F.A.L. Auto Co., Chicago, Illinois (1913–1915). Succeeded Reliable-Dayton Motor Car Co. Also "F.A.L. Greyhound," 1915. Touring cars.

FALCAR
USA 1909–1915
F.A.L. Motor Co., Chicago, Illinois.
See "F.A.L."

FALCON
CDN 1921
Gove Motor Car Co., Tilbury and Thorolt, Ontario

FALCON
D 1921–1926
Falcon Automobilwerke GmbH, Sontheim (1921–1922). Falcon-Werke AG, Ober-Ramstadt (1922–1926). 1.3- and 1.5-litre cars.

FALCON
GB 1958–1964
Falcon Shells Ltd., Waltham Abbey, Essex (1958–1959). Epping, Essex (1959–1961). Falcon Cars Ltd., Epping, Essex (1961–1962). Hatfield, Essex (1962–1964). Sports cars.

FALCON
USA 1905
F.W. Flynn, Youngstown, Ohio. Bay City, Michigan.

FALCON
USA 1907–1909
Falcon Engineering Co., Chicago, Illinois. Formerly Larsen Machine Co. 7-passenger touring cars.

FALCON
USA 1910
Falcon Motor Car Mfg. Co. Inc., Philadelphia, Pennsylvania.

FALCON
USA 1913–1914
Falcon Cyclecar Co., Cleveland, Ohio; Staunton, Virginia. Cyclecars.

FALCON
USA 1922
Halladay Motors Corp., Newark, Ohio. Former "Halladay." In hands of receiver March 1921.

FALCON
USA 1922
Moller Motor Car Co., Lewistown, Pennsylvania. Roadsters.

FALCON
USA 1960–1969
Ford Motor Co., Dearborn, Michigan.
See "Ford."

FALCON-KNIGHT
USA 1927–1928
Falcon Motors Corp., Detroit, Michigan. Subsidiary of "Willys-Overland." Absorbed by "Willys-Overland" 1928.

FALKE
D 1899–1908
Fahrrad- und Automobilwerke Albert Falke & Co. (1907–1908). Falke Motorfahrzeuge Albert Falke & Co., Mönchengladbach (1907–1908). Voiturettes; light cars used Fafnir engines.

FALLS
USA 1913
Falls Garage Co., Chagrin Falls, Ohio.

FALLS
USA c. 1924
Falls Motors Corp., Sheboygan Falls, Michigan. Mostly engines, few complete cars. Also built racing models.

F.A.M.
I 1911–1915
Fabbrica Automobili e Motori per Marina, Modena.

FAM
I 1949; 1952
Fabbrica Auto Motoveicoli, Pesaro. Small car prototypes.

F.A.M.
USA 1908
See "French-American."

FAMA
D 1924
Fama GmbH, Kiel. Light 2-seater.

FAMOUS
USA 1906–1909
Famous Mfg. Co., East Chicago, Illinois. Highwheelers. Became "Champion."

FAN-CHUA
PRC c. 1970
Shanghai.

FANCIULLINI
I 1955
Minicar.

FANNING
USA 1901–1903
Fanning Mfg. Co., Chicago, Illinois. Electric and air-cooled gasoline cars.

FARGO
USA 1929
Chrysler Corporation, Detroit, Michigan. Station wagon.

FARLEY
GB 1949
Light car.

FARMACK
USA 1915–1916
Farmack Motor Car Corp., Chicago, Illinois. Roadsters.

FARMAN
F c. 1902
H. Farman et Cie., Paris. Light cars.

FARMAN
F 1920–1931
Automobiles Farman, Billancourt/Seine. 6.6-litre touring and sports cars.

FARMAN-MICOT
F 1898
Farman, Micot et Cie., St. Maurice/Seine. Light cars.

FARMER-MOBILE
USA 1907

Summit Carriage-Mobile Co., Waterloo, Iowa.
See "Summit."

FARMER'S AUTO
USA 1905
Farmer's Auto Motor Car Co., Sheffield, Kansas.
See "Caps."

FARMOBIL
GR 1962–1967
Thessaloniki. Air-cooled small offroad vehicles.

FARMOBILE
USA 1907–1909
Farmobile Mfg. Co., Columbus, Ohio. Offshoot of Oscar Lear Auto Co. Prototype.

FARMOBILE
USA 1914
Farmobile Co., San Francisco, California.

FARNER
USA 1922–1923
Farner Motor Car Co., Streator, Illinois. 6-cylinder assembled cars.

FARNUM
USA 1901
C.H. Farnum, Baraboo, Wisconsin.

FARRELL
USA 1894
William Farrell, Jamestown, North Dakota. Three-wheeler.

FARUS
BR 1982–1991
Farus Industria de Veiculos Esportivos Ltda., Belo Horizonte, Minas Gerais. Sports cars. 41 cars built in 1984.

FAS
I 1906–1912
Fabbrica Automobili Standard, Torino.

FASA-RENAULT
E 1951–c. 1979
Fasa-Renault, Valladolid. "Renault" (F) license.

FASCINATION
USA c. 1971
Highway Aircraft Corp., Sidney, Nebraska. Sports cars.

FAST
I 1907
Fabbrica Automobili Siena Toscana.

FAST
I 1919–1925
Fabbrica Automobili Sport Torino (1919–1923). Fabbrica Automobili Sport Torino di Ing. Orasi (1923–1925), Torino. Sports cars.

FASTO
F 1926–1929
Ateliers Mecaniques de St. Eloy, St. Eloy-les-Mines, Puy-de-Dome; St. Ouen/Seine. 4- and 6-cylinder family cars.

FATA
I 1921–1925; 1931–1935
Fabbrica Automobili Torinese Aurea, Torino.

FAUBER
USA 1900–1904
Fauber & Marr, Elgin, Illinois. Fauber Automobile Co., Indianapolis, Indiana. Steam car. Became "Marr."

FAUBER BI-CAR
USA 1914
W.H. Fauber, Indianapolis, Indiana. Cyclecar.

FAUGÉRE
F 1898–1901
Faugére, Ochin et Dangleterre, Corbeil/Somme. Sté. des Automobiles Légéres, Paris. 3 hp 2-cylinder horizontal engine.

FAULKNER-BLANCHARD
USA 1910
Faulkner-Blanchard Motor Car Co., Detroit, Michigan. E.J. Cook, designer. Touring cars.

FAULTLESS
USA 1914
Cyclecar.
See "Saginaw."

FAUN
D 1924–1927
Faun-Werke AG, Nürnberg. Touring and sports cars.

FAURE
F 1941–1947
Pierre Faure, Paris. Electric cars.

FAUSTINO
I
See "Odetti."

FAVEL
F 1941–1944
Ets. Favel, Fabrication de Vehicules Automobiles. Electriques Legeres, Marseilles. Electric cars.

FAVIER
F 1924
Sté. Favier, Tullins/Isere.

FAVORIT
CS 1928–1933
Fa. Favorit, stavba motoru a vozidel G. Kroboth, Sternberk. Light cars.
See "Kroboth" (CS).

FAVORIT
D 1908–1909
Favorit Motorwagen Fabrik Carl Hübscher, Berlin. Three-wheelers.

FAW
CHI 1991–present
First Automobile Works, Changchun. "Audi" (D) license. Built also "Hongqui."

FAWCETT-FOWLER
GB 1907–1909
Fawcett, Preston & Co. Ltd., Liverpool. Steam car.

FAWICK
USA 1910–1912
Fawick Motor Car Co., Sioux Falls, South Dakota.

FAWICK FLYER
USA 1907
Thomas L. Fawick, Milwaukee, Wisconsin.
See "Silent Sioux."

FAY
USA 1912
Greenville Metal Products Co., Greenville, Pennsylvania. Subsidiary of Salisbury Axle Co.

FAZ
I
See "Zena."

F.D.
B 1921–1925
Automobiles F.D., Roulers.

F.D.
GB 1911
Vining Tractor & Motor Manufacturing Co., London. Front-wheel-drive prototype.

FEDDEN
GB 1939–1947
Designed by Sir Roy Fedden, aeronautical engineer.

FEDELIA
USA 1913–1914
J.H. Sizelan Co., East Cleveland, Ohio. Cyclecar.

FEDERAL
AUS 1925
Five-seater touring.

FEDERAL
USA 1900–1902
Federal Motor Vehicle Co., Brooklyn, N.Y. Designed by C.L. King. Steam car.

FEDERAL AUTO BUGGY
USA 1906–1910
Federal Automobile Co., Chicago, Illinois (1906–1908). Industrial Automobile Co., Elkhart, Indiana (1909). Became Rockford Automobile & Engine Co., Rockford, Illinois, 1909. Motor buggy and highwheelers.

FEE-AMERICAN
USA 1908–1909
Fee Motor Car Co., Detroit, Michigan.

FEENY
USA 1914
Feeny Mfg. Co., Muncie, Indiana. Cyclecar.

FEERRAR
USA 1895
J.C.W. Feerrar, Lock Haven, Pennsylvania.

F.E.G.
D
See "Erdmann."

FEI
BR 1968
Prof. Ing. Rigoberto Solery, São Paulo. Amphibian prototype.

FEJES
H 1923–1928
Magyar Lemezmotor és Gépgyár, Budapest. Simply 1.2-litre 4-cylinder cars made of pressed and welded sheet-iron.

FELBER
A 1952–1954
Felber & Co., Wien. Three-wheeler minicar. About 400 cars were built.

FELBER
CH 1971–1982
W.H. Felber, Haute Performance Morges, Morges (Lausanne). Sports car and replica.

FELDAY
GB 1966–1967
Felday Engineering Ltd., Dorking, Surrey. Sports cars.

FELDMANN
D 1905–1912
Westfalische Automobilgesellschaft B. Feldmann & Co., Soest. Voiturette and tourer.

FEND
D 1948–1953
Fend Kraftfahrzeug GmbH, Rosenheim. Three-wheelers.

FENG-HUANG
PRC c. 1958–1974?
Shanghai Motor Vehicle Plant, Shanghai. 6-cylinder 150 hp cars.

FENIX
E 1901–1904
E. Domingo Tamaro y Roig, Barcelona. About 25 light cars were made.

FENN
USA 1904
Fenn-Sadler Machine Co., Hartford, Connecticut.

FENNY
USA c. 1905
Frank Fenny, Derby, Connecticut.

FENTON
USA 1905
Fenton Automobile Co., Fenton, Michigan.

FENTON
USA 1913–1914
Fenton Engineering Co. Fenton Cyclecar Co., Fenton, Michigan. Cyclecars.
See "Signet."

FERBEDO
D 1923–1924
Ferdinand Betthäuser, Nürnberg. Three-wheelers, cyclecars. In 1925 renamed to "Tom."

FERGUS
GB USA 1915–1922
J.B. Ferguson Ltd., Belfast (1915–1916). Fergus Motors of America, Newark, New Jersey (1920–1922). O.D. Cars Ltd., Belfast (1921). 6-cylinder sedan.

FERGUS
USA 1920–1923
Fergus Motors of America, Inc., Newark, New Jersey. Prototype shown 1916. Production started 1920.

FERGUS
USA 1949
Fergus Motors Inc., New York, N.Y. Restyled "Austin" (GB) A40. Prototype stage only.

FERGUSON
USA 1902
Ferguson Buggy Co., Ann Arbor, Michigan.

FERGUSON
GB 1915
Josef B. Ferguson Ltd., Belfast, N. Ireland.

FERGUSON
GB 1961–1972
Harry Ferguson. Sports cars.

FERMI
I 1949–1953
Treviso. Minicars "Fermi-Micro" and "Lucertola."

FERNA
D
See "H.H."

FERNANDEZ
F
See "La Sirene."

FEROLDI
I 1912–1924
Officine Feroldi, Torino. 20/30 hp four of 3.3-litre capacity.

FERON ET VIBERT
F 1905–1907
Feron et Vibert, Soissons/Aisne. Conventional touring cars.

FEROX
GB 1914
Ferox Light Car Co., Paisley. Light car.

FERRA
CS 1932
Ferra, Kladno. Light car prototype.

FERRARI
I 1946–present
Auto Costruzione Ferrari (1946–1960). Societa Esercizio Fabbriche Automobili e Corse Ferrari (1960–1966). Ferrari SpA, Esercizio Fabbriche Automobili e Corse, Maranello (1967–present). High-performance sports cars.

FERRARIS
I 1973
Romeo Ferraris. Sports car.

FERRER
USA 1966
Bottier Engineering, Camden, New Jersey. Ferrer Motors Corp., Miami, Florida. Reworked "Volkswagen" chassis with fiberglass body.

FERRIS
USA 1920–1922
Ohio Motor Vehicle Co., Cleveland, Ohio. Succeeded Ohio Trailer Co. 6-cylinder cars.

FERRO
I 1935
Autorimessa Ferro, Genova. Three-wheeled prototype only.

FERT
I 1905–1906
Antonietti e Ugolini, Torino. 3.8-litre 4-cylinder 24 hp cars.

FERVES
I 1968–1971
Ferves Srl, Torino. 4 × 4 cars.

FESZTIVAL
H 1960
Szabadi Kálmán, Budapest. 300 cc minicar prototype.

FETZGER
USA 1910
Fetzger Automobile Mfg. Co., Galion, Ohio.

FEWMAL
USA 1914
Fewmal Motors Co., California. Motorette.

FEY
USA 1897–1905
Lincoln H. Fey, Northfield, Minnesota. Touring cars.

FEYENS
B 1898
T. Feyens, Bruxelles. Voiturette.

FEYENS
B 1937–1939
Ateliers Francois Feyens, Auderghem.

F.F.
B 1924
Automobiles F.F., Vilvorde.

F.H.
E 1956–1960
Fabrica Hispana, Barcelona. 197 cc and 324 cc minicars.

FIAL
I 1906–1909
Fabbrica Italiana Automobili Legnano, Legnano. Light cars.

FIAM
I 1923
Alessandria.

FIAM
I 1921–1926
Fabbrica Italiana Automobili e Motori, Brescia; Torino. 706 cc light cars.

FIAT
I 1899–present
Fabbrica Italiana Automobili Torino (1899–1918). Fiat SpA, Torino (1918–present). Passenger and sports cars.

FIAT
USA 1909–1918
Fiat Co., Poughkeepsie, N.Y. Italian origin. Sued "Oldsmobile," "S.G.V." and "Daniels" on radiator design 1916.

FIAT ANSALDI
I 1905–1906
FIAT- Ansaldi SA, Torino. 3-litre 4-cylinder cars.
See "Brevetti Fiat."

FIBERFAB
D 1971–1982
Karosserie Fiberfab, J. Kuhnle, Ilsfeld-Auenstein bei Heilbronn. Plastics-bodied sports cars.

FIBERFAB
USA 1966–1982
Fiberfab, Inc., Minneapolis, Minnesota. Kit cars.

FIBERSPORT
USA 1953–1954
Fibersport, Inc., Bloomington, Indiana. Fiberglass sports roadsters.

FIBROMIRELI
P 1989–1994
Fibromireli, Mirando do Corvo. Plastic-bodied cars.

FICHTER
USA 1910
R.M. Fichter, Sutter, California.

FIDÉLIA
F 1905–1906
Voitures Fidélia, Angers/Maine-et-Loire. Steam cars.

FIDELIA
USA 1914
J.H. Sizelan Co., Cleveland, Ohio. Tandem cyclecars.

FIDELIO
D
See "Ehrhardt."

FIDELITY
USA 1909
Fidelity Motor Car Co., Chicago, Illinois.

FIDES
I 1905–1911
SA Fabbrica Automobili Marca Brasier, Roma (1905–1908). SA Fabbrica Automobili Brevetti Enrico, Torino (1908–1911). "Brasier" (F) license; own 4-cylinder sv engines.

FIEDLER
D 1899–1900
Berliner Electromobil- und Accumulatoren-Gesellschaft, Berlin. Electric cars.

FIELD
USA 1885–1887
E.F. Field. Field & Crabshaw Machine Co., Lewiston, Maine. Gave the Stanleys inspiration. Steam cars.

FIELD
USA 1910
Field Automobile Mfg. Co., Lincoln, Nebraska.

FIELD
USA 1924
Field Motor Co., Rice Lake, Wisconsin.

FIELD & BUTTERWORTH
USA c. 1905
Frank B. Field & R. Butterworth, Sommerville, Massachusetts.

FIERTLER
I 1949
Officine dell Comm. Luigi Fiertler, Reggio Calabria. Microcar "Lupetta."

F.I.F.
B 1909–1914
Automobiles F.I.F., Bruxelles. Light sports cars.

FIFTY-FIFTY
USA 1914
Sheppard Mfg. Co., Chicago, Illinois. Cyclecar.

FIGARI
I 1925–1926

Gian Vittorio Figari & Prof. Francesco Bonavoglia, Milano. 840 cc 4-cylinder 2-stroke prototype.

FIGINI
I 1899–1907
Ditta Luigi Figini & C., Milano. 1-, 2- and 4-cylinder light cars.

FILECCIA
I 1904
Fileccia & Figli, Palermo.

FILIPINETTI
CH 1966–1973
Georges Filipinetti, Grandson. Sports cars.

FILLOW
USA 1901
Fillow Auto Co., Danbury, Connecticut.

FILOQUE
F 1902
Filoque Pere, Bourgtheroulde/Eure. Voiturette.

FILTZ
F 1899–1903
Sté. des Moteurs et Voitures Automobiles Filtz, Neuilly/Seine. Light cars.

FIM
I 1975–1982
FIM, Angri (Salermo). Three-wheelers.

FIMER
I 1947–1949
Fabbrica Italiana Motoveicoli e Rimorchi, Milano. 250 cc minicar.

FINA
USA 1953–1955
Perry Fina, New York, N.Y. Convertibles with "Ford" chassis and "Cadillac" power.

FINAL CONCEPT
USA 1990s
Final Concept, Port Charlotte, Florida. Kit cars.

FINCH
USA 1903–1904
Michigan Yacht & Power Co., Detroit, Michigan. Also called "Finch-Limited."
See "Pungs-Finch."

FINCH & HOCKING
AUS 1992–present
Finch & Hocking, Mt. Barker. Replicas.

FINCHLEY
GB 1957
Single-seater light car.

FINDLAY
USA 1910–1912
Findlay Motor Co., Findlay, Ohio. Absorbed by General Motors, 1912.

FINDLAY
40 USA 1909–1910
Findlay Carriage Co., Findlay, Ohio.

FINLAYSON
AUS 1900–1908
Finlayson Bros. & Co. Pty. Ltd., Dovenport, Tasmania. Steam and gasoline cars.

FIORE
I 1974–c. 1976
Carrozzeria Fiore, Napoli. "Fiat" based small cars.

FIORETTI
I 1980
Autofioretti Srl, Roma.

FIREBALL
GB 1969–c. 1975
J.B. Developments (1969–1971). F.J. Boyle, Aldershot, Hampshire (1971–c. 1975). Sports cars.

FIREBOMB
USA 1955–1956
Dual Motors Corp., Detroit, Michigan. Sports car.
See "Dual-Ghia."

FIREFLY
GB 1902–1904
Firefly Motor & Engineering Co. Ltd., Croydon, Surrey. Shaft-driven light cars.

FIRESTONE
USA 1908
Columbus Buggy Co., Columbus, Ohio. Highwheeler.

FIRESTONE-COLUMBUS
USA 1909–1915
Columbus Buggy Co., Columbus, Ohio. 1914 became New Columbus Buggy Co.

FIRTH
USA 1911
Firth Motor Car Co., Mansfield, Ohio. Misspelling of "Forth."

FISCHER
A 1963–1966
Helmut Fischer, Wien. Sports car prototypes.

FISCHER
CH 1909–1919
Fischer-Wagen AG, Zürich. Sleeve-valve 16/22 hp cars. About 200 were made.

FISCHER
D 1902–1905
Fischer & Co., Pfälzische Motoren- und Automobilfabrik, Hassloch. Small vehicles.

FISCHER
D 1912–1913
Westautohaus Alex Fischer & Co., Berlin. Electric cars.

FISCHER
USA 1900–1905
S.M. Fischer, Chicago, Illinois. Fischer Motor Vehicle Co., Hoboken, New Jersey. Mostly gas-electric trucks. Trucks only after 1904.

FISCHER
USA 1914
C.J. Fischer Co., Detroit, Michigan. A light car, formerly known as "Fischer-Detroit" cyclecar.

FISH
USA 1906–1907
Fish Automobile Co., Bloomington, Illinois.

FISHER
CDN 1914–1915
Fisher Motor Car Co. Ltd., Walkerville, Ontario. "Tudhope" in everything but name.

FISHER
GB 1990s
Fisher Sports Cars, Marden, Kent. Sports kit cars.

FISHER
USA 1840–1869
J.K. Fisher, New York, N.Y. Both vehicles resembled locomotives.

FISHER
USA 1904
Fisher Automobile Co., Mooresville, Indiana.

FISHER
USA 1914–1920
Fisher Motor Corp., New York, N.Y.

FISHER
USA 1917

F.E. Fisher, Baltimore, Maryland. Three-wheeler.

FISK
USA c. 1905
G.E. Fisk, Springfield, Massachusetts.

FISKE
USA c. 1905
Fred S. Fiske, East Providence, Rhode Island.

FISSON
F 1895–1898
L. Fisson et Cie., Paris. Based on the "Benz" (D) design.

FISSORE
I 1970s
Carrozzeria Fratelli Fissore, Savigliano (Cuneo). "Fiat" based cars. Coachbuilders since 1930.

FITCH
USA 1909
Fitch Gear Co., Rome, N.Y. Formerly "Maxwell-Fitch."

FITCH
USA 1949–1951
Sport & Utility Motors Inc., White Plains, N.Y. Sports, street or track cars.

FITCHBURG
USA c. 1905
Fitchburg File Works, Fitchburg, Massachusetts

FITCH PHOENIX
USA 1961–1969
John Fitch & Co., Inc., Falls Village, Connecticut. Modified "Chevrolet" Corvair with body by Intermeccanica (I).

FITT
USA 1904
James Fitt, Rochester, N.Y.

FITZGIBBON
USA 1913
Fitzgibbon & Crisp, Trenton, New Jersey. Prototype.

FIVE-BORO
USA 1924–1927
Moller Works, Hegerstown, Maryland. Taxicabs.

F.J.T.A.
I 1907–1927
Fabbrica Junior Torinese d'Automobili, Torino.
See "F.A.T.A."

FKFS
D 1936–1939
Forschungsinstitut für Kraftfahrzeugwesen und Fahrzeugmotoren in Stuttgart, Stuttgart. Streamlined cars designed by Prof. Wunnibald Kamm.
See "Kamm."

F.L.
F
See "Otto."

FL
I 1952
Fratelli Laureati, Acoli Piceno.

FLAC
DK 1915
Mammen & Drescher, Jyderup. Only 25 cars were produced.

F.L.A.G.
I 1905–1908
Fabbrica Ligure Automobili Genova, Genova. Solid-built touring cars.

FLAGLER
USA 1914
Flagler Cyclecar Co., Chicago, Illinois; Cheyboygan, Wisconsin. Cyclecar.

FLAID
B 1920
Ateliers Depireux, Liege. Light car.

FLAIR
USA 1901
Henry Flair, St. Louis, Missouri. Two cars built, one gasoline, one steam.

FLANDERMOBILE
USA 1901
Flandermobile Co., Anderson, Indiana.

FLANDERS
USA 1909–1912
Flanders Motor Co., Detroit, Michigan. Absorbed 1912 by Maxwell and U.S. Motor Company.

FLANDERS ELECTRIC
USA 1911–1913; 1914–1915
Flanders Mfg. Co., Pontiac, Michigan. Became Flanders Electric Co. (1914–1915). From October 1913 to March 1914 the "Flanders" automobile carried the name of "Tiffany."

FLANDRIA
B 1953
Minicar prototype.

FLAPPER
USA 1922
New York, N.Y. Camping car.

FLEETBRIDGE
GB 1904–1905
J.T. Bentley, London. Light cars.

FLEETWOOD KNIGHT
CDN 1924
L.J. Davis, Kingston, Ontario.

FLEISCHMANN
D c. 1987
Fleischmann-Tuning, Flörsheim-Dalsheim. Tuning.

FLEMING
USA 1901
Fleming Motor Vehicle Co., Ossining, N.Y.

FLETCHER
GB 1966–1967
Norman Fletcher (Sales & Developments) Ltd., Walsall, Staffs. Sports cars. Formerly "Ogle" design.

FLETCHER
USA 1895
Levi Fletcher, Hollis, Maine. Steam car.

FLETCHER
USA 1954
Fletcher Aviation Corp., Rosemead, California. 4 × 4 vehicles.

FLEUR DE LYS
GB 1989
Fleur de Lys Automobile Mfg. Ltd., Newark, Nottinghamshire. Replicars.

F.L.H.
D 1931–1933
Fahrzeugbau Luther und Heyer GmbH, Berlin. Three-wheeler.

FLINDERS
USA 1983
Flinders University. Electric car prototype.

FLINN
1904
Richard J. Flinn, W. Roxbury, Massachusetts. Steam car.

FLINT
USA 1902–1903
Flint Automobile Co., Flint, Michigan. Founded by A.B.C. Hardy. Also called "Flint Roadster."
See "Hardy."

FLINT
USA 1924–1927
Flint Motor Co., Long Island City, N.Y. Elizabeth, New Jersey. Flint, Michigan. Handmade prototypes shown at Hotel Commodore January 1923. First production cars started October 1923 (1924 models). Subsidiary of Durant Motors. 36,754 cars were made.

FLINT-LOMAX
USA 1905
Flint-Lomax Electric Mfg. Co., Denver, Colorado. Shown at 1905 Denver Auto Show.

FLINTRIDGE
USA 1957
Flintridge Motor Manufacturing Corp., Los Angeles, California. Sports cars using "DKW" (D) components. About 15 were built.
See "Darrin."

FLIPPER
F 1978–1984?
Flipper SARL, Villejuif. 50cc three-wheelers.

FLIRT
I 1913–1914
Fortis Levis Iucunda Rapida Transeat di Ing. P. Pestalozza, Torino. 2.7-litre 4-cylinder cars.

FLORENTIA
I 1903–1912
Fabbrica di Automobili Florentia, Firenze. Under license from "Rochet Schneider." 4.4-, 6.6- and 9.9-litre engines.

FLORI
USA 1900
George Flori, St. Louis, Missouri.

FLORIO
I 1906
Palermo.

FLORIO
I 1911–1914; 1914–1916
Florio Automobili di G. Beccaria & C., Torino. 3- and 5-litre engines. From 1914 as "Beccaria."

FLOYD-WARREN
USA c. 1918
Floyd V. Warren, Ludlow, Vermont.

FLYER
USA 1913–1914
Flyer Motor Co., Elizabeth, New Jersey. Mt. Clemens, Michigan. Cyclecars.

FLYING DUTCHMAN
USA 1908
N.C. Gauntt, North Yakima, Washington.

FLYING FEATHER
J
See "Suminoe."

FLYING SCOTSMAN
GB
See "Scotsman."

FLYING STAR
F 1906
Voitures Flying Star, Lyon.

FLYNN
USA 1905
Walter F. Flynn, Youngstown, Ohio.
See "Falcon."

FMR
D 1948–1964
Regensburger Stahl- und Metallbau. Fahrzeug- und Maschinenbau GmbH, Regensburg. Three-wheelers.
See "Messerschmitt."

F.N.
B 1899–1935
Fabrique Nationale d'Armes de Guerre, Liege. 100 voiturettes in 1900; light and large touring and sports cars.

F.N.M.
BR 1959–c. 1972
Fabrica Nacional de Motores SA, Rio de Janeiro. "Alfa Romeo" (I) license.

FOCACCIA
I 1970
Cervia. Small car prototype.

FOCHESATO
F 1994
Fochesato Preparation, Limonest. "Ford" (D/GB) tuning.

F.O.D.
I 1924–1927
Fonderie Officine De Benedetti, Torino. Cyclecar.

FOERS
GB 1992–c. 1994
J.A. Foers Engineering Co. Rotherham. 4 × 4 vehicles.

FOGLIETTI
I 1958–1960
Automobili Foglietti, Milano. Sports cars.

FOHA
A 1986
Foha Autocraft, Paschin. Tuning.

FOIDART & ROSENTHAL
B 1900
Établissements Foidart & Rosenthal, Bruxelles. Voiturette.

FOLGER
D 1985–c. 1990
Hans Günter Folger, Karosserie-Styling, Paderborn. Tuning.

FOLGORE
I 1900–1902
Sebastiano Castagneri, Alessandria. Light cars.

FOLLIS
F 1968- 1973?
Automobiles Follis Freres, Craponne/Rhone. Sports cars.

FONCK
F 1920–1925
Sté. des Automobiles René Fonck, Fraisse-Unieux/Loire. High-quality cars built in 4-, 6- and 8-cylinder models.

FONDU
B 1906–1912
Automobiles Charles Fondu, Vilvorde, Bruxelles. 1.7-, 2.1- and 4.8-litre engines. Built as the "Russo-Baltique" in Russia.

FONLUPT
F 1920–1921
Établissements Fonlupt, Levallois-Perret/Seine. 4-cylinder 2.1-litre and 8-cylinder 4.2-litre cars.

FONTANA
I 1950
Carrozzeria Fontana, Bassano del Grappa. Sports car. Primarily a coachbuilder.

FOOS
USA 1910
Foos Gas Engine Co., Springfield, Ohio. Experimental cars.

FORBES
USA 1896
Joseph N. Forbes, Cromanton, Florida.

FORD
AUS 1925–present

Ford Motor Company of Australia Ltd., Geelong; Broadmeadows, Victoria. First assembled was the Model T, and Model A's had Australian-made bodies on American chassis. All later Australian Fords had small body variations from their American counterparts.

FORD
BR 1967–present
Ford-Willys do Brasil SA, Sao Bernardo do Campo. The company resulted from a 1967 merger between the Willys and Ford interests in Brazil. "Renault" (F), "Willys" (USA) and "Ford" (USA) were assembled.

FORD
CDN 1912–present
Ford Motor Co. of Canada, Ltd., Windsor, Ontario

FORD
D 1931–present
Ford-Werke AG, Köln. Ford started assembling the Model T in Berlin in 1925 and Model A in 1927. In a new factory in Cologne the production began in 1931. Later cars of own design, from 1968 some models identical with British Ford.

FORD
F 1947–1954
Ford S.A.F., Poissy/Seine-et-Oise. Post-war French Ford succeeded the Matfords. Own designs later. From November, 1954, production was continued under the name of "Simca."

FORD
GB 1911–present
Ford Motor Co. Ltd., Manchester (1911–1931). Dagenham, Essex (1932–to date). Ford Advanced Vehicles Ltd., Slough, Bucks (1964–1966). Right-hand-drive versions of the American Ford until 1932, when the first true British Ford, the Model Y, was introduced (built also in Cologne, Germany). Own designs later.

FORD
USA 1901
The Henry Ford Co., Detroit, Michigan. Succeeded Detroit Automobile Co. Became Cadillac Automobile Co.

FORD
USA 1903–present
The Ford Motor Co., Dearborn, Michigan. Absorbed Lincoln Motor Car Co. 1922.
See "Mercury," "Falcon," "Continental," "Lincoln," "Edsel." Passenger and sports cars.

FORDHAM
GB
See "Wright."

FORD ITALIANA
I 1964–1967
Ford Italiana SpA, Roma. Passenger cars.

FORD 1901 REPLICA
USA 1968
Horseless Carriage Corp., Ft. Lauderdale, Florida. A ¾ scale replica of 1901 "Ford."

FORDMOBILE
USA 1903
The Fordmobile Company, Detroit, Michigan.
See "Ford."

FORD-MONTIER
F 1923–1932
Garage Montier, Paris. Sports cars.

FORD TRANSFORMEE
B 1924–1925
F. De Wandre, Bruxelles. Modified Model T "Ford."

FORE RIVER
USA 1903
Fore River Shipbuilding Co., Quincy, Massachusetts.

FOREST
USA 1905–1906
Forest Motor Car Co., Boston, Massachusetts. Five-seater tourer.

FOREST
USA 1908–1909
Forest Automobile Co., St. Louis, Missouri.

FOREST CITY
USA 1905
Forest City Motor Car Co., Massillon, Ohio. Became "Jewell" 1906.

FORMACAR
USA 1969
Centaur Engineering, Mount Clemens, Michigan. Sports car prototype.

FORMAN
GB 1904–1906
Forman Motor Mfg. Co. Ltd., Coventry, Warwickshire. 2- and 4-cylinder cars.

FORM CAR
USA 1966
Formcar Constructors Inc., Orlando, Florida.

FORMULA 27
GB 1990s
Formula 27 Sports Cars Ltd., Brimscombe, Gloucestershire. Kit cars.

FORNAGE
F 1994
Fornage, Reims. "Lancia" (I) tuning.

FORREST
GB 1907–1916
J.A. Wade & Co. Ltd., Liverpool. Light cars.

FORSTER
CDN 1920–1922
Forster Motor Mfg. Co., Ltd., Montreal, Quebec. Streamlined six-cylinder cars. Also called "Forster Six."

FORSTER
GB 1922
Forster Light Car Co. Ltd., Richmond, Surrey. Light car.

FORSTER SIX
CDN
See "Forster."

FORSYTH
USA c. 1896
George Forsyth, Franklin, Minnesota.

FORSYTH
USA c. 1905
William R. Forsyth, Lynn, Massachusetts.

FORTH
USA 1910
Forth Motor Car Co., Mansfield, Ohio.

FORT PITT
USA 1908–1909
Fort Pitt Motor Mfg. Co., New Kensington, Pennsylvania. 9.1-litre 6-cylinder engine.
See "Pittsburgh."

FORTUNE
USA 1860
Thomas L. Fortune, Atchison, Kansas. Steam wagon.

FORT WAYNE
USA 1903

Fort Wayne Auto Mfg. Co., Ft. Wayne, Indiana.

FOSS
CDN 1897
George Foote Foss, Sherbrooke, Quebec.

FOSS
USA c. 1905
Walter O. Foss, Taunton, Massachusetts. Two 12 hp automobiles were built.

FOSS-HUGHES
USA 1908
Foss-Hughes Co., Philadelphia, Pennsylvania.

FOSSUM
N 1906–1907
Marcus Hansen Fossum, Oslo. 2-cylinder air-cooled and 1-cylinder water-cooled engines.

FOSTER
USA 1896
Foster & Brown Co., Westbrook, Maine. Steam wagon.

FOSTER
USA 1901–1904
Foster & Co. Foster Automobile Mfg. Co., Rochester, N.Y. Gasoline and electric cars.

FOSTER
USA 1901
Improved Gasoline Motor & Automobile Company, Haverhill, Massachusetts.

FOSTER
USA 1906
Foster Motor Car Co., New Haven, Connecticut.

FOSTER
USA 1908
W.O. Foster Co., Newton, Iowa. Highwheeler.

FOSTER STEAM
USA 1904
Atzberger Automobile Co., Allegheny, Pennsylvania. From Foster Automobile Mfg. Co., Rochester, N.Y.

FOSTLER
USA 1904–1905
Chicago Motorcycle Co., Chicago, Illinois.

FOSTORIA
USA 1904
Fostoria Foundry Co., Fostoria, Ohio.

FOSTORIA
USA 1906–1907
Fostoria Motor Car Co., Fostoria, Ohio. Succeeded "Detroit-Oxford."

FOSTORIA
USA 1915–1916
Fostoria Motor Co. Fostoria Light Car Co., Fostoria, Ohio. Became Seneca Motor Car Co. in December 1916
See "Seneca."

FOTH
D 1906–1907
Carl Foth Maschinenfabrik, Dömitz. Voiturette.

FOUCH
USA 1914–1915
James R. Fouch, Los Angeles, California. Roadsters.

FOUCHER ET DELACHANAL
F 1907–1900
Foucher et Delachanal, Paris. 2-cylinder horizontal engine.

FOUILLARON
F 1900–1914
G. Fouillaron, Levallois-Perret/Seine. Expansible-pulley transmission was used on many models.

FOURNESS
GB 1788
Robert Fourness, Edinburgh. Steam car.

FOURNIER
F 1913–1924
SA Anciens Établissements Fournier, Levallois-Perret/Seine. Friction transmission.

FOURNIER
USA
See "Searchmont."

FOURNIER-MARCADIER
F 1963–c. 1974
Fournier et Marcadier, Lyon (1963–1967); Mions, Rhone (1967–c. 1974). Light touring and sports cars.

FOURNIER-SEARCHMONT
USA 1902–1903
Fournier-Searchmont Co., Saratoga Springs, N.Y.; Philadelphia, Pennsylvania. Succeeded Searchmont Motor Car Co. Became Searchmont Automobile Co.
See "Searchmont."

FOUR SEASONS
GB c. 1970
Four Seasons Buggy Co., London. Dune buggy kit car.

FOUR TRACTION
USA 1907–1909
Four Traction Automobile Co., Mankato, Minnesota.
See "Kato."

FOUR WHEEL DRIVE
USA 1902–1907
Four Wheel Drive Wagon Co., Milwaukee, Wisconsin.

FOX
F 1912–1914; 1919–1923
M.L. van der Eyken, Neuilly/Seine (1912–1914). Puteaux/Seine (1919–1923). Five models ranging from 9 hp to 18/20 hp.

FOX
USA 1904
Charles A. Fox, Syracuse, N.Y.

FOX
USA 1921–1923
Fox Motor Car Co., Philadelphia, Pennsylvania. Air-cooled cars. Introduced at Hotel Commodore, New York City, January, 1922.

FOYE
USA 1901
Foye Hubmotor & Automobile Co., Jersey City, New Jersey. Carriage with hub motors. Designed by Carl Bergman.

FOY-STEELE
GB 1913–1916
S.M.C. Syndicate Ltd., London. 4-cylinder monobloc.

F.R.
F 1927–1928
Fehr & Rougouchin, Paris. Three-wheelers.

FRADA
CS 1948
František Adámek, Modřany. 97 cc minicar prototype.

FRAM
I 1906
Fabbriche Rotabili, Avantreni, Motori, Genova; Roma.
See "Cantono" and "SALR."

FRAMO
D 1932–1939
Metallwerke Frankenberg GmbH. Framo-Werke GmbH, Frankenberg i. Sa. Three-wheelers.

FRANCE JET
USA 1961
France Jet Motors, Ltd., New York, N.Y. Fiberglass-bodied two-seaters.

FRANCIOLI
I 1911–1915
Novara.

FRANCISCO-MARTIN
USA 1915
Francisco-Martin Motor Co., Newport, Michigan.

FRANCKE
USA 1904
George O. Francke Auto Co., Milwaukee, Wisconsin. Touring car.

FRANCO
I 1907–1914
Automobili Franco, Sesto San Giovanni, Milano. 4-cylinder 6.8-liter engine.

FRANCO-AMERICAN
USA 1903
Automobile Co. of America, Manion, New Jersey. Formerly "Gasmobile."

FRANCO-AMERICAN
USA 1907
Franco-American Car Co., Los Angeles, California. French motor with steel cylinders and four-wheel brake.

FRANCON
F 1922–1925
Truelle et Cie., Rueil Malmaison/Seine-et-Oise (1922–1925). St. Ouen/Seine (1925). Light cars.

FRANKE
CH 1975–1978
Franke & Co., Neuhausen. Sports car and dune buggy.

FRANKEL & KIRCHNER
A 1954
Three-wheeler.

FRANKFORD
USA 1922
Frankford Motors Co., Philadelphia, Pennsylvania. Designed by Lee Oldfield.

FRANKFORT
USA 1917
Frankfort Motor Car Co., Frankfort, Indiana. Incorporation reported February 1917.

FRANKLIN
USA 1902–1934
H.H. Franklin Co. Franklin Automobile Co., Syracuse, N.Y. Founded 1893 Absorbed New York Motor Car Co. Air-cooled cars.

FRANTZ
USA 1901–1902
Rev. H.A. Frantz, Allentown, Pennsylvania. Frantz Automobile Co., Cherryville, Pennsylvania. Steam cars.

FRANZ
CH
See "Wetzikon."

FRASER
GB 1911
Douglas S. Fraser & Sons Ltd., Arbroath, Angus. Steam cars.

FRASER
GB 1967–1968
Alan Fraser Engineering Co., Hildenborough, Kent. Sports cars.

FRAYER-MILLER
USA 1904–1910
Oscar Lear Automobile Co., Columbus, Ohio (1904–1907); Springfield, Ohio (1907–1909). Touring cars.

FRAZEE
USA 1903
George T. Frazee, Osage, Iowa. Runabouts.

FRAZEN
USA 1951–1962
Ray Green Co., Toledo, Ohio. Fiberglass sports roadsters.

FRAZER
GB 1981
Frazer Cars, Sywell, Northampton. Modified "Austin" Metro.

FRAZER
USA 1947–1951
Graham-Paige Motors Corp., Detroit and Willow Run, Michigan. Absorbed by Kaiser-Frazer Corporation, Willow Run, Michigan, February 1947. Production began in June 1946.
See "Kaiser."

FRAZER NASH
GB 1924–1960
Frazer Nash Ltd. (1924–1925). William G. Thomas & Frazer Nash Ltd., Kingston on Thames,. Surrey (1925–1926). A.F.N. Ltd., Isleworth, Middlesex (1926–1960). Sports cars.

FRAZIER
USA 1914
W.S. Frazier & Co., Aurora, Illinois. Cyclecar. Also called "Sprite."

FRAZIER-ELKHART
USA 1915
O.Z. Frazier, Elkhart, Indiana.

FREDERICKSON
USA 1914
Frederickson Patents Co., Chicago, Illinois. Tandem cyclecar.

FREDERIKSEN
DK
See "Anglo-Dane."

FREDONIA
USA 1895
Fredonia Mfg. Co., Fredonia, N.Y.

FREDONIA
USA 1902–1904
Fredonia Automobile Co., Youngstown, Ohio. Carriages, experimental cars from 1896.

FREDRICKSON
USA 1909
H.E. Fredrickson Automobile Co., Omaha, Nebraska.

FREEDMAN
USA c. 1905
William Burtz, Fremont, Nebraska. 7 hp car.

FREEMAN
USA 1901
J.W. Freeman, Joplin, Missouri. Steam car.

FREEMAN
USA 1920
Freeman Motor Car Co., Omaha, Nebraska; Cleveland, Ohio. Proposed production: 50 passenger cars and 500 trucks.

FREE-WAY
USA 1970s
H-M Vehicles, Minnesota. Electric and gasoline-powered three-wheelers.

FREIA
D 1921–1927
Kleinautobau AG, Greiz/Vogtland (1921–1923). Freia Automobil AG,

Greiz (1923–1927). Three-wheelers and shaft-driven light cars.

FREJUS
I
See "Diatto."

FREMONT
USA 1920–1922
Fremont Motors Corp., Fremont, Ohio. 6-cylinder cars.

FRENAY
B 1914
Automobiles Frenay, Liege. Light two-seater.

FRENCH
USA 1899–1900
Thomas French, Andover, Maine. Later United States Motor Carriage Co. Steam car.

FRENCH
USA 1905
French Automobile Co., Rumford Falls, Maine; Clinton, Massachusetts.

FRENCH
USA 1913–1914
Earl French, Washington, D.C. Cyclecar.

FRENIER
USA 1912
Frenier Automobile Co., Rutland, Vermont.

FRERA
I 1905–1913
S.A. Corrado Frera & Co., Tradate. Air-cooled light cars.

FREZE
SU 1899–1905
Piotr Alexandrovich Freze, Sankt Peterburg. "De Dion-Bouton" license.

FRICK
GB 1904–1906
A. Dougill & Co. Ltd., Leeds. Friction drive.

FRICK
USA 1955
Bill Frick Motors, Rockville Centre, N.Y. Sports coupe prototype.

FRIDDLE
USA 1915
Friddle Motor Car Co., Tacoma, Washington.

FRIEDMAN
USA 1900–1903
National Sewing Machine Co., Belvedere, Illinois. Became "Ideal" 1903. Runabouts.
See "Eldredge."

FRIEDMANN-KNOLLER
A 1904
Armaturenfabrik Alexander Friedmann, Wien. Steam car. Built in co-operation with Weyr & Richmond, Paris.

FRIEND
USA c. 1900
Friend Mfg. Co., Gasport, N.Y.

FRIEND
USA 1920–1921
Friend Motor Corp., Pontiac, Michigan. Succeeded "Olympian." Bankruptcy reported May 1922.

FRIES
USA 1895
Frederick Fries, Reading, Pennsylvania. Steam surrey.

FRIGERIO
I 1905
Ing. Carlo Frigerio & C., Milano.

FRISBIE
1901

FRISBIE-HOEFT
USA 1909
R.A. Frisbie, Cromwell & Middletown, Connecticut. Roadsters.

FRISKY
GB 1957–1964
Henry Meadows (Vehicles) Ltd. (1957–1958). Frisky Cars Ltd. (1958–1959). Frisky Cars (1959) Ltd., Wolverhampton, Staffs (1959–1961); Sandwich, Kent (1961–1962). Frisky Spares and Service Ltd., Queensborough, Kent (1963–1964). Minicars with 197 cc, 249cc, 328 cc and 492 cc 2-stroke engines.

FRISWELL
GB 1906–1907
Friswell Ltd., London. Light car.

FRITCHLE
USA 1904–1920
Fritchle Auto & Battery Co., Denver, Colorado. Fritchle Electric Co. 1919. Gas-electricars.

FRM
CS 1936
Fischer-Reiman-Motory, Praha. Streamlined car prototype.

FROGEYE
GB 1993–present
Frogeye Car Company Ltd., Dryde, Isle of Wight. Replicars.

FRONTAWAY
USA 1917
Millington Motor Car Co., Chicago, Illinois. Absorbed Millington Auto Engineering Co. Front-drive conversions. Built runabouts, but mostly trucks.

FRONT DRIVE
USA 1905
Automobiles Front Drive Mfg. Co., St. Louis, Missouri.

FRONTENAC
CDN 1931–1933
Dominion Motors Ltd., Toronto, Ontario. Discontinued production December 1933.

FRONTENAC
CDN 1959–1960
Ford Motor Company of Canada Ltd., Windsor, Ontario.

FRONTENAC
USA 1906–1913
Abendroth & Root Mfg. Co., Newburgh, N.Y. 40-50 cars built 1906, 100 in 1907.

FRONTENAC
USA 1921–1925
Frontenac Motor Corp., Indianapolis, Indiana. Speed cars by Chevrolet Brothers.

FRONTMOBILE
USA 1917–1918
Bateman Mfg. Co. Safet Motor Co. Camden Motors Co., Greenloch, New Jersey. Front-wheel-drive car. Some lists erroneously carry this make as "Bateman."

FRONT WHEEL DRIVE
USA 1926
Positive Traction Motors Corp., Brookline, Massachusetts.

F.R.P.
USA 1914–1916
Finley Robinson Porter Co., Port Jefferson, Long Island, N.Y. 5 to 10 hand-made cars. Became "Porter" (1919–1922).

FRUA
I 1956–1983
Carrozzerie Pietro Frua, Borgo S. Pietro. Sports cars.

FRYKMAN
USA 1908–1909
August Frykman, Souris, North Dakota. Runabout.

F-S
USA 1911–1922
F-S Motors Co., Milwaukee, Wisconsin. Runabout.

FSM
PL 1955–present
Fabryka Samochodow Malolitrazowych, Bielsko-Biala. Small cars.
See "Fiat Polski," "Syrena."

FSO
PL 1951–present
Fabryka Samochodow Osobowych (1951–1996). Daewoo-FSO Motor Sp. Z.o.o., Warszawa (1996–present). Passenger cars.
See "Fiat Polski," "Warszawa," "Polonez."

FSR
PL 1972–c. 1996
Fabryka Samochodow Rolniczych, Poznan.
See "Tarpan."

FTA
I
Fabbrica Toscana di Automobili, Firenze.
See "Florentia."

FUCHS
A 1922–1923
Inzerdorfer Industriewerke Hans Fuchs AG, Wien. Light cars.

FUFFI
CH 1971
Sports car prototype.

FUGITIVE
GB 1986
The Unique Vehicle Co. Ltd., Newbury, Berkshire. Sports car.

FUJI CABIN
J 1957–1958
Fuji Motors Corp., Tokyo. 85 three-wheelers were made.

FUJIOKA
USA 1922–1923
Fujioka Motor Car Co., Los Angeles, California. For export to Japan.

FUKANG
PRC 1992–1997
Shenlong Automobile Corporation, Shiyan, Hubei. "Citroën" (F) based cars. From 1997.
See "Shenlong."

FULDAMOBIL
D 1950–1969
Elektromaschinenbau Fulda GmbH, Fulda. Nordwestdeutsche Fahrzeugbau GmbH, Wilhelmshaven (1954–1955). Three-wheeler.

FULGURA
D
See "Bergmann."

FULLER
USA 1908–1910
Angus Automobile Co., Angus, Nebraska. Touring cars.

FULLER
USA 1909–1910
Fuller Buggy Co., Jackson, Michigan. Became Jackson Automobile Co. 1911. Highwheelers and touring cars.

FULLER
USA 1914
Fuller Electric Car Co., Detroit, Michigan. Electric car.

FULMEN
E 1921
Ernesto Rodriguez Iranzo, Barcelona. Cyclecar.

FULMINA
D 1913–1926
Fulmina-Werk Carl Hofmann GmbH (1913–1921). Fulminawerk GmbH, Mannheim (1921–1926). 2.5- and 4.4-litre engines.

FULTON
USA 1900–1901
Fulton Machine Works, Chicago, Illinois.

FULTON
USA 1908–1909
Fulton Motor Car Co., New York, N.Y.

FULTON
USA 1908
Connecticut Motor Works, New Haven, Connecticut. Also called an Air-Cooled Cyclecar.

FULTON
USA 1920
Fulton Motor Truck Co., Farmingdale, N.Y.

FULTON & WALKER
USA 1900–1901
Fulton & Walker Co., Philadelphia, Pennsylvania.

FUN HUGGER
USA 1968–c. 1972
Fun Hugger Co., San Bernardino, California. Dune buggy.

FURGASON
USA 1910
Furgason Motor Car Co., Lansing, Michigan.
See "Clarkmobile."

FURIA
BR 1972
Sports car prototype.

FURTMAYR
D 1989
J. Furtmayr, Romaldini GmbH, München. "Fiat" (D) based conversion.

FUSCALDO
I 1912–1913; 1920–1921
Societa Automobili Brevetti Fuscaldo. Rhomboid wheel placement.
See "Rombo," "Chiribiri," "Serpentina" (USA).

FUSI-FERRO
I 1948–1949
Societa Fusi-Ferro, Torino; Como; Milano. 1.1-litre straight-8 60 hp engined six-seater aerodynamic saloon prototype.

FUXING
PRC 1994–present
State Operated Quinchuan Machinery Factory, Shaanxi. Minicars.

F.V.E.
I 1900
Milano.

F.W.D.
USA 1910–1912
The Four Wheel Drive Auto Co., Clintonville, Wisconsin.
See "Badger" (F.W.D.). Formerly "Z & B." Touring cars.

GABRIEL
F 1912–1914
Gabriel Campana, Paris. 4.5-litre conventional cars.

GABRIEL
USA 1910–1912
Gabriel Carriage Co. Gabriel Auto Co., Cleveland, Ohio. Cars and trucks.

GABRY
I 1963
Aeronautica Macchi Spa, Milano. 150 cc minicar prototype.

GAD
PL 1952
Stefan Gajecki, Warszawa. 496 cc 23 hp sport car prototype.

GADABOUT
GB 1948
Suyllow Coach Building Co., Walsall. Three-wheeler.

GADABOUT
USA 1913–1916
Gadabout Motor Corp., Newark, New Jersey. Cyclecars. Wicker body. First announced August 1913.

GADABOUT
USA 1945–1946
Detroit Industrial Designers, Detroit, Michigan. Ray Russel, Grosse Pointe, Michigan. Three-seat roadster prototype.

GADOUX
F
  See "Omega Six."

GAETH
USA 1898; 1902–1903
Paul Gaeth, Cleveland, Ohio. Experimental steam car.

GAETH
USA 1902–1904
Paul Gaeth, Cleveland, Ohio. Steam cars.

GAETH
USA 1904–1910
Gaeth Automobile Co., Cleveland, Ohio. Became Stuyvesant Motor Car Co., 1910.

GAGE
USA 1900
A.S. Gage, West Gardner, Massachusetts. One steam car produced for owner's use.

GAGE
USA 1914
Gage Mfg. Co., Los Angeles, California. Cyclecar.

GAGEMOBILE
USA 1902
W.M. Gage, Saratoga Springs, N.Y. Built-to-order cars.

GAGGENAU
D 1905–1911
Süddeutsche Automobilfabrik GmbH (1905–1910). Benz-Werke Gaggenau GmbH vorm. Süddeutsche. Automobilfabrik, Gaggenau (1911). Large 8.8-litre tourers.

GAILLARDET
F 1899
5 hp three-wheelers.
  See "Doctoresse."

GAINSBOROUGH
GB 1902–1903
Gainsborough Motor Engineering Co. Ltd., Gainsborough, Lincs. 17 hp horizontal 4-cylinder engine.

GAITAN
E 1953
Gaitan, Sevilla. Three-wheeler prototype.

GALASSI
I 1945
Zeno Galassi. Minicar.

GALBA
F 1929–1931
Sté. Sylla, Courbevoie/Seine (1929–1930). Voiturettes Huascar, Courbevoie/Seine (1931). 564 cc 2-stroke engine.
  See "Huascar."

GALE
USA 1901
Gale Mfg. Co., Albion, Michigan.

GALE
USA 1904–1907
Western Tool Works, Galesburg, Illinois. Light runabout. Succeeded by Robson Mfg. Co., 1908.

GALE FOUR
USA 1920
Gale Motors Co., Indianapolis, Indiana. McCurdy-Hercules Corp., Evansville, Indiana.

GALILEO
I 1904
Officine Galileo, Firenze. Electric car.

GALLET ET ITASSE
F 1900–1901
Gallet et Itasse, Boulogne-sur-Seine. Voiturette.

GALLIA
F
  See "Regina."

GALLIA
I 1905–1907
Societa Italiana Vetture Elettriche, Torino. Electric car.
  See "SIVE."

GALLIA ELECTRIC
USA 1906–1908
Gallia Electric Carriage Co., New York, N.Y.

GALLINARI
I 1906–1908
Cantieri Gallinari, Livorno.

GALLIOT
F 1908
Sté. d'Allumage Electrique et d'Accessoires, Paris. Tandem two-seater steered from the rear seat.

GALLOWAY
GB 1921–1928
Galloway Motors Ltd., Tongland, Kirkcudbright (1921–1922); Heathall, Dumfries (1923–1928). Light cars.

GALLOWAY
USA 1908–1911
William Galloway Station, Waterloo, Iowa. Bought Mason-Maitag Motor Car Co.
  See "Arabian."

GALT
CDN 1911–1912
Canadian Motors Limited, Galt, Ontario. Roadsters and touring cars.

GALT
CDN 1913–1915
Galt Motor Company, Galt, Ontario. Gasoline-electric car.

GALY
F 1954–1957
Automobiles Galy, Forges et Ateliers de la Vence et de la. Fournaise, Paris. 175 cc or 280 cc small coupe.

G.A.M.
F 1930
Établissements G.A.M., St. Etienne. Cyclecar with tandem seating.

GAMAGE
GB 1903–1904; 1914–1915
A.W. Gamage Ltd., London. Light cars.

GAMC-BALDI
I c. 1960s
GAMC-Baldi, San Remo. Mini car.

GAMMA
A 1965
Werner Holbl, Wien. Sports coupe prototype.

GAMMA
F 1921–1922
Sté. des Automobiles Gamma, Courbevoie/Seine. Conventional small cars.

GAMMONS
USA c. 1905
Samuel C. Gammons, Bridgewater, Massachusetts. 12 hp automobile.

GANZ
CH
See "Rapid."

G.A.R.
F 1922–1931
Cyclecars G.A.R., Clichy/Seine. Gardahaut et Cie., Asnieres/Seine. Cyclecars and small sports cars.

GAR
I 1924–1926
Alceo Verza Automobili Gar, Milano.
See "CAR."

GARABELLO
I
Cyclecar.

GARANZINI
I 1925–1926
Fabbrica Automobili Oreste Garanzini, Milano. Small cars.

GARBACCIO
CH 1913
Amphibian vehicle.

GARBÁTY
D 1924–1927
Autowerk Garbáty, Mainz. Light cars.

GARCIN
F
See "B.G.S."

GARDNER
F 1898–1900
Frank L. Gardner, Paris. Few gasoline cars were made.

GARDNER
USA 1865
John C. Gardner, Hingham, Massachusetts. Steam vehicle.

GARDNER
USA 1896
Gardner Motor Co., Ltd., New Orleans, Louisiana.

GARDNER
USA 1910
Brown Cooton Gin Co., New London, Connecticut. Roadsters.

GARDNER
USA 1920–1931
Russel E. Gardner & Sons. Gardner Motor Car Co., St. Louis, Missouri. Russel Gardner formerly made "Banner" buggies and "Banner" highwheelers, 1910. 6- and 8-cylinder engines.

GARDNER-SERPOLLET
F
See "Serpollet."

GAREAU
CDN 1909–1910
Gareau Motor Car Co. Ltd., Montreal, Quebec. Three tourers were built.

GARFIELD
USA 1904–1905
Garfield Automobile Co., Chicago, Illinois.

GARFORD
USA 1908; 1911–1914
Garford Motor Car Co., Cleveland, Ohio. Built chassis for "Studebaker," "Cleveland," "Rainier," "Ardsley," "Gaeth" and "Royal." Acquired by "Studebaker" 1906. Sold to and absorbed by Willys-Overland 1912 (Garford Co., Division of Willys-Overland Co., Elyria, Ohio 1913). Large touring cars.

GARICAR
USA 1909
W.M. Pease, Aberdeen, South Dakota.

GARRARD
GB 1904
Shaft-driven light car.

GARRETT
USA 1909
Garrett Machine Works, Garrett, Indiana. Highwheeler.

GARRIGA
E 1923
Auto Academia Garriga, Brcelona. Small sports cars.

GARRISON
USA 1914
Garrison Machine Works, Dayton, Ohio. Cyclecar.

GARSTANG
USA 1899
Ira Garstang, Alton, Illinois. Gasoline car.

GARVIN
USA 1901
Garvin Machine Co., New York, N.Y.

GARY
USA 1909
Alfred C. Gary, Muskegon, Michigan.

GARY
USA 1909
Gary Taxicab Co., Chicago, Illinois. Taxicabs.

GARY SIX
USA 1914
Gary Automobile & Mfg. Co., Gary, Indiana. 6-cylinder cars. Trucks until 1927.

GAS-AU-LEC
USA 1905–1906
Vaughn Machine Co. (1905). Corwin Mfg. Co. (1906), Peabody, Massachusetts. Gasoline-electric car.

GAS-ELECTRIC
USA 1928
Mitten Management, Philadelphia, Pennsylvania. Taxicabs.

GASI
D 1921
Fritz Gary & Edmund Sielaff, Gasi-Motorradwagen GmbH, Berlin. Three-wheeler.

GASLIGHT
USA 1960–1961
Gaslight Motors Corp., Detroit, Michigan. Replica of 1902 "Rambler."

GASMOBILE
USA 1899–1902
Automobile Co. of America, New York, N.Y. (1899–1900); Marion, New Jersey (1900–1902). 1-, 3-, 4- and 6-cylinder models.

GASOLINE MOTOR CARRIAGE
USA 1897
Sintz Gas Engine Co., Grand Rapids, Michigan.

GATEAU
F 1984–c. 1996
Automobiles Gateau, Division Automobile d'Yvars S.A., Yvre-sur-Seine; Saint Gilles, Croix de Vie. City car.

GATES
USA 1928–1930
A.J. Gates Co., Detroit, Michigan.

GATFORD
NL
See "Gatso."

GATSBY
USA 1982
Gatsby Coachworks, Ltd., San Jose, California. Sports car and replica.

GATSO
NL 1948–1950
M. Gatsonides, Heemstede. 3.9-litre streamlined coupe.

GATTER
CS 1928
Vilibald Gatter, Autopodnik, Zákupy u České Lípy. Light cars.

GATTS
USA 1905
Alfred Parma Gatts, Hamersville, Ohio. Runabout.

GAUBSCHAT
D 1953–1956
Helmut Gaubschat Elektrowagen GmbH, Berlin. Electric car.

GAUTHIER
F 1904–1937
Gauthier et Cie., La Garenne-Colombes (1904–1932). G. Gauthier, Blois/Loir-et-Cher (1933–1937). About 350 air- and water-cooled cars were made.

GAUTIER
F 1902–1903
Charles Gautier et Cie., Courbevoie/Seine. Voiturette and 30 hp tourers.

GAUTIER-WEHRLÉ
F 1894–1896 (steam); 1896–1900 (gasoline); (electric)
Rossel Gautier et Wehrlé (1894–1897). Societe Continentale, Paris (1897–1900). Voiturette and steam, electric and gasoline cars.

GAWLEY
USA 1895
T.R. Gawley, Aurora, Nebraska. One built for Chicago Times-Herald Race.

GAY
USA 1905
Calvin Gay, Worcester, Massachusetts. 8 hp automobile.

GAYLORD
USA 1910–1913
Gaylord Motor Car Co., Gaylord, Michigan. Passenger car that converted to a truck.

GAYLORD
USA 1955–1957
Gaylord Cars Ltd., Chicago, Illinois. 3 luxury two-seaters, styled by Brooks Stevens and produced by the Karosserie Spohn (D).

GAZ
SU/RUS 1932–present
Gorkovskii Avtomobilnii Zavod, Gorki. Passenger cars. Started assembling the Model A "Ford" (USA).
See "Pobeda," "Volga," "ZIM." Luxury 7-passenger sedan "Chaika." ("Seagull") powered by a 5.5-litre V-8 motor was built from 1958 to 1965.

GAZELLE
GB 1945–1946
Rochester, Kent. Small car prototype.

GAZELLE
NL 1959–1975
N.V. Gazelle Truckbouw, Aalten. Small car.

G.B.
GB 1922–1924
George Baets, London. Three-wheeler.

G.B. MOTORS
GB 1970
G.B. Motors, Birmingham. Sports car and dune buggy kit.

G.C.
F 1908
Automobiles G.C., H. Guyot et Cie., Paris.

GD
GB 1990s
Gardner Douglas Sports Cars, Bottesford, Nottingham. Sports kit cars.

G.E.A.
S 1905
AB Gustav Ericssons Automobilfabrik, Stockholm. Very large 6-cylinder car.

GEARHART
USA 1911–1912
Glenn D. Gearhart, Houston, Texas. Three-wheelers.

GEARLESS
USA 1907–1909
Gearless Transmission Co. (1907–1908). Gearless Motor Car Co. (1908–1909), Rochester, N.Y. Used planetary cone friction drive.
See "Olympic."

GEARLESS
USA 1919–1922
Gearless Motor Corp., Pittsburgh, Pennsylvania. Steam car. Built by Duncan MacDonald.

GEARLESS STEAMER
USA 1919
The Peterson-Culp Gearless Steam Automobile Co., Denver, Colorado.

GEBER
USA 1904
Geber Automobile Mfg. Co., Pittsburgh, Pennsylvania.

G.E.C.
USA 1898; 1902–1905
General Electric Co., West Lynn, Massachusetts (1898). Schenectady, N.Y. (1902–1905). Electric experimental car developed by Prof. Elihu Thompson.

GECKO
GB 1967
Stuart Smith. 200 cc city car prototype.

GEDDES
I 1942
Giorgio Geddes, Lucca.

GEER
USA 1901
R. Geer, St. Louis, Missouri. Steam car.

GEERING
GB 1899
T. Geering & Son, Rolvenden, Kent. Light car.

GEHA
D 1910–1923
Elektromobilfabrik Gebhardt & Harborn (1910–1917). Elitewerke AG, Berlin (1917–1923). Electric three-wheeler.

GEIGER
USA 1919
Ray Geiger, Covington, Indiana. Speedster.

GEIJER
N 1921
A/S C. Geijer & Co., Oslo. About 20 cars built.

GELLERAT
F 1864
Gellerat & Cie., Paris. Steam car.

GELRIA
NL 1900–1902
Gelria Machine- en Motorenfabriek, Arnhem. About 30 cars built.

G.É.M.
F 1907–1909
Sté. Générale d'Automobiles Electro-Mécaniques, Puteaux/Seine. Gasoline-electric cars.

GEM
GB 1968–1974
Grantura Plastics Ltd., Blackpool, Lancs. Sports car.

GEM
USA 1917–1919
Gem Motor Car Co., Jackson, Michigan. Grand Rapids, Michigan. Touring cars.

GEMBALLA
D 1985–c. 1996
Gemballa Automobilinterieur GmbH, Leonberg. Tuning.

GEMINI
I 1983
Electric car.

GENDRON
F 1924–1928
Sté. Genfron, Paris. Light sports cars.

GENERAL
GB 1902–1905
General Motor Car Co. Ltd., London (1902–1903); Mitcham, Surrey (1903–1905). Sports and racing cars.

GENERAL
USA 1902–1903
General Automobile & Mfg. Co. General Automobile Co., Cleveland, Ohio. Succeeded Hansen Automobile Co. "Studebaker" bid in all property, machinery, parts and real estate. Reported October 1903.

GENERAL ELECTRIC
USA 1898–1900
General Electric Automobile Co., Philadelphia, Pennsylvania; Manayunk, Pennsylvania.

GENERAL ELECTRIC
USA 1902–1904
General Electric Co., Schenectady, N.Y. Four-cylinder gasoline-electric car.

GENE
USA 1904
Gene.
See Auto Co., Rochester, N.Y.

GENE
USA 1911–1912
Gene.
See Motor Co., Batavia, N.Y. 8-passenger touring cars with 6-cylinder 11.1-litre engine. Limousine was listed at $10,000.

GENESTIN
F 1926–1929
P. Genestin, Fourmies/Nord. Light cars.

GENEVA
USA 1901–1904
Geneva Automobile & Mfg. Co., Geneva, Ohio. Built both steam and gasoline cars. Became Cleveland. Auto Cab Co., Cleveland, Ohio.

GENEVA
USA 1914
Geneva Auto Specialty & Repair Co., Geneva, Indiana. Cyclecars.

GENEVA
USA 1916–1917
Schoeneck Co., Harvey, Illinois. Roadsters.

GENEVA
USA 1899; 1920–1921
Geneva Wagon Co., New York, N.Y.

GENEVIEVE
USA 1903
Neustadt-Perry Co., St. Louis, Missouri.
See "Neustadt."

GENI
USA c. 1970
Geni Power, Inc., Portland, Oregon. Steam car.

GENIE
USA 1959–1969
British Motor Car Importers, San Francisco, California. Sports cars.

GEO
USA 1989–present
Geo/Chevrolet Motor Division, GM Corp., Warren, Michigan. Passenger car.

GEORGES IRAT
F 1921–1946
Automobiles Georges Irat SA, Chatou/Seine (1921–1929); Neuilly/Seine (1929–1934); Levallois-Perret/Seine (1935–1946). Touring and sports cars.
See "Irat."

GEORGES RICHARD
F
See "Brasier."

GEORGES ROY
F 1906–1929
Automobiles Georges Roy, Bordeaux. Touring cars.

GEORGES VILLE
F 1904–1909
Sté. d'Industries Mécanique, Paris. Cars intended for town use.

GEORGE WHITE
USA 1909
The George White Buggy Co., Rock Island, Illinois. Highwheeler.

G.E.P.
F 1913–1914
Automobiles G.E.P., Gennevilliers/Seine. Friction transmission and chain fine drive.

GEPARD
D 1970
Helmut Kretschmann, Gepard-Fahrzeugbau, Bonn-Beuel. Sports car prototype.

GEPARD
PL 1993–1996

Fabryka Samochodow Gepard, Mielec. Sports car replica.

GERALD
GB 1920
Gerald Cyclecar Co., Birmingham. Cyclecar.

GERAMITA
USA 1982
Geramita, Clifton, New Jersey. "Cobra" replica.

GÉRARD
F 1927
Automobiles Gérard, Clichy/Seine. Light cars.

GERBER
CH 1972
Sports car.

GERION
E 1972
"Bugatti" replica.

GERMAIN
B 1897–1914
SA des Ateliers Germain, Monceau-sur-Sambre. Improved "Panhard."

GERMAN-AMERICAN
USA 1902–1903
German-American Automobile Co., New York, N.Y. Petition in bankruptcy by employees reported November, 1902. Runabouts.

GERONIMO
USA 1917–1920
Geronimo Motor Car Co., Enid, Oklahoma. Touring cars.

GEROPA
NL 1922
Garage- en Reparatie-Inrichting "Geropa," Amsterdam.

GERSIX
USA 1920–1921
Gersix Mfg. Co., Seattle, Washington. Gerlinger Motor Co., Portland, Oregon. Mostly truck production.

GETABOUT
USA 1901
George T. Turner Co., Philadelphia, Pennsylvania.

GETAWAY
USA 1968–1974
D.M.CO., East Derry, New Hampshire. Dune buggy.

GETTY
USA 1986–1993
Getty Design, Santa Ana, California. Sports car.

GF
E 1996
Grupo Fiero, Arganda del Rey. Sports cars.

GFG
D 1986–1997
Gerhard Feldevert & Co., Gronau-Epe. "Mercedes-Benz" 540 K replica and tuning.

GFH
CH 1954
Grandjean, Ferry & Hauri, Biel. Sports car prototype.

GHENT
USA 1917–1918
Ghent Motor Co., Ottawa, Illinois. Built by S.G. Gay Co. Building sold to A.L. Richards for $ 5,382, January, 1919. 4-, 6- and 8-cylinder assembled cars.

GHIA
I 1954–1980s
Carrozzeria Ghia, Torino. Sports cars and prototypes. Coachbuilders since 1915.

GHIOLDI
I 1912–1922
Guglemo Ghioldi & C.
  See "FIAL."

GIANNINI
I 1963–c. 1989
Giannini Automobili SpA, Roma. "Fiat" based sports cars. About 2,500 cars built in 1974.

GIAUR
I 1950–1954
Officina Meccanica Bernardo Taraschi, Teramo. Sports and competition cars.
  See "Taraschi."

GIBBONS
GB 1921–1926
Gibbons & Moore, Chadwell Heath, Essex. Sports and racing cars.

GIBBS
USA 1901
American Tractor Co., Elizabethport, New Jersey. Steam car.

GIBBS
USA 1903–1905
Gibbs Engineering & Mfg. Co., Glendale, N.Y. Electric car.

GIBSON
USA 1899
Charles D.P. Gibson, Jersey City, New Jersey. Steam car.

GIDDINGS & STEVENS
USA 1900–1901
Giddings & Stevens Motor Vehicle Co., Rockford, Illinois.

GIDEON
DK 1913–1920
R. Kramper & Jorgensen, Horsens. 129 passenger and commercial vehicles were made.

GIESBERGER
F 1921
Gyroscope-balanced 2-wheeled car.

GIFFORD-PETIT
USA 1907–1908
Gifford-Pettit Mfg. Co., Chicago, Illinois.

GIGLIATO
J 1987–1997
Gigliato Design Co. Ltd., Kohhoku-ku, Yokohama. Sports cars.

GIGNOUX
F 1907
B. Gignoux, Lyon. 10 light cars.

GILBERN
GB 1959–1974
Gilbern Sports Cars (Components) Ltd., Pontypridd, Glamorgan. About 1100 sports cars were made.

GILBERT
GB 1901
Ralph Gilbert & Son, Birmingham. Light car.

GILBERT
USA 1902
C.S. Gilbert, St. Joseph, Missouri. Runabout.

GILBERT
USA c. 1905
T. Henry Gilbert, Salem, Massachusetts. 5 hp car.

GILBERT-PATRIOT
USA 1974
Electric city car.

GILBURT
GB 1904–1906
Gilburt Motor Car Co. Ltd., London. Light cars.

GILCHRIST
GB 1920–1923
Light cars.

GILCO
I 1948–1955
Gilberto Colombo, Milano. Sports car.

GILCOLT
GB 1972
This car was based on the "Reliant" Regal three-wheeler.

GILDA
RA 1957
Rosati y Christoforo, Buenos Aires. Six-seater with water-cooled V-4 57 hp engine.

GILERA
B 1920
M. Gillet, Libramont. Light car.

GILL
GB 1958–1961
Gill Getabout Cars Ltd., London. Two-seater coupe.

GILL
USA 1908
A.J. Gill, Portland, Oregon.

GILLET
B 1992–1995
Gillet Automobiles SA, Namur. Sports car.

GILLET-FOREST
F 1900–1907
Sté. Gillet-Forest, St. Cloud/Seine. Large, curved gilled-tube radiator.

GILLET-HERSTAL
B 1928–1929
Cyclecars.

GILLETT
GB 1926–1927
British Ensign Motor Ltd., London. The smallest car of the company. About 25 cars were made.

GILLETTE
USA 1916
Gillette Motors Co., Mishawaka, Indiana. 1915 succeeded American Simplex Co. mfg. of "Amplex." Company formed by King C. Gillette (Gillette Razors). Receiver appointment announced September 1917
    See "Amplex."

GILMORE
USA 1901–1904
G.A. Gilmore, Detroit, Michigan.

GILMORE ELECTRIC
USA 1904
Gilmore Electric Co., Boston, Massachusetts.

GILROY
USA c. 1917
Gilroy, California.

GILSON
CDN 1920–1921
Gilson Mfg. Co., Guelph, Ontario.

GILYARD
GB 1912–1916
Barkerend Engineering Co., Bradford, Yorks. Cyclecar.

GINETTA
GB 1957–present
Walklett Bros., Woodbridge, Suffolk (1957–1962). Ginetta Cars Ltd., Witham, Essex (1962–1972). Ennerdale Racing, Canterbury, Kent (1970–1971). Ginetta Cars Ltd., Sudbury, Suffolk (1972–present). Scunthorpe, South Humberside. Sports cars.

GINK
NL 1899
    See "Hinde," "Van Gin."

GIOM
CS 1973; 1984
Peter Chudý, Piešťany. Sports car prototypes.

GIORGIA
I 1971
Giorgia, Milano. "Delage" (F) replicars.

GIRARD
USA c. 1905
H.A. Girard, Lawrence, Massachusetts. 3.5 hp automobile.

GIRARDOT
F
    See "G.E.M."

GIRINO
I 1951
Milano. Minicar prototype.

GIRLING
GB 1913–1914
Girling Motor Ltd., Bedford. Three-wheeler.

GITANE
GB 1962
G.F. Plant Ltd., Wolverhampton, Staffs. 6 small sports cars were made.

GITHENS
USA 1900–1902
Githen Brothers Inc., Chicago, Illinois. Steam runabout.

GIZMO
USA 1998–present
Neighborhood Electric Vehicle Co., Eugene, Oregon. Small electric cars.

G.J.G.
USA 1909–1915
George J. Grossman. G.J.G. Motor Car Co., White Plains, N.Y. Runabout.

GL
I
    See "Landini."

GLADIATOR
F 1896–1920
Société Gladiator, Pré-St. Gervais (1896–1909). Puteaux/Seine (1910–1920). Voiturette and tonneau; 1.7-, 2.2-, 2.7- and 4.1-litre models.

GLAS
D 1955–1968
Hans Glas GmbH, Isaria Maschinenfabrik, Dingolfing. Small cars.

GLASPAC
BR 1984–1987
Glaspac Ltda., Sto Amaro, São Paulo. Replicars.

GLASSIC
USA 1966–1972; 1972–1975
Glassic Industries, Inc., West Palm Beach, Florida. Fiberglass replica of 1930 Ford roadster or phaeton on "International" Scout chassis.

GLASSPAR
USA 1950–1955
Glasspar Co., Santa Ana, California. 200 fiberglass-body roadsters were made.

GLEASON
USA 1909–1913
Kansas City Vehicle Co., Kansas City, Missouri. Former "Kansas City" car. Became "Bauer" 1914.

GLEN
CDN 1920–1921
Scarborough Beach, Ontario. Cyclecar.

GLENWOOD
USA 1922
Glenwood Motor Car Corp., Findlay, Ohio.

GLIDE
USA 1903–1920
Bartholomew Co., Peoria, Illinois. First models called "Glidemobile."
See "Bartholomew."

GLISENTI
I 1900
Ditta Glisenti, Brescia.

GLOBE
GB 1904–1907
Hitchon Gear & Automobile Co. Ltd., Accrington, Lancs. About 25 cars were made.

GLOBE
GB 1913–1916
Tuke & Bell Ltd., London. Cyclecar.

GLOBE
USA 1910
Globe Motor Car Co., Detroit, MI.

GLOBE
USA 1915
Globe Motor Car Co., Canton, Ohio.

GLOBE FOUR USA 1920–1922
Globe Motors Co., Cleveland, Ohio. Announced September, 1920.

GLORIETTE
A 1932–1936
Hans Pitzek, Wien. Small cars.

GLOVER
CDN 1908
William R. Dobbie, Pincher Creek, Alta.

GLOVER
GB 1912–1913
Glover Bros., Coventry, Warwickshire. Cyclecar.

GLOVER
USA 1902
George T. Glover, Chicago, Illinois. Auto-buggy.

GLOVER
GB/USA 1920–1921
Glover Motor Car Co., New York, N.Y. Car built for export to England (sold by Glovers Motors Ltd., Leeds, Yorks.). Also called "Glover-American."

GLÜCK
PL 1925–1926
Adam Glück, Warszawa. Prototype.

G.M.
F 1924–1928
Gendron et Cie., Paris. Light cars.

GMACHMEIR
D 1975
Sports car prototype.

GMC
USA 1912–present
General Motors Corporation, Detroit, MI. Primarily trucks, but some cabs c. 1922, and truck-based station wagons since 1935. General Motors Corp. in business from 1908; GMC nameplate appeared 1912.

GM LE SABRE
USA 1951
General Motors Corporation, Detroit, Michigan. Experimental car prototype.

GMÜR
CH 1914
Gmür et Cie., Schänis. Electric cars.

G.N.
GB 1910–1925
G.N. Ltd., Hendon, Middlesex (1910–1920). G.N. Motors Ltd., London (1920–1923). G.N. Ltd., London (1923–1925). Cyclecars.

G.N.
GB 1912
F.W. Berwick & Co. Ltd., London. Prototype.

GNESUTTA
I 1900
Officina Meccanica E. Gnesutta, Milano. Light car prototype.

G.N.L.
GB
See "Newey."

GNOM
CS 1924–1936
Freise a spol., továrna automobilu, Gnom', Nový Jičín. "Gnom"-Kleinautowerke Fritz Hückel, Šenov u Nového Jičína. Light cars.

GNOM
D 1949–1950
FG. Ingenieurbüro Fahrzeug- und Gerätebau Gick, Berlin.

GNOME
F
See "Gracile."

GNOME
GB 1925–1926
Gnome Cars Ltd., London (1925–1926). Nomad Cars Ltd., London (1926). 343 cc light two-seater. "Nomad" is a name of same car.

GNOME ET RHONE
F 1919
Sté. des Moteurs Gnome et Rhone, Paris. High-quality cars.

GOABOUT
USA 1901–1902
Standard Mfg. Co., Kokomo, Indiana.

GOBEL
USA 1911
Konrad Gobel, Oakland, California.

GOBRON
F
See "Gobron-Brillie."

GOBRON-BRILLIE
F 1898–1930
Sté. Gobron-Brillie, Boulogne-sur-Seine (1898–1918). Automobiles Gobron, Levallois-Perret/Seine (1919–1930). Roadsters and touring cars.

GOBY
USA 1914
Motor Engineering Co., Cleveland, Ohio. Cyclecar.

GODDARD
USA 1904
Williams Foundry & Machine Co., Akron, Ohio.

GODDARD
USA 1908
Goddard Brothers, Conneaut, Ohio.

GODDEU
USA 1897–1898
Louis Goddeu, Winchester, Massachusetts. Tandem cyclecar.

GODIVA
GB 1900–1901
Payne & Bates Ltd., Coventry, Warwickshire. 2-cylinder front-mounted 9 hp engine.

GOGGOMOBIL
D 1955–1969
See "Glas."

GOGGOMOBIL
E 1962–1966
Munguia Industrial SA, Bilbao. "Goggomobil" (D) license.

GÖHRKE
D 1931
Three-wheeler.

GOLDEN
USA 1915
Golden Motor Car Co., Chicago, Illinois.

GOLDEN EAGLE
USA 1906
Atlanta, Georgia.

GOLDEN GATE
USA 1894
A. Schilling & Sons., Santa Maria, California. Three-wheelers.

GOLDEN STATE
USA 1902–1903
Golden State Automobile Co., San Jose, California. Succeeded Christman Motor Carriage Co.

GOLDEN STATE
USA 1904–1906
Ross M.G. Phillips, Los Angeles, California. Runabouts.

GOLDSCHMIDT-DIRECT
B
See "Direct."

GOLF
USA 1956
Charles Golf, Texarkana, Texas. Five-passenger sports cars.

GOLIATH
D 1928–1963
Goliath-Werke Borgward & Co. (1928–1932). Hansa-Lloyd u. Goliath-Werke Borgward & Tecklenborg (1932–1936). Hansa-Lloyd Goliath-Werke Carl F.W. Borgward (1937–1938). C.F.W. Borgward Automobil- und Motoren Werke GmbH, Bremen. (1938–1963). Passenger and sports cars.

GOLIATH
I
See "Sertum."

G.O.M.
I 1974–1976
Three-wheeler.

GOOD BROTHERS
CDN 1899–1902
Berlin (Kitchener).

GOODCHILD
GB 1914–1915
F.B. Goodchild & Co. Ltd., London. Light car.

GOODEMOBILE
USA c. 1907
Horace C. Goode, Connelly Springs, North Carolina. Motor buggy.

GOODNOW
USA 1905
James E. Belger, Natick, Massachusetts. Steam car.

GOODRICH
USA 1903
Raymond Goodrich, Hartford, Connecticut. Steam car.

GOODRICH
USA c. 1904
Foley & Williams Mfg. Co., Cincinnati, Ohio. Motor buggy.

GOODSPEED
USA 1922
Commonwealth Motors Co., Joliet, Illinois. Phaeton.

GOODWIN
USA 1913
Goodwin Car Co., Chicago, Illinois.

GOODWIN
USA c. 1905
J.P. Goodwin, Marblehead, Massachusetts. 3.5 hp automobile.

GOODYEAR
GB 1924
American Auto Agency Ltd., Manchester. Similar to Ford Model T.

GORDANO
GB 1946–1950
Gordano Motor Co. Ltd., Bristol. Sports cars.

GORDINI
F 1951–1957
Automobiles Gordini, Paris. Sports and racing cars.

GORDON
CZ 1996–present
Gordon Cars a.s., Rokycany; Žamberk. Sports car replica.

GORDON
GB 1824–1830
David Gordon, Steam car.

GORDON
GB 1903–1904
Gordon Cycle & Motor Co. Ltd., London. Voiturette.

GORDON
GB 1912–1914
East Riding Engineering Works, Beverly, Yorks. Cyclecars.

GORDON
GB 1954–1958
Vernons Indusries Ltd., Bidston, Cheshire. Three-wheeler.

GORDON; GORDON-KEEBLE
GB 1960–1961; 1964–1967
Gordon Automobile Co. Ltd., Slough, Bucks (1960–1961). Gordon-Keeble Ltd., Eastleigh, Hampshire (1964–1965). Keeble Cars Ltd., Southampton (1965–1967). 66 sports cars were made between 1964 and 1967.

GORDON
USA 1948
H. Gordon Hansen, San Lorenzo, California. Rhomboid wheel placement. One prototype.

GORE
USA c. 1837
John Gore, Brattleboro, Vermont. Steam vehicle.

GORGONI
I 1946
Dr. Ing. Alberto Gorgoni, Roma. Rhomboid wheel placement.

GORHAM
J 1920–1922
Jitsuyo Jodosha Seizo Co., Osaka. Three-wheelers.

GÖRICKE
D 1907–1908
Bielefelder Maschinen-und Fahrradfabrik, August Göricke, Bielefeld. Three-wheeler.

GÖRKE
D 1927
Three-wheeled cyclecar.

GORM
DK 1917
Karl J. Smidt, Copenhagen. 2 cars powered by Perkins, 14 cars by JAP engines.

GOSHEN
USA 1905–1907
Goshen Motor Works, Goshen, Indiana.

GOTHAM
USA 1911–1915
Gotham Motor Car Co., New York, N.Y. About 50 cars built.

GOTTSCHALK
D 1900–1901

Berliner Motorwagen-Fabrik Gottschalk & Co. KG, Berlin. Small cars.

GÖTZ
D 1932
Fa. Götz, Villingen. Three-wheeler.

GOUJON
F 1896–1901
E. Goujon, Neuilly-sur-Seine. "Benz" (D)-like vehicles.

GOULD
USA c. 1905
Charles Gould, Lowell, Massachusetts. 4 hp automobile.

GOULD
USA 1970s
Gould, Inc., Rolling Meadows, Illinois. Electric cars.

GOVE
USA 1921
Gove Motor Truck Co., Detroit, Michigan. Truck company which built a four-cylinder, air-cooled car.

GOZZY
J 1981
Replicars.

GP
GB 1968–1995
GP Vehicles Ltd., Isleworth, Middlesex. Dune buggy and sports car kit.

GP BUGGIES
GB 1967–present
GP Buggies, South Ascot, Berkshire. Dune buggy.

G.R.A.C.
F 1970–1972
Automobile G.R.A.C., Valence/Drome. Sports car.

GRACIELA
RA 1957–1961
D.I.N.F.I.A., Camino San Roque, Cordoba. Developed from the "Justicialista."

GRACILE
GB 1905–1907
Gracile Motor Car Co. Ltd., London.

GRADE
D 1921–1926
Grade Automobilwerk AG (1921–1925). Grade Automobil AG, Bork bei Brück (1925–1926). Air-cooled 2-cylinder 2-stroke 808 cc engine.

GRÄF & STIFT
A 1907–1938
Gräf & Stift (1907–1908). Wiener Automobilfabrik AG vorm. Gräf & Stift, Wien (1908–1938). 5.9- and 8-litre touring cars.

GRÄFFORD
A 1936–1938
Wiener Automobilfabrik AG, Wien. "Ford" (USA) V-8 built under license.

GRAHAM
USA 1899–1900
Graham Equipment Co., Boston, Massachusetts. Steam car.
See "Compound" and "Graham-Fox."

GRAHAM
USA 1903
Graham Bros. Graham Automobile & Launch Co., Chicago, Illinois. Electric cars.

GRAHAM
USA 1930–1941
Graham-Paige Motors Corp., Detroit, Michigan. Succeeded "Graham-Paige."

GRAHAME-WHITE
GB 1920–1924
The Grahame-White Co. Ltd., Hendon, Middlesex. Light cars.

GRAHAM-FOX
USA 1901–1904
Graham-Fox Co., New York, N.Y. Middletown, Connecticut. 1904 merged with Eisenhuth Horseless Vehicle Co.
See "Compound."

GRAHAM MOTORETTE
USA 1902–1903
Charles Sefrin Motor Carriage Co., Brooklyn, N.Y. Runabout.

GRAHAM-PAIGE; GRAHAM
USA 1928–1941
Graham-Paige Motors Corp., Detroit, Michigan. Touring cars. Succeeded "Paige," Paige Detroit Motor Company.

GRAMM
CDN 1913
Gramm Motor Truck Co., Walkerville, Ontario. Truck company to have built cyclecars with air-cooled two-cylinder engines.

GRAMM
USA 1902
Benjamin A. Gramm, Chillicothe, Ohio.
See "Logan."

GRAMME
F 1901
Sté. des Accumulateurs Compound, Levallois-Perret/Seine. Electric three-wheeler.

GRAND
USA 1912
Grand Rapids Motor Truck Co., Detroit, Michigan.

GRAND DUCHES
USA 1982
See "Classic Roadsters."

GRANDEUR
USA 1979–c. 1983
Grandeur Motor Car Corp., Pompano Beach, Florida. Sports cars and replicars.

GRANITE FALLS
USA 1912
Granite Falls Machine Shop, Granite Falls, Minnesota.
See "Lende."

GRANT
USA 1864
John J. Grant, Cleveland, Ohio. Steam vehicle.

GRANT
USA 1896–1897
W. Wallace Grant, Brooklyn, N.Y. Long Island City, N.Y. Runabout.

GRANT
USA 1900
Grant Brothers, Boston, Massachusetts.

GRANT
USA 1912–1922
Grant Bros. Automobile Co., Detroit, Michigan. Grant Motor Co., Findlay, Ohio. 1916 became Grant Motor Car Corp., Cleveland, Ohio. Touring cars.

GRANT
USA 1913–1914
Grant Cyclecar Co. Grant Motor Co., Detroit, Michigan. Cyclecar.

GRANTA
GB 1906
Granta Motor Co., London. Double chain drive.

GRANTURA
GB c. 1970s
Grantura Plastics Ltd. Dune buggy and Jeep-type small cars.

GRAVES & CONGDON
USA 1909
Graves & Congdon Co., Amesbury, Massachusetts. Highwheeler. Became "Crown."

GRAY
CDN 1905
William Gray, Chatham, Ontario.

GRAY
USA c. 1905
C.H. Gray, Cambridge, Massachusetts. 6 hp automobile.

GRAY
USA 1908
H. Liggett Gray, New York, N.Y. Steam car prototype.

GRAY
USA 1916
Gray Taxicab Co., Sunnyvale, California.

GRAY
USA 1922–1926
Gray Motor Corp. Gray Mfg. Co., Detroit, Michigan. Touring cars.

GRAY & COUCH
USA
Gray & Couch Motor Vehicle Co., Stoneham, Massachusetts.
See "Crouch."

GRAY-DORT
CDN 1915–1924
Gray-Dort Motors Ltd., Chatham, Ontario. Famed coachbuilders, William Gray & Sons.

GRAY LIGHT CAR
USA 1920
Gray Light Car Corp., Longmont, Idaho; Denver, Colorado. Two cars produced. Used Harley-Davidson engines.

GRAYHOUND
USA c. 1910
Chris Hove, Minden, Nebraska.

GRAZIOSA
A 1899–1901
Graziosa Fahrradwerke Benedikt Albl & Co., Graz. Voiturette.

GREAT ARROW
USA 1904–1908
George N. Pierce Co., Buffalo, N.Y. Renamed "Pierce-Arrow" 1909.

GREAT EAGLE
USA 1910–1915
U.S. Carriage Co., Columbus, Ohio. Touring cars. Trucks only after 1915.

GREAT SIX
USA 1907
Gearless Transmission Co., Rochester, N.Y.
See "Gearless."

GREAT SMITH
USA 1907–1911
Smith Automobile Co., Topeka, Kansas. Formerly "Smith" from 1904.

GREAT SOUTHERN
USA 1912–1914
Great Southern Automobile Co., Birmingham, Alabama; Montgomery, Alabama. Touring cars and roadsters.

GREAT WESTERN
USA 1907–1908
Great Western Motor Car Co., San Diego, California.

GREAT WESTERN
USA 1904–1916
Great Western Mfg. Co., LaPorte, Indiana. Model Automobile Co., Auburn, Indiana (1908–1909); Peru, Indiana. Great Western Auto Co., Kalamazoo, Michigan; Peru, Indiana (1909–1916). Reported March 1916 Claude Andrews (receiver) to continue business. Touring cars and roadsters.

GREELFY
USA 1903
E.N. Miller, Greeley, Colorado. Runabout.

GREEN
USA c. 1905
Samuel M. Green, Holyoke, Massachusetts. 4 hp automobile.

GREEN
USA 1913
Green Mfg. Co., Cobleskill, N.Y.

GREEN BAY
USA 1878
E.P. Cowles, Wequiock, Wisconsin. Steam car.

GREENDUCK
USA c. 1901
Los Angeles, California.

GREENE
USA c. 1905
F.P. Greene, Malden, Massachusetts. 6 hp automobile.

GREENE
USA 1916
Greene Motor Car Co., Newark & Paterson, New Jersey. 6-wheel vehicle.

GREENLEAF
USA 1902
Green Leaf Cycle Co. Green Leaf Automobile Co., Lansing, Michigan. Surrey.

GREEN MINI BUG
USA 1968
Green Leaf Cycle Co. Green Motors Inc., Livonia, Michigan.

GREENVILLE
USA 1912–1914
See "Fay," "Empire."

GREENWOOD
USA 1978–1989
John Greenwood Sales Inc., Troy, Michigan. Greenwood Automotive Performance, Sanford, Florida. Sports cars.

GREER
USA 1916–1917
Greer College of Motoring. Greer Auto Co., Chicago, Illinois.

GREER
USA 1901
H.R. Greer, St. Louis, Missouri. Steam car.

GREEVES
GB c. 1957
Handicapped carriage.

GREGG
USA 1916
Elmore E. Gregg. Motors Co. of Philadelphia, Pittsburgh, Pennsylvania.

GRÉGOIRE
F 1903–1924
Grégoire et Cie. SA des Automobiles Grégoire, Poissy/Seine-et-Oise. Fast small and larger cars.

GREGORY
USA 1920–1922
Gregory-Crann Motor Co., Kansas City, MO, 1920–1922. Front Drive Motor Co., Kansas City, MO, 1922. A "Scripps-Booth" with front drive.

GREGORY
USA 1948
Ben F. Gregory. Gregory Front Drive Motor Cars, Kansas City, Missouri. Rear-engined front-wheel drive prototype.

GREMEL
USA 1916
H.G. Gremel, Detroit, Michigan. Car made up of the parts of 102 different automobiles.

GRENSFELDER
USA 1901
J.M. Grensfelder, St. Louis, Missouri. Runabout.

GRENVILLE
GB 1875
Experimental steam car.

GREPPI
I 1974–1975
Dune buggy and sports cars kit.

GREUTER
USA 1898
Charles R. Greuter, Holyoke, Massachusetts. Became "Holyoke."

GREWE-SCHULTE-DERNE
D 1954–1956
Grewe, Schulte & Derne, Lünen/Westfalen. Three-wheeler.

GREYHOUND
USA 1909
Burdick Motor Car Co., Eau Claire, Wisconsin.

GREYHOUND
USA 1914–1916
Greyhound Cyclecar Co. Greyhound Motor Co. States Motor Car Co., Toledo, Ohio; Kalamazoo, Michigan. Initially a cyclecar (1914–1915).

GREYHOUND
USA 1918–1919
American Motor Vehicle Co., Lafayette, Indiana. Formerly built "American Junior."

GREYHOUND
USA 1919–1920
Greyhound Motor Car Co. Greyhound Motors, New York, N.Y. E. Warren, Rhode Island.

GRICE
GB 1927
G.W.K. Ltd., Maidenhead, Berks. Three-wheelers.

GRIDI
D 1923–1924
Gridi Kraftfahrbau AG, Saulgau/Württemberg. Small cars with 1-cylinder 865 cc engine.

GRIFFIN
GB 1975–c. 1980
Nomad Sales, Burnham-on-Crouch, Essex. Sports cars.

GRIFFIN
USA 1909
Fredonia Iron Works, Fredonia, Kansas. Auto-buggy.

GRIFFIN
USA 1930
R.A. Griffin, San Diego, California. Three-wheeler.

GRIFFIN
USA 1930–1931
Gardner Motor Co., St. Louis, Missouri. Front wheel drive.
See "Gardner."

GRIFFITH
GB 1821–1825
Julius Griffith, Brahmah. Steam cars.

GRIFFITH
USA 1964–1966
Griffith Motor Car Co., Syoset, Long Island, N.Y. (1964–1965). Griffith Motors, Plainview, Long Island, N.Y. (1965–1966). 285 sports cars were made.

GRIFFITH INTERNATIONAL
GB 1981
Griffith International Ltd., London. "Toyota" (J) Celica sports cars with convertible body by Tickford.

GRIFFITHS
USA 1899
W.H. Griffiths, Boston, Massachusetts. Steam runabout.

GRIFFON
F 1906–1910; 1921–1924
SA des Cycles Griffon, Courbevoie/Seine. Voiturette; cyclecars.

GRIMALDI
I 1906
Grimaldi & C., Milano.

GRINNALL
GB 1982–1995
Grinnall Cars, Stourport, Worcestershire. Sports cars.

GRINNELL
USA 1912–1916
Grinnell Electric Automobile Co., Detroit, Michigan. Electric cars. Former "Phipps-Grinnell."

GRISARD
CH 1899–1900
Grisard et Cie., Geneve. "Egg" license.

GRISWOLD
USA 1905–1906
Griswold Mfg. Co., Quincy, Massachusetts.

GRISWOLD
USA 1906
Runabout.

GRISWOLD
USA 1907–1909
Griswold Motor Car Co. Griswold Motor & Body Co., Detroit, Michigan.

GROFF & RUNKLE
USA 1902
Groff & Runkle Motor Vehicle Co., Columbus, Ohio.

GROFRI
A 1922–1927
Grofri-Werk AG, Atzgerdorf. 6-cylinder 12/45 hp cars, later "Amilcar" (F) based models.

GRONNINGER
NL 1898–1899
Groninger Motorrijtuigenfabriek, Groningen. Heavy dos-a-dos cars.

GRONOS
CH 1972
Iwan & Dieter Gronostay, Reinach, Basel. Sports car prototype.

GROPA
GB
See "Nomad."

GROSE
GB 1899–1900
Grose Ltd., Northampton. Light car.

GROUSSET
F 1904–1905

Atelier de Mécanique et d'Automobiles Grousset et Fils, Firminy/Loire. 12 cars for local clients.

GROUT
USA 1898–1915
Grout Bros. Grout Brothers Automobile Co. Grout Automobile Co., Orange, Massachusetts. Steam to 1905; gasoline vehicles from 1903. Became "Red Arrow" (1915).

G.R.P.
F 1924–1928
G. et R. Paul, Paris. Touring and sports cars.

GRP
PI c. 1988–present
GRP Systems & Fabricators Incorporated, Makati, Manila. Plastic bodied cars.

GRUBB
USA 1902
Light Cycle Co., Pottstown, Pennsylvania.
See "Light Steamer."

GRUBE
USA 1900
Grube Carriage Works, Rahway, New Jersey.

GRUMAN
USA c. 1905
Carl A. Gruman, Worcester, Massachusetts. 4 hp automobile.

GRUMETT
U 1972
Esposito S.A., Montevideo. "Vauxhall" (GB) Viva based cars.

GRUNO
NL 1899
Rijwielfabriek "Gruno," Winschoten. Three-wheeler.

GRYFF
CH 1977; 1983
Jean-Pierre Läubin, Allschwil, Basel. Sports car prototype.

GS
GB 1975–c. 1980
GS Cars, Warmley, Bristol. Sports cars.

G.S.M.
ZA/GB 1958–1966
Glass Sports Motor Co. Pty. Ltd., Cape Town (1958–1962). G.S.M. Cars Ltd., West Malling, Kent (1960–1964).

G.S.M. Pty. Ltd., Paarden Eiland, C.P. (1963–1966). Sports cars.

G.T.B.
USA 1968–c. 1973
Denk Plastics Inc., Chester, Pennsylvania. Dune buggy.

GT CENTRON
GB 1971
Sports car prototype.

GTD
GB 1988–present
GT Developments Ltd., Poole, Dorset. Sports cars and replicars.

GTD
GB 1990s
GTD Supercards, Sutton Coldfield, West Midlands. Sports kit cars.

G.T.M.
GB 1966–1990
Cox & Co. (Manchester) Ltd. (1966–1969). G.T.M. Kit Cars, Hazel Grove, Cheshire (1969–1990). GTM Engineering, Nottingham. Loughborough, Leicestershire. "Mini"-powered mid-engined sports/GT car.

GUANCI
USA 1982–?
Guanci Automobiles, Inc., Woodstock, Illinois. Sports cars.

GUANGZHOU
PRC 1988–present
Guangzhou-Peugeot Automobile Corp. Ltd., Jishan, Huang-pu. "Peugeot" (F) license.

GUARALDI
I 1904
Automobili Guaraldi, Lodi.

GUARANTY
USA 1917–1918
Guaranty Motors Co., Cambridge, Massachusetts.

GUEPARDO
E
See "Artes."

GUERRAZ
F 1900–1902
Voitures Legeres Louis Guerraz, Levallois-Perret/Seine. Light cars.

GUICHARD & PECK
USA 1899
Guichard & Peck, Walla Walla, Washington.

GUIDETTI
I 1971
Sports car prototype.

GUILDFORD
GB 1920
Griffith's Engineering Works, Guildford, Surrey. Cyclecar.

GUILICK
F 1914–1929
G. Guilick et Cie., Maubeuge/Nord. Assembled cars.

GUILLIERME
F 1906–1910
Automobiles Guillierme, Paris. Shaft drive and 4-cylinder "Ballot" engine.

GULDSTRAND
USA 1995
Guldstrand Automobiles, Culver City, California. Sports cars.

GULF & WESTERN
USA 1983
Electric car.

GULLWING
USA 1981–1994
Gullwing Car Inc., Gardena, California. Replicars.

GUNDAKER
USA 1982
Gundaker Fabrication, Metuchen, New Jersey. Sports car.
See "Vandetta."

GÜNTER
D 1972
J. Günter, Berlin. One-seater minicar prototype.

GURGEL
BR 1966–present
Macan Ind. E Com. Ltda. (1966–1968). Gurgel Veiculos Ltda., Rio Claro, São Paulo (1969–present). Fiberglass-bodied sports cars.

GURLEY
USA 1899–1901
Tom W. Gurley, Meyersdale, Pennsylvania.

GURNEY
GB 1825–1830
Goldworthy Gurney, London; Bath. Steam cars.

GURYEV
SU c. 1830
Vasilii Petrovich Guryev. Steam carriage.

GUTBROD
D 1949–1954
Gutbrod Motorenbau GmbH, Plochingen. 2-stroke 593 cc and 663 cc light cars.

GUTKNECHT
CH 1959
Werner Gutknecht, Wohlen, Bern. Sports car prototype.

GUTMANN
D 1985–1994
Karl Gutmann, Automobiltechnik, Breisach. Tuning.

GUY
CDN 1911
Matthew Guy Carriage & Automobile Co., Oshawa, Ontario. Brintnell Motor Car Co., Toronto, Ontario. 30 hp tourer.

GUY
F 1904–1916
H. Guillemin et Cie. (1904–1909). E. Nicolas et Cie., Courbevoie/Seine (1909–1916). Touring and sports cars.

GUY
GB 1919–1925
Guy Motors Ltd., Wolverhampton, Staffs. V-8 luxury cars.

GUYOT SPECIALE
F 1925–1931
Ets. Albert Guyot et Cie., Clichy/Seine. Sports car.

GUYSON
GB 1974–1975
"Jaguar" E Type powered sports cars.

GUY VAUGHAN
USA 1910–1913
W.A. Wood Automobile Mfg. Co., Kingston, N.Y. Vaughan Motors Co. (1912–1913). Name was to be changed to "Vaughan" for 1914.

G.V.
USA 1907
General Vehicle Co., Long Island City, N.Y. Absorbed Vehicle Equipment Co. May, 1908. Wright-Martin bought plant.

GWALIA
GB 1922
Stanfield Ltd., Cardiff. Light car.

G.W.K.
GB 1911–1931
G.W.K. Ltd., Datchet, Bucks. (1911–1914). Maidenhead, Berks. (1914–1931). Cyclecars and light cars.

GWYNNE
GB 1922–1929
Gwynne's Engineering Co. Ltd., London (1922–1925). Gwynne Cars Ltd., London (1925–1929). Tourer.

GYROSCOPE
USA 1900
Western Wheel Works, Chicago, Illinois. Three-wheeler. On display in New York City November 1900. Also called "Tri Moto."

GYROSCOPE
USA 1908–1909
Gyroscope Co. Inc., New York, N.Y. Rotary type engine. Patents sold to "Page-Adrian."

GYROSCOPE
USA 1908
Blomstrom Mfg. Co., Detroit, Michigan.

GYROSCOPE
USA 1914
Blomstrom Automobile Co., Detroit, Michigan. Built by Lion Motor Car Co., Adrian, Michigan.

H

HAARGAARD
DK 1952
Haargaard. Three-wheeler prototype.

HAASE
USA 1902–1904
Northwestern Automobile Co. Haase Brothers, Milwaukee, Wisconsin.
See "H.B." highwheeler.

HABAG
D 1924
Hamburger Auto-Bau-Gesellschaft mbH, Hamburg. Light car.

HABERER
USA 1910–1913
Cincinnati, Ohio.
See "Cino."

HABIG
USA 1919
Harry Habig, Cincinnati, Ohio. Light sports car.

HACKETT
USA 1916–1919
Hackett Motor Car Co., Jackson, Michigan; Grand Rapids, Michigan. Succeeded "Argo." Became "Lorraine," Lorraine Motor Car Co.

HACKLEY
USA 1905
George T. Hackley, Los Angeles, California.

HADFIELD-BEAN
GB
See "Bean."

HAFER ELECTRIC
USA 1903–1904
Hafer Brothers, Los Angeles, California.

HAG
D 1922–1927
Hessische Automobil-Gesellschaft AG, Darmstadt (1922–1925). Waggonfabrik Gebr. Gastell, Mainz-Mombach (1925–1927). 1.3-litre OHC engine.

HAGAMAN
USA 1895
J.D. Hagaman, Adrian, Michigan.

HAGEA
D 1922–1924

Dipl.-Ing. O. Bischoff & M. Althoven GmbH, Berlin. Emil Heinicke AG, Hagea-Vertriebs-Gesellschaft, Berlin. Small cars.

HAGEN
D 1903–1908
Accumulatorenwerke Gottfried Hagen, Kalk bei Köln. Electric cars built also under names (see) "KAW" and. "Urbanus."

HAGENLOCHER
USA 1896
Henry Hagenlocher, Erie, Pennsylvania. Runabout.

HAG-GASTELL
D
See "HAG."

HAGMANN & HAMMERLY
USA 1902–1905
Hagmann & Hammerly, Chicago, Illinois.

HAHN
USA 1902
Hahn Automobile Co., Pueblo, Colorado.

HAIN
USA 1898–1902
Ralph B. Hain, Mishwaka, Indiana. Los Angeles, California.

HAINES & GRUT
AUS 1904
Haines & Grut, Melbourne, Victoria. Highwheeler.

HAINS
USA 1913
Ross M. Hains, Los Angeles, California.

HAI-YAN
PRC 1976–1979
Hai-Yan Automobile Works, Shanghai. Small cars.

HAKAR
CS 1950–1957
Alois Rieger, Hradec Králové. Sports cars.

H.A.L.
USA 1916–1918
H.A. Lozier & Co., Cleveland, Ohio (1915). Reorganized as H.A.L. Motor Car Co., 1916. Assets reported auctioned April 1918. Touring cars.

HALF BREED
USA 1916
Wiley Griffin, McCracken, Kansas. Assembled from two production cars. One off.

HALL
GB 1918–1919
H.E. Hall & Co., Tonbridge, Kent. Landaulette and taxicabs.

HALL
USA 1903–1904
Hall Motor Carriage Co., Dover, New Jersey. Became Hall Motor Vehicle Co. 1903.

HALL
USA 1905–1906
Specht & Kuntz, St. Louis, Missouri. Two cars built.

HALL
USA 1914–1916
Hall Cyclecar Mfg. Co., Waco, Texas. Cyclecars. 1915 became Hall Motor Car Co.

HALL
USA 1950
T.P. Hall, San Diego, California.

HALLADAY
USA 1907–1922
Streator Motor Car Co., Streator, Illinois (1907–1914). A.C. Barley Mfg. Co., Streator, Illinois (1914–1917). Halladay Motor Car Co. (1917–1918). Halladay Motor Co. (1918–1920), Attica, Ohio. Halladay Motors Corp. (1920–1922), Newark, Ohio. Became "Falcon." Touring cars.

HALLAMSHIRE
GB 1900–1905
Durham, Churchill & Co. Ltd., Sheffield, Yorks. Light cars.

HALL & MARTIN
GB
See "Martin."

HALLER
USA 1910
George Haller, Louisville, Kentucky.

HALLETT
USA 1914
Chester P. Hallett, Casselton, North Dakota.

HALL GASOLINE TRAP
USA 1895
John W. Hall & Sons., Jacksonville, Illinois.

HALLOCK
USA 1915
Hallock Engineering Co., Cleveland, Ohio.

HALSEY
USA 1901–1907
Halsey Motor Vehicle Co., Philadelphia, Pennsylvania.

HALSEY
USA 1904
James T. Halsey, New York, N.Y. Steam car.

HALSEY & DIMOCK
USA 1904
Woodruff W. Halsey & Edward J. Dimock, Elizabeth, New Jersey. Buckboard.

HALSEYLEC
GB c. 1955–1959
Eric Brandon, Halsey's Electric Co. Ltd. Only 2 sports cars were built.
See "Cliden."

HALVERSON
USA 1908
A. Halverson, New York, N.Y.

HAMBLINETTA
GB c. 1971
Prof. Rawcliff, University of Bristol, Bristol. Electric car prototype.

HAMBRECHT
CDN 1907
Herman Hambrecht, Berlin (Kitchener).

HAMBRICK
USA 1905–1906
J.W. Hambrick, Huntington, West Virginia. Hambrick Motor Car Co., Parkersburg, West Virginia. Also known as "Grey Goose."

HAMBRICK
USA 1908
Hambrick Motor Car Co., Washington, Indiana.

HAMILTON
GB 1921–1925
D.J. Smith & Co. Ltd., Wickford, Essex. Light two-seater.

HAMILTON
USA 1909
Columbia Carriage Co., Hamilton, Ohio.

HAMILTON
USA 1917
Hamilton Motor Car Co., York, Pennsylvania.

HAMILTON
USA 1917–1918
Hamilton Motors Co., Grand Haven, Michigan. Absorbed Alter Motor Car Co. Mostly trucks.

HAMILTONIAN
USA 1909
Hamilton Motor Car Co., Greensburg, Indiana. 6-cylinder cars.

HAMLEN
GB
See "Lenham."

HAMLIN
USA 1834
Cyrus Hamlin, Portland, Maine. Steam wagon.

HAMLIN
USA 1901
Ralph Hamlin, Los Angeles, California. Runabout.

HAMLIN
USA 1930
Hamlin Motor Co., Harvey, Illinois. Front-wheel drive prototype. Company failed before starting production.

HAMLIN-HOLMES
USA 1919–1930
Hamlin-Holmes Motor Car Co., Harvey, Illinois; Detroit, Michigan. Front-wheel drive. 38 cars built.

HAMMEL
DK 1886
Albert F. Hammel & Urban Johansen, Kobenhavn. 2-cylinder carriage.

HAMMER
AUS c. 1903
Mount Torreus, South Australia.

HAMMER
USA 1904–1906
Hammer Motor Co., Detroit, Michigan. Succeeded Hammer-Sommer Automobile Carriage Co. Touring cars.

HAMMER-SOMMER
USA 1902–1904
Hammer-Sommer Automobile Carriage Co., Detroit, Michigan. Became Hammer Motor Co.
See "Hammer" and "Sommer."

HAMMETT STEAM CARRIAGE
USA 1900
M.M. Hammett, Boston, Massachusetts.

HAMMETT
USA 1914
E.A. Hammett, Lincoln, Nebraska. Cyclecar.

HAMMOND
GB 1919–1920
Whitworth Engineering Co. Ltd., London. Light cars.

HAMMOND
USA 1901
Fred L. Hammond, Lewiston, Maine. Steam car.

HAMMOND & THIEDE
D c. 1985
Hammond & Thiede, Würzburg-Heidingsfeld. Tuning.

HAMPDEN
USA 1899–1901
Hampden Automobile & Launch Co., Springfield, Massachusetts; Chicopee Falls, Massachusetts. J.F. Duryea's interim project.

HAMPTON
GB 1911–1933
Hampton Engineering Co., Hampton-in-Arden, Warwicks (1911); Birmingham (1912–1919); Stroud, Glos. (1919–1925). Stroud Motor Manufacturing Co. Ltd. (1926). Hampton Cars (London) Ltd. (1927–1930). Safety Suspension Car Co. Ltd., Stroud, Glos. (1931–1933). Touring and sports cars.

HANAS VAHAAR
IND
See "Fuldamobil" (D).

HANAUER
USA 1901
Charles Hanauer Cycle Co., Cincinnati, Ohio.

HANCHETT
USA 1900
George T. Hanchett, New York, N.Y.

HANCOCK
GB 1830–1838
Walter Hancock, London; Windsor; Stratford. Steam cars.

HANCOCK
USA 1901
William C. Hancock, Concord, Massachusetts. Electric cars.

H & F
USA 1910
H & F Electromobile Co., Detroit, Michigan. Electric car.

HANDLEY
USA 1923
Handley Motors Inc., Kalamazoo, Michigan. Purchased by "Checker Cab" 1923.

HANDLEY KNIGHT
USA 1920–1923
The Handley-Knight Co., Kalamazoo, Michigan. Used "Willys-Knight" engine. Became "Handley."

H. & R.
USA 1915
H. & R. Machine & Garage Co., Ridgewood, New Jersey. Runabout.

HANDS
GB 1921–1924
G.W. Hands Motor Co., Birmingham. Light cars.

HANDSOME
PRC 1994–?
Beifan Haishen Auto Corp., Chang-Chun. Minicars.

HANEL
CS 1948
Miloš Hanousek, Dobruška. 500 cc minicar prototype.

HANISSARD
F c. 1921
Cyclecar.

HANOMAG
D 1924–1939
Hannoversche Maschinenbau AG vorm. Georg Egerstorff, Hannover. Light and touring cars.

HANOVER
USA 1921–1927
General Gas-Electric Co. Hanover Motor Car Co., Hanover, Pennsylvania. Purchse of "Parenti" plant in Buffalo, N.Y. reported June 1922. About 800 cars were made.

HANSA
D 1906–1939
Hansa Automobil-Gesellschaft mbH, Varel (1906–1914); Bielefeld (1913–1914). Hansa-Lloyd-Werke AG, Varel (1914–1929); Bremen (1929–1931). Hansa-Lloyd und Goliath-Werke A

Borgward & Tecklenborg,. Bremen (1931–1937). Hansa-Lloyd Goliath-Werke Carl F.W. Borgward, Bremen (1937–1939). Light and touring cars.

HANSA-LLOYD
D 1921–1929
Hansa-Lloyd-Werke AG, Bremen. Luxury cars.

HANSEN
USA 1895
Chicago Carriage Motor Co., Chicago, Illinois.

HANSEN
USA 1902
Hansen Automobile Co., Cleveland, Ohio. Gasoline runabout.

HANSEN
USA 1906
Four Wheel Drive Wagon Co., Milwaukee, Wisconsin.

HANSEN-WHITMAN
USA 1907
Hansen Auto & Machine Works, Pasadena, California. Runabout.

HANSON
USA 1917–1923
George W. Hanson (1916). Hanson Motor Co., Atlanta, Georgia. Company incorporated 1916. Production to have started May, 1917 with 100 per day scheduled.

HANS VAHAAR
IND 1960s
"Fuldamobil" (D) license.

HANZER
F 1900–1903
Hanzer Freres, Petit-Ivry/Seine. Voiturette.

HARA
CS 1932
Halasta, Rakovník. 2-cylinder car prototype.

HARABAS
PI 1972–1975
General Motors Co., Manila. Light passenger car/delivery van.

HARBER
USA 1904
Harber Bros., Bloomington, Illinois.

HARBORN
D 1907–1908
Victor Harborn, Weissen.

See bei Berlin. Three-wheelers. *See* "Bef," "Geha" and "Elite."

HARBOROUGH
GB 1964
Harborough Construction Co., Harborough. Electric town car prototype.

HARDIE
USA 1896
American Air Power Co., New York, N.Y.

HARDIE
USA 1900
Hardie-Lynes Foundry & Machine Co., Birmingham, Alabama.

HARDING
CDN 1911–1912
Harding Motor Car Co., London, Ontario. Runabouts.

HARDING
USA 1899
Harding Mfg. Co., Nashville, Tennes.

HARDING
USA 1916–1917
Harding Motor Car Co., Cleveland, Ohio. Twelwe-cylinder motor, 7-seater touring cars.

HARDINGE
USA 1903–1904
Hardinge Co., York, Pennsylvania. Six-wheeler. Two built. Became "York-Pullman."

HARDY
USA 1902–1903
Flint Automobile Co., Flint, Michigan. Former "Flint" and "Roadster."

HARE
USA 1918
Holding company for "Mercer," "Locomobile," "Simplex"; no "Hare" car.

HARIMAU
MAL 1972–1975
Johore Bahu. Light passenger car/deliver van.

HARISCOTT
GB 1920–1921
Harrison, Scott & Co., Bradford, Yorks. Small sports car.

HARISS
USA c. 1930s
H.R. Hariss, Grosse Pointe, Michigan. Steam prototype.

HARKNESS
USA 1904
Harkness Automobile Co., Flushing, N.Y. Sports car.

HARLÉ
F
See "Sautter-Harlé."

HARLEQUIN
GB 1990s
Harlequin Autokits Ltd., Stroud, Gloucestershire. Kit cars.

HARPER
GB 1898–1900; 1905–1906
John Harper & Thomas Mowatt, Aberdeen, Scotland. Experimental cars; landaulette based on the 1-cylinder "Cadillac" (USA).

HARPER
GB 1921–1926
A.V. Roe & Co. Ltd., Manchester. Three-wheeler.

HARPER
USA 1907–1908
Harper Buggy Co., Columbus City, Indiana. Gasoline runabout.

HARRIGAN
USA 1922
Harrigan Motor Corp., Cleveland, Ohio.

HARRIS
USA 1891; 1896
George T. Harris, Washington, D.C. Baltimore, Maryland. Steam vehicles.

HARRIS
USA 1900
Peter Harris, Manchester, Rhode Island.

HARRIS
USA 1936
Benjamin F. Harris III, Chicago, Illinois. Sporting one-seater.

HARRIS-LEON LAISNE
F
See "Leon Laisne."

HARRISON
USA 1905–1907
Harrison Wagon Co., Grand Rapids, Michigan.

HARRIS SIX
USA 1923
U.S. Tractor & Machinery Co. Wisconsin Automotive Corp., Menasha, Wisconsin. 6-cylinder assembled cars.

HARROLDS
USA 1905
Harrolds Motor Car Co., New York, N.Y.

HARROUN
USA 1905
R.W. Harroun, Chicago, Illinois.

HARROUN
USA 1917–1922
Ray Harroun, Detroit, Michigan. Harroun Motors Corp., Wayne, Michigan. 1135 cars were built.

HARRUFF
USA 1930
J.W. Harruff, Toledo, Ohio.

HART
GB 1900–1901
E.W. Hart & Co., Luton, Beds. Electric car.

HART
USA 1904–1905
Frederick Hart, Poughkeepsie, N.Y. Steam car.

HART
USA 1953–1954
Los Angeles, California.

HARTFORD
USA c. 1914
Hartford Motor Car Co., Hartford, Conecticut.

HARTFORD-APPERSON
USA 1916
Hartford-Apperson Motor Co., Hartford, Connecticut.

HARTGE
D 1985–1998
Hartge Motorsport, Kohl Automobile GmbH, Aachen. Hartge GmbH, Beckingen. Tuning.

HARTLEY
USA 1896–1898
Hartley Power & Supply Co., Chicago, Illinois. A steam unit adaptable to horse-drawn vehicle.

HARTMAN
USA 1900
W.G. Hartman, Portland, Oregon. Steam carriage.

HARTMAN
USA 1914–1918
George W. Hartman, Red Bluff, California. About 20 cars built.

HARTMANN
D 1993–present
Hartmann-Motorsport, Stuttgart. Tuning.

HARTNETT
AUS 1951–1957
Hartnett Motor Co., Melbourne, Victoria. 120 light 594 cc cars were made.

HARTWELL
USA c. 1905
Edward Hartwell, Lynn, Massachusetts. 4 hp car.

HARVARD
USA 1908
Pioneer Motor Car Co., York, Pennsylvania.

HARVARD
USA 1915–1921
Pioneer Motor Car Co., Troy, N.Y. 1918 became Harvard-Pioneer Motor Car Co., Troy, N.Y., Hudson Falls, N.Y. 1920 became Harvard-Pioneer Motor Car Co., Hyattsville, Maryland. Open two-seaters.

HASBROUCK
USA 1899–1902
Hasbrouck Motor Co., Newark, New Jersey. Hasbrouck Motor Works, Piermont, N.Y. Gasoline vehicles.

HASCHKE
USA 1904
J.E. Haschke, Chicago, Illinois. Electric car.

HASCHO
D 1924
Schollmeyer & Halbritter, Mühlhausen/Thür. Light car.

HASELTINE
USA 1916
Believed to be "Heseltine" misspelled.

HASLBECK
D c. 1985
Gebrüder Haslbeck GmbH, Mühldorf am Inn. Tuning.

HASSAL
USA 1907
Hassal Iron Works, Colorado Springs, Colorado.

HASSLER
USA 1917
Hassler Motor Car Co., Indianapolis, Indiana. Roadster.

HASSLER MOTOR BUGGY
USA 1898
R.H. Hassler, Indianapolis, Indiana.

HASTINGS
USA 1902
T.K. Hastings, New York, N.Y. Steam touring car.

HASTINGS
USA 1910
Hastings Motor Car Co., Detroit, Michigan.

HATAZ
D 1921–1925
Hataz Kleinautofabrik Hans Tautenhahn, Zwickau. Small cars with Steudel engines.

HATCH
USA c. 1905
Estes J. Hatch, Montpelier, Vermont. 5 hp automobile.

HATFIELD
USA 1907–1908
Hatfield Motor Vehicle Co., Cortland, N.Y. Advance Motor Vehicle (1908), Miamisburg, Ohio. Highwheelers.
See "Buggyabout."

HATFIELD
USA 1916–1924
Cortland Cart & Carriage Co., Sidney, N.Y. Operated in receivership July 1924. 1,554 cars were made.

HATHAWAY
USA c. 1905
E.F. Hathaway, Dorchester, Massachusetts. Built three automobiles.

HATHAWAY
USA c. 1981
Hathaway Motor Company, Santee, California. Replicars.

HATHORN
USA 1914
C.E. Hathorn, Davenport, Iowa. Cyclecar.

HAUSER
D 1998–present
Hauser GmbH, Eichenau. Sports cars.

HAUSHALTER
USA 1910
H.P. Haushalter, Milwaukee, Wisconsin.

HAUTIER
F 1899–1905

Sté. Hautier, Paris. Electric and gasoline cars.

HAVANA
USA 1905
Havana Automobile Co., Paterson, New Jersey. Some large touring cars were built by the Mack Brothers Motor Car Co., Allentown, Pennsylvania.

HAVERHILL
USA c. 1905
E.F. Sweet, Haverhill, Massachusetts. 8 hp automobile.

HAVENS
USA 1906
Herbert Havens, Denver, Colorado.

HAVERS
USA 1911–1914
Havers Motor Car Co., Port Huron, Michigan. Touring cars.

HAVILAND
USA 1895–1896
Dr. Frank M. Haviland, New York, N.Y.

HAVOC
USA 1914
Havoc Cyclecar Mfg. Co., Rochester, N.Y. Cyclecar.

HAWA
D 1923–1925
Hannoversche Waggonfabrik AG, Hannover. Small electric cars.

HAWK
GB 1983
Faye Caerleon Ltd., Cwmbran, Gwent, Wales. Replicars.

HAWK
GB 1990s
Hawk Cars Ltd., Frant, East Sussex. Kit cars.

HAWK
USA 1914
Hawk Motor Car Co. Hawk Cyclecar Co., Detroit, Michigan. Cyclecar.

HAWKINS
USA 1905–1906
Hawkins Automobile & Gas Engine Co., Houston, Texas.

HAWKINS
USA 1914
Hawkins Cyclecar Co., Xenia, Ohio.

Cyclecar. January 1915 directors sued to close company.
See "Xenia."

HAWLEY
USA 1906–1908
Hawley Automobile Co., Constantine, Michigan (1906–1907); Mendon, Michigan (1907–1908). Runabout and tonneau.

HAY & HOTCHKISS
USA 1898–1899
Walter Hay. Hay & Hotchkiss Co., New Haven, Connecticut. Stanhope. Original car extant, 1950.

HAY-BERG
USA 1907–1908
Hay-Berg Motor Car Co., Milwaukee, Wisconsin. Roadsters.

HAYDEN
USA c. 1905
Douglas Hayden, South Natick, Massachusetts.

HAYDEN DART
ZA 1997–present
Dart Engineering cc, Montague Gardens. Sports cars.
See "Dart."

HAYDOCK
USA 1906–1908
D.W. Haydock Motor Car Mfg. Co., St. Louis, Missouri. Front-wheel drive.
See "Cosmopolitan."

HAYN
USA 1901
Western Gas Engine Co., Mishawaka, Indiana.

HAYNES
USA 1894; 1904–1925
Haynes Automobile Co., Kokomo, Indiana. Touring cars.

HAYNES-APPERSON
USA 1895–1905
Haynes-Apperson Co., Kokomo, Indiana. Rear-mounted horizontally-opposed 2-cylinder 3.1-litre engine.

HAZ; HAZARD
D c. 1969–1983
Rudolf Kühn KG, Hamburg. Dune buggy and sports car kit.

HAZARD
USA 1914–1915
Hazard Motor Mfg. Co., Rochester, N.Y.

HAZELTON
USA 1908
M.W. Hazelton, Oneonta, N.Y. Steam car.

H-B
USA 1908
H. Brothers, Chicago, Illinois. Highwheeler.
See "Haase."

H-C
USA 1916
H-C Motor Car Co., Detroit, Michigan.

H.C.E.
GB 1912–1913
H.C.E. Cars, London (1912). Harold Wood, Essex (1913). Cyclecar.

H.C.S.
USA 1920–1925
Harry C. Stutz. H.C.S. Motor Car Co., Indianapolis, Indiana. Became H.C.S. Cab Mfg. Co. 2,175 cars were made. Taxicabs built 1925–1927.

H.E.
GB 1920–1931
Herbert Engineering Co. Ltd., Reading, Berks. Sports tourer.

HEADLAND
GB 1897–1900
Headlands Patent Electric Storage Battery Co. Ltd., London. Electric car.

HEADLAND
USA 1895
Harry Headland, Freedom, Pennsylvania.

HEALEY
GB 1946–1954
Donald Healey Motor Co. Ltd., Warwick. Sports cars.

HEALEY
GB 1985–1993
Healey Motor Company Ltd., Slimbridge, Gloucestershire. Replicars.

HEALEY
USA c. 1905–c. 1916
Healey & Co., New York, N.Y.

HEALEY
USA 1953–1955
Nash Motors, Kenosha, Wisconsin.
See "Nash-Healey."

HEALY
USA 1888

Caleb E. Healy, New London, Ohio. Steam carriage.

HEALY
USA 1900
Healy Bros., Madera, California.

HEALY
USA 1910–1911
Healy & Co., New York, N.Y. Electric car. Also gasoline car in 1910.

HEBE
E 1920–1921
Fabrica Espanola de Automoviles Hebe, Barcelona. Light cars.

HECK
CH 1972
Peter Heck. Sports car prototype.

HEDAG
D 1905–1938
Hamburger Elektrische Droschken Aktien-Gesellschaft, Hamburg. Electric car.

HEDEA
F 1913–1914
A. Accary, Paris. Light cars. Also known as the "Accary."

HEIFNER
USA 1919–1922
L.M. Heifner Mfg. Co. Heifner-Douglas-Perkins Co., Chester, Pennsylvania. Heifner Motor Car Co., Geneva, Ohio. Roadsters.

HEIKENSKJÖLD
S 1918
G. Heikenskjöld. 13 hp light car.

HEILBRONNER
D 1900
Heilbronner Fahrzeugfabrik, Heilbronn.

HEILMAN
USA 1907
John C. Heilman, Cincinnati, Ohio. Runabout.

HEIM
D 1921–1926
Heim & Cie., Badische Automobilfabrik, Mannheim. Sports and touring cars.

HEINE-VELOX
USA 1905–1906; 1921–1923
Heine Velox Motor Co., San Francisco, California (1905–1906). Heine-Velox Engineering Co. (1921–1923). Touring cars.

HEINIS
F 1925–1930
Établissements Charles Heinis, Neuilly/Seine. 4-cylinder SCAP engines and the straight-8 Lycoming of 5-litres.

HEINKEL
D 1955–1958
Ernst Heinkel AG, Stuttgart. Heinkel Fahrzeugbau GmbH, Speyer. Three-wheelers.

HEINKEL I
IRL 1958–1961
Dundalk. Minicars based on the "Heinkel" Kabine (D).

HEINLE & WEGELIN
D 1897–1903
Motorfahrzeug-Werke Heinle & Wegelin, Oberhausen-Augsburg. Three-wheelers.

HEINZELMAN
USA 1908
Heinzelmann Bros. Carriage Co., Belleville, Illinois. Highwheelers.

HELBÉ
F 1905–1907
Leveque et Bodenréder, Boulogne-sur-Seine. Light assembled cars.

HELD
USA c. 1905
Alfred G. Held, Rockville, Connecticut.

HELEM
F 1998–present
R.J Racing, Téloché. Sports cars.

HELICA
F 1921
Propeller powered cyclecar.

HELICAK
RI c. 1975
Djakarta. Three-wheelers.

HELIOS
CH 1906–1907
Automobiles Helios, Zürich. 18/24 hp cars.

HELIOS
D 1924–1926
Helios Automobilbau AG, Köln. Horizontally-opposed 2-cylinder 972 cc engine.

HELIOS
S 1901–1902
AB Södertälje Verkstader, Södertälje. Rear-engined vis-à-vis.

HELLMANN
D 1902–1903
Ing. W. H. Hellmann, Berlin. Three-wheelers.

HELO
D 1924–1925
"Helo"-Kraftfahrzeugbau Herrmann & Lommatzsch, Berlin. Three-wheelers.

HELVETIA
F 1899–1900
Compagnie des Voitures Electriques Helvetia, Combs-la-Ville/Seine-et-Marne. Electric cars designed by a Swiss, Jacques Fischer-Hinnen who went to Prague in 1900 to design electric cars which were built by Frantisek Křižík.
See "Křižík" A/CS.

HEMSTREET
USA 1901
Hemstreet, Niobrara, Nebraska. 18 hp steam car.

HENDEE
USA 1910
Hendee Mfg. Co., Springfield, Massachusetts. Runabout.

HENDEL
USA 1903–1904
William Hendel & Son, Red Wing, Minnesota.

HENDERSON
USA 1912–1914
Henderson Motor Car Co., Indianapolis, Indiana. June 1912 introduction announcement. July 1914 liquidation notice. Touring cars.

HENDRICKSON
USA 1902
Magnus Hendrickson, Chicago, Illinois.

HENLEY
USA 1899
Henley-Kimball Co., Boston, Massachusetts. Steam car.

HENNEGIN
USA 1908
Commercial Automobile Co., Chicago, Illinois. Highwheeler.

HENNESSEY
USA 1996–present
Hennessey Motorsports, Houston, Texas. "Dodge" Viper based sports cars.

HENNEY
USA 1921–1931
Henney Motor Co., Freeport, Illinois. Custom convertible sedans. Owned by Moline Plow Co.

HENNEY-KILOWATT
USA 1960–1964
The Henney Motor Co., Bloomington, Illinois. Division of Eureka Williams Corp., Canastota, N.Y. Experimental electric cars. About 100 were made.

HENON
F
See "S.U.P."

HENRIETTA
USA 1901
Henrietta Motor Co., New York, N.Y. Steam car.

HENRIOD
CH 1896–1898
Henriod Freres, Bienne. Steam and gasoline cars.

HENRIOD
F 1898–1908
Henriod et Cie., Neuilly/Seine. Light water- and air-cooled cars.

HENRY
USA 1899
John C. Henry, Denver, Colorado. Electric carriage.

HENRY
USA 1910–1912
D.W. Henry. Henry Motor Car Co., Muskegon, Michigan. Bankrupt 1912. 1909 succeeded Gary Motor Car Co.

HENRY GREY
USA 1912
Henry Grey, Los Angeles, California. One car produced.

HENRY J
USA 1950–1954
Kaiser-Frazer Corp., Willow Run, Michigan. 126,000 cars were made. Cars were assembled in J, NL and IL.
See "Allstate."

HENSCHEL
D 1899–1906
Berliner Maschinenfabrik Henschel & Co., Berlin. Electric and gasoline cars.

HE-PING
PRC 1958–1974 ?
Automobile Repair Works, Tientsin, Hopei. The first models resembled the "Plymouth" (USA) of the period.

HÉRALD
F 1901–1906
Sté. Hérald, Levallois-Perret/Seine. Voiturette.

HERBERT
GB 1916–1917
Herbert Light Car Co., London. Light car.

HERCULES
CH 1902–1903
Hercules AG, Menziken. Chain-driven cars.

HERCULES
D 1932–1934
Nürnberger Hercules-Werke AG, Nürnberg. Three-wheelers.

HERCULES
E 1922
Juan Antonio Orus. Cyclecar.

HERCULES
USA 1902
Smith Stamping Factory, Milwaukee, Wisconsin. Electric car.

HERCULES
USA 1906–1907
James MacNaughton Co., Buffalo, N.Y. Electric car.

HERCULES
USA 1914–1915
Hercules Motor Car Co. Hercules Automobile Co. Hercules Sales Co., New Albany, Indiana. Kentucky Wagon Mfg. Co., Louisville, Kentucky. Former "Crown" and "Ohio Falls" cars.

HERCULES
USA 1919
The Hercules Corp., Evansville, Indiana. Electric car.

HERDMAN SPARTAN
CH 1977–c. 1980
Herdman Cars, Sportcar Center, Hornussen. Sports cars.

HERFF-BROOKS
USA 1914–1916
Herff-Brooks Corp., Indianapolis, Indiana. Absorbed Marathon Motor Works.
See "Marathon" (1908–1914). Touring cars.

HERITAGE
USA 1989–c. 1993
Heritage Motor Cars Inc., Miami, Florida. Replicars.

HERKIMER
USA 1903–1904; 1910
James A. Clark Co., Utica, N.Y.

HERMAN
USA 1900
M.P. Herman, Harrisburg, Pennsylvania. Steam car.

HERMES
BI 1906–1909
SA Hermes, Bressoux, Liege. Hermes Italiana SA, Napoli. Sports cars.

HERMES
GB
See "Accles-Turrell."

HERMES
USA 1913
Hermes Motor Car Co., Cincinnati, Ohio.

HERMES
USA 1920
Tsacomas Desmos, New York, N.Y. Built for export to Greece only.

HERMES ITALIANA
I 1906–1908
Hermes Italiana, Roma; Napoli.

HERMES-SIMPLEX
D 1904–1906
E.E.C. Mathis, Sté. Alsacienne de Construction Mécanique, Graffenstaden. Sports roadster.

HERMITAGE
USA 1912
Hermitage Motor Co., Nashville, Tennes.
See

HERMON
GB 1936
Hermon Car Co. Ltd., Orpington, Kent; Bolney, Sussex. Light cars.

HERO
D 1933
"Hero"-Werke Fr. E. Rothe, Gera/Thür. Three-wheeler.

HERON
GB 1904–1905
Heron Motor Co., Birmingham. Conventional 10, 12 and 14 hp cars.

HERON
GB 1924–1926

Strode Engineering Works, Herne, Kent. Light car with plywood body and an engine mounted on a subframe.

HERON
GB 1961–1965
Heron Plastics Ltd., London. Sports kit cars.

HERON
GB 1987
Heron Power, Crowley, West Sussex. Three-wheeler.

HERRESHOFF
USA 1880
Herreshoff Engine Co., Providence, Rhode Island. Steam car.

HERRESHOFF
USA 1909–1914
Herreshoff Motor Co., Detroit, Michigan. Later Herreshoff Motor Car Co. Touring cars.

HERRESHOFF LIGHT CAR
USA 1914
Herreshoff Motor Co., Troy, N.Y. Herreshoff Light Car Co., Mechanicsville, N.Y.

HERRMANN
USA 1905
Herrmann Automobile Co., Tell City, Indiana

HERSCHELL-SPILLMAN
USA 1901–1904; 1907
Herschell-Spillman Mfg. Co., North Tonawanda, N.Y. Touring cars.

HERSCHMANN
USA 1901–1903
Columbia Engineering Works, Brooklyn, N.Y. Commercial Automobile Co., New York, N.Y. Steam car.

HERTEL
USA 1895–1900
Max Hertel, Chicago, Illinois. Reorganized 1898 as Oakman Motor Vehicle Co., Greenfield, Massachusetts. By 1899 there was no mention of "Hertel" in "Oakman" publicity.

HERTZ
USA 1925–1927
Yellow Cab Mfg. Co., Chicago, Illinois. Formerly "Ambassador." General Motors control in 1925. A "Drive It Yourself" rental car.

HERZ & SCHRÖTER
A 1921–1922
Autowerke Herz & Schröter, Wien. Light car.

HERZOG
D 1981
Herzog Sportwagen GmbH, Duren. Sports car.

HERZOG
D
See "Conte."

HESELTINE
USA 1916–1917
Heseltine Motor Corp., Buffalo, N.Y. Succeeded "Gadabout."

HESS
USA 1902
Hess Steam Vehicle Co., Philadelphia, Pennsylvania. Steam vehicle. Charcoal burner manufacturer.

HESSE
USA 1895
Gregory C. Hesse, New York, N.Y.

HEULIEZ
F 1925–present
Groupe Henri Heuliez, Colombes. Prototypes, sports cars.

HEUSCHMID
D c. 1987
Heuschmid Tuning, Benningen. Tuning.

HEWITT
USA 1906–1907
William Hewitt Motor Co., New York, N.Y. Formerly Standard Motor Construction Co.
See "Standard." (1904–1905) and "United States Long Distance."

HEWITT-ADAMS
GB
See "Hewitt," "Adams."

HEWITT-LINDSTROM
USA 1990–1902
Hewitt-Lindstrom Electric Co., Chicago, Illinois. Electric car.

HEXE
D 1905–1907
Achenbach & Co., Hamburg. 2- and 4-cylinder cars.

HEYBOURN
GB 1914
A.W. Heybourn & Co., Maidenhead, Berks. Cyclecar.

HEYMAN
USA 1901–1904; 1907
Edward Heyman, Boston, Massachusetts. Five-cylinder rotary motor.

HEYMANN
USA 1898–1904
Heymann Motor Vehicle and Mfg. Co., Melrose, Massachusetts.

HF
D 1985–1987
HF Auto-Spezial-Service, Offenbach am Main. Tuning.

H.F.
USA 1902
H.F. Construction Co., New London, Connecticut.

H.F.G.
GB 1920–1921
Portass & Son Ltd., Sheffield, Yorks. Light car.

H.H.
D 1906–1907
Hüttis & Hardebeck Motorwagenfabrik, Aachen. 10, 24 and 28 hp models. Brand-name "Ferna" was also used.
See "Hüttis & Hardebeck."

HIAWATHA
USA 1903–1904
Hiawatha Mfg. Co., Hiawatha, Kansas.

HIBBARD & BUSH
USA 1902
W.L. Hibbard & W.J. Bush, Fond du Lac, Wisconsin. Runabout.

HICKEY TRAIL-BLAZER
USA 1961–?
Trail-Blazer, Downey, California. Four-wheel drive cross-country vehicle.

HICKS
USA 1899–1900
John C. Hicks. Hicks Motorcycle Co., Chicago, Illinois. Five-wheeler. Fifth wheel in center of rear axle for driving.

HICO
USA 1900
John C. Hicks, Chicago, Illinois. Believed to be "Hicks" (5-wheeler) misspelled.

HIDALGO
I 1969
Aerostyle C. Sports car prototype.

HIDIEN
F 1898–1902
E. Hidien, Chatillon-sur-Indre. Some 20 voiturettes were made.

HIDLEY
USA 1901
Hidley Automobile Co., Troy, N.Y. Steam car.

HIGDON
USA 1905–1907
John C. Higdon, St. Louis, Missouri. Seven cars built. Sold 980 motor buggies.

HIGDON & HIGDON
USA 1896
John L. Higdon, Kansas City, Missouri.

HIGHGATE
GB 1903–1904
Highgate Motor Co., London. Light car.

HIGHLAND
AUS 1894
Annandale, N.S.W.

HIGHLANDER
USA 1919–1922
Frankfort Motor Car Co., Indianapolis, Indiana. Midwest Motor Co., Kansas City, Missouri.

HIGH TECH
F 1995
High Tech Automobiles, Langres. Sports cars.

HILDEBRAND
D 1922–1924
Martin Hildebrand Automobilwerke AG, Singen. Small three-seater.

HILDEBRAND
USA 1895; 1897 (1900–1901?)
J.A. Hildebrand. R.F. McMullin Co., Chicago, Illinois.

HILL
USA 1868–1870; 1885
James F. Hill, Fleetwood, Pennsylvania. Steam/gasoline buggy.

HILL
USA 1900
C.C. Hill Automobile Co., Chicago, Illinois.

HILL
USA 1901
J.J. Hill Co., Knightsville, Rhode Island. Became "Rhode Island."

HILL
USA 1904–1908
Hill Automobile Co. Hill Motor Car Co., Haverhill, Massachusetts.

HILL & STANIER
GB 1914
R. Hill, Stanier & Co., Newcastle-upon-Tyne. Cyclecar.

HILL CLIMBER
USA 1904–1905
Hill Climber Auto Mfg. Co., San Francisco, California.

HILLE
D 1898
Hille-Werke AG, Dresden. Three-wheeler.

HILLEN
NL 1912–1914
V.A. Hillen & Co., Jutphaas.

HILLER
D 1924–1927
Hiller Automobilfabrik AG, Berlin. "Ego" cars were assembled.

HILL LOCOMOTOR
USA 1896; 1901
Hill & Cummings, Chicago, Illinois.

HILLMAN
GB 1907–1978
Hillman-Coatalen Motor Car Co. Ltd., Coventry (1907–1909). Hillman Motor Car Co. Ltd., Coventry (1910–1946); Ryton-on-Dunsmore, Warwickshire (1946–1970); Linwood, Glasgow (1963–1970); Chrysler UK Ltd., Ryton-on-Dunsmore, Warwickshire; Linwood, Glasgow (1970–1978). Passenger cars.

HILLSDALE
USA 1908
Hillsdale Motor Co., Hillsdale, Michigan.

HILTON
USA 1920–1921. Motor Sales & Service Co., Riverton, New Jersey. Introduced August 13, 1920. 4-cylinder coupe.

HINDE
NL 1899
See "Van Gink."

HINDUSTAN
IND 1951–present
Hindustan Motors Ltd., Uttarpara, Hooghly, West Bengal. "Morris" (GB) based vehicles.

HINES
USA 1908–1910
Moehlhauser Machine Co. National Screw & Tack Co., Cleveland, Ohio. Touring cars.

HINMAN
USA 1906
J.A. Hinman, ? 2-cylinder 16 hp car.

HINO
J 1953–1968
Hino Motors Ltd., Tokyo. "Renault" (F) 4CV built first, later own design. In 1967 Hino joined the "Toyota" group.

HINSTIN
F 1920–1926
SA des Établissements Jacques Hinstin, Maubeuge/Nord. Light cars.

HIRANO
J 1936–1940
Nagoya. Three-wheelers.

H.I.S.A.
B I.
See "Hermes."

HISPANO-ALEMAN
E 1970
BMW Importados, Madrid. "Lotus" (GB) based sports car with BMW (D) engine.

HISPANO-ARGENTINA
RA 1940–1941
Hispano-Argentina Fabrica de Automoviles SA, Buenos Aires. 6-cylinder Diesel-engine powered large cars; small cars.

HISPANO-SUIZA
E 1904–1944
SA Hispano-Suiza, Barcelona. High-quality touring and sports cars.

HISPANO-SUIZA
F 1911–1938
Sté. Francaise Hispano-Suiza, Levallois-Perret/Seine (1911–1914); Bois-Colombes/Seine (1914–1938). High-quality touring cars.

HISPARCO
E 1925–1928
P. del Arco y Compania, Madrid. Small sports car.

HITCHCOCK
USA 1909
Hitchcock Motor Car Co., Warren, Michigan.

HITCHON-WELLER
USA
See "Globe."

H.K.
F 1907
AS de Kostka, Paris. Light cars.

H.L.
F 1912–1914
Hainsselin et Langlois, St. Cloud/Seine-et-Oise. 2.1-, 2.6- and 3-litre cars.

H.L.B.
GB 1914
H.L.B. Motors, London. Steam car.

H-M
USA 1982
H-M Vehicles, Inc., Burnsville, Minnesota. Gas and electric car.

H.M.C.
GB 1913
Hendon Motor Cycle Co. Ltd., London. Cyclecar.

H.M.C.
GB 1993–present
H.M.C. Sportscars Ltd., Stroud, Gloucestershire. Sports car.

HME
D 1994
HME Elektroautomobile, Passau. Electric cars.

HOBART BIRD
GB c. 1904
Three-wheeler.

HOBBIE ACCESSIBLE
USA 1908–1910
Hobbie Automobile Co., Hampton, Iowa. Highwheelers.

HOBBS
USA 1903
John O. Hobbs. Self-starting. Became "Lorraine."

HOBBYCAR
F 1992–1995
Hobbycar S.A., Thenay. 4 × 4 vehicles.

HODGETTS
USA 1908
W.J. Hodgetts, Wallingford, Connecticut. 7-passenger touring car.

HODGSON
GB 1924–1925
Hodgson Motors, Leeds, Yorks. Sports cars.

HODGSON
USA 1902
Dr. A.J. Hodgson, Waukesha, Wisconsin. Runabout.

HODKINS
USA 1913
Pierce N. Hodkins, Glucester, Massachusetts. Steam vehicle.

HOFELE
D 1995–1997
Hofele-Design, Donzdorf. Tuning, convertibles.

HOFER
D 1971
Max Hofer, Munchen. "Volkswagen" (D) 1500/1600 based sports car.

HOFFMAN
D 1901–1904
Hoffman Automobile Mfg. Co., Cleveland, Ohio. Steam car. Formerly Hoffman Bicycle Co. Became "Royal Tourist." Name changed to Royal Motor Car Co. Later gasoline cars.

HOFFMAN
USA 1931
Roscoe C. Hoffman, Detroit, Michigan. Front-wheel drive.

HOFFMANN
D 1954–1955
Jakob Osswald Hoffmann, Lintorf. Minicars, very similar to the "BMW" Isetta. 110 were built.

HOFFWEBER
USA 1914
Hoff Motor Co., Detroit, Michigan.

HOFLACK
B 1901
Francois Hoflack, Ypres. Voiturette.

HOFMANN
USA 1909
Josef Hofmann, Aiken, South Carolina.

HOFMANN & CZERNY
A 1906–1910
Continental Musik-Werke Hofmann & Czerny, Wien. Voiturette.

HOFSTETTER
BR 1986–1994
Hofstetter Tecnodesign, , Ind. e Com. de Veiculos Ltda., São Paulo. Sports cars.

HOLBEIN
D 1949
Small car.

HOLBORN
GB
See "McLachlan."

HOLBROOK
USA 1912
Holbrook-Armstrong Co., Racine, Wisconsin.

HOLCAR
GB 1897–1905
M. Holroyd-Smith, London. V-2 and V-4 engines.

HOLCOMB
USA 1913
American Box Ball Co., Indianapolis, Indiana.

HOLDEN
AUS 1948–present
General Motors, Holden's Pty. Ltd., Melbourne, Victoria; Woodville, S.A. Passenger cars. American and British General Motors products were assembled first.

HOLDEN
USA 1914
George B. Holden. Indian Cycle Co., Springfield, Massachusetts. Cyclecar.

HOLDEN
USA 1915
Clarence Holden, Comanche, Texas. Three-wheeler.

HOLDSWORTH
GB 1903–1904
Light Car & Motor Engineering Co. Ltd., Birmingham. Light car.

HOLKA-DKW
CH 1935–1945
Ernst Göhner, Holka AG, Altstätten. "DKW" (D) license. 1674 cars were made.

HOLLAND
USA 1898–1908
Sam Holland, Park River, North Dakota. Runabout.

HOLLAND
USA 1902–1903
Holland Automobile Co., Jersey City, New Jersey. Also built "Boisselot."

HOLLAND
USA 1910
Holland Automobile Mfg. Co., Holland, Michigan.

HÖLLER
A 1971–1973
Gerhard Höller, Kraubath. Sports car kit.

HOLLEY
USA 1897; 1900–1904
George M. Holley. Bovaird & Sefang Mfg. Co. Holley Bros. (Holley Motor Co.), Bradford, Pennsylvania. Became Bradford Motor Works.

HOLLIER
USA 1915–1921
Lewis Spring & Axle Co., Jackson, Michigan; Chelsea, Michigan. 1922 Hollier Automobile Co. 3,643 cars were made. 1914 built "Briscoe" chassis.

HOLLIS
USA 1922
Hollis Tractor Co., Tiffin, Ohio. Electric car. First car built in Hollywood, California.

HOLLOWAY
USA 1901
Henry Holloway, Gilroy, California. Steam car.

HOLLY
USA 1913–1915
Holly Motor Co., Mt. Holly, New Jersey.
See "Otto-Mobile."

HOLMES
USA 1900
Frank C. Holmes, Binghamton, N.Y.

HOLMES
USA 1902
Robert Holmes & Sons, Danville, Illinois. Steam car.

HOLMES
USA 1906–1908
Holmes & Childs Motor Co. Holmes Motor Vehicle Co., East Boston, Massachusetts.

HOLMES
USA 1917–1923
Holmes Automobile Mfg. Co., Canton, Ohio. Air-cooled. 4,201 cars were built.

HOLMES GAS TRICYCLE
USA 1895
Lyman S. Holmes, Gloversville, N.Y.

HOLSMAN
USA 1902–1912
Holsman Automobile Co., Chicago, Illinois; Plano, Illinois. Highwheelers. 6,348 cars were made.

HOLSON
USA 1901–1904
A.B. Holson, Chicago, Illinois.

HOLSON ELECTRIC
USA 1904–1905
Holson Motor Patents Co., Grand Rapids, Michigan.
See "Autolet" electric.

HOLT
USA 1899
Pliny E. Holt, Stockton, California.

HOL-TAN
USA 1908
Hollander & Tangeman, New York, N.Y. Roadsters. Built by Moon Motor Car Co. Company formerly New York "Fiat" Dealer.

HOLTOM
USA 1919; 1934
Clyde Cars Co., Clyde, Ohio. New York, N.Y. Also built "Clydesdale" trucks.

HOLTZER-CABOT
USA 1892–1895
Holtzer-Cabot Electric Co., Brookline, Massachusetts. Built-to-order electric vehicles. 1892 car built for Fiske Warren.

HOLZER
D 1993–1996
Holzer Motorsport, Augsburg. Tuning.

HOLYOKE
USA 1899–1903
Holyoke Motor Works. Holyoke Automobile Co., Holyoke, Massachusetts. Runabouts. Became Matheson Motor Car Co.
See "Matheson."

HOLZAPFEL
USA c. 1905
F.E. Holzapfel, Springfield, Massachusetts.

HOMARK
GB 1983
Homark Workshop, Poole, Dorset. "Ford" (USA) T-Type replicars.

HOMER-LAUGHLIN
USA 1916–1918
Homer-Laughlin Engineering Corp., Los Angeles, California. Four-wheel drive.

HOMESTEAD
USA 1900
Homestead Motor Vehicle Co., Homestead, Pennsylvania.

HOMMEL
F 1994–present
Automobiles Michel Hommel, Loheac. Sports cars.

HONDA
J 1962–present
Honda Motor Co. Ltd., Tokyo. Passenger and sports cars.

HONEY BEE
USA 1959
Swift Mfg. Co., El Cajon, California. Fiberglass-bodied three-wheelers.

HONG-QI
PRC 1958–present
No. 1 Automobile Plant, Changchun, Kirin, Manchuria. FAW — First Automobile Works, Changchun, Jiin.

HÖNIG
CS 1926
Ing. Frantisek Hönig a spol., Hodonín. 2-seater electric car.

HOOCKS
D 1928
Hoocks & Co., Köln. Three-wheeler.

HOOD
USA 1899–1901; 1908–1910
R.O. Hood. Simplex Motor Vehicle Co., Danvers, Massachusetts. Steam and gasoline cars.

HOOKER
USA c. 1905
Lyman S. Hooker, St. Johnsbury, Vermont. 4 hp automobile.

HOOPER
GB 1986–present
Hooper & Co. Ltd., London. Luxury cars based on "Bentley" and "Rolls-Royce." Coachbuilders since 1909.

HOOSIER LIMITED
USA 1907–1908
Coppock Motor Car Co., Decatur, Indiana.
See "Decatur."

HOOSIER SCOUT
USA 1914
Warren Electric & Machine Co., Indianapolis, Indiana. Cyclecar.

HOOVER
USA 1913–1914
H.H. Hoover, St. Louis, Missouri. Cyclecars.

HOPE
DK 1983–1984
Hope Automobil Industri A/S, Hadsund. Electric cars.

HOPKINS
USA 1902–1903
Hopkins Motor Carriage Co., Wellington, Massachusetts. E.P. Hopkins, New York, N.Y.

HOPPE & KROOSS
D 1929
Maschinenfabrik Hoppe & Krooss, Cuxhaven. Amphibian vehicle.

HOPPE & STREUR
USA 1935
Allen M. Hope & Allyn F. Streur, Hollywood, California. Streamlined prototype.

HOPPENSTAND
USA 1948–1949
Hoppenstand Motors Inc., Greenville, Pennsylvania. Aluminum-bodied small cars.

HÓRA-AURORE
H 1898
Hóra Nándor Müvek, Budapest. Voiturette. Later vans for post offices.

HORACK
USA 1902
Kittery, Maine.

HORBICK
GB 1902–1909
Horsfall & Bickham Ltd., Pendleton, Manchester. 2-, 4- and 6-cylinder tourers.

HORCH
D 1909–1939
A. Horch & Co., Köln (1900–1902). Reichenbach/Vogtland (1902–1904). Motorwagenwerke AG, Zwickau (1904–1939). Wide range from 2-cylinder 5 hp light cars to the V–12 6-litre coupe.

HORLEY
GB 1904–1907
Horley Motor & Engineering Co., Horley, Surrey. Light two-seater.

HÖRMANN
D 1985–present
Ing. E. Hörmann Motorsport, Kempten/Allgäu-St. Mang; Haldenwang. Tuning.

HORMIGER
E 1909–1912
Alvar Gonzalez, Gijon, Asturias. Light cars with marine engines.

HORNET
GB 1905–1907
Horner & Sons, London. Light car.

HORNET
USA 1970–1977
American Motors Corp., Detroit, Michigan.

HORNSTED
D GB.
See "Moll" (D).

HORSELESS CARRIAGE
USA 1901
Horseless Carriage Co., Barberton, Ohio.

HORSEY HORSELESS
USA 1899
Uriah Smith, Battle Creek, Michigan. "Haynes-Apperson" with horse head and rigged with reins.

HORSTMANN
GB 1914–1929
Horstmann Cars Ltd., Bath, Somerset. Light and sports cars.

HORSTMOBILE
USA 1973
1920s car replica.

HORTEK
PL 1950
Light car prototype.

HORTON
USA 1910
Horton Autoette Mfg. Co., Detroit, Michigan.

HOSKINS
USA 1920
G.J. Hoskins & Sons, Los Angeles, California. Touring cars.

HOSKYNS
GB 1988–1993
Hoskyns Group plc, London. Electric cars designed by Karl Joe Schwarzkopf-Bowers.

HOSTACO
NL c. 1955
"Fuldamobil" (D) license.

HOT-CAR
I 1972
Milano. Dune buggy.

HOTCHKISS
F 1903–1955
Hotchkiss et Cie. (1903–1936). Automobiles Hotchkiss, St. Denis, Seine (1936–1955). Sports and racing cars with 18.8-litre engine in 1905; later smaller touring and sports cars.

HOTCHKISS
GB 1920
Hotchkiss et Cie., Coventry, Warwickshire. Prototype only.

HOTZENBLITZ
D 1988–c. 1996
Hotzenblitz-Mobile GmbH & Co. KG, Ibach. Electric cars.

HOUARD
B 1900
Houard Cie., Gent. Voiturette.

HOUGHTON
USA 1900–1901
Houghton Automobile Co., West Newton, Massachusetts. Steam car.

HOULBJERG
DK 1913–1921
C. Houlbjerg, Odense. Ballot engine. About 30 cars were made.

HOUPT
USA 1909–1910
Harry S. Houpt Mfg. Co., New York, N.Y. Factory at Bristol, Connecticut. 1010 became New Departure Mfg. Co. Afterwards "Houpt-Rockwell."

HOUPT-ROCKWELL
USA 1910–1912
New Departure Mfg. Co., Bristol, Connecticut. Succeeded "Houpt."

HOUSE
USA 1898–1899; 1901
The Steam Car Co., Bridgeport, Connecticut. Steam car.

HOUSE
USA 1906
Harry House, Cheyenne, Wyoming.

HOUSER
USA 1906
Orville Houser, Chilicothe, Ohio.

HOUSE STEAMER
USA 1867

Henry A. & James House, Bridgeport, Connecticut. Steam car. Henry A. House built also "Lifu" steam trucks in England.

HOWARD
GB 1913
Howard Motor Works, Sutton, Surrey. Cyclecar.

HOWARD
USA 1895–1903
The Howard Cycle Co., Trenton, New Jersey. Became Howard Automobile Co.
See "Howard Steamer."

HOWARD
USA 1901
Grant-Ferris Co., Troy, N.Y.

HOWARD
USA 1903–1908
Howard Automobile Co., Yonkers, N.Y. Succeeded Trojan Launch & Autoworks, Troy, N.Y.

HOWARD
USA 1908
Howard Motor Works, Yonkers, N.Y. Sold assembled or unassembled cars.

HOWARD
USA 1911
Howard Automobile Co., Jackson, Michigan; Macon, Georgia.

HOWARD
USA 1913–1914
Central Car Co., Connersville, Indiana. Also Howard Motor Car Co. Succeeded Lexington Motor Car Co. as Lexington-Howard Co. Large 6-cylinder cars.
See "Lexington" (1909–1928).

HOWARD
USA 1911; 1916–1917; 1919
A.Howard Co., Galion, Ohio. Open five-seater with 6-cylinder 5-litre engine.

HOWARD
USA 1928–1929
Howard Motors Corp., Detroit, Michigan. Howard Motor Internaional Co., New York, N.Y. Former Acme Brass Co. 6-cylinder cars.

HOWARD STEAMER
USA 1901–1902
Howard Automobile Co., Trenton, New Jersey. Succeeded Howard Cycle Co.

HOWE
USA c. 1905
Leonard H. Howe, Dorchester, Massachusetts. 8 hp automobile.

HOWELL
USA 1900
Wisconsin Wheel Works Co. Racine, Wisconsin.
See "Mitchell."

HOWETT
GB 1913
Fowler's Garage, Birmingham. Cyclecar.

HOWEY
USA 1907–1908
Howey Motor Car Co., Kansas City, Missouri. Highwheelers.

HOWICK
USA
See "Fenton," "Elgin."

HOWMET T.X.
USA 1968
Howmet Corp., New York, N.Y.

HOYT
USA 1899–1901
A.H. Hoyt, Penacook, New Hampshire. Steam cars.

H.P.
F 1913
Cyclecar.

H.P.
GB 1926–1928
Hilton-Peacey Motors, Woking, Surrey. Cyclecars.

H.P.M.
USA c. 1921
H.P.M. Motors, Inc., New York, N.Y.
See "Moller."

H.R.G.
GB 1936–1956
H.R.G. Engineering Co. Ltd., Tolworth, Surrey. Only 156 sports cars were built.

HRUBON
F 1980–c. 1985
Sté. Hrubon, Guebviller. 50cc minicars.

HS
D 1994–?
HS Automobilbau International AG, ?. "AC" (GB) Cobra replicars.

H.S.M.
GB 1913–1915
H.S.M. Motors, London. Three-wheeler.

H.T.
D 1925
Hans Thiele, Kraftfahrzeugbau, Berlin. Light car.

H.T.V.
USA 1968–1973
Bermoco Inc., Berkeley, California. Dune buggy.

HUASCAR
F
See "Galba."

HUB
USA 1899–1900
Hub Motor Co., Chicago, Illinois. Electric car.

HUB
USA 1906
Hub Automobile Co., Boston, Massachusetts.

HUB
USA 1907
Hub Motor Car Exchange, Dorchester, Massachusetts. Runabout.

HUBBARD
GB 1904
Three-wheeler.

HUBER
USA 1894
Ide-Sprung-Huber Automobile Co., Oxford, Michigan.

HUBER
USA 1903–1907
Huber Automobile Co., Detroit, Michigan.

HUBER
USA 1909
Emil Huber, Davenport, Iowa. Runabout prototype.

HUBERT
USA c. 1905
Moise J. Hubert, Spencer, Massachusetts. 2.7 hp automobile.

HUDEC
A/CS 1902
Bohumil Hudec, továrna na velocipedy, motocykly a automobily, Čáslav. Voiturette with DeDion engine.

HUDEČEK
CS 1924
Ladislav Hudeček, Praha. Light car.

HUDLASS
GB 1897–1902
Phoenix Motor Works, Southport, Lancs. First car of Felix Hudlass' own design; later models followed "Benz" (D) principles.

HUDSON
GB 1991–?
Hudson Components Cars WKG, Norwich. Three-wheelers.

HUDSON
USA 1899–1902
Hudson Gas Motor & Vehicle Mfg. Co., Saratoga Springs, N.Y.

HUDSON
USA 1909–1957
Hudson Motor Car Co., Detroit, Michigan. Company founded February 24, 1909. Started production July. First 1,100 cars were 1909 models. Merged with Nash-Kelvinator Corp. into American Motors Corp. 1954.

HUDSON STEAM
USA 1904
C.J. Hudson, Cobington, Georgia.

HUDSON STEAMER
USA 1901–1902
Beau Chamberlain Mfg. Co., Hudson, Michigan. Also known as "Bean-Chamberlain."

HUEBNER
USA 1914
O.E. Huebner, Brooklyn, N.Y. Electric cyclecar.

HUENE
USA 1901
E.A. Huene, Barberton, Ohio.

HUESTIS
USA c. 1905
Thomas B. Huestis, Bristol, Rhode Island. 4 hp car.

HUET
F 1935
Light car.

HUFFIT
F 1914
Huffit Cyclecars Co., Paris.

HUFFMAN
USA 1920–1925
Huffman Bros. Motor Co., Elkhart, Indiana. In August, 1920 stockholders asked receivership charging mismanagement and fraud. 690 cars were built.

HUGHES & ATKIN
USA 1899–1904
Hughes & Atkin Auto Carriage Co., Providence, Rhode Island. 18 steam cars built.
See "Rhode Island."

HUGOT
F 1897–1899; 1905
Voiturettes.

HUGOT ET PECTO
F
See "Hugot."

HUMBEE
J 1950–1962
Mitsui Seiki Kogyo Co. Ltd., Tokyo. Three-wheelers.

HUMBER
GB 1898–1978
Humber Ltd., Beeston, Notts. (1898–1908). Coventry (1898–1946). Ryton-on-Dunsmore, Warwickshire (1946–1970). Chrysler UK Ltd., Ryton-on-Dunsmore, Warwickshire (1970–1978). Passenger cars.

HUMBLE
AUS 1903
Humble & Sons, Geelong, Victoria. Four-seater tonneau.

HUMMER
USA 1991–present
AM General Corporation, Wayne, Michigan; South Bend, Indiana. 4 × 4 cars.

HUMMING BIRD
USA 1946
Talmadge Judd, Kingsport, Tennes.
See Small Convertible Coupe.

HUMO
NL 1920
N.V. Automobiel- en Viegtuigfabriek "Humo," Heemstede.

HUMPHREY
USA 1899
John D. Humphrey, New Britain, Connecticut.

HUMPHRIS
GB 1908–1909
Humphris Gear & Engineering Co. Ltd., Eastleigh, Hampshire. Patent gearbox in the rear axle.

HUNGERFORD ROCKET
USA 1929
Hungerford Brothers, Elmira, N.Y. Powered by either the usual engine or by a rocket.

HUNT
USA 1905
Hunt Automobile Co., San Diego, California.

HUNT
USA 1936–1940
J. Roy Hunt, Los Angeles, California. Steam cars.

HUNT & OSEN
USA 1900–1901
Osen & Hunt, San Jose, California. Runabout.

HUNTER
USA 1900
Hunter Gun & Cycle Works, Fulton, N.Y.

HUNTER
USA 1920–1921
Hunter Motor Car Co., Harrisburg, Pennsylvania. At least one chassis completed November 1920.

HUNTER
USA c. 1981
Chuck Hunter, Vintage Motor Works, Sonoma, California. Replicars.

HUNTER ELECTRIC
USA 1899–1903
Rudolph M. Hunter, Philadelphia, Pennsylvania. Last models built by Electric Vehicle Co.

HUNTER & STEUR
USA 1935
E.F. Hunter & Allyn F. Steur.

HUNTINGBURG
USA 1902–1903
Huntingburg Wagon Works, Huntingburg, Indiana. Runabout.

HUNTINGTON
USA 1906–1907
Huntington Automobile Co., Huntington, N.Y.
See "Merciless."

HUNT SPECIAL
USA 1910

Hunt & Hunt Automobile Specialists, San Diego, California. Built one five-passenger touring car.

HUOBAN
PRC 1997–present
Jiaxing Auto Design & Development Co. Ltd., Jiaxing, Zhejiang. Taxicabs.

HUPMOBILE
USA 1908–1941
Hupp Motor Car Co., Detroit, Michigan. Started delivering cars September 1908. Bought Chandel Factory and absorbed "Chandler" 1929. Operation suspended January 1936 to June 1937. End of production mid-summer, 1940.

HUPP-YEATS
USA 1910–1918
Hupp-Yeats Electric Car Co. Hupp Corp., Detroit, Michigan. June 1911 five Hupp Companies consolidated, except Hupp Motor Car Co. 1912, R.C.H. Corp. Electric cars.

HURACAN
E 1958
Barcelona. 197 cc minicars.

HURLINCAR
GB 1913–1916
Hurlin & Co. Ltd., London. Light cars.

HURMID
GB
 See "Hurst."

HURON
GB 1970–1972
Huron Auto Race Developments Ltd., Enfield, Middlesex (1970–1971); Cobham, Surrey (1971–1972). Sports cars.

HURON
USA 1911
Huron Motor Car Co., Detroit, Michigan.

HURRICANE
A 1971–1972
Custoka Kunststoffakarosserien, Kranbath. Sports cars.

HURST
D 1946–1950
Arthur Friedrich Hurst, Stuttgart; Mannheim. 250 cc minicars for handicapped persons.

HURST
GB 1900–1907
G. Hurst, London (1900–1906). Hurst & Middleton Ltd., London (1906–1907). 2-, 4- and 6-cylinder cars.
 See "Hurmid."

HURST & LLOYD
GB 1897–1900
Hurst & Lloyd, London. 2-cylinder tonneau.

HURTAN
E 1998–present
Talleres J. Hurtado SL, Maracena, Granada. Sports car replica.

HURTU
F 1896–1930
Compagnie des Autos et Cycles Hurtu, Albert/Somme; Neuilly/Seine; Rueil/Seine-et-Oise. Voiturette and light cars.

HUSELTON
USA 1911–1914
Edgar C. Huselton Co., Butler, Pennsylvania. 13 touring cars were built.

HUSQVARNA
S 1943
Husqvarna Vapenfabriks AB, Husqvarna. Three-wheelers.

HUSSEY
USA 1903
Hussey Automobile & Supply Co., Detroit, Michigan. Runabouts with tilting steering wheel.

HUSTLER
GB 1978–c. 1980
Interstyl, Moreton-in-Marsh, Gloucestershire. "Austin/Morris" Mini-Moke based small car.

HUTCHINS & BERLOW
USA c. 1905
Hutchins & Berlow, Dorchester, Massachusetts. 16 hp automobile.

HUTSON
GB 1984–1996
The Hutson Motor Co. Ltd., Bradford, West Yorkshire. Replicars.

HÜTTIS & HARDEBECK
D
Hüttis & Haardebeck, Aachen.
 See "H.H."

HUTTO
USA 1905
M.C. Hutto, Jacksonville, Florida. A few touring cars were made.

HUTTON
GB 1900–1905; 1908
J.E. Hutton Ltd., Northallerton, Yorks (1900–1902). Thames Ditton, Surrey (1903–1905). D.Napier & Son Ltd., London (1908). Voiturette and light cars.

HUVO
CH 1972
Hudec & Vondrák, Biel. Dune buggy.

HVM
CS 1948
Miloslav Hokes, Mělník & Miloslav Vejvoda, Přívazy. 250 cc minicar prototype.

H.W.M.
GB 1950–1956
H.W. Motors Ltd., Walton-on-Thames, Surey. Sports and racing cars.

H.W.O.
USA 1915–1917; 1921–1923
HWO Motors Corp., Chicago & Waukegan, Illinois (1915–1917). Milwaukee, Wisconsin (1920–1923).
 See "Ogren."

HYATTSVILLE
USA 1912
 See "Independence."

HYBRICON
USA 1983
Electric car.

HYDE
USA 1904
W.W. Hyde Co., Milwaukee, Wisconsin.

HYDRAMOTIVE
USA 1961–1962
Hydramotive Corp., Charlotte, North Carolina. Small diesel-engine car. One produced.

HYDRO
USA 1919
Hydro Motor Car Co., Cincinnati, Ohio.

HYDRO-CAR
USA 1901–1902
Automobile Dept., American Bicycle Co., Chicago, Illinois. Sometimes misspelled "Hydra-Car." Became "Toledo." Runabout.

HYDROCAR
USA 1917
George Monnot, Canton, Ohio. Amphibian.

HYDRO-CARBON
USA 1901–1903
Friedman Automobile Co., Chicago, Illinois.
See "Friedman."

HYDRO-IMP
USA 1948
Centerscope Products Inc., Glendale, California. Buckboard.

HYDROMETER
USA 1917
Automobile Boat Mfg. Co., Seattle, Washington. Amphibian car.

HYDROMOBIL
D 1903–1907
Pittler Hydromobil-Gesellschaft mbH, Berlin. Prototype with hydraulic transmission.

HYDROMOBILE
USA 1902
American Hydromobile Works, Winchester, Ohio.

HYDROMOTOR
USA 1914–1917
Automobile Boat Mfg. Co., Seattle, Washington. Became Hydromotor Car Mfg. Co. Indian Motor & Mfg. Co., Indianapolis, Indiana.

HYDRO STEAM
USA 1919
Hydro Engineering Co., Cincinnati, Ohio.

HYLANDER
USA 1919–1922
Midwest Motor Co., Kansas City, Missouri.
See "Highlander."

HYMMEN
D 1900; 1910
Maschinenfabrik Theodor Hymmen, Bielefeld. Light cars made to order.

HYSLOP
USA 1914
Hyslop & Clark, Toledo, Ohio. Cyclecar.

HYTHE
GB
See "New Century."

HYUNDAI
ROK 1967–present
Hyundai Industries Co. Ltd., Seodaemoonku, Seul. Hyundai Motor Co., Jongro Ku, Seoul. Passenger cars.

IAME
RA
IAME Industrias Aeronauticas y Mecanicas Estado, Cordoba.
See "Justicialista," "Institec."

I & F
USA 1910
I & F Motor Car Co., New Britain, Connecticut.

IATO
I 1985–1993
Iato SpA, Nusco. 4 × 4 vehicles.

IBERIA
E 1913–1914
Barcelona. Cyclecar.

IBIS
F 1907
Automobiles Ibis, Levallois-Perret/Seine. Light cars.

ICM
USA 1990s
ICM Industries, Burbank, California. Kit cars.

IDEAL
E 1915–1922
Taklleres Hereter SA, Barcelona. Touring and sports cars.

IDEAL
USA 1902–1904
Richmond & Holmes Co., St. Johns, Michigan.

IDEAL
USA 1902
Ideal Automobile Mfg. Co., New Castle, Indiana.

IDEAL
USA 1902–1903
B & P Co., Milwaukee, Wisconsin. Light two-seater.

IDEAL
USA 1903–1909
Ideal Motor Vehicle Co., Chicago, Illinois.

IDEAL
USA 1905–1906
Ideal Motor Car Co., Cleveland, Ohio.

IDEAL
USA 1906
Ideal Steam Automobile Co., S. Berwick, Maine. Steam car.

IDEAL
USA 1907–1908
Bethlehem Automobile Co., Bethlehem, Pennsylvania.

IDEAL
USA 1908
Godfrey Lund, Stanton, Nebraska. Auto-buggy.

IDEAL
USA 1908–1909
Ideal Mfg. Co., Portsmouth, Ohio.

IDEAL
USA 1909–1911
Ideal Electric Co., Chicago, Illinois. Electric cars. 1910 Borland-Grannis Co.

IDEAL
USA 1914
The Ideal Cyclecar Shop, Buffalo, N.Y. Cyclecar.

IDEAL LIGHT CAR
USA 1915–1916
Ideal Light Car Co., Columbus, Ohio.

IDEAL RUNABOUT
USA 1907
Ideal Runabout Mfg. Co., Buffalo, N.Y.

IDEN
GB 1904–1907
Iden Motor Car Co. Ltd., Coventry, Warwickshire. Front-wheel drive car in 1907.

IENA
I 1922–1925
Industria Economica Nazionale Automobili di Tommasi & Rizzi, Lodi. 1.1-litre light car.

IES
RA 1987
Modified "Citroën" (F) 2 CV.

IFA
DDR 1948–1956
Industrieverwaltung Fahrzeugbau, Zwickau (1948–1951); Eisenach (1952–1956). Two-stroke passenger cars.

IFG
USA 1990s
IFG Co., Chino, California. Kit cars.

IGALA
WAN 1975–c. 1978
Lagos. "Volkswagen" (D) 1600 license.

IGNIS
I 1963
Ignis, Comerio. "Hino" (J) Contessa license.

I.H.C.
USA 1907–1911
International Harvester Co., Chicago, Illinois. Highwheeler.
See "International." Both names apply to same vehicle.

I.H.C.
USA 1911
Independent Harvester Co., Plano, Illinois. Air-cooled highwheeler. Similar to "Holsman" highwheeler. Four-cylinder engine. Also called "Independent Harvester."

IHRIG
USA 1905
See "Goshen."

I.K.A.
RA 1958–1983
Industrias Kaiser Argentina, Buenos Aires.
See "Kaiser Carabela" and "Torino."

IKAR
BG 1972
Plovdiv. Sports car prototype.

IKARA
AUS
See "Bolwell."

IKENGA
GB 1969
Sports car prototype.

ILFORD
GB 1902–1903
Ilford Motor Car & Cycle Co., Ilford, Essex. Light car.

ILLINGA
AUS 1974–1975
Illinga Co., Melbourne. Two sports cars with Leyland V-8 engine were made.

ILLINOIS
USA 1905
Illinois Auto-Motor Co., Chicago, Illinois. 8-cylinder 35/40 hp car.

ILLINOIS
USA 1907
Moline Pump Co., Moline, Illinois. 20 hp runabout.

ILLINOIS
USA 1910–1914
Overholt Co. Illinois Automobile Co., Galesburg, Illinois. Roadsters. Succeeded "Overholt" highwheeler.

ILLINOIS
USA 1914
Illinois Cyclecar Co., Kankakee, Illinois. Cyclecar.

ILLINOIS ELECTRIC
USA 1897–1901
Illinois Electric Vehicle & Transportation Co., Chicago, Illinois.

ILORE
CS 1948
Viliam Rösch, Plzeň. 200 cc minicar prototype.

IL PAMPERO
GB 1914
J. Barron Ackroyd, Leeds. Cyclecar.

ILSE
D 1926
Stolberg-Hütte, Wernigerode/Harz. Light car.

ILYIN
SU 1910–1912
Sankt Peterburg. "La Buire" (F) license. Assembled also "Russo-Buire" in 1912.

IMC
FL 1986
International Motor Company, Vaduz. Small Jeep-type car.

IMESA
E 1983–present
Industrias Motrices Espanolas S.A., Pologono de Sabon-Arteixo. "Seat" based cars.

IMHOF
D 1932
Paul Imhof, Welschensteinbach. Three-wheeler.

IMHOF
USA 1900
J.I. Imhof, Racine, Wisconsin. Runabout.

IMMERMOBIL
D 1905–1907
Max Eisenmann & Co., Hamburg. DeDion engined voiturette.

IMMISCH
GB 1894–1897
Acme & Immisch Electric Works Ltd., London. Electric car.

IMP
CDN 1913
Holden-Morgan Co. Ltd., Toronto, Ontario.

IMP
I 1960–1963
Intermeccanica Puch, Torino. Sports cars.

IMP
USA 1914
Imp Cyclecar Co. W.H. McIntyre Co., Auburn, Indiana. Cyclecars designed by William B. Stout. Subsidiary of W.H. McIntyre Co. In hands of creditors' committee January 1915.

IMP
USA 1949–1951
International Motor Products Co., Glendale, California. 7 hp plastic bodied auxiliary cars.

IMPERIA
B 1906–1949
Automobiles Imperia, Liege; Nessonvaux (1906–1929). SA des Automobiles Imperia-Excelsior, Nessonvaux (1929–1949). Touring and sports cars.

IMPERIA
D 1924–1925; 1935
Imperia-Werk AG, Bad Godesberg. Streamlined three-wheeler.

IMPERIAL
GB 1900–1905
Imperial Autocar Manufacturing Co. Ltd., Manchester. Light cars.

IMPERIAL
GB 1904–1905
The Anti-Vibrator Co. Ltd., Croydon, Surrey. Electric car.

IMPERIAL
GB 1914
Implitico Ltd., London. Cyclecar.

IMPERIAL
USA 1900
Imperial Automobile Co., Chicago, Illinois.

IMPERIAL
USA 1900–1901
Philadelphia Motor Vehicle Co., Philadelphia, Pennsylvania.

IMPERIAL
USA 1903–1905
Rodgers & Co., Columbus, Ohio. Air-cooled cars 1904. Electrics 1905.

IMPERIAL
USA 1903–1905
Imperial Automobile Co., Detroit, Michigan. Electric cars.

IMPERIAL
USA 1906–1908
Imperial Motor Car Co., Williamsport, Pennsylvania. 5.5-litre Rutenber engine. Reported in hands of receivers October 1908.

IMPERIAL
USA 1908–1916
Imperial Automobile Co., Jackson, Michigan. Touring cars. Merged with "Marion" (1904–1915) in Mutual Motors Corp.

IMPERIAL
USA 1909
Imperial Motor Car Co., Hamilton, Ohio.

IMPERIAL
USA 1955–1975; 1981–1983
Chrysler Corp., Detroit, Michigan. Formerly "Chrysler Imperial." Emerged as separate make 1955.

IMPETUS
F 1899–1903
Max Hertel, Automobiles Impetus, Pornichet/Loire-Inferieure. Light cars.

IMP-MCINTYRE
USA 1915
W.H. McIntyre, Auburn, Indiana.

IMPROVED
USA 1901
Improved Gasoline Motor & Automobile Company, Haverhill, Massachusetts.
See "Foster."

IMV
YU 1955–c. 1986
IMV, Industrija Motornih Vozil, Novo Mesto. "DKW" (D) and "Fiat" (I) license.

IMZA
TR 1999
Jetpa Motors Co., Gunesli, Istanbul. Light car prototype. Production planned in Siirt factory from 2002, 100,000 cars per year.

INACAR
GB 1971
Handicapped three-wheelers.

INCAMP
E 1952
Bilbao. Minicar, only 12 were made.

INCONTRI
I 1905
Societa Italiana noc Trolley Automotori, Napoli

INDEPENDENCE
USA 1912
Independence Motor Co., Hyattsville, Maryland. H.O. Carter organized new company to take over plant of defunct Carter Motor Car Corp.

INDEPENDENCE
USA 1915
Independence Motor Car Co., Lima, Ohio; Atlanta, Georgia.

INDEPENDENT
USA 1903
Independent Automobile Mfg. Co., Sioux Falls, South Dakota.

INDEPENDENT HARVESTER
USA 1910–1911
Independent Harvester Co., Plano, Illinois.
See "I.H.C."

INDER
GB 1898
Henry J. Inder, Dartmouth. Three-wheeler prototype.

INDESTOR
I 1974
Torino. Dune buggy.

INDIAN
USA 1905–1927
Hendee Manufacturing Co., Springfield, Massachusetts. Roadsters.

INDIAN
USA 1909–1910
Indian Motor & Mfg. Co., Indianapolis, Indiana. Indian Motor Car Co., Franklin, Indiana.

INDIAN
USA 1920
Indian Motorcycle Co., Springfield, Massachusetts. Prototypes only. Plant built to build car. Sold to Wire Wheel Co., then to "Rolls-Royce" (USA).

INDIAN
USA 1927
Indian Motorcycle Co., Springfield, Massachusetts. Midget car prototype only.

INDIANA
USA 1901
Indiana Motor & Vehicle Co., Indianapolis, Indiana.

INDIANA
USA 1904
Indiana Scale & Truck Co., Bluffton, Indiana.

INDIANAPOLIS
USA 1899
Indianapolis Automobile and Vehicle Co., Indianapolis, Indiana. Formerly C.H. Black Co.
See "Black."

INDIAN TRICAR
USA 1905
Hendee Mfg. Co., Springfield, Massachusetts.

INDIGO
S 1998–present
Jösse Car AB, Arvika. Sports cars.

INDIO
U 1969–?
General Motors Uruguaya S.A., Montevideo. Simple passenger car/light van.

INDUCO
F 1922–1925
Automobiles Induco, Puteaux/Seine. About 20 cars were built.

INDUHAG
D 1922–1924
Industrie- und Handels-Gesellschaft mbH, Düsseldorf. Three-wheeler.

INFINITI
J 1989–present
Nissan Motors Ltd., Chuo-ku, Tokyo. Name for "Nissan" luxurious cars.

INGERSOLL-MOORE STEAMER
USA 1885–1895
Ingersoll-Moore, Bloomington, Illinois. Built a 4-wheel 2-seat vehicle 1888, 3-wheel and 6-wheel vehicles 1899. A car for the 1895 Chicago Times-Herald Race was designed but not completed by race day.

INGOT
USA 1915
Ingot Automobile Co., Calumet, Michigan.

INGRAM-HATCH
USA 1914–1917
Ingram-Hatch Co. Ingram-Hatch Motor Corp. Ingram-Hatch Motor Car Co., Rosebank, Staten Island, N.Y. Paraffin-burning 4-cylinder engine.

INMAN
USA 1946
Frank Inman, Goose Creek, Texas.

INNES
AUS 1905
Sydney, N.S.W.

INNES
USA 1920–1921
American Motors Export Co., Jacksonville, Florida. Roadsters.

INNOCENTI
I 1960–present
Societa Generale per l'Industria Metallurgica e Meccanica, Milano. Innocenti Milano SpA, Rozzano (Milano). "Austin" and "Austin-Healey" (GB) license. 1972 owned by the British Leyland Co. 1976 owned by the "De Tomaso" and in 1990 by "Fiat."

INNOTECH
CZ 1992–present
Innotech International s.r.o., Jaroměř. 400–750 hp sports cars.

INNOVARI
USA 1996
United States Steel Corporation. Front-wheel-driven experimental car.

INSTITEC
RA 1954–1955
Industrias Aeronauticas y Mecanicas Estado (IAME), Cordoba. 2-cylinder 2-stroke front-wheel drive car; "Justicialista" Sport powered by a "Porsche" (D) engine; some cars had an air-cooled 3-litre V-8 engine.
See "IAME."

INTER
F 1953–1956
S.N.C.A.N., Lyon. Three-wheelers.

INTERMECCANICA
I 1956–1976
Costruzione Automobili Intermeccanica, Torino. Sports car.

INTERMECCANICA
USA 1976–present
Automobiles Intermeccanica, Santa Ana, California. "Porsche" replica.

INTERNATIONAL
GB 1898–1904
International Motor Car Co., London. Light cars with French and German design influence.

INTERNATIONAL
USA 1899–1900
International Auto Co. International Auto & Vehicle Co., Boston, Massachusetts.

INTERNATIONAL
USA 1899–1904
International Power Co., Hartford, Connecticut; Providence, Rhode Island. Steam car.

INTERNATIONAL
USA 1900–1901
International Power Vehicle Co. International Motor Carriage Co., Stamford, Connecticut.
See "Klock."

INTERNATIONAL
USA 1907–1911
International Harvester Co., Chicago, Illinois; Akron, Ohio. Experimental 1901. Trucks after 1911. Also known as "I.H.C.," "International Auto Buggy," "Auto Wagon" and "Farmer's Auto."

INTERNATIONAL
USA 1909
International Automobile Co., Chicago, Illinois. Surrey.

INTERNATIONAL
USA 1914
International Cyclecar Co., New York, N.Y.
See "Economycar."

INTERNATIONAL
USA 1961–1980
International Harvester Co., Chicago, Illinois. 4 × 4 vehicles.

INTERNATIONALE
NL 1942
Internationale Automobiel Mij, Den Haag. Very light electric three-wheeler.

INTERSTATE
USA 1909–1919
Interstate Automobile Co., Muncie, Indiana. 1914 reorganized as Interstate Motor Co. Roadsters. 8,182 cars built.

INTERSTYL
GB 1978
William Towns, London. City car prototype.

INTERURBAN
USA 1905
F.A. Woods Auto Co., Chicago, Illinois. Front-wheel drive electric car.

INTREPID
USA 1903–1905
Rotary Motor Vehicle Co., Boston, Massachusetts.
See "Rotary." The name "Intrepid" used in advertisements and catalogue.

INTROZZI
I c. 1981
Officine Introzzi, Lipomo (Como). "Fiat" based special bodied cars.

INTRUDER
USA 1995
Mosler Automotive, Riviera Beach, Florida. High performance sports cars.

INVACAR
GB 1971–1975
Three-wheelers for handicapped. About 2500 cars built in 1974.

INVADER
GB 1971
Dune buggy.

INVICTA
GB 1900–1905
H.E. Richardson, London. Voiturette.

INVICTA
GB 1913–1914
Clark's Engineering Works, Leamington, Warwickshire. Cyclecar.

INVICTA
GB 1925–1938; 1946–1950
Invicta Cars, Cobham, Surrey (1925–1933); London (1933–1938). Invicta Car Development Co. Ltd., Virginia Water, Surrey (1946–1950). Sports cars.

INVICTA
I 1906
Stabilimento Meccanico Carlo Mantovani & Cia., Torino. Side-chain drive light cars.

IOTA
GB 1947–1952
Iota Racing Cars Ltd., Bristol. Sports cars.

IOWA
USA 1908–1909
Iowa Motor Car Co., Kellogg, Iowa.

IPE
D 1919–1921
Ipe Auto-Gesellschaft mbH, Berlin. Light cars.

IRADAM
PL 1925–1939
Inz. Adam Gluck-Gluchowski, Krakow. Rear-engine car prototypes.

IRAT
F 1946–1953
See "Georges Irat." Prototypes only.

IRIS
GB 1905–1915
Legros & Knowles Ltd., London (1905–1907). Iris Cars Ltd., London (1907–1909). Aylesbury, Bucks. (1909–1915). Crudely engineered machines.

IRMSCHER
D 1968–present
Irmscher GmbH, Remshalden-Grunbach. Tuning.

IROQUOIS
CDN 1906
Iroquois Motor Car Mfg. Co., Welland, Ontario.

IROQUOIS
USA 1903–1907
John S. Leggett Mfg. Co., Syracuse, N.Y. Became Iroquois Motor Co. February, 1905, and moved to Seneca Falls. Runabouts and touring cars.

IROQUOIS STEAMER
USA 1906–1908
Iroquois Iron Works, Buffalo, N.Y. One car built by W. Grant King.
See "King Steamer."

ISCA
I 1954
Industria Sanmarinese Costruzioni Automezzi, Milano.

ISDERA
D 1983–present
Isdera Styling Design und Racing GmbH, Leonberg-Warmbronn. Sports cars.

ISETTA
I 1953–1955
Iso SpA, Torino. Three-wheelers.
See "BMW" (D) and "V.E.L.A.M." (F).

ISHIKAWAJIMA
J 1916–1927
Ishikawajima Dockyard & Engineering Co. Ltd., Tokyo. Large sedan.

ISIS
CS 1923–1928
Ing. Frantisek Beutelschmidt a Ing. Ružička, Praha. Karel Krčil, Praha. About 20 sports cars with 1.1 and 1.5-litre engines were made.

ISIS
I 1960–1961
See "De Tomaso."

ISO
I 1953–1979
Autoveicoli S.p.A., Bresso (Milano) 1953–1974. Varedo (1974–1979). Sports cars.

ISOTTA FRASCHINI
I 1900–1949
Soc. Milanese d'Automobili Isotta Fraschini & C. (1900–1904). Fabbrica Automobili Isotta Fraschini (1904–1949), Milano. Large sports and touring cars.

ISOTTA FRASCHINI
I 1996
Isotta Fraschini Automobili, Cherasco. Sports cars with aluminium chassis and body.

ISOS
I 1954
Small car.

ISPANO-FRANCIA
F 1913–1920
V.P. Pelladeux, Biarritz. Voiturette.

I.S.S.I.
I 1953–1954
Istituto Scientifice Sperimentale Industriale SpA, Milano. Three-wheelers "Microbo."

ISUZU
J 1953–present
Isuzu Motors Ltd., Tokyo. Passenger cars.

I.T.
I 1950–1951
Italmeccanica, Torino. Sports cars.

ITALA
I 1904–1934
Itala Fabbrica Automobili (1904–1929). Itala (1929–1931). Itala Societa Anonima Costruzioni Automobilistiche — SACA (1931–1934), Milano. Touring and sports cars.

ITAL DESIGN
I 1991
Ital Design Srl, Moncalieri. Sports car "Nazca." Coachbuilders since 1968.

ITALIA
I 1907–108
Fabbrica Automobili Gallottini & Figlio, Bologna.

ITALJET
I 1972
Italjet Sas, S. Lazzaro di Savena, Bologna. Dune buggy.

ITALMECCANICA
I
See "I.T."

ITALSUISSE
CH 1960–1966
Carrosserie Italsuisse, Geneve-Carrouge. Sports car prototypes.

IVA
CS 1948
Alfréd Sequart, Praha. 125 cc minicar prototype.

IVANHOE
CDN 1903–1905
Canada Cycle & Motor Co., Toronto, Ontario. Electric cars.

IVEL
GB 1899–1906
Dan Albone, Biggleswade, Bedfordshire. Four-seater vis-à-vis.

IVERNIA
GB 1920
4.8-litre prototype.

IVERSON
USA 1902
J.E. Iverson & Co., Milwaukee, Wisconsin.

IVM
D 1998–present
IVM Technical Consultants, München. "Callaway" (USA) based sports cars.

IVOR
GB 1912–1916
Ivor Motors Ltd., London. 12/14 hp Ballot engined prototype.

IVRY
F 1906; 1912–1914
Automobiles Ivry, Ivry/Seine. Tricar; conventional cars.

IZARO
E 1920
Construcciones de Automoviles Izaro Srl, Madrid. 600 and 750 cc light cars.

IZH
SU/RUS 1967–present
Izhevskii Mashinostroitelnii Zavod. PO IzhMash, Izhevsk. Modified "Moskvitch."

IZZER
USA 1910
Irvington Izzer, Irvington, N.Y.

IZZER
USA 1910
Myer Carriage & Buggy Co., Peru, Indiana. Three runabouts were built.

J

JACK ENDERS
F 1914–1920
Enders Jack et Cie., Asnieres/Seine. Light car.

JACK FROST
USA 1903
Kammann Mfg. Co., Chicago, Illinois. Electric car.

JACKS
USA 1899–1900
Jacks Autobain Co., Napa, California. Runabout and roadster.

JACKSON
GB 1899–1915
Yorkshire Motorcar Mfg. Co. Ltd., Bradford, Yorks. (1899–1900). Reynold-Jackson & Co. Ltd., London (1903–1915). Cyclecars and light cars.

JACKSON
USA 1897
Byron Jackson Machine Works, San Francisco, California. Steam carriage.

JACKSON
USA c. 1905
Fritz W. Jackson, Barre, Vermont. 12 hp automobile.

JACKSON
USA 1903–1923
Jackson Motor Carriage Co. Jackson Automobile Co., Jackson, Michigan (1903–1919). Reorganized as Jackson Motor Corp. 1919. Absorbed Fuller Buggy Co. 1910. Absorbed with "National" and "Dixie-Flyer" into Associated Motor Industries. Renamed "National" (Model 651) 1923.
See "Duck," "Jaxon" and "Orlo." 21,567 cars were made.

JACKSON & KIMMYS
GB 1904
Three-wheeler.

JACOBSEN
DK 1902
G.V.J. Jacobsen, Kobenhavn. Light car.

JACQUEMONT
F 1922–1925
Automobiles Jacquemont, Paris. Cyclecars.

JACQUES MULLER
F 1920–1922
Jacques Muller, La Garenne-Colombes/Seine. Shaft-driven cyclecar.

JACQUET FLYER
USA 1920
Jacquet Flyer Motor Corp. of America, Belding, Michigan. 6.2-litre sports cars.

JAEGER
DK 1907
Aarhus.

JAEGER
USA 1932–1933
Jaeger Motor Car Co., Belleville, Michigan. Sports coupes.

JAF
F 1907
Jean-Auguste Feral. Voiturette.

J.A.G.
GB 1950–1952; 1954–1956
J.A.G. Cars, Thames Ditton, Surrey. R.G.S. Automotive Components Ltd., Windsor, Berks. Some 50 sports cars were built.

JAGO
GB 1971–c. 1993
Geoff Jago Custom Automotive, Chichester, Sussex. Jeep-type car and dune buggy.

JAGUAR
GB 1945–present
Jaguar Cars Ltd., Coventry, Warwickshire. High-performance touring and sports cars.
See "S.S."

JAMES
USA 1829–1833

William T. James, New York, N.Y. 6 steam cars were built.

JAMES
USA 1904
Alfred James Foundry Co., La Crosse, Washington.

JAMES
USA 1909–1911
J. & M. Motor Car Co., Lawrenceburg, Indiana. Motor buggy. Succeeded "Dearborn."

JAMES
USA 1914
Irving James, Los Angeles, California. Two cyclecars made.

JAMES & BROWNE
GB 1901–1910
Martineau & Browne (1901–1902). James & Browne Ltd., London (1902–1910). Horizontal engines.

JAMIESON
USA 1899–1900
Robert W. Jamieson, Rochester, N.Y. Steam carriage.

JAMIESON
USA 1902
M.W. Jamieson Co., Warren, Pennsylvania. Gasoline runabout.

JAMOS
A 1964
Rudolf Moser, Wien. Sports coupe powered by a 643 cc 2-cylinder Steur-Puch engine.

JAN
DK 1915–1918
Jan Hagemeister, Kobenhavn. Light cars.

JANÉMIAN
F 1920–1923
M. Janémian, Bievres/Seine-et-Oise. Cyclecars.

JANERY
USA c. 1905
John B. Janery, Uxbridge, Massachusetts. 3 hp automobile.

JANKEL
GB 1960–present
The Jankel Group, Weybridge, Surrey. Hand-built motor cars based on "Rolls-Royce," "Bentley," "Jaguar," "Range Rover," "Mercedes-Benz" (D), "BMW" (D), "Audi" (D), etc.

JANNEY
USA 1907
Janney Motor Co., Flint, Michigan. Absorbed by "Buick" 1907.

JANSEN
NL 1900–1901
B.A. Jansen, 's-Hertogenbosch. Voiturette.

JANSSENS
B 1902–1910
Ateliers A. Janssens, St. Nicholas. Front-wheel drive town car.

JANVIER
F 1903–1904
V. Janvier, Paris. 6-wheel car with front two steered axles.

JANVIER
F 1926–1928
Janvier, Sabin et Cie., Chatillon-sur-Bagneux/Seine. Sports cars.

JAPPIC
GB 1925
Jarvis and Sons, London. Chain-driven cyclecar.

J.A.R.
GB c. 1914
Cyclecar.

JARC
GB 1955
Jarc, Middlesex. Small car.

JARO
CS 1926–1927
Jaro, továrna automobilních vozidel, Jaroměřice. Light car.

JARRET
F 1968–1972
Jarret Frères, Paris. Electric three-wheeler.

JARVIS
USA 1902
Jarvis Engine Machine Co., Lansing, Michigan. Steam carriage.

JARVIS-HUNTINGTON
USA 1912
Jarvis Machine & Supply Co. Jarvis-Huntington Automobile Co., Huntington, West Virginia. 8-passenger touring cars.

JASZKOWIAK
USA 1902–1908
Frank Jaszkowiak, Bismarck, North Dakota. Gasoline wagon and touring car.

JAWA
CS 1934–1939; 1956–1958
Zbrojovka Ing. Fr. Janeček. Závody 9. Května, n.p., Praha. Two-stroke 2-cylinder cars. Minicar prototypes only in 1956–1958.

JAXON
USA 1902–1903
Jackson Automobile Co., Jackson, Michigan. Steam car.
See "Jackson."

JAY
USA 1907–1908
Webb-Jay Motor Co., Chicago, Illinois.
See "Webb-Jay" steam.

JAY CARTER
USA 1975
Steam car based on "Volkswagen" 1500 Variant chassis.

JAYCO
USA 1982
Jayco, Inc., Middlebury, Indiana. Sports car "Questor."
See "Questor."

JAY-EYE-SEE
USA 1914
J.I. Case Threshing Machine Co., Racine, Wisconsin.
See "Case."

J.B.
GB 1913
Turner Manufacturing Co., Wolverhampton. Cyclecar.

J.B.
GB 1926
Jones, Burton & Co. Ltd., Liverpool. Medium-sized car prototype.

J.B.A.
GB 1982–c. 1993
J.B.A. Engineering Ltd., Standish, Nr. Wigan. Replicars.

J.B.M.
GB 1947–1950
James Boothby Motors Ltd., Horley, Surrey; Crawley, Sussex. Light two-seater.

J.B. MINOR
AUS 1949
Jeffrey Brothers, Brisbane. Three-wheeler prototype.

J.B.R.
E 1921–1923
Jose Boniquet Riera, Barcelona. Cyclecars and light cars.

J.B.S.
GB 1913–1915
Light car.
  See "Bagshaw."

JDM
F 1987–1988
Simpa Cie., Avrille. City cars with Diesel motors.

J.D.S.
GB
  See "Deasy," "Siddeley-Deasy."

JEAN BART
F 1907
Automobiles Jean Bart, Nanterre/Seine. Renamed "Prosper-Lambert."

JEAN GRAS
F 1924–1930
SA des Automobiles Jean Gras, Lyon. Small sports cars. About 200 were made.

JEANNEAU
F 1974–present
Constructions Nautiques Jeanneau, Les Herbiers/Vendee. Two-seater "Microcar."

JEANNIN
USA 1908
Jeannin Auto Mfg. Co., St. Louis, Missouri. Highwheeler.

JEANPERRIN
F 1900
Jeanperrin Freres, Gray/Haute-Saone. Four-seater vis-à-vis.

JEANS
USA c. 1905
Charles L. Jeans, North Reading, Massachusetts. 3.5 hp automobile.

JEANTAUD
F 1881; 1893–1906
A. Jeantaud, Paris. Electric cars.

JEECY-VEA
B 1925–1926
Motos Jeecy-Vea, Bruxelles. Light cars.

JEEP
USA 1941–present
Willys-Overland, Inc. (1941–1953). Willys Motors, Inc. (1953–1963). Kaiser-Jeep Corp. (1963–1970). Jeep Corporation (1970–1987), Toledo, Ohio. Jeep-Eagle Division, Chrysler Corporation, Detroit, Michigan (1987–1998). During the Second World War the car was an Army general purpose vehicle. Similar cars built by the Ford Motor Co. and American Bantam Car Co., 1941–1945.

JEFE
RA 1956
Casa Fehling, Buenos Aires.

JEFFERY
USA 1914–1917
Thomas B. Jeffery Co. Nash Motors Co., Kenosha, Wisconsin. Succeeded "Rambler" (1902–1913). Company bought by Charles W. Nash in July 1916. Car renamed "Nash." Touring cars.

JEG
BR 1973–1984
Dacunha Veiculos & Mecanica S.A. QT Engenharia e Equipamentos Ltda., Sao Bernardo do Campo. 4 × 4 Jeep-type car.

JEHLE
FL 1978–present
Xaver Jehle Car & Motor Enginering, Schaan. Sports car.
  See "Saphier."

JEM
USA 1922
John E. Meyers, New York, N.Y. Also known as "Jem Special."

JEM
GB 1971
Sports car prototype.

JENARD
GB 1956
G.A. Elsmore, Yeovil, Somerset. Sports car.

JENATZY
B 1898–1903
Camille Jenatzy, Bruxelles. Electric and gasoline-electric cars.

JENKINS
USA 1900–1901
Francis Jenkins Auto Co., Washington, D.C. Steam, electric and gasoline vehicles.

JENKINS
USA 1907–1912
J.W. Jenkins Motor Car Co., Rochester, N.Y. Touring cars and roadsters.

JENNIGS
GB 1913–1915
Jennings Chalmers Light Car Co., Birmingham. Cyclecars.

JENNIS
USA 1903–1905
P. Jennis, Philadelphia, Pennsylvania. Two cars were built.

JENSEN
DK 1984
Steen Jensen. Electric three-wheeler prototype.

JENSEN
GB 1936–1976; 1983–present
Jensen Cars Ltd., West Bromwich, Staffs. Sports cars. 1972–1976 built the "Jensen-Healey"; 10,926 made.

JENSEN & PEDERSEN
DK 1900
M. Jensen & J. Pedersen, Kobenhavn. One car produced.

JENSEN-HEALEY
GB 1972–1976
Jensen Motors Ltd., West Bromwich, Staffs.

JERSEY CITY
USA 1919
Wrong name for "Argonne."

JET
CH 1979
A. Barmettler, Buggy- und Sportwagen-Vertrieb, Buochs/NW. Sports cars.

JET
E 1955
Madrid. 197cc minicars.

JETMOBILE
USA 1952
Richard Harp, Frederick, Maryland. Three-wheelers.

JEWEL
GB 1921–1939
John E. Wood, Bradford, Yorks. Cyclecars.

JEWEL
USA 1906–1910

Forest City Motor Car Co., Massillon, Ohio. 1909 reorganized as Jewel Motor Car Co. 1909 became Croxton-Keeton Motor Car Co. Name changed to "Croxton-Keeton." Two-seater with 2-stroke 1-cylinder engine; 5.8-litre 4-cylinder from 1908.

JEWEL ELECTRIC
USA 1911
Jewel Electric Co., Chicago, Illinois.

JEWELL
USA 1905–1906
Forest City Motor Car Co., Massillon, Ohio. Roadsters. Became "Jewel."

JEWETT
USA 1901–1902
Jewett Motor Carriage Co., Jewett, Ohio.

JEWETT
USA 1922–1927
Jewett Motors Inc., Detroit, Michigan. Subsidiary of Page-Detroit Motor Car Co. Introduced January, 1922. 115,879 cars were made.

J.H.N.
USA 1903
Neustadt-Perry Co., St. Louis, Missouri. Kit cars.

JIANGBEI
PRC 1987–present
Jiangbei Machinery Factory, Jilin, Longtan. "Subaru" (J) and "Opel" (D) based cars.

JIDE
F 1969–1974
Jacques Durand, Chatillon-sur-Thouet, Deux Sevres. Sté. des Automobiles Jide, Cherves-de-Cognac. Sports car.
See "Scora."

JIKRA
CS 1937
Jindřich Kraucher, Praha. Sports car.

JILEK
USA 1903
Joseph Jilek, Devils Lake, North Dakota

JIMENEZ
F c. 1995
Jimenez Motor SA, Monteux. 560 hp and 380 km/h sports cars.

JIMINI
GB 1975–c. 1981
Jimini Automotive Ltd., Woking, Surrey. Mini/Moke based small Jeep.

JIN-BU
PRC 1958–c. 1981
H'sin-Chien Mechanical Works, Chungking, Sechuan. 2-door sedan.

JINGGANGSHAN
PRC 1958–c. 1977 ?
Peking No. 1 Automobile Plant, Peking. Small rear-engined saloon; 4-cylinder radial air-cooled engine later.

JINLEI
PRC 1997
Beijing Golden-Thunder Classic Motors Co. Ltd., Peking. "Austin Healey" (GB) replica.

JIOTTO
J 1989–present ?
Fuji Heavy, Tokyo. Sports cars with 585 hp motors.

JK
CS
See "Mono JK."

J.L.
GB 1920
A.E. Creese, London. Sporting light cars.

J.M.
CDN 1990s
J.M. Design Auto Sport, Lac Carre, Quebec. Kit cars.

JM
CH 1913
Geneve.

J.M.B.
GB 1933–1935
J.M.B. Motors Ltd., Ringwood, Hampshire. Three-wheeler.

JOAGAR
BR 1948; 1957
Joaquim Garcia, Jaboticabal, São Paulo. Small car prototypes.

JOEL
GB 1899–1902
National Motor Carriage Syndicate Ltd., London. Electric car.

JOERNS
USA 1910
Joerns Bros., St. Paul, Minnesota. Motor buggies.

JOHNARD
GB 1976–1978
Johnard Vintage Car Repairs Ltd., Blanford, Dorset. Replica.

JOHNEX
CDN 1990s
Johnex Motorsports, Brampton, Ontario. Kit cars.

JOHN O'GAUNT
GB 1902–1904
William Atkinson & Sons, Lancaster. Light car.

JOHNSON
USA 1902
Johnson-Jennings Co., Cleveland, Ohio.

JOHNSON
USA 1902–1907
Johnson Gasoline Motor Co., Manchester, New Hampshire.

JOHNSON
USA 1903; 1918
Ernest Johnson, Beverly, Massachusetts. Cyclecars.

JOHNSON
USA 1905–1912
Johnson Service Co., Milwaukee, Wisconsin. Steam and gasoline cars.
See "Elite" (1909–1910) and "Empress."

JOHNSON
USA 1911
Johnson Bros., Philadelphia, Pennsylvania. Steam car.

JOHNSON
USA 1912
T.J. Johnson, Pelican Rapids, Minnesota.

JOHNSON
USA 1913
Daniel E. Johnson, Hartford, Connecticut.

JOHNSON MOBILE
USA 1959
Horton Johnson Inc., Highland Park, Illinois. One prototype (copy of a 1904 car) produced.

JOHNSON STEAMER
USA 1896
Charles W. Johnson, Uniontown, Pennsylvania. Reportedly built one car a day until fire destroyed the company plant.

JOKER
DK 1972
O. Sommer A/S, Kobenhavn. Prototype.

JOMAR
USA 1954–1960
Saidell Sports Racing Cars, Manchester, New Hampshire. Sports cars.

JOMO
GB 1967–1969
K. Vickery, Redditch, Worcs. Sports cars.

JONAS
USA 1904
Jonas Automobile Works, Milwaukee, Wisconsin.

JONES
USA 1899
Joseph W. Jones, New York, N.Y. Steam carriage.

JONES
USA 1899
Isaac B. Jones, Xenia, Ohio.

JONES
USA 1901
Henry J. Jones, Portland, Maine. Steam carriage.

JONES
USA 1902
A.B. Jones, Bridgeport, Connecticut.

JONES
USA 1905
Lewis Jones Machine Works, Philadelphia, Pennsylvania.

JONES
USA 1905
L.R. Jones, Stamford, Connecticut. Two cars were built.

JONES
USA 1910
William Newton Jones, New England, North Dakota. Motor buggy.

JONES
USA 1913
J.L. Jones, Leslie, Georgia. Roadsters.

JONES
USA 1914–1920
Jones Motor Car Co., Wichita, Kansas. Manufacture began November, 1914. Reported creditors asked receiver August, 1920. 3,902 cars were made.

JONES-CORBIN
USA 1902–1907
Jones-Corbin Co. Jones-Corbin Automobile Co., Philadelphia, Pennsylvania. Reported reorganized December, 1903. Became "Sovereign." Matthews Motor Co., Camden, New Jersey. Runabouts.

JONSSON
S 1921
Alfred Jonssons Motorfabrik, Lidköping. 2-cylinder paraffin engine.

JONZ
USA 1909–1912
American Automobile Mfg. Co. Jonz Automobile Co., Beatrice, Nebraska. 1911 absorbed American Automobile Mfg. Co., Kansas City, Missouri and moved to New Albany, Indiana. Became Crown. Motor Car Co., Louisville, Kentucky.
  See "Crown." 2-stroke. 2, 3 and 4-cylinder engines with 20, 30 and 40 hp respectively.

JOPLIN
USA c. 1905
William A. Joplin, Lawrence, Massachusetts. 4 hp automobile.

JORDAN
USA 1916–1931
Jordan Motor Car Co., Cleveland, Ohio. 6-cylinder 5-litre, and 8-cylinder 4.4- and 5.3-litre engines. 78,780 cars were made.

JOSESO
RA 1959
IAMA SA, Industria Argentina de Microautomoviles, Rio Gallegos. Minicar.

JOSWIN
D 1920–1926
Josef Winsch, Abt. Joswin-Motorwagenfabrik, Berlin. 6.5- and 7.3-litre engines.

JOU
F 913–1926
Automobiles A. Jou, Suresnes/Seine. Conventional 4-cylinder car.

JOUFFRET
F 1920–1928
H. Demeester, Colombes/Seine. Voiturette.

JOURDAIN
F 1920
Automobiles Jourdain, Tours. Cyclecar.

JOUSSET
F 1924–1926
Louis Jousset, Bellac/Haute-Vienne. Sporting light cars.

JOUVE
F 1913
Jouve et Cie., Paris. Cyclecar.

JOVI
USA 1990s
Jovi Ltd., Ft. Lauderdale, Florida. Kit cars.

JOWETT
GB 1906–1954
Jowett Motor Manufacturing Co. Ltd. (1906–1919). Jowett Cars Ltd., Bradford, Yorks. (1919–1954). Passenger and sports cars.

JOYMOBILE
NL 1953–1954
Washmobile Holland Co., Amsterdam. 4-cylinder Diesel engine powered prototype.

J.P.
F 1905
J. Prunello, Dumas et Cie., Puteaux/Seine. Gnome engines.

J.P.
GB 1950–1954
Joseph Potts Ltd., Bellshill, Lanarks. Sports cars.

JPB
P 1985
JPB Artefacto Ltda., Armando da Costa Jeronimo, Lin da Averha. "Bugatti" replicars.

J.P.L.
USA 1914
J.P.L. Cyclecar Co., Detroit, Michigan. La Vigne Motor Co., Detroit, Michigan. Cyclecars designed by J.P. La Vigne.
  See "La Vigne."

JPR
GB 1987–1993
JPR Cars Ltd., N. Chichester, W. Sussex. Replica.

J.P. WIMILLE
F 1946–1950

S.E.T.A.M., Courbevoie/Seine (1946–1947). Ford S.A.F., Poissy/Seine-et-Oise (1947–1949). Compagnie Parisienne d'Automobile, Paris (1949–1950). An advanced rear-engined closed sports two-seater.

JPX
BR 1994–present
JPX do Brasil, Pouso Alegre. 4 × 4 cars.

JUCHTAJDĚRDA
CS 1948
Ing. Jiří Pohl, Libněves. Two minicar prototypes: with 100 cc Jawa and 615 cc "Aero-Minor" engine.

JUDD
USA 1900–1901
Judd-Comiskey Motor Vehicle Co., New York, N.Y.

JUHAN
CS 1949
Jaroslav Juhan, Praha. 48 cc three-wheelers for handicapped persons.

JUHÖ
D 1922
Julius Höflich AG, Fürth. Two-seater cyclecar.

JULES
CDN 1911–1912
Jules Motor Car Co. Ltd., Guelph, Ontario. Small touring car.

JULIAN
USA 1918; 1925
Julian Brown Development Co., Syracuse, N.Y. Radial-engined prototype. Although production was contemplated, Brown could not obtain the financing necessary.

JULIEN
F 1925–1926
G. Julien, Blois/Loire-et-Cher. Single-seater cyclecar.

JULIEN
F 1946–1949
Sté. Nouvelle des Automobiles M.A. Julien, Paris. 352 cc small car.
See "M.A.J."

JUNIOR
E 1955–1956
Distribuidora Marcom, Junior S.L., Barcelona. 197cc three-wheelers.

JUNIOR
I 1905–1909
Fabbrica Junior Torinese d'Automobili, Torino. Voiturette and sports cars.

JUNIOR
USA 1917–1922
Sypher Mfg. Co., Toledo, Ohio. Juvenile cars.

JUNIOR
R USA 1924
John R. Raskob, Lockport, N.Y. Touring car.

JUNIOR SPORTS
GB 1920–1921
Aluminium & General Foundry Co., London. Light car.

JURISCH
D 1956–1957
Jurisch GmbH, Wappelshofen bei Nürnberg. Three-wheeler.

JUSSY
F 1898–1900
SA des Ets. Jussy, Saint-Etienne/Loire. Light cars.

JUSTICIALISTA
RA 1951–1955
IAME, Cordoba.
See "IAME," "Institec."

JUTTA
USA 1974
Small car prototype.

JUVENILE
USA 1906–1907
The American Metal Wheel & Auto Co., Toledo, Ohio. Electric cars.
See "American Juvenile Electric."

JUWEL
B 1922–1927
Societe des Autos Juwel, Herstall; Waremme. 1100 cc tourer.

JYANE
IR 1970
Small car.

K.A.C.
DK 1914
A. Jacobsen, Kobenhavns Automobil Central, Kobenhavn. Roadsters and touring cars.

KAHA
D 1920–1922
Elektromobilwerk Kaha GmbH, Wasseralfingen/Württbg. Electric cyclecar.

KAINZ
A 1900–1901
Josef Kainz, Wien. Voiturette.

KAISER
D 1911–1913
Justus Christian Braun, Premier-Werke AG, Nürnberg. Electric and gasoline cars.

KAISER
D 1935–1937
Kaiser-Fahrzeugbau, Oschersleben. Aerodynamic three-wheelers.

KAISER
USA 1947–1955
Kaiser-Frazer Corp., Willow Run, Michigan. First cars in late 1946. Passenger cars.

KAISER CARABELA
RA 1958–1962
Industrias Kaiser Argentina (IKA), Buenos Aires. "Kaiser" (USA) Manhattan manufactured in (RA).

KAISER JEEP
USA
See "Jeep."

KAISIS
CY 1975
"Clan" (GB) based sports cars.

KAK SPECIAL
CS 1946
Koller a spol., Bratislava. Sports car.

KALAMAZOO
USA 1903–1904
Michigan Buggy Co., Kalamazoo, Michigan.
See "Michigan."

KALMAR
S 1967–1969
Kalmar Verkstads AB, Kalmar. Light car with "Daf" (NL) components.

KAMA
SU/RUS 1988–present
Kamaz, Naberezhnie Chelni. Small cars.

KAMEI
D 1980–present
Kamei GmbH & Co. KG, Wiesbaden. Tuning.

KAMM
D 1936–1939
Prof. Wunnibald Kamm, Stuttgart. Streamlined cars.
See "FKFS."

KÄMPER
D 1905–1906
Heinrich Kämper Motorenfabrik, Berlin. Taxicabs.

KAN
A/CS 1911–1915
Královéhradecká továrna automobilu, Alois Nejedly, Kukleny. About 400 light cars with 1-cylinder 7 hp and 2-cylinder 11 hp engines were made.

K & M
1908
Kreider Machine Co., Lancaster, Pennsylvania. Highwheeler.

KANE-PENNINGTON
USA 1894–1900
Thos. Kane & Co. Anglo-American Rapid Vehicle Co., Racine, Wisconsin. Stock sold, little production.
See "Pennington."

KANSAS CITY
USA 1906–1908
Kansas City Motor Car Co., Kansas City, Missouri. Former "Caps." Became "Gleason"; touring cars.

KANSAS CITY HUMMER
USA 1904–1905
Hummer Motor Car Co., Kansas City, Kansas. Motor buggy.

KANSAS CITY WONDER
USA 1909
Wonder Motor Car Co., Kansas City, Missouri.
See "Wonder."

KANZLER
USA 1979
Replicars.

KAPI
E 1950–1958
Automoviles Kapi, Barcelona. Small cars.

KAPPE
USA 1895
W.J.H. Kappe, Quincy, Illinois.

KARBACH
USA 1905–1907
Karbach Automobile & Vehicle Co., Omaha, Nebraska.

KARENJY
RM 1985–?
Insitut Malgache d'Innovation, Fianarantosa. 4 × 4 cars with plastic body.

KARMANN
D 1955–1974
Wilhelm Karmann GmbH, Osnabruck. Sports cars on "Volkswagen" chassis.

KARNER
A 1929
Anton Karner, Wien. Cyclecars.

KARNS KAR
USA 1895–1905
Chester Karns, Everett, Pennsylvania. Runabouts.

KATO
USA 1907–1913
Four Traction Automobile Co., Mankato, Minnesota. 4-wheel drive 5–7-seater.

KAUFFMAN
USA 1909–1912
Advance Motor Vehicle Co., Miamisburg, Ohio. Reorganized as Kauffman Motor Car Co. Formerly. "Buggy-about."
See "Hatfield."

KAUZ
D
See "Ansbach."

KAVAN
USA 1905
Kavan Mfg. Co., Chicago, Illinois. A $200 runabout.

K.A.W.
D
See "Hagen."

KAYSER
D
See "Primus."

KCC
ZA 1982–present
KCC Kit Car Center Pty. Ltd., Jet Park Boksburg. Sports cars and replicas.

KD
SU 1972
Vladimir Yeltishev, Moskva. Sports car prototype.

K-D
USA 1912–1914
K-D Motor Co., Brookline, Massachusetts. K-D is Knight-Davidson. Crescent valve invented by Margaret E. Knight.

KDF
D
See "Volkswagen."

KEARNS
USA 1909–1916
Kearns Motor Car Co. Inc., Beavertown, Pennsylvania. Highwheelers; Trucks and fire engines after 1911. 1912 located in Rockville Center, New York. 1,151 cars were made.

KEARNS MOTOR BUGGY
USA 1908–1909
Kearns Motor Buggy Co., Beavertown, Pennsylvania. Became "Kearns."

KEATING
USA 1899–1901
Keating Automobile & Wheel Co., Middletown, Connecticut. Gas and electric cars.

KEENELET
GB 1904
Keene's Automobile Works Ltd., London. Steam cars.

KEENE STEAMOBILE
USA 1900–1901
Trinity Cycle Mfg. Co., Keene, New Hampshire. Sold to Steamobile Co. of America. Became "Steamobile."

KEEN STEAMLINER
USA 1870s; 1940–1944; 1955–1968
Charles F. Keen Mfg. Co., Madison, Wisconsin. Thermal Kinetics Corp., Rochester, N.Y. Steam vehicles. 1946–1948 "Plymouth" converted to steam power.

KEETON
CDN 1912–1915
Keeton Motors Ltd., Brantford, Ontario.

KEETON
USA 1912–1914
Keeton Motor Co., Chicago, Illinois; Detroit, Michigan. Became American Voiturette Co.
See "Car-Nation" cyclecar. Bankruptcy reported October 1914; Touring cars.

KEETON TOWN CAR
USA 1908
Keeton Town Car Works, Detroit, Michigan.

KEINATH
D 1949; 1970–present
Auto Keinath GmbH, Dettingen. Three-wheelers; Sports cars and tuning.

KEITEL
D 1921
Hans Keitel. About 6 streamlined cars were produced.

KELLENERS
D 1986–present
Kelleners Sport, Dinslaken. Tuning.

KELLER
USA 1948–1949
Keller Motors Corp., Huntsville, Alabama. Succeeded "Bobbi-Kar." Two models only: station wagon and coupé. with soft or hard top. About 18 cars made.
See "PLM" (USA/B).

KELLER ELECTRIC
USA 1899; 1903
J. Keller Electric Works, Canton & Cleveland, Ohio. Electric carriages.

KELLER KAR
USA 1914–1915
Keller Cyclecar Co., Chicago, Illinois. Cyclecar.

KELLEY
USA c. 1905
Joseph G. Kelley, Cambridge, Massachusetts. 8 hp automobile.

KELLISON
USA 1960–1963
Kellison Engineering & Mfg. Co. Kellison Car Co., Folsom, California.

KELLOGG
USA c. 1905
Harry W. Kellogg, Greenfield, Massachusetts. 4 hp automobile.

KELLY
USA 1884
John B. Kelly, Blyth, Ontario. Steam car.

KELLY
USA 1895; 1901
William Kelly, Detroit, Michigan. Gasoline cars.

KELLY
USA 1904
Ernest R. Kelly, Wilmington, Delaware.
See "Acadia."

KELLY
USA 1905
Kelly-Bridgett Co., Danville, Illinois.

KELLY
USA c. 1905
Charles Kelly, Boston, Massachusetts. 4 hp automobile.

KELLY
USA 1991
Kelly Motors Ltd., Fort Collins, Colorado. Sports car.

KELLY STEAM
USA 1902
O.S. Kelly Co., Springfield, Ohio.

KELMARK
USA 1972–1989
Kelmark Engineering, Inc., Okemos, Michigan. Sports car kit.

KELSEY
USA 1902
C.W. Kelsey Co., Philadelphia, Pennsylvania.

KELSEY
USA 1913–1914
Kelsey Car Corp., Connersville, Indiana.

KELSEY
USA 1920–1924
Kelsey Motor Co., Newark, New Jersey. Friction-drive cars and taxi cabs; 601 cars were made.

KELSEY & TILNEY
USA 1897
C.W. Kelsey & I.S. Tilney, Chestnut Hill, Pennsylvania. Experimental runabout.

KELSEY MOTORETTE
USA 1910–1912
C.W. Kelsey Mfg. Co., Hartford, Connecticut. Three-wheelers. Also called "Motorette."

KELVIN
GB 1904–1906
Bergius Car & Engine Co., Glasgow. About 15 passenger cars were built.

KEMA
NL 1899
Gebr. Kema, Rijwielfabriek en -reparatie-inrichting, Rotterdam. Light cars.

KEMP
USA 1907
John Kemp, Quincy, Massachusetts.

KEMPTEN
D 1900–1901
Süddeutsche Fahrzeugfabrik, Kempten. Voiturette.

KENDALL
GB 1912–1913
Kendall Motors Ltd., Birmingham. Cyclecar.

KENDALL
GB 1945–1946
Grantham Productions Ltd., Grantham, Lincs. 594 cc light cars.

KENDALL
USA 1897
Kendall Carriage Co., Camden, New Jersey.

KENDALLVILLE
USA 1910
Kendallville Buggy Co., Kendallville, Indiana. 5-passenger touring car.

KENMORE
USA 1910–1912
Kenmore Mfg. Co., Chicago, Illinois. Semi-highwheelers.

KENNEDY
CDN 1909–1910
Kennedy Mfg. Co., Preston, Ontario.

KENNEDY
GB 1907–1910
Hugh Kennedy & Co., Glasgow. Very few made only.

KENNEDY
GB 1914–1916
Kennedy-Skipton & Co. Ltd., Leicester. Light car.

KENNEDY
USA 1898–1903
C.W. Kennedy, Philadelphia, Pennsylvania. Electric cars.

KENNEDY
USA 1900; 1905
Kennedy Automobile Co., Cortland, N.Y.

KENNEDY
USA 1915–1917
W.J. Kennedy Mfg. Co., Los Angeles, California.

KENSINGTON
USA 1899–1904
Kensington Automobile Mfg. Co., Buffalo, N.Y. Formerly Kensington Bicycle Co. Electric and steam 1899–1902, gasoline 1902–1904.

KENT
USA 1901
A.W. Kent, Marietta, Ohio. Steam car.

KENT
USA 1916–1917
Kent Motors Corp., Newark, New Jersey. Formerly exporters to Latin America. June 1917 bankruptcy reported. November 1917 officials indicted for using mails to defraud.

KENTER
D 1924–1925
A.Kenter Werkzeugmaschinen und Kraftfahrzeug AG, Berlin; Leisnig. The factory in Leisnig was bought by Max Curth who produced the "Macu" cars in 1925.
See Macu.

KENT'S PACEMAKER
USA 1899–1901
Colonial Automobile Co., Boston, Massachusetts. Runabout.

KENTUCKY
USA 1914–1915
Kentucky Wagon Works, Louisville, Kentucky. Electric car.
See "Dixie Flyer."

KENTUCKY KAR
USA 1916
Kentucky Wagon Works, Louisville, Kentucky.
See "Dixie Flyer."

KENWELL/KENWILL
USA 1912–1914
Connecticut. 7 cars were made.

KENWORTHY
USA 1920–1922
Kenworthy Motor Corp., Mishawaka, Indiana. First shown at 1920 Chicago Auto Show. 4-, 6- and 8-cylinder cars.

KEOHWA
ROK 1980s
"Jeep" (USA) license.

KEPLER-BEERY
USA 1903–1904
Kepler-Beery Motor Car Co., Dayton, Ohio.

KERMATH
USA 1907
Kermath Motor Car Co., Detroit, Michigan. One four-seater runabout was made.

KERNMOBILE
USA 1902
Brooklyn, N.Y.

KERO-CAR
USA 1909
Kero-Car Motor Co., Dayton, Ohio. Gasoline, kerosene or alcohol as fuel.

KEROMOTOR
USA 1900–1901
Keromotor Co., Newark, New Jersey.

KEROSENE MOTOR SURREY
USA 1900
Kerosene Oil Engine Co., New York, N.Y.

KERRY
USA 1905
Kerry Co., London. Three-wheelers.

KERSTING
D 1950
Prof. Walter M. Kersting Modellwerkstatt, Waging/Oberbayern. Minicar with wooden body.

KERSTON
USA 1917
Harry Kerston, Detroit, Michigan. Gas-electric car.

KESSELL
USA 1899
Frank E. Kessell, Massillon, Ohio.

KESSLER
USA 1920–1921
Kessler-Detroit Motor Car Co. Kessler Motor Co., Detroit, Michigan. Touring cars. Also called "Kessler-Super-Charge 4."

KESS-LINE 8
USA 1922
Kess-Line Motors, Detroit, Michigan. Became "Balboa."

KESTREL
GB 1914
Bristol Road Motor Garage Co., Gloucester. Light car.

KÉVAH
F 1920–1924
Établissements Kévah, Paris. Light cars.

KEWET
DK 1990–present
Kewet Industries, Hadsund. Electric cars.

KEYS
USA 1914
Keys Bros., Council Bluffs, Iowa.

KEYSTONE
USA 1899–1901
Keystone Motor & Mfg. Keystone Wagon Co., Reading, Pennsylvania. Formerly Keystone Motor Cycle Co. Became Searchmont Motor Co.

KEYSTONE
USA 1900
Keystone Motor Co., Philadelphia, Pennsylvania. Wagonette.

KEYSTONE
USA 1914–1915
H.C. Cook & Bros., Pittsburgh, Pennsylvania. 55hp Rutenber 6-cylinder engine.

KEYSTONE SIX
USA 1909–1910
Munch-Allen Motor Car Co., Du Bois, Pennsylvania. Formerly Munch Motor Car Co., Yonkers, N.Y.

KEYSTONE STEAMER
USA 1899–1900
Keystone Match & Machine Co., Lebanon, Pennsylvania.

KHRUSHCHEV
SU 1912
Orel. Simple motor carriage.

KIA
ROK 1973–present
Kia Motors Corporation Ltd., Seoul. Passenger cars.

KIBLINGER
USA 1907–1908
W.H. Kiblinger Company, Auburn, Indiana. 613 highwheelers were built.
See "McIntyre."

KICK
NL 1987–c. 1994
Kick Design, Helmond. Sports car.

KICO
D 1924
Kieling & Co., Frankfurt am Main. Light cars.

KIDDER
USA 1898–1903
W.P. Kidder, Jamaica Plain, Massachusetts. Kidder Motor Vehicle Co., New Haven, Connecticut. Steam and gasoline cars.
See "Springer."

KIDDY
F 1921–1922
Ateliers Lecourbe, Paris. 397 cc light car.

KIEFT
GB 1950–1961
Kieft Car Constructions Ltd., Bridgend, Glam (1950–1952). Kieft Cars Ltd., Wolverhampton, Staffs (1953–1956); Birmingham (1956–1963). Sports and racing cars.

KIENER
F 1957
Christian Kiener, Paris. Front-wheel drive prototype.

KIKOS
F 1985
Société Francaise Kikos, Antibes. Sports cars.

KILBOURN
USA 1909
Marshall Co., Kilbourn, Wisconsin.

KILO SPORT
GB 1984
The Thousand Workshop, Bodmin, Cornwall. Replica.

KIM
SU 1930–1947
Moskovskii Zavod Imeni KIM, Moskva. "Ford" (USA) Type A assembled, later built as "GAZ." 1940–1942 about 500 KIM-10 cars very similar to "Opel" (D) Kadett/Olympia were built. After WWII "Opel" (D) assembled in a new factory "MZMA" called "Moskvitch."
See "GAZ" and "Moskvitch."

KIMBALL
USA 1888
Fred M. Kimball, Boston, Massachusetts. Electric tricycle.

KIMBALL
USA c. 1905
Herbert L. Kimball, Lynn, Massachusetts. 4 hp automobile.

KIMBALL
USA 1910–1912
Electric runabout. Custom body builder after 1912.

KIMPEL
USA 1914
George W. Kimpel, Cleveland, Ohio. Cyclecars.

KINDALL
USA 1903
A.J. Kindall, Bluffton, Indiana. 10 hp steam car.

KINDER
USA c. 1905
C.H. Kinder, Roxbury, Massachusetts. 4.5 hp automobile.

KINESHMA
RUS 1998–present
Avtoagregat, Moskva. Minicars.

KING
GB 1904
King & Co., Leicester. Light cars.

KING
USA 1896
Charles B. King, Detroit, Michigan. Claimed to be Detroit's first car.

KING
USA 1899–1900
A.W. King, Chicago, Illinois. Gasoline powered runabout.

KING
USA 1911–1924
King Motor Car Co., Detroit, Michigan; (1911–1923); Buffalo, N.Y. (1923–1924). Charles B. King incorporated company in 1911. Built "King Light. Car" 1914; 18,951 cars were built.

KING & BIRD
GB 1903
King & Bird, Mansfield, Notts. Dog cart.

KINGFISHER
GB 1993
Kingfisher Kustoms, Smethwick Warley, W. Midlands. Light 4 × 4 car.

KING MIDGET
USA 1948–1969
Midget Motors Supply Co., Athens, Ohio. About 5,000 buckboard-type vehicles were produced.

KING-REMICK
USA 1910
A.O. Dunk Autoparts Mfg. Co., Detroit, Michigan. Runabouts.

KINGSBURGH
GB 1901–1902
Kingsburgh Motor Construction Co., Edinburgh. 12 hp light cars.

KINGSBURY
USA 1900
Harry T. Kingsbury, Keene, New Hampshire. Naphtha-fueled automobile.

KINGSBURY
USA 1915
Kingsbury Gas-Electric Motor Car Co., Great Falls, Montana.

KINGSBURY JUNIOR
GB 1919–1922
Kingsbury Engineering Co. Ltd., London. Light two-seater.

KING STEAM CAR
USA 1904
Osgood, Indiana.

KING STEAMER
USA 1902
W. Grant King, Buffalo, N.Y.

KING STEAMER
USA 1904
Gilbert M. King, Providence, Rhode Island.

KINGSTON
USA 1907
Kingston Motor Car Co., Kingston, N.Y. Name changed to "Allen-Kingston" 1907. Transferred to Bristol. Engineering 1908.

KINNEAR
USA 1913
Kinnear Mfg. Co., Columbus, Ohio. Four-wheel drive. Built F.W.D. racer 1913.

KINNEY
USA 1922
Boston, Massachusetts.

KINSLEY BENNETT
USA 1907
Hartford, Connecticut.

KIRBY
USA c. 1905
Charles A. Kirby, Revere, Massachusets. 3 hp automobile.

KIRK
USA 1903–1904
Kirk-Snell Co., Toledo, Ohio.

KIRKHAM
USA 1906
Kirkham Motor Car Co., Bath, Maine.

KIRK-LATTY
USA 1903
Kirk-Latty Mfg. Co., Cleveland, Ohio.

KIRKSELL
USA 1907
Dr. James Selkirk, Aurora, Illinois. 50 hp prototype only, built in shop of C.C. Hinckley.

KIRK-SNELL
USA 1902
See "Yale."

KIRSCH
USA 1905–1916
Peter Kirsch, Decatur, Indiana.

KISSEL
USA 1919–1931
Kissel Motor Co., Hartford, Wisconsin. Formerly "Kissel Kar." Finely crafted cars. 21,503 cars were built.

KISSEL KAR
USA 1906–1909
Kissel Motor Car Co., Hartford, Wisconsin. Name shortened to "Kissel" 1919.

KISSEL-SILVER
USA 1918–1919
C.T. Silver Co., New York, N.Y. Special design Kissels. Also known as "Silver-Kissel."

KITE
USA 1903
Kite Bros., Ft. Scott, Kansas.

KITTO
USA 1903–1911
Simplicities Auto Co., Middletown, Connecticut. William H. Kitto, English car dealer. One car built.

KK
D 1986
KK-Automobil GmbH, Heilbronn. "Fiat" (I) Panda based cars.

KLAUS
F 1894–1899
Th. Klaus, Boulogne-sur-Seine; Lyon. Three-wheelers.

KLEIBER
USA 1924–1929
Kleiber Motor Truck Co., San Francisco, California. 815 touring cars were made. Built trucks to 1930.

KLEINE WOLF
D 1950–1951
Georg Wolf, Niebüll. Minicar with fiberglass body.

KLEINSCHNITTGER
D 1950–1957
Kleinschnittger Werk, Arnsberg/Westfalen. Small cars.

KLEINSTWAGEN BELGE
B 1952
Ets. De Reuck, Gand. Small car prototype.

KLEPFER
USA 1912–1914
Klepfer Bros., Depew, N.Y.

KLEMM
USA 1917
E.R. Klemm, Chicago, Illinois.

KLIEMT
D 1899–1900
C. Kliemt Wagenfabrik, Berlin. Electric cars.

KLINE
USA 1909–1911
B.C.K. Motor Car Co., York, Pennsylvania; Bath, N.Y. Reorganized 1911 as Kline Motor Car Co. Name changed to "Kline Kar."

KLINE KAR
USA 1911–1923
Kline Motor Car Corp., York, Pennsylvania. Opened Richmond, Virginia factory late 1912. Name changed to. Kline Kar Corp. 1918; 3,717 cars were made.

KLING
USA 1900–1901
Kling Cycle Mfg. Co., Harrisburg, Pennsylvania.

KLINGENBERG
D 1899–1900
Prof. Georg Klingenberg, Technische Hochschule, Berlin. Allgemeine Automobil-Gesellschaft, Berlin. One-cylinder car, later built by the "NAG."

KLINK
USA 1907–1910
Klink Motor Car Mfg. Co., Dansville, N.Y. Touring cars.

KLOCK
USA 1900–1901
Percy L. Klock, Stamford, Connecticut. Former National Motor Carriage Co. Absorbed by International. Motor Car Co.; Gasoline stanhope.

KLONDIKE
USA 1916–1920
W.H. Kohlmeyer, Logansville, Wisconsin. Touring cars.

KLOSTERMANN
D c. 1978
Harald Klostermann Pkw-Sonderaufbauten, Kamen. Sports car.

KM
GB 1954–1955
Prototype.

KNAP
B/F 1898–1909
Sté. des Constructions Liegeoise d'Automobile, Liege (B) (1898–1900). SA des Moteurs Knap, Troyes, Aube (F) (1904–1909). Voiturettes and three-wheelers.

KNAPP
USA 1906
Bert E. Knapp, San Jose, California.

KNECHT
USA 1905
John Knecht, West Salisbury, Pennsylvania. Steam car.

KNICKERBOCKER
USA 1901–1903
Ward-Leonard Electric Co., Bronxville, N.Y. Runabouts.
See "Century Tourist."

KNICKERBOCKER
USA 1905
Knickerbocker Friction Drive Auto-

mobile Co., Worcester, Massachusetts.

KNIGHT
USA 1900–1902
Frank D. Knight & Son, Hudson, Massachusetts. Steam cars.

KNIGHT & KILBOURNE
USA 1906–1909
Knight & Kilbourne Co., Chicago, Illinois.
See "Silent Knight."

KNIGHT OF THE ROAD
GB 1902
Light car.

KNIGHT OF THE ROAD
GB 1913–1914
Knight Brothers, Chelmsford, Essex. 5-seater tourer.

KNIGHT-SPECIAL
USA 1917
Watson & Stoekle, New York, N.Y. Touring cars.

KNIGHTSWOOD
GB 1914
Glasgow. One three-wheeler built.

KNÖLLER
D 1924
Karl Knöller Automobilfabrik, Ravensbrück bei Fürstenberg. Three-wheelers and four-wheelers.

KNOTT
USA c. 1905
George R. Knott, Agawam, Massachusetts. 5 hp automobile.

KNOW
USA 1900
Know Automobile Co., New York, N.Y.

KNOWLES
USA 1904
Knowles Automobile Mfg. Co., Buffalo, N.Y. Former "Kensington."

KNOWLES KHAKI FLYER
USA 1901
Kensington Automobile Mfg. Co., Buffalo, N.Y.

KNOX
USA 1900–1914
Knox Automobile Co., Springfield, Massachusetts. Re-organized 1914 as Knox Motors Corp. 10,835 cars were made.

KNUDSEN
USA 1899
Karsten Knudsen, Chicago, Illinois. Electric car.

KNUDSEN
USA 1948
Knudsen Mfg. & Design Co. Inc., Buffalo, N.Y. Prototypes only.

KNUDSEN
USA 1981–1985
Baroque Motorcars, Omaha, Nebraska. Luxury replicars.

KOBOLD
D 1920
Kobold Kleinauto GmbH, Berlin. Small car.

KOBUSCH
USA 1906
Kobusch Automobile Co., St. Louis, Missouri. Merged with St. Louis Car Co. 1906.
See "American Mors."

KOCH
D 1969
Studio Koch, Bad Homburg. Dune buggy.

KOCH
F 1898–1901
Koch Freres, Paris. 6 hp phaeton.

KOCO
D 1921–1926
Kleinauto- und Motorenwerke Koch & Co. (1921–1922). Koco-Werke GmbH, Erfurter Kleinauto- und Motorenbau, Erfurt (1922–1926). Small three-seater cars.

KODIAK
D 1984–1990
Speed + Sport Motor GmbH, Ostfildern. Sports cars.

KOEB-THOMPSON
USA 1910–1911
Koeb-Thompson Motors Co., Leipsig, Ohio. Touring cars.

KOECHLIN
F 1910–1913
S. Gerster et Cie., Courbevoie/Seine. 3-litre touring and sports cars.

KOEHLER
USA 1897
H.W. Koehler, Detroit, Michigan. Electric carriage.

KOEHLER
USA 1910–1912
H.J. Koehler Co., Newark, New Jersey. Announced February 1910. Trucks only after 1912.

KOENIG
D c. 1985–1992
Koenig Specials GmbH-Car Tuning, München. Tuning.

KOHL
USA 1900–1902
Edward Kohl, Cleveland, Ohio. Kohl Automobile Co., Whitney Point, N.Y. Gasoline carriages.

KOHOUT
A/CS 1905
První moravská továrna motorových kol a vozu, Petr Kohout a spol., Brno. Voiturette.

KOLBEN NW
A/CS 1900
Kolben & Co., Praha. Electric vehicle. Gasoline car built in 1907.
See "EAS."

KOLLSTED
USA c. 1905
George Kollsted, Providence, Rhode Island. 12 hp automobile.

KÖLN
D 1907
Motorfahrzeugfabrik "Köln," Uren, Kotthaus & Co., Köln. 24/40 hp landaulet.

KOMET
D 1922–1924
Komet Autofabrik Buchmann & Co., Leisnig. Light car.

KOMET
USA 1898
Keith Bros., Elkhart, Indiana.

KOMET
USA 1911
Elkhart Motor Co., Elkhart, Indiana.
See "Sterling."

KOMNICK
D 1907–1927
Elbinger Maschinenfabrik F. Komnick; (1907–1922). Automobilfabrik Komnick AG, Elbing (1922–1927). Touring cars.

KONDOR
D 1900–1902

Kondor Fahrradwerke AG vorm. Liepe & Breest, Brandenburg. 5 hp light cars.

KÖNIG
D 1985
König Starline, Beilstein. Tuning.

KONIGSLOW
USA 1902–1904
Otto Konigslow, Cleveland, Ohio.
 See "Ottokar."

KONINGS
NL 1901–1902
Maschinefabriek P. Konings, Swalmen. Voiturette.

KONOLLMAN
USA 1900
H. Konollman, Philadelphia, Pennsylvania.

KOPPEL
B 1901–1903
Compagnie Belge de Velocipedes, Liege. Voiturette.

KOPPIN
USA 1914
Koppin Motor Car Co., Fenton, Michigan. Cyclecar. Succeeded "Fenton" cyclecar.

KORFF
USA 1952
Walter H. Korff, Burbank, California.

KORN & BREIDING
USA 1901
Korn & Breiding, Sterling, Illinois.

KORN ET LATIL
F 1901–1902
A. Korn et Latil, Paris. Light front-wheel-drive voiturette.

KORTE
GB 1903–1905
Rice & Co. Ltd., Leeds, Yorks. 4- or 6-seater front-wheel-drive tonneau.

KÖRTING
D 1922–1924
Wilhelm Körting Automobilbau, Wülfrath/Rheinland. 4-cylinder Selve engines.

KORVENSUU
FIN 1913
Hans Lindström, Mynämäki. 2-cylinder light car.

KORYT
CS 1949–1952
Ludvík Korytář, Šternberk. Minicar prototype.

KOSMATH
USA 1916
Kosmath Co., Detroit, Michigan.
 See "Pennsy."

KOS MOS
USA 1909
KosMos Electric Runabout Co., New York, N.Y. Electric car.

KOUGAR
GB 1977–1990
Kougar Cars, Storcourt Wells Ltd., Uckfield, Sussex. Sports cars.

KOVER
F 1951–1952
Sté. Industrielle de Livry, Paris. Very small two-seater.

KOVER CAPILLA
E 1951–1952
Kover Capilla, Barcelona. 200 cc 6 hp minicars based on the "Kover" (F).

KRAFT
USA 1896; 1901
J.F. Kraft, St. Louis, Missouri. Steam runabout.

KRAFTFAHRZEUG-WERKE-BRANDENBURG
D 1906
Kraftfahrzeug-Werke Brandenburg a. H. Steam car;
 See "KWB."

KRAJAN
CS 1948
Jan Kraman, České Budějovice. 250 cc minicar prototype.

KRAJÁNEK
CS 1948
Frantisek Grulich, Seloutky. 175 cc minicar prototype.

KRAJČOVIČ
CS 1949
Ján Krajčovič, Trnava. Streamlined sports car prototype.

KRAJEWSKI-PESANT
USA 1898–1900
Krajewski, Pesant & Co., Brooklyn, N.Y. Gasoline vehicle prototype.

KRAL
A 1921–1923
Felix Kral, Wien. Cyclecar.

KRAMER
USA 1920
E.M. Kramer, Peoria, Illinois. Steam car.

KRASNII PUTILOVEC
SU 1933
Mashinostroitelnii Zavod "Krasnii Putilovec," Leningrad (Sankt Peterburg). 8-cyl. in-line engine, six 7-seater limousines were built.

KRASTIN
USA 1902–1904
Krastin Automobile Mfg. Co. Krastin Automobile Co., Cleveland, Ohio. Runabouts.

KRAUSE
CS 1925
W. Krause a spol., továrna automobilu, Rumburk. Light car.

KRAUSE
DDR 1961–1997
Louis Krause, Krankenfahrzeugfabrik, Leipzig (1961–1966). VEB Krankenfahrzeuge, Leipzig (1966–1970). VEB Fahrzeugbau und Ausrustungen, Brandis (1970–1990). Fahrzeugbau und Ausrustungen GmbH, Brandis (1990–1997). Three-wheelers.

K.R.C.
GB 1922–1924
White, Holmes & Co. Ltd., London. Light cars.

KREJBICH
CS 1948
Václav Krejbich, Praha. 350 cc minicars.

KREMER
c. 1985
E. & M. Kremer GmbH, Porsche Racing, Köln. Tuning.

KREUGER
USA 1904–1905
Kreuger Mfg. Co., Milwaukee, Wisconsin.

KRIEGER
F 1897–1909
Compagnie Parisienne des Voitures Electriques (Systeme Krieger). Paris (1897–1907). Compagnie Parisienne des Voitures Electriques, Colombes (1907–1909). Electric vehicles.

KRIEGER
I 1905–1913

Societa Italiana Automobili Krieger; (1905–1906). Societa Torinese Automobili Elettriche STAE (1907–1913), Torino. Electric vehicles.

KRIM-GHIA
USA 1966
Krim-Ghia Import Co., Detroit, Michigan. Limited production of sports cars bodied by the Carrozzeria Ghia (I).

KRIT
USA 1909–1916
Krit Motor Car Co. Puritan Machine Co., Detroit, Michigan. Organized September 3, 1909. "Packard" bought plant April 1916.

KŘIŽÍK
A/CS 1895; 1900
Ing. Frantisek Křižík, Praha. Electric cars.

KROBOTH
CS 1930
Gustav Kroboth, stavba motoru a vozidel, Šternberk. Advanced designed light cars using a 500 cc 1-cylinder engine, tubular backbone frame and transverse semi-elliptic suspension at front and rear.
See "Favorit" and "Kroboth" (D).

KROBOTH
D 1954–1955
Fahrzeug- und Maschinenbau Gustav Kroboth Seestall am Lech/Landsberg. Three-wheeler.
See "Kroboth" (CS).

KROHN
USA 1916
Louis J. Krohn, Oakland, California. About 7 cars were built.

KRONOS
A 1905–1907
Siegfried Schick, Bruck an der Mur. Voiturette.

KROPP
USA c. 1908
James A. Kropp, Lansing, Michigan.

KROTZ
USA 1903–1904; 1908–1911
Krotz Mfg. Co., Springfield, Ohio (1903–1904); Defiance, Ohio (1908–1911). Electric cars.

KRUEGER
USA 1904–1909
Krueger Automobile Co., Milwaukee, Wisconsin.
See "Eclipse."

KRÜGER
D
See "Electra."

KRUPKAR
GB
See "Morrison."

KRUSE
D 1899–1901
Gebr. Kruse, Hamburg. Electric and steam cars.

KÜHLSTEIN
D 1898–1902
Kühlstein Hofwagenbau, Berlin. Electric cars.

KÜHN
D 1927–1929
Otto Kühn, Halle/Saale. About 20 cars were built.

KULAGE
USA 1896
J.J. Kulage, St. Louis, Missouri.

KUNMING
PRC 1960–c. 1973
Kunming Motor Vehicle Plant, Kunming, Yunnan.

KÜNSTLER
D 1925
Automobilfabrik Paul Künstler, Heidelberg-Schlierbach. Three-wheeler.

KUNZ
USA 1897–1905
John L. Kunz (1897), Appleton, Wisconsin. Kunz Automobile Co. (1901). Kunz Automobile & Motor Co. (1902). Speedwell Automobile Co. (1902–1903). J.L. Kunz Machine Co. (1904), Milwaukee, Wisconsin. Company built cars 1902 and changed name to Speedwell Automobile Co. No cars built 1903 or 1904. Cars built again under Kunz name 1905. Runabouts. Engines only after 1905.

KUPFER
USA 1914
A.M. Kupfer Corp., Los Angeles, California. Cyclecar.

KURIER
CS 1948
Karol Strejc, Bratislava. 250 cc minicar prototype.

KUROGANE
J 1935–1962
Nippon Nainenki Seiko Co. Ltd. (1935–1959). Tokyu Kurogane Kogyo Co. Ltd., Tokyo (1959–1962). Three-wheelers; 4,800 four-wheel-drive cars were also made.

KURTIS
USA 1948–1955
Kurtis-Kraft Inc., Glendale, California. Kurtis Corp., Los Angeles, California. After building 34 sports cars in 1949, Frank Kurtis sold the entire operation to Earl Muntz, who produced the "Muntz Jet." Kurtis later produced other models of his "Kurtis Kraft."

KURTZ AUTOMATIC
USA 1920–1925
Kurtz Motor Car Co., Cleveland, Ohio. Pre-selector gearshift control; 675 cars were built.

KÜWE
c. 1985
KüWe special-tuning, Essen. Tuning.

K.V.S.
F 1976–1985
K.V.S., Chassieu. 125cc minicars.

KWB
D
See "Kraftfahrzeug-Werke-Brandenburg."

KYMA
GB 1903–1905
New Kyma Motor Car Co. Ltd., London. Three-wheeler.

KYOCERA
J 1994–present
Kyocera Corporation, Kyoto. Electric cars.

KYOHO
J 1937–1940
Three-wheelers.

KYOSAN
J 1930s
Air-cooled 2-stroke small cars.

KYOTE
USA 1968–1972
Dean Jeffries Automotive Styling, Hollywood, California. Dune buggy.

L

LABOR
F 1907–1912
Weyher et Richemond, Pantin/Seine. Conventional 4-cylinder landaulette.

LA BUIRE
F 1904–1930
Chantiers de la Buire (1904–1905). Societe des Automobiles de la Buire (1905–1909). Societe Nouvelle de La Buire-Automobiles, Lyon (1910–1930). Touring cars.

LA BULLE
F c. 1963
Henri Viard, Paris. Plastic bodied city car prototype.

LA CITADINE
F 1972
Electric citycar prototype.

LACOBA
GB
  See "Lacoste et Battman" (F) and "Jackson" (GB).

LACONIA
USA 1900; 1912
Laconia Car Co., Laconia, New Hampshire.

LACONIA
USA 1914
H.H. Buffum, Laconia, New Hampshire. Cyclecar.

LACOSTE ET BATTMANN
F 1897–1913
Lacoste et Battmann, Paris. Quadricycles; touring cars were marketed also under aliases as Napoleon (1903), Regal (1903), Gamage (1903), Speedwell (1904), Cupelle (1905), Lacoba (1906) and Simplicita (1910).

LACOUR
F 1912–1914
Lacour et Cie., Paris. Cyclecar.

LACRE
GB 1904–1905
Lacre Motor Car Co., London. Electric car.

LACROIX & LAVILLE
F 1898–1900
About 17 three-wheelers were built.

LA CUADRA
E 1900–1901
E. de la Cuadra y Cia., Barcelona. Electric cars.

L.A.D.
GB 1913–1926
Oakleigh Motor Co., London (1913–1914). L.A.D. Productions Ltd., Farnham, Surrey (1923–1926). Three-wheelers.

LADA
SU/RUS 1967–present
Volzhskii Avtomobilnii Závod, Togliatti. "Fiat" (I) license.
  See "VAZ."

LADAS
GB
  See "Bowen."

LA DAWRI
USA c. 1962
La Dawri Coach Craft, Long Beach, California. Mostly special bodies.

LADBROKE
GB 1973–1986
Ladbroke Avon Ltd., Warwick. "Jaguar" conversions.

LA DIVA
F 1902
Jules Zimmerman et Cie., Paris. Voiturette.

LAD'S CAR
USA 1912–1914
Niagara Motor Car Corp., Niagara Falls, N.Y. Runabout.

LA DURANCE
F 1908–1910
L. Conchy, Sisteron, Basses-Alpes. Light three-wheelers.

LADY
GB 1899
Henry Cave, Coventry, Warwickshire. Light car.

LA FAUVETTE
F 1904
La Locomotion Moderne, Paris. Light cars.

LAFAYETTE
USA 1904
Lafayette Automobile Co., Detroit, Michigan.

LAFAYETTE
USA 1921–1924
Lafayette Motor Co., Mars Hill, Indiana. Lafayette Motors Corp., Indianapolis, Indiana. 1924 reorganized as part of Nash Motors, then moved to Milwaukee, Wisconsin. Also a "Nash" subsidiary; 1,859 cars were made.

LAFAYETTE
USA 1934–1939
Nash Motors Corp., Kenosha, Wisconsin. 42,260 cars were built.

LAFAYETTE
USA 1982
Lafayette Bay Co., Inc., Wyazata, Minnesota. "Bugatti" (F) replica.

LAFER
BR 1974–1990
Lafer S.A., São Paulo. "MG" replicars.
  See "MP Lafer."

LAFITTE
F 1923–1928
SA de Constructions de Voiturettes Th. Lafitte, Paris. 3-cylinder 736 cc light car.

LA FLECHE
F 1912–1913
Guders Jack, Asnieres/Seine. Tandem-seated cyclecar.

LA FLEURANTINE
F 1906
J. Lagarde et Cie., Fleurance/Gers. Three-wheeler.

LAFORZA
USA 1989
Laforza Automobile Inc., Hayward, California. 4 × 4 car.

LA FRANCAISE
F
  See "Diamant."

LA FRANCE
USA 1903–1905
Pleasure cars shown at Madison Square Garden 1903. Reported bankrupt January 1904. Revived later as American La France Fire Engine Company; Touring cars.

LA GAULOISE
F 1907
Sté. des Voiturettes la Gauloise, Issy-les-Moulineaux/Seine.

LA GAZELLE
F 1913–1920
M. Tzaut, Neuilly/Seine. Light cars.

LAGERQUIST
USA 1909
Lagerquist Carriage Co., Des Moines, Iowa. Highwheelers.

LAGONDA
GB 1906–1963
Lagonda Motor Co. Ltd. Lagonda Ltd., Staines, Middlesex. Lagonda Ltd., Feltham, Middlesex. Aston-Martin-Lagonda Ltd., Newport Pagnell, Bucks. Sports and touring cars.

LAGO-TALBOT
F
See "Darracq."

LA GRACIEUSE
B 1899
La Societé Electricité Mécanique Automobile, Bruxelles. Voiturette.

LA HAULT
B 1886
Frederic de la Hault, Bruxelles. Three-wheeler.

LAHER
USA 1960–1963
Laher Spring & Electric Car Corp., Oakland, California; Memphis, Tennessee.
See Electric cars.

LAIDLAW ELECTRIC
USA 1903
James Laidlaw, Jersey City, New Jersey.

LAIGLE
F 1902–1903
Laigle Paquet et Cie., Amiens.

LAIRD
USA 1899
Robert Laird, Hanford, California. Electric carriage.

LA JOYEUSE
F 1907–1908
Voitures Legeres Taine, Paris. Light cars.

LAKEWOOD
USA 1920
Lakewood Engineering Co. Electric car.

LA LICORNE
F
See "Corre."

LA LOCOMOTRICE
B 1904–1905
Sté. La Locomotrice, Liege. "Rochet-Schneider" under license.

LA LORRAINE
F 1899–1902
Charles Schmid, Bar-le-Duc/Meuse. Small vis-à-vis.

LA MARNE
F 1920
Brun et Forest, Chalons/Marne. Touring car.

LA MARNE
USA/CDN 1919–1920
La Marne Motor Car Co., Cleveland, Ohio. Later moved to Ontario, Canada (1921) as Anglo-American Motors Inc; Touring cars.

LAMB
USA 1899
Lamb Mfg. Co., Chicopee Falls, Massachusetts. Gasoline carriage.

LAMB
USA 1905
Lamb Boat & Engine Co., Clinton, Iowa.

LAMB & VEDDER
USA 1901
Lamb & Vedder Co. Lamb & Co., Adrian, Michigan. Gasoline runabout.

LAMB ELECTRIC
USA 1901–1902
Lamb & Co., Grand Rapids, Michigan.

LAMBERT
F 1902–1906
Lamber et Cie., Paris. Small cars.

LAMBERT
F 1926–1953
Automobiles Lambert, Macon (1926–1931); Reims (1931–1936; 1940–1945); Giromagny, Belfort (1948–1953). Front-wheel-cars; electric two-seater; sports cars.

LAMBERT
GB 1914
Leslie Lambert, Drumchapel, Scotland. Amphibian cyclecar.

LAMBERT
USA 1891
John W. Lambert, Ohio City, Ohio. Three-wheeler. One-cylinder engine by John B. Hicks modified from a three-cylinder engine. Offered for sale at $550 February 1891.

LAMBERT
USA 1903
Lambert-Marion Co., St. Louis, Missouri.

LAMBERT
USA 1906–1917
Union Automobile Co., Union City, Indiana. 1905 became Lambert Automobile Co., Anderson, Indiana.
See "Union."

LAMBERT & WEST
GB
See "Warren-Lambert."

LAMBERT-HERBERT
GB 1914
Lambert-Herbert Light Car Co. Light car.

LAMB-KAR
GB c. 1950
Lamb-Kar Co., Fordham, Cambridgeshire. Three-wheelers similar to the "Bond" Minicar.

LAMBORGHINI
I 1963–present
Automobili Lamborghini, Cento (1963–1964); Sant' Agata Bolognese (1964–present). High-performance sports cars.

LAMBRETTA
F 1981
City car.

LAMBRO
I 1952
125 cc three-wheelers.

LA MINERVE
F 1901–1906

Sté. La Minerve, Billancourt, Seine. Voiturette.

LAMM
D 1993–1998
Lamm Design GmbH, Kappelrodeck-Waldulm. Tuning.

LAMMAS-GRAHAM
GB 1936–1938
Lammas Ltd., Sunbury-on-Thames, Middlesex. 3.7-litre touring cars.

LAMOND
USA 1907
George LaMond, Grafton, North Dakota.

LA MORALY
F 1956
Rear-engined small car.

LAMOREUX
USA 1914
Charles Lamoreux, Dunseith, North Dakota.

LA MOUCHE
F
See "Teste et Moret."

LA MOUETTE
F 1909
Joanny Faure, Lyon. Two-seater raceabout.

LAMPLOUGH
GB c. 1975
Replicars.

LAMPO
USA 1915
Adams & Montant Co., New York, N.Y.

LA NATIONALE
F 1899
Sté. La Nationale, Paris. 4 hp gasoline or paraffin engine.

LANCAMOBILE
USA 1900–1901
James H. Lancaster Co., New York, N.Y. Electric and gasoline runabouts.

LANCASTER
GB 1902–1903
E.H. Lancaster & Co. Ltd., Sunderland, Co. Durham. Light car.

LANCER
AUS 1961–c. 1964
BMC Australia Pty., Ltd., Zetland, N.S.W. "Wolseley" (GB) based cars.

LANCHESTER
GB 1895–1956
Lanchester Engine Co. Ltd., Birmingham (1895–1904). Lanchester Motor Co., Birmingham (1904–1913); Coventry (1931–1956). Quality touring and sports cars.

LANCIA
I 1906–present
Fabbrica di Automobili Lancia & C. (1906). Lancia S.p.A., Torino. Touring and sports cars.

LANDA
E 1916–1927
Talleres Landaluce, Estrecho, Madrid (1916–1922). Sociedad Espanola de Automoviles Landa, Madrid (1923–1927). Sports and touring cars.

L. & E.
USA 1924–1934
Lundelius & Eccleston, Los Angeles, California. Prototypes.

LANDGREBE
D 1921–1924
C.O. Landgrebe, Dresden. Three-wheeler, similar to the "Phänomobil."

L & H
D 1991–present
L & H Automobile, Frankfurt am Main. Tuning.

LANDINI
I 1920–1921
Vetturette G.L. Landini. SA Industrie Automobilistiche Novarese di Cameri, Cameri. Light cars.

LANDON
USA 1926–1927
Jack Landon, Los Angeles, California.

LAND ROVER
GB 1948–present
Land Rover Ltd., Solihull, West Midlands. 4 × 4 cars.
See "Rover."

LANDRY
USA 1913
J.A. Landry Motor Car Co., New Orleans, Louisiana.

LANDRY ET BEYROUX
F
See "M.L.B."

LANE
USA 1900–1911
Lane Bros. Co. Lane Motor Vehicle Co., Poughkeepsie, N.Y. Steam cars. First car in summer 1900. Five cars sold that year. 733 cars were made.

LANE
USA c. 1905
Ernest I. Lane, Hingham, Massachusetts. 18 hp automobile.

LANE
USA 1915
Lane Light Car Mfg. Co., Wichita Falls, Texas. Light cars.

LANE & DALEY
USA 1902
Lane & Daley Co., Barre, Vermont. Steam car.

LA NEF
F 1901–1903
Lacroix et de Laville, Agen/Lot-et-Garonne. Three-wheelers.

LANGAN
USA 1898
Louis Langan, St. Louis, Missouri. Runabouts.

LANG & SCHARMANN
USA 1907–1909
George J. Lang & Otto T. Scharmann, Marshfield, Wisconsin. Touring cars.

LANGEL
CH 1969
Jacques Langel, La Chaux-de-Fonds. Sports car prototype.

LANICH
USA 1908
Arthur S. Lanich, Baraboo, Wisconsin. Highwheeler.

LANPHER
USA 1906–1916
Lanpher Motor Buggy Co., Carthage, Missouri. Often misspelled "Lampher."

LANSDEN
USA 1901–1910
The Lansden Co., Birmingham, Alabama (1901–1903); Newark, New Jersey (1906–1910). Electric cars. Continued with trucks. Basis of General Motors Corporation electric trucks.

LANZA
I 1898–1903
Sta. Automobili Michele Lanza (1895–1898). Fabbrica Automobili Lanza, Torino (1898–1903). The first gasoline-engined 4-wheeler made in Italy.

LA PERLE
F 1913–1927
Louis Lefevre, Boulogne-sur-Seine. Cyclecars.

LA PETITE
USA 1905
Detroit Automobile Mfg. Co., Detroit, Michigan. Became Marvel Motor Car Co.
 See "Marvel" and "Paragon."

LA POINTE
USA 1948
Albert A. La Pointe, W. Hartford, Connecticut.

LA POINTE-SIMPLEX
USA 1903
Hodge Iron Works, Houghton-Hancock, Michigan.

LA PONETTE
F 1900–1925
Sté. des Automobiles La Ponette, Chevreuse/Seine-et-Oise. Light two-seater.

LA PORTE
USA 1895
La Porte Carriage Co., La Porte, Indiana.

LA RAPIDE
GB 1920
La Rapide Cyclecar Co., London. Cyclecar.

LARCHMONT
USA 1920
Larchmont Motors Corp., Newark, Delaware.

LARCOM
USA c. 1905
Fred Larcom, Lexington, Massachusetts. 6 hp automobile.

L'ARDENNAISE
F 1901
H. Lessieux et Cie., Rethel/Ardennes. Light cars.

LARMANGEAT
F 1867
Steam car.

LARMAR
GB 1946–1951
Larmar Engineering Co. Ltd., Ingatestone, Essex. Handicaped minicars.

LA ROCHE
USA 1905
La Roche Automobile Co., Dover, Delaware.

LAROS
I 1932
S.A. Fratelli Pellegati, Milano. Small 4-cylinder cars.

LA ROULETTE
F 1912–1913
Cyclecars La Roulette, Courbevoie/Seine. Cyclecar.

LARRIEU
F 1897
M. Larrieu & Ets. Jiel-Laval, Bordeaux. Rhomboid wheel placement.

LARSEN
USA 1908–1909
John M. Larsen. Larsen Machine Co., Chicago, Illinois. Became "Falcon."

LARSON
USA 1966–?
Larson Boat Works, Little Falls, Minnesota.

LARSSON
USA 1909
Henry W. Larsson, Los Angeles, California. Recreational vehicle.

LA SAETTA
USA 1955
Testaguzza Brothers, Detroit, Michigan. 15 sports cars were made.

LA SALLE
USA 1927–1940
Cadillac Division, General Motors Corp., Detroit, Michigan. Passenger cars.

LA SALLE-NIAGARA
USA 1905–1907
La Salle-Niagara Automobile Co., Niagara Falls, N.Y. Touring cars.

LASER
USA 1974–1983
"Porsche" (D) replicars.

LASHER
USA 1895
R.E. Lasher, St. Louis, Missouri.

LA SIRENE
F 1900–1902
Fernandez et Cie., Paris. Cie. "La Sirene," Paris. 5 hp light cars.

LASSEN
D 1931
Hamburg. Three-wheeler.

LA TORPILLE
B 1901
Sté. L'Automobile, Vleurgat-lez-Bruxelles. Voiturette.

LA TORPILLE
F 1907–1923
Leonce et Camille Bobrie, Saumur/Maine-et-Loire. Tandem two-seater cyclecar.

LA TORPILLE
F 1912–1913
Perrin et Cie., Annonay/Ardeche. Three-wheelers.

LA TROTTEUSE
F 1913–1914
St. Remy/Seine-et-Oise. Light cars.

LAUER
D 1922
Automobilfabrik Lauer & Sohn GmbH, Merseburg/Leipzig. 5/15 hp small car.

LAUER
USA 1894
John Lauer, Detroit, Michigan.

LAUGHLIN
USA 1916
Homer-Laughlin Engineering Corp., Los Angeles, California. Front-wheel drive.
 See "Homer Laughlin."

LAUNCESTON
GB 1920
Launceston Engineering Co. Ltd., London. Four-seater touring car.

LAUREL
USA 1916–1917
Laurel Motor Car Co., Richmond, Indiana.

LAUREL
USA 1917–1921
Laurel Motors Corp., Anderson, Indiana.

LAURENCE-JACKSON
GB 1920
Laurence-Jackson Ltd., Wolverhampton, Staffs. Light car with JAP engine.

LAURENT
F 1901
Laurent et Cie., Vierzon, Cher. Light voiturette.

LAURENT
F 1907–1908
Laurent et Cie., St. Etienne, Loire. 4-cylinder medium-sized cars.

LAURIN & KLEMENT
A/CS 1905–1925
Laurin & Klement, továrna motorových kol a vozů, Mladá Boleslav (1905–1907). Laurin & Klement, A.G., Motorfahrzeugfabrik, Jungbunzlau (1907–1918). Laurin & Klement, akc. spol., továrna automobilu, Mladá Boleslav (1907–1925). Voiturettes, passenger and sports cars.
See "Škoda"(CS/CZ).

LAUTH
USA 1905
J. Lauth & Co., Chicago, Illinois.

LAUTH-JUERGENS
USA 1907–1909
Lauth-Juergens Motor Car Co., Chicago, Illinois. Touring cars. Trucks only after 1909.

L'AUTOMOTRICE
F 1901–1907
Sté. l'Automobile (1901–1903). Sté. l'Automotrice, Bergerac/Dordogne (1904–1907). Voiturette.

L'AUTOVAPEUR
F 1905–1906
Sté. l'Autovapeur, Paris. Steam cars.

LA VA BON TRAIN
F 1900
Larroumet et Lagarde, Agen/Lot-et-Garonn. Three-wheelers.

LA VALKYRIE
F 1905–1907
Sté. Parisienne de Construction Automobile La Valkyrie, Montrouge/Seine. 1.7- and 2.3-litre cars.

LA VIGNE
USA 1913–1914
La Vigne Cyclecar Co., Detroit, Michigan. Cyclecars.
See "J.P.L.," "La Petite," "Marvel" and "Paragon."

LAVIL
I 1969–1982
Lavil SpA, Milano. Small cars.

LA VIOLETTE
B 1913–1920
Sté. Joseph Valentin Laviolette, Liege.

LA VIOLETTE
F 1910–1914
Franc et Cie., Levallois-Perret/Seine. Light cars.

LA VOIE
CDN 1923
Lavoie Automobile Devices Ltd., Montreal, Quebec. One was made.

LAW
USA 1901–1902; 1904
Frederick A. Law, Hartford, Connecticut. Inventor constructed several successful gasoline autos which became "Pope" gasoline cars. Then he incorporated in 1904 with several cars which were already built.
See below.

LAW
USA 1905–1907
Lawa Automobile Corp., Bristol, Connecticut. Company dissolved March 1907.

LAWIL
I 1969–1972
Lawil SpA Costruzioni Meccaniche e Automobilistiche, Milano. Sports cars and city cars.

LAWLER
USA 1948–1950
Lawler Steamobile, South Gate; Huntington Park, California. Steam cars.

LAWRENCE
USA c. 1904
Harry Lawrence, Staten Island, N.Y. Three-wheeler.

LAWRENCE & HOLLISTER
USA 1902
Lawrence & Hollister, New Haven, Connecticut.

LAWRENCE-JACKSON
GB 1920
Cyclecar.

LAWSON
USA 1895
Welch & Lawson, New York, N.Y.
See "Welch & Lawson."

LAWSON
USA 1900
Western Wheel Works, Chicago, Illinois.

LAWSON MOTOR WHEEL
GB
See "Dougill."

LAWTER
USA 1909
Safety Shredder Co., New Castle, Indiana. Touring cars.

LAYMAN-LOWY
USA 1916
Layman-Lowy Motor Car Co., New York, N.Y. Prototype.

LAYTON
GB 1960
Layton Sports Cars, Blackpool.

L.B.
F 1925
Lucien Borel, Villefranche de Lauraguais/Hte-Garonne. Cyclecars.

LC
BR 1991–1994
L'Auto Craft, Montadora de Veiculos Especiais Ltda., Barra do Pirai, Rio de Janeiro. Replicars.

L.C.E.
USA 1914–1916
L.C. Erbes, Jackson, Michigan; Waterloo, Iowa. Former "Cutting."

LEA
SK 1999
WUSAM, a.s., Zvolen. Electric minicar prototype.

LEACH
USA 1899–1901
Leach Motor Vehicle Co., Everett, Massachusetts. Steam cars.

LEACH
USA 1909
Charles Leach, Lima, Ohio.

LEACH
USA 1920–1923
Leach Motor Car Co. Leach-Biltwell Motor Car Co., Los Angeles, California. 6-cylinder touring cars.

LEADER
CDN 1901
The Leader Mfg. Co., Toronto, Ontario.

LEADER
GB 1905–1909
Charles Binks Ltd (1905–1906). New Leader Cars Ltd., Apsley, Nottingham (1906–1909). Cars ranged from a small two-seater to the 60 hp V-8.

LEADER
NL 1904–1905
Bosch, Zijlstra & Rupp, Arnhem. Voiturette.

LEADER
USA 1905–1912

Columbia Electric Co., McCordsville, Indiana (1905-1906). Leader Manufacturing Co., Knightstown, Indiana (1906-1912). Runabouts and touring cars.

LEA-FRANCIS
GB 1904-1906; 1920-1935; 1937-1953; GB; 1960; 1989-present Lea & Francis Ltd (1904-1935); Lea-Francis Cars Ltd., Coventry, Warwickshire (1937-1960); Studley, Warwickshire (1989-present)
Passenger and sports cars.

LEAR
USA 1904-1909
Oscar Lear, Columbus, Ohio.
See "Frayer-Miller."

LEAR
USA 1968-1969
Lear Motor Co., Reno, Nevada. Experimental steam cars.

LEBANON
USA 1906-1907
Lebanon Motor Works, Lebanon, Pennsylvania. Absorbed "Upton" 1904-1907.

LEBED
SU 1916-1917
Jaroslavl. 4.5-litre 6-seater tourer.

LEBLANC
USA c. 1905
Joseph LeBlanc, Lewiston, Maine.

LE BLANT
F 1894
Steam car.

LE BLON
F 1898-1900
Le Blon Freres, Paris. Light cars.

LE BRUN
F 1898-1900
Automobiles Le Brun, Montrouge/Seine. Four-seater vis-à-vis.

L.E.C.
GB 1912-1913
London Engine Co., Southall, Middlesex. Cyclecar.

LE CABRI
F 1924-1925
Automobiles Le Cabri, Asnieres/Seine. 5 hp and 7hp 4-cylinder cars.

LECAS
I
See "Todeschini."

LECK
USA 1897
John Leck, Santa Ana, California. Gasoline wagon.

LECKLIDER
USA 1902; 1906
A.E. Lecklider, Toledo, Ohio. Runabouts.

LE COMPTE
USA 1913-1914
George W. Le Compte Co., New York, N.Y. Cyclecar.

LECOY
GB 1921-1922
Lambert Engineering Co. Ltd., Harrow, Middlesex. Light cars.

LECTRA
USA 1993
Electric cars.

LEDA
F 1908
Thorand, Thiem et Cie., Paris. Light cars.

LE DAUPHIN
F 1941-1942
Andre L. Dauphin, Paris. Electric car.

LEDL
A c. 1973-1990;
Ledl Automobilerzeugung Kunststoffprodukte, Tattendorf. Dune buggy and sports cars.

LEDOUX
CDN 1914
Ledoux Carriage Company Ltd., Montreal, Quebec. Aluminum bodies.

LEE
USA c. 1905
H.K. Lee, Hartford Engine Works, Hartford, Connecticut.

LEE
USA 1910-1911
Diamond Mfg. Co., Detroit, Michigan.

LEE & LARNED
USA 1863
Lee & Larned, New York, N.Y. Steam fire engine.

LEE & PORTER
USA 1905
Lee & Porter Mfg. Co., Buchanan, Michigan.

LEEDS
RA 1960-1964
Leeds, Industrias Platenses Automotrices, La Plata. 324cc minicars.

LEEGER
CH 1886
Tägerwilen. Steam car.

LEESDORFER
A 1898-1900
Leesdorfer Automobilwerke, Leesdorf. Amedee "Bolee" (F) license.

LEFEBVRE
B 1900
S.A. des Cycles et Automobiles C. Lefebvre et Cie., Ciney. Voiturette.

LEFERT
B 1902
J. Lefert, Ghent. Electric cars.

LEGAT
F 1921
Propeller powered car.

LEGEND
GB 1990s
Legend Motor Company, Hanbury, Worcestershire. Sports kit cars.

LEGGATTI
D 1990-1994 ?
Leggatti Automobilbau Cohnen und Sommersell GmbH, Düsseldorf. Replicars.
See "Torrelaro" (E/U).

LEGGETT
USA 1903-1905
J.S. Leggett Mfg. Co. (1903). J.S. Leggett Automobile Co. (1904-1905), Syracuse, N.Y.
See "De Long," "Iroquois."

LEGIA
B 1900
Sté. Deprez-Joassart, Herstal. Voiturette.

LEGNANO
I 1908
See "FIAL."

LEGRAND
F 1901
3 hp light car.

LEGRAND
F 1913
Albert Legrand, Paris. 4-cylinder monobloc engine.

LEGROS
F 1900–1913
René Legros, Fécamp/Seine-Inférieure. 2- and 4-stroke light cars.

LEGROS & KNOWLES
GB 1905–1907
C.A. Legros & Guy Knowles. Became "Iris."

LE GUI
F
See "Guy."

LEHMBRUCH
D 1908
Three-wheeler.

LEHR
USA 1905; 1908–1909
Lehr Agricultural Co., Fremont, Ohio.

LEICHTAUTO
D 1924
Leichtauto Gesellschaft mbH, Berlin. Light cars.

LEIDART
GB 1936–1938
Leidart Cars Ltd., Pontefract, Yorks. American Ford V-8 engine.

LEIFA
D 1924–1925
Leifa-Automobil GmbH, Berlin. Two-cycle two-cylinder engine.

LEIGHTON
USA 1910
Leighton Auto Co., Brockton, Massachusetts.

LEINWATHER & BLAZEK
D 1985
Leinwather & Blazek GmbH, Recklinghausen. Tuning.

LEISEN
CH 1875–1905
Jacques von Leisen, Geneve. Steam three-wheelers.

LEIST
USA 1911
Leist Automobile Mfg. Co., Michigan City, Indiana.

LEITNER
SU 1901; 1911
A. Leitner & Co., Riga, Latvia. "De Dion Bouton" (F) license.

L'ELEGANTE
F 1903–1907
J.B. Mercier, Paris. DeDion engine.

LE JEAL
USA 1900–1906
Le Jeal Cycle & Mobile Works, Erie, Pennsylvania. Runabouts.

L.E.M.
I 1974
Laboratorio Elettronico Mobile. Experimental electric city car prototype built by the Carrozzeria G. Michelotti, Orbassano.

LE MAIRE & PAILLOT
B 1896
Herstal. Voiturette.

LE MANS
GB 1996. Le Mans Sports Car Co., Westbury, Wiltshire. "Jaguar" D-Type replicars.

LE MARNE
USA/CDN
See "La Marne."

LE MEHARI
F 1927
F. Reynaud, Nouzonville/Ardennes. Cyclecar.

LE METAIS
F 1904–1910
Voiturettes Le Metais, Levallois-Perret/Seine.

LEMP ELECTRIC
USA 1897–c. 1902
Hermann Lemp, Lynn, Massachusetts. Electric carriages.

LEMS
GB 1903
London Electromobile Syndicate, London. Electric car.

LENAWEE
USA 1904
Church Mfg. Co., Adrian, Michigan. Tonneau.
See "Murray."

LENDE
USA 1902–1909
Lende Automobile Mfg. Co., Minneapolis, Minnesota. Touring cars.

LENGERT
USA 1896
Lengert Co., Philadelphia, Pennsylvania.
See "Barrow" electric.

LENHAM
GB 1976–1985
Lenham Motor Company Ltd., Harrietsham, Kent. Sports cars.

LENOIR
F 1860–1863
Jean Joseph Etienne Lenoir, Paris. Gas engine cart.

LENOX
USA 1911–1918
Lenox Motor Car Co., Hyde Park, Massachusetts; Lawrence, Massachusetts. Succeeded "Martell." Touring cars.

LENOX
USA 1920
A.G. Delamater, New York, N.Y. For export only.

LENOX ELECTRIC
USA 1908–1909
Maxim & Goodridge, Hartford, Connecticut.
See "Maxim-Goodridge."

LENTZ
I 1906–1908
Societa Italiana Automobili Marca Oria Lentz, Milano. 14/16hp and 20/24 hp cars.

LEO
CH/D/H 1989–?
Tecoplan GmbH, St. Gallen; München and Ingolstadt; Kiskunhalas. Light cars.

LEO
GB 1913
Cyclecar.

LEONARD
GB 1904–1906
J.J. Leonard & Co., London. 6hp De-Dion engine powered light car.

LEONARD
USA c. 1907
W.H. Leonard, Salisbury, North Carolina.

LÉON BOLLÉE; MORRIS-LÉON BOLLÉE
F 1895–1933
Automobiles Léon Bollée (1895–1924). Morris Motors Ltd., Usines Léon Bollée (1925–1931). Sté. Nouvelle Léon Bollée, Le Mans (1931–1933). Leon Bollee was a son of Amedee Bollee, pioneer of steam road vehicles in France. Leon invented a new name for his light

gasoline cars — a voiturette. Small and full-sized cars were made.

LEON DUSSEK
F 1906–1907
Chain and shaft drive 4-cylinder cars.

LEONE
I 1949–1950
Officine Elettromeccaniche Vincenzo Leone, Torino. Small sports car.

LÉON LAISNE; HARRIS-LÉON LAISNE; HARRIS
F 1920–1937
L. Laisne et Cie., Lille (1920–1927). Automobiles Harris-Léon Laisne, Nantes (1927–1931). Automobiles Harris, Nantes (1931–1937) Touring cars with unconventional suspension.

LEON RAMBERT
F 1934
Clermont-Ferrand. 175 cc and 250 cc ultra-light cars.

LEON RUBAY
USA 1923–1924
Rubay Co., Cleveland, Ohio. A line of town cars by famous body builder. Also called "Rubay."

LEONTINA
I c. 1973
Pettenella Ferruccio Carrozzeria, Torino. "Alfa-Romeo" (I) 1750 replica.

LEOTARD
F 1980–c. 1984
Christian de Leotard, Paris. "Renault" 5 based 6-wheeled cars.

LEPAPE
F 1896–1901
Hippolyte Lepape, Paris. 3-cylinder radial engine.

LEPHBRIDGE
CDN 1908–1909
Lephbridge Motor Car Co., Lephbridge, Alberta.

LE PIAF
F 1951
Sté. Industrielle de Livry, Livry-Gargan/Seine. Simple minicar.

LEPOIX
F 1975
Louis Lepoix, Paris. Electric three-wheeler prototype.

LEPPO
USA 1895
Leppo Bros., Belleville, Ohio.

LEPRECHAN
GB
See "Autogear."

LE ROITELET
F 1921–1923
Paris. Cyclecar.

LE ROLL
F 1922
Delauné, Bergé et Boudéne, Paris. 900 cc light car.

LEROUX
USA 1918
Marquette Motor Sales Co., Chicago, Illinois. Steam car.

LEROUX-PISART
B 1919–1921
Sté. Leroux-Pisart, Bruxelles. Passenger cars.
See "SOMEA."

LEROY
CDN 1901–1907
Milton H. Good & Nelson Good, Kitchener, Ontario. Experimental cars 1899–1900. 32 cars built. Patterned after "Oldsmobile."

LESCH
D 1922
Ing. Paul Lesch, Leipzig. Three-wheeler.

LESCINA
USA 1916
Lescina Automobile Co., Newark, New Jersey. First cars assembled at Chicago, Illinois. Touring cars.

LESLIE
USA 1916
Leslie Motor Car Co., Detroit, Michigan.

L'ESPERANCE
USA 1911
L'Esperance Motor Co., Detroit, Michigan. Incorporated early 1911 with $10,000.

LESPINASSE
F 1909
Automobiles et Moteurs L. Lespinasse, Cauderan/Gironde. 4- and 6-cylinder cars.

LESSEPS
F 1913
Experimental car.

LESSHAFT
D 1925–1926
Lesshaft & Co., Berlin. Three-wheeler.

LESSNER
SU 1905–1910
Mashinostroitelnii Zavod G.A. Lessnera, Sankt Peterburg. "Canstatt-Daimler" (D) license.

LESTER
GB 1913
Lester Engineering Co., London. Cyclecar.

LESTER
GB 1949–1955
H. Lester, Knebworth, Herts. (1949); Thatcham, Berks. (1949–1951). H. Lester Cars Ltd., Thatcham, Berks. (1951–1954). The Monkey Stable, London (1954–1955). Sports and racing cars.

LESTER
USA 1901
L.P. Lester, Newton, Kansas.

LETAR
F 1894
Steam car.

LETHIMONNIER
F
See "Sultane."

LE TIGRE
F 1920–1923
R. Merville, Asnieres/Seine. Light car powered by a Fiat (I) engine.

LEVENN
F 1900
Ernst et Cie., Paris. Voiturette.

LEVER
USA 1930–1933
Lever Motors Inc., Quapaw, Oklahoma. Formerly "Elcar." Others proposed to have been built by Kissel Inc. in 1933.
See "Elcar" and "Kissel."

LEWIS
AUS 1898–1902
Lewis Cycle Works, Adelaide, South Australia. Air-cooled engine and wheel or tiller steering.

LEWIS
GB 1923–1924
Abbey Industries Ltd., London. Cyclecar.

LEWIS
USA 1894–1899
George W. Lewis, Chicago, Illinois.

Won prize for friction drive device in Chicago Times-Herald Race.

LEWIS
USA 1895; 1899–1900
Lewis Wagon Co. Lewis Motor Vehicle Co., Philadelphia, Pennsylvania.

LEWIS
USA 1901
Lewis Cycle Co., Brooklyn, N.Y.

LEWIS
USA 1913–1916
L.P.C. Motor Co. (Lewis, Petard & Cram), Racine, Wisconsin. Later Lewis Motor Co. Absorbed by Mitchell-Lewis Motor Co. 1915. Touring cars.

LEWIS AIROMOBILE
USA 1937
Lewis-American Airways, Inc., Rochester, N.Y.

LEWIS ELECTRIC
USA 1893–1895
J.D. Perry Lewis, St. Louis, Missouri.

LEXINGTON
USA 1909–1927
Lexington Motor Car Co., Lexington, Kentucky (1910). Moved to Connersville, Indiana. Absorbed by Howard Motor Car Co. 1913 and reorganized as Lexington-Howard Co. Reorganized as Lexington Motor Co. 1917. Properties acquired by "Auburn" 1926. 38,148 cars were built.
See "Howard."

LEXMAUL
D 1985–1995
Lexmaul, Opel Tuning, Rödermarkt-Oberroden. Tuning.

LEXUS
J 1989–present
Toyota Motor Corporation, Toyotashi, Aichi-ken. Luxury cars of "Toyota."

LEY
D 1905–1929
Rudolf Ley AG, Arnstadt i. Th.
See "Loreley."

LEYAT
F 1913–1921
Marcel Leyat, Meursault/Cote d'Or. Propeller powered car.

LEYLAND
GB 1920–1923
Leyland Motors Ltd., Leyland, Lancs. Luxury touring cars.

LE ZÈBRE
F 1909–1932
SA Le Zèbre, Suresnes; Puteaux/Seine. Light cars.

LIBELLE
A 1952
Libelle Fahrzeugbau- und Vertriebsgesellschaft, Innsbruck. 200 cc three-wheelers.

LIBELLE
D 1920–1922
Kleinautofabrik GmbH, Sindelfingen. Cyclecars.

LIBELLULA
I 1952
Fratelli Boselli, Milano. Three-wheelers.

LIBÉRIA
F 1900–1902
G. Dupont, Plessis-Trévise/Seine-et-Oise. Conventional light car.

LIBERTA
B 1972
Liberta Engineering SA, Liege. Sports car kit.

LIBERTY
USA 1910
Belmont Automobile Mfg. Co., New Haven, Connecticut.

LIBERTY
USA 1914
Joseph A. Anglada. Liberty Motor Co., New York, N.Y. Cyclecar.

LIBERTY
USA 1916–1923
Liberty Motor Car Co., Detroit, Michigan. Bought by Columbia Motors Co. 1923. 36,962 cars were made.

LIBERTY BRUSH
USA 1911–1912
Brush Runabout Co., Detroit, Michigan. Became United States Motor Co., Brush Division.

LIBERTY LIGHT CAR
USA 1920–1921
Liberty Mfg. Co., New York, N.Y.

LIBERTY-MUTUAL
USA 1960–1961
Liberty-Mutual Insurance Co., Boston, Massachusetts. Experimental safety car.

LIDKÖPING
S 1923
Lidköping Mek. Verkstad, Lidköping. Light four-seater.

LIDOVKA
CS 1948
Zdeněk Pilát, Praha. Small car prototype.

LIEGE
GB 1998–present
Liege Motor Company, Fladbury, Worcestershire. Two-seater sports cars.

LIFU
GB 1899–1902
The Steam Car Co. (House's System) Ltd., London. Steam cars.

LIGHT
GB 1993–1996
Light Car Company Ltd., St. Neots, Cambridge. Sports car.

LIGHT
USA 1905
Kavan Mfg. Co., Chicago, Illinois.
See "Kavan."

LIGHT
SIX/USA 1914
Light Motor Car Co., Detroit, Michigan.

LIGHTSPEED
GB 1973–1987
Lightspeed Panels, Whitby, North Yorks. Kit cars.

LIGHT STEAMER
USA 1901–1902
Light Cycle Co., Pottstown, Pennsylvania.

LIGIER
1969–c. 1994
Guy Ligier Sport S.A., Abrest. Automobiles Ligier, Vichy/Allier. Sports car prototype and mini cars.

LILA
J 1923–1925
Jitsuyo Jidosha Seizo Co., Osaka. 10hp light cars.

LILIPUT
D 1904–1907
Bergmanns Industriewerke (1904–1905). Süddeutsche Automobilfabrik GmbH, Gaggenau (1905–1907). 567 cc light cars.
See "VCS."

LILIPUTIAN
USA 1902
Turner Automobile Co., Ltd., Philadelphia, Pennsylvania.
  See "Turner."

LIMA
USA 1915
C.E. Miller & F.M. McGraw. Lima Light Car Co., Lima, Ohio.

LINCOLN
AUS 1919–1924
Lincoln Motor Car Co., Sydney, N.S.W.

LINCOLN
GB 1920
Three-wheeler.

LINCOLN
USA 1904; 1908–1909
Lincoln Motor Vehicle Co., Lincoln, Illinois. Highwheelers.

LINCOLN
USA 1912–1913
Lincoln Motor Car Works, Chicago, Illinois. Highwheeler. Company built cars for "Sears" (Sears Roebuck) late 1911 and into 1912. Also built trucks.

LINCOLN
USA 1914
Lincoln Motor Car Co., Detroit, Michigan. Cyclecar. Successor to American Voiturette Co.

LINCOLN
USA 1920–present
Lincoln Motor Co., Detroit, Michigan. Purchased by Ford Motor Co. 1922. Luxury passenger cars.

LINCOLN ELECTRIC
USA 1900
Lincoln Electric Co., Cleveland, Ohio.

LINCOLN ZEPHYR
USA 1935–1942
Ford Motor Co., Detroit, Michigan.
  See "Zephyr."

LIND
USA 1974
Lind Motor Car Co., Onancock, Virginia. Replica.

LINDBERG
USA 1981–1984
Lindberg Engineering, Tollhouse, California. Replica kit.

LINDCAR
D 1922–1925
Lindcar Auto AG, Berlin. Light cars with plywood body.

LINDSAY
GB 1906–1908
Lindsay Motor Car Co. Ltd., Woodbridge, Suffolk. Three-wheelers and light cars.

LINDSAY
USA 1902–1903
Lindsay Automobile Parts Co. Lindsay-Russel Co., Indianapolis, Indiana. Electric cars. Mfg. of running gears and parts.

LINDSLEY
USA 1908–1909
J.V. Lindsley & Co., Chicago, Illinois. J.V. Lindsley Auto Chassis Co., Dowagiac, Michigan. Highwheelers. Became Dowagiac Motor Car Co.

LINETT
A 1921–1928
Linett-Automobilfabriks GmbH, Wien. Cyclecars.

LINGENFELTER
USA 1997–present
Lingenfelter Performance, Decatur, Indiana. "Chevrolet" Corvette based sports cars.

LINGTON
GB 1920
Lington Engineering Co. Ltd., Bedford. Cyclecar.

LINON
B 1900–1914
Ateliers Linon, Ensival-Verviers. More than 2,000 cars were built.

LINSER
A/CS; 1906–1908
Christian Linser, Liberec. 12 hp voiturette.

LION
USA 1909–1912
Lion Motor Car Co., Adrian, Michigan. Founded when Page Gas Engine Co. bought gyroscope patents. Owned by Blomstrom Mfg. Co. Assets sold to A.O. Dunk Auto. Parts Mfg. Co. reported February 1913.
  See "Page" and "Gyroscope."

LION-PEUGEOT
F 1906–1913
Les Fils de Peugeot Freres, Beaulieu-Valentigney (1906–1910). SA des Automobiles et Cycles Peugeot, Audincourt (1910–1913). Voiturette and touring cars.

LIPMAN
USA 1901; 1911
Lipman Mfg. Co., Beloit, Wisconsin.

LIPPI
I 1959
C. Lippi, Bologna.

LIPSCOMB
GB 1903–1905
English Motor Car Co. Ltd., London. Assembled cars with DeDion-Bouton (F) engine.

LIPSIA
D 1922–1924
Lipsia Automobilfabrik GmbH, Schleussig bei Leipzig. 6/20 hp and 6/30 hp cars.

LIQUID AIR
USA 1899–1900
Liquid Air Power and Automobile Co. Ltd., Boston, Massachusetts.

LISTER
GB 1954–1959
Brian H. Lister (1954–1956). B.H. Lister Ltd., Cambridge (1956–1959). Sports and racing cars.

LISTER
GB 1986–present
Lister Cars Ltd., Leatherhead, Surrey. Sports cars.

LITTLE
USA 1912–1913
Little Motor Car Co., Flint, Michigan. 1913 absorbed with "Republic" into Chevrolet Motor Co.

LITTLE DETROIT
USA 1910
De Mot Car Co., Detroit, Michigan.
  See "De Motcar."

LITTLE DETROIT SPEEDSTER
USA 1913–1914
Detroit Cyclecar Co., Detroit, Michigan. Cyclecar.
  See "Detroit Speedster."

LITTLE FOUR
USA 1904
McLachlen & Brown. Little Four Automobile Mfg. Co., Detroit, Michigan.

LITTLE KAR
USA 1911
Little Motor Kar Co., Arlington, Texas.

LTTLE KAR
USA 1920–1922
Little Motor Kar Co., Grand Prairie, Texas; Dallas, Texas. Reported officers arrested for fraud April 1920.
See "Texmobile."

LITTLEMAC
USA 1930–1932
Thompson Motor Corp., Muscatine, Iowa. Touring cars.

LITTLE MYSTERY
USA 1929
Kenneth L. Morehouse, Detroit, Michigan.

LITTLE PRINCESS
USA 1913–1914
Princess Cyclecar Co., Detroit, Michigan. Cyclecars.

LITTLE RED DEVIL
USA 1904
St. Louis, Missouri. Runabout.

LITTLE SCOTSMAN
GB
See "Scotsman."

LITTLE SIX
USA 1913
Republic Motor Co. of Michigan, Detroit, Michigan.
See "Little," Little Motor Car Co., Flint, Michigan.

LITTLE STEAMER
USA 1900–1903
David M. Little, Salem, Massachusetts.

LIUZHOU
PRC 1989–c. 1993
Liuzhou Minicar Factory, Liuzhou, Guangxi. Small car.

LIVER
GB 1900–1901
William Lea Motor Co. Ltd., Liverpool. Based on the "Benz" (D).

LIVERPOOL
USA c. 1905
Harry J. Liverpool, Boston, Massachusetts. 4 hp automobile.

LLOYD
D 1906–1914; 1950–1963
Norddeutsche Automobil- und Motoren AG (1906–1914). Lloyd-Motorenwerke GmbH, Bremen (1950–1963). Electric cars; touring and light cars.

LLOYD
GB 1936–1951
Lloyd Cars Ltd., Grimsby, Lincs. Ultra light open two-seater.

LLOYD & PLAISTER
GB 1900–1911
Lloyd & Plaister, London. 10, 16, 20 and 40 hp cars.

LM
F 1971–1973
G. Thelin, Savigny. Dune buggy.

L.M.
GB 1905–1922
William Cunningham, Clitheroe, Lanc. (1905–1919). Little Midland Car Co. Ltd., Blackburn, Lancs. (1919–1920); Preston, Lancs. (1920–1922). Light cars.

L.M.
USA 1912
L.M. Motor Co., Brooklyn, N.Y. Two built; formerly "B.L.M."

L.M.B.
GB 1960–1962
L.M.B. Components Ltd., Guildford, Surrey. Sports cars.

LMX
I 1968–1972
Michele Liprandi, Torino; Milano (1968–1970). LMX Automobili Srl, Torino (1970–1972). Sports cars.

LO CASCIO
I 1905–1913
Societa Imprese Elettriche e di Automobili Giuseppe Lo Cascio & C., Napoli. Electric and gasoline cars.

LOCKE
USA 1902
Locke Regulator Co., Salem, Massachusetts. Steam engines only.
See "Puritan."

LOCKWOOD
GB 1921–1922
Lockwood's Garage, Eastbourne, Sussex. Miniature cars.

LOCOMOBILE
CDN 1902
National Cycle & Automobile Co., Hamilton, Ontario.

LOCOMOBILE
USA 1899–1929
Locomobile Co. of America, Bridgeport, Connecticut. Before 1902 at Newton, Massachusetts and Westfield, Massachusetts. Purchased "Stanley" patents 1899. Absorbed Overmann Automobile Co. 1902. Controlled by Hare's Motors 1920–1922, Durant Motors 1922–1929. Steam 1899–1903, gasoline 1902–1929.

LOCOMOTOR
USA 1900–1901
America Locomotor Mfg. Co., Connelsville, Pennsylvania. Runabouts.

LOEB
D 1909–1917
Loeb & Co., Berlin.
See "Luc," "Dinos."

LOGAN
USA 1904–1908
Logan Construction Co., Chillicothe, Ohio. Formerly Motor Storage and Mfg. Co. Air and water-cooled cars to 1906, later air-cooled cars only. After 1908 trucks only.

LOGAN
USA 1914
Northwestern Motorcycle Works, Chicago, Illinois. Cyclecar.

LOGICAR
DK 1983–1985
Prototypes.

LOHNER
A 1896–1906
Jacob Lohner & Co., Wien. Gasoline-electric cars.

LOHR
USA 1911
Lohr Motor Co., Elkhart, Indiana. Touring cars.

LOIDIS
GB 1900–1904
A. Dougill & Co. Ltd., Leeds, Yorks. Light car.

LOLA
GB 1958–c. 1973
E. Broadley, Bromley, Kent (1958). Lola Cars Ltd., Bromley, Kent; Byfleet, Surrey (1958–1961); Bromley, Kent (1961–1965); Slough, Bucks. (1965–1970); Huntingdon (1970–c. 1973). Sports and racing cars.

LOMAR
I 1985
Three-wheeler.

LOMAS
GB 1966–1968
Lomas Racing, Knutsford, Cheshire. Sports and racing cars.

LOMAX
GB/E 1980–c. 1997
Lomax Motor Co. Ltd., Bewdley, Worcs. (1980–1993). Fabricacion Europea de Automoviles, S.L., Madrid. Replicars.

LOMAX
USA 1913–1914
Lomax Motor Car Co., Lomax, Illinois.

LOMAX FLINT
USA 1905
Denver, Colorado.
See "Flintlo."

LOMBARD
F 1927–1929
Bollack, Netter et Cie., Argenteuil/Seine-et-Oise; Puteaux/Seine. Sporting voiturette.

LOMBARD
USA 1898–1900
A.O. Lombard, Waterville, Maine.

LOMBARDA
I 1911–1915
See "Esperia," "SAL."

LOMBARDI
I 1969–1974
Carrozzeria Francis Lombardi, Vercelli. "Fiat" based cars. Coachbuilders since 1947.

LONDONIA
GB
See "Owen."

LONDON SIX
CDN 1922–1924
London Motors Ltd., London, Ontario. About 100 6-cylinder cars were made.

LONE STAR
USA 1919–1922
Lone Star Motor Truck & Tractor Assn., San Antonio, Texas. Lone Star Motor Co., El Paso, Texas. Touring cars.

LONG
USA 1908
Harry Long, Aneta, North Dakota. Two cars built.

LONG
USA 1922–1926
R.H. Long & Co. Long Motor Sales, Framingham, Massachusetts. Company built "Bay State" 1922–1924.

LONG
USA 1939
Long's Motor Service, Spartanburg, South Carolina. Roadster.

LONG DISTANCE
USA 1901–1903
U.S. Long Distance Automobile Co., Marion, New Jersey. Runabouts.
See "United States Long Distance."

LONGEST
USA 1906
Longest Bros. Co., Louisville, Kentucky.

LONGHORN
USA 1938
Oliver Albert, Gonzales, Texas. Sports car prototype.

LONG ISLAND
USA 1901–1904
Long Island Motor Vehicle Co., Brooklyn. N.Y.

LONG STEAM CAR
USA 1875–1882
George A. Long, Hinsdale, New Hampshire (1875–1878); Northfield, Massachusetts (1880–1882). Only known "Long Steam Car" is in Smithsonian collection.

LONGTIN
B 1902–1904
Longtin et le Hardy de Beaulieu, Jette St. Pierre. Voiturette.

LONSDALE
AUS 1982
Passenger car prototype.

LONSDALE
GB 1900
Monk & Lonsdale, Brighton, Sussex. Light car.

LOOMIS
USA 1896–1904
Gilbert J. Loomis (1896–1897). Loomis Automobile Co. (1898–1904), Westfield, Massachusetts. About 50 cars built.

LOOS
USA 1907
George Loos, Grafton, North Dakota. 12 hp runabout.

LORD BALTIMORE
USA 1913
Lord Baltimore Automobile Co., Baltimore, Maryland. Touring cars.

LORELEY
D 1906–1927
Rudolf Ley AG, Arnstadt.
See "Ley."

LORENC
B 1903–1904
Transmission Lorenc, Bruxelles. Front-wheel drive.

LORENZ & RANKL
D 1985–1988
Lorenz & Rankl GmbH & Co. Fahrzeugbau KG, Wolfratshausen. Tuning and replicars.

LORINSER
D 1983–present
Sport-Service Lorinser GmbH, Waiblingen. Tuning.

LORRAINE; LORRAINE-DIETRICH
F
See "De Dietrich."

LORRAINE
USA 1907–1909
Lorraine Automobile Mfg. Co., Chicago, Illinois. Large cars with a 5.1-litre engine.

LORRAINE
USA 1920–1921
Lorraine Car Co., Richmond, Indiana.

LORRAINE
USA 1920–1922
Lorraine Motors Corp., Grand Rapids, Michigan. Formerly "Hackett." David Buick employed by company.

LORYC
E 1920–1924
Talleres Lacy y Ribas Srl, Palma de Mallorca. Small sports cars.

LOS ANGELES
USA 1914
Los Angeles Cyclecar Co., Los Angeles, California; Buffalo, N.Y. Cyclecar. L.E. French, designer.

LOST
USA 1963–1964
Lost Cause Motors, Louisville, Kentucky.

LOSURE
USA 1906
Zan Losure, Van Buren, Indiana.

LOTEC
D 1986–1995
Lotec, Kurt Lotterschmidt, Kolbermoor. Sports car.

LOTHIAN
GB 1920
W.J.M. Auto Engineering Ltd., London. 10 hp light car.

LOTIS
GB 1908–1912
Sturmey Motors Ltd., Coventry, Warwickshire. Tourer.

LOTUS
GB 1952–present
Lotus Engineering Co., London (1952–1959). Lotus Cars Ltd., Lotus Components Ltd., Cheshunt, Herts. (1959–1966). Lotus Cars Ltd., Hethel, Norwich (1966–present). Sports cars.

LOUBIERES
F 1951–1953
Compagnie Normande d'Études. Gasoline-electric cars.

LOUET
F 1902–1908
Sté. des Automobiles Louet, Paris (1902–1904). E. Louet et Badin, Auxerre/Yonne (1904–1908). 3-cylinder vertical engine.

LOUIS CHENARD
F 1920–1932
Automobiles Louis Chenard, Colombes/Seine. Small family cars.

LOUISVILLE
USA 1911
Electric Vehicle Co., Louisville, Kentucky. Electric car.

LOUTZKY
D 1899–1900
Gesellschaft für Automobilwagenbau GmbH, Berlin. 3 hp small cars.

LOVE
USA c. 1905
Robert Love, West Warren, Massachusetts. 6 hp automobile.

LOVEJOY
USA 1895
Elmer F. Lovejoy, Laramie, Wyoming.

LOWELL-AMERICAN
USA 1908–1909
Lowell-American Automobile Co., Lowell, Massachusetts. Built motors and supplied automobile plans as early as 1902.

LOWELL AUTOMOTOR
USA 1902
Lowell Motor Co., Lowell, Massachusetts. Runabout.

LOWERY
USA 1895
V.L.D. Lowery, Eaton, Illinois

LOWY
USA 1916
Layman-Lowy Motor Car Co., New York, N.Y.
See "Layman-Lowy."

LOYD-LORD
GB 1923–1924
Loyd-Lord Ltd., London. 2-stroke air-cooled supercharged engine.

LOZA
B 1925
Rhomboid wheel placement, prototype.

LOZIER
USA 1898; 1901
Lozier Motor Co., Plattsburg, N.Y. Steam car.

LOZIER
USA 1905–1918
Lozier Motor Co., Plattsburg, N.Y.; Detroit, Michigan (1910). After steam experimentation, built gasoline marine engines and launches only 1901–1905. First car exhibited Madison Square Garden January 1905; 3,570 cars were made.

LOZIER
USA 1922
Lozier Motor Co., New York, N.Y. 6-cylinder touring car.

L.P.C.
USA 1913
L.P.C. Motor Co., Racine, Wisconsin.
See "Lewis."

L.R.
GB 1983–c. 1993
L.R. Roadsters Co., Newmarket, Suffolk. Replicars.

L-S
PL 1936
Wystawie Przemyslu Mechanicznego i Elektrycznego. Panstwowe Zaklady Inzynerii, Warszawa. Prototype of 3.9 litre V8 engine car "Lux Sport."

L.S.D.
GB 1920–1924
Sykes & Sugden Ltd., Huddersfield, Yorks. (1920–1923). L.S.D. Motor Co. Ltd., Mirfield, Yorks. (1923–1924). Three-wheelers.

L-T
S 1923
A.R. Lindström, Torsby. 20 hp air-cooled car.

LUAZ
SU/UA 1967–present
Mashinostroitelnii i Traktornii Zavod Kommunar, Zaporozhie. Lutskii Avtomobilnii Zavod, Lutsk. Small 4 × 4 vehicle.

LUC
D 1909–1914
Loeb & Co. GmbH, Berlin. 2.6- and 3-litre models.
See "Dinos."

LUCANIA
GB
See "Oppermann."

LUCAR
GB 1914
Lucar Ltd., London. Light car.

LUCAS
GB 1974–1983
Joseph Lucas (Industries) Ltd., Birmingham. Electric cars.

LUCCIOLA
I 1947–1948
G. Pennacchio, Milano. 250cc minicars.
See "Pennacchio."

LUC COURT
F 1899–1936
Sté. des Ans. Établissements Luc Court et Cie., Lyon. Sports and touring cars.

LUCERNA
CH 1907–1909
A.-H. Grivel, Luzern. Assembled car with an Aster engine.

LUCERTOLA
I 1948–1949
See "Fermi."

LUCIA
CH 1904–1908
L. Picker, Moccand et Cie., Chene-Bougeries. About 100 cars were made; acquired by "Sigma."

LUCIEN BOLLACK
F 1929–1930
Lucien Bollack, Paris. 4.3- and 5-litre Lycoming engines.

LUCK UTILITY
USA 1912–1914
Cleburn Motor Car Mfg. Co., Cleburn, Texas. $2,000 five-seater.

LÜDERS
D 1904
Maschinenfabrik für Automobilbau Emil Lüders KG, Berlin. Very few cars were made.
See "Elite."

LUDWIG
USA 1914
Ludwig Motor Car Co., Detroit, Michigan.

LUETH
USA 1903
Lueth Bros., Kankakee, Illinois.

LUFBERY
F 1898–1902
C.E. Lufbery, Chaunay/Aisne. Chain-drive and tiller steering.

LUGLY
F 1921
SA des Automobiles Lugly, Courbevoie/Seine. Touring car.

LUGO ELECTRIC
USA 1891
Electric Road Carriage Co., Boston, Massachusetts.

LUITWIELER
USA 1909
Luitwieler Pumping Engine Co., Rochester, N.Y.

LU-LU
USA 1914–1915
Kearns Motor Truck Co., Beavertown, Pennsylvania. Cyclecars.

LUMMA
D 1997–present
Horst Lumma, Winterlingen. Convertibles.

LUNANT
F 1900–1914
Sté. des Constructions de Cycles et Automobiles Lunant, Lyon. Electric and gasoline cars.

LUNKENHEIMER
USA 1900–1902
Lunkenheimer Brass Works. Lunkenheimer Motor Vehicle Co., Cincinnati, Ohio.

LURQUIN-COUDERT
F 1906–1914
Lurquin et Coudert, Paris. Three-wheelers and cyclecars.

LUSK
USA 1942
Bill Lusk, Cicero, Illinois. "Cycle bus."

LUTECE
F 1906
G. Cochot, Colombes/Seine. Voiturette.

LUTONIA
GB
See "Hart."

LUTWEILER
USA 1909
Lutweiler Pumping Engine Co., Rochester, N.Y.

LUTZ
USA 1898
G.H. Lutz, San Antonio, Texas. Steam car.

LUTZ
USA 1917
Lutz Steam Car Co., Buffalo, N.Y. Steam car.

LUTZMANN
D 1893–1898
Friedrich Lutzmann, Dessau. Vis-à-vis; production rights bought by "Opel" ("System Lutzmann").

LUVERNE
USA 1903–1917
Luverne Automobile Co., Luverne, Minnesota. 570 cars were made.

LUWO
D 1922–1923
Kleinautobau Ludwig & Wolzogen & Co. KG, München. Small cars.

LUX
D 1897–1902
Lux-Werke (1897–1898). Lux'sche Industriewerke AG, Ludwigshafen (1898–1902). Gasoline and electric cars.

LUX
I 1906–1907
Fabbrica di Automobili e Cicli "Lux," Torino. Light cars.

LUXFORD
USA 1928
New York, N.Y. Taxicab on the Model A "Ford" chassis.

LUXIOR
F 1912–1914
Berthaud et Moreau, Vincennes/Seine. Conventional 4-cylinder cars.

LUXOR
USA 1900
C.R. Harris, Williamsport, Pennsylvania. Gasoline chariot.

LUXOR CAB
USA 1924–1927
Luxor Cab Mfg. Co., Hagerstown, Maryland (1924); Framingham, Massachusetts (1924–1927).
See "Moller," "Standish."

L.W.C.
USA 1915–1917
Columbia Taxicab Co., St. Louis, Missouri.

LYBE
USA 1895
D.I. Lybe, Sidney, Iowa.

LYKKE
USA 1901
A. Lykke, Grand Island, Nebraska.

LYMAN
USA 1903–1904
C.F. Lyman, Boston, Massachusetts. Touring cars.

LYMAN & BURNHAM
USA 1903–1905
Lyman & Burnham, Boston, Massachusetts. Successor to Binney & Burnham. Built by Fore River Ship & Engine Co., Quincy, Massachusetts. Concurrent with "Lyman." Five-seater rear-entrance tonneau.

LYNN
USA 1903
Lynn Automobile Co., Lynn, Massachusetts.

LYNN HIGHWHEEL
USA 1908
Lynn Car Co., Everett, Massachusetts.

LYNX
GB 1969–present
Lynx Motor Company, Northiam, Sussex. Lynx Motors International Limited, St. Leonards-on-Sea, Sussex. "Jaguar" D-Type replicars.

LYON
USA 1902
E.H. Lyon, New York, N.Y. Steam car.

LYON
USA c. 1903
George L. Lyon, Durham, North Carolina. 8 hp highwheeler.

LYON
USA 1911
Lyon Motor Car Co., Adrian, Michigan.
See "Lion."

LYONS
USA c. 1905
William Lyons, Lewiston, Maine. 3.5 hp automobile.

LYONS-ATLAS
USA 1912–1914
Lyons-Atlas Co., Indianapolis, Indiana.
See "Lyons-Knight" 1912–1915.

LYONS-KNIGHT
USA 1914–1915
Lyons-Atlas Co., Indianapolis, Indiana. Successor to Atlas Engine Co. 1912 and Atlas Motor Car Co., Springfield, Massachusetts. Sleeve-valve Knight engines.

M

MACAGNO
I
See "SAL," "Esperia."

MACCHI
I 1951
Varese.

MACDONALD
USA 1922–1925
MacDonald Steam Automotor Car Co. MacDonald Steam Automotive Corp., Garfield, Ohio. About 48 steam cars built.

MACDUFF
USA 1903
J.B. MacDuff, Brooklyn, N.Y. Propeller powered runabout.

MACERONE & SQUIRE
GB 1832; 1834–1835; 1841
Francis Macerone & John Squire, London. Steam cars.

MACHIAVELLI
USA c. 1988
Machiavelli Motors of Miami Inc., Key Biscaine, Florida. Sports cars.

MACINNIS
USA 1909–1911
MacInnis Bros., Toledo, Ohio. Electric cars.

MACK
USA 1908
Perry Mack, Milwaukee, Wisconsin. Air-cooled car.

MACKENZIE
GB 1896
Mackenzie & Sons, London. Electric car.

MACKENZIE
USA 1914
H. Jordan MacKenzie, New Orleans, Louisiana. Cyclecar.

MACKENZIE & MCARTHUR
USA 1895
MacKenzie & McArthur Co., New Haven, Connecticut.

MACKER
USA 1902
Macker Automobile Co., Westborough, Massachusetts.

MACKEY
USA 1902–1903
J.C. Mackey Automobile Co., Detroit, Michigan.

MACKLE-THOMPSON
USA 1903
Mackle-Thompson Automobile Co., Elizabeth, New Jersey. Runabout.

MACLEOD
USA 1895
W. MacLeod, New York, N.Y. Surrey.

MACNAUGHTON
USA 1906
James MacNaughton Co., Buffalo, N.Y. Electric car.

MACOMBER
USA 1917
Walter G. Macomber Motors Co., Los Angeles, California. Formerly supplied motors for "Eagle" cyclecar.

MACON
USA 1915–1917
All Steel Motor Car Co. Macon Motor Car Co., Macon, Massouri. Touring cars.

MACQUE
AUS 1913
Allan Macqueen, South Melbourne, South Victoria. Cyclecars.

MACU
D
See "Kenter."

MACY-ROGER
USA 1895–1896
Roger-American Mechanical Carriage Co., New York, N.Y. Entered Chicago Times-Herald Race.

MADA
D 1947
Maschinenfabrik G. Danger GmbH, Säckingen/Rhein. Small cars.

MADELVIC
GB 1898–1900
Madelvic Motor Carriage Co. Ltd., Granton, Edinburgh. Electric car.

MADI
1986
Minicar.

MADISON
GB 1981–1983
GP Concessionaires. Replicars.

MADISON
USA 1915–1919
Madison Motor Co. Madison Motors & Tractors Corp. Madison Motors Corp., Anderson, Indiana. Reorganized as Madison Motors Co. 1916. Used old "Rider-Lewis" and "Nyberg" plant; 453 cars were made.

MADOU
F 1922–1925
Automobiles Madou, Paris. Sports cars.

MADSEN
DK 1972
Alfred Madsen. Dune buggy.

MADSEN
USA 1901–1904
L.P. Madsen, Council Bluffs, Iowa. Chain-drive runabout.

MAE
D 1993–1995
Müller-Auto-Entwicklung, Esslingen. Tuning.

MAF
D 1908–1921
Markranstädter Automobil-Fabrik Hugo Ruppe (1908–1911). Markranstädter Automobil-Fabrik vorm. Hugo Ruppe GmbH, Markranstädt (1911–1921). Air-cooled engines.

MAFFEIS & FIGLIO
I 1904
Milano.

MAG
H 1912–1935
Magyar Általános Gépgyár R.T., Budapest. 4- and 6-cylinder passenger cars.

MAGALI
F 1905–1906
Gazon et Cie., Levallois-Perret/Seine. 10hp and 30hp cars.

MAGDA
CS 1936–1955
Jaroslav Vlček, Praha. Sports and racing cars.

MAGENTA
GB 1972–c. 1981
Lightspeed Panels, Whitby, North Yorkshire. Sports car.

MAGGIORA
I 1905
Automobili Maggiora, Padova. 4hp and 8hp light cars.

MAGIC
USA 1914
Fisher Motor Corp., New York, N.Y. Pilots built with Mondex Magic engines.

MAGLIOLA
I 1911–1915
A. Magliola & F., Novara.

MAGNET
D 1921–1926
Motoren-Fabrik Magnet GmbH. Magnet-Motoren AG, Berlin. Three-wheelers.

MAGNETIC
GB 1921–1926
Magnetic Car Co. Ltd., London. 2.6- and 5.2-litre cars.

MAGNETIC
USA 1921–1922
Owen Magnetic Motor Co. A gas-electric vehicle.
See "Crown Magnetic."

MAGNOLIA
USA 1902–1903
Magnolia Automobile Co., Riverside, California.

MAGNOLIA
USA c. 1908
Tom Dean, Magnolia, Minnesota.

MAGNUM
GB 1990s
Magnum Engineering, Compton Verney, Warwickshire. Sports kit cars.

MAGRAW
GB 1979
Magraw Engineering Ltd., Bromley, Kent. Sports cars.

MAGUIRE
USA 1895
Maguire Power Generating Co., Chicago, Illinois.

MAHAG
D 1970
MAHAG, München. Dune buggy.

MAHANA
USA 1910
J.B. Mahana, Poultney, Vermont.

MAHINDRA
IND 1968–present
Mahindra & Mahindra Ltd., Worli, Bombay. "Jeep" (USA) license.

MAHLER
CH 1913–1914
Mahler & Co., Oensingen. Light cars.

MAHONING
USA 1904–1905
Mahoning Motor Car Co., Youngstown, Ohio. Air-cooled car.

MAHS
USA 1903–1904
W.H. Mahs, Detroit, Michigan. Large tourers.

MAIBOHM
USA 1916–1922
Maibohm Motors Co., Racine, Wisconsin; Sandusky, Ohio. Formerly Maibohm Wagon Co. Became Arrow Motors.
See also "Courier"; 4,195 cars were made.

MAICO
D 1955–1958
Maico-Werke GmbH, Pfäffingen. Small sports and passenger cars.

MAIER
D 1964
Peter Maier-Asboe, Berlin. Plastic bodied coupe.

MAIFLOWER
GB 1919–1921
Maiflower Motor Co. Ltd., Gloucester. Improvers of the Model T "Ford" (USA).

MAILLARD
F 1900–1903
M. Maillard, Incheville/Seine-Inferieure. Light cars.

MAINE
USA 1915–1918
See "Hartman."

M.A.I.S.
TR 1971
Motorlu Araclar Imal ve Satis A.S. "Renault" (F) license.

MAIS
USA 1911
Mais Motor Truck Co., Indianapolis, Indiana. Roadster.

M.A.J.
F
See "Julien."

MAJA
A 1907–1908
Österreichische Daimler-Motoren AG, Wiener-Neustadt. 4-cylinder chain-driven cars.

MAJA
D 1923–1924
Maja-Werk für Motor-Vierrad-Bau AG, München. 500 cc BMW engine.

MAJER
A/CS c. 1913
M. Majer, Psáre pri Kozárovciach. Light car for producer's own use.

MAJERUS
USA 1909
J.B. Majerus, Goodhue, Minnesota.

MAJESTIC
F 1926–1930
Automobiles Majestic, Paris. 3-litre 6-cylinder engine.

MAJESTIC
GB
See "Whitehead-Thanet."

MAJESTIC
USA 1909
Milwaukee Auto Engine and Supply Co., Milwaukee, Wisconsin.

MAJESTIC
USA 1916
Majestic Motor Corp., Chicago, Illinois. 4-cylinder 30 hp touring cars.

MAJESTIC
USA 1917
Majestic Motor Co., New York, N.Y. Touring cars.

MAJESTIC
USA 1925–1927
Larrabee-Deyo Motor Truck Co., Binghampton, N.Y. Taxicabs.

MAJOCCHI
I 1898–1906
Officine Fratelli Majocchi, Milano.

MAJOLA
F 1911–1928
J. Majola, St. Denis/Seine (1911–1920); Chatou/Seine-et-Oise (1920–1928). Sports cars.

MAJOR
F 1920–1921; 1932
Cyclecars Major, Paris. Cyclecars.

MALAXA
RO 1945
Malaxa, Bucuresti & IAR, Brasov. Rear-engined 3 cyclinder light car prototype.

MALCOLM
USA 1900
C.P. Malcolm & Co., Oxford, Michigan. 1-, 2- and 4-cylinder cars.

MALCOLM
USA 1914
Malcolm-Jones Detroit Co. Malcolm-Jones Cyclecar Co., Detroit, Michigan. Cyclecar. Malcolm Cyclecar Co., Plymouth, Michigan, successor.

MALCOLM
USA 1915–1916
Malcolm Motor Car Co., Detroit, Michigan. Successor to "Malcolm" cyclecar.

MALCOLMSON
USA 1905–1906
Alexander Malcolmson, Detroit, Michigan.

MALDEN
USA 1898; 1902
Malden Automobile Co., Malden, Massachusetts. Steam cars.

MALEVEZ
B 1902–1904
Malevez et Michotte, Namur. 9 hp light cars.

MALICET & BLIN
F 1911
Sté. Malicet et Blin, Aubervilliers/Seine. Light cars.

MALLALIEU
GB 1976–1981
Mallalieu Engineering Ltd., Abingdon, Oxfordshire. Replicars.

MALLEY
USA c. 1905
G.H. Malley, Boston, Massachusetts. 3.5 hp automobile

MALLIARY
F 1901
G. Malliary, Puteaux/Seine. Voiturette.

MALONE
GB 1990s
Malone Designs, West Putford, Nr. Holsworthy, Devon. Sports kit cars.

MALTBY
USA 1900–1902
Maltby Automobile Co., Brooklyn, N.Y.; Matawan, New Jersey. Gasoline runabout.

MALTERNER
USA 1903
Silas Malterner, Canton, N.Y. Steam vehicle.

MALUTKA
SU 1947; 1964
Minicar prototypes built in Leningrad.

MALVERNIA
GB
See "Santler."

MANCHESTER
GB 1904–1905
Bennett & Carlisle Ltd., Manchester. Prototype.

MANCHESTER
USA 1901–1904
Manchester Locomotive Works, Manchester, New Hampshire. Steam car.

M & C
USA 1913
National Contracting Co., New York, N.Y. Electric car.

MANDERBACH
D 1928–1938
Louis Manderbach & Co. Fahrzeugfabrik, Wissenbach/Dillkreis. Three-wheelers. Light delivery vans 1950–1956.

M & L
USA 1998
M & L Autospecialists, Two Rivers, Wisconsin. Sports cars.

MANEXALL
USA 1921
Manufacturers & Exporters Alliance, New York, N.Y.
See "Cyclomobile."

MANGIAPAN
I 1917
Societa per Costruzione Meccaniche, Milano.

MANHATTAN
USA 1903–1904
Manhattan Automobile Co., New York, N.Y. Both gas and electric cars.

MANHEIM
USA 1902
Manheim Automobile Co., Manheim,

Pennsylvania. High-wheeled electric stanhope.

MANIC
CDN 1969–1971
Ecurie Manic Inc. Les Automobiles Manic, Granby, Quebec. Sports cars.

MANISTEE
USA 1902
Manistee Motor Car Co., Manistee, Michigan. Runabout.

MANLIUS
USA 1910
Manlius Motor Co., Manlius, N.Y. Roadsters.

MANN
USA 1895
Mann Press Co., Gladbrook, Iowa.

MANN & MARSHALL
USA c. 1905
Albert Mann & Edward Marshall, Bridgeport, Connecticut. 7.5 hp automobile.

MANNESMANN
D 1923–1929
Mannesmann Motoren-Werke & Co (1923–1926). Mannesmann-Automobil-Werk KG, Remscheid (1927–1929). Light cars; 3.4- and 5.2-litre supercharged models.

MANNING
USA 1901
George Manning, Lewiston, Maine.

MANNING
USA 1932
Don Manning, Lockport, Illinois. Midget car.

MANOCAR
F 1953
Ets. Manom, Saint-Ouen. 125 cc three-wheeler prototype.

MANON
F 1903–1905
H. Chaigneau, Paris. Light car.

MANROSS
USA 1908
Frederick Newton Manross, Bristol, Connecticut. Gasoline touring runabout.

MANS
B 1899–1905
Leon Mans et Cie., Forest-Bruxelles. Three-wheelers and voiturettes.

MANSFIELD
USA 1901, 1903
See "Darlin," "Shelby."

MANSURY & SMITH
USA 1903
See "Goodrich."

MANTA
USA 1973–present
Manta Cars Ltd., Santa Ana, California. Sports car kit.

MANTELLI
I 1960
Carrozzeria Mantelli, Torino. 4-door limousines based on the "Fiat" 500.

MANTON
USA 1866
Joseph P. Manton, Providence, Rhode Island. Steam car.

MANTOVANI
I 1903–1906
Stabilimento Meccanico Carlo Mantovani & C., Torino.

MANTZEL
D 1962; 1966
Albrecht-Wolf Mantzel. Sports coupe.

MANX TOW'D
USA 1966–1972
B.F. Meyers Co., Fountain Valley, California. Dune buggy.

MAPLEBAY
USA 1907
Maplebay Mfg. Co., Crookston, Minnesota. Runabout.

MARATHON
F 1954–1955
Automobiles Marathon, Paris. "Trippel" (D) based small cars.

MARATHON
USA 1908–1914
Marathon Motor Car Co., Cincinnati, Ohio. Southern Motor Works, Nashville, Tennessee. Name changed to Marathon Motor Works 1912. Absorbed by Herff-Brooks Corp. Bankruptcy reported June 1914. Touring cars.

MARATHON
USA 1920
Marathon Motor Export Co., Elkhart, Indiana. For export only.

MARATHON SIX
USA 1909
Marathon Automobile Co., Cincinnati, Ohio.

MARAUDER
GB 1950–1952
Wilks, Mackie & Co. Ltd., Dorridge, Warwickshire (1950–1951). Marauder Car Co. Ltd., Kenilworth, Warwickshire (1951–1952). 15 sports cars were built.

MARAUDER
USA 1975–1993
Marauder & Co., Potomac, Illinois. Sports cars.

MARAZZI
I 1983–c. 1988
Marazzi Carrozzeria SpA, Caronno Pertusella. Sports car.

MARBLE-SWIFT
USA 1903–1905
Marble-Swift Automobile Co., Chicago, Illinois. Runabouts and touring cars.

MARBON
GB 1966–1967
Marbon Chemical Division, Borg-Warner Group. Sports car prototype.

MARCADIER
F 1963–c. 1977
Automobiles Marcadier, Mions. Sports cars.

MARCA TRE SPADE
I 1908
Torino. 16/24 hp conventional cars.
See "Bertoldo."

MARCHAND
I 1898–1909
Orio & Marchand (1898–1900), Piacenza. F. lli Marchand (1900–1905). Marchand (1905–1906). Marchand-Dufaux (1906–1909), Genova. Very large and high bodywork, wide range of engines.

MARCOS
GB 1959–present
Speedex Castings and Accessories Ltd. (1959–1961). Monocoque Chassis & Body Co. Ltd. (1961). Marcos Cars Ltd., Luton, Beds. (1962–1963); Bradford-on-Avon, Wilts. (1963–1970); Westbury, Wilts. (1970–present). Sports cars.

MARCUS
A/CS 1889
Siegfried Marcus, Märky, Bromovsky a Schulz, Adamov. Austro-Hungarian automobile pioneer. His first atmospheric gas motor ran in Wien, 1860.

MARCUS
GB 1920
London. Cyclecar.

MARDEN
F 1975–1988
Sogalon S.A., Neuilly/Seine; Ofranville. Electric and gasoline city cars.

MARENDAZ
GB 1926–1936
D.M.K. Marendaz Ltd., London (1926–1932). Marendaz Special Cars Ltd., Maidenhead, Berks (1932–1936). Sports cars.

MARENGO
I 1907–1909
Automobili Marengo, Genova. Small cars.

MARGUERITE
F 1922–1928
Marguerite, Courbevoie/Seine. About 250 sports cars were built.

MARIE
F 1907
Bayeux. Single-seater car.

MARIENFELDE
D
See "M.M.B."

MARINO
I 1920–1930
Marino SA, Alberto & Giacomo Marino, Padova (1920–1929). Auto Officine Meccaniche Marino di Marino Luigi (1929). Marino Luigi & Dalla Costa Silvio (1931). Auto Officine Meccaniche Marino, Padova (1931). Sports cars.

MARION
USA 1901
Marion Automobile Co., Marion, Ohio.

MARION
USA 1904–1915
Marion Motor Car Co., Indianapolis, Indiana. Marion-Handley Mutual Motors Corp., Jackson, Michigan. Marketed in 1912 with "Overland" and "American Underslung" by John N. Willys in American Motors Corp. Reorganized 1914 with "Imperial" in Mutual Motors Corp. May 1912 assets sold to J.I. Handley. Became "Marion-Handley." 9,663 cars were made (incl. "Marion-Handley").

MARION-FLYER
USA 1910
Hartman Motor Car Co., Omaha, Nebraska. Touring roadster.

MARION-HANDLEY
USA 1916–1919
Mutual Motors Corp., Jackson, Michigan. Became "Handley-Knight."

MARION-OVERLAND
USA 1910
Willys-Overland Co., Toledo, Ohio.

MARITIME
CDN 1913
Maritime Motor Car Co. Ltd., Goldbrook, New Brunswick.

MARK
USA 1902
Harry J. Mark, New York, N.Y.

MARKETEER
USA 1954
Electric Marketeer Mfg. Co., Redlands, California. Electric cars.

MARKETOUR
USA 1964–c. 1974
Marketour Electric Cars, Long Beach, California. Electric three-wheelers.

MARKETTE
USA 1967–1968
Westinghouse Electric Corp., Pittsburgh, Pennsylvania. One electric car made.

MARKS-MOIR
AUS 1923–1924
Marks Motor Construction Co., Sydney, N.S.W.

MARK III
USA 1968
Auto Craft Northwest, Portland, Oregon. Sports cars.

MARLAND
F 1969–1977
Marland Sarl, Issy-les-Moulineaux, Hauts-de-Seine. Dune buggy and replicars. 462 cars built in 1973, 527 cars in 1974.

MARLBORO
USA 1900–1903
Marlboro Automobile Co. Marlboro Automobile & Carriage Co., Marlboro, Massachusetts. Steam car.
See "Walker."

MARLBOROUGH
F/GB 1906–1926
Malicet et Blin, Aubervilliers, Seine (1906–1924). T.B. Andre & Co. Ltd., London (1909–1926). Touring and sports cars.

MARLBOROUGH
NZ 1919–1926
John North Birch, Blenheim, South Island; Gisborne, North Island.

MARLBOROUGH-THOMAS
GB 1923–1924
T.B. Andre & Co., Weybridge, Surrey. 5.8-litre 4-cylinder cars.

MARLIN
GB 1974–present
Paul P. Moorhouse, Mutley, Plymouth, Devon. Marlin Engineering, Crediton, Devon. Sports cars and replicars.

MARMON
USA 1902–1933
Nordyke & Marmon Co., Indianapolis, Indiana. Reorganized 1926 as Marmon Motor Car Company. 115,211 cars were made. Also produced a low-priced car called the "Roosevelt."

MAROCCHI
I 1900–1901
Fratelli Marocchi, Milano. Three-wheeler.

MAROT-GARDON
F 1899–1902
Ph. Marot, Gardon et Cie., Corbie/Somme. Three-wheelers and light cars.

MAROT-GINTRAC
F 1905
Bordeaux. 35/40 hp engines.

MARQUETTE
USA 1912
Marquette Motor Co., Saginaw, Michigan. Organized by General Motors in 1909 to consolidate "Rainier" and "Welch-Detroit." Built both cars into 1911. 40–45 hp engines. Company

renamed Peninsular Motor Co. April 1912.

MARQUETTE
USA 1930
Buick Motor Co., Flint, Michigan. 35,007 passenger cars were built.

MARQUEZ
BR 1979–1981
Marquez Ind. e Com. De Veiculos Ltda., Matao. Sports cars.

MARQUEZ
F 1930
Automobiles L.F. Marquez, Paris. Expensive streamlined sports car.

MARQUIS
USA 1954
Plasticar, Doylestown, Pennsylvania. Sports cars.

MARR
USA 1903–1904
Marr Auto Car Co., Detroit, Michigan. Runabouts built by Fauber & Marr, Elgin, Illinois.

MARR
USA 1914
Marr Automobile Co., Detroit, Michigan. Walter L. Marr had been chief engineer for "Buick." One cyclecar extant in Flint, Michigan museum.

MARRIOTT
AUS 1902
Marriott & Co., Melbourne, Victoria.

MARS
A/CS 1912
Slatiňanská továrnma automobilu R.A. Smekal, Slatiňany. Light cars.

MARS
D 1906–1908
Mars-Werke AG, Nürnberg. Friction drive.

MARS
USA 1966–1972
Electric Fuel Propulsion, Inc., Ferndale, Michigan. One experimental car built and tested 1966. Nine cars ordered and tested by utility companies 1967–1968. Mars II built in "Renault" R-10 body shell.

MARSEEL; MARSEAL
GB 1919–1925
Marseal Motors Ltd., Coventry, Warwickshire. Orthodox light cars.

MARSH
USA 1899
Marsh Brothers. Marsh Motor Carriage Company, Brockton, Massachusetts. Steam car. One prototype after three years' work.

MARSH
USA 1905–1906
American Motor Co., Brockton, Massachusetts. Organized by Marsh Brothers. Built motor cycles 1900–1905. Absorbed by Waltham Mfg. Co.

MARSH
USA 1907–1908
Frederick D. and Winfred Marsh, Detroit, Michigan. Highwheelers.

MARSH
USA 1920–1923
Marsh Motors Co., Cleveland, Ohio.

MARSHALL
GB 1897–1902
Marshall & Co., Manchester.
See "Belsize."

MARSHALL
GB 1919–1920
P.F.E. Marshall, Gainsborough, Lincs. Coventry-Climax engines.

MARSHALL
USA 1920–1922
Marshall Motor Car Co., Chicago, Illinois. Touring car.

MARSHALL
USA 1924
Norwalk Motor Car Co., Martinsburg, West Virginia. "Norwalk" sold under "Marshall" name.
See "Norwalk."

MARSHALL-ARTER
GB 1912–1915
Marshall-Arter Ltd., London. Light cars.

MARSHALLTOWN
USA 1909
Marshalltown Buggy Co., Marshalltown, Iowa.

MARSONETTO
F 1965–1969
Ateliers Marsonetto, Lyon/Rhone. Sports car.

MARTA
H 1910–1914
Magyar Automobil Részvény Társaság Arad, Arad. About 650 passenger cars and hire cars were made.

MARTEL
USA 1925–1927
Elcar Co., Elkhart, Indiana. Taxicab.

MARTELL
USA 1908–1910
MartelMotor Car Co., Jamaica Plain, Massachusetts. Became "Lenox."

MARTES
I 1951–1956
Danilo Tesini, Verona. Built 3 or 4 cars.

M' ARTHUR
USA 1895
A.W. M' Arthur, Rockford, Illinois.

MARTI
TR 1990–present
Tüvasas, Izmir. Electric city cars.

MARTIGNONI
I
See "Cattaneo Guido."

MARTIN
CDN c. 1900
Martin Carriage Works, Chatham, Ontario

MARTIN
F 1975–1993
Martin Automobiles, Olonne-sur-Mer. Replicars.

MARTIN
GB 1905–1906
Hall & Martin, East Croydon, Surrey. Four-seater tonneau.

MARTIN
GB 1974–1993
Martin Engineering Co., Plymouth, Devon. Replicars.

MARTIN
USA 1898–1900
Martin Motor Wagon Co., Buffalo, N.Y.

MARTIN
USA 1900
A.J. Martin, Buffalo, N.Y.

MARTIN
USA 1903
M.B. Martin, Grand Rapids, Michigan.

MARTIN
USA 1905
Palmer & Christie, New York, N.Y.

MARTIN
USA 1907
Al Martin, Atlanta, Georgia. 6 hp runabout.

MARTIN
USA 1910
Martin Carriage Works, York, Pennsylvania. Runabouts.

MARTIN
USA 1920–1922
Martin Motor Co. Martin Motor & Trailer Corp., Springfield, Massachusetts. Also a three-wheel Scootmobile.

MARTIN
USA 1928–1932
James V. Martin Aeroplane Co., Garden City, N.Y. Three- and four-wheeled streamlined rear-engined cars.

MARTIN ET LETHIMMONIER
F
See "Sultane."

MARTINETTE
D 1921–1922
Volta-Werken, Berlin. About 100 light cars were built.

MARTINETTE
USA 1954
Martin Development Laboratories, Rochelle Park, N.Y. Three-wheelers. Firm sold to Bassons Industries Corp. in 1955.
See "Bassons Star."

MARTINI
CH 1897–1934
Martini et Cie., Frauenfeld (1897–1903); St. Blaise-Neuchatel (1903–1906). Sté. Nouvelle des Automobiles Martini, St. Blaise-Neuchatel (1906–1934). Touring and sports cars.

MARTINOT ET GALLAND
D 1898/1899
Ateliers de Construction de Bitschweiler, Thonn, Alsace. 1-cylinder horizontal engine and solid tires.

MARTINS
DK 1944
Martins Konstruktioner. Rear-engined small car prototype.

MARTIN STATIONETTE
USA 1954
Commonwealth Research Corp., New York, N.Y. Three-wheeler. J.V. Martin designer.

MARTIN-T
USA 1956–1964
Tanner Motor Co., Saginaw, Michigan.

MARTIN-WASP
USA 1919–1925
Martin Wasp Co., Bennington, Vermont.
See "Wasp."

MARUTI
IND 1981–present
Maruti Udyog Ltd., Neu Delhi. "Suzuki" (J) license.

MARVEL
F 1905–1908
Automobiles Marvel, Paris.

MARVEL
USA 1907
Marvel Motor Car Co., Detroit, Michigan. Succeeded Detroit Auto Mfg. Co; Runabout.

MARVIA
RI 1993
P.T. Marvia Graha Motor, Jakarta Pusat. Replica kit.

MARYLAND
USA 1900
Maryland Automobile Mfg. Co., Cumberland, Maryland. Steam car.

MARYLAND
USA 1900–1901
Maryland Automobile & Mfg. Co. Maryland Automobile Co., Luke, Maryland; Westernport, Maryland. Steam cars.

MARYLAND
USA 1907–1910
Sinclair Scott Co., Baltimore, Maryland. Succeeded "Ariel" September 1906. First shown New York, January 1907; Touring cars and roadsters.

MARYLAND
USA 1914
Maryland Electric Automobile & Mfg., Baltimore, Maryland. Electric car.

MARYLAND
USA 1922
Maryland Motor Car Co., Frederick, Maryland.

MARYSVILLE
USA 1905
Marysville Motor Car Co., Marysville, Ohio.

MASCOT
S 1920
Raverken, Hälsingborg. Cyclecars.

MASCOTTE
GB 1919–1921
Mascotte Engineering Co. Ltd., London. Light cars.

M.A.S.E.
F 1921–1924
Manufacture d'Autos, Outillage et Cycles, St. Etienne/Loire. Light car.

MASERATI
I 1914–present
Officine Alfiermi Maserati, Bologna (1914–1937). Societa Anonima Officine Alfieri Maserati, Modena (1940–1975). Maserati S.p.A., Modena (1975–present). High performance sports and touring cars.

MASON
USA 1898–1899
William B. Mason. Mason Steam Regulator Co., Milton, Massachusetts. Steam car. Similar to "Stanley."

MASON
USA 1906–1914
Mason Motor Car Co., Des Moines, Iowa (1906–1910); Waterloo, Iowa (1910–1914). First auto venture of Fred Duesenberg. Became Mason Automobile. Co. Reorganized 1910 as Maytag-Mason Motor Co. 1,515 cars.

MASON
USA 1907
Puritan Machine Co., Boston, Massachusetts.

MASON-MOHLER
USA 1914
Mason Motor Co., Waterloo, Iowa. Car used Mason-Duesenberg engine.

MASON-SEAMAN
USA 1914
Mason-Seaman Transportation Co., New York, N.Y. Gas-electric taxicabs.

MASON TOURIST KING
USA c. 1918
Newark, New Jersey. Phaeton.

MASS
F 1903–1923
Automobiles Mass (L. Pierron), Courbevoie/Seine. Voiturettes.
See "Pierron."

MASSACHUSETTS
USA 1899
John C. Welch, Lynn, Massachusetts.

MASSACHUSETTS
USA 1901
Massachusetts Steam Wagon Co., Pittsfield, Massachusetts. Steam car.

MASSACHUSETTS
USA c. 1905
Massachusetts Auto Car Co., Leominster, Massachusetts. 7 hp gasoline car.

MASSIE
USA 1903
Massie & Sons., Quincy, Illinois.

MASSILLON
USA 1909
W.S. Read Co., Massillon, Ohio. Roadsters.

MASTER
USA 1917–1918
Master Motor Car Co., Cleveland, Ohio.

MASTERBILT SIX
USA 1926
Govreau-Nelson Engineering Works, Detroit, Michigan.

MASTRA
GB 1935
Prototype.

MASTRETTA
MEX 1997
Tecnosport S.A., Mexico City. Sports cars.

MATAS
E 1919–1922
Matas y Cia., Barcelona. Light car.

MATCHLESS
GB 1913–1924
H. Collier & Sons Ltd., London. Three-wheeler.

MATFORD
F 1934–1946
SA Francaise Matford, Strasbourg; Asnieres/Seine. Name from "MAThis" (F) and "FORD" (USA/GB).

MATHESON
USA 1903–1913
Mastheson Motor Car Co., Grand Rapids, Michigan; Holyoke, Massachusetts. Merged with Holyoke Motor Works. Moved to Wilkes-Barre, Pennsylvania 1905. Touring cars and runabouts.

MATHEWS
USA 1907–1908
Mathews Motor Co., Camden, New Jersey. Succeeded "Jones-Corbin."
   See "Sovereign."

MATHEWS
USA 1912–1914
John L. Mathews, Lidgerwood, North Dakota. Two cars were built.

MATHIEU
B 1902–1904
Usines Eugene Mathieu, Louvain. Four-seater tonneau.

MATHIS
D/F 1898–1903; 1910–1914; 1919–1935; 1945–1950; E.E.C. Mathis, Strasbourg (1898–1914). SA Mathis, Strasbourg (1919–1950)
Sports and touring cars.

MATHIS
I 1912
Fratelli Pellini, Milano

MATHIS
USA 1931
Durant Motors, New York, N.Y.; Lansing, Michigan. Limited production under French "Mathis" license.

MATHOMOBILE
B 1980–1993
Mathomobile Replicars, Bruxelles. "Bugatti" (F) replica. 13 cars built in 1981.

MATICH
AUS 1965–?
Matich Cars, Castlecove, N.S.W. Sports car.

MATRA
F 1965–1984
Matra Sports Srl, Romorantin/Loir-et-Cher (1965–1984). Sports cars.

MATRA-SIMCA
F 1969–1984
Société Mécanique Aeronautique et Traction. Matra-Simca, Division Automobile, Velizy-Villacoublay. Sports cars and city cars.

MATTHES
D 1985
Matthes Söhne GmbH, Frankfurt. Tuning.

MATTHEWS
USA
   See "Sovereign."

MATTHEY ET MARTIN
F 1924–1925
Matthey et Martin, Paris. Light car.

MATTIG
D 1986
Mattig-Tuning, Hauzenberg. Tuning.

MAUDSLAY
GB 1902–1923
Maudslay Motor Co. Ltd., Coventry, Warwickshire. Steam carriage in 1835. Touring cars.

MAUMEE
USA 1906–1907
Maumee Motor Car Works, Toledo, Ohio. Absorbed Wolverine Auto & Commercial Vehicle Co., and transferred to Craig-Toledo Motor Co. Bankrupt 1907.
   See "Wolverine" and "Craig-Toledo."

MAURER
D 1908–1909; 1923–1924
Johanna Maurer (1908–1909). Automobilfabrik Ludwig Maurer, Nürnberg (1923–1924). Light cars.

MAURER-UNION
D 1900–1910
Nürnberger Motorfahrzeug-Fabrik "Union" (1900–1908). Automobilwerke Union AG, Nürnberg (1908–1910). Friction-driven cars.

MAUSER
D 1923–1927
Mauser-Werke AG, Oberndorf. Two-wheel vehicle.

MAUVE
F 1923–1924
Cyclecars Mauve, Levallois-Perret/Seine. Anzani engine.

MÁVAG
1936–1942
Állami Gépgyár Mávag, Budapest. License-built German "Ford"; 7-seater limousine of own design. About 600 cars were made, either as private cars or taxicabs.

MAVERICK
USA 1953–1955
Maverick Motors, Mt. View, California.

7 three-passenger cars on "Cadillac" chassis were made.

MAX
F 1927–1929
Mourlot et Cie., Billancourt/Seine. Cyclecars.

MAX
NL 1988–1993
Max Motors B.V., Helmond. Sports cars.

MAXEN
USA 1904; 1913
Roy McCartney, Cedar Rapids, Iowa. Electric cars.

MAXIM
GB 1902–1905
London General Automobile Co. Ltd., Londo. 16 hp 2-cylinder conventional cars.

MAXIMAG
CH 1923–1928
SA Motosacoche, Geneve. Light sports cars.

MAXIM ELECTRIC
USA 1913–1914
Maxim Munitions Co., Cedar Rapids, Iowa.

MAXIM-GOODRIDGE
USA 1908
Maxim-Goodridge Co., Hartford, Connecticut. Electric car.
 See "Lenox."

MAXIM MOTOR TRICYCLE
USA 1894–1895
American Projectile Co., Lynn, Massachusetts (1894). Maxim Mfg. Co., Hartford, Connecticut (1895). Three-cylinder tricycle.

MAXIM TRI-CAR
USA 1911–1914
Blushnell Press Co., Thompsonville, Connecticut (1911–1912). Maxim Tri-Car Mfg. Co., Port Jefferson, N.Y. (1913–1914).

MAXMOBILE
CDN 1900
D.A. Maxwell, Waterford, Ontario.

MAXWELL
USA 1904–1925
Maxwell Motor Co., Detroit, Michigan. Reorganized 1921 as Maxwell Motor Corp. Formerly Maxwell. Briscoe Motor Co; Touring cars and roadsters.

MAXWELL-BRISCOE
USA 1904–1913
Maxwell Briscoe Motor Co., Tarrytown, N.Y.
 See "Maxwell." Became unit of United States Motor Co. 1910. This is the early name for "Maxwell."

MAXWELL-FITCH
USA 1905; 1909
Maxwell & Fitch Co., Rome, N.Y. Prototypes only.

MAXWERKE
D 1899–1903
Elektrizitäts- und Automobil-Gesellschaft Harff & Schwarz AG, Köln. Electric cars.

MAY
GB 1989–1993
May Corporation (Europe) Ltd., Harpenden, Hertfordshire. Sports cars.

MAYA
GB
 See "Camber."

MAYBACH
D 1921–1941
Maybach Motoren-Werke GmbH, Friedrichshafen. Large luxury touring cars.

MAYER
D 1899–1900
Hugo Mayer, Berlin. Voiturette.

MAYER
USA 1899–1901
Simon Mayer, Chicago, Illinois. Runabout.

MAYER SPECIAL
USA 1903–1907
Louis Mayer, Mankato, Minnesota. V-8 powered.

MAYFAIR
GB 1900–1907
Sports Motor Car Co. Ltd (1900–1901). G.L.M. Dörwald & Co., London (1906–1907).

MAYFAIR
USA 1925
Mayfair Mfg. Co., Boston, Massachusetts. A fabric-bodied stretched-out "Ford."

MAYFLOWER
GB 1995–present
Mayflower Corporation plc, High Wycombe, Buckinghamshire. Passenger and sports car prototypes and projects.

MAYMAN
AUS 1903
Mayman Co., South Yarra, Victoria.

MAYNARD
USA c. 1905
E.D. Maynard, Lynn, Massachusetts. 4 hp automobile.

MAYRETTE
D 1927–1930 (1921–1924?)
Kleinfahrzeugbau Karl Mayr, München. Light cars.

MAYTAG
USA 1910–1915
Maytag-Mason Motor Co., Waterloo, Iowa. Successor to Mason Automobile Co. Became Mason Motor Car Co.
 See "Mason"; 765 cars were made.

MAZDA
J 1960–present
Toyo Kogyo Co. Ltd., Hiroshima. Passenger and sports cars.

MAZEL
E 2000
Mazel Ingenieros SA, Abrera. Sports car prototype.

M.B.
F 1921
Maurice Badaroux. Sports cars.

M.B.
GB 1919–1921
Merrall-Brown Motors Ltd., Bolton, Lancs. Cyclecars.

MB
I 1925
Motta & Baudo, Torino.
 See "Motta & Baudo." Light car.

M.B.
USA 1908–1911
Motor Buggy Mfg. Co., Minneapolis, Minnesota. Roadsters.

M.B.M.
CH 1959–1962
Garage Monteverdi, Binningen (Basel). Sports and racing cars.

MBP
I
 See "BMP."

M.C.A.
D 1962–1964
M.C.A. Automobile Ulrich Otten, Bremen. Fiberglass-bodied coupe and roadster on "Volkswagen" chassis.

M.C.C.
GB
See "Vapomobile."

MCCABE
USA c. 1905
McCabe, Somerville, Massachusetts. 4 hp car.

MCCAN
USA 1902
D.C. McCan, New York, N.Y.

MCCANDLESS
GB 1954–1957
R. and W.A.C. McCandless (Engineers) Ltd., Belfast. Sports and racing cars.

MCCLINTOCK
USA 1904
McClintock, Kansas City, Missouri.

MCCLUER
USA 1891
Marshall McCluer, Spring Lake, Michigan.

MCCORD
USA 1913
McCord Automobile Co., Chicago, Illinois. Touring cars.

MCCORMACK
USA 1921–1922
McCormack Bros. Motor Car Co., Birmingham, Alabama. Steam car.

M.C.C. SIX
USA 1913
M.C.C. Co., Detroit, Michigan. Touring cars.

MCCUE
USA 1908–1911
McCue Co., Hartford, Connecticut. Automobile and carriage fittings from December 1904. Very few touring cars and runabouts were built.

MCCULLOUGH
USA 1899–1900
W.T. McCullough Automobile Co., Boston, Massachusetts. Also Back Bay Cycle & Motor Co. Became U.S. Motor Vehicle Co. Two-seater light cars.

MCCURD
GB 1923–1927
McCurd Lorry Mfg. Co. Ltd., Hayes, Middlesex. Light cars.

MCCURDY
USA 1922
Hercules Corp. McCurdy-Hercules Corp., Evansville, Indiana.
See "Gale 4."

MCDUFFEE
USA 1905
McDuffee Automobile Co., Dayton, Ohio.

MCEWEN
USA 1913
Norman S. McEwen, Nashville, Tennessee. Cyclecars.

MCFARLAN
USA 1910–1928
McFarlan Carriage Co. McFarlan Motor Corp., Connersville, Indiana. Reorganized as McFarlan Motor Car Co. 3,639 cars were made.

MCGILL
USA 1921–1922
McGill Motor Car Co., Ft. Worth, Texas. Touring cars.

MCHARDY
USA 1904
McHardy-Peterson Car Works, Detroit, Michigan.

MCHARG
USA c. 1900
A.V.A. McHarg, Edgewater, New Jersey.

MCINTOSH
AUS 1893
McIntosh & Co., Picton, N.S.W.

MCINTYRE
USA 1909–1915
W.H. McIntyre, Toledo, Ohio. W.H. McIntyre Co., Auburn, Indiana. Formerly "Kiblinger." Absorbed Motor Car Co. of America 1912. Made "Imp" cyclecar 1914; 1,699 cars were made.

MCKAY
CDN 1911–1914
Nova Scotia Carriage Co., Kentville, Nova Scotia. Tourer and torpedo. Similar to "Penn."

MCKAY
USA 1900–1902
Stanley Mfg. Co., Boston, Massachusetts. Steam cars. Succeeded "Stanley-Whitney" steam.

MCKENZIE
GB 1913–1926
Thomas McKenzie (1913–1920). McKenzie Motors Ltd., Birmingham (1920–1926). Light cars.

MCLACHLAN
GB 1899–1900
E.A. McLachlan (1899). McLachlan Engine Co., London (1900). Three-wheelers and light cars.

MCLAREN; MCLAREN-ELVA
GB 1964–c. 1972
Bruce McLaren Motor Racing Ltd., Slough, Bucks. (1964–present). Elva Cars (1961) Ltd., Rye, Sussex (1965–1966); Croydon, Surrey (1966–1968). Trojan Ltd., Croydon, Surrey (1969–c. 1972). Sports cars. F1 racing cars to date.

MCLAREN
GB 1993–1998
Mc Laren International Ltd., Woking, Surrey. 550 hp sports cars.

MCLAUGHLIN
CDN 1908–1922
McLaughlin Motor Car Co. Ltd., Oshawa, Ontario. Based on "Buick" components.

MCLAUGHLIN
USA c. 1905
John A. McLaughlin, Quincy, Massachusetts. 8 hp automobile.

MCLAUGHLIN
USA 1926
George McLaughlin, Bangor, Maine. Propeller-powered car.

MCLAUGHLIN-BUICK
CDN 1923–1942
McLaughlin Motor Car Co. Ltd., Oshawa, Ontario. Succeeded "McLaughlin."

MCMULLIN
USA 1900–1901
McMullin Power & Construction Co., Chicago, Illinois. Phaeton.

MCMURTY
USA 1896
A.L. McMurty, Chester, Pennsylvania. Steam car.

MCNABB
USA 1910
See "Billy Four."

MCPHAIL
USA 1906
John McPail, Dorchester, Massachusetts. Runabout.

MCQUAY-NORRIS
USA 1933–1934
McQuay-Norris Mfg. Co., St. Louis, Missouri. 6 cars built on "Ford" chassis.

MCQUESTEN
USA 1901–1902
George McQuesten, Boston, Massachusetts. Steam car. Became "Binney & Burnham."

MEAD
USA 1912
Mead Engine Co., Dayton, Ohio. Rotary valves.

MEADE
I 1970
Tom Meade, Modena. Sports car.

MÉAN
B 1966–1972
Méan Motor Engineering SA, Liège-Guillemins (1966–1971). Liberta Engineering SA, Liège (1972–1975). Sports cars. From 1972.
See "Liberta."

MEBEA
GR 1970–1976
Mebea, Athens. Three-wheeler.

MÉCANIQUE ET MOTEURS
B 1903–1906
Société Mécanique et Moteurs, Liège. 3- and 4-cylinder cars.

MECCA
USA 1914
Mecca Motor Car Co., Teaneck, New Jersey. Cyclecar.

MECCA
USA 1915–1916
Times Square Automobile Co., New York, N.Y. Built by Princess Motor Car Co., Detroit, Michigan. Touring cars.

MECHALEY
USA 1903
Mechaley Bros., Stamford, Connecticut. Steam and gasoline cars built to order.

MECHANICS
USA 1925–1928
Los Angeles, California.

MECKY
USA 1901–1902
A. Mecky, Philadelphia, Pennsylvania.

MED-BOW
USA 1907–1908
Med-Bow Automobile Co., Springfield, Massachusetts.
See "Springfield."

MEDCRAFT
USA
See "Springfield."

MEDEA
GB 1912–1916
Mead & Deakin, Birmingham. Cyclecars.

MEDIA
USA 1899–1900
Media Carriage Works, Media, Pennsylvania. Electric runabouts.

MEDICI
GB
See "Leonard."

MEDINGER
GB 1913
Medinger Car & Engine Co., Southall, Middlesex. Cyclecar.

MEDUZA
PL 1958
Wytwornia Sprzetu Komunikacyjnego, Mielec. Only one small car was built.
See "WSK."

MEGA
F 1992–present
Mega Aixam Automobiles, Aix-les-Bains. 4 × 4 cars.

MEGY
F 1901–1903
L. Megy, Paris. Both clutch and brake were operated by moving the steering wheel up or down.

MEISELBACH
USA 1904–1909
Meiselbach Typewriter Co., North Milwaukee, Wisconsin. Highwheelers.

MEISENHELDER
USA 1919–1924
Meisenhelder Motors, York, Pennsylvania. Roadsters based on "Paige."

MEIWA
J c. 1952–1960
Meiwa Automobile Mfg. Co. Up to 7-passenger three-wheelers.

MELDI
I 1927–1933
Officina Meccanica Giuseppe Meldi, Torino. 12 cars made.

MELEN
GB 1913–1914
F. & H. Melen Ltd., Birmingham. Light car.

MELKUS
DDR 1959–1990
Heinz Melkus Sportwagenbau KG, Dresden. Sports cars.

MELLER
SU 1902–1906
Sankt Peterburg.

MEL SPECIAL
USA 1918–1924
Mel Striger, Pottstown, Pennsylvania. Sports cars.

MEMPHIS
USA 1904–1905
Memphis Motor Carriage Co., Memphis, Tennessee. Steam car.

MENARD
CDN 1908–1910
Windsor Carriage & Wagon Works, Windsor, Ontario. Highwheelers.

MENDELSSOHN
F
See "Passy-Thellier."

MENDIP
GB 1914–1922
Mendip Engineering Co., Chewton Mendip, Somerset (1914). Mendip Motor and Engineering Co. Ltd., Bristol (1914–1921). New Mendip Engineering Co. Ltd., Melksham, Wilts. (1922). Light cars.

MENGES
USA 1902
Menges Engine Co., Memphis, Tennessee.

MENGES
USA 1908
Menges Motor Carriage Co., Grand Rapids, Michigan. A.L. Menges ex-designer of "Harrison." 8-seater touring car.

MENIX
CH 1982
Beat Menzi, Dulliken bei Olten. Sports car prototype.

MENKENNS
USA 1937
Willie Menkenns, Hillsboro, Oregon. Propeller-powered car.

MENLEY
GB 1920
Menley Motor Co., Stoke-on-Trent, Staffs. Cyclecar.

MENOMINEE
USA 1902; 1915
Menominee Electric Mfg. Co., Menominee, Michigan. Electric car.

MENON
I 1897–1902
Officina Velocipedi Carlo Menon, Roncade (TV). Approx. 20 made.

MENTASCHI
I 1924
Mentaschi & C., Lambrate (Milano). Electric car, prototype only.

MENUS-VAN HORN
USA 1902
Menus-Van Horn Motor Co., Boston, Massachusetts.

MÉRAY
H 1928–1935
Méray Motorkerékpárgyár Rt., Budapest. Three-wheelers with 500 cc JAP engine.

MERCANTILE
USA 1905
Mercantile Motor Co., Jersey City, New Jersey. Gasoline and steam vehicles.

MERCEDES
D 1901–1926
Daimler Motoren-Gesellschaft, Bad Canstatt (1901–1903); Stuttgart (1903–1926). Touring and sports cars.

MERCEDES
USA 1904–1909
Daimler Mfg. Co., Long Island City, N.Y.
 See "American Mercedes."

MERCEDES-BENZ
D 1926–present
Daimler-Benz AG, Stuttgart (1926–1998). DaimlerChrysler AG, Stuttgart (1998–present). Passenger and sports cars.

MERCER
USA 1910–1926; 1931
Mercer Automobile Co. Walter Automobile Co., Trenton, New Jersey (1910–1926). Mercer Motors Corp., Elkhart, Indiana (1931). Formerly "Roebling-Planche."
 See "Walter." With "Locomobile" and "Crane-Simplex" into Hare's Motors Inc. 12,893 cars were made.

MERCER COBRA
USA 1964
Copper Development Asso. Inc., Detroit, Michigan. Sports car.

MERCILESS
USA 1906–1907
Huntington Automobile Co., Long Island, N.Y. 10-litre 6-cylinder engine.

MERCUR
D
 See "Ego."

MERCURY
CDN 1921
Canadian Automobile Corp., Lachine, Quebec.

MERCURY
GB 1905
Ivanhoe Motor Co., London. 24hp cars.

MERCURY
GB 1914–1923
Medina Engineering Co. Ltd (1914–1920). Mercury Cars (Production) Ltd., Twickenham, Middlesex (1920–1923). Light car.

MERCURY
USA 1903–1904
Mercury Machine Co., Philadelphia, Pennsylvania. Steam cars.

MERCURY
USA 1913–1914
Mercury Cyclecar Co. Michigan State Automobile School, Detroit, Michigan. Cyclecars. Bankruptcy reported September 1914.

MERCURY
USA 1918–1920
Mercury Cars Inc., Hollis, N.Y. Touring cars with the Weidely engines.

MERCURY
USA 1920
Mercury Motor Car Co., Cleveland, Ohio. Duesenberg engine.

MERCURY
USA 1939–present
Lincoln Mercury Division, Ford Motor Co., Dearborn, Michigan. Passenger cars.
 See "Ford" and "Lincoln." Introduced August 26, 1938.

MERCURY SPECIAL
USA 1946
Paul Omohundro, Los Angeles, California. Aluminum-bodied prototypes only.

MEREDITH
USA 1895
E. Meredith, Batavia, Illinois.

MEREDITH
USA 1913–1914
George W. Meredith, Detroit, Michigan.

MERIT
USA 1921–1922
Merit Motor Co., Cleveland, Ohio. Touring cars.

MERKEL
USA 1905–1907
Merkel Mfg. Co. Merkel Motor Co., Milwaukee, Wisconsin. Air- or water-cooled engines.

MERKEL
USA 1914
J.F. Merkel, Milwaukee, Wisconsin. Cyclecar.

MERLIN
GB 1913–1914
New Merlin Cycle Co., Birmingham. Light car.

MERLIN
GB 1981–1984
Thoroughbred Cars Ltd., Southend-on-Sea, Essex. Replicars.

MERRILL
USA 1905
Frank H. Merrill, Plainfield, New Jersey.

MERRY OL'
USA 1958–1962
American Air Products Corp., Ft. Lauderdale, Florida. Replica 1904 "Oldsmobile."

MERY
USA c. 1899
Michael L. Mery, Chico, California.

MERZ
USA 1914
Merz Cyclecar Co., Indianapolis, Indiana. Cyclecars. Receiver reported appointed July 1914. January 1915 receiver sold assets for $1,200. Creditors received 20%.

MERZ & STINCHI
I
  See "SIMS."

MESERVE
USA 1901–1904
W.F. Meserve, Canobie Lake, New Hampshire; West Derry, New Hampshire. Custom built steam cars only.

MESSENGER
USA 1914
Brasie Motor Car Co., Minneapolis, Minnesota.
  See "Brasie."

MESSERER
USA 1899–1901
Stephen Messerer Automobile Co., Newark, New Jersey. Stanhope.

MESSERSCHMITT
D 1953–1962
Regensburger Stahl- und Metallbau GmbH (1953–1956). Fahrzeug- und Maschinenbau GmbH, Regensburg (1956–1962). Three- and four-wheeled small cars.
  See "FMR."

MESSIER
F 1926–1931
Georges Messier, Montrouge/Seine. Compressed-air pneumatic suspension.

METALINE
GB 1990s
Metaline Ltd., Wisbech, Cambs. Kit cars.

MÉTALLURGIQUE
B 1898–1928
SA L'Auto Métallurgique, Marchienne-au-Pont. Touring and sports cars.

METCALFE
USA 1902
R.H. Metcalfe, Patchogue, N.Y. 3 hp gasoline-engined runabout.

METEOR
B 1905–1906
Felix Hecq, Bruxelles. Cars powered by "De Dion" (F) engines.

METEOR
CDN 1949–1961; 1969–present
Ford Motor Co. of Canada, Ltd., Windsor, Ontario. Identical to "Ford" (USA) except for its special grille and trim.

METEOR
GB 1903–1905
Pritchett & Gold Ltd., Feltham, Middlesex. Electric and gasoline cars.

METEOR
USA 1900–1901
Springfield Cornice Works. Howell & Meehan Co., Springfield, Massachusetts. Became Automotor Co; Runabouts.

METEOR
USA 1902–1903
Meteor Engineering Co., Reading, Pennsylvania. Succeeded Reading Steam Vehicle Co., and Steam Vehicle Co. of America. Steam cars.
  See "Reading Steam Carriage."

METEOR
USA 1904–1905
Lemon Automobile & Mfg. Co., St. Louis, Missouri.

METEOR
USA 1904–1906
Worthington Automobile Co., New York, N.Y. Absorbed Berg Automobile Co. 1905.
  See "Berg" and "Worthington."

METEOR
USA 1907–1910
Meteor Motor Car Co., Bettendorf, Iowa (1907–1909); Davenport, Iowa (1909–1910). Touring cars.

METEOR
USA 1909–1927
Meteor Motor Car Co., Indianapolis, Indiana; Shelbyville, Indiana. Cars to 1916. Special order to 1930. Then ambulances and hearses. Coachbuilders to date.

METEOR
USA 1915–1930
Meteor Motor Car Co., Piqua, Ohio. Sedans.

METEOR
USA 1919–1922
Meteor Motors Inc., Philadelphia, Pennsylvania. Sport touring cars.

METEORITE
GB 1912–1924
Meteorite Motors Ltd. (1912–1921). Meteorite Cars Ltd., London (1921–1924). Cyclecars and light cars.

METEOR SPORTS
USA 1956
Meteor Sports Cars, Denver, Colorado.

METISSE
GB 1990s
Metisse Cars Ltd., St. Mary Hill, Mid-Glamorgan. Sports kit cars.

METROODZER
USA 1905
Rood & Metzer, Hartford, Connecticut. Buckboard.

METROPOL
USA 1913–1914
Metropol Motor Co., Port Jefferson, N.Y. Outgrowth of "Only."

METROPOLITAN
GB 1901
Metropolitan Motor Mfg. Co., London. Light car.

METROPOLITAN
USA 1922–1923
Metropolitan Motors Inc., Kansas City, Missouri. Touring cars.

METROPOLITAN
USA 1954–1961
American Motors Corp., Kenosha, Wisconsin. Three-seater coupe or convertible, built by "Austin" (GB). for sale by American Motors.

METRO-TYLER
GB 1922–1923
Metro-Tyler Ltd., London. 550 cc cyclecars.

METZ
NL 1909
Amsterdam. Three-wheelers.

METZ
USA 1909–1921
Metz Co., Waltham, Massachusetts. Succeeded Waltham Mfg. Co.
  See "Waltham-Orient." Became.

Waltham Motor Mfrs. Inc. See "Waltham" (1922); 40,082 cars were made.

METZGER
USA 1910
Metzger Motor Car Co., Detroit, Michigan. Company incorporated September 20, 1909.
 See "Everitt."

MEVEA
GR 1970s
Mevea, Athenai. "Reliant" (GB) based 3- and 4-wheelers.

MEYER
USA c. 1901
J.A. Meyer, San Francisco, California. Built several gasoline cars.

MEYER
USA 1919
A.J. Meyer Corp., Chicago, Illinois. Touring cars.

MEYERS
USA 1931
Roy J. Meyers, Los Angeles, California. Roadster.

MEYERS-MANX
USA 1964–1972
B.F. Meyers & Co., Newport Beach, California. Dune buggy.

MEYRA
D 1950–1956
Wilhelm Meyer, Krankenfahrzeugfabrik, Vlotho/Wester. Light car.

MF
I 1972
MF Elaborazione, Biella-Chiavezza. "Lancia" Fulvia Coupe based sports car.

M.G.
GB 1924–present
Morris Garages Ltd., Oxford (1924–1928). M.G. Car Co. Ltd., Abingdon, Berks. (1929–1970). Austin-Morris Division, British Leyland Motor Corp. Ltd., Abingdon, Berks. (1970–1980). Rover Cars, Canley, Coventry (1992–present). Touring and sports cars.

M.G.P.
F 1912
Automobiles Jean Margaria, St. Cyr/Seine. 12 hp light car.

M.H.C.
USA 1917
Michigan Hearse & Motor Co., Grand Rapids, Michigan.

MIAMI
USA 1901–1902
Miami Cycle Co., Middletown, Ohio. Steam car.

MIARI E GIUSTI
I 1896–1899
Miari, Giusti & C., Brevetti Bernardi, Padova. Three-wheeler.

MICHAELSON
USA 1914
Michaelson Motor Co. Brasie Motor Car Co., Minneapolis, Minnesota. Cyclecar.

MICHALAK
D 1985
Bernd Michalak Automobildesign, Wiesbaden. Tuning.

MICHEL IRAT
F 1929–1930
Automobiles Michel Irat SA, Paris. 1,086 cc light car.

MICHELOTTI
I 1960s–1980s
Studio Stile Carrozzeria G. Michelotti, Orbassano. Prototypes, sports and touring cars. Coachbuilders since 1949.

MICHIGAN
USA 1903–1908
Michigan Automobile Co., Kalamazoo, Michigan. Formerly Blood Bros.
 See "Blood." Continued making transmissions.

MICHIGAN
USA 1904
Michigan Motor & Machine Co., Detroit, Michigan.

MICHIGAN
USA 1904
Michigan Automobile Co., Grand Rapids, Michigan.

MICHIGAN
USA 1903–1907; 1911–1913
Michigan Buggy Co., Kalamazoo, Michigan. 1912 reorganized as Michigan Motor Car Co. Also called "Mighty Michigan." Runabouts and touring cars.

MICHIGAN
USA 1916
Michigan Hearse & Motor Co., Grand Rapids, Michigan. 6-cylinder limousine.

MICHIGAN SIX
USA 1910
Michigan Motor Car Mfg. Co., Rochester, Michigan. Concurrent with Michigan Buggy Co; Roadsters.

MICHIGAN STEAMER
USA 1907–1909
Michigan Steam motor Co., Pontiac, Michigan. Steam car. Changed from Belknap Motor Co., Detroit, Michigan. Reported May 1907.

MICROBO
I
 See "ISSI."

MICROCAR
D 1970
Jürgen Junginger, Berlin. Minicar prototype.

MICROCAR
F 1983–c. 1996
Departement Automobile des Constructions Nautique Jeanneau,. Les Herbiers. Electric minicars.

MICRON
F 1925–1930
Automobiles Micron, Castanet-Tolosane, Toulouse. Very small cyclecar.

MIDAS
GB c. 1978–1989
Midas Cars, Corby, Northants. Sports cars. About 500 were built.
 See "D. & H" and "Mini-Marcos."

MIDDLEBRIDGE
GB 1988–1990
"Reliant" Scimitar GTE based sports cars.

MIDDLEBY
USA 1908–1913
Middleby Automobile Co., Reading, Pennsylvania. Succeeded Duryea Power Co. Added "Reading" (1910–1913) September 1910. Property auctioned May 1913. Roadsters.

MIDDLETOWN
USA 1909–1911
Middletown Buggy Co., Middletown, Ohio. Highwheeler.
 See "Ohio" and "Crescent." Company became Crescent Motor Co.

MIDGET
USA 1915

Midget Cyclecar Co., Springfield, Massachusetts. Cyclecars.

MIDGET
USA 1947
Greenfield-Lippman, Buffalo, N.Y.

MIDGLEY
USA 1901–1905
Midgley Mfg. Co., Columbus, Ohio.

MIDLAND
USA 1908–1913
Midland Motor Car Co., Moline, Illinois. Roadsters. 2,954 cars were built. Succeeded "Deere-Clark."
See "Colby."

MIDLAND
USA 1909–1912
Midland Machine Works, Muskogee, Oklahoma.

MIDLAND
USA 1918–1919
Midland Motor Car & Truck Co., Oklahoma City, Oklahoma.

MIDSTATES
USA 1990s
Midstates Classic Cars, Hooper, Nevada. Kit cars.

MIDTEC
GB 1990s
Midtec Sportscars Ltd., Leicester. Kit cars.

MIDWAY
USA 1910
Mountain Bros. Co., Los Angeles, California.

MIDWEST
USA 1918–1920
Midwest Motor Co., Kansas City, Missouri.

MIELE
D 1911–1914
Miele & Cie., Maschinenfabrik, Gütersloh. 6/17hp and 9/22 hp cars.

MIER
USA 1908–1909
Mier Carriage & Buggy Co., Ligonier, Indiana. Highwheeler.
See "Izzer" and "Star."

MIERLEY
USA 1902
A.W. Mierley, Davenport, Iowa.

MIESSE
B 1896–1926
J. Miesse et Cie., Bruxelles. Steam and gasoline cars.

MIESSE
GB 1902
Miesse Steam Motor Syndicate Ltd., London. Steam car.

MIEUSSET
F 1903–1914
Ateliers de Construction Mécanique et d'Automobiles Mieusset, Lyon. Double chain-drive.

MIGHTY-MICHIGAN
USA 1912–1913
Michigan Buggy Co., Kalamazoo, Michigan.
See "Michigan."

MIGHTY MITE
USA 1953
Mid-America Research Corp., Wheatland, Pennsylvania. 4 × 4 cars.

MIGNON
F 1908
C.E. Chepke, Paris. Voiturettes.

MIGNONETTE
F 1900
Wehrlé et Godard-Desmarest, Neuilly/Seine.

MIGNONETTE-LUAP
F 1899–1900
Jiel-Laval et Cie., Bordeaux. Voiturette.

MIGNOT
B 1890
M. Mignot, Bruxelles. Steam three-wheeler.

MIKASA
J 1957–1961
Okamura Mfg. Co. Ltd., Tokyo. Front-wheel drive small cars.

MIKKELSON
USA c. 1914
Hans Mikkelson, Bottineau, North Dakota. 12 hp automobile.

MIKROMOBIL
D 1922–1924
Automobil-Gesellschaft Thomsen KG (1922–1924). Mikromobil AG, Hamburg (1924). Light cars.

MIKRUS
PL 1958–1960
Wytwornia Sprzetu Komunikacyjnego, Mielec. Mini cars.
See "WSK."

MILAC
USA 1916
Lithwaite-Hussy Co., Los Angeles, California. Sports and racing cars.

MILANO
I 1906–1907
Sta Milanese dell'Industria Meccanica, Milano. Water-cooled brakes.

MILBURN
USA 1915–1923
Milburn Carriage & Wagon Co., Toledo, Ohio. Electric cars.

MILDÉ
F 1898–1909
Mildé et Cie., Levallois-Perret/Seine. Electric cars.

MILES
GB 1910–1912
Joubert Miles, Sharpness, Gloucestershire. Three-wheelers.

MILITARY
USA 1907
V.L. Emerson, Cincinnati, Ohio.

MILLBURY
USA c. 1905
Millbury Machine Co., Millbury, Massachusetts. 10 hp automobile.

MILLER
USA 1900–1902
George C. Miller Carriage Co., Cincinnati, Ohio. George Miller, Kenton, Ohio. Miller Storage Battery Electric Co., Bellefont, Ohio. Electric cars.

MILLER
USA 1901
Tom Gurley, Meyersdale, Pennsylvania. Steam surrey.

MILLER
USA 1901–1902
J.W. Miller, Trail & Orville, Ohio. Built several gasoline vehicles.

MILLER
USA 1902
Miller Bros., Amesbury, Massachusetts.

MILLER
USA 1902–1903
Charles E. Miller, New York, N.Y. Gasoline tonneau.

MILLER
USA 1905–1906
Miller Carriage Co., Goshen, N.Y.

MILLER
USA 1910
Vernon Miller, Brice, Ohio.

MILLER
USA 1911–1914
Miller Motor Car Co. Kosmath Co., Detroit, Michigan. Touring cars.

MILLER
USA 1912
Miller Machine Co., Defiance, Ohio.

MILLER
USA 1928; 1932
Harry A. Miller Inc., Los Angeles, California. Speedsters.

MILLER-QUINCY
USA 1922–1924
E.M. Miller Co., Quincy, Illinois. Few large sedans and limousines were built.

MILLER SPECIAL
USA 1917; 1923; 1930
Harry A. Miller Inc. H.A. Miller Mfg. Co. (Kirchoff Body Works), Pasadena, California; Los Angeles, California.

MILLER STEAMER
USA 1902
Charles E. Miller, New York, N.Y. Also built gasoline vehicles.

MILLERSVILLE
USA 1910
Millersville Machine Co., Millersville, Ohio. Runabout.

MILLION
USA 1896
Robert J. Million, Monticello, Indiana. Gasoline motor buggy.

MILLOT
CH 1906–1907
Sté. des Automobiles Millot, Zürich. 4- and 6-cylinder cars.

MILLOT
F 1901–1902
Millot Freres, Gray/Hte-Saone. 6 hp tonneau.

MILLS
USA 1895
M.B. Mills, Chicago, Illinois.

MILLS & SERLS
USA 1895
Mills & Serls Co., Chicago, Illinois.

MILLS ELECTRIC
USA 1917
Mills Electric Co., Lafayette, Indiana.

MILLS STEAMER
USA 1876
Isaac Mills, Jr., Pittsburgh, Pennsylvania.

MILMOR
GB 1959–1968
H. Milborrow, London. Sports-racing cars.

MILNE STEAMER
USA 1901
Frank Milne, Everett, Massachusetts. Steam vehicles built to order.

MILNES
GB 1901–1902
G.F. Milnes & Co. Ltd., Wellington, Shropshire. Chassis built by the "Daimler (D).

MILTON
GB 1920–1921
Bedford Motor Co., Edinburgh. Light car.

MILTON
USA 1914
Milton Mfg. Co., Los Angeles, California.

MILWAUKEE
USA 1901
Milwaukee Automobile & Brass Specialty Co., Milwaukee, Wisconsin.

MILWAUKEE
USA 1904
Milwaukee Motor Mfg. Co., Milwaukee, Wisconsin.

MILWAUKEE
USA 1906
Eagle Automobile Co., Milwaukee, Wisconsin. Two-seater, prototype only.

MILWAUKEE
USA 1914
Milwaukee Cyclecar Co., Milwaukee, Wisconsin. Cyclecar.

MILWAUKEE STAR
USA 1903
Milwaukee Auto Engines and Supply Co., Milwaukee, Wisconsin. Tonneau.

MILWAUKEE STEAM
USA 1900–1902
Milwaukee Automobile Co., Milwaukee, Wisconsin. W.H. McIntyre, later of Auburn, Indiana, connected with company.
See "McIntyre."

MIMIKRY
D 1931
Der Deutsche Wirtschaftsbund e.V., Berlin.

MINCH
USA 1909
Philip J. Minch, Cleveland, Ohio. Electric roadster.

MINELLI
CH 1998–present
Minelli AG, Pfäffikon. Sports car replica.

MINERVA
B 1899–1939
S. de Jong et Cie (1899–1902). Minerva Motors SA (1903–1934). Société Nouvelle Minerva, Anvers (1934–1935). Large and expensive touring cars.

MINEUR
B 1924
Automobiles Mineur, Marchienne-au-Port. "Ford" (USA) Type T based cars.

MINI
GB 1970–present
Austin-Morris Division, British Leyland Motor Corporation Ltd., Longbridge, Birmingham. Cowley, Oxford. Austin-Rover Group Ltd., Canley, Coventry (1988–present). Pioneer of the transverse engine configuration. Individual make from 1970; previously marketed under the "Austin" and "Morris" names.

MINI BUG
USA 1968–1972
Green Motors Inc., Livonia, Michigan. Dune buggy.

MINICAR
CS 1948
Ing. Rudolf Vykoukal, Praha. Small car prototype.

MINICAR
USA 1969
Minicars, Inc., Goleta, California. One 3-passenger car was built.

MINICAT
F 1979
Minicat Distribution, Nantes. City cars.

MINI COMTESSE
F 1975–c. 1985
Sté. ACOMA, d'Angers. Mini car.

MINI-EL
DK 1985–present
El-Trans A/S, Randers. Electric cars.

MINIJEM
GB 1966–1976
Jem Developments Ltd., London (1966–1968). Fellpoint Ltd., Penn, Bucks. (1968–1971). High Performance Mouldings, Cricklade, Wilts. (1971–1976). About 350 small sports cars were built.

MINIKIN
USA 1986
Three-wheelers.

MINIMA
F 1911
Ets Leroy, Levallois-Perret/Seine. Voiturette.

MINIMA
I 1935
Antonio Passarin, Milano.

MINI-MARCOS
GB 1971–1979
See "D. & H." and "Midas."

MINI MOKE
GB/AUS 1960–1982; I/P 1990–present
Automotive Engineering & Manufacturing, Wales. Moke Automobile SpA, Morazzone. Small open cars.

MINIMUS
D 1921–1924
Minimus-Fahrzeug GmbH, Pasing. Cyclecar.

MINI-SCAMP
GB 1970–c. 1981
Robert Madry Scamps, Brookwood, Surrey. Small off-road vehicle.

MINISSIMA
GB 1973
City car prototype.

MINI-T
USA 1968–1973
Berry Plastics, Long Beach, California. Dune buggy.

MINI-VAN
USA 1973–1979
Mini-Van Inc., Conaga Park, California. Fiberglass body.

MINIVOLKS
USA 1968–1973
Dunbar's Inc., Framingham, Massachusetts. Dune buggy.

MINNEAPOLIS
USA 1914–1915
Minneapolis Motor Car Co., Minneapolis, Minnesota.

MINNEAPOLIS
USA 1914
Minneapolis Motor Co., Minneapolis, Minnesota. Cyclecars.

MINNOW
GB 1951–1952
Bonallack & Sons Ltd., London. Three-wheeler.

MINO
USA 1914
Mino Cyclecar Co., New Orleans, Louisiana. Cyclecar.

MINOTAUR
GB 1990s
Minotaur Sports cars, Sheerness, Isle of Sheppey, Kent. Kit cars.

MINUTOLI — MILLO
I 1902–1903
Minutoli Millo & C., Vorno (Lucca). Prototype only.

MIOLANS
F 1910
Valade et Guillemand, Neuilly/Seine. Light car.

MIPAL
CS 1948
PAL, n.p., Kraslice. 250 cc minicar prototype.

MIRA
F 1906
Neuilly/Seine. Light car with DeDion engine.

MIRABILIS
I 1906–1907
Giuseppe de Maria, Torino. Light voiturette.

MIRAGE
GB 1969–1971
John Weyr Automotive Engineering Ltd., Slough, Bucks. Sports and racing cars.

MIRAGE
GB 1990s
Mirage Replicars Ltd., Wellingborough, Nordhants. Replicars and sports kit cars.

MIRAGE
I 1970–1972
Officina Stanguellini, Modena. Sports cars and dune buggy.

MIRAGE
USA 1997–present
Euro-Works, Kettering, Ohio. Sports kit cars.

MIRDA
CS 1948
Václav Vejvoda, Praha. 250 cc minicar prototype.

MISSION
USA 1914
Mission Motor Car Co., Los Angeles, California.

MISSION
USA 1921; 1923
West Coast Automobile Mfg. Co., Los Angeles, California.

MISTRAL
B 1932
M. Houdret, Bruxelles. Sports car prototype.

MITCHELL
USA 1902–1903
Wisconsin Wheel Co., Racine, Wisconsin. Became "Pierce-Racine."

MITCHELL
USA 1903–1923
Wisconsin Wheel Works. Mitchell Motor Car Co., Racine, Wisconsin. 1910 merged with Mitchell & Lewis Co. Absorbed L.P.C. Motor Co. ("Lewis") and reorganized 1916 as Mitchell Motors Inc. "Lewis" plant purchased by "Nash" 1923; 86,966 cars were made.

MITCHELL
USA 1914
Mitchell Automobile Co., Chicago, Illinois. Cyclecars.

MITSUBISHI
J 1917–1921; 1959–present
Mitsubishi Kobe Dockyard Works, Kobe (1917–1921). Mitsubishi Heavy Industries Ltd., Tokyo (1959–1970). Mitsubishi Motors Corp., Tokyo (1970–to date) Passenger and sports cars.

MITSUI
J 1952–1962
Mitsui Precision Machinery & Eng. Co. Ltd. 285 cc three-wheelers.

MITSUOKA
J 1993–present
Mitsuoka Motors Co., Ltd., Fuchucho, Neigun, Toyama-ken. Replicars.

MIURA
BR 1974–1993
Besson Gobbi S.A., Divisao Miura, Porto Alegre. Sports cars.

MIVAL
I 1954
Three-wheeler.

M.J.G.
USA 1910
Allen-Kingston Co., New York, N.Y.
See "Allen-Kingston."

MK
D 1981–present
MK Motorsport, Autohaus Krankenberg GmbH, Gaggenau; Ötigheim. Tuning.

M.L.B.
F 1894–1902
Cie des Moteurs et Autos M.L.B., Hondouville/Eure; Passy/Seine. Voiturette and 4-seater enclosed cab.

M.L.T.
F 1900
Molas, Lamielle et Tessier, Paris. 20hp 4-cylinder single-acting engine actuated by compressed air.

MM
I 1939
Mario Mazzetti & Alfonso Morini. One car built.

MM
I 1967
Michelotti-Maniero. 4.7-litre Ford (USA) engine powered sports car prototype.

M.M.B.
D 1899–1902
Motorfahrzeug- und Motorenfabrik Berlin AG, Berlin. 12 hp cars.

M.M.C.
GB 1897–1908
The Great Horseless Carriage Co. Ltd (1897–1898). The Motor Manufacturing Co. Ltd., Coventry, Warwicks. (1898–1907); London (1907–1908). Touring cars.

M.M.C.
USA 1910
Manlius Motor Co., Manlius, N.Y.
See "Manlius."

M.M.F.
F 1912
Muller, Mignot et Cie., Levallois/Seine. 2.1-litre cars.

M.M.W.
D 1901–1905
Magdeburger Motor- und Motorfahrzeug-Werke GmbH (1901). Magdeburger Motorwerke Max Stang & Co., Magdeburg (1902–1905). Voiturettes.

MOBBEL
D
See "Piccolo."

MOBILE
GB 1903–1907
Mobile Motor & Engineering Co. Ltd., Birmingham. Four-seater tonneau.

MOBILE
USA 1900–1903
Automobile Co. of America, Tarrytown, New York. Steam cars. Started by purchasing (with "Locomobile") one-half interest in Stanley Motor Carriage Co.

MOBILETTE
USA 1965–1974
Mobilette Electric Cars, Long Beach, California. Electric car.

MOCHET
F 1951–1958
Charles Mochet, Puteaux/Seine. 125cc and 175 cc minicars.

MÖCKWAGEN
D 1924
Gebr. Möck, Tübingen. 5/20 hp light cars.

MODEL
USA 1902
Steam Vehicle Co. of America, New York, N.Y. Steam car.

MODEL
USA 1903–1909
Model Gas & Gasoline Engine Co. (1903–1904). Model Gas Engine Works, Auburn, Indiana (1904–1906). Model Automobile Co., Peru, Indiana (1906–1909). 825 cars were made.

MODERN
USA 1906–1909
Modern Tool Co., Erie, Pennsylvania.
See "Payne Modern."

MODISTACH
AUS 1903
Tanunda, S.A.

MODOC
USA 1909–1911; 1914
Chicago Motor Car Co., Chicago, Illinois. Mail order car for Montgomery Ward & Co.

MODULO
I 1994
Italian Car di R. Spampinato, Ronco Briantino (Milano). Tandem three-wheeler.

MOEHN
USA 1895–1896
J.N. Moehn, Milwaukee, Wisconsin.

MOGLIA
I 1925
Edmondo Moglia.

MOHAWK
USA 1903–1904
Mohawk Automobile & Cycle Co., Indianapolis, Indiana. Tonneau.

MOHAWK
USA 1914–1915
Mohawk Motor Co., Boston, Massachusetts. Cyclecar.

MOHAWK
USA 1914–1915
Mohawk Cyclecars. Mohawk Motor Corp., New Orleans, Louisiana.

MOHAWK-MANON
F
See "Manon."

MOHLER
USA 1901
A.B. Mohler, Kokomo, Indiana.

MOHLER & DE GRESS
USA 1901–1904
Mohler & De Gress, Astoria, Long Island, N.Y. First built 1896 in Mexico City, Mexico, then brought to Astoria, N.Y.

MOHR
D 1990–1994

Mohr Automobile GmbH, Straubenhardt. Sports car replicas.

MOHS
USA 1967–1978
Mohs Seaplane Corp., Madison, Wisconsin. "Vehicles of Compelling Interest." All cars built to order. Production 3 or 4 cars a year.

MOKE
I 1990–1994
Moke Automobili SpA, Morazzone. Small cars.

MOLIN
S 1900
C.J. Molin, Eskilstuna. Voiturette.

MOLINE
USA 1904–1913
Root & Vandervoort. Moline Automobile Co., East Moline, Illinois. Became "Moline-Knight."

MOLINE-KNIGHT
USA 1914–1919
Moline Automobile Co., East Moline, Illinois. Formerly "Moline." Became "R & V Knight." January 1918 Root & Vandervoort Engineering Co. 8,968 cars were built (1904–1919).

MÖLKAMP
D 1923–1926
Möllenkamp-Werke AG für Fahrzeugbau, Düsseldorf; Köln. 1.5- and 2.6-litre models.

MOLL
D 1922–1925
Moll-Werke AG, Chemnitz. Light cars.

MOLLA
F 1922
Molla et Cie., Paris. Cyclecar.

MOLLE
F 1907–1910
Emile Molle, Riom, Puy-de-Dome. Nine 2-stroke 1.5-litre cars were made.

MOLLENHOUR
USA 1908
A.T. Mollenhour, Mentone, Indiana.

MOLLER
USA 1920–1922
Moller Motor Co. Moller Motor Car Co., Lewiston, Pennsylvania. Became "Falcon." Roadsters. Also built taxicabs.

MOLLIE
USA c. 105
Patrick J. Custy, Meriden, Connecticut. 4.5 hp automobile.

MOLSHEIM
USA 1975
California. "Bugatti" (F) replicars.

MOM
F 1906–1907
Ateliers de Constructon Mécanique, Paris. Voiturette.

MOMO
I 1911–1915
F. & C. Momo, Milano.

MOMO
USA 1971–1972
Momo Corp., Forest Hills, N.Y. Sports GT cars.

MONACO
I 1907
Societa per Motori e Automobili, Busto Arsizio.

MONARCH
CDN 1946–1961
Ford Motor Co. of Canada Ltd., Windsor, Ontario. Identical to the "Mercury" (USA) except for grille.

MONARCH
GB 1912–1914
R. Walker & Sons, Tyseley, Birmingham. Light car.

MONARCH
GB 1925–1928
Monarch Motor Co. Ltd., Castle Bromwich, Birmingham. Assembled cars.

MONARCH
USA 1902–1909
Monarch Motor Vehicle Co., Chicago, Illinois. Monarch Motor Car Co., Aurora, Illinois; Franklin Park, Illinois. Monarch Motor Mfg. Co., Chicago, Illinois. Runabouts.

MONARCH
USA 1903
Sold by P.J. Dasey Co., Chicago, Illinois.
See "Morlock."

MONARCH
USA 1903–1904
Milwaukee Motor Mfg. Co., Milwaukee, Wisconsin. Runabouts.

MONARCH
USA 1906
Joseph S. Heller, New York, N.Y. Small runabout.

MONARCH
USA 1908
Monarch Machine Co., Des Moines, Iowa. Motor buggy.

MONARCH
USA 1908–1909
Monarch Motor Car Co., Chicago Heights, Illinois. Highwheeler. Company formed March 1906 to use patents of J.J. Boucher. Four models shown at 1907 Chicago Show. Touring cars and stanhope.

MONARCH
USA 1914–1917
Monarch Motor Car Co., Detroit, Michigan (1914–1916). Carter Bros. Co., Hyattsville, Maryland (1916–1917). Eight and twelve-cylinder cars. R.C. Hupp, president.

MONCRIEFF
USA 1901–1902
J.A. Moncrieff, Pawtucket, Rhode Island. Steam cars.

MONDEX-MAGIC
USA 1914–1915
Aristos Co., New York, N.Y. Built 40 and 60 hp touring cars.

MONDIAL
I 1950
Fratelli Boselli, Milano. Three-wheeler.

MONET-GOYON
F 1921–1926
Établissements Monet et Goyon, Macon/Saone-et-Loire. Three-wheelers and light cars.

MONGO
I 1969
Aldo Sessano, Torino.

MONICA
F 1971–1976
Compagnie Francaise de Produits Métallurgiques, Balbigny/Loire. 2.6-litre Martin V-8 engined sports car.

MONITOR
F 1920–1921
Charles Rouquet et Cie., Suresnes/Seine. Cyclecar.

MONITOR
USA 1909–1911

Monitor Automobile Works, Chicago, Illinois (1909–1910). Became Monitor Auto Co., Janesville, Wisconsin (1910–1911). Highwheel and standard vehicles. Also dual purpose car.

MONITOR
USA 1915–1922
Cummins-Monitor Co., Columbus, Ohio. Reorganized 1916 as Monitor Motor Car Co. Liquidation reported. January 1922; 5,890 cars were made.

MONK & LONSDALE
GB
See "Lonsdale."

MONNIER
F 1908
Monnier et Cie., Juvisy-sur-Orge. Light cars.

MONO
D 1909–1912
Mono-Werke Roger & Niebuhr, Automobil- und Maschinenfabrik, Hamburg. 6/16hp model.

MONO JK
CS 1950–1955
Július Kubinsky, Brno. "Tatra" 603 based sports car prototype.

MONOS
D 1928–1930
Monos Fahrzeug-Ges. MbH, Berlin. Three-wheeler.

MONOTRACE
F 1924–1930
Ateliers du Rond Point, Sainte Etienne/Loire. 2-wheeled car with 2 small auxiliary wheels.

MONROE
USA 1914–1923
Monroe Automobile Co. Stratton Motors Corp., Monroe Division, Flint, Michigan. Reorganized 1918 as William Small Co., Indianapolis, Indiana. Sold 1923 to "Premier." Became "Stratton-Premier." 14,344 cars were made.

MONSEN
USA 1908–1910
Monsen Automobile Garage, Chicago, Illinois.

MONTAGE
GB 1981–1987
The Unique Vehicle and Accessory Co. Ltd., Newbury, Berks. Sports car.

MONTANA SPECIAL
USA 1920
Luverne Automobile Co., Luverne, Minnesota.
See "Luverne."

MONTE CARLO
MC 1992–1993
Monte Carlo Automobile S.A.M., Monte Carlo. Sports cars.

MONTEVERDI
CH 1967–1994;
Automobile Monteverdi AG, Binningen-Basel. Luxury high-performance sports car.

MONTGOMERY-WARD
USA 1898
Montgomery-Ward & Co., Chicago, Illinois. Two electric cars built, both used for advertising and not offered. for sale.
See "Wardway."

MONTIER
F 1923–1932
Garage Montier, Paris. Sporting versions on the Model T "Ford" (USA).

MONTU
I 1900
Officina Meccanica Montu, Alessandria.

MONVISO
I 1950
Stabilimento Monviso, Torino. Sports car. Primarily a coachbuilder.

MOODY
USA 1903–1905
Charles L. Moody, Elgin, Illinois.

MOOERS
USA 1900–1901
Louis P. Mooers, New Haven, Connecticut. Louis P. Mooers later was designer for "Peerless," "Moon," "Geneva" and "Excelsior."

MOON
USA 1905–1929
Joseph W. Moon Buggy Co., St. Louis, Missouri. Moon Motor Car Co. 1905. Reorganized 1928 with same name. Windsor Corp. formed to take over production of straight eight cars. Name changed to "Windsor" 1930. Factory built "Ruxton" 1930. Last of Moon assets distributed 1966. 59,485 cars were made.

See "Diana," "Hol-Tan" and "Windsor."

MOORE
USA 1902–1903
H.S. Moore. Moore Auto Co., Cleveland, Ohio.

MOORE
USA 1906
Moore Automobile Co., Walla Walla, Washington.

MOORE
USA 1906–1908
Moore Automobile Co., New York, N.Y. Factory at Bridgeport, Connecticut.

MOORE
USA 1916–1921
Moore Motor Co., Minneapolis, Minnesota. Reorganized 1919 as Moore Motor Vehicle Co., Danville, Illinois. Used "Pontiac" chasis and Wayne Works Body. Company sold out at auction December 22, 1920 for $54,807. 1,186 cars were made.

MOORE AUTOMOBILE SLEIGH
USA 1902
W.E. Moore, Goodwin's Mills, Maine.

MOORE AUTOPLANE
USA 1925–1933
Virgil B. Moore, Los Angeles, California.

MOORE-CAR
USA 1917
W.G. Moore, Indianapolis, Indiana.

MOORESPRING
USA 1888–1890; 1895
Ingersoll Moore, Bloomington, Illinois.

MOORE STEAMER
USA 1902–1903
Charles J. Moore Mfg. Co., Westfield, Massachusetts. This company did build steamers but it is believed they were sold under "Westfield" name.

MOOSE JAW STANDARD
CDN 1916–1918
Moose Jaw, Saskatchewan. 6-cylinder Continental engine.

MOPS
D 1924–1925
Schmidt & Bensdorf GmbH, Mannheim. Three-wheeler.

MORA
USA 1906–1911
Mora Motor Car Co., Newark, N.Y. Bankrupt October 1910. Property sale November 15, 1911, 9 acres, 50 cars and parts. Plant sold for $120,000.

MORASSUTI
I 1953
One car registered.

MORAVAN
CS 1956
Moravan, n.p., Otrokovice. 350 cc minicar prototype.

MORE
USA 1902
Rochester, N.Y.

MOREHOUSE
USA 1902
Fisher Morehouse, Naples, N.Y.

MORETTI
I 1945–1990
Fabbrica Automobili Moretti SpA (1945–1961). Moretti Fabbrica Automobili e Stabilimento Carrozzeria S.A.S., Torino (1962–1990). "Fiat" based sports cars. Coachbuilders since 1926. 3,292 cars built in 1973, 1071 cars in 1974.

MORGAN
D 1924–1925
Morgan Auto-AG, Berlin. Rhomboid wheel placement.

MORGAN
GB 1905–1907
Morgan & Co. Ltd., Leighton Buzzard, Beds. 5.8-litre conventional cars.

MORGAN
GB 1910–present
Morgan Motor Co. Ltd., Malvern Links, Worcs. Sports cars.

MORGAN
USA 1897
Morgan Construction Co, Worcester, Massachusetts. Steam carriage.

MORGAN
USA 1900–1902
Morgan Motor Co., Brooklyn, N.Y.

MORGAN
USA 1914
W.M. Steele, Worcester, Massachusetts. Cyclecars.

MORISSE
F 1899–1914
P. Morisse et Cie., Etampes/Seine-et-Oise. Voiturette.

MÖRITZ
D 1935
Josef Möritz, München. Three-wheeler.

MORLOCK
USA 1903
Sold by P.J. Dasey Co., Chicago, Illinois. Built by Morlock Automobile Co., Buffalo, N.Y.
See "Monarch." Succeeded Spaulding Automobile Co. Runabouts.

MORRIS
GB 1913–1983
W.R.M. Morris Ltd. (1913–1919). Morris Motors Ltd. (1919–1970). Austin-Morris Division, British Leyland Motor Corp. Ltd., Cowley, Oxford (1970–1983). Passenger cars.

MORRIS & SALOM
USA 1894–1897
Morris & Salom, Philadelphia, Pennsylvania. Electric cars. Became Electric Carriage & Wagon Co. (Hansom Cabs for New York City).
See "Electrobat."

MORRIS COMMERCIAL
GB 1930–1931
Morris-Commercial Cars Ltd., Birmingham. 4.3-litre 6-cylinder cars.

MORRIS-LÉON BOLLÉE
F
See "Léon Bollée."

MORRISON
GB 1904–1905
Krupkar Ltd., London. Three-wheelers.

MORRISON
USA 1891–1902
William Morrison, Des Moines, Iowa. Early U.S. electric vehicle. 1891 vehicle sold to Harold Sturges.
See "Sturges" electric.

MORRISON
USA 1935
Willard L. Morrison, Buchanan, Michigan. Sedans.

MORRISS
GB 1908–1911
H.E. & F. Morriss, London. Steam car.

MORRISS-LONDON
USA 1923–1925
Century Motor Co., Elkhart, Indiana. Export car for England.

MORS
F 1895–1925; 1941–1943
Société d'Électricité et d'Automobiles Mors (1895–1907). Société Nouvelle des Automobiles Mors, Paris (1908–1943). Touring and sports cars.

MORSE
USA 1903–1904
William W. Morse, Newark, New Jersey. Kerosene-engined runabout.

MORSE
USA 1904
Morse Motor Co., Brookline, Massachusetts.

MORSE
USA 1904–1906
Morse Motor Vehicle Co. Morse Automobile Co., Springfield, Massachusetts. Steam car. Incorporated late 1904.

MORSE
USA 1910–1916
Easton Machine Co., South Easton, Massachusetts. Morse Motor Car Co., Brookline, Massachusetts. Touring cars.

MORSE
USA 1914–1916
Frank H. Morse. Morse Cyclecar Co., Pittsburgh, Pennsylvania. Front-wheel drive cyclecars.

MORSE-RADIO
USA 1909–1910
Morse-Radio Automobile Co., Springfield, Massachusetts. Roadsters.

MORSE STEAMER
USA 1901
J.S. Morse, Newton, Massachusetts.

MORT
USA 1917–1924
Meteor Motor Car Co., Piqua, Ohio. Funeral coaches and limousines on "Meteor" chassis.

MORTENSEN
DK 1904
L. Mortensen, Fredericia. 6hp voiturette.

MORTON
USA 1904–1905
Raleigh A. Morton, San Jose, California.

MORVI
IND 1911–1912
Morvi Motor Works, Morvi State. Only one was made.

MOSER
CH 1914–1924
Moteurs Moser, St. Aubin, Neuchatel. Cyclecars.

MOSKVITCH
SU/RUS; 1947–present
Moskovskii Zavod Malolitrazhnikh Avtomobilei, Moskva. Passenger cars.
See "AZLK," "MZMA," "Aleko."

MOSLER
USA 1996–1997
Mosler Automotive, Riviera Beach, Florida. Sports cars.
See "Consulier," "Intruder."

MOSS
GB 1981–1993
Moss Motor Company, Sheffield. Moss Cars (Bath) Ltd., Bath, Avon. Replicars.

MOSSBERG
USA 1899–1901
Frank Mossberg Co., Attleboro, Massachusetts.

MOTA
USA 1953
Banning Electric Products Corp., New York, N.Y. Fiberglass-bodied gas/electric hybrid.

MOTEC
D 1989–present
Motec GmbH, Manching. Stretched limousines.

MOT ET SARALEGUI
F 1902
Voiturette.

MOTETTE
CDN 1900–1903
Canadian Motors Ltd., Toronto, Ontario.

MOTOBECANE
F 1955; 1961
Motobecane, Paris. 125 cc minicar prototype.

MOTOBLOC
F 1902–1930
G. Carde, Fils et Cie. SA Motobloc, Bordeaux.

MOTO-COR
I
Motovetturetta Carrozzata Originale Resistentissima, Torino. Three-wheelers.
See "AM" Cyclecar di Armino Mezzo.

MOTOFLITZ
D 1949
Rear-engined small car prototype.

MOTO-KAR
USA 1938
Moto-Skoot Mfg. Co., Chicago, Illinois. Three-wheeler.

MOTOMECCANICA
I 1922
Ing. Pavesi, Milano.
See "Aratrice."

MOTOR BOB
USA 1914
E.N. Bowen, Buffalo, N.Y. Runabouts.

MOTOR BUGGY
USA 1908
Motor Buggy Co., Ft. Wayne, Indiana. Highwheeler.

MOTOR CAR
USA 1903
Church Mfg. Co., Adrian, Michigan.
See "Murray."

MOTOR CAR
USA 1906
Believed to be company name of Motor Car Co., Detroit, Michigan.
See "Cartercar."

MOTOR CHAIR
USA 1915–1916
Motor Chair Sales & Operation Co., Chicago, Illinois. Three-wheelers.

MOTORETTE
USA 1911–1914
C.W. Kelsey Mfg. Co., Hartford, Connecticut. Three-wheelers.
See "Kelsey-Motorette."

MOTORETTE
USA 1946–1948
Motorette Corp., Buffalo, N.Y.

MOTOR HORSE
USA 1897
Joseph Barsaleaux, Sandy Hill, N.Y.
See "Barsaleaux."

MOTORMOBILE
F
See "Vilain."

MOTORMOBILE
USA 1901
Carl E. Lipman, Beloit, Wisconsin.

MOTORSPORTS INTERNATIONAL
USA 1990s
Motorsports International, El Cajon, California. Kit cars.

MOTO SCOOTER
E 1951–1959
Moto Scooter SA, Madrid. Three-wheelers.

MOTOTRI CONTAL
D 1907
Max Eisenmann & Co., Hamburg. Three-wheelers.

MOTTA & BAUDO
I 1925
Paolo Motta & Antonio Baudo, Torino. Light car prototype.
See "MB."

MOTZ
USA 1900
Charles A. Motz, Akron, Ohio.

MOUETTE
F 1923–1925
Automobiles Mouette, Paris. 1.1 and 1.5 liter conventional cars.

MOUNT PLEASANT
USA 1914
Mount Pleasant Motor Co., Mount Pleasant, Michigan.
See "M.P.M."

MOURRE
F 1921–1923
Antoine Mourre, Paris. Cyclecars.

MOUSTIQUE
B 1925
Ateliers Luffin, Etterbeek-Bruxelles. Light car prototype.

MOVEO
GB 1931–1932
Moveo Car & Engineering Co., Preston, Lancs. 3-litre sports coupe.

MOVER
USA 1902
B & F Mover Co., Chicago, Illinois.

MOVILUTIL
E 1959
Movilutil. 2 + 2 seater 15 hp small car prototype.

MOYEA
USA 1903–1904
Moyea Automobile Co., New York, N.Y.; Pittsfield & Springfield, Massachusett. Touring cars.

MOYER
USA 1910–1915
H.A. Moyer. Moyer Automobile Co., Syracuse, N.Y. 1904 became Consolidated Motor Co. Absorbed by Alden-Sampson. Mfg. Co.

MOZOTA
F 1906
A. de Mozota, Paris.

MP LAFER
BR 1974–1990
Lafer S.A. Ind. e Com., São Paulo. "MG" (GB) replica.
See "Lafer."

M.P.M.
USA 1915–1916
M.P.M. Motor Car Co., Mount Pleasant, Michigan. Formerly called "M.P."
See "Mount Pleasant."

M.P.M.
USA 1920
M.P. Moller Motor Co., Lewiston, Pennsylvania. Separate from "M.P.M.," Mount Pleasant, Michigan.

M.R.
RO 1945
A.S.A.M., Bucuresti & I.A.R., Brasov. 6-passenger 3-cylinder air-cooled 30 hp prototype.

M.S.
F 1923–1925
Automobiles M.S., Sevres/Seine-et-Oise (1923–1924). Sté. Nouvelle des Automobiles M.S., Suresnes/Seine (1924–1925). Cyclecars.

M.S.L.
GB 1911–1912
Motor Showrooms Ltd., London. Assembled cars.

M.T.
E 1957
Maquinaria y Elementos de Transporte SA, Nervion. About 10 three-wheeled 125cc minicars built.

MTM
D 1993–1995
MTM GmbH, Wettstetten. Tuning.

MTS
D 1981–1989
MTS GmbH, Weinstadt-Endersbach. Tuning.

MTX
CS/CZ 1991–present
MTX spol. s r.o., Praha. Sports cars. Racing and rally cars from 1969.

MUELLER
USA 1909–1910
Mueller Motor Car Co., Milwaukee, Wisconsin. Highwheelers.

MUELLER-BENZ
USA 1895
H. Mueller Mfg. Co., Decatur, Illinois. Later built "Mueller-Trap."

MUELLER-NEIDHART
S 1952
Light car.

MUIR
USA 1900
John S. Muir, South Norfolk, Connecticut. Compressed air powered vehicle.

MUK-WAGEN
D
See "Reissig."

MULFORD
USA 1915; 1922
Mulford Motors Co., New York, N.Y. Cars built by racing driver Ralph Mulford.

MÜLLER
A 1913–1914
Wien. Cyclecar.

MULTIMACO
F 1970
Multimaco, Courbevoie/Seine. Dune buggy.

MULTIPLEX
USA 1912–1913
Multiplex Mfg. Co., Berwick, Pennsylvania.

MULTIPLEX
USA 1952–1954
Multiplex Manufacturing Co., Berwick, Pennsylvania. 3 sports cars made.

MUMFORD
GB 1973–1993
Mumford Engineering Ltd., Nailsworth, Stroud. Three-wheeler, convertibles.

MUNCH-ALLEN
USA 1910
Munch-Allen Motor Car Co., DuBois, Pennsylvania.
See "Keystone."

MUNCIE
USA 1903
Muncie Wheel & Jobbing Co., Muncie, Indiana.

MUNGUIA
E 1961–1967
Munguia Industrial SA, Bilbao. "Goggomobil" (D) based minicars. About 5,200 vehicles were built.

MUNSING
USA 1908–1910
Munsing Mfg. Co., Hoboken, New Jersey.

MUNSING
USA 1913
New York, N.Y.

MUNSON
USA 1896–1900
The Munson Co., La Porte, Indiana. Gas-electric runabout.

MUNTZ JET
USA 1950–1955
Muntz Motor Works, Chicago, Illinois; Evansville, Indiana.

MURAD
GB 1948–1949
Murad Machine Tool Co. Ltd. Murad Developments Ltd., Aylesbury, Bucks. 1.5-litre saloon.

MURDAUGH
USA 1900–1905
Murdaugh Automobile Co., Oxford, Pennsylvania. Runabout.

MURDOC
GB 1784
William Murdock, Birmingham. Steam car.

MURENA
I
See "Intermeccanica."

MURENA
USA 1969
Murena Motors Inc., New York, N.Y. Luxury station wagon with Ford V-8 engine and Italian bodywork.

MURILLO
USA 1906–1907
Murillo Motor Car Co., Marion,

Indiana. Became Coppock Motor Car Co.
See "Decatur."

MURLOCK
USA 1903
Murlock Automobile Mfg. Co., Buffalo, N.Y.

MURPHY SPECIAL
USA 1906
Murphy Auto Construction Co., Minneapolis, Minnesota.

MURRAY
USA 1896
Oliver C. Murray, Homer, N.Y. Runabout.

MURRAY
USA 1902–1903
Church Mfg. Co., Adrian, Michigan. Runabouts. Became "Lenawee."

MURRAY
USA 1916–1921
Murray Motor Co. Murray Motor Car Co., Pittsburgh, Pennsylvania; Newark, New Jersey. Built intermittently by J.J. McCarthy. Succeeded "Murray."

MURRAY-MAC
USA 1921–1929
Murray Motor Car Co., Atlantic, Massachusetts.

MUSCATEER
USA 1968–1973
Muscat Corp., Forest Lake, Minnesota. Jeep-type off-road amphibian vehicle.

MUSTAD
N 1917
Clarin Mustad, Gjovik. 6-wheeled car.

MUSTANG
USA 1948–1949
Mustang Engineering Corp., Renton, Washington. Six-passenger cars (2 + 4) were made.

MUSURUS
F 1921–1922
Janvier, Sabin et Cie., Chatillon-sur-Bagneux/Seine. Few cars built for a wealthy Turkish enthusiast, Musurus Bey.

MUTEL
F 1902–1906
Mutel et Cie., Paris. Built to special orders.

MUTUAL
USA 1915
Mutual Motor Car Co., Buffalo, N.Y.

MUZOLA
F 1922
Sports cars.

MV
I 1952; 1958–1959
Meccanica Verghera, Cascina Costa di Samarate (Novara). Sports cars.

M.V.M.
GB 1956
Manor View Motors, Catel, Guernsey, C.I. Sports car.

MVS
F 1984–present
Manufacture de Voitures de Sport, Cholet; Coueron. Sports car.
See "Venturi."

M.W.
D
See "Wegmann."

M.W.D.
D 1911–1922
Motor-Werke GmbH, Dessau. Touring cars.

M.W.F.
A 1905–1907
Maschinen- und Waggonbaufabrik AG, Simmering. 8/10 hp DeDion engines.

MWM
I 1967
Motor World Machines, Giorgio Neri & Piergiorgio Marazzi, Modena.

MYERS
USA 1901
Thomas Myers, New York, N.Y.

MYERS
USA 1911
F.M. Myers, Atlanta, Georgia. Roadsters.

MYMSA
E 1957
Motores y Motos SA, Barcelona. About twelve 175 cc three-wheelers were built.

MYRON
CS 1934
Myron, továrna automobilu a leteckych motoru, Zlín. 2-cylinder 2-stroke 800 cc engined small car prototype.

MYSTERY CAR
USA 1925
Chicago, Illinois. 5-passenger phaeton.

MYSTERY CAR ELECTRIC
USA 1935
Oakland, California. Electric three-wheeler.

MYTHOLM
GB 1899–1902
Brown & Buckton (1899–1900). Yorkshire Motor Car Mfg. Co. Ltd., Hipperholme, Yorks. (1900–1902). Light car.

MYTHOS
D 1995
Mythos, Baden-Baden. "Bugatti" (F) replica.

MZMA
SU 1947–1969
Moskovskii Zavod Malolitrazhnikh Avtomobilei, Moskva.
See "Moskvitch," "AZLK."

NACIONAL
E 1929–1932
Fabrica Nacional de Automoviles, Barcelona. 2.8- and 3.9-litre sports cars.
See "Nacional Pescara."

NACIONAL
MEX 1949–1952
Fabrique DM-Nacional, Mexico City. 15 convertible bodied cars.

NACIONAL CUSTALS
E 1919
Sr. Custals, Barcelona. Based on "Ideal" design.

NACIONAL-G
E 1939–1940
Natalio Horcajo (Tecnico Industrial), Zaragoza. 700 cc light cars.

NACIONAL PESCARA
E
See "Nacional."

NACIONAL RG
E 1948
Ramon Guillaumes, Nacional R.G., Barcelona. 740 cc light car prototype.

NACIONAL SITGES
E 1933–1937
Sitges. Based on "Peugeot" (F) design.

NACKE
D 1901–1913
Automobilfabrik E. Nacke, Coswig/Sachsen. 5.2- and 6.8-litre chain-driven touring cars.

NADIG
USA 1891–1896
Henry Nadig & Sons, Allentown, Pennsylvania. Gasoline carriage. Built "Eureka" trucks in Allentown from 1905–1906.

NAFA
D 1923
Norddeutsche Automobilfabrik AG, Hamburg. Light car.

NAG
D 1902–1934
Allgemeine Elektrizitäts-Gesellschaft (1902–1908). Neue Automobil-Gesellschaft (1908–1915). Nationale Automobil-Gesellschaft, Berlin (1915–1934). Touring cars.

NAGANT
B 1900–1928
Nagant Freres. SA des Automobiles Imperia-Excelsior, Liege. 2-, 2.6-, 4.2-litre touring and sports cars.

NAGARI
AUS 1970–1974
Graeme & Campbell Bolwell, Frankston. Sports cars.

NAGEL
USA c. 1905
Fred A. Nagel, Massachusetts. 18 and 30 hp automobiles.

NAIG
D 1909–1911
Neue Automobil-Industrie GmbH, Berlin. Voiturette.

NAMAG
D 1906–1914
Norddeutsche Automobil- und Motoren-Aktiengesellschaft, Bremen.
See "Lloyd," "Hansa-Lloyd."

NAMCO
GR c. 1978–1983
Namco, Thessaloniki. "Citroën" (F) based small car.

NAMELESS
GB 1908–1909
Nameless Motor Car Co., London.

NAMI
SU 1927–c. 1989
Zavody Spartak, Nauchnii Avto-Motornii Institut, Moskva. Passenger and sports car prototypes. First Soviet passenger cars NAMI–1 built 1927–1930, 512 being produced.
See "NATI."

NANCE
USA 1911
Nance Motor Car Co., Philadelphia, Pennsylvania. Touring cars. Became "Touraine."

NANCIENNE
F 1900–1903
Sté. Nancienne d'Automobiles, Nancy. Alcohol-fueled cars.

NAOMI
J 2000
Ohno Toshihiko, Kashima, Ibaraki. 235 kW Wankel motor powered sports car.

NAPIER
GB 1900–1924
D. Napier and Son Ltd., London. Large limousines.

NAPIER
USA 1904–1905
Napier Motor Co. of America, Roxbury, Massachusetts. Assembled, not manufactured in USA.
See "American Napier."

NAPOLEON
USA 1916–1919
Napoleon Automobile Mfg. Co., Napoleon, Ohio. Reorganized 1917 as Napoleon Motors Co., Traverse City, Michigan. 4- and 6-cylinder cars. Trucks only 1920–1922.

NARDI
I 1947–1959
Nardi & Danese (1947–1951). Officine Enrico Nardi & C (1951–1959), Torino. Sports cars.

NARDI MONACO
I 1932
Enrico Nardi & Augusto Monaco, Torino. Sports cars.

NARDO
D 1990–1993
V.M. Exclusiver Fahrzeugbau GmbH, Bergisch-Gladbach. Sports cars.

NASH
USA 1917–1942
Nash Motors Co., Kenosha, Wisconsin. Succeeded Thomas B. Jeffery Co. Became Nash-Kelvinator Corp. 1936. Merged with Hudson Motor Car Co. to form American Motors Corp. 1954. Touring cars.

NASH AUTO-CAR
USA 1906–1911

Nash Auto-Car Co., Detroit, Michigan.

NASH-HEALEY
USA 1951–1955
Nash Motors Co., Kenosha, Wisconsin. Built in England for U.S. market. 506 cars sold.

NATHAN
GB 1965–1970
Roger Nathan Racing Ltd., London. Sports cars with wooden frame.

NATI
SU 1930–1933
Nauchnii Avto-Traktornii Institut, Moscow. Passenger car prototypes.
See "NAMI."

NATIONAL
GB 1904–1912
Rose Bros., Gainsborough, Lincs. Light sports cars.

NATIONAL
USA 1898–1900
National Motor Carriage Co., Stamford, Connecticut.

NATIONAL
USA 1899–1901
National Motor Co., St. Louis, Missouri.

NATIONAL
USA 1900
National Automobile Co., Wilmington, Delaware.

NATIONAL
USA 1902–1903
National Automobile & Motor Co., Oshkosh, Wisconsin.

NATIONAL
USA 1903
National Automobile Co., Providence, Rhode Island. Electric and steam vehicles.

NATIONAL
USA 1900–1924
National Automobile & Electric Co., Indianapolis, Indiana. Reorganized as National Motor Vehicle Co. 1902. Electric. Reorganized as National Motor Car & Vehicle Co. 1916. Merged with "Dixie Flyer" and "Jackson" into Associated Motors Corp. 1922; 23,558 cars were made.

NATIONAL
USA 1914
National Cyclecar Co., Detroit, Michigan. Cyclecar.

NATIONAL ROAD CAR
USA 1903–1906
National Sewing Machine Co., Belvidere, Illinois.
See "Eldredge."

NATIONAL STEAM
USA 1899–1900
National Transportation Co., Boston, Massachusetts.

NAVAJO
USA 1954
Navajo Motor Car Co., New York, N.Y. Sports cars using Mercury V-8 engine.

NAVARRE
USA 1921
A.C. Schulz. Package Machinery Co., Springfield, Massachusetts. Possibly only prototype built.

NAW
D
Norddeutsche Automobil-Werke, Hameln/Weser.
See "Colibri."

NAYLOR
GB 1984
Naylor Cars plc, Bradford, West Yorkshire. "MG" replica.

NAZZARO
I 1911–1923
Fabbrica Automobili Nazzaro & C. (1911–1916). S.A. Automobili Nazzaro (1919–1923), Torino. Touring and sports cars.

N.B.
I/GB; 1913–1915
Newton Bennett, John Newton Fabbrica Automobili, Torino. Conventional, well-made cars.

NCF
GB 1990s
NCF Motors Ltd., Great Whittington, Newcastle-upon-Tyne. Kit cars.

N.C.G.
GB 1979
N.C.G. Design Ltd., New Milton, Hampshire. Sports cars.

NEALE
GB 1897
Douglas Neale, Edinburgh. Electric car.

NEANDER
D 1934–1939
Neander-Motorfahrzeuge, Düren-Rölsdorf, Rheinland. Cyclecars and light sports cars designed by Ernst Neumann-Neander.

NEBRASKA
USA 1914
Nebraska Cyclecar Co., Omaha, Nebraska. Cyclecar.

N.E.C.
GB 1905–1920
New Engine Co. Ltd., London. Town cars with horizontal underfloor engine.

NECKAR
D 1959–1969
Neckar Automobilwerk AG, Heilbronn. "Fiat" (I) based cars.

NEDOMA-NADJER
USA 1921
Experimental 5-cylinder car.

NEFF
CDN 1899
Benton Neff, Humberstone, Ontario.

NEFTEL
USA 1902–1903
Neftel Automobile Co., Brooklyn, N.Y. Gasoline-electric car.

NEGRE
F 1897
H. Negre, Amiens/Somme. Steam car.

NEIL
USA 1902
S.S. Neil, Tyrone, Pennsylvania.

NEILSON
USA 1906–1907
Neilson Motor Car Co., Detroit, Michigan. Typographical error in contemporary journals.
See "Nielson."

NEIMANN
D 1929–1932
Dipl.-Ing. Neimann & Co., Köln. Three-wheeler.

NELSON
USA 1905

T.K. Nelson Motor Co., Harlan, Iowa. Touring cars.

NELSON
USA 1905
Nelson, New Britain, Connecticut.

NELSON
USA 1917–1921
E.A. Nelson Motor Car Co., Detroit, Michigan. Absorbed by Gray Motor Co. 1919 reorganized as Nelson Motor Car Co. 1920 reorganized as E.A. Nelson Automobile Company. 1,028 cars were made.

NELSON-BRENNAN-PETERSON
USA 1914–1915
Detroit, Michigan.

NEMALETTE
D 1923–1925
Netzschkauer Maschinenfabrik Franz Stark & Söhne, Netzschkau. Three-wheeler.

NEMBO
I 1966
Modena. Sports car.
See "Neri & Bonacini."

NEMBO
I 1970
Burgert Srl, Dobbiaco. Sports kit cars.

NENNDORF
D 1924
Herbert Nenndorf GmbH, Stettin.

NERGAL
I 1970
Glasurit Italiana Soc., Roma. Sports car prototype designed by Aldo Sessano.

NERUS
GB 1969–1971
Checkpoint Engineering Ltd., Hastings, Sussex. Sports cars.

NESKOV-MUMPEROW
USA 1921–1922
Neskov-Mumperow Motor Car Co., St. Louis, Missouri.
See "St. Louis."

NESSELSDORFER
A/CS 1897–1920
Nesselsdorfer Wagenbau-Fabriks-Gesellschaft vorm. K.k. priv. Wagenfabrik Schustala & Co., Nesselsdorf (1897–1918). Kopřivnická vozovka, a.s., Kopřivnice (1919–1920). First passenger gasoline car in Central Europe. Hans Ledwinka and Edmund Rumpler as main designers. The Type S of 1906 with a 3.3-litre 4-cylinder engine can be regarded as founding the make's worldwide reputation.
See "NW." Name changed to "Tatra" (CS/CZ) in 1920.

NESTOR
PL 1996–present
J.A.K., Katowice. Kit cars.

NETAM-L-CAR
NL 1941–1942
N.V. Nederlandsche Tank-Apparaten en Maschinefabriek, Rotterdam. Electric cars.

NEUHAUS & PAUER
A 1900
Neuhaus & Pauer, Wien. Electric car.

NEUMANN-NEANDER
D
See "Neander."

NEUSS
D 1900
Jos. Neuss, Berlin. Cars to special order. Mainly coachbuilders.

NEUSTADT
USA 1904–1912
J.H. Neustadt Co. Neustadt Auto & Supply Co., St. Louis, Missouri.

NEUSTADT-PERRY
USA 1901–1907
Neustadt-Perry Co., St. Louis, Missouri. Formerly J.H. Neustadt Co. (steamers). Running gear for other companies. Gasoline and steam cars.
See "Neustadt."

NEVADA
USA 1908
Nevada Motor Car Co., Reno, Nevada.
See "Desert Flyer" and "Reno."

NEVILLE
USA 1908–1914
Thomas Neville, Oshkosh, Wisconsin.

NEWARK
USA 1901–1903
Newark Motor Vehicle Co., Newark, New Jersey.

NEW BRITISH
GB 1921–1923
Charles Willetts Junr. Ltd., Cradley Heath, Staffs. Light cars.

NEW CARDEN
GB 1924–1925
7 hp cyclecars.

NEW CASTLE
USA 1907–1908
New Castle Automobile Co., New Castle, Pennsylvania.

NEW CENTURY
GB 1902–1904
Suffield & Brown, London. Steam and gasoline car.

NEW CENTURY
GB 1902–1904
Hoyle Brothers & Co. Ltd., Brighouse, Yorks. Light car.

NEWCOMB
USA 1906
Newcomb Motor Co., Long Island, N.Y. Steam car.

NEW ENGLAND
USA 1898
New England Motor Carriage Co., Waltham, Massachusetts. Steam car.

NEW ENGLAND
USA 1899–1901
New England Electric Vehicle & Transportation Co., Camden, New Jersey.

NEW ERA
USA 1900
New Era Motor Co., Boston, Massachusetts.

NEW ERA
USA 1901–1902
Automobile & Marine Power Co., Camden, New Jersey. Tiller-steered runabouts.

NEW ERA
USA 1912
New Era Motor & Mfg. Co., Lansing, Michigan.

NEW ERA
USA 1916
New Era Engineering Co., Joliet, Illinois. Became Elgin Motor Car Co. $660 tourer.
See "Elgin" (1916–1924).

NEW ERA
USA 1933–1934
New Era Motors Corp., New York, N.Y. Sedan.

NEWEY
GB 1913–1921

Gordon Newey Ltd., Birmingham. Assembled cars.

NEW HAVEN
USA 1899
New Haven Carriage Co., Hartford, Connecticut.

NEW HAVEN
USA 1902–1903
New Haven Carriage Co., New Haven, Connecticut. Absorbed by Electric Vehicle Co.

NEW HOME
USA 1898–1901
Grout Bros., Orange, Massachusetts. Steam car.
See "Grout."

NEW HUDSON
GB 1912–1924
New Hudson Cycle Co. Ltd., Birmingham. Small two-seaters.

NEW IMPERIAL
GB 1914
New Imperial Cycles Ltd., Birmingham. Light car.

NEW LONDON
USA 1895
New London Specialty Co., New London, Ohio.

NEW MAP
F 1938–1949
P. Martin, Lyon. Small cars.
See "Rolux."

NEWMOBILE
GB 1906–1907
Newmobile Ltd., London. 24hp 6-cylinder cars.

NEW MONARCH
USA 1903
Milwaukee Motor & Mfg. Co., Milwaukee, Wisconsin.
See "Monarch."

NEW ORLEANS
GB 1900–1910
Burford, Van Toll & Co. (1900–1901). New Orleans Motor Co. Ltd. (1901–1905). Orleans Motor Co. Ltd., Twickenham, Middlesex (1905–1910). Voiturette; landaulette. From 1905 "Orleans."

NEW ORLEANS
USA 1914
New Orleans Cyclecar Co., New Orleans, Louisiana. Cyclecar.

NEW PARRY
USA 1911–1912
The Motor Car Mfg. Co., Indianapolis, Indiana. Former "Parry."

NEW PICK
GB
See "Pick."

NEW PITTSBURGH
USA 1915
Motors Co. of Pittsburgh, Pittsburgh, Pennsylvania.
See "Pennsy."

NEWPORT
USA 1903
Newport Engineering Works, Newport, Rhode Island.

NEWPORT
USA 1920
Newport Motors Inc., New York, N.Y.

NEW POWER
USA 1897
New Power Co., New York, N.Y.

NEW ROCHELLE
USA 1903
New Rochelle Motor Car Co., New Rochelle, N.Y.

NEW SOUTH
USA 1910
New South Automobile Co., Augusta, Georgia.

NEWTON
I 1914–1915
Fabbrica Automobili John Newton, Torino.
See "N.B."

NEW WAY
USA 1905–1907
New Way Motor Co., Lansing, Michigan. Seven cars built.

NEW YORK
USA 1900–1901
New York Automobile Co., New York, N.Y.

NEW YORK
USA 1900–1902
New York Automobile Co., Syracuse, N.Y. Transferred to H.H. Franklin Co.

NEW YORK
USA 1907
New York Car & Truck Co., Kingston, N.Y.

NEW YORK & OHIO
USA 1899–1900
The New York & Ohio Co., Warren, Ohio.
See "Packard."

NEW YORK SIX
USA 1927–1929
Automotive Corp. of America, Moline, Illinois. Car built in Richmond, Indiana, by the Automotive Corp. of America, Baltimore, Maryland. Parent corp. of G.W. Davis Motor Car Co., Richmond, Indiana. New car announced 1929.

NEW YORK STEAM
USA 1900–1901
New York Motor Vehicle Co., Middletown, Connecticut.
See "Volomobile."

NF
GB 1990s
NF Auto Developments, Lindridge Lane, Staplehurst. Kit cars.

NG
GB 1978–1991
N.G. Cars Design Ltd., New Milton, Hants; Lymington, Hampshire. Vintage-style bodied kit and sports cars.

NIAGARA
USA 1900–1902
Niagara Automobile Co., Niagara Falls, N.Y.

NIAGARA
USA 1902
Niagara Motor Vehicle Co., Buffalo, N.Y. Electric car. Asked voluntary dissolution, reported November 1902.

NIAGARA
USA 1903–1905
Wilson Automobile Mfg. Co., Wilson, N.Y. LaSalle-Niagara Auto Co., Niagara Falls, N.Y. Runabouts.

NIAGARA
USA 1915–1916
Wilson-Niagara Co., Wilson, N.Y.

NIAGARA FOUR
USA 1915–1916
Mutual Motor Car Co. Niagara Automobile Co., Buffalo, N.Y. Former "Mutual"; Touring cars.

NIBBIO
I 1935; 1955

Conte Giovanni Lurani Cernuschi, Milano. Sports cars.

NICHOLS
USA 1908
D.P. Nichols & Co., Boston, Massachusetts.

NICHOLS
USA 1925
Arthur Nichols, Waltham, Massachusetts. Roadsters.

NICHOLS & SHEPARD
USA 1910–1911
Nichols & Shepard & Co., Battle Creek, Michigan. Built tractors after 1911.

NICLAUSSE
F 1906–1914
J. et A. Niclause, Paris. Landaulette.

NIC-L-SILVER PIONEER
USA 1959
Nic-L-Silver Battery Co., Santa Ana, California. Experimental electric car.

NIELSON
USA 1906–1907
Nielson Motor Car Co., Detroit, Michigan. Runabouts.

NIESNER
A 1905–1914
Josef Niesner, Mechanische Werkstätte, Wien. Voiturette.

NIKE
E 1917–1919
E. Alejandro Riera S. en C., Barcelona. Five 12/15 hp cars were made.

NIKKEI-TARO
J
  See "N.J."

NILES
USA 1903
Automobile & Gas Engine Co., Niles, Michigan.

NILSSON
S 1900
Lambert Nilsson, Köping. Voiturette prototype.

NINON
F 1930; 1946
G. Vincent, Nantes. Three-wheelers; minicar prototype.

NISSAN
J 1937–1943; 1960–present
Nissan Motor Co. Ltd., Yokohama. Passenger and sports cars.

NIZZA
D 1968
Gebr. Burgert, Merklingen. Plastic bodied coupe.

N.J.
J 1954–1956
Nippon Keijidosha Co., Kawaguchi, Saitama.
  See "Nikkei-Taro."

NOBEL
GB
  See "Fuldamobil" (D).

NOBLE
USA 1902
Noble Automobile Mfg. Co., Cleveland, Ohio. Runabout and touring car.

NOBLE
USA 1914
Warren Noble, Buffalo, N.Y.

NOBLE
USA 1960
Satellite Corp. of America, Wiscaset, Maine.

NOCKE
D 1905
Prototype.

NOEL
F 1913–1921
Lucien Noel, Courbevoie/Seine. Tandem-seated cyclecar.

NOEL BENET
F 1900
Noel Benet, Offranville/Seine-Maritime. Two-seater voiturette.

NOEL DUPLEX
USA 1923
J.C.N. Noel Motor Car Co., Jersey City, New Jersey.

NOMA
USA 1919–1923
Noma Motor Corp., New York, N.Y. Roadsters; 614 cars were made.

NOMAD
GB 1967–1974
Nomad Cars, Hastings, Sussex. Sports and racing cars.

NOMAD
GB 1981
J.A. Foers Engineering, Rotherham, South Yorkshire. Kit cars.

NO NAME
GB
  See "Horley."

NORCROSS
USA 1865
United Electrical Mfg. Co., Norcross, Georgia. Touring cars.

NORDEC
GB 1949
North Downs Engineering Co., Whyteleafe, Surrey. Sports cars.

NORDEN
S 1902–1906
AB Södertälje Verkstäder, Södertälje. Two-seater buggy by the "Northern" (USA) license.

NORDENFELT
B 1906–1909
Liege. Barriquand et Marre engines.

NORDHUSIA
D 1925–1926
Kurt Schmidt, Motorfahrzeuge, Nordhausen.

NORDYKE
USA
Company name of Nordyke & Marmon Co., Indianapolis, Indiana, not name of car.
  See "Marmon."

NORFOLK
GB 1904–1905
Blackburn & Co., Cleckheaton, Yorks. Light cars.

NORIS
D 1902–1904
Süddeutsche Motorwagen-Industrie Noris Gebr. Bauer, Nürnberg. 6-, 12- and 14hp cars.

NORMA
GB 1912–1914
Norma Motor & Engineering Co. Ltd., London. Shaft-driven light car.

NORMAN-LIONEL
USA 1904–1905
Norman Motor Sleigh Co., Boston, Massachusetts. Motor sleigh, shown at New York City Auto Show.

NORRIS
GB 1914
Stockport Garage Co., Stockport, Cheshire. Light car.

NORSK
N 1908–1911
Norsk Automobil & Vognfabrik AS, Oslo. 8hp friction drive tourer.

NORSK GEIJER
N 1926–1930
AS C. Geijer & Co., Oslo. About 20 cars with Lycoming engine and hydraulic brakes. Later straight-8 65 hp cars.

NORTAN
D c. 1995
Nortan Special Cars, Mettmann. 300 hp sports cars.

NORTH BRITISH
GB
See "Drummond."

NORTH EAST
USA c. 1905
North East Automobile Co., Boston, Massachusetts. 5 hp automobile.

NORTHERN
USA 1902–1909
Northern Mfg. Co., Detroit & Port Huron, Michigan. Organized by J.D. Maxwell and C.B. King. Reorganized as Northern Motor Car Co. 1906. Absorbed by "E.M.F." 1908. Touring cars.

NORTH-LUCAS
GB 1923
Robin Hood Engineering Works, London. 5-cylinder air-cooled motor.

NORTH STAR
GB 1920–1921
North Star Works, London. Cyclecars.

NORTHWAY
USA 1921–1922
Northway Motors Corp., Boston, Massachusetts; Natick, Massachusetts.

NORTHWESTERN
USA 1904
Northwestern Automobile Co., Milwaukee, Wisconsin.
See "Haase."

NORTHWESTERN
USA 1914
Northwestern Automobile Mfg. Co., Seattle, Washington.

NORTHWESTERN
USA 1914
Northwestern Cyclecar Co., Chicago, Illinois. Cyclecars.

NORTON
GB 1913
Tom Norton Ltd., Llandrindod Wells, Radnorshire. Cyclecars.

NORTON
USA 1895
F.G. Norton, Waukegan, Illinois.

NORTON
USA 1901–1902
James J. Norton, Lowell, Massachusetts. Runabouts.

NORTON
USA 1903
W.P. Norton, Torrington, Connecticut. Steam cars.

NORVELL
USA 1946
Jack Norvell, Los Angeles, California.

NORWALK
USA 1911–1916 and 1920–1922
Norwalk Motor Car Co., Martinsburg, West Virginia; Norwalk, Ohio. 2,121 cars were made. Succeeded "Auto-Bug."

NOSTALGIA
GB 1990s
Nostalgia Cars, Honiton, Devon. Kit cars.

NOTA
AUS 1971–1974?
Nota Engineering Pty. Ltd., Parramatta, N.S.W. Light sports cars.

NOTHELLE
D 1967–1993
Nothelle GmbH, Mülheim. Tuning.

NOVA
B 1914
Gustave Van Wilderode, Tirlemont. Prototype.

NOVA
GB 1971–1978
Automotive Design & Development Ltd., Woolston, Southampton. Sports car kit.

NOVA
GB 1978–1994
Nova Sports Cars Ltd., Bradford, Yorkshire; Dewsbury, West Yorkshire. Sports cars.

NOVA
GB 1987–1993
TFS Ltd., Mirfield. Sports cars.

NOVARA
USA 1917
Herreshoff Mfg. Co., Bristol, Rhode Island. Sports cars only.
See "Herreshoff."

NOVIOMAGNUM
NL 1887
Van Rijn, Nijmwegen. Steam car prototype.

NOWA
D 1924–1926
Nowa-Werk, Potsdam. Light cars.

N.P.
GB 1923–1925
S.L.C. Co. Ltd., Newport Pagnell, Bucks. cars were made.

NR
D 1997–present
NR-Automobile, München. "Volkswagen" Beetle conversions.

NSU
D 1905–1977
Neckarsulmer Fahrradwerke AG, Neckarsulm (1905–1910). Neckarsulmer Fahrzeugwerke AG, Neckarsulm; Heilbronn (1910–1931). NSU-Werke AG, Neckarsulm (1958–1969). Audi NSU Auto-Union AG, Neckarsulm (1969–1977). Touring and sports cars. The first Wankel-engined cars in 1963.

NSU-FIAT
D 1929–1967
NSU-Automobil AG (1929–1959). Neckar Automobilwerk AG, Heilbronn (1959–1967). "Fiat" (I) based cars.
See "Neckar."

NUFMOBIL
D 1924
Nufmobil GmbH, Freiberg. Three-wheeler.

NUG
D 1921–1925
Nug-Kraftfahrzeugwerke Niebaum, van Horn & Co., Herford. 960 cc small cars.

NUGENT
USA 1909–1910
Nugent Automobile Works, New York, N.Y.

NU-KLEA
USA 1959–1960
Nu-Klea Automobile Co., Lansing, Michigan. Small electric cars.

NUVOLARI
D
See "EAM."

NW
A/CS 1897–1920
Nesselsdorfer Wagenbaufabriks-Gesellschaft, Nesselsdorf (1897–1918). Kopřivnická vozovka, a.s., Kopřivnice (1919–1920).
See "Nesselsdorfer" and "Tatra" (CS; CZ).

NWF
D 1954–1955
Nordwestdeutsche Fahrzeugbau GmbH, Wilhelmshaven/Mariensiel. "Fuldamobil" license.

NYBERG
USA 1903–1904
Nyberg-Waller Automobile Works, Chicago, Illinois.

NYBERG
USA 1911–1913
Nyberg Automobile Works, Anderson, Indiana. Succeeded "Rider-Lewis" February 28, 1911. Became "Madison." 4- and 6-cylinder cars.

NYE
USA c. 1905
Joseph K. Nye, Fairhaven, Massachusetts. 7 hp automobile.

NYFFENEGGER
CH 1964–1965
Eugen Nyffenegger, Aesch bei Birmensdorf. Sports car prototype.

OAKLAND
CDN 1931
General Motors Products of Canada Ltd., Oshawa, Ontario.

OAKLAND
USA 1907–1931
Oakland Motor Car Co., Pontiac, Michigan. Succeeded Pontiac Buggy Co. Purchased by General Motors 1909. Division of G.M. Corp. 1917. Introduced "Pontiac" 1926. Became Pontiac Motor Division 1932.
See "Pontiac."

OAKMAN
USA 1899–1900
Oakman Motor Vehicle Co., Greenfield, Massachusetts.

OAKMAN-HERTEL
USA 1898
Oakman Motor Vehicle Co., Greenfield, Massachusetts. Became "Oakman" 1899.

OAK SIX
USA 1917
Oak Mfg. Co., Chicago, Illinois.

OBC
S 1974
OBC A.B., Klippan. Plastic bodied sports car prototype with BMW (D) motor and Porsche (D) gearbox.

OBER
USA c. 105
Hersey S. Ober, Lynn, Massachusetts. 3 hp automobile.

OBERLIN
USA 1902–1903
O.S. Oberlin, McKeesport, Pennsylvania.

O'BRIEN
USA 1900
O'Brien & Sons, San Francisco, California. Electric car.

OCELOT
USA 1968–1973
Sand Chariots, Fullerton, California. Dune buggy.

OČENÁŠEK
CS 1900; 1907; 1920
Ludvík Očenášek, elektrotechnická továrna a strojírna, Praha. Prototypes with rotation engine.

O' CONNOR
USA 1916
O' Connor Corp., Chicago, Illinois. Touring cars.

O.C.R.
USA 1968–1972
Orange County Recreation Enterprises, Santa Ana, California. Dune buggy.

OCTO
F 1921–1928
L. Vienne, Courbevoie/Seine. Light cars.

OCTO-AUTO
USA 1912
Experimental 8-wheeler built by Milton O. Reeves. Used "Overland." body and chassis. Running gear by Reeves.
See "Reeves."

OD
D 1932–1938
Fahrzeug- und Armaturenfabrik Willy Ostner, Dresden. Three-wheeler.

ODD-VW-ARK
USA 1970
Automotive Design Associates, Inc., Monroe, Connecticut. Sports cars.

ODELOT
USA 1915
Lawrence Stamping Co., Toledo, Ohio. Spells Toledo backwards. Bucket-seat raceabout.

ODENBRETT
USA 1897
George L. Odenbrett, Milwaukee, Wisconsin.

ODENSEMOBIL
DK 1905
Odense. 2-cyl. voiturette.

ODERO
I 1905
Livorno.

ODERO-RAGGIO-PRINA
I 1905
Savona.

ODETTI
I 1922–1925
Fabbrica Automobili Faustino Odetti, Milano. Light cars.

OEKOMOBIL
CH 1982–present
Peraves, Winterthur. 2-wheeled vehicles.

OETTINGER
D 1946–present
Oettinger GmbH & Co. KG, Friedrichsdorf. Tuning.

OFELDT
USA 1899–1902
F.W. Ofeldt & Sons, Brooklyn, N.Y (1899–1900). Ofeldt Automobile & Steam Launch Co., Newark, New Jersey (1901–1902). Steam carriages.

OFELIA
DK 1887
Hans Johan Johansen. First Danish car, very similar to "Daimler" (D) of 1886.

OFFENHAUSER
USA 1934–1938
Offenhauser Engineering Co., Los Angeles, California. Racing and sports cars.

OFFICINE DI SESTO S. GIOVANNI
I
See "Camona Giusani Turinnelli."

O'GARA
USA 1983–1987
O'Gara Coachworks, Simi Valley, California. Stretched limousine.

OGLE
GB 1961–1964
David Ogle Ltd., Letchworth, Herts. Sports cars (about 70), prototypes, coachworks for "Reliant."
See "Fletcher."

OGO
CH 1970
Otto Grossweiler. Sports car prototype.

OGONTZ
USA 1916
Ogontz Motor Car Co., Sandusky, Ohio.

OGREN
USA 1915–1923
Ogren Motor Car Co., Chicago, Illinois. Racers only, 1914–1917. Became "H.W.O." 1916 reorganized as Ogren Motor Works, Waukegan, Illinois. 1917 reverted to Ogren Motor Car Co. Moved to Milwaukee, Wisconsin. 306 cars were made.

OHIO
USA 1899–1902
Ohio Automobile Co., Warren, Ohio. Synonym for "Packard."
See "Packard."

OHIO
USA 1909–1915
Jewel Carriage Co. Ohio Motor Car Co., Cincinnati, Ohio; Carthage, Ohio. 1912 absorbed by Northway Motor & Mfg. Co. Became Crescent Motor Co.

OHIO
USA 1913–1915
Crescent Motor Co., Cincinnati, Ohio.

OHIO
USA 1909–1912
Ohio Motor Car Co., Carthage, Ohio.

OHIO ELECTRIC
USA 1910–1918
Ohio Electric Carriage Co. Ohio Electric Car Co., Toledo, Ohio. Electric cars.

OHIO FALLS
USA 1913–1914
Ohio Falls Motor Co., New Albany, Indiana. Succeeded "Jonz." Also built "Pilgrim."

OHLMEYER
AUS 1904
Ohlmeyer & Co., Tanunda, S.A. Light cars.

OHMIC
J c. 1952
356 cc small sports car prototype.

OHMPHUNDRA
USA 1946
Los Angeles, California.

OHTA
J 1922; 1934–1957
Ohta Jidosha Seizosho Co. Ltd (1922; 1934–1935). Kosoku Kikan Kogyo Co. Ltd. (1935–1945). Ohta Jidosha Kogyo Co. Ltd., Tokyo (1947–1957). Passenger cars.

OKA
SU/RUS; 1989–1994
Small cars.
See "SMZ."

OKEY
USA 1896–1907
Okey Automobile Co. Okey Motor Car Co., Columbus, Ohio. Runabouts.

OKLAHOMA SIX
USA 1917–1918
Midland Motor Car & Truck Co., Oklahoma City, Oklahoma.

OLDFIELD
USA 1924
Oldfield Motors Corp., Los Angeles, California; Detroit, Michigan. Sports cars.

OLDFIELD CYCLECAR
USA 1914
L.W. Oldfield, Minneapolis, Minnesota.

OLD MILL
GB 1914
Albert Lambourne Ltd., Brighton, Sussex. Quality light cars.

OLDS
USA 1896–1897
P.F. Olds & Son Engine Works, Lansing, Michigan. After building steam cars in late 1880s and early 1890s, turned to gasoline car. One built 1896, four more built 1897.

OLDS ELECTRIC
USA 1899–1901
Olds Motor Works, Detroit, Michigan; Lansing, Michigan.
See "Oldsmobile."

OLDSMOBILE
USA 1897–present
Olds Motor Vehicle Co., Lansing, Michigan. Formerly P.F. Olds & Son Engine Works. 1899 reorganized as Olds Motor Works, Detroit, Michigan. Moved to Lansing after 1901 fire. Became a unit of General Motors Corp. 1908, a division 1917.
See "Viking" (1929–1930).

OLDS 1901 REPLICA
USA 1968
Horseless Carriage Corp., Ft. Lauderdale, Florida. A ¾ scale replica of original "Oldsmobile."

OLI
CS 1948
Josef Hadinec, Hořice. 125 cc small car prototype.

OLIVE
USA 1901
Olive Wheel Co., Syracuse, N.Y. Steam car.

OLIVER
USA 1905
Oliver Trackless Car Co., South Bend, Indiana. 700 cc five-seater.

OLIVER
USA 1906
Oliver Electric Vehicle Co., Cleveland, Ohio. Electric car.

OLIVIERI
I 1901–1905
Palermo.

OLLEARO
I 1934
Fabbrica Motoleggere Ollearo, Torino.

OLSON
USA 1900–1905
Ivan W. Olson, Chicago, Illinois. Gas, electric and steam to 1903; gas and steam 1903–1905.

OLSON
USA 1908
C.J. Olson Buggy & Carriage Mfg. Co., Pittsboro, Indiana.

OLSSON
USA 1900–1905
Ivan W. Olsson, Chicago, Illinois. Built to order.

OLTCIT
RO 1981–1994
Socetatea Mixta Oltcit S.A., Craiova. "Citroën" (F) based car. From 1994 name changed to (*see*) "Oltena." From 1995 *see* "Rodae."

OLTENA
RO 1994–1995
Automobile Craiova S.A., Craiova.
  See "Oltcit" and "Rodae."

OLYMPIA
AUS 1930
Melbourne, Victoria.

OLYMPIAN
USA 1917–1920
Olympian Motors Corp., Pontiac, Michigan. Succeeded Pontiac Chassis Co. Became Friend Motor Co.
  See "Friend"; 2,070 cars were made.

OLYMPIC
USA 1909
Gearless Transmission Co., Rochester, N.Y. Gear-driven companion car to "Gearless."

OM
I 1918–1934
Officine Meccaniche gia Miani, Silvestri & C.A. Grondona, Comi & Co (1918–1928). OM Fabbrica Bresciana di Automobili, Brescia (1928–1934). Sports and passenger cars. Also one rhomboid wheel placement car designed by "Fuscaldo."

OMAHA
USA 1899
Omaha Gas Engine & Motor Car Co., Omaha, Nebraska.

OMAHA
USA 1912–1913
Omaha Motor Co., Omaha, Nebraska. Touring cars. Temporarily used plant of T.F. Stroud Co.

OMAI
I 1988–1993
Omai SaS, C. da Gagliarda di Ortona. 4 × 4 cars.

OMAR
USA 1908–1910
  See "Browniekar."

OMB
I 1906–1913
Officina Meccanica Beccaria.
  See "Florio."

OMEGA
A 1913–1914. "Premier" (D) assembled cars.

OMEGA
CS 1923
Čs. zbrojovka, Brno. 2-stroke light cars.
  See "Z."

OMEGA
D 1921–1922
Omega Kleinautobau GmbH, Berlin. Light cars.

OMEGA
D
  See "Premier."

OMEGA
F 1900
Kreutzberger Freres, Paris. Voiturette.

OMEGA
F 1922–1930
Automobiles Omega-Six, Boulogne-sur-Seine. 3-litre 6-cylinder sports cars.

OMEGA
GB 1925–1927
W.J. Green Ltd., Coventry, Warwickshire. Three-wheelers.

OMEGA
USA 1966–1967
Suspensions International Corp., Charlotte, North Carolina. Sports cars using Ford V-8 engine.

OMIKRON
D 1922–1925
Omikron Kleinautobau GmbH (1922–1924). Berlin-Forster Automobilfabrik GmbH, Berlin (1924–1925). Small cars.

OMNIA
NL 1907–1911
Houwing & Co., Stompwijk (1907–1908). NV Omnia Motoren, Voorburg (1908–1911). Passenger and hire cars. Not more than 100 cars built.

OMNIMOBIL
D 1904–1910
Aachener Stahlwarenfabrik AG, Aachen. Construction kit used by some German manufacturers to produce cars under their own name.

OMNOBIL
D 1922
Deutsche Elektromobil- und Motorenwerke AG, Wasseralfingen. Electric cars.

OMT
I 1907–1913
Officine Meccaniche Torinesi, Torino. Built "Victrix."

ONECA
E 1970s
Pamplona. "Seat" based 7-seater limousines.

O'NEIL
USA 1903
John O'Neil, Lawrence, Massachusetts. 3-cylinder 20 hp car.

ONE OF THE BEST
GB
See "Adams."

ONFRAY
F 1901–1905
Cie Francaise de Cycles et Automobiles, Paris. Light tonneau.

ONLY
USA 1909–1913
Only Motor Car Co., Port Jefferson, N.Y. Race-type torpedo.

ONNASCH
D 1924
Traugott Onnasch, Köslin/Pommern. Three-wheelers.

ONONDAGA
USA 1906
Cronin Automobile Co., Syracuse, N.Y.

ONYX
GB 1990s
Onyx Sports Cars, Grimsby, Lincolnshire. Sports kit cars.

O.P.
F 1921–1924
Automobiles O.P., Levallois-Perret/Seine. Three-wheelers.

OPEL
D 1898–present
Adam Opel (1898–1928). Adam Opel AG, Rüsselsheim (1928–present). Passenger and sports cars. Member of the General Motors Corp. since 1929.

OPERATIONS PLUS
USA 1990s
Operations Plus, Santa Anna, California. Kit cars.

OPES
I 1946–1948
Officine di Precisione e Stampaggio, Torino. "Ninfea" cars and three-wheelers.

OPESSI
I 1935–1936
Pierino Opessi, Torino. Three-wheeler prototype.

OPHIR
USA 1901
Century Motor Vehicle Co., Syracuse, N.Y. Steam car.

OPPERMAN
GB 1956–1959
S.E. Opperman Ltd., Boreham Wood, Herts. "Unicar" light cars.
See "Stirling" (GB) 1956–1959.

OPPERMANN
GB 1898–1907. London
Electric cars and taxicabs.

OPUS
D 1995–1997
Opus-Performance, Kempten. Tuning.

OPUS-H.R.F.
GB 1966–1973
Rob Walker Corsley Garage Ltd., Warminster, Wilts. (1966–1970). H.S.P. Motor Co., Bristol (1970–1973). Sports and fun cars.

ORACLE
B 1997–present
Oracle, Lokeren. Sports cars.

ORAVA
SO 1939–1942
Orava, slovenská úč. spol. pre výrobu a predaj strojov, elektrotechnického zariadenia a automobilov, Bratislava. "Praga" (CS) cars and trucks assembled in the first Slovak Republic.

ORCUTT
USA 1899
Edward L. Orcutt, Somerville, Massachusetts. Steam cars.

OREGON
USA 1916
Beaver State Motor Car Co., Gresham, Oregon.
See "Beaver."

OREL
F 1905–1914
Automobiles Orel, Argenteuil/Seine-et-Oise. Voiturette.

ORIA
I
See "Lentz."

ORIAL
F 1923–1924
Cyclecar.

ORIENT
USA 1899–1907
Waltham Manufacturing Co., Waltham, Massachusetts. In 1899–1901 the company produced two-passenger runabouts equipped with either a 3 or 5 hp water-cooled engine. During 1903 and 1904 air-cooled cars using 20 hp engine were built. 1905 name changed to "Waltham-Orient." 5,889 cars were made.

ORIENTAL-DETROIT
USA 1910
Oriental-Detroit Co., Birmingham, Michigan.

ORIENT-EXPRESS
D 1895–1903
Bergmanns Industriewerke, Gaggenau. Light 3- and 4-wheelers. Also marketed as "Bergmann."

ORIO & MARCHAND
I
Piacenza.
See "Marchand."

ORIOLE
USA 1910
Giddings & Lewis Mfg. Co., Fond Du Lac, Wisconsin.

ORION
A/CS; 1906–1909
Vilém Michl, Slaný. Light cars with underfloor engine.

ORION
GB 1914
Cyclecar.

ORION
I
See "Societa Italo-Svizzera Costruzioni Meccaniche."

ORION
SU 1971
Viktor Kurganskii, Sadki, Poltava. Sports car prototype.

ORIX
E 1952–1954
Juan Ramirez, Barcelona. Small cars. About 12 prototypes were built.

ORLEANS
GB
See "New Orleans."

ORLO
USA 1904
Jackson Automobile Co., Jackson, Michigan. Touring cars.
See "Jaxon" and "Jackson."

ORLOFF
D 1925
Streamlined aluminum body.

ORMOND
USA 1904–1905
United Motor & Vehicle Co., Boston, Massachusetts. Steam car.

ORPINGTON
GB 1920–1924
Smith & Milroy Ltd., Orpington, Kent. Model T "Ford" components.

ORR
USA 1915
Orr Motor Co., Yazoo City, Mississippi.

ORSA
I 1971–1976
Officina Realizzazioni Sarde Automobili, Piero Attilo Rivolta. Barberi, Cagliari (Torino). Replicars.

ORSON
USA 1910–1911
Orson Automobile Co., New York, N.Y. Brightwood Motor Mfg. Co. Drenco Machine Co., Springfield, Massachusetts. 100 cars built for wealthy capitalists. Also called "Millionaire's Car."

ORYX
D 1907–1922
Berliner Motorwagen-Fabrik GmbH (1907–1909). Oryx-Motorenwerke, Zweigniederlassung der Dürkoppwerke AG, Berlin (1909–1922). 1.6-litre cars.

O-S
USA 1914–1916
Owen-Schoeneck Co., Rock Island, Illinois.

OSBORN
USA 1899
Pioneer Iron Works, Clarksburg, West Virginia.

OSBORN
USA 1906
Alden E. Osborn, New York, N.Y. Three-wheelers.

OSCA
I 1947–1966
Officina Specializzata Costruzione Automobili, Fratelli Maserati, Bologna. Sports cars.

O.S.C.A.
I 1999–present
G.M.P. Automobili Srl, Caronno Pertusella. Sports cars.

OSCAR
DK 1983–1987
Ole Sommer A/S, Naerum. Replica. About 20 cars produced yearly.

OSCAR
GB 1969–1970
Oscar Car Co., Lambourn, Berks; Aldershot, Hampshire. Sports cars.

OSCAR-LEAR
USA 1903
Oscar Lear Automobile Co., Columbus, Ohio.
See "Frayer-Miller."

OSEN & HUNT
USA 1898
Osen & Hunt, San Jose, California. Light car.

OSHKOSH
USA 1878
Oshkosh, Wisconsin. Steam vehicle.

OSI
I 1961–1968
Officine Stampaggi Industrali, Torino. Sports cars.

OSTERBERG & SUTTON
USA 1900
Fred Osterberg & Frank Sutton, New York, N.Y. Electric car.

OSTERFIELD
GB 1907–1909
Douglas S. Cox, London. 4- and 8-cylinder cars.

OSTERMANN
D 1985–1994
Speedster Ostermann, Munster; Ibbenbüren. Sports cars.

OSTWALD
D 1931
Fritz Ostwald, Sprendingen. Three-wheeler with rear-wheel steering.

OSWALD
USA 1900
W.E. Oswald, Kalamazoo, Michigan. 4.5 hp car.

OSWALD
USA 1910
Oswald Automobile Co., Bay City, Michigan.

OSWALD
USA 1918
H.A. Oswald Engineering Co., Grand Haven, Michigan. Touring cars.

OTAS
I 1968–1971
Officina Trasformazioni Automobili Sportive di Franco Giannini, Torino. Sports cars.

OTAV
I 1905–1908
Officine Türkheimer per Automobili e Velocipedi, Torino. Voiturette.

OTI
F 1959
Office Technique International, Paris. Three-wheeler prototype designed by Paul Villeple.

OTOMO
J 1924–1927
Hakuyosha Ironworks Ltd., Tokyo. About 35 passenger cars built each month.

OTOSAN
TR 1959–present
Otosan OtomobilSanayi A.S., Kadiköy, Istanbul. Passenger cars.
See "Anadol."

OTOSANTARU
J
See Auto Sandal.

O.T. SIX
USA 1909
Owen Thomas Motor Car Co., Janesville, Wisconsin. Air-cooled cars. Three body styles, six-cylinder rotary valve engine.

OTTO
D 1923–1924
Otto-Werke GmbH, München. Few passenger cars were built.

OTTO
F 1901–1914
Sté. Generale des Voitures Automobiles Otto, Paris. Light cars.

OTTO
USA 1909–1911
Otto Gas Engine Co. Ottomobile Co., Philadelphia, Pennsylvania; Mt. Holly, New Jersey. Touring cars.
See "Ottomobile."

OTTO-CROSS
USA 1968–1972
Auto Craft Inc., Portland, Oregon. Dune buggy.

OTTOKAR
USA 1902–1904
Otto Konigslow, Cleveland, Ohio.

OTTOLINI
I 1900–1901
Fabbrica Automobili Ignazio Ottolini, Milano. 5hp 1-cylinder cars.

OTTO-MOBILE
USA 1899
Bayersdorfer Dumbleton & Co., Omaha, Nebraska. Prototype only.

OTTOMOBILE
USA 1912
Holly Motor Co., Mt. Holly, New Jersey. Succeeded bankrupt Otto Gas Engine Co.

OURS
F 1906–1909
SA des Automobiles Ours, Paris. Touring cars.

OUTING
USA 1910
Outing Motor Co., Detroit, Michigan.

OUZOU
F 1900–1901
Emile Ouzou et Cie., Levallois-Perret/Seine; Poisy/Seine. Voiturette.

OVENDEN
USA 1898
W.C. Ovenden, West Boylston, Massachusetts. Steam car. One sold.

OVERHOLT
USA 1909
The Overholt Co., Galesburg, Illinois. Highwheelers. Became "Illinois."

OVERLAND
USA 1903–1926; 1939
Standard Wheel Co., Division of Parry Mfg. Co., Terre Haute, Indiana (1903–1907). Overland Automobile Co., Terre Haute and Indianapolis, Indiana (1907–1908). Willys-Overland Co. (1908–1936). With "Marion" and "American" in American Motor Sales Co. 1912. Became "Whippet" 1926–1930.

OVERLAND
GB c. 1984
Overland Vehicles, Fareham, Hampshire. 4 × 4 car based on "Land Rover."

OVERMAN
USA 1899–1904
Overman Wheel Co. (1899–1900). Overman Automobile Co., Chicopee, Massachusetts (1901–1904). Steam and gasoline cars.

OVOD
RUS 1999–present
Obukhov Engineering. "Volvo" (S) based 4 × 4 luxury coupe.

OWATONNA
USA 1895–1896
D.J. Ames, Owatonna, Minnesota.

OWATONNA
USA 1903
Virtue & Pound Mfg. Co., Owatonna, Minnesota. 9hp gasoline car.

O-WE-GO
USA 1914
O-We-Go Car Co., Owego, N.Y. Tandem two-seater cyclecars. Company started March 1914. Failed and put in receivers' hands by December 1914.

OWEN
GB 1899–1935
Automobile Transport Co. Orleans Car Co., London. Voiturette; gasoline-electric cars.

OWEN
USA 1898
R.M. Owen Carpet & Rug Mfg. Co., Cleveland, Ohio. Experimental cars only.

OWEN
USA 1899–1901
Owen Motor Carriage Co. Owen Motor Co., Cleveland, Ohio. Gasoline carriage.

OWEN
USA 1910–1912
Owen Motor Car Co., Detroit, Michigan. Touring cars.

OWEN
USA 1914
Owen Motor Car Co., Toledo, Ohio.

OWEN-MAGNETIC
USA 1914–1922
R.M. Owen Co., New York, N.Y. 1915 Baker, Rauch & Lang Co., Cleveland, Ohio. 1919 International Fabricating Co., Wilkes-Barre, Pennsylvania. 1920 Owen-Magnetic Motor Car Corp., Wilkes-Barre, Pennsylvania. Had magnetic transmission. 974 cars were made.

OWENS
USA 1900
H.E. Owens. Thomas Mfg. Co., Springfield, Ohio. Steam car.

OWENSBORO
USA 1903
Owensboro Wagon Co., Owensboro, Kentucky.

OWEN-SCHOENECK
USA 1915–1916
The Owen-Schoeneck Co., Chicago, Illinois. 5.2-litre touring cars.

OWEN THOMAS
USA 1908–1910
Owen Thomas Motor Car Co., Janesville, Wisconsin.
See "O.T. Six." Both names apply to same vehicle. Company advertised car as "O.T. Six."

OWOSSO
USA 1902; 1910
Owosso Buggy Co., Owosso, Michigan.

OXFORD
CDN 1913–1915
Oxford Motor Cars & Foundries Co., Montreal, Quebec. Well-made 4- and 6-cylinder models.

OXFORD
USA 1900
Oxford Automobile Co., Everett, Massachusetts. Steam cars.

OXFORD
USA 1900–1901
Oxford Automobile Co., Augusta, Maine. Steam cars.

OXFORD
USA 1905–1906
Detroit-Oxford Mfg. Co., Oxford, Michigan. Touring cars. Became "Fostoria."
See "Detroit-Oxford."

OYAK
TR 1969–present
Oyak Renault Otomobil Fabrikalari A.S., Findikli, Istanbul. "Renault" (F) license.

OYLER
USA 1900
Oyler Mfg. Co., Minneapolis, Minnesota.

PABIAN
USA 1897
Bob Pabian, Prague, Nebraska. 1-cylinder water-cooled small car.

PACIFIC
USA 1900–1904
Pacific Motor Co. Pacific Motor Vehicle Co., Oakland, California. Runabouts.

PACIFIC
USA 1913
Seattle Car & Foundry Co., Renton, Washington.

PACIFIC
USA 1914
Pacific Cyclecar Co., Seattle, Washington. Cyclecar.

PACIFIC
USA 1914
Portland Cyclecar Co., Portland, Oregon. Cyclecar.
See "Portland."

PACIFIC SPECIAL
USA 1911–1913
Cole California Car Co., Oakland, California. Roadster and tourer.

PACKARD
USA 1895–1896
Lucius B. Packard, Salem, Massachusetts. One vehicle built.

PACKARD
USA 1899–1958
New York & Ohio Co., Warren, Ohio. 1890 two experimental cars. 1900 Ohio Automobile Co., Warren, Ohio. 1902 reorganized as Packard Motor Car Co. and moved to Detroit, Michigan. Merged with Studebaker Corp. 1954 as Studebaker-Packard Corp.
See "Clipper." Passenger cars.

PACKET
USA 1914
Pacific Cyclecar Co., Seattle, Washington. Cyclecars. Misspelled; "Pacific."

PACKET
USA 1914
Scripps-Booth Cyclecar Co., Detroit, Michigan. Cyclecar.
See "Scripps-Booth."

PACKETT
USA 1914–1918
Brasie Motor Car Co. Packett Motor Car Mfg. Co., Minneapolis, Minnesota.
See "Brasie." Name for "Brasie" roadster. Mostly trucks after 1916.

PACO
USA 1908–1909
Pietsch Auto & Marine Co., Chicago, Illinois. Highwheelers and runabouts.

PADUS
I 1906–1908
S.A. Fabbrica Automobili Padus, Torino. Voiturette.

PAG
BR 1988–1993
Projets d'Avant Garde Ltda., Santana do Parnaiba. Minicars.

PAG
D
See "Priamus."

PAGANI
I 1998–present
Pagani Automobili Srl, Modena. Sports cars.

PAGE
USA 1906–1908
Page Motor Vehicle Co., Providence, Rhode Island. Air-cooled car.

PAGE
USA 1909
J.I. Page, Owosso, Michigan.

PAGÉ
USA 1921–1924
Victor Pagé Motors Corp., Stamford, Connecticut. Raymond Engineering Co., Farmingdale, N.Y. Liquidation reported January 1924. No cars sold.

PAGE-ADRIAN
USA 1907–1909
Page Gas Engine Co., Adrian, Michigan. Experimental air-cooled car. Company organized August 1906. Built two-cycle cars. Bought Bloomstrom "Gyroscope" patents 1909. Became "Lion" 1909. 1916 made windshields.

PAGENHARDT
USA 1886
Pagenhardt Brothers, White Post, Virginia. Steam vehicle.

PAGENKOPF
USA 1906
William Pagenkopf, Goldfield, Nevada.

PAGE-TOLEDO
USA 1910–1911
Toledo Motor Co., Toledo, Ohio. Succeeded "Pope-Toledo."

PAIGE
USA 1900
F.E. Paige, Batavia, N.Y.

PAIGE
USA 1911–1928
Paige-Detroit Motor Car Co., Detroit, Michigan. 1927 purchased by Graham-Bros. 1928 became Graham-Paige Motors Corp. Formerly called "Paige-Detroit."
See "Jewett" and "Graham-Paige." 353,487 cars were made (both "Paige" and "Paige-Detroit").

PAIGE-DETROIT
USA 1909–1910
Paige-Detroit Motor Car Co., Detroit, Michigan.
See "Paige." Became "Paige."

PAINE
USA 1914
H.S. Paine, Westerville, Ohio. Cyclecar.

PAISANO
USA 1968
V.W.C. Specialty Co., Kermit, Texas. Dune buggy.

PAL
IND c. 1944–present
The Premier Automobiles Ltd., Bombay. "Fiat" (I) license.
See "Premier."

PALEČEK
CS 1924
Paleček a spol., Praha. Friction-drive light car.

PALLADIUM
GB 1912–1925
Palladium Autocars Ltd., London. Touring cars.

PALM
CDN 1918–1919
Distributed by E.W. Brown Motors Ltd., Milburn, Victoria. Basically Canadian Model T "Ford."

PALM
GB
See "Palmerston."

PALMER
USA 1899
Frank & Ray Palmer, Mianus, Connecticut. Runabout. Later
See "Palmer Light Car."

PALMER
USA c. 1905
George H. Palmer, Attleboro, Massachusetts. 6 hp vehicle.

PALMER
USA 1906
Palmer Automobile Mfg. Co., Cleveland, Ohio; Ashtabula, Ohio. Highwheelers.

PALMER
USA 1912–1913
Palmer Motor Car Co., Ecorse, Michigan. Combined with Partin Mfg. Co. Became "Partin-Palmer." Runabouts.

PALMER LIGHT CAR
USA 1914–1915
Palmer Bros., Cos Cob, Connecticut.

PALMERS DE GROOTE
B 1877; 1880; 1897
Charles Palmers de Groote, Stevoort; Herstal. Steam three-wheelers; first Belgian gasoline car in 1897.

PALMER-SINGER
USA 1908–1914
Palmer & Singer Mfg. Co., Mt. Vernon, N.Y. Company former agents for Matheson and Simplex cars. Car built by "Matheson" 1908. New factory at Long Island City, N.Y. 1911. 1914 became Singer Motor Co.
See "Singer."

PALMERSTON
GB 1920–1923
Palmerston Motor Co. Ltd., Bournemouth, Hampshire.
See "Palm."

PAMCOR
PI 1963–1992
Philippine Automotive Manufacturing Corporation, Manila. "Chrysler" (USA) and "Mitsubishi" (J) license.

PAN
USA 1919–1921
Pan Motors Co., St. Cloud, Minnesota. Company promoted by Samuel Conner Pandoled who was ultimately convicted for fraud. Approximately 737 cars built.

PAN-AM
USA 1902–1903
Pan American Automobile Co. Pan-American Motor Co., Mamaroneck, N.Y. Also called "Pan American." Became Commercial Motor Co., Marion, New Jersey. Touring cars.

PAN AMERICAN
USA 1917–1922
Pan American Motors Corp., Decatur, Illinois. Former "Chicago Light 6." Reported liquidated January 1922. 2,200 cars were made.

PANAUTO ITALIANA
I 1962
Aeromare de Gardolo.

PANDA
USA 1955–1956
Small Cars Inc., Kansas City, Kansas. Two-passenger small cars.

P & S
USA 1904
Palmer & Singer Mfg. Co., Long Island City, N.Y.
See "Palmer-Singer." Both names apply to same vehicle.

P & S MAGIC
USA 1913–1914
Wrong name for "Palmer-Singer" with Magic engine.

PÁNEK
CS 1921
B.Pánek, Rakovník. 12 hp cyclecars.

PANHARD
F 1889–1967
Panhard et Levassor (1889–1898). Société des Anciens Établissements Panhard et Levassor (1899–1965). SA Andre Citroën, Paris (1965–1967). Touring cars; air-cooled cars after 1945.

PANKOTAN
USA 1940
Paul Pankotan, Miami, Florida. Autoboat.

PANORMITAN
I 1907
Fabbrica Siciliana d'Automobili. Sports car prototype.

PANOZ
USA 1996–present
Panoz Auto Development, Braselton, Georgia. Sports cars.

PANTHER
D 1902–1904
Panther Fahrradwerke Oskar Vormbaum, Magdeburg. Three-wheelers.

PANTHER
GB 1906–1908
F.M. Russell & Co. Ltd., London. 14 hp light cars.

PANTHER
GB 1972–1990
Panther Westwinds Ltd., Walton-on-Thames, Surrey; Weybridge, Surrey. Sports car. 150 cars built in 1974. 6-wheeled "Super Six" in 1977. 2 cars were built. 1990 bought by the Jindo Group (ROK). Since 1993 built by "SsangYong" (ROK).

PANTHER
GB 1984–1993
The Panther Car Co. Ltd., Byfleet, Surrey; Harlow, Essex. Sports car.

PANTHER
I 1954–1957
Panther Diesel SpA, Milano. Industria Sanmarinese Costruzione Automobili, Milano. Diesel-powered small cars.
See "ISCA," "RUMI."

PANTHER
USA 1909
Panther Car Co., Boston, Massachusetts.

PANTHER
USA 1962–1963
Panther Automobile Co., Bedford Hills, N.Y. Sports cars.

PANTHÈRE
F 1922–1923
904 cc light cars.

PANTZ
F 1900–1901
Charles Pantz, Pont-à-Mousson/Meurthe-et-Moselle. Tiller steering.

PAPP
A 1979; 1986
Stefan Papp, Villach/Kärnten. Sports car prototypes.

PAPPENBURGER
D 1954
Three-wheeler.

PARADISE
USA 1968–1973
Paradise Inc., Paradise, California. Dune buggy.

PARAGON
GB 1913–1914
K. Portway & Co., Manningtree, Essex. Cyclecar.

PARAGON
USA 1906
Detroit Automobile Mfg. Co., Detroit, Michigan. Roadsters.
See "La Petite." Became "Marvel."

PARAGON
USA 1920–1921
Paragon Motor Car Co., Connellsville, Pennsylvania (Febr. 1920). Paragon Motor Co., Cumberland, Maryland (May 1921).

PARAMOUNT
GB 1950–1956
Paramount Cars (Derbyshire) Ltd. (1950–1952). Meynell Motor Co. Ltd., Melbourne, Derbyshire (1952–1953). Paramount Cars (Leighton Buzzard) Ltd., Linsdale, Bucks. (1953–1956). Roadsters.

PARAMOUNT
USA 1923–1924
Paramount Motors Corp., Azusa, California. 3 all-weather coupes were made.

PARAMOUNT
USA 1927–1931
Moller Co., Hagerstown, Maryland. Taxicabs.

PARANT
F 1906–1907
Parant Freres, Neuilly/Seine. Touring car.

PARDESSUS
USA 1905
R. Pardessus, New London, Connecticut.

PARENT
F 1913–1914
Paul Faitot (Automobiles Parent), Maisons-Alfort, Seine. 704cc and 905 cc light cars.

PARENTI
USA 1920–1923
Parenti Motors Corp., Buffalo, N.Y. Plywood unit built body and frame. Plant sold 1922 to Hanover Motor Car Co., Hanover, Pennsylvania. Touring cars.

PARENT-LACROIX
F 1900–1903
Parent et Lacroix, Villefranche/Rhone. Voiturette.

PARISIA
GB
See "Owen."

PARISIENNE
F 1899–1903
Sté. Parisienne E. Couturier et Cie., Paris. Voiturette.

PARIS-RHONE
F 1947–1950
Lyon. Electric three-wheeler.

PARIS SINGER
GB 1900
Paris Singer Ltd., London. Light car.

PARKER
CDN 1922
Parker Motor Car Co. Ltd., Montreal, Quebec. Formerly "Forster" 1920–1922.
See "Royal Six."

PARKER
GB 1897
Electric car.

PARKER
GB 1901–1902
Thomas H. Parker, Wearwell Motor Co., Wolverhampton, Staffs. Steam car.

PARKER
USA 1825
T.W. Parker, Edgar County, Illinois. Steam three-wheeler.

PARKER
USA 1936
Harry S. Parker, Ellsworth, Maine. One car produced.

PARKIN
USA 1903–1908
Parkin & Son, Oxford & Philadelphia, Pennsylvania.

PARKSHODRO
IR 1986
Iran National Industrial Company, Teheran. 4 × 4 vehicle.

PARNACOTT
GB 1913–1920
A.E. Parnacott, Penge, Kent. 1.5-litre car.

PARR
GB 1901–1902
J. Parr & Co. Ltd., Leicester. Light car.

PARRADINE
GB 1985–1993
Parradine Motor Co. plc, Appleby, South Humberside. Sports car.

PARROTT
USA c. 1905
F.E. Parrott, Lynn, Massachusetts. 3 hp automobile.

PARRY
USA 1896; 1900
Parry Bros., Indianapolis, Indiana.

PARRY
USA 1910–1912
Parry Automobile Co., Indianapolis, Indiana. Became Motor Car Mfg. Co. Called "New Parry" 1911. Touring cars.
See "Pathfinder."

PARSONS
USA 1900
J.H. Parsons. McClean & Kendall Co., Wilmington, Delaware. Steam car.

PARSONS
USA 1905–1906
Parsons Electric Motor Carriage Co., Cleveland, Ohio. Electric car.

PARTIN
USA 1913
Partin Mfg. Co., Chicago, Illinois. Became "Partin-Palmer."

PARTIN-PALMER
USA 1913–1917
Partin Mfg. Co., Chicago, Illinois.

Partin-Palmer Motor Car Co., Chicago, Illinois manufacturers 1914. Reorganized as Commonwealth Motors Co. April 1915. In 1917 name changed to "Commonwealth"; 1,874 cars were made.

PARVA
I 1950
Fratelli Grignani, Torino. Minicar prototype.

PARVILLÉ
F 1927–1929
Edouard Parvillé, Paris. Electric car.

PASCAL
F 1902–1903
Automobiles Pascal, Paris. Large chain-drive tonneau.

PASHLEY
GB 1953
W.R. Pashley Ltd., Birmingham. Three-wheelers.

PASING
D 1902–1904
Automobilwerk Pasing Albert Regensteiner, Pasing. Voiturette.

PASQUALIN
I 1951–1952
Pasqualin-Giannini, Padova.

PASQUET
F 1898
Louis Pasquet, Charlo-Saint-Mard. Rhomboid wheel placement.

PASQUINI
I 1978–1982
Studio Paolo Pasquini, Castenaso (Bologna). City cars.

PASSAT
D 1952
Passat Werk, Krefeld. Light car prototype.

PASSE PARTOUT
F
See "Reyrol."

PASSONI
I 1905–1906
Maurizio Passoni, Torino. Voiturette.

PASSY-THELLIER
F 1903–1907
Sté. Passy-Thellier, Levallois-Perret/Seine. Sports cars.

PASTORA
USA 1913
One registered in Michigan 1916.

PASTOURIE
F 1949
Light cars.

PAT
CS 1948
Adolf Patrman, Turnov. 125 cc small car prototype.

PATERSON
USA 1895
William Paterson, Chicago, Illinois.

PATERSON
USA 1908–1923
W.A. Paterson Carriage Co. W.A. Paterson Co., Flint, Michigan. 12,652 cars were made.

PATHFINDER
USA 1899
Pathfinder Mfg. Co., Chicago, Illinois.

PATHFINDER
USA 1912–1917
Motor Car Mfg. Co. Pathfinder Automobile Co., Indianapolis, Indiana. Succeeded Parry Mfg. Co. 1917 reorganized as Pathfinder Motor Co. of America. 4-, 6- and 12-cylinder touring cars.

PATIN
F 1898–1900
Cie Électrique O. Patin, Paris. Electric car.

PAT-PAF
A/CS 1907
Pražská automobilní továrna — Prager Automobil-Fabrik, Praha. Passenger cars.
See "Praga."

PATRI
F 1923–1925
Établissements Patri, Paris. Cyclecars.

PATRIA
D 1899–1901
Weyersberg, Kirschbaum & Co. AG, Solingen. Voiturette.

PATRICK
USA 1916
Seattle, Washington.

PATRIOT
USA 1920
Patriot Mfg. Co., Havelock, Nebraska. Formerly Hebb Motors Co., Lincoln, Nebraska. Mostly trucks.

PATTERSON-GREENFIELD
USA 1916–1919
C.R. Patterson & Son, Greenfield, Ohio. Roadsters.

PATTON
USA 1890
Gas-electric car.

PAUL
USA 1900
J.E. Paul, Eureka, California. Gasoline carriage.

PAULET
F 1922–1925
Sté. Mécanique du Rhone, Marseilles. 3.9-litre 6-cylinder high-quality cars.

PAUL VALEE
F 1955
Three-wheeler prototype.

PAV
CS 1919
Petrášek a Věchet, Kukleny. Voiturette.

PAWI
D 1921
Paul Viktor Wilke, Berlin. 1.6-litre cars.

PAWTUCKET
USA 1897
Pawtucket Motor Carriage Co., Pawtucket, Rhode Island. Electric carriages.

PAWTUCKET
USA 1901–1902
Pawtucket Steam Boat Co., Pawtucket, Rhode Island. Steam car.

PAXTON
USA 1951–1953
Paxton Engineering Co., Los Angeles, California. Steam and air-cooled cars.

PAYDELL
GB 1924–1935
Paydell Engineering Co., Hendon, Middlesex.

PAYKAN
IR
See "Peykan."

PAYNE-MODERN
USA 1907–1909
Modern Tool Co., Erie, Pennsylvania.

See "Modern" 1906–1909; touring cars.

PAYZE
GB   1920–1921
Payze Light Car Co. Ltd., Cookham, Berks. 10 hp Coventry-Simplex engine.

P.B.
F   1955
Pierre Brissonnet. Three-wheelers.

PCHELKA
RUS   1999–present
Avtoagregat. Minicars.

P.D.A.
GB   1912–1913
Pickering, Darby & Allday Ltd., Birmingham. Cyclecars.

PEARSALL-WARNE
GB
  See "Warne."

PEARSON-COX
GB   1909–1916
Pearson & Cox Ltd., Shortlands, Kent. Steam car.

PEARSON-COX
GB   1913
Cyclecar.

PECK
CDN   1911–1913
Peck Electric Ltd., Toronto, Ontario. Electric cars.

PECK
USA   1897–1899
Barton L. Peck, Detroit Horseless Carriage Co., Detroit, Michigan. Gasoline carriage.

PECKHAM
USA   1915
Peckham Motor Car Co., Toledo, Ohio.

PECORI
I   1891
Enrico Pecori, Como. Steam tricycle.

PECQUEUR
F   1828
Oneisiphore Pecqueur, Lyon? Steam carriage with differential.

PEDALMOBILE
USA   1912
Pedalmobile Mfg. Co., Indianapolis, Indiana. Later "Herff-Brooks."

PEDERSEN
USA   1922
L.C. Pedersen Motor Car Co., Inc., Chicago, Illinois. Mail order cyclecars.

PEDRO
USA   1902–1903
Franco-American Automobile Co., Marion, New Jersey.
  See "Franco-American."

PEEL
GBM   1962–1966
Peel Engineering Co. Ltd., Peel, Isle of Man. Gas and electric 3-wheelers.

PEER GYNT
D   1925
Dickmann AG, Berlin. Small cars.

PEERLESS
GB   1957–1960
Peerless Cars Ltd., Slough, Bucks. 325 sports cars were made.

PEERLESS
USA   1899
Liquid Air Power & Automobile Co., New York, N.Y.
  See "Liquid Air."

PEERLESS
USA   1900–1901
Peerless Long Distance Steam Carriage Co., Washington, D.C. Steam car.

PEERLESS
USA   1900–1931
Peerless Mfg. Co., Cleveland, Ohio. 1902 reorganized as Peerless Motor Car Co.; 1925 as Peerless Motor Car Corp.; Respected luxury cars. 108,116 made.

PEET
USA   1900–1901
Dr. A.J. Peet & Dr. William T. Jenkins, Brooklyn, N.Y. Steam cars.

PEET
USA   1923–1926
Peet Motor Corp., Hollis, N.Y.

PEGASO
E   1951–1958
Empresa Nacional de Autocamiones SA, Barcelona. Expensive sports cars.

PEGASO
E   1991–1994
Los Clasicos Pegaso S.A., Madrid. Sports cars.

PEGASSE
F   1924–1925
M. Arboval, Boisguilbert. Cyclecar.

PEGASUS
USA   1902
Pegasus Automobile Company, Harvey, Illinois. Prototypes only.

P 80
PL   1957–1958
Jozef Przybylski, Warszawa. 250 cc 12 hp three-wheeler prototype.

PEILLON
F   1899–1900
Boulogne-sur-Seine. Voiturette.

PE-KA
D   1924–1925
Pe-Ka Fahrzeugfabrik, Dresden. PE-KA Fahrzeugbau GmbH, Karlsruhe in Baden. P. Raebel GmbH Fahrzeugbau, Berlin. Ultra-light 3-wheeler (70 kg).

PEKING
PRC   1960–present
Dong Fang Hong Works, Peking. Passenger cars.
  See "Bei-Jing."

PELHAM
GB
  See "Bayley & Lambert."

PELIKAN
D   1923
Jakob Baumann, Ludwigshafen/Rhein.

PELL
GB   1990s
Pell Automotive, West Yorks. Kit cars.

PELL
USA   1910
David W. Pell. Pell Motor Car Co., Oswego, N.Y.

PELLAND
GB   1978–c. 1982
Pelland Engineering, King's Lynn, Norfolk. Sports cars.

PELLETIER
USA   1906
Pelletier-Duquesne Motor Co., Jamestown, N.Y. Formerly "Duquesne" Motor Car Co.

PENDLETON
USA   1899–1905
Trumbull Mfg. Co., Warren, Ohio. Touring cars.

PENDLETON
USA   1914
Pendleton Cyclecar Mfg. Co., Culver City, California. Cyclecar.

PENELLE
F 1900–1901
B. Penelle, Melun/Seine-et-Marne. "Benz" (D)-like car.

PENINSULAR
USA 1912–1913
Peninsular Motor Co., Saginaw, Michigan. Formerly "Marquette."

PENN
USA 1908
Dr. Shakespeare Penn, Washington, D.C. One three-wheeler produced.

PENN
USA 1911–1912
Penn Motor Car Co., Pittsburgh and New Castle, Pennsylvania. Roadsters.

PENNACCHIO
I 1947–1948
Vettura Lucciola, Milano.

PENNANT
USA 1924–1925
Barley Motor Car Co., Kalamazoo, Michigan. Taxicabs.

PENNEY
USA 1899
J.W. Penney & Sons, Mechanic Falls, Maine.

PENNEY
USA 1901
H.D. Penney, Woonsocket, Rhode Island. Steam carriage.

PENNINE
GB 1914
Halifax. Cyclecar.

PENNINGTON
USA/GB; 1894–1895; 1896–1899; 1899–1902
E.J. Pennington, Cleveland, Ohio (1894–1895). Great Horseless Carriage Co. Ltd., Coventry, Warwicks. (1896–1897). Pennington and Baines, London (1898–1899). Pennington Motor Co. Ltd., London (1899). Anglo-American Rapid Vehicle Co., New York, N.Y.; Philadelphia, Pennsylvania (1899–1902). Three- and four-wheeled cars.

PENNSY
USA 1916–1917
Pennsy Motor Corp. of Pittsburgh, Pittsburgh, Pennsylvania. Formerly "Kosmath." Became "Pennsylvania." Touring cars.

PENNSYLVANIA
USA 1895–1900
Pennsylvania Steam Vehicle Co., Carlisle, Pennsylvania. Steam car.

PENNSYLVANIA
USA 1900–1901
Pennsylvania Horseless Carriage Co., Washington, D.C.

PENNSYLVANIA
USA 1907–1911
Pennsylvania Auto-Motor Co., Bryn Mawr, Pennsylvania. Touring cars.

PENNSYLVANIA
USA 1918–1919
Pennsylvania Electric Vehicle Co. Pennsylvania Motor Car Co., Pittsburgh, Pennsylvania.

PENNSYLVANIA ELECTRIC
USA 1905–1906
Pennsylvania Electric Vehicle Co., Philadelphia, Pennsylvania.

PENTE
H 1938; 1946–1947
Weiss Manfred Acelmüvek, Budapest. Csepel, Budapest. Small car prototypes.

PENTON
USA 1928
Penton Motor Co., Cleveland, Ohio.

PEOPLES
USA 1900–1902
Peoples Automobile Co., Cleveland, Ohio. Became Troy Automobile & Bicycle Co., Troy, Ohio. Runabouts.

PEOPLES CAR
AUS 1947
Peoples Car (Australia) Ltd. Light car prototype.

PEORIA
USA 1904
Peoria Automobile Co., Peoria, Illinois.

PEREGRINE
GB 1961
Peregrine Cars Ltd., Waltham Abbey, Essex. Sports cars.

PEREIRA
P 1975
Pereira e Teles, Cascais. Dune buggy.

PERFECT
USA 1906
Saint Anne Kerosene Motor Co., Saint Anne, Illinois.

PERFECTA
I 1899–1903
Automobili Perfecta, Torino.
See "Bender & Martiny."

PERFECTION
USA c. 1905
George P. Marx, New York, N.Y. 20 hp automobile.

PERFECTION
USA 1907–1908
Perfection Automobile Works, South Bend, Indiana. Became "Ricketts."

PERFEKT
A/CS 1909
Fr. Petrášek, Kukleny. Voiturette.

PERFETTI
I 1922–1923
Automobili Perfetti, Milano. The driver sat in the center of the body, with a passenger on each side and one behind.

PERFEX
GB 1920–1921
Perfex Manufacturing Co. Ltd., Bournemouth, Hampshire. Medium-sized assembled cars.

PERFEX
USA 1912–1913
Perfex Co., Los Angeles, California. Roadsters.

PERKINS
USA 1906
Perkins Mfg. Co., Springfield, Massachusetts. Experimental car. Produced as "Bailey" 1907.

PERKINS
USA 1914–1915
Masnick-Phipps Mfg. Co., Detroit, Michigan. Cyclecars.

PERL
A 1921–1927; 1951
Automobilfabrik Perl AG, Liesing. Perl-Auhof-Automobil-Bestandteile- und Karosserie-Fabrik, Liesing. Light cars; minicars.

PERMAX
USA 1914–1915
Union Car Co., Los Angeles, California. 2-seater roadsters.

PERREAU
F 1923–1925

Automobiles Perreau, Epinay/Seine. 7 hp Ruby engine.

PERRET
USA 1896; 1900
Frank Perret, New York, N.Y. Electric cars.

PERRY
GB 1913–1916
Perry Motor Co. Ltd., Tyseley, Birmingham. Tourer.

PERRY
USA 1896
O.H. Perry Mfg. Co., Boston, Massachusetts.
See "Boston-Haynes-Apperson" designed and built by O.H.Perry 1898.

PERRY FINA SPORT
USA 1953
New York, N.Y.

PERRY-LEWIS
USA 1895
J.D. Perry Lewis Electric Wagon Co., St. Louis, Missouri. Electric car.

PERRYMOBILE
USA 1942–1945
The Perrymobile Co., Los Angeles, California.

PERRY STEAMER
USA 1945
Perry-Braver Motor Co., Los Angeles, California.

PERSU
RO 1922
Aurel Persu, Bucuresti. Streamlined rear-engined experimental car.

PESAGUS
USA 1902
Pesagus Automobile Co., Harvey, Illinois. Typographical error.
See "Pegasus."

PESTO
D 1972
Peter Stoy, Berlin. Dune buggy kit.

PESTOURIE ET PLANCHON
F 1922
Small car with wooden chassis and body.

PET
D 1977
PET GmbH, Kaiserslautern. "KdF" replicars.

P.E.T.
USA 1913–1914
P.E. Teats Cyclecar Co., Detroit, Michigan. Cyclecars.

PETELER
USA 1900
Adolph Peteler, New Orleans, Louisiana. Gasoline automobile.

PETER-MORITZ
D 1921–1925
Automobilwerke Peter-Moritz, Eisenberg/Thuringen (1921–1923); Naumburg/Saale (1923–1925). Two-seater cyclecars.

PETER PAN
USA 1914–1915
Randall Co., Norfolk Downs, Massachusetts. Randall Motor Car Co., Wollaston, Massachusetts. Cyclecars.

PETERS
USA 1915
Walton-Ludlow Auto Engineering Co., Philadelphia, Pennsylvania. Became "Peters Tricar."

PETERS
USA 1921–1922
Peters Motor Car Co., Pleasantville, N.Y.; Trenton, New Jersey. Peters Autocar Co., Bethlehem, Pennsylvania. Became Peters Motor Car Division of Romer Motors Corp.

PETERSON
USA 1909
P.O. Peterson, Chaffee, North Dakota. 10 hp runabout.

PETERSON
USA c. 1914
Peterson, Kenmare, North Dakota. 12 hp runabout.

PETERS TRICAR
USA 1916
Peters Tricar Corp., Philadelphia, Pennsylvania

PETERS-WALTON-LUDLOW
USA 1916
Peters-Walton-Ludlow Auto Engineering Co., Philadelphia, Pennsylvania. Cyclecar.

PETIT
F 1909
Tarare/Rhone. Voiturette.

PETRA
CS 1919
Fr. Petrášek, Královéhradecká továrna automobilu, Kukleny. Voiturette.

PETRÁŠEK
CS 1926–1933
Ing. Frantisek Petrášek, Hradec Králové. Voiturette.

PETREL
USA 1908–1912
Petrel Motor Car Co., Kenosha, Wisconsin. Formerly "Earl" 1907. Combined with Beaver Mfg. Co. in Fuller & Stowell Motors Co; Roadsters.

PETRINI
I 1948
Vincenzo Petrini, Vercelli/Asti.

PETROMILLI
I 1922
Petromilli, Torino.
See "CIP."

PETROMOBILE
USA 1900
Kidder Motor Vehicle Co., New Haven, Connecticut.
See "Kidder."

PETROMOBILE
USA 1902
Petromobile Co., Brooklyn, N.Y.

PETTER
GB 1895–1898
Jas. B. Petter & Sons (1895–1896). Hill & Boll, Yeovil, Somerset (1897–1898). Light cars.

PEUGEOT
F 1889–present
Les Fils de Peugeot Frères, Beaulieu-Valentigney (188–1897). SA des Automobiles Peugeot, Audincourt (1897–1910). SA des Automobiles et Cycles Peugeot, Lille (1902–1908); Audincourt (1910–1926); Sochaux (1910–1926). SA des Automobiles Peugeot, Sochaux (1928–present). Passenger and sports cars.

PEUGEOT CROIZAT
I 1905–1907
S.A. Brevetti Automobili Peugeot, Vittorio Croizat (1905–1906). Peugeot-Croizat SA, Torino (1906–1907). "Peugeot" (F) license.

PEUGEOT ITALIANA
I 1924–1929
S.A. Italiana Cicli e Automobili Peugeot, Milano.

PEYKAN
IR 1967–present
Iran National Industrial Manufacturing Co., Teheran.
See "Hillman" (GB). Sometimes written as "Paykan."

PFA
PL 1923–1924
Poznanska Fabryka Automobilowa, Liwoszna. Coupe prototypes.

PFEIL
D 1928
Motor GmbH, Bleckendorf. Cyclecar.

PFLÜGER
D 1900
Vereinigte Accumulatoren- und Electrizitätswerke Dr. Pflüger & Co., Berlin. Small electric cars.

PGE
I 1976–1982
Progetti Gestione Ecologiche, Milano. Electric cars.

PHAETON
USA 1977–1979
Phaeton Coach Corporation, Dallas, Texas. Stretched limousines.

PHÄNOMEN
D 1907–1927
Phänomen-Fahrradwerke Gustav Hiller (1907–1910). Phänomen-Werke Gustav Hiller AG, Zittau/Sachsen (1910–1927). Three-wheelers.

PHANTOM
USA 1982
Phantom Vehicle Co., Costa Mesa, California. Sports car kit.

PHANTOM CORSAIR
USA 1939
Rust Heinz, Pasadena, California. One car produced.

PHÉBÉ
B 1900
See "Pittevil."

PHEBUS
F 1899–1903
Noe Boyer et Cie., Suresnes/Seine. Voiturette.

PHEBUS
F 1921
Cyclecars Phebus, Lyon. Cyclecar.

PHELPS
USA 1903–1905
Phelps Motor Vehicle Co., Stoneham, Massachusetts. Became "Shawmut" 1905–1909. Touring cars.

PHENIX
F 1912–1914
Automobiles Phenix, Puteaux/Seine. 10, 12 and 15hp light cars.

PHIANNA
USA 1917–1922
Phianna Motor Co., Newark, New Jersey (1917–1918). Succeeded "S.G.V." 1919 became M.H. Carpenter Co., Long Island City, N.Y. (1919–1922). Touring and town cars.

PHILADELPHIA
USA 1899–1900
Philadelphia Motor Carriage Co., Philadelphia, Pennsylvania. Electric car.

PHILADELPHIA
USA 1900–1901
Philadelphia Motor Vehicle Co., Philadelphia, Pennsylvania.

PHILADELPHIA
USA 1911
Philadelphia Electric Co., Philadelphia, Pennsylvania. Electric car.

PHILBRICK
USA 1900
H.B. Philbrick, Hartford, Connecticut. 2 electric carriage prototypes were built.

PHILBRICK STEAMER
USA 1887
Andrew J. Philbrick, Beverly, Massachusetts.

PHILION
USA 1892
Achille Philion, Akron, Ohio. Steam car.
See "Achille Philion" steamer.

PHILIPSON
S 1946
Gunnar Philipson, Augustendal. 2-cylinder 700 cc 2-stroke engine.

PHILLIPS
USA c. 1905
George F. Phillips, Quincy, Massachusetts. 8 hp automobile.

PHILLIPS
USA 1979–1986
Phillips International Trade Corporation, Margate, Florida. Replica.

PHILOS
F 1912–1913
SA Nouvelle des Automobiles Philos, Lyon. Altos, Ballot, Ruby and SCAT engines were used.

PHIPPS
USA 1912
Phipps Electric Automobile Co., Detroit, Michigan. Electric car.

PHIPPS-GRINNELL
USA 1909–1911
Phipps-Grinnell Automobile Co., Detroit, Michigan. Electric car.
See "Grinnell" electric.

PHOENIX
BR 1987–1993
LHM Industrias Mecanicas Ltda., Rio de Janeiro. Replica.

PHOENIX
ET 1955–1956
Cairo Motor Co. Ltd., Cairo; Alexandria. Small car designed by Raymond Flower.
See "Frisky" (GB).

PHOENIX
GB 1902–1904
Phoenix Motor Works, Southport, Lancs. 3-cylinder cars.

PHOENIX
GB 1903–1928
Phoenix Motor Co., London (1903–1911). Ascot Motor and Mfg. Co., Letchworth, Herts. (1911–1928). Three-wheelers; voiturette; light cars.

PHOENIX
GB 1985
Phoenix Automotive, Blockley, Gloucestershire. Light car.

PHOENIX
GB 1990s
Phoenix Automotive, Westbury, Wiltshire. Kit cars.

PHOENIX
USA 1899–1900
Phoenix Motor Vehicle Co., Cleveland, Ohio.

PHOENIX
USA 1905
D.C. Stover Automobile Co., Freeport, Illinois.
See "Stover."

PHOENIX
USA 1966
John Fitch & Co., Inc., Falls Village, Connecticut.
See "Fitch Phoenix." Both names apply to same vehicle.

PHOENIX
USA 1999–present
Phoenix Automotive, Westbury, Wiltshire. Kit cars.

PHÖNIX
H 1905–1915
Phönix Autógyár (1905–1910). Autó-, Malom- és Gépgyár, Budapest (1911–1915). Based on the "Cudell" (D). Later production of "MAG" cars.

PHOOLTAS
IND 1986–1993
Phholtas Transmotives Pvt. Ltd., Patna. Small 4 × 4 cars.

PHRIXUS
F
See "O.P."

PIAGGIO
I 1951–1956
Piagio SpA, Genova. Three-wheelers "Ape."

PIANIGIANI
I 1924–1934
Guido Pianigiani, S. Quirico d'Orcia (Siena).

PICCOLO
D 1904–1912
A. Ruppe & Sohn AG (1904–1910. Apollo-Werke AG, Apolda (1910–1912). Air-cooled light cars.
See "Apollo," "MAF."

PICK; NEW PICK
GB 1898–1925
J.H. Pick & Co. (1898–1908). New Pick Motor Co. Ltd. (1908–1915). Pick Motor Co Ltd., Stamford, Lincs. (1915–1925). Light sports cars.

PICKARD
USA 1909–1912
Pickard Bros., Brockton, Massachusetts. Touring cars and runabouts.

PICKER-MOCCAND
CH
See "Lucia."

PICKFORD
USA 1905–1906
Llewellyn Pickford, Palmerton, Pennsylvania. Touring cars.

PICKLE
USA 1906
Fred Pickle, Greenville, Michigan.

PIC-PIC
CH 1906–1924
Sté. des Automobiles à Geneve (1906–1910). Piccard-Pictet et Cie., Geneve (1910–1924). Large and expensive touring cars.

PIEDMONT
USA 1908
Piedmont Buggy Co., Monroe, North Carolina. Motor buggy.

PIEDMONT
USA 1917–1922
Piedmont Motors, Lynchburg, Virginia. 2,470 cars were made. Also built cars for "Bush," "Lone Star" and "Alsace."

PIEPER
B 1899–1903
Sté. des Établissements Pieper, Liege. Voiturette.

PIERCE
USA 1895
Pierce Engine Co., Racine, Wisconsin.

PIERCE-ARROW
USA 1901–1938
Pierce-Arrow Motor Car Co., Buffalo, N.Y. Formerly George N. Pierce Co. Under "Studebaker" control 1928–1933. Reorganized 1933 as Pierce-Arrow Motor Car Co. 85,474 cars were made.

PIERCE-CROUCH
USA 1895
Pierce-Crouch Engine Co., New Brighton, Pennsylvania.
See "Crouch."

PIERCE ELECTRIC
USA 1900–1904
Dr. Ray V. Pierce, Newark & Bound Brook, New Jersey. Electric runabouts.

PIERCE GREAT ARROW
USA 1904–1909
George N. Pierce Co., Buffalo, N.Y. Formerly "Pierce Motorette" 1901–1903. Became "Pierce-Arrow." 1909–1938.

PIERCE MOTORETTE
USA 1901–1903
George N. Pierce Co., Buffalo, N.Y. Used De Dion engine. Became "Pierce Great Arrow."

PIERCE-RACINE
USA 1904–1911
Pierce Engine Co., Racine, Wisconsin. 1903 merged with Wisconsin Wheel Co. 1909 absorbed by Pierce Motor Co. Bought by J.I. Case Threshing Machine Co. 1910. Name changed to "Case" 1911. 2,211 cars were made.
See "Mitchell."

PIERCE STEAM
USA 1895
W.A. Pierce, Sistersville, West Virginia. Steam tricycle.

PIERRE
USA 1898
Frank Edson, Pierre, South Dakota. Motor carriage.

PIERRE ROY
F 1902–1908
Pierre Roy, Grand Montrouge/Seine. 14/20 and 24/30 hp models.

PIERRON
F
See "Mass."

PIGEON
CDN 1990s
Garage Pigeon, Ste-Julienne, Quebec. Kit cars.

PIGGINS
USA 1908–1910
Piggins Bros., Racine, Wisconsin. Touring cars. Trucks only after 1910.

PILAIN
F 1902–1920
SA des Automobiles Pilain, Lyon. Expensive and excellent machines.

PILAIN
F 1930–1935
E. Pilain, Levallois-Perret/Seine. 919cc light car.

PILCAR
CH 1977–1978
Pilcar, Chene-Bourg. Electric city cars.

PILGRIM
GB 1906–1914
Pilgrim's Way Motor Co. Ltd., Farnham, Surrey. Large town cars.

PILGRIM
GB 1985
Pilgrim Cars, Henfield, Sussex. Replica.

PILGRIM
USA 1900
Pilgrim Motor Co., Somerville, Massachusetts. Steam car.

PILGRIM
USA 1899–1900
Pilgrim Motor Vehicle Co., Somerville, Massachusetts.

PILGRIM
USA 1913–1914
Ohio Falls Motor Co., New Albany, Indiana. Touring cars. Also built "Ohio Falls."

PILGRIM
USA 1915–1918
Pilgrim Motor Car Co., Detroit, Michigan. Designed by W.H. Radford formerly with "Warren" 1913–1914. Later designer for "Balboa." R.C. Aland designed 1916 model.

PILGRIM
USA 1916–1917
Pilgrim Motor Co., Portland, Maine.

PILLING
USA c. 1905
Alfred J. Pilling, Lynn, Massachusetts. 3 hp automobile.

PILLINGS
USA 1904
George T. Pillings, Williamsport, Pennsylvania. Steam carriages.

PILLIOD
USA 1915–1916
Pilliod Motor Car Co., Toledo, Ohio. Company formed March 1915. Bankrupt June 1916. Touring cars.

PILOT
D 1923–1928
Pilot-Wagen AG, Bannewitz bei Dresden (1923–1924). Sächsische Waggonfabrik, Werdau (1924–1928). Passenger cars.

PILOT
GB 1909–1914
Motor Schools Ltd. (1909–1911). Pilot Motors & Friction Cars Ltd., London (1911–1914). Friction-drive light cars.

PILOT
USA 1909–1924
Pilot Motor Car Co., Richmond, Indiana. 5,282 cars were made.

PILTON
USA c. 1905
Henry Pilton, Marlboro, Massachusetts. 9 hp automobile.

PINART
B 1901
Ernest Pinard, Bruxelles. Voiturette.

PINEO
USA c. 1905
Henry A. Pineo, West Quincy, Massachusetts. 6 hp automobile.

PINGUIN
D 1953–1954
Rotenburger Metallwerke Rudolf Stierlen KG, Rotenburg. Ruhr Fahrzeugbau, Herne. About 12 three-wheelers were built.

PINGUIN
D 1991
Fridez & Maass, Stuttgart. Electric cars.

PININFARINA
I 1960
Carrozzeria Pininfarina, Grugliasco (Torino). Prototype PF "X" with rhomboid wheel placement. Coachbuilders from 1930. Limited-production cars built on the standard "Fiat," "Lancia" and "Alfa Romeo" chassis to date.

PINNACE
GB
See "Norma."

PINOY
PI 1975
Francisco Motor Corp., Rizal. Light cars and taxicabs.

PIO
D 1950
Bruno Piotrowski, Hamburg. 400 cc 12 hp three-wheeler prototype.

PIONEER
AUS 1897
Australian Horseless Carriage Syndicate, Melbourne. Probably the first internal-combustion-engine cars built in AUS.

PIONEER
USA 1896–1899
J.A. Meyer, San Franisco, California. Three experimental cars built.

PIONEER
USA 1898
Patrick Sullivan, Detroit, Michigan. Runabout.

PIONEER
USA 1907–1912
Pioneer Car Co. Inc., El Reno, Oklahoma. Pioneer Car Mfg. Co., Oklahoma City, Oklahoma. Runabouts.

PIONEER
USA 1910
Pioneer Motor Co., Marquette, Michigan.

PIONEER
USA 1913
Pioneer Motor Co., Muskogee, Oklahoma.

PIONEER
USA 1914
American Manufacturing Co., Chicago, Illinois. Cyclecars.

PIONEER
USA 1959–1960
Nic-L-Silver Battery Co., Santa Ana, California. Electric cars.
See "Nic-L-Silver."

PIONIER
PL 1953
Mieczyslaw Lukawski, Warszawa. 500 cc 23 hp light car prototype.

PIPE
B 1898–1922
Compagnie Belge de Construction Automobile, Bruxelles. Touring and sports cars.

PIPER
GB 1966–1976
Campbells Garages, Hayes, Kent (1966–1967). Piper Cars Ltd., Wokingham, Berks. (1967–1971). Embrook Engineering Ltd., Wokingham, Berks. (1971–1972). Piper F.M. Ltd., Ashford, Kent (1972–1976). About 150 sports cars were made.

PIPER
USA 1982
Piper Automobile Co., Salina, Kansas. Replicars.

PIPER & TINKER
USA 1895–1899
J.W. Piper & G.M. Tinker, Waltham, Massachusetts. Three cars built.

PIRANHA
USA 1967
AMT Corporation, Phoenix, Arizona.

PIRATE
USA 1905–1907
Breese & Lawrence, Brroklyn, N.Y.
See "B.L.M."; B.L.M. Motor Car Co., Brooklyn, N.Y. Bankrupt. October 1907.

PISA
USA 1990s
Pisa Corp., Phoenix, Arizona. Kit cars.

PISKORSKI
USA 1901
Dan J. Piskorski, St. Louis, Missouri. Steam runabout.

PISTEUR
CH 1982
Bernard Pisteur, Meyrin-Geneve. Sports car replica.

PITCAIRN
USA 1934
Autogiro Co. of America, Philadelphia, Pennsylvania. Flying automobile.

PITT
GB 1902–1903
Pitt Yorkshire Machine Co., Liversedge, Yorks. Prototype.

PITTEVIL
B 1900
S.A. de Fabrication de Velocipedes et Automobiles, Anvers. Voiturettes.
See "Phébé."

PITTLER
D
See "Hydromobil."

PITTSBURGH
USA 1897–1899
Pittsburgh Motor Vehicle Co., Pittsburgh, Pennsylvania. Organized 1896, two cars built by 1898.
See "Autocar" (1897–1911).

PITTSBURGH
USA 1905
Pittsburgh Automobile Co., Pittsburgh, Pennsylvania.

PITTSBURGH
USA 1905–1908
Pittsburgh Machine Tool Co., Allegheny, Pennsylvania. Steam cars.

PITTSBURGH
USA 1905–1911
Pittsburgh Motor Vehicle Co., Pittsburgh, Pennsylvania. Electric cars.

PITTSBURGH
USA 1908–1911
Ft. Pitt Motor Manufacturing Co. General Engineering Co., New Kensington, Pennsylvania. 1911 Pittsburgh Motor Car Co.

PITTSBURGH
USA 1912
Chester Engineering Co., Chester, Pennsylvania.

PITTSFIELD
USA 1907
Pittsfield Motor Carriage Co., Pittsfield, Massachusetts. Became Stilson Motor Car Co.

PIVOT
F 1904–1907
Automobiles Pivot, Puteaux/Seine. Touring and town cars.

PIXLEY
USA 1909
G.H. Pixley Co., Boston, Massachusetts.

PIZAZZ
USA 1968
Tomco Division, Milwaukee, Wisconsin. Dune buggy.

PL
D 1985
Peter Lorenz. Sports car prototype.

PLANCHE
USA 1908–1909
John A. Roebling & Sons Co. Roebling-Planche Co., Trenton, New Jersey.
See "Roebling-Planche," "Walter" and "Mercer" (1909–1925).

PLANET
D 1907
Planetwerke Max Blohm & Co., Berlin. Planetary gear.

PLANET
GB 1904–1905
Automobile Engineering Co. Ltd., London. Touer and tonneau.

PLANET
USA 1914
Planet Motor Works, Minneapolis, Minnesota. Cyclecar.

PLASS
USA 1900
Plass Motor Wagon Co., Pierre, South Dakota.

PLASS MOTOR SLEIGH
USA 1895
Reuben H. Plass, Brooklyn, N.Y.

PLASTIC
H 1987–1988
Plastic Design Studio, Budapest. Dune buggy.

PLASTI-CAR
USA 1954
Plasti-Car Inc., Doylestown, Pennsylvania. Two-seater fiberglass-bodied cars with "Renault" (F) 4CV engine.

PLATE
I 1947
Luigi (Gigi) & Enrico Plate, Milano.

PLAYBOY
USA 1946–1951
Playboy Motor Car Corp., Buffalo, N.Y. About 90 convertible minicars were built.

PLAYBOY
USA 1968–1973
Playboy Mfg. Co., San Mateo, California. Dune buggy.

PLEASANTON
USA 1903
Pleasanton Iron Works, Pleasanton, California.

P.L.M.
USA/B 1954–1955
Poelmans, Merksen, Anvers.
See "Keller" (USA).

PLUMMER
USA 1913
National Business Exchange, Washington, D.C. All-purpose car.

PLUTO
D 1924–1927
Automobilfabrik Zella-Mehlis GmbH, Zella-Mehlis (1924–1927). Pluto Automobilfabrik AG, Zella-St. Blasii (1927). "Amilcar" (F) under license.

PLUTON
F 1901
Sté. Industrielle d'Automobile Pluton, Levallois-Perret/Seine. Spider or tonneau body.

PLYMOUTH
CDN 1932–2000
Chrysler Corp. of Canada, Windsor, Ontario.

PLYMOUTH
USA 1910
Plymouth Motor Truck Co., Plymouth, Ohio. Experimental car. Several produced, afterwards trucks only.

PLYMOUTH
USA 1928–2000
Plymouth Motor Co., Chrysler Corp., Detroit, Michigan. Introduced July 28, 1928 at Madison Square Garden, New York, N.Y.
See "Chrysler," "De Soto," "Dodge" and "Imperial."

P.M.
B 1921–1926
Sté. Auto-Mécanique P.M., Liege. Touring cars.

PMC
GB 1912–1913
See "Premier." Three-wheeler.

P.M.C.
USA 1908
C.S. Peets Mfg. Co., New York, N.Y. Highwheelers.

PNEUMATIC
USA 1896–1899
Pneumatic Carriage Co. Inc. (1896). New York Auto Truck Co. (1899), New York, N.Y. All units built by A.H. Hoadley at American Wheelock Vehicle Co., Worcester, Massachusetts. Compressed air powered.

PNEUMOBILE
USA 1914–1915
Cowles-McDowell Pneumobile Co. Pneumobile Motor Car Co., Chicago, Illinois; Anderson, Indiana. Touring cars.

POBIEDA
SU 1946–1958
Závod Imieni Molotova, Gorki.
See "GAZ" and "ZIM."

POCCARDI
I 1960s
Carrozzeria Poccardi, Grugliasco. Station wagons and sports cars. Coachbuilders since 1945.

POCOCK
USA 1899
Francis A. Pocock, Philadelphia, Pennsylvania. Electric cars.

PODEUS
D 1910–1914
Paul Heinrich Podeus, Wismar i.M. Tourer.

PODVINECZ & HEISLER
H c. 1900
Podvinecz Daniel & Heisler Vilmos, Budapest. Light cars.

POHL
D 1932
Dipl.-Ing. Herbert Pohl, Dresden. Three-wheeler.

POINARD
F 1952
Three-wheeler.

POIRIER
F 1928–1959
Établissements G. Poirier, Fondettes/Indre-et-Loire. Three-wheelers for handicapped persons.

POKORA
CS 1937
Josef Pokora a spol., Kostelec nad Labem. Sports car prototype.

POKORNEY
USA 1904–1906
H. Pokorney. Richards Automobile & Gas Engine Co., Guthrie, Indiana.
See "Tricolet."

POLHEMUS & THOMAS
USA 1902
Polhemus & Thomas, New Brunswick, New Jersey.

POLLAND
USA c. 1905
P.E. Polland, Waltham, Massachusetts. 7 hp automobile.

POLONIA
PL 1924
M. Karpowski, Warszawa. 45hp 6-cylinder six-seater prototype.

POLSKI-FIAT
PL 1932–1939; 1968–present
Fabryka Samochodow Osobowych, Warszawa. "Fiat" (I) based cars.

POLYMOBIL
D 1904–1909
Polyphon Musikwerke AG, Wahren. "Oldsmobile" (USA) Curved Dash under license.
See "Dux."

POLYPHON
D
See "Dux."

POMEROY
USA 1902
Pomeroy Motor Vehicle Co., Brooklyn, N.Y. Runabouts.

POMEROY
USA 1920–1924
Pomeroy Aluminum Manufacturers Inc., Cleveland, Ohio (1920–1922). Aluminum Co. of America, Buffalo, N.Y. (1923–1924). 7-passenger sedan.

PONCIN
F 1990–c. 1994
Vehicules Poncin SA, Sedan. 4 × 4 and 6 × 6 vehicle.

POND
USA 1905
L.W. Pond Machine & Foundry Co., Worcester, Massachusetts.

PONDER
USA 1923
Ponder Motor Mfg. Co., Shreveport, Louisiana. 6-cylinder Continental engine. Succeeded "Bour-Davis."

PONTIAC
CDN 1933–present
General Motors of Canada Ltd., Oshawa, Ontario.

PONTIAC
USA 1906
Pontiac Motor Vehicle Co., Pontiac, Michigan.

PONTIAC
USA 1907–1909
Pontiac Buggy Co. Pontiac Spring & Wagon Co., Pontiac, Michigan; Rockford, Illinois. Highwheeler.

PONTIAC
USA 1910
Pontiac Motor Car Co., Pontiac, Illinois.

PONTIAC
USA 1915
Pontiac Chassis Co., Pontiac, Michigan. Chassis only. Became Olympian Motors Co.

PONTIAC
USA 1926–present
Oakland Motor Car Co. Pontiac Motor Car Co., Pontiac, Michigan. Pontiac Motor Division, General Motors Corp. succeeded "Oakland" and Oakland Motor Car Co. 1932. Passenger cars.

PONTICELLI
F 1984
4 × 4 vehicle prototype.

PONTUS
D 1995–1997
Pontus Racing, Remscheid. Tuning.

POP
D 1991–1997
Pop-Automobile GmbH, Mannheim. Convertibles and electric cars.

POPE
F 1933–1934
L.A. Pope, Paris. Front-wheel-drive coupe.

POPE
USA c. 1905
H.M. Pope, Springfield, Massachusetts. 4 hp automobile.

POPE-HARTFORD
USA 1904–1914
Pope Mfg. Co., Hartford, Connecticut. 4,733 cars were made.

POPE-ROBINSON
USA 1903–1904
Pope-Robinson Co., Hyde Park, Massachusetts. Succeeded J.T. Robinson Co. ("Robinson"). Purchased by "Buick."
See "Robinson."

POPE-TOLEDO
USA 1904–1909
Pope Motor Car Co., Toledo, Ohio. Succeeded "Toledo." Became Toledo Motor Car Co. Touring cars.

POPE TRIBUNE
USA 1904–1908
Pope Manufacturing Co., Hagerstown, Maryland. Touring cars.

POPE WAVERLEY
USA 1903–1908
Pope Motor Car Co., Indianapolis, Indiana. Electric cars.
See "Waverley" electric (1908–1916).

POPP
CH 1898
Lorenz Popp, Basel. Two- and four-seater on "Benz" (D) lines.

POPPY
USA 1917
Eisenhuth Motor Co., Los Angeles, California. Five-cylinder, self-starting, no transmission.

POPULAIRE
USA 1904
American Automobile & Power Co., Boston, Massachusetts. Also known as "American Populaire."

PORSCHE
A/D 1948–present
Porsche Konstruktions-GmbH, Gmund (Austria) (1948–1950). Dr. Ing. h.c. F. Porsche KG, Stuttgart-Zuffenhausen (1950–present). Sports cars.

PORSCHE
USA c. 1905
William Porsche, Holyoke, Massachusetts. 3 hp automobile.

PORTARO
P 1974–present
Sociedade Electro-Mecanica de Automoveis Ltda., Lisbon. "ARO" (RO) based 4 × 4 vehicles.

PORTER
USA 1900–1901
Porter Automobile Co., Allston, Massachusetts. Steam cars.

PORTER
USA 1919–1922
American & British Mfg. Co., Bridgeport, Connecticut. Finley Robertson Porter Co., Port Jefferson, N.Y. Touring cars. Succeeded "F.R.P."

PORTHOS
F 1906–1914
Sté. Generale des Automobiles Porthos, Billancourt/Seine. 10,857 cc sports-racing car; touring cars.

PORTLAND
GB 1904
International Motor Co. Ltd., London. 850 and 1400 cc engines.

PORTLAND
USA 1914
Lewis L. Thompson, Portland Cyclecar Co., Portland, Oregon. Cyclecars.
See "Pacific" cyclecar.

PORTSMOUTH
USA 1912
Portsmouth Automobile & Machine Co., Portsmouth, Ohio.

POSEJPAL & ZWETSCKE
CS 1924
Posejpal & Zwetschke, autosprávkárna, Kolín. Cyclecars.

POST
USA 1909
Charles Bushnell Post, New London, Ohio. Air-cooled gasoline automobile.

POSTAL
USA 1907–1908
Postal Automobile & Engineering Co., Bedford, Indiana. Runabouts. Became Buggy Car Co., Cincinnati, Ohio.

POSTE
USA 1899
Poste Bros. Buggy Co., Columbus, Ohio.

POSTERT
D 1986–1997
Postert-Tuning, Oberhausen; Essen. Tuning.

POTTER
USA c. 1905
Clinton E. Potter, Providence, Rhode Island.

POWELL
USA 1918
Bill Powell, Chicago, Illinois. 11 hp automobile.

POWELL
USA 1954–1956
Powell Sportswagon, Compton, California. 2400 Sports Wagons were built.

POWER
USA 1901
W.M. Power, Montclair, New Jersey. Gasoline car prototype.

POWER
USA c. 1905
Fred E. Power, Framingham, Massachusetts. 6 hp automobile.

POWERCAR
USA 1909–1911
Powercar Automobile Co., Cincinnati, Ohio. Touring cars.

POWER CAR
USA 1959
Power Car Division, Springfield, Massachusetts. Juvenile and adult fun car.

POWERDRIVE
GB 1956–1958
Powerdrive Ltd., London. Three-wheeler.

PRACTICAL
USA 1906–1909
Practical Auto Co., Genoa, Illinois. Practical Automobile Co., Aurora, Illinois.
See "Culver" (1906–1909).

PRADO
USA 1920–1922
Prado Motors Corp., New York, N.Y. About 10 expensive touring cars were made with Curtiss OX-5 engine.

PRAGA
A/CS; 1907–1947
Automobilní oddělení První českomoravské továrny na stroje (1907–1929). Auto-Praga, Českomoravská Kolben-Daněk (1929–1945). AZKG, n.p.; Praha (1945–1947). Passenger cars.
See "PAT-PAF."

PRALL
USA 1897
W. Edgar Prall, Washington, D.C. Rotary engine.

PR & D
CDN 1981–1993
Prototype Research & Development Ltd., Campbellford, Ontario. Replica.

PRATT
USA 1907
Pratt Chuck Works, Frankfort, N.Y. Six-wheeler.

PRATT
USA 1911–1915
Elkhart Carriage & Harness Mfg. Co., Elkhart, Indiana. Formerly "Pratt-Elkhart" 1909–1911. Became "Elcar," Elcar Motor Co. 1,084 cars were made ("Pratt" and "Pratt-Elkhart" together).

PRATT-ELKHART
USA 1909–1911
Elkhart Carriage & Harness Mfg. Co., Elkhart, Indiana. Became "Pratt" 1911–1915.

PRAUL
USA 1895
John E. Praul Motocycle Co., Philadelphia, Pennsylvania. Rotary gasoline engine.

PRAY
USA c. 1905
Joseph F. Pray, Brookline, Massachusetts. 20 hp automobile.

PRECISION
USA 1990s
Precision Design, Escondido, California. Kit cars.

PREFERRED
USA 1920
Preferred Motor Car Co., Louisville, Kentucky. Prototype.

PREFEX
USA 1912–1914
Prefex Co., Los Angeles, California. Believed to be "Perfex" misspelled.

PREINER
H 1875
Preiner Ferenc. Steam carriage.

PREMIER
A/CS; 1913
Fahrrad- und Motorradfabrik, Eger (Cheb). Light cars.

PREMIER
D 1913–1914
Justus Christian Braun Premier-Werke AG, Nürnberg. Sports cars.

PREMIER
GB 1906–1907; 1912–1913
Premier Motor Co. Ltd., Birmingham. Three-wheelers and cyclecars.

PREMIER
IND 1955–present
The Premier Automobile Ltd., Bombay. "Fiat" (I) under license.
See "PAL."

PREMIER
USA 1902–1926
Premier Motor Mfg. Co., Indianapolis, Indiana. 1915 reorganized as Premier Motor Car Co. 1916 Premier Motor Corp. 1921 Premier Motor Car Corp. 1923 reorganized as Premier Motors Inc. Purchased "Monroe" 1923. Merged with "Stratton."
See "Stratton-Premier." 11,400 cars were made.

PREMOCAR
USA 1920–1923
Preston Motors Corp., Birmingham, Alabama. One model used 4-cylinder Rochester Duesenberg engine. 6-cylinder model called "Magic Six." Blue Sky Law indictment reported October 1923. 563 cars were made.

PRESCOTT
USA 1901–1905
Prescott Automobile Mfg. Co., Passaic, New Jersey. Steam runabouts.

PRESCOTT
USA c. 1905
Crawford E. Prescott, Hudson, Massachusetts. 14 hp automobile.

PRESTIGE
USA 1982
Prestige Classics, Wayzata, Minn. Replicas.

PRESTO
D 1901–1927
Presto-Werke Günther & Co. (1901–1907). Presto-Werke AG, Chemnitz (1907–1927). Touring cars.

PRESTON
USA 1917–1920
Preston Motors Corp., Birmingham, Alabama. Became "Premocar."

PRESTON
USA 1936
Ben Preston, Wichita, Kansas. Roadster.

PRIAMUS
D 1901–1923
Kölner Motorwagenfabrik GmbH. vorm. Heinrich Brunthaler (1901–1903). Motorfahrzeugfabrik Köln, Uren, Kotthaus & Co. (1904–1909). Priamus Automobil-Werk GmbH (1909–1921). Priamus-Werke AG für Fahrzeugbau, Köln (1921–1923). Voiturette; medium-sized cars.

PRIBIL
USA 1936–1937
Pribil Safety Aircraft Co., Saginaw, Michigan. Streamlined prototype.

PRICE
USA 1907–1908
W.C. Price, Chicago, Illinois. Runabout shown at 1907 Chicago Auto Show.

PRIDEMORE
USA 1914
Pridemore Machine Works, Northfield, Minnesota. Cyclecar.

PRIGG
USA 1914

H. Paul Prigg Co., Andreson, Indiana. Cyclecars.
See "Real."

PRIMA
F 1906–1909
Sté. des Automobiles Prima, Levallois-Perret/Seine. Voiturette.

PRIMO
USA 1910–1915
Primo Motor Co., Atlanta, Georgia. Touring cars. Reported bankrupt July 1915.

PRIMUS
D 1899–1903
Pfälzische Nähmaschinen- und Fahrräderfabrik vorm. Gebr. Kayser, Kaiserslautern. Voiturette.

PRIMUS
I 1905
Alessandria.

PRINCE
I 1921–1923
Automobili Costruzioni di V. Carena e Mazza, Torino. Cyclecar.

PRINCE
J 1952–1969
Tama Motors Co. (1952). Prince Motors Co., Tachikawa (1952–1954). Fuji Precision Machinery Co. Ltd. (1954–1961). Prince Motors Ltd. (1961–1966). Prince Motors Ltd. (Division of Nissan Motors Co.), Tokyo (1966–1969). Passenger cars.

PRINCEPS
GB 1902–1903
Princeps Autocar Co., Northampton. Light car.

PRINCEPS
GB 1920
Light car.

PRINCESS
GB 1922–1923
Streatham Engineering Co. Ltd., London. Light car.

PRINCESS
GB
See "Vanden Plas."

PRINCESS
USA 1904–1905
Royal Automobile Co., Chicago, Illinois.
See "Royal Princess."

PRINCESS
USA 1914
Princess Cyclecar Co., Detroit, Michigan. Cyclecar. Former "Little Princess." Notice of dissolution reported September 1914.

PRINCESS
USA 1914–1918
Princess Motor Car Co., Detroit, Michigan. Succeeded "Princess" cyclecar. Touring cars.

PRINCESS RUNABOUT
USA 1904
Neustadt-Perry Co., St. Louis, Missouri.

PRINCETON
USA 1923–1924
Durant Motors Corp., Muncie, Indiana. Car resembled "Flint" (1924–1927). Sport touring cars.

PRINETTI & STUCCHI
I 1898–1902
Milano. Voiturettes designed by Ettore Bugatti.
See "Stucchi."

PRIOR
USA c. 1905
George A. Prior, Hartford, Connecticut.

PRITCHARD
AUS 1977
Steam car prototype designed by Ted Pritchard.

PRITCHETT & GOLD
GB 1903–1904
Pritchett & Gold Ltd., Feltham, Middlesex. Electric car.

PROBE
GB 1969–1971
Adams Probe Motor Co., Bradford-on-Avon, Wilts. (1969–1971). Caledonian Probe Motor Co., Irvine, Ayrshire (1971). Very low coupe.

PROCTOR
USA 1907
Albert Proctor, Gloucester, Massachusetts. Runabouts.

PRODAL
USA 1909–1911
Motor Car Repair Co., New York, N.Y.

PROD'HOMME
F 1907–1908
Établissements Prod'homme, Ivry-Port/Seine. 2- and 4-cylinder cars.

PROGRESS
GB 1898–1903
Progress Cycle Co. Ltd., Coventry, Warwickshire. DeDion or MMC engine.

PROGRESS
GB 1934
Haynes Economy Motors Ltd., Manchester. Three-wheeler.

PROGRESS
PRC 1958–c. 1971
Hsinchien Machine Works, Chung-King. Passenger cars.
See "Jin-Bu."

PROJECTA
GB 1914
Percival White Engineering Works, London. Cyclecar.

PROJEKTZWO
D 1992–present
Projekt Zwo automobildesign GmbH, Utting. Tuning.

PROMBRON
SU 1922–1923
Pervoi Bronne-Tanko-Avtoremontnii Zavod, Fila. 5 cars were assembled from the "Russo-Baltique" parts.
See "BTAZ."

P.R.O.S.C.A.
USA 1990s
P.R.O.S.C.A., Santa Clarita, California. Kit cars.

PROSPECT
USA 1902; 1907–1908
Wottring Bros., Prospect, Ohio. Gas runabouts.

PROSPERITY
USA 1933
Allied Cab Mfg. Co., Elkhart, Indiana. Taxicabs.

PROSPER-LAMBERT
F 1901–1906
Sté. Prosper-Lambert, Nanterre/Seine. Touring cars.

PROTEK
D 1949–1951
Protek-Gesellschaft für Industrieentwicklungen, Stuttgart. Light cars designed by Hanns Trippel.
See "Trippel."

PROTEUS
GB 1983–present

Proteus Cars Ltd., Bolton, Lancs. Replica.

PROTEUS
ZA 1956
Sports cars built in Johannesburg.

PROTON
MAL 1983–present
Perusahaan Otomobil Nasional Berhad, Shah Alam, Selangor. "Mitsubishi" (J) license.

PROTOS
D 1900–1926
Motorenfabrik Protos Dr. Alfred Sternberg (1900–1904). Motorenfabrik Protos GmbH (1904–1908). Siemens-Schuckert-Werke GmbH, Automobilwerk Nonnendamm, Berlin (1908–1926). Touring cars.

PROUTY
USA 1897
Enoch Prouty, Chicago, Illinois. Gasoline three-wheeler.

PROUTY
USA c. 1905
L.W. Prouty, South Framingham, Massachusetts. 5 hp automobile.

PRO-V
USA 1990s
Pro-V Co., Lemon Grove, California. Kit cars.

PROVINCIAL
GB 1904–1905
Provincial electric Construction Co. Ltd., Liverpool. Light car.

PRUNEL
F 1900–1907
Société des Usines Prunel, Puteaux/Seine. Voiturettes.

PRVENAC
YU 1959
M. Nestorovic, Beograd. Rhomboid wheel placement.

P-T
USA 1901–1902
P-T Motor Co., New York, N.Y. Gasoline runabouts.

P.T.V.
E 1956–1962
Sociedad de Automoviles Utilitarios S.A., Manresa. About 5000 minicars with 250cc Ausa engine were built.

PUBLIX
USA/CDN 1947–1948
Publix Motor Car Co., Buffalo, N.Y.; Fort Erie, Ontario. Three-wheelers.

PUCH
A 1906–1925
Johann Puch, Erste Steiermarkische Fahrrad-Fabriks-AG (1906–1914). Puchwerke AG, Graz (1914–1925). Touring cars.

PUCKETT
USA 1990s
Puckett Auto Works, Santee, California. Kit cars.

PUCKRIDGE-KINMONT
AUS 1904
Port Lincoln, S.A.

PUG
USA 1968
Brice Mfg. Co., Minneapolis, Minnesota. Jeep-type off road vehicle.

PUGH
USA 1901
William J. Pugh, Davenport, Iowa. Three cars were built.

PULCINO
I
Antonio Artesi, Palermo.
See "Artesi."

PULGA
E 1952
Juan Llabres & Vicente Mas, Onteniente. Three-wheeler prototype.

PULI
H/D 1986–c. 1997
Hódgép — Mezögazdasági Gépgyártó Kft., Hódmezövásárhely. Eco Drive AG, Stäfa. Gasoline and electric minicars mainly for export to France.

PULLAR
USA c. 1905
James G. Pullar, Hartford, Connecticut.

PULLCAR
GB 1906–1908
Pullcar Works, Preston, Lancashire. A very early example of front-wheel-drive.

PULLMAN
USA 1903
Broomell, Schmidt & Steacy Co., York, Pennsylvania. Six-wheeler.

PULLMAN
USA 1907–1908
Pullman Auto Carriage Co. Pullman Motor Car Co., Chicago, Illinois. Reorganized as Pullman Motor Vehicle Co. (in addition to the York, Pennsylvania "Pullman"). Built by Model Automobile Co., Peru, Indiana. Known also as "Pullman Flyer."

PULLMAN
USA 1905–1917
York Motor Car Co., York, Pennsylvania. Succeeded "York," York Automobile Co. Became Pullman Motor Car Co. 1910; 23,384 cars were made.

PULSAR
GB 1974–c. 1980
Mirage Developments Ltd., Biggin Hill, Kent. Sports car.

PULSE
USA 1986
Three-wheelers.

PUMA
BR 1964–1994
Sociedade de Automoveis Luminari Ltda. (1964–1966). Puma Veiculos e Motores Ltda, São Paulo (1966–1983). Alfa Metais Veiculos Ltda., Curitiba (1983–1994). Sports car.

PUMA
I c. 1982–1996
Stabilimento Puma, Guidonia. Puma di Adriano Gatto, Roma. Dune buggy and sports car.

PUMA
ZA 1987–1993
Puma Marketing Pty. Ltd., Pretoria. Sports cars.

PUNGS-FINCH
USA 1904–1910
Pungs-Finch Auto and Gas Engine Co., Detroit, Michigan. Acquired Sintz Gas Engine Co. Touring cars and roadsters.

PUP
USA 1948–1949
Pup Motor Car Co., Spencer, Wisconsin. Two-seat roadsters.

PURICELLI
I 1951
One sports car registered.

PURITAN
USA 1902–1905

Locke Regulator Co., Salem, Massachusetts. Steam cars. Later Puritan Motor Car Co.

PURITAN
USA 1913–1914
Puritan Motor Co., Chicago, Illinois. Cyclecars.

PURITAN
USA 1917
Puritan Motors Co., Framingham, Massachusetts.

PURMAX
USA 1915
Union Car Co., Los Angeles, California. Frequent typographical error.
See "Permax."

PURVIS
AUS 1974
Sports cars.

PUTNAM
USA 1901
R.S. Putnam, Mendon, Michigan.

PUZYREV
SU 1899; 1909–1914
B.P. Puzyrev, Sankt Peterburg. Very few cars were made.

P. VALLEE
F 1952–1957
Société Colas, Blois/Loir-et-Cher. 125 cc little two-seater.

PW
NL 1947
Prototype.

PYOTT
USA 1876
L.T. Pyott, Philadelphia, Pennsylvania. Steam carriage.

PYRAMID
GB 1914
Payne's Engineering Co., London. Cyclecar.

PYRO-PNEUMATIC
USA 1895
P.E. McDonnel & W.A. Brennan, Chicago, Illinois. Auto-buggy.

QC
GB 1901
Horner & Sons, Aldgate. Light car.

QSC
GB
See "Quantum."

QUADRANT
GB 1906–1907
Quadrant Cycle Co. Ltd., Birmingham. 14/16 and 20/22 hp cars.

QUAGLIOTTI
I 1904
Auto Garage Carlo Quagliotti, Torino. DeDion and Aster engines.

QUAKERTOWN
USA 1902–1904
Quakertown Automobile Mfg. Co., Quakertown, Pennsylvania.

QUANTUM
GB 1988–present
Quantum Sports Cars, Lye West, West Midlands; Stourbridge, West Midlands. Sports cars.

QUANTUM
USA 1962–1963
Automotive Development Corp., Seymore, Connecticut. Quantum Corp., Rockland, Maryland. Rebodied "Saab" (S).

QUASAR-UNIPOWER
GB 1968
Universal Power Drives Ltd., Perivale, Middlesex. City car prototype.

QUEEN
CDN 1901–1903
Queen City Cycle & Motor Works, Toronto, Ontario. Runabout.

QUEEN
USA 1904–1906
C.H. Blomstrom Motor Co., Detroit, Michigan. Runabouts. About 1,500 cars were made. Reported merged with DeLuxe Motor Car Co., October 1906.

QUENTIN
F 1908–1912
Quentin et Cie., Levallois-Perret/Seine. Light cars.

QUESTROM
USA c. 1905
A.I. Questrom, Swampscott, Massachusetts. 2.5 hp automobile.

QUEVRIN
F 1974
Electric city car prototype.

QUICK
USA 1899–1900
H.M. Quick Mfg. Co. Paterson, New Jersey (1899–1900). Quick Mfg. Co., Newark, New Jersey (1900). Runabouts. Absorbed by Remington Automobile and Motor Co., Lion, N.Y.

QUINBY
USA 1899–1900
J.M. Quinby & Co., Newark, New Jersey. Electric carriages for special order and export. Built bodies for "Simplex," "S.G.V." and others.

QUINCY
USA 1906
Quincy Automobile Co., Quincy, Illinois.

QUINCY-LYNN
USA 1975–1988
Quincy-Lynn Enterprises, Inc., Phoenix, Arizona. Three-wheelers.

QUINLAN
USA 1904
M.W. Quinlan, Jr., Brookline, Massachusetts.

QUINSLER
USA 1904
Quinsler & Co., Boston, Massachusetts. Runabouts.

QUO VADIS
F 1900–1902

Laurent et Touzet, Lyon. Front-wheel-driven light cars.

QUO VADIS
F 1921–1923

Automobiles Quo Vadis, Courbevoie/Seine. Cyclecars.

RÁBA
H 1912–1925; 1941
Magyar Waggon és Gépgyár Részvénytársaság, Györ. "Praga" (CS) cars under license. "Mars" car of their own design in 1941.

RABAG-BUGATTI
D 1922–1926
Rheinische Automobilbau AG, Düsseldorf; Mannheim. Sports cars.

RABER & LANG
USA 1909
Raber & Lang Co., Soith Bend, Indiana. At least two cars were made.

RABOEUF
F 1914
M. Raboeuf, Amiens. Light car.

R.A.C.
USA 1910–1911
Diamond Automobile Co., South Bend, Indiana. Succeeded "Diamond" 1910.

RACABOY-KIRCHNER
F 1972
Racaboy & Kirchner. Gasoline and electric car.

RACCA
I 1900
Officine di Pastore & Racca (Marcelo Racca), Torino.

RACINE
USA 1895
Racine Motor Vehicle Co., Racine, Wisconsin.

RACINE
USA 1909–1911
Racine Boat Mfg. Co., Detroit, Michigan.

RACINE-SATTLEY
USA 1910–1911
Racine-Sattley Co., Racine, Wisconsin.

RACINE WAGON
USA 1902
Racine Wagon & Carriage Co., Racine, Wisconsin.

RACING DYNAMICS
D 1993–1994
Racing Dynamics, Remscheid. Tuning.

RADBOURNE
GB c. 1969
Radbourne Racing Ltd., London. Sports cars with "Fiat" (I) engine.

RADFORD
USA 1895
W.J. Radford, Oshkosh, Wisconsin.

RADFORD
USA 1903
A.L. Radford, Boston, Massachusetts. Two cars were made.

RADFORD LIGHT CAR
USA 1914
W.H. Radford, Detroit, Michigan.
  See "Pilgrim."

RADIA
F
  See "L'Automotrice."

RAE
USA 1898; 1902
Rae Motor Cycle Co., Chicago, Illinois. Electric cars.

RAE
USA 1909
Rae Electric Vehicle Co., Boston, Massachusetts; Springfield, Vermont. Electric car.

RAF
A/CS; 1907–1913
Reichenberger Automobil-Fabrik, Reichenberg (Liberec). Passenger cars with sleeve-valve Knight engines. In 1913 merged with "Laurin & Klement."

RAF
CZ 1995–present
RAF a.s., Plzeň. Sports replicars.

RAF
D 1952–1954
Rheinische Automobil-Fabrik, Henhofer & Co., Ludwigshafen.
  See "Champion."

RAFALE
F c. 1956
Sports car prototype.

RAFFARD
F 1881
3- and 4-wheeled electric cars.

RAGGE
BR 1991–1994
Ragge Industrial Ltda., Duque de Caxias. Plastic bodied small cars.

RAGLAN
GB 1899
Raglan Cycle Co., Coventry, Warwickshire. Prototype.

RAGO
U 1967
Waldemar & Carlos Rago, Montevideo. 325 cc 14 hp sports coupe. About 12 were built.

RAILSBACH
USA 1914
R.M. Railsbach, Saginaw, Michigan. Cyclecar.

RAILTON
GB 1933–1949
Railton Cars, Cobham, Surrey (1933–1940). Hudson Motors Ltd., London (1940–1949). Luxurious and sports cars.

RAILTON
GB 1989–1993
Railton Motor Co. Ltd., Alcester, Warwickshire. Sports cars.

RAIMONDI
I 1898
Fabbrica Biciclette e Automobili Ippolito Raimondi, Parma. One belt-driven light car was built.

RAINIER
USA 1905–1911
Rainier Motor Car Co., Flushing, N.Y. Chassis made by "Garford" to 1907. Reorganized 1907; moved to Saginaw, Michigan 1908; bought by General Motors 1909. Combined with "Welch-Detroit" into "Marquette." Touring cars.

R.A.L.
B 1908–1914
Garages Raskin & Aigret, Liege. Passenger cars.

RALEIGH
GB 1905; 1916; 1933–1936
Raleigh Cycle Co. Ltd., Nottingham. Three-wheelers.

RALEIGH
USA 1921–1922
Raleigh Motors Inc., Bridgeton, New Jersey (1921); Reading, Pennsylvania (1921–1922). Touring cars.

RALF STETYZ
PL 1926–1928
Tow. Akc. Konstrukcji Mostowych "Rudski," Warszawa. A small series of cars powered by Continental (USA) engines.

RALLY
F 1921–1933
Automobiles Rally, Colombes/Seine. Sporting voiturettes.

RAMAPAUGH
USA 1901–1902
Charles A. Ball, Paterson, New Jersey. Three steam cars built for $10,000 each.
See "Ball."

RAMBLER
USA 1900–1903
Rockaway Bicycle Co., Rockaway, N.Y.
See "Rockaway."

RAMBLER
USA 1902–1913
Thomas B. Jeffery Co., Kenosha, Wisconsin. Became "Jeffery"; 33,512 cars built.

RAMBLER
USA 1950–1969
Nash Motors Co. (1950–1954), Kenosha, Wisconsin. American Motors Corp. (1954–1969), Detroit, Michigan. Passenger cars.
See "Nash" and "Hudson." Discontinued 1969.

RAMBLER 1902 REPLICA
USA 1959–1960
American Air Products Corp., Ft. Lauderdale, Florida. Gaslight Motors Corp., Lathrup Village, Michigan.

RAMSES
ET 1959–1973
Egyptian Light Transport Manufacturing Co., Cairo. "Frisky" (GB) under license; about 1,200 were built. Small cars with "NSU" (D) motors from 1960. 2,376 cars built 1963–1969.

RAMUS
F 1900
Ateliers de Constructions Mécaniques Ramus Freres, Chambery/Savoie. Voiturette.

RANDALL
USA 1902–1903
G.N. Randall, Meadville, Pennsylvania. Steam car.

RANDALL
USA 1903–1905
J.V. & C. Randall & Co., Newton, Pennsylvania. Three-wheeler.

RANDALL
USA 1905
Charles J. Randall, San Jose, California. Gasoline runabout.

RANDALL
USA 1910
Randall Motor Car Co., Ft. Wayne, Indiana.

R & D
B 1921
Richard & D'Haegalaer, Liege. Cyclecars.

R & D
USA 1990s
R & D Design Concepts, Omaha, Nebraska. Kit cars.

RAND & HARVEY
USA 1899–1900
Rand & Harvey, Lewiston, Maine. Steam runabouts.

RANDS
USA 1906–1907
Rands Mfg. Co., Detroit, Michigan. Touring cars.

R & V KNIGHT
USA 1920–1924
Root & Vandervoort Engineering Co., East Moline, Illinois. Succeeded Moline Automobile Co.
See "Moline" and "Moline-Knight"; 3,799 cars were made.

RANGER
B 1970–1972
General Motors Continental SA, Anvers. "Opel" (D) and "Vauxvall" (GB/ZA) based cars.

RANGER
CH 1970–1972
General Motors Suisse S.A., Biel. The same as "Ranger" (B).

RANGER
GB 1913–1914
Ranger Cyclecar Co. Ltd., Coventry, Warwickshire. Cyclecar.

RANGER
GB c. 1975
Three-wheeler and kit car.

RANGER
USA 1907–1910
Ranger Motor Works, Chicago, Illinois. Highwheelers and runabouts. Bankruptcy reported November 1910.

RANGER
USA 1920–1922
Southern Motors Mfrs. Association, Houston, Texas. Touring cars. First car distributed September 1920.

RANGER
ZA 1968–1970
General Motors South Africa Pty. Ltd., Port Elizabeth. The same as "Ranger" (B) and (CH).

RANLET
USA 1900
Ranlet Automobile Co., St. Johnsbury, Vermont. 4-cylinder car.

RAOUVAL
F 1899–1902
Sté. Mécanique Industrielle d'Arzin, Arzin/Nord. Four-seater tonneau.

RAPID
CH 1899–1900

Zürcher Patent-Motorwagen-Fabrik Rapid, Zürich. Three-wheelers.

RAPID
CH 1946
Rapid Motormäher AG, Dietikon, Zürich. 34 light cars were built.

RAPID
I 1904–1921
Societa Torinese Automobili Rapid (S.T.A.R.), Torino. Touring cars.

RAPID
USA 1903
Rapid Motor Car Co., Grand Rapids, Michigan. Touring cars.

RAPIER
GB 1933–1940
Lagonda Ltd., Staines, Middlesex (1933–1935). Rapier Cars Ltd., London (1935–1940). Sports cars.

RAPPORT
GB 1977–1980
Rapport International, London. Sports car.

RASKIN
B
See "R.A.L."

RATIER
F 1926–1928
Montrouge/Seine. Voiturettes and sports cars.

RATIONAL
GB 1901–1906
Heatly-Gresham Engineering Co. Ltd., Royston, Herts. 17 10 hp cars were made.

RATIONAL
GB 1910–1911
K.J. McMullen, Brimpton, Berks. Light cars.

RATTLER
USA 1968–1973
B & N Rattler Club, Springfield, Ohio. Dune buggy.

RAUCH & LANG
USA 1905–1932
Rauch & Lang Carriage Co., Cleveland, Ohio. Electric cars. Merged with "Baker" into Baker, Rauch and Lang Co. 1915. Built "Owen Magnetic" 1916–1919. 1920 reorganized as Rauch & Lang Inc., at Chicopee Falls, Massachusetts. Absorbed. Rubay Co. 1924. 1930 used "Willys-Knight" chassis. Built "Raulang" electric taxicabs.

RAUCH & LANG
USA 1929–1930
Rauch & Lang Inc., Chicopee Falls, Massachusetts. G.E. Co., Schenectady, N.Y. Gas-electric car.

RAULANG
USA
See "Rauch & Lang."

RAVASI
I 1947
Giulio Ravasi, Milano. Front-wheel drive small car prototype with 3-cylinder 4-cycle. 750 cc engine.

RAVEL
F 1868
Joseph Ravel, Neuilly/Seine. Liquid-fuelled light steam car.

RAVEL
F 1900–1902
SA des Automobiles Louis Ravel, Neuilly/Seine. 5 hp V-twin engine light car.

RAVEL
F c. 1902
Joseph & Edouard Ravel, Neuilly/Seine. 15 hp 2-cylinder 2-stroke engine.

RAVEL
F 1923–1928
SA des Automobiles Ravel, Besancon/Doubs. Touring cars.

RAWLSON
GB 1971–c. 1974
Rawlson Ltd., Dover, Kent. Sports car.

RAWNSLEY
USA 1906
Hollon Rawnsley, Sanford, Maine. Runabout.

RAY
USA 1901
W.A. Ray, Auburn, Maine. Steam stanhope.

RAYFIELD
USA 1911–1912
Rayfield Motor Car Co., Springfield, Illinois; Chrisman, Illinois. No connection with Rayfield Motor Co. Former "Springfield." Touring cars.

RAYFIELD
USA 1912–1915
Rayfield Motor Co., Springfield & Chrisman, Illinois. Cyclecars. Sued Great Western Auto Co. of Peru, Indiana for failure to build cars.

RAYMOND
F 1923–1925
An assembled car with Ford T engine.

RAYMOND
USA 1905; 1908
Hillsdale Motor Co., Hillsdale, Michigan.

RAYMOND
USA 1912–1913
Raymond Engineering Corp., Hudson, Massachusetts; Lincoln Park, Massachusetts. Light roadster.

RAYMOND MAYS
GB 1938–1939
Shelsley Motors Ltd., Bourne, Lincs. 2.6-litre Standard V-8 engined sports cars.

RAYTON FISSORE
I 1978–c. 1994
Rayton Fissore SpA, Cherasco. Sports and 4 × 4 car. "Fissore" coachbuilders since 1930.

R.C.H.
USA 1911–1914
Hupp Corp., Detroit, Michigan. Reorganized 1912 as R.C.H. Corp. Touring cars and roadsters.

REA
USA 1901–1902
Rea Machine Co., Rushville, Indiana.

R.E.A.C.
F 1953–1954
750cc sports cars.

READ
USA 1791
Nathan Read, Danvers, Massachusetts. Steam car.

READ
USA 1913–1914
Read Motor Car Co., Detroit, Michigan. Touring cars.

READING
GB 1902
Reading Steam Carriage Co., London. Steam car.

READING
USA 1910–1913

Middleby Automobile Co., Reading, Pennsylvania. Roadsters.
See "Middleby" (1908–1913).

READING
USA 1917
Reading Chassis & Motor Co., Reading, Pennsylvania.

READING-DURYEA
USA 1904–1905
Waterloo Motor Works, Waterloo, Iowa.

READING STEAMER
USA 1901–1902
Steam Vehicle Co. of America, Reading, Pennsylvania; New York, N.Y. 1902 absorbed by Meteor Engineering Co.
See "Meteor" (1902–1903)

REAL
USA 1914
H. Paul Prigg Co. Real Cyclecar Co., Anderson, Indiana. Five cyclecars built. Became "Real Light Car."

REAL LIGHT CAR
USA 1914–1915
Real Light Motor Car Co., Converse, Indiana. Bankrupt December 1915.

REBER
USA 1901–1903
Reber Mfg. Co., Reading, Pennsylvania. Became Acme Motor Car Co.
See "Acme" and "S.G.V."

REBOUR
F 1905–1908
Automobiles Rebour, Puteaux/Seine. Touring cars. In Spain sold as "Catalonia."

REBUS
I 1909
Enrico Restelli & Felice Buzio, Milano.

RECH
USA 1900
Jacob Rech & Sons, Philadelphia, Pennsylvania. Steam runabout.

RECH-MARBAKER
USA 1906
Rech-Marbaker Co., Philadelphia, Pennsylvania. Electric car.

RECORDMOBIL
A 1920
Recordmobil-Werke, Wien. Cyclecars.

RED ARROW
USA 1914

Red Arrow Automobile Co., Orange, Massachusetts. Former "Grout."

RED BUD
USA 1916
Lafayette, Indiana. Cyclecars.

RED BUG
USA 1928
Automotive Standards Inc., Newark, New Jersey. Electric slat cars. Also built "Red Bug Jr."

RED DIAMOND
USA 1920–1921
Red Diamond Motors, Atlanta and Athens, Georgia.

RED JACKET
USA 1904–1905
O.K. Machine Works, Buffalo, N.Y.

RED PATH
CDN 1903
Berlin (later Kitchener), Ontario. Toronto, Ontario.

RED ROVER
USA 1901
Automobile Co. of America, New York, N.Y. 3-cylinder 10 hp engine.

RED SHIELD
USA 1911
Red Shield Hustler Power Co., Detroit, Michigan.

RED WING
USA 1909
Red Wing Boat Mfg. Co., Red Wing, Minnesota.

REED
USA 1909
Believed to be company name of W.S. Reed Co., Massillon, Ohio.
See "Massillon."

REED & BROWN
USA 1860; 1862
John A. Reed & Joseph Renshaw Brown, New York, N.Y. Steam carriages.

REES
USA 1921
Rees Motor Corp., Attica, Ohio. Touring cars.

REESE
USA 1887–1904
S. Reese Machine & Tool Works, Plymouth, Pennsylvania. Three-wheelers.

REESE MIDGET
USA 1921
Sheldon F. Reese Co., Huron, South Dakota. Runabouts.

REEVES
USA 1896–1898; 1905–1912
Reeves Pulley Co., Columbia, Indiana. First cars multi-passenger "Motocycles." Experimental only after.
See "Octo-Auto" and "Sexto-Auto."

REFORM
A 1906–1907
Thein & Goldberger, Wien. 8 hp engine.

REGAL
CDN 1910
Walkerville, Ontario. 30 hp touring car or runabout.

REGAL
CDN 1914–1917
Canadian Royal Motor Car Co., Kitchener, Ontario. Light-weight touring cars.

REGAL
F 1903
O.C. Selbach, Paris. Light two-seater.

REGAL
USA 1908–1918
Regal Motor Car Co., Detroit, Michigan. 52,544 cars built and sold. Plant reported auctioned off May 1918.

REGAL
USA 1990s
Regal Roadsters, Ltd., Madison, Wisconsin. Kit cars.

REGAL T-BIRD
USA c. 1980–1986
Regal T-Bird Limited, Madison, Wisconsin. Replicars.

REGAS
USA 1903–1905
Regas Automobile Co., Rochester, N.Y. Runabouts.

REGENT
D 1903–1904
Maschinenfabrik W. Stutznäcker, Dortmund.

REGESTER
USA 1900
T.L. Regester, Rock Island, Illinois.

REGINA
F 1903–1908

Société l'Électrique, Paris. Petrol and electric cars.

REGINA
F 1922–1923
Automobiles Regina, Paris. Three-wheelers.

REGINETTE
F 1922
Paris. Cyclecar.

REGIS
GB 1985–1993
Regis Automotive, Bognor Regis, West Sussex. Sports car.

REGNER
F 1905–1906
Daniel Regner, Paris. Voiturette.

REID
USA 1895
Charles G. Reid, Chicago, Illinois. Two electric three-wheelers.

REID
USA 1904–1905
See "Wolverine."

REILLY
USA 1902–1903
James Reilly Repair & Supply Co., New York, N.Y. Steam surrey.

REINERTSON
USA 1902
Rex Reinertson, Milwaukee, Wisconsin. Runabouts.
See "Rex Buckboard."

REINHARD
F 1911–1914
Sté. de Construction des Moteurs Reinhard, Lyon. 2- and 3-litre sleeve-valve engines.

REISACHER-JULIEN
F 1900
Ets Reisacher-Julien, Marseilles. Reisacher engines and Julien bodies.

REISSIG
D 1912–1914
Automobilwerk "Siegfried" Arno Köhl-Krüger, Plauen-Reissig. 9/26 hp cars.
See "MUK-Wagen."

REJO
GB 1958–1965
Rejo Cars, London. Sports car.

REKORD
D 1905–1908
Internationale Automobilzentrale Dr. Mengers & Bellmann, Berlin. 6 to 80 hp engines.

RELAY
USA 1903–1904
Relay Motor Car Co., Reading, Pennsylvania. Three-cylinder, water-cooled, overhead valve Wyoma engine.

RELIABLE
USA 1906
Dayton-Mashey Co., Chicago, Illinois. Became "Reliable-Dayton."

RELIABLE-DAYTON
USA 1906–1909
Reliable-Dayton Motor Car Co., Chicago, Illinois. Highwheelers. Became F.A.L. Motor Co.
See "F.A.L."

RELIANCE
USA 1904–1906
Reliance Auto Mfg. Co. Reliance Motor Car Co., Detroit, Michigan. 1906 reorganized as Reliance Truck Co. Passenger car business carried on by Crescent Motor Car Co.
See "Crescent." Also built "Reliance-Detroit."

RELIANT
GB 1952–present
Reliant Engineering Co. (Tamworth) Ltd.; Reliant Motor Co. Ltd., Tamworth, Staffs. Reliant Cars Ltd., Tipton, West Midlands; Burntwood. Sports cars and three-wheelers.

RELOT
USA 1921–1922
George Hannum.

RELYANTE
F/GB 1903
Relyante Motor Works, London. French machines of different makes imported to GB.

REMAG
D 1924
Richter & Maak GmbH, Chemnitz. Sports cars.

REMAL-VINCENT
USA 1923
Remal-Vincent Steam Car Co., Oakland, California. Steam cars.

REMI-DANVIGNES
F 1935–1939
Remi-Danvignes et Cie., Paris. Sports cars.

REMINGTON
USA 1895
Remington motor Vehicle Co., Utica, N.Y. Experimental car.

REMINGTON
USA 1900–1904
Quick Mfg. Co., Newark, New Jersey. Remington Automobile & Motor C., Ilion, N.Y. (1900–1901); Utica, N.Y. (1901–1904).

REMINGTON
USA 1910–1913
Remington-Standard Motor Co., Charleston, West Virginia.

REMINGTON
USA 1914–1915
Remington Arms Co. Remington Motor Co., Rahway, New Jersey. Cyclecars.

REMINGTON
USA 1915–1916
Remington Motor Car Co., Kingston, N.Y. Touring cars. Planned by Philo E. Remington.

REMINGTON DART
USA 1909–1910
Remington Automobile Co., Philadelphia, Pennsylvania. Runabouts.

REMINGTON STANDARD
USA 1900–1901
Remington Automobile & Motor Co., Ilion, N.Y.

RENAISSANCE
CDN 1979
La Vicomte Classic Coachbuilders, Inc., St. Sauveur des Monts, Quebec. Replicars.

RENAULT
F 1898–present
Renault Frères (1898–1909). SA des Usines Renault (1909–1945). Régie Nationale des Usines Renault, Billancourt (1945–present); Flins (1952–present); Havre-Sandouville (1963–present). Passenger and sports cars.

RENAUX
F 1901–1902
Sté. l'Énergie, Paris. Light cars.

RÉNÉ BONNET
F 1962–1964
Réné Bonnet, Champigny-sur-Seine. Sports cars.

RENFERT
D 1924–1925
Josef Renfert, Motorfahrzeugfabrik, Beckum. 2-cycle 2-cylinder cars.

RENFREW
GB 1904
Scottish Motor Carriage Co. Ltd., Glasgow. 16/20 hp five-seater tourer.

RENNIE
GB 1907
Rennie Motor Manufacturing Co., Brighton, Sussex. 4- and 6-cylinder assembled cars.

RENO
USA 1908
Nevada Motor Car Co., Reno, Nevada. See "Desert Flyer" and "Nevada."

RENOWN
USA
See "Palm."

RENVILLE
USA 1911
Motor Buggy Mfg. Co., Minneapolis, Minnesota. 10 cars were made.

REO
USA 1905–1936
R.E. Olds Co., Lansing, Michigan. Name changed 1904 to Reo Motor Car Co. R.M. Owen was selling agent. 344,912 cars were made. Trucks only after 1936.

REPLICAR
E 1993
Comauto S.A., Quart de Poblet. "Porsche" (D) replica.

REPLICAR
USA 1977–1995
Replicars Inc., West Palm Beach, Florida. Replicas.

REPTON
GB 1904
Repton Engineering Works, Repton, Derbyshire. Three-wheeler.

REPUBLIC
USA 1901–1902
Republic Motor Vehicle Co., Minneapolis, Minnesota. Electric cars.

REPUBLIC
USA 1910–1916
Republic Motor Car Co., Hamilton, Ohio; Tarrytown, N.Y. Touring cars. Built "Little" in 1913.

RESTELLI
I 1907–1923
Officina Meccanica Isola Bella, Milano. Sports car.

REUTER
USA 1900–1901
Reuter Automobile Co., Davenport, Iowa.

REUTER
USA 1905–1906
Reuter Motor Car Co., Trainer, Pennsylvania.

REVELLI
I 1941
Mario Revelli, Torino. Three-wheeled electric car, 2 prototypes built.

REVERE
USA 1918–1926
ReVere Motor Car Co., Logansport, Indiana. 1923 reorganized as ReVere Motor Co. 247 cars were made.

REVILLE
AUS 1950
Reville Motor Company, Canberra. Front-wheel drive car prototype.

REVOL
F 1923–1925
J.F. Revol, Fontenay-aux-Roses/Seine. Cyclecar.

REVOZ
SLO 1991–present
Revoz d.d., Novo Mesto. "Renault" assembling.

REX
CS 1935
Josef Holuša, továrna na radiátory, Dolní Benešov. Light car.

REX; REX-SIMPLEX
D 1901–1923
Deutsche Automobil-Industrie Friedrich Hering (1901–1904). Deutsche Automobil-Industrie Hering & Richard (1904–1908). Automobilwerk Richard & Hering AG (1908–1921). Elitewagen AG, Ronneburg (1921–1923). Sports and touring cars.

REX
EST 1996–present
Kit Grupp Ltd., Tallinn. Kit cars.

REX
GB 1901–1914
Birmingham Motor Manufacturing and Supply Co. Ltd., Birmingham (1901–1902). Rex Motor Manufacturing Co. Ltd., Coventry, Warwicks. (1902–1914). Three-wheelers, light and touring cars; built under names "Ast-Rex," "Airex," "Rexette," "Rex-Remo" and "Rex-Simplex" (no connection with the German marque).

REX
USA 1908–1909
Rex Automobile Car Co., Indianapolis, Indiana.

REX
USA 1914
Rex Machine Works, Brooklyn, N.Y. Cyclecar. Not related to "Rex" of Wyandotte, Michigan.

REX
USA 1914
Rex Motor Co., Ford City (Wyandotte), Michigan. Front-wheel drive cyclecar.

REX
USA 1919–1920
Rex Motor Car Co., New Orleans, Louisiana.

REX BUCKBOARD
USA 1903
Pennsylvania Electrical & R.R. Supply Co., Pittsburgh, Pennsylvania. Designed by Rex Reinertsen.

REXER
F
See "Weyher et Richemond." Steam cars.

REX-SIMPLEX
D
See "Rex."

REYA
USA 1917
Reya Motor Co., Napoleon, Ohio. See "Napoleon" cars built into 1919.

REYMOND
F 1901
Automobiles Reymond et Cie., Chalons-sur-Saone. 12hp light car.

REYNARD
GB 1931
Reynard Car & Engineering Co. Ltd., London. Sports cars.

REYONNAH
F 1951–1954
Robert Hannoyer, Paris. 175cc folding cars.

REYROL (PASSE-PARTOUT)
F 1901–1930
Société des Automobiles Reyrol, Neuilly/Seine (1901–1906); Levallois-Perret/Seine (1907–1930). Voiturette.

R.G.
RA 1991–1993 ?
R.G. Sport, Ruben Garcia, Buenos Aires. Sports car.

R.G.S.-ATALANTA
GB 1947–1958
R.G.S. Automobile Components Ltd., Windsor, Berks. Sports cars.

R.H.
F 1927–1928
Établissements Raymond-Hebert, Levallois-Perret/Seine. Small sports cars.

RHÉDA
F 1898–1899
Sté. des Automobiles Rhéda, Paris. Three-wheelers.

RHENAG
D 1924–1926
Rhenania Motorenfabrik AG, Berlin; Mannheim. Sports cars.

RHINO
D
See "Vesta."

RHODE
GB 1921–1935
Rhode Motor Co., Birmingham. Touring and sports cars.

RHODE ISLAND
USA 1899–1900
Hughes & Atkin, Providence, Rhode Island.

RHODE ISLAND
USA 1904
Rhode Island Electromobile Co., Providence, Rhode Island. Electric car.

RHODE ISLAND AUTO CARRIAGE
USA 1900–1901
Rhode Island Auto Carriage Co., Olneyville, Rhode Island.
See "Hill."

RHODES
USA c. 1905
Melvin P. Rhodes, Lynn, Massachusetts.

RHONE
I 1917
Societa Italiana Motori Gnome e Rhone, Torino.

RHONSON
F 1948
Henry Lanoy, Paris. Three-wheeler prototype.

R.H.P.
D c. 1995
Robert Hillmann Products, Wolfratshausen. Replicars.
See "Spiess."

RIBBLE
GB 1904–1908
Jackson & Kinnings, Southport, Lancs. Three-wheelers.

RIBETTI
I 1906; 1924
Ribetti, Duccio & Colombato, Torino.
See "Rotor."

RIBOUD
F 1976
Three-wheeler.

RICART
E 1922–1928
Ricart y Perez, Barcelona. Sports cars.

RICART-ESPANA
E 1928–1929
Industrial Nacional Metalurgica, Barcelona. 2.4-litre 6-cylinder sports cars.

RICE
USA 1858
Richard D. Rice, Hallowell, Maine. Steam carriage.

RICHARD
USA 1914–1919
M. Richard Automobile Co. Richard Automobile Mfg. Co., Cleveland, Ohio. Touring cars. Also known as "Ri-Chard."

RICHARDS
USA 1896–1903
Walter Richards, Trenton, New Jersey. Gasoline cars.

RICHARDS
USA 1902
Mark Richards, Aurora, Illinois.

RICHARDS
USA 1910
Richards Iron Works, Manitowoc, Wisconsin.

RICHARDSON
GB 1903–1907
J.R. Richardson & Co. Ltd., Saxilby, Lincs. Tubular frames and shaft drive.

RICHARDSON
GB 1919–1922
C.E. Richardson & Co. Ltd., Sheffield, Yorks. Cyclecars.

RICHARDSON
USA c. 1899
C.Fred Richardson & Son, Athol, Massachusetts.

RICHARDSON
USA c. 1905
F.A. Richardson, Leominster, Massachusetts. 7 hp automobile.

RICHELIEU
USA 1922–1923
Richelieu Motor car Co. United Auto Body Corp., Asbury Park, New Jersey. Touring cars. Became "Barbarino."

RICHLAND
USA 1899
Richland Buggy Co., Mansfield, Ohio.

RICHMOND
USA 1902–1903
Richmond Automobile & Cycle Co., Richmond, Indiana. Steam car.

RICHMOND
USA 1905
T. Richmond, Jessup, Iowa. Amphibious three-wheeler.

RICHMOND
USA 1904–1917
Wayne Works, Richmond, Indiana. 1,348 cars were made.

RICHMOND
USA 1916
Richmond Motor Co., Custer, Michigan.

RICHTER
USA 1902
Henry Richter, Brazil, Indiana.

RICKENBACKER
USA 1922–1927
Rickenbacker Motor Co., Detroit, Michigan. Introduced at 1922 New York Auto Show. 27,419 cars were made.

RICKETTS
USA 1909–1911
Ricketts Automobile Works, White Pi-

geon, Michigan; South Bend, Indiana. Touring cars.
See "Diamond."

RICKMAN
GB 1985–1993
Rickman Engineering Ltd., New Milton, Hampshire. Sports and 4 × 4x car.

RICKMOBILE
USA 1948
Rickmobile Co., San Francisco, California. Motorized rickshaw for export.

RICORDI
I 1898–1902
Giuseppe Ricordi, Milano.

RICORDI & MOLINARI
I 1905–1906
Societa Italiana Costruzioni Meccanica Automobili, Milano. 8hp tonneau.

RIDDEL
USA 1900
William Riddel, San Francisco, California.

RIDDLE
USA 1916–1926
Riddle Manufacturing Co., Ravenna, Ohio. Sedans.

RIDER-LEWIS
USA 1908–1911
Rider-Lewis Motor Car Co., Muncie & Anderson, Indiana. Property reported attached October 1910. February 1911 reported sold for $38,500. Plant went to Madison Motors Corp. Touring cars and roadsters.

RIDLEY
GB 1901–1907
Ridley Autocar Co. Ltd., Coventry, Warwicks. (1901–1904). Ridley Motor Co. Ltd., Paisley, Renfrewshire (1906–1907). About 10 light two-seaters were built.

RIDLEY
GB 1914
Thorofare Motors Ltd., Woodbridge, Suffolk. Light cars.

RIEGEL
F 1902
Transformations Automobiles Riegel, Paris. 10hp fore-carriage.

RIEJU
E 1954–1956
Rieju y Juanda SA, Figueras, Gerona. Mini cars.

RIESS-ROYAL
USA 1922
Riess Motor Inc., York, Pennsylvania.

RIETTI
CH 1910
Zürich.

RIGAL
GB 1902–1903
Rigal Motor Co., London. DeDion engine.

RIKAS
D 1922–1923
Rikas Automobil-Werke, Berlin. Light cars.

RIKER
USA 1897–1902
The Riker Motor Vehicle Co., Elizabethport, New Jersey. Electric cars. 1894 experimental (Riker Motor Co., Brooklyn, N.Y.). Merged 1900 with Electric Vehicle Co., Hartford, Connecticut. Also gas autos 1901–1902.

RILA
BG 1967–1985
Balkan, Lovec. "Moskvitch" (SU) license.

RILEY
GB 1898–1969
Riley Cycle Co. Ltd. (1898–1912). Riley (Coventry) Ltd., Coventry, Warwickshire (1912–1948). Riley Motors Ltd., Abingdon, Berks. (1948–1969). Passenger and sports cars.

RILEY & COWLEY
USA 1902
Riley & Cowley, Brooklyn, N.Y. Steam cars.

RING
USA c. 1905
C.A. Ring, Waltham, Massachusetts. 2.5 hp automobile.

RINSPEED
CH 1976–present
Frank M. Rinderknecht, Rinspeed AG, Zürich; Zumikon. Tuning.

RIOTTE
USA 1895; 1899
Riotte & Hadden Mfg. Co., New York, N.Y. U.S. Long Distance Automobile Co., Jersey City, New Jersey. Experimental kerosene-powered motor carriages.

RIP
F 1908–1912
SA des Voitures Automobiles Rip, Rive-de-Gier/Loire. Transverse coil springs at front and rear.

RIPERT
F 1899–1902
Automobiles Ripert, Marseilles. 6 and 12hp cars.

RIPPER
USA 1903
Ripper Motor Carriage Co., Buffalo, N.Y. Runabouts. October 1903, V.E. Ripper disappeared.

RISK
USA c. 1905
Winthrop A. Risk, Providence, Rhode Island. 4.5 hp automobile.

RITCHIE
USA 1899
William Ritchie, Hamilton, Ohio. Gasoline carriage.

RITTER
B 1972
Garage de la Cloche S.A., Jemeppe. Dune buggy.

RITTER
USA 1896–1901
C.E. Ritter, Milton, Pennsylvania. Steam cars.

RITTER
USA 1912
Ritter Automobile Co., Madison, Wisconsin. 4-cylinder cars.

RITZ
USA 1914–1915
Ritz Cyclecar Co., New York, N.Y. Cyclecars. Built by Driggs-Seabury Ordnance Co. Became "Sharon" Cyclecar.

RIVAL
USA 1914
T.F. Lang. Wichita Motor Co., Wichita Falls, Texas. Cyclecars.
See "Wichita Falls."

RIVAT ET BOUCHARD
F 1900
Rivat et Bouchard, Lyon. Voiturette.

RIVAZ
CH 1804; 1807; 1809–1813
Isaac de Rivaz, Sitten. Atmospheric gas motor powered vehicle.

RIVELAINE
F 1980
50 cc engine powered city car.

RIVETT SPECIAL
USA 1912
Claude Rivett, Syracuse, N.Y. Runabout.

RIVIERA
USA 1907
Milton H. Schnader, Lebanon, Pennsylvania. 2-cylinder 20 hp cars. Became "Schnader."

RJD
GB 1990–1994 ?
Robert Jankel Design, Weybridge, Surrey. Sports cars.

R.L.C.
GB 1920–1921
Argyll (London) Motor & Enginering Co. Ltd., London. Light cars.

R.L. MORGAN
USA 1897
Morgan Construction Co., Worcester, Massachusetts.
   See "Morgan."

RM CLASSICS
ZA 1980s
RM Classics, Port Elizabeth. Replicars.

RMA
D 1984–c. 1994
Rheinauer Maschinen- und Armaturenbau GmbH, Kehl/Rhein. Amphibian.
   See "Amphi Ranger."

RMB
GB 1973–c. 1981
RMB Motors, Barwell, Leics. "MG" TF replica.

R.M.C.
USA
   See "Regal."

R MOTORSPORT
USA 1990s
R MotorSport, Rochester, N.Y. Kit cars.

R.N.W.
GB 1951
R.N.W. Products Ltd., Farnham, Surrey. Two-seater minicars.

R-O
USA 1911
R.M. Owen & Co., Lansing, Michigan.
   See "Owen."

ROA
E 1958
Industrais Motorizadas Onieva SA, Madrid. Three-wheeler prototype, similar to the "BMW" Isetta (D).

ROACH
USA 1899
W.E. Roach, Philadelphia, Pennsylvania.

ROACH & ALBANUS
USA 1899–1900
Roach & Albanus, Fort Wayne, Indiana.

ROADABLE
USA 1946–1947
Southern Aircraft, Garland, Texas. Ted Hall designed three-wheel car/plane. One produced.

ROAD CART
USA 1896
R.S. Scott, Flint, Michigan.

ROADER
USA 1911–1912
Roader Car Co., Brockton, Massachusetts. Runabouts.

ROAD KING
USA 1908
   See "Monarch."

ROADRUNNER
USA 1904
Roadrunner Automobile & Power Co., Los Angeles, California.

ROAD RUNNER
USA 1908
Road Runner Auto Co., Los Angeles, California. Four-wheel drive car prototype.

ROAD RUNNER
USA 1963
Cyclone Sales Co., Los Angeles, California. "Chevrolet" Corvair based cars.

ROADSTER
USA 1902–1903
Flint Automobile Co., Flint, Michigan.
   See "Flint."

ROAMER
USA 1914
H.J. Roamer Co., Taunton, Massachusetts. Cyclecars.

ROAMER
USA 1915
Adams & Montant, New York, N.Y. Also spelled "Romer."

ROAMER
USA 1917–1929
Romer Co. (Adams & Montant), New York, N.Y. Barley Mfg. Co., Streator, Illinois. Succeeded Streator Consolidated Corp. Renamed Barley Motor Car Co. at Kalamazoo, Michigan 1917. 1923 reorganized as. Roamer Motor Car Co. Touring cars. 11,643 cars were made.

ROARING TWENTIES
USA 1991
Twenties Motor Car Company, Addison, Illinois. Replicars.

ROBB
USA 1901
Dr. Malcolm Robb, St. Louis, Missouri.

ROBE
USA 1914–1915
W.B. Robe & Co., Portsmouth, Ohio. Cyclecars.

ROBE
USA 1923
W.B. Robe & J.D. Strong, Nansemond, Virginia. Robe Motor Corp., Norfolk, Virginia. Touring cars.

ROBERTS
USA 1884
J.H. Roberts, Providence, Rhode Island. Steam automobile.

ROBERTS
USA 1897
S.W. Roberts, Chicago, Illinois. Electric cars.

ROBERTS
USA 1904
O.G. Roberts, Columbus, Ohio.

ROBERTS
USA 1915
Roberts Motor Co., Sandusky, Ohio. 6-cylinder 60 hp cars.

ROBERT SERF
F 1926–1933
Automobiles Robert Serf, Colombey-les-Belles/Meurthe-et-Moselle. Light cars.

ROBERTSON
GB 1900–1902
William Robertson & Sons Ltd., Dundee, Scotland. Voiturette.

ROBERTSON
GB 1915–1916
James Robertson, Manchester. Cyclecars.

ROBERTSON
USA 1895
G.W. Robertson, Mt. Vernon, Indiana.

ROBERTSON
USA 1921
Robertson Co., San Antonio, Texas. Prototypes.

ROBERTS SIX
CDN 1921
Canadian Automobile Corp., Lachine, Quebec. Only a prototype was built.

ROBIE
USA 1914
Robie Cyclecar Co., York, Pennsylvania; Chicago, Illinois; Detroit, Michigan. Cyclecars.

ROBINET
F 1906–1907
F. Robinet et Cie., Nantes/Loire-Inférieure. Wooden frame with two seats in tandem. The driver sat in the rear seat.

ROBIN HOOD
GB 1990–1993
Robin Hood Engineering, Sherwood, Nottingham. Sports cars.

ROBINSON
GB 1907
Charles Robinson, Kettering, Northamptonshire. Three made only.

ROBINSON
USA 1900–1902
J.T. Robinson, Co., Hyde Park, Massachusetts. Runabouts. Formerly "Bramwell-Robinson"; 1898–1899. 1901 renamed Robinson Motor Vehicle Co. Became "Pope-Robinson."

ROBINSON
USA 1910
Robinson Motor Car Co., Detroit, Michigan.

ROBINSON
USA 1914
Charles Robinson, Los Angeles, California. Three-wheeler.

ROBINSON & HOLE
GB 1906–1907
Robinson & Hole Ltd., Thames Ditton, Surrey. Ordinary machines with 2.8 litre motor.

ROBINSON & PRICE
GB 1905–1906; 1913
Robinson & Price Ltd., Liverpool. Cyclecars.

ROB ROY
GB 1922–1926
Kennedy Motor Co. Ltd., Glasgow. Light cars.

ROBSON
USA 1909
Robson Mfg. Co., Galesburg, Illinois. Runabouts.

ROBY
USA 1899
George L. Roby, Albion, Michigan.

ROC
GB
See "Wall."

ROCH-BRAULT
F 1898–1899
Sté. Francaise d'Automobile Roch-Brault et Cie., Paris. Few examples of gasoline cars.

ROCHDALE
GB 1957–1975
Rochdale Motor Panels and Engineering Ltd., Rochdale, Lancs. Sports cars.

ROCHE
USA 1924–1925
Lifton R. Roche, Los Angeles, California. Two-cycle engine, four-wheel drive.

ROCHESTER
USA 1901–1902
Rochester Cycle Mfg. Co. Rochester Gasoline Carriage & Motor Co., Rochester, N.Y. Steam runabouts.

ROCHESTER SPECIAL
USA 1910
C.P. Smith & Co., Rochester, N.Y.

ROCHET; ROCHET-PETIT
F 1899–1905
Compagnie Générale des Cycles et Autos. Sté. Rochet, Paris. 4hp tonneau.

ROCHET FRÈRES
F 1898–1901
Rochet Frères et Cie., Lyon. Light vis-à-vis.

ROCHET-PETIT
F
See "Rochet."

ROCHET-SCHNEIDER
F 1894–1932
SA des Établissements Rochet-Schneider, Lyon. Light tonneau; 4.5-litre touring cars.

RÖCK
H 1905–1918
Röck István Gépgyár, Budapest. Some "Csonka" cars were made. 21/35 and 22/50 hp cars built under "Lloyd" (D) license.

ROCKAWAY
USA 1902–1904
Rockaway Automobile Co., Rockaway, New Jersey. Mohler & DeGress, Long Island City, N.Y. Runabouts.

ROCK CREEK
USA 1906
Rock Creek Auto & Wagon Works, Alexandria, Virginia.

ROCKEFELLER YANKEE
USA 1949–1953
Rockefeller Sports Car Corp., Rockville Center, Long Island, N.Y. Sports cars using Ford V-8 engine.

ROCKET
USA 1903
Samuel D. Sturgis, Los Angeles, California. 4-cylinder 24 hp touring car.

ROCKET
USA 1913–1914
Rocket-Batterman & Booth. Scripps-Booth Cyclecar Co., Detroit, Michigan. Cyclecars. Became "Scripps-Booth," Scripps-Booth Motor Co.

ROCKET
USA 1948
Hewson Pacific Corp., Los Angeles, California. 3-passenger cars.

ROCK FALLS
USA 1919–1925
Rock Falls Mfg. Co., Sterling, Illinois. Touring cars.

ROCK HILL
USA 1910
Rock Hill Buggy Co., Rock Hill, South Carolina. Became "Anderson."

ROCKLIFF
USA 1901
Charles Rockliff, Brooklyn, N.Y.

ROCKNE
CDN 1932–1933
Studebaker Corp. of Canada Ltd., Walkerville, Ontario. Started December 27, 1932.

ROCKNE
USA 1932–1933
Rockne Motors Corp., Detroit, Michigan; South Bend, Indiana. Subsidiary of Studebaker Corp.; 36,041 cars were made.

ROCKNEY
USA 1910
Bennett E. Rockney, Portland, North Dakota. Runabout.

ROCKWELL
USA 1910–1911
Connecticut Cab Co., Bristol, Connecticut. Name of taxicabs marketed by the New Departure Mfg. Co. who built the "Houpt-Rockwell."

ROCOIT
USA 1909
Rocoit Motor Car Co., Beloit, Wisconsin; Rockford, Illinois.
  See "Lipman."

ROCOURT-MERLIN
F 1900
Ets Rocourt et Merlin Fils, Marseilles. Abeille engines.

RODAE
RO 1995–present
Rodae Automobile S.A., Craiova. Formerly "Oltcit."
  See "Oltena." "Daewoo" (ROK) based cars from 1996.

RODEFELD
USA 1909–1917
A.H. Rodefeld, Richmond, Indiana. About 12 passenger cars and 12 trucks were made.

RODFORD
USA c. 1905
H.S. Rodford, Boston, Massachusetts. 30 hp automobile.

RODGERS
USA 1903–1904
Rodgers & Co.
  See "Imperial."

RODGERS
USA 1921
Scientific Automotive Corp., New York, N.Y. 4-cylinder 36 hp automobile.

RODLEY
GB 1954–1955
Rodley Automobile Co. Ltd., Leeds, Yorks. Minicars.

ROEBLING-PLANCHE
USA 1909
Roebling-Planche Motor Co., Trenton, New Jersey. Touring cars. Became "Meteor."

ROGER
F 1888–1896
Emile Roger, Paris. "Benz" (D) manufactured.

ROGER
GB 1920–1924
Thomas Roger & Co. Ltd., Wolverhampton, Staffs. About 100 light cars were built.

ROGER
USA 1895
Roger-American Mechanical Carriage Co., New York, N.Y. Built for Chicago Times-Herald Race. Became "Macy-Roger."

ROGERS
CDN 1984
Rogers Inter Auto, Vancouver, B.C. Three-wheelers with "Polski-Fiat" (PL) 850 cc engine.

ROGERS
USA 1899–1900
W.S. Rogers Steamobile Co., Boston, Massachusetts. Steam cars.

ROGERS
USA 1901–1904
W.S. Rogers Automobile Co., Beloit, Wisconsin.

ROGERS
USA 1911–1912
Ralph Rogers, Ralston, Nebraska. Rogers Motor Car Co., Omaha, Nebraska. Highwheelers.

ROGERS & HANFORD
USA 1899–1902
The Rogers & Hanford Co., Cleveland, Ohio. Surrey.

ROGERS & THATCHER
USA 1903
Rogers & Thatcher, Cleveland, Ohio. Runabout.

RÖHR
D 1928–1935
Röhr Automobilwerke AG (1928–1930). Neue Röhrwerke AG, Ober-Ramstadt (1930–1935). Passenger cars. Type "Junior" (1933–1935) under "Tatra" (CS) license.

ROLAND
D 1907
Kraftwagen-Gesellschaft Roland, Berlin. Voiturette.

ROLAND
D 1926
Bertling, Dessau. Small two-seaters.

ROLAND
USA 1915
Roland Gas-Electric Vehicle Corp., New York, N.Y.

ROLLAND-PILAIN
F 1906–1931
SA des Établissements Rolland-Pilain, Tours. Large touring cars.

ROLLFIX
D 1926–1936
Rollfix-Eilwagen GmbH. Rollfix-Werke Frederic Schröder KG, Wandsbek bei Hamburg. Three-wheelers.

ROLLIN
USA 1924–1925
Rollin Motors Co., Cleveland, Ohio. 5,750 cars were built. Formerly "Zeder." Subsidiary of Cleveland Tractor Co. Reported bankrupt January 1926. Rollin White (founder) son of Thomas White, founder of White Co.

ROLLING
F
  See "Dupressoir."

ROLLO
GB 1911–1913
Rollo Car Co. Ltd., Birmingham. Cyclecars.

ROLLSMOBILE
USA 1959–1960
Starts Manufacturing Co., Ft. Lauderdale, Florida. ⅔ scale replica of 1901 "Oldsmobile."

ROLLS-ROYCE
GB 1904–present
Royce Ltd. (1904–1906). Rolls-Royce Ltd., Manchester (1906–1908). Rolls-Royce Ltd., Derby (1908–1945). Rolls-Royce Ltd. (1946–1971). Rolls-Royce

Motors (1971) Ltd., Crewe, Cheshire (1971–present). "The Best Car in the World."

ROLLS-ROYCE
USA 1920–1935
Rolls-Royce of America Inc., Springfield, Massachusetts. Bought factory of Wire Wheel Corp. of America, formerly built by Hendee Mfg. Company. Production announced July 1920. 1,703 "Silver Ghosts" and 1,241 "New Phantoms" were made.

ROLUX
F 1951–1952
Société Rolux, Clermont-Ferrand. About 300 mini cars were built.
See "New Map."

ROM
IL 1966–1982
Rom Carmel Industries Ltd., Haifa. Small cars.

ROMA
I 1905–1910
Societa Automobili Roma di Ricardo Memmo, Roma.

ROMANAZZI
I 1953
Carrozzeria Romanazzi, Bari. 3-passenger three-wheelers based on the Vespa scooter.

ROMANELLI
CDN 1970
Romanelli Motors Ltd., Montreal, Quebec. Sports car.

ROMBO
I 1920–1921
Societa Automobili Brevetti Fuscaldo, Brescia. Rhomboid wheel placement.

ROMER
USA 1921
Romer Motors Corp., Danvers, Massachusetts; Taunton & Boston, Massachusetts. Absorbed "Peters" cyclecar, Trenton, New Jersey.

ROMETSCH
D 1950–1961
Karosserie Rometsch, Berlin. About 500 Rometsch-bodied convertibles and coupes on the "Volkswagen" chassis. Coachbuilders from 1924.

ROMI
BR 1956–1961
Americo Emilio Romi, Santa Barbara d'Oeste. 3,090 minicars based on the "Iso" Isetta (I) were built.

RONART
GB 1985–1994
Ronart Cars Ltd., Bretton, Peterborough, Cambs. Sports cars.

RONDINE
I
See "Adami."

RONTEIX
F 1906–1914
J. Ronteix, Levallois-Perret/Seine. Light cars.

ROO
AUS 1917–1919
Roo Motor Car Manufacturing Co., Sydney, N.S.W. Two light cars were made.

ROOSEVELT
USA 1929–1930
Marmon Motor Car Co., Indianapolis, Indiana. Production: 4,132 cars.

ROOTS & VENABLES
GB 1896–1904
Roots Oil Motor & Motor Car Co., London. Three-wheelers and light cars.

ROPER
USA 1860s–1896
Sylvester H. Roper, Roxbury, Massachusetts. Ten two-, three- and four-wheel steam vehicles built by Sylvester Roper and exhibited from the 1860s to the 1890s throughout New England and the Midwest.

ROPER-CORBET
GB 1911–1912
Prototype.

ROSELLI
I 1899–1904
Emanuel di A. Roselli, Torino.

ROSE NATIONAL
GB
See "National."

ROSENBAUER
USA 1900–1901
Rosenbauer Automobile & Power Co., Milwaukee, Wisconsin.

ROSENGART
F 1928–1955
Automobiles L. Rosengart, Neuilly-sur-Seine (1928–1937). Société Industrielle de l'Ouest Parisienne, Paris (1927–1955). Touring and sports cars.

ROSS
CDN 1911–1914
Ross Motor Car Co., Ltd., Toronto, Ontario.

ROSS
USA 1915–1918
Ross Automobile Co., Detroit, Michigan. Roadsters. Formerly Ross & Young Machine Co.

ROSS & KRAMER
USA 1904
Ross & Kramer Automobile Co., Chicago, Illinois.

ROSSEL
F 1898–1899
Edouard Rossel, Lille. "Daimler" (D) design.

ROSSEL
F 1903–1926
F. Rossel et Cie; SA des Automobiles Rossel, Sochaux-Montbeliard/Doubs. 12-litre cars in 1907; touring cars.

ROSSELLI
I 1899–1904
Emmanuel A. Rosselli Fabbrica Italiana di Automobili, Torino. Voiturettes.
See "Emmanuel."

ROSSI & SEGRE
I 1897
Torino.

ROSSLER
USA 1906–1907
C. Rossler Mfg. Co., Buffalo, N.Y. Speedwagon builders planned to build light runabout 1906.

ROSS STEAMER
USA 1906–1909
Louis S. Ross, Newtonville, Massachusetts.

ROTARIAN
USA 1921
Bournonville Rotary Valve Motor Co., Hoboken, New Jersey. Became "Rotary Six."

ROTARY
USA 1903–1905

Rotary Motor Vehicle Co., Boston, Massachusetts. Touring cars.
See "Intrepid."

ROTARY
USA 1906
Rotary Motor Car Co. of America, New York, N.Y. Steam car.

ROTARY
USA 1921–1923
Bournonville Rotary Valve Motor Co., Hoboken, New Jersey. 5-litre 6-cylinder engines.
See "Rotarian."

ROTHSCHILD
USA c. 1905
Rothschild & Son, Boston, Massachusetts. 24 hp automobile.

ROTHWELL
GB 1901–1916
Eclipse Machine Co. Ltd., Oldham, Lancashire. Tourer.

ROTOR
I 1905
Societa Automobili Rotor (Ribetti, Ducco, Colombatto), Torino.

ROTRAX
GB 1993
Adam Rotrax Ltd., Bradford-on-Avon, Wiltshire. 4 × 4 car.

ROUGH
GB 1899–1900
R. Rough & Co., Hereford. Friction transmission.

ROUNDS
USA 1901
George E. Rounds, Plymouth, Massachusetts. Two steam cars were made.

ROUSSEL
F 1908–1914
Établissements Roussel, Charleville/Ardennes. 10 and 12hp light cars.

ROUSSEY
F 1949–1950
Roussey Freres, Meudon/Seine-et-Oise. Little four-seater sports saloon.

ROUSSON
F 1910–1914
Rousson et Chamoix, Feurs/Loire. 1.5- and 3.6-litre cars.

ROUXEL
F 1899
Rouxel et Cie., Boulogne-sur-Seine. Voiturette.

ROVENA
USA 1926
Rovena Motor Co., Kansas City, Missouri. Front drive.

ROVER
GB 1904–present
The Rover Co. Ltd., Coventry, Warwickshire (1904–1940); Birmingham (1919–1925); Solihull, Warwickshire (1945–present). Passenger cars.
See "Land Rover."

ROVIN
F 1946–1959
Robert de Rovin, Saint-Denis/Seine; Colombes/Seine. Small cars.

ROWAN
USA 1967–1969
Rowan Controller Co., Westminster, Maryland; Oceanport, N.Y. Electric cars.

ROWE
USA 1908; 1919
Rowe Motor Co., Waynesboro, Pennsylvania.

ROWELL
USA 1902
A.E. Rowell, Auburn, Maine. Surrey.

ROY
USA c. 1905
Fred L. Roy, Adams, Massachusetts. 4 hp automobile.

ROYAL
USA 1904–1909
Royal Motor Works, Augusta, Maine.

ROYAL
USA 1904–1910
Royal Motor Car Co., Detroit, Michigan.

ROYAL
USA 1905
Royal Automobile Co., Chicago, Illinois. Electric cars. Also called "Royal Queen Electric." Also built "Princess" gasoline cars.

ROYAL
USA 1913
Royal Motor Car Co., Elkhart, Indiana. Touring car.

ROYAL
USA 1914
Crescent Motor Co., Cincinnati, Ohio. Companion to "Ohio" (1913–1915).

ROYAL
USA 1915
Royal Cyclecar Co., Bridgeport, Connecticut. Cyclecars.

ROYAL AMSTON
USA 1915
Charles M. Ams, Amston, Connecticut. Also called "Ams-Sterling." Pilot model only.

ROYALE
GB 1996–present
Royale Motor Company, Preston, Lancashire. Sports car replica.

ROYAL ENFIELD
GB 1901–1905
Royal Enfield Cycle Co. Ltd., Redditch, Worcs. Light cars with DeDion engines.

ROYAL MARTEL
USA 1925–1927
Royal Martel Taxi Corp., Elkhart, Indiana. About 200 taxicabs were made.

ROYAL PRINCESS
USA 1904–1905
Royal Automobile Co., Chicago, Illinois.
See "Princess." Both names apply to same vehicle.

ROYAL RUBY
GB 1913–1914; 1927
Royal Ruby Cycle Co., Manchester. Cyclecar, and three-wheeler.

ROYAL SIX
CDN 1921–1923
Parker Motor Car Co. Ltd., Montreal, Quebec.

ROYAL STAR
B 1904–1910
Sté. de Construction Mecaniques. SA Royal Star, Anvers. 1-, 2-, 4- and 6-cylinder cars.
See "SAVA."

ROYAL TOURIST
USA 1904–1911
Royal Motor Car Co., Cleveland, Ohio. Reorganized as Royal Tourist Car Co. 1909; Consolidated Motor Car Co. 1911. Succeeded "Hoffman" (1900–1904).

ROYAL WINDSOR
CDN 1911
See "Dominion."

ROYCE
GB 1904
Royce Ltd., Manchester. 1.8-litre prototypes.

ROYDALE
GB 1907–1909
Roydale Engineering Co. Ltd., Huddersfield, Yorks. Conventional machines of 18, 20 and 25 hp.

RSL
USA 1969–?
RSL Corporate, Cleveland, Ohio.

R.T.C.
GB 1922–1923
Rene Tondeur Co. Ltd., Croydon, Surrey. Cyclecars.

RU-AN
A 1921–1922
Anton Rumpler & Leopoldine Ringer, Wien. Cyclecars.

RUBAY
USA 1922–1924
Rubay Co., Cleveland, Ohio.
See "Leon-Rubay."

RUBINO
I 1920–1923
Officine di Netro, Netro.

RUBURY-LINDSAY
GB
See "R.L.C."

RUBY
F 1910–1922
Godefroy et Leveque, Levallois-Perret/Seine. Friction transmission and chain final drive.

R U CAR
USA 1990s
R U Car Crafters, Sand Springs, Oklahoma. Kit cars.

RUDGE
GB 1912–1913
Rudge-Whitworth Ltd., Coventry, Warwickshire. Cyclecars.

RUDOLPH
D 1998–present
Rudolph Perfect Roadster, Mechernich. Sports car replica.

RUDOLPH
USA 1901
William F. Rudolph, Philadelphia, Pennsylvania.

RUF
D 1983–present
Ruf Automobile GmbH, Pfaffenhausen. Tuning.

RUGBY
USA 1923–1928
See "Star."

RUGER
USA 1968–1972
Sturm, Ruger & Co. Inc., Southport, Connecticut. Replica of mid-twenties tourer for $13,000.

RUGGERI
I 1950–1955
Milano. Sports cars.

RUGGLES
USA 1905
F.A. Ruggles, Ware, Massachusetts.

RUHL
B 1901
S.A. des Automobiles Ruhl, Dison-lez-Verviers. Voiturettes.

RULER
USA 1917
Ruler Motor Car Co., Aurora, Illinois. Frameless car.

RULEX
GB 1904
R.L. Motor Engineering Co. Ltd., London. Light cars.

RUMI
I 1954
Bergamo.
See "ISCA."

RUMPF
B 1899–1901
Sté. le Progres Industriel, Bruxelles. Voiturettes.

RUMPLER
D 1921–1926
Rumpler Motoren-Gesellschaft mbH, Berlin. Streamlined cars.

RUMREICH
A/CS 1899
František Rumreich, Ivančice u Brna. One car for builder's own use.

RUPF
USA c. 1905
E.L. Rupf, Lawrence, Massachusetts. 6 hp automobile.

RUPPE
D
See "Piccolo."

RUSH
D 1996–present
Autohaus Achim Gorgus, Straubenhardt. "Lotus" (GB) replica.

RUSHMOBILE
USA 1901–1908
Brecht Automobile Co., St. Louis, Missouri. Steam cars.
See "Brecht."

RUSKA
NL 1981–1993
Ruska Automobielen B.V., Amsterdam. Replica and dune buggy.

RUSSEL
USA 1921
Russel Wheel & Foundry Co., Detroit, Michigan. Touring cars.

RUSSELL
USA 1902
Russel, Brunswick, Maine.

RUSSELL
CDN 1905–1916
Canada Cycle & Motor Car Co., Toronto, Ontario. Changed to Russell Motor Car Co. 1911.

RUSSELL
USA 1903–1904
Russell Motor Vehicle Co., Cleveland, Ohio. Vehicle invented by Dr. C.W. Russell, Springfield, Ohio.

RUSSELL
USA 1946
Raymond Russell, Detroit, Michigan. Run by oil pressure.

RUSSELL-DEIBLER
USA 1908–1909
Frank Russell Moccasin Co., Ripon, Wisconsin.

RUSSELL-KNIGHT
CDN 1910–1915
Canada Cycle & Motor Car Co. Russell Motor Car Co., Toronto, Ontario. Plant acquired by "Willys-Overland" reportedly in November 1915.

RUSSELL-SPRINGFIELD
USA 1903
C.W. Russell Co., Springfield, Ohio. Runabouts.

RUSSO-BALTIQUE
SU 1909–1915
Russko-Baltiskij Vagonnij Zavod, Riga. "Fondu" (B) built under license at first, own constructions later. 512 cars were

built. Very successful at long-distance rallies to Europe.
See "Prombron" after 1915.

RUSSO-BUIRE
SU 1912
Zavod Ilyin, Sankt Peterburg. "La Buire" (F) under license.

RUSSON
GB 1951–1952
Russon Cars Ltd., Stanbridge, Beds. Minicars.

RUST
USA c. 1908
Charles W. Rust, Oakland, California.

RUSTAN
USA c. 1902
Manley Rustan, Aneta, North Dakota.

RUSTON-HORNSBY
GB 1919–1924
Ruston & Hornsby Ltd., Lincoln. 2.6- and 3-litre conventional cars.

RUTENBER
USA 1902
Rutenber Mfg. Co., Logansport, Indiana.

RUTH
USA 1907
Ruth Automobile Co., North Webster, Indiana. Highwheelers.

RUTHERFORD
GB 1907–1911
Highclere Motor Car Syndicate Ltd., Newbury, Berks. Steam cars.

RÜTTGER
D 1920–1921
Carl Rüttger Motorpflug- und Automobilwerke, Berlin. Prototypes only.

RUWISCH
D 1950
Three-wheelers.

RUXTON
USA 1929–1930
New Era Motors Inc., New York, N.Y. Front wheel drive. New Era projected 12,000 cars to be built at unnamed plants in 1929, but only prototypes built that year. Most cars produced at "Moon" plant in 1930. About 500 built.

R.W.
GB 1993
R.W. Kitcars Ltd., Melton Mowbray, Leicestershire. Sports car kit.

RWN
D 1929–1931
Motorfahrzeugfabrik Rudolf Weide, Nordhausen/Harz. Three-wheelers.

RYAN
USA 1990s
Ryan Motors, Seal Beach, California. Kit cars.

RYCSA
RA
See "Gilda."

RYDE
GB 1904–1906
Ryde Motors Ltd., West Ealing, Middlesex. 3-cylinder cars.

RYDER
USA 1896–1897; 1900
California Automobile Co., San Franicsco, California. Gasoline powered cars.

RYJAN
F 1920–1926
Grillet, Chatou/Seine-et-Oise (1920–1925); Nanterre/Seine (1925–1926). Conventional ouring cars.

RYKNIELD
GB 1903–1906. Ryknield Engine Co. Ltd (1903–1905). Ryknield Motor Co. Ltd., Burton-on-Trent, Staffs. (1906). Small cars.

RYLEY
GB 1901–1902
Ryley, Ward & Bradford, Coventry, Warwickshire. Light cars.

RYLEY
GB 1913
J.A. Ryley, Birmingham. Cyclecar.

RYNER-WILSON
GB 1920–1921
Ryner-Wilson Motor Co. Ltd., London. 6-cylinder 2.3-litre prototype.

RYTECRAFT
GB 1934–1940
British Motor Boat Mfg. Co. Ltd. (1934–1939). B.M.B. Engineering, London (1939–1940). 250cc "Scootacar" mini cars.

S.1.
DK 1949–1950
E. Sommer, Copenhagen. Light car.
See "Sommer."

SAAB
S 1950–present
Svenska Aeroplan AB (1950–1965). Saab Aktiebolag (1965–1968). Saab-Scania Aktiebolag, Lindköping (1968–present). Passenger cars and sports car, up to 1967 with 2-stroke engines.

SABA
I 1925–1928
Societa Automobili Brevetti Angelino, Milano. Central backbone frame and 4-wheel drive and steering.

SABELLA
GB 1906–1914
Sabella Motor Car Co. Ltd., London. Cyclecars.

SABLATNIG-BEUCHELT
D 1925–1926
Buechelt & Co., Grünberg. 1.5-litre small car.

SABRA
IL 1960–1974
Autocars Co. Ltd., Haifa. "Reliant" (GB) based cars.

SACA
B 1924–1927

Automobiles SACA, Etterbeek-Bruxelles. "Ford" (USA) assembled.

SACHSENRING
DDR 1956–1959
VEB Sachsenring Automobilwerk, Zwickau. About 1,400 cars with 2.4-litre engine were produced.

SÄCHSISCHE ACCUMULATORENWERKE
D c. 1900
Sächsische Accumulatorenwerke AG, Dresden. Electric car.

SÄCHSISCHE WAGGONFABRIK WERDAU
D
See "Pilot."

SADD
USA c. 1905
Sadd Motor Car Co., Boston, Massachusetts. One 9 hp automobile was built.

SAF
D
Süddeutsche Automobil-Fabrik, Gaggenau.
See "Bergmann" (Gaggenau), "Liliput."

S.A.F.
F 1908–1912
Sté. Anon. Des Ateliers du Furan, Sainte-Étienne/Loire. Three-wheelers.

S.A.F.
S 1921–1922
AB Svenska Automobilfabriken, Bollnäs. Assembled cars.

SAFARI
USA 1968–1972
Safari Enterprises Inc., Gardena, California. Dune buggy.

SAFETY
USA 1901–1902
Safety Steam Automobile Co., Boston, Massachusetts; Ipswich, Massachusetts. Steam cars.

SAFETY FIRST
USA 1914–1916
Safety First Motor Car & Truck Co., Kalamazoo, Michigan; Plainwell, Michigan.

SAFIR
CH 1907–1908
Automobilfabrik Safir, Zürich. Passenger cars.

SAF-T-CAB
USA 1926–1928
Saf-T-Cab Corp., Cleveland, Ohio. Taxicabs.

S.A.G.
CH
See "Pic-Pic."

SAGA
F 1981–1993
C.L. Duprez, Paris. Saga Sarl, Laons. Replicars.

SAGE
F 1900–1906
Ateliers P. Sage, Paris. Gasoline-electric cars.

SAGER
CDN 1910
United Motors Ltd., Welland, Ontario. 30hp touring cars.

SAGINAW
USA 1914
Saginaw Motor Car Co., Saginaw, Michigan. Also called "Saginaw Speedster."
See "Detroit."

SAGINAW
USA 1914–1915
Valley Boat & Engine Co., Saginaw, Michigan. Cyclecars.

SAGINAW EIGHT
USA 1916
Lehr Motor Co., Saginaw, Michigan. Became "Yale."

SAIDD
I
S.A. Italiana Darracq.
See "SIAD," "Darracq Italiana."

SAIER
D 1987–1997
Automobilbau Alexander Saier, Engstingen. Replicars.
See "AS."

SAIGON
VN 1986
Ho-Chi-Minh Town. "Citroën" (F) based light car prototype.

ST. JOE
USA 1908
St. Joe Motor Car Co., Elkhart, Indiana. Succeeded Shoemaker Automobile Co. Became Sellers Automobile Co.
See "Sellers" and "Shoemaker."

ST. JOHN
USA 1902–1903
S.H. St. John & Son, Canon City, Colorado. One experimental runabout produced.

ST. LAURENCE
GB 1899–1902
Light cars.

ST. LOUIS
USA 1898–1907
St. Louis Motor Carriage Co. St. Louis Motor Car Co., St. Louis, Missouri. 1905 moved to Peoria Heights, Illinois. Affairs wound up and plant sold for $10,000, reported December 1907. 1,793 cars were made.

ST. LOUIS
USA 1899–1900
St. Louis Gasoline Motor Co., St. Louis, Missouri.

ST. LOUIS
USA 1900–1901
St. Louis Automobile & Supply Co., St. Louis, Missouri. Electric car.

ST. LOUIS
USA 1900
St. Louis Auto Supply Co., St. Louis, Missouri.
See "Dyke."

ST. LOUIS
USA 1905
St. Louis Car Co., St. Louis, Missouri. Few built. Became "American Mors."

ST. LOUIS
USA 1921
John M. Neskou, St. Louis, Missouri.

ST. LOUIS
USA 1923
St. Louis Automotive Co., St. Louis, Missouri. Five built.

ST. VINCENT
GB 1903–1908
William McLean (St. Vincent Cycle & Motor Works), Glasgow.

SAIPAC
IR 1972–c. 1976
Société Iranniene de Production des Automobiles Citroën. "Citroën" (F) license. 15,340 cars built in 1974.

SAL
I 1905–1913
Societa Automobili Lombarda di

Giovanni Macagno, Bergamo. "Esperia" car, 67 made.
See "Esperia."

SAL
I 1920
Societa Automobili Lombarda, Milano.

SALEEN
USA 1988–1993
Saleen Autosport, Anaheim, California. Sports cars.

SALISBURY
USA 1895–1896
Horseless Carriage Co., Chicago, Illinois. Three-wheel electric cars. Designed by Wilber S. Salisbury.

SALMON
GB 1914
Baguley Cars Ltd., Burton-on-Trent, Staffs. Light cars.

SALMSON
F 1921–1957
Société des Moteurs Salmson, Billancourt/Seine. Sports and touring cars.

SALMSON ITALIANA
I 1923
Reggio Emilia.

SALOMON
F 1931
Ultra light car designed by Jules Salomon.

SALR
I 1906–1913
S.A. Ligure Romana, Roma.
See "Cantono," "FRAM," "Soc. Romana."

SALSBURY
USA 1947–1948
Salsbury Motors, Inc., Pomona, California.

SALTER
USA 1909–1915
William A. Salter Motor Co., Kansas City, Missouri. Salter Motor Car Co., Centropolis, Kansas. 1910 Salter Motor Mfg. Co. Touring cars.

SALVA
I 1906–1907
Societa Anonima Lombarda Vetture Automobili, Milano. Big 4-cylinder 60/70 hp cars.

SALVADOR
E 1916
Industrias Salvador, Barcelona. Cyclecar.

SALVADOR
USA 1914
Salvador Motor Co., Boston, Massachusetts. Cyclecars.
See "S.J.R."

SALVATOR
F
See "Underberg."

SALVE
B 1908
Herstal.

SALVO
GB 1906
Swan & Co., London. 24/30 hp limousine.

SALZMAN
USA 1897; 1910
George S. Salzman, Boston, Massachusetts.

SAM
I 1924–1928
Societa Automobili e Motori, Legano (Milano). Sporting voiturette.

SAM
I
Genova.
See "Marengo."

SAM
PL 1954–1956
Small sports car designed by Antonin Weiner.

SAMAS
I 1968–c. 1975
Societa Albese Meccanica Autoveicoli Speciali, Ricca d'Alba (Cuneo). 4 × 4 cars.

SAMCA
I 1947
Societa Applicazioni Meccanici Costruzione Automobilistiche, Camillo Monguido & Renato Vitto, Parma. "Atomo" three-wheeler.

SAMCOR
ZA 1994–present
Samcor Ltd., Pretoria. "Ford" (GB) and "Mazda" (J) based cars.

SAMEM
I 1939
S.A. Motocarri Elettrici Moretti, Giovanni Moretti. Electric cars.

SAMPSON
USA 1904; 1911
Alden-Sampson Mfg. Co., Pittsfield, Massachusetts (1904). United States Motor Co., Detroit, Michigan (1911). Absorbed "Crestmobile" and "Consolidated."

SAMSON
USA 1919
Samson Tractor Co., Janesville, Wisconsin. Known for their "Whole Family Car."

SAMUELS
USA 1899
A.A. Samuels, Moline, Ohio. Electric cars.

SAN
IND 1998
Locomotive and Wagon Mfg. Co. Ltd., Bangalore. Sports cars.

SAN ANTONIO
USA 1910
Commercial Motor Car Co., San Antonio, Texas.

SANCHIS
F 1906–1912
Enrique Sanchis, Paris; Courbevoie/Seine. Voiturettes.

SANDERS
USA c. 1905
F.S. Sanders, Cliftondale, Massachusetts. 6 hp automobile.

SANDFORD
F 1922–1939
S. Sandford, Paris. Three-wheelers.

S & M
USA 1913
S & M Motor Co. (Strobel & Martin), Detroit, Michigan. Became "Benham"; Touring cars.

S & M SIMPLEX
USA 1904–1907
Smith & Mabley Mfg. Co., New York, N.Y. Became Simplex Automobile Co.
See "Simplex." 226 cars were made.

SAND PIPER
USA 1968–1973
Kellison, Inc., Lincoln, California. Dune buggy.

SANDRINGHAM
GB 1902–1905
Frank Morriss, King's Lynn, Norfolk. "Daimler" based cars.

SANDRINGHAM
GB   c. 1981–?
SMC Engineering (Bristol) Ltd., Hambrook, Bristol. "Land-Rover" based 6 × 6 passenger car.

SAND ROVER
USA   1968–1973
Poty Enterprises, Santa Fe Springs, California. Dune buggy.

S. & S.
USA   1924–1930
Sayers & Scovill Co., Cincinnati, Ohio.

SAND SHARK
USA   1968–1974
Diana Imports, Royal Oak, Michigan.

SANDUSKY
USA   1902–1904
Sandusky Automobile Mfg. Co. Sandusky Automobile Co., Sandusky, Ohio. Succeeded Ohio Gas Engine Co. Became "Courier." Runabouts.

SANFORD
USA   c. 1905
George W. Sanford, Thomaston, Massachusetts. 4 hp automobile.

SAN FU
PRC   1980s
San Fu Motors.

SAN GIORGIO
I   1905–1909
S.A.I. Costruzione Automobili Terrastri e Marittimi San Giorgio, Genova. License "Napier" (GB).

SAN GIUSTO
I   1922–1925
Off. Mec. Di Cesare Beltrami, Guglielmo Ghioldi & Guido Ucelli, Trieste.
  See "FIAL," "Vaghi."

SAN REMO
USA   c. 1978
Ogner Motors, Ltd., Westlake Village, California. Convertibles only.

SANTA MATILDE
BR   1977–present
Cia. Industrial Sta. Matilde, Rio de Janeiro. Sports cars.

SANTANA
E   1958–present
Santana Motors SA, Madrid. 4 × 4 vehicle.

SANTAX
F   1922–1924
Cyclecars.

SANTLER
GB   1898–1924
C. Santler & Co., Malvern Link, Worcs. Three-wheelers and light cars.

SANTOS-DUMONT
USA   1902–1904
Columbus Motor Vehicle Co., Columbus, Ohio. Former "Columbus." Touring cars. Became "Dumont."

SAPHIER
FL   1981
AR-Studio Xavier Jehle, Schaan. Sports car.
  See "Jehle."

S.A.R.A.
F   1923–1930
Sté. des Autos a Refroidissiment par Air, Courbevoie/Seine; Puteaux/Seine. Air-cooled 1.8-litre cars.

SARALEGUI
F
  See "Mot et Saralegui."

SARAP
F   1970–1977
SARAP, Sundhouse. Dune buggy.

SARATOGA TOURIST
USA   1901
D.B. Smith Co., Utica, N.Y. Also built "Elite" steam car.

SARONI
USA   1879–1880
Professor Henry S. Saroni, St. Paul, Minnesota. Steam vehicles.

S.A.S.
F   1927–1928
Automobiles S.A.S., Paris. 4- and 6-cylinder saloons.

SASCHA
A   1913
Graf Alexander Kolowrat, Wien. Cyclecar.

S.A.T.A.M.
F   1941
Ets Satam, La Courneuce/Seine. Electric coupe.

SATURN
USA   1985–present
Saturn Corporation, Troy, Michigan. Passenger cars.

SAUER
D   1921–1922
Sauer Motoren-Werke GmbH, Hamburg. 10/30 hp cars.

SAURER
CH   1897–1914
Adolphe Saurer AG, Arbon. Passenger cars, later trucks only.

SAURWINE
USA   1901
Louis Saurwine, Slatington, Pennsylvania.

SAUTEL ET SECHUD
F   1902–1904
Sautel et Sechaud, Gentilly/Seine. Three-wheelers.

SAUTTER-HARLÉ
F   1907–1912
Sté. Sautter, Harlé et Cie (1907–1908). Harlé et Cie., Paris (1908–1912). 2- and 4-cylinder cars.

S.A.V.A.
B   1910–1923
Sté. Anversoise pour Fabrication des Voitures Automobiles, Anvers. Passenger cars.
  See "Royal Star."

SAVAGE
USA   1912
M.W. Sawage Factories, Minneapolis, Minnesota.
  See "Dan Patch."

SAVAGE
USA   1914
Savage Motor Car Co., Detroit, Michigan. One touring car was built.

SAVER
GB   1912
Saver Clutch Co. Ltd., Manchester. Prototype.

SAVIANO
USA   1960
Saviano Vehicles, Inc., Warren, Michigan. Jeep-type vehicles.

SAVIGLIANO
I   1895
Steam car.

SAVIO
I   1966–c. 1975
Stabilimento G. Savio, Borgo S. Pietro

(Torino). Light Jeep-type cars. Coachbuilders since 1919.

SAVOIA
I 1916–1918
Ing. G. Pedretti, Milano.

SAVONUZZI
I
See "SVA."

SAW
PRC 1992–present
Second Auto Works, Shenlong Automobiles Corp., Shiyan. "Citroën" (F) based cars.

SAWYER
USA 1856
Elijah Sawyer, Fitchburg, Massachusetts. Steam vehicle.

SAWYER
USA c. 1905
Sawyer Motor Car Co., Somerville, Massachusetts. 10 hp vehicle.

SAXON
USA 1913–1922
Saxon Motor Co., Detroit, Michigan. Reorganized 1915 as Saxon Motors Corp. 92,694 cars were made.

SAYERS
USA 1917–1924
Sayers & Scovill Co., Cincinnati, Ohio. Became Hess & Eisenhart Co. Touring cars with Continental engines.

S.B.
D 1920–1924
Slaby-Beringer Automobilgesellschaft mbH, Berlin. Electric cars.

SB
I 1921
Silvani & Botta, Milano.
See "Silvani."

SBARRO
CH 1971–present
Ateliers d'Études de Construction Automobiles Sarl, Les Tuileries. De Grandson (1971–1972). Sté. de Fabrications d'Automobiles Sbarro, Gressy (1973–1985). ACA Atelier de Construction Automobile, Franco Sbarro Les Tuilleries-de-Grandson (1986–present). Sports cars, luxury cars, replicars.

S.B.K.
S 1904–1906
Svenska Belysning-Kraft AB, Tidaholm. Motor buggy.

S.B.M.
USA 1902
Shaeffer, Bunce & Marvin, Lockport, N.Y. Steam cars.

SCA
I 1899–1901
Societa Costruzioni Automobili, Roma.

SCACCHI
I 1911–1915
Fabbrica Automobili Caesar, Scacchi & C., Chivasso (Torino). 20/30 hp medium-sized cars.

SCALDIA
B
See "Moskvitch" (SU).

SCAMP
GB 1969–1978
Connaught Garage, Brookwood, Surrey. Small terrain 4- and 6-wheeled vehicles. 53 cars built in 1974.

SCAMPOLO
D 1933; 1950–1961
Kraftfahrtechnische Versuchsbau (Walter Komossa & Willy. Arnolds), Recklinghausen. Three-wheelers; sports cars.

SCANIA
S 1902–1912
Maskinfabriks AB Scania, Malmö. 2-cylinder Kamper engines; about 30 4-cylinder cars were made.

SCANIA-VABIS
S 1914–1929
AB Scania-Vabis, Södertälje. 20 and 60hp cars.

S.C.A.P.
F 1912–1929
SA des Automobiles S.C.A.P., Billancourt/Seine; Boulogne-sur-Seine; Courbevoie/Seine. Sports cars.

S.C.A.R.
F 1906–1915
Sté. de Construction Automobile de Reims (Rayet, Lienart. et Cie.), Witryles-Reims/Marne. From 1.3- to 6-litre models.

SCARAB
USA 1932–1936; 1946
Stout Engineering Laboratories, Stout Motor Corp., Detroit, Michigan. Rear-engined streamlined eight.

SCAT
I 1906–1923
Societa Ceirano Automobili Torino, Torino. Absorbed by "SPA."

SCEPTRE
USA c. 1978
Sceptre Motor Car Company, Goleta, California. Sports car.

S.C.H.
B 1927
Light sports cars.

SCHAAP
USA 1900
Schaap Cycle Co., Brooklyn, N.Y. Gasoline tricycle. Also called "Automote."

SCHACHT
USA 1904–1913
G.A. Schacht Mfg. Co., Cincinnati, Ohio. Schacht Motor Car Co. 1909–1913. Continued after 1913 with trucks. Became Schacht Motor Truck Co. 9,256 cars were made.

SCHAEFER
USA 1909
W.E. Schaefer Mfg. Co., Berlin, Wisconsin.

SCHAI
CH 1969
Toni Schai, Sargans. Sports car prototype.

SCHARF GEARLESS
USA 1913–1914
Scharf Gearless Motor Car Co., Westerville, Ohio. Cyclecars.
See "Paine."

SCHASCHE
A 1929
Alois Schasche, Wien. Cyclecar prototype.

SCHÄTZ
D c. 1999
Schätz Tuning, München. Tuning.

SCHAUDEL
F
See "Motobloc."

SCHAUM
USA 1900–1903
Schaum Automobile Mfg. Co., Baltimore, Maryland. Motors and vehicles built to special order. Runabouts.

SCHEBERA
D
See "Cyklon."

SCHEBLER
USA 1908–1909
Wheeler & Schebler, Indianapolis, Indiana. Reportedly built a V-12 roadster.

SCHEELE
D 1899–1910
Heinrich Scheele (1899–1906). Kölner Elektromobil-Gesellschaft H. Scheele, Köln (1906–1910). Electric cars.

SCHEIB
D 1975–present
Automobilbau Scheib GmbH, Ansbach/Bayern. Replicars.

SCHEIBLER
D 1900–1907
Motorenfabrik Fritz Scheibler (1900–1903). Scheibler Automobil-Industrie GmbH, Aachen (1903–1907). Flat-twin engines and friction drive.

SCHELLING
USA c. 1917
Alexander Schellink, Santa Rosa, California.

SCHERMERHORN
USA 1922
C.E. Schermerhorn, Philadelphia, Pennsylvania. Camping car.

SCHEVENINGER
NL 1907
Scheveningsche Rijtuig- en Automobielfabriek, Scheveningen.

SCHILLING
D 1905
V. Chr. Schilling, Suhl Voiturette with Fafnir engine.

SCHILLING
USA 1893
Schilling & Son, San Francisco, California. Gasoline powered tricycle.

SCHINDLER
USA 1895
A.J. Schindler, Chicago, Illinois.

SCHLIG
USA 1904–1905
Schlig Automobile Works. Schlig & Moore Automobile Works, Evanston, Illinois. Two cars were built.

SCHLOEMER
USA 1892
Frank Toepfer Machine Shop, Milwaukee, Wisconsin. Runabout.

SCHLOSSER
CS 1924
Karl Schlosser, továrna automobilu, Liberec. Few light cars were made.

SCHLOSSER
USA 1910–1912
W.H. Schlosser Mfg. Co., New York, N.Y. 7.7-litre 4-cylinder engine.

SCHMID
CH 1922–1939
Schmid, Zürich. Sports cars.

SCHMIDLIN
F 1925–1926
Construction Jean Schmidlin, Paris. 985 cc light cars.

SCHMOTZ
DDR 1974
Rudolf Schmotz, Rodleben. Sports car prototype.

SCHNADER
USA 1907
Milton H. Schnader, Reading, Pennsylvania.
See "Riviera."

SCHNEEBERGER
CH 1987
Replicars.

SCHNEIDER
CH 1965–1967
Karl Schneider, Holzmannshaus. Sports coupe prototypes.

SCHNEIDER
F
See "Brillie" and "Th. Schneider."

SCHNEIDER
USA 1902–1904
J.P. Schneider, Detroit, Michigan.

SCHNEIDER
USA c. 1905
F. Schneider, Lawrence, Massachusetts. 6 hp automobile.

SCHNEIDERS
D 1928
Schneiders, Köln-Mühlheim. Three-wheelers.

SCHNERR
USA 1916
San Francisco, California.

SCHNITTKE
D 1954
Kurt Schnittke. Three-wheelers.

SCHNITZER
1979–present
Schnitzer GmbH, Freilassing. Tuning.
See "AC Schnitzer."

SCHÖCHE
D 1897
Steam car.

SCHOENECK
USA 1914–1916
Schoeneck Co., Chicago, Illinois.
See "O-S" and "Geneva."

SCHOENING
USA 1895
J.W. & C.J. Schoening, Oak Park, Illinois. Kerosene carriage.

SCHOLTE
NL
See "Electricit."

SCHOLZE
USA 1901–1903
Scholze Gas Engine Co., Pawtucket, Rhode Island.

SCHÖNNAGEL
D 1924
Automobil- und Motoren-Versuchs-Werkstätten Ing. H. Schönnagel, Berlin. Light car prototype.

SCHRAM
USA 1913–1914
Schram Motor Car Co., Seattle, Washington. 6-cylinder 6.2-litre engine.

SCHROEDER
USA c. 1904
Charles and Joe Schroeder, Syracuse, Nebraska. Touring car.

SCHUCKERT
D 1899–1900
Elektrizitäts-AG vorm. Schuckert & Co., Nürnberg.
See "Siemens-Schuckert."

SCHULER
USA 1924
Schuler Motor Car Co., Slinger, Wisconsin. Roadsters.

SCHULTZ
USA 1901–1903
John L. Schultz, New York, N.Y.

SCHULZ
D 1904–1906

Maschinenfabrik G. Schulz, Magdeburg. 18hp and 28 hp models.

SCHULZ
D 1985
Schulz-Automobile, Korschenbroich. Tuning.

SCHURICHT
D 1921–1925
Automobilwerk Walter Schuricht, München (1921–1924). Bayerisches Automobilwerk AG, Pasing (1924–1925). Small 2–3-seater cars.

SCHURMAN
USA c. 1905
E.M. Schurman, Everett, Massachusetts. 2.5 hp automobile.

SCHÜSSLER
D 1985
Schüssler Autotechnik, Kerpen-Sindorf. Tuning.

SCHÜTTE-LANZ
D 1922–1923
Schütte-Lanz Kleinautomobil GmbH, Zeesen bei Königswusterhausen. Small cars.

SCHUYLER
USA 1899
Wilton J. Schuyler, Ocenaside, California.

SCHWARTZ
USA 1899–1900
Schwartz Automobile & Carriage Co., Philadelphia, Pennsylvania.

SCHWINN
USA 1896–1902
Arnold Schwinn & Co., Chicago, Illinois. Electric cars.

SCHWORM
USA 1888
Melville F. Schworm, Massillon, Ohio. Steam automobile.

SCIMITAR
USA 1959
Brooks Stevens Associates, Milwaukee, Wisconsin.

SCIOTO
USA 1910–1911
Scioto Motor Car Co., Chillicothe, Ohio. Became Arbenz Motor Co.
See "Arbenz."

SCIREA
I 1914–1927
Officine Arturo Scirea, Milano (1914–1915); Monza (1924–1927). Cyclecars.
See "Turkheimer," "OTAV."

SCIONERI
I 1955–c. 1970s
Carrozzeria Scioneri, Savigliano/Cuneo. Sports cars. Coachbuilders since 1944.

SCIROCCO
D 1969
Kohlmus GmbH, Munchen. Sports coupe.

SCLAVO
I 1911–1914
Automobili Eridano Sclavo, Torino.

SCOIATTOLO
I 1969–1982
Scoiattolo SpA, Riva del Garda. Jeep-type minicars.

SCOOTACAR
GB 1957–1964
Scootacars Ltd., Leeds, York. Three-wheelers.

SCOOTER CAR
USA 1947
2-passenger vehicles.

SCOOTMOBILE
USA 1922
See "Martin."

SCOOTMOBILE
1947–1952
Norman Anderson, Corunna, Michigan. Three-wheeler prototype.

SCORA
F 1974–1977

SCORA
Lapleau. Sports cars. Designed by Jacques Durand.
See "Jide."

SCORPION
GB 1972–1975
Innes Lee Motors Ltd., Telford, Salop. Sports cars.

SCORPION
USA 1954
San Francisco. Glass-fibre bodied sports roadster prototype.

SCOTIA
GB 1907
Glasgow. 17/20 hp engine.

SCOTSMAN
GB 1922–1923
Scotsman Motor Car Co., Glasgow. About 10 light cars built.

SCOTSMAN
GB 1929–1930
Scotsman Motors Ltd., Edinburgh. About 30–40 cars powered by Sara (F) and Meadows (GB) engines.

SCOTT
F 1912
Scott et Cie., Paris. 2.1- and 3.7-litre models.

SCOTT
USA 1900–1904
Ashley Scott & Tod Cooper Co. Scott-Cooper Mfg. Co. J.A. Scott Motor Works, St. Louis, Missouri. Built three vehicles. Absorbed by Scott Automobile Co.
See "Scott Electric."

SCOTT
USA 1901–1904
Scott Iron Works, Baltimore, Maryland.

SCOTT & CLARK
USA 1912–1913
Scott & Clark Corp., Norwich, Connecticut.

SCOTT ELECTRIC
USA 1898–1901
St. Louis Electric Automobile Co. (1898–1900). Scott Automobile Co. (1900–1901). Bought out Scott-Cooper Co. and continued "Scott" production.

SCOTTISH ASTER
GB
See "St. Vincent."

SCOTT-NEWCOMB
USA 1920–1921
Standard Engineering Corp. Scott-Newcomb Steam Motor Co., St. Louis, Missouri. Steam cars.
See "Standard-Steam."

SCOTT SOCIABLE
GB 1921–1925
Scott Autocar Co. Ltd., Bradford, Yorks. Three-wheelers.

SCOUT
GB 1904–1923
Dean and Burden Bros. Ltd. (1904–1908). Scout Motors Ltd., Salisbury, Wilts. (1908–1921). Whatley & Co., Pewsey, Wilts. (1921–1923). Touring cars.

SCOUT
USA 1914
Scout Cyclecar Co., Muskogee, Oklahoma. Cyclecars.

SCRAMBLER
USA 1968–c. 1974
Action Age, Cleveland, Ohio. All-terrain six-wheel vehicles.

SCRIPPS
USA 1911
Scripps Motor Car Co., Detroit, Michigan.

SCRIPPS-BOOTH
USA 1914–1922
The Scripps-Booth Co., Detroit, Michigan. Succeeded "Rocket" cyclecar. Absorbed Sterling Motor Co. and reorganized as Scripps-Booth Corp. Joined General Motors Corp., 1917. About 37,800 cars were made.

SCRIPPS-BOOTH
USA 1914
Scripps-Booth Cyclecar Co., Detroit, Michigan. Cyclecar. January 1915 Puritan Machine Co. bought cyclecar parts business.

SEAB
F 1981
City cars.

SEABROOK
GB 1920–1928
Seabrook Bros. Ltd., London. 4-cylinder 12hp engines with aluminum pistons and cylinder heads.

SEABROOK
USA 1912
Regal Motor Car Co., Detroit, Michigan. English export model of "Regal."

SEAGRAVE
USA 1914
Seagrave Fire Apparatus Co., Columbus, Ohio. Prototypes only.

SEAL
GB 1912–1924
Haynes & Bradshaw (1912–1920). Seal Motors Ltd., Manchester (1920–1924). Three-wheelers.

SEARCHMONT
USA 1900–1903
Searchmont Motor Co., Philadelphia, Pennsylvania. 1902 became Fourier-Searchmont Co. 1904 became Searchmont Automobile Co.

See "Keystone" and "Chadwick." Touring cars.

SEARS
USA 1901
Sears Bros., Indianapolis, Indiana. Steam cars.

SEARS
USA 1908–1912
Sears, Roebuck & Co., Chicago, Illinois. Lincoln Motor Car Works of Chicago took over production 1911. Highwheelers and runabouts.

SEAT
E 1950–present
Sociedad Espanola de Automoviles de Turismo SA (1950–1982). Seat SA, Barcelona (1982–present). "Fiat" (I) based cars until 1982, later own construction.

SEATON-PETTER
GB 1926–1927
British Dominions Car Co. Ltd., Yeovil, Somerset. High, roomy four-seaters with 1.3-litre 2-stroke engines.

SEAZ
SU/RUS 1990–present
Serpukhovskii Avtomobilnii Závod, Serpukhov. Small (invalid) cars.
See "SMZ."

SEBRING
USA 1910–1912
Sebring Motor Car Co. (1910). Sebring Automobile Co. (1911), Sebring, Ohio. Touring cars.

SEBRING GT 2
USA 1967
Universal Plastics, San Carlos, California. Sports cars.

SEBRING
USA 1972–1978
Sebring Vanguard Inc., Sebring, Florida. Electric cars.

SEBRING-SPYDER
D 1997–present
Horst Frischkorn, Urbach. "Porsche" RSK replica.

SECK
D 1898
Willi Seck, Dresden. Friction drive.

2ND CHANCE
USA c. 1993
2nd Chance Classic Inc., Gibbon, Nebraska. Replicars.

SECQUEVILLE-HOYAU
F 1919–1924
SA des Anciens Ets Secqueville-Hoyau, Gennevilliers/Seine. High-quality and expensive light cars.

SECURUS
D 1906
Securus-Automobilbau, Max Ortmann, Berlin. Three-wheelers.

SEDGWICK
USA 1899–1901
I.H. Sedgwick, Richmond, Indiana. Large touring carriages.

SEELIGER
USA 1904
Emil Seeliger, Lockhart, Texas. One gasoline carriage was produced.

SEELY
USA 1901–1902
Seely Mfg. Co., Pittsburgh, Pennsylvania.

SEELY
USA 1905
F.L. Seely, Princeton, New Jersey. Steam car.

SEEMAG-SEEBACH
CH 1922
Zürich. Passenger cars.

SEENEY
USA 1914
Seeney Mfg. Co., Muncie, Indiana. Cyclecars. It was merely a typo for the "Feeny."

SEETSTU
GB 1906–1907
James McGeoch & Co., Paisley, Renfrewshire. 6 or 7 three-wheelers were built.

SEFRIN
USA 1904–1905
Charles Sefrin Motor Carriage Co., Brooklyn, N.Y.

SEFTON
GB 1903
Liverpool & Manchester Motor Manufacturing Co., Liverpool. Voiturette prototype.

SEIDEL
USA 1908–1909
Seidel Buggy Co., Richmond, Indiana. Highwheeled motor buggy.

SEIDEL-AROP
D 1925–1926

Arop Automobilbau GmbH, Berlin. Frameless car prototype.

SEIG
USA 1899
C.H. Seig Mfg. Co., Milwaukee, Wisconsin.

SEKINE
USA 1923
Sekine & Co. (Japan). Austin M. Wolf, New York, N.Y. One-wheel drive vehicles for export to Japan.

SEKURA
DK 1985
Sports car prototype.

SEKURUS
D 1906
Sekurus-Mobilbau Max Ortmann, Berlin. Three-wheelers.

SELDEN '1877'
USA 1906
Electric Vehicle Co., Hartford, Connecticut. One car built as court exhibit for defense in Selden patent case. Another car built by George Selden's sons in Rochester, N.Y., for the same purpose.

SELDEN
USA 1907–1914
Selden Motor Vehicle Co., Rochester, N.Y. Absorbed Buffalo Gas Motor Car Co. 7,424 cars were made. Continued with trucks.

SELF
S 1916; 1919; 1922
Axel H. and Per Weiertz, Svedala. Light car prototypes.

SELF-CONTAINED
USA 1896
Self Contained Equipment Motor Vehicle Co., Dorchester,. Massachusetts.
See "Walkins."

SELLERS
USA 1909–1912
Sellers Automobile Co., Elkhart, Indiana. Succeeded St. Joe Motor Car Co. Later moved to Hutchinson,. Kansas. In 1919 became Central States Engineering Co. Touring cars.

SELLEW-ROYCE
CDN 1911
Sellew Motors Limited, Toronto, Ontario.

SELMA
USA 1900
Selma Automobile Co., Selma, California.

SELVE
D 1923–1929
Selve-Automobilwerke AG, Hameln/Weser. 2-, 2.3-, 2.8- and 3.1-litre touring cars.

S.E.M.
F
See "Morisse."

S.E.M.
USA 1914
Sharp Engineering & Mfg. Co., Detroit, Michigan. Became "Sharp."

SEMAG
CH 1920
Seebacher Maschinenbau AG, Zürich. 11 hp light cars.

SEMPLE
USA 1846
General James Semple, Springfield, Illinois. Steam vehicle.

SENATOR
USA 1907–1910
Victor Automobile Co., Ridgeville, Indiana. Touring cars.

SENATOR
USA 1912
Senator Motor Car Co., Pittsburgh, Pennsylvania. Touring cars and roadsters.

SENECA
USA 1917–1924
Seneca Motor Car Co., Fostoria, Ohio. Succeeded "Fostoria" (1915–1916). 5,084 cars were made.

SENECHAL
F 1921–1929
Senechal et Cie., Courbevoie/Seine (1921–1925). Sté. Industrielle et Commerciale, Gennevilliers/Seine (1925–1929). Sporting voiturettes and sports cars.

SENG ET HENRY
F 1901–1902
Light cars.

SENSAUD DE LAVAUD
F
See "De Lavaud."

SEN SEENEY
USA 1898–1901
Dr. E.M. Sen Seeney, St. Louis, Missouri. Runabout.

SEQUOIA
USA 1914
Sequoia Motor Car Co., San Leandro, California. Electric car.

SEQUOIA
USA 1926
Gilbert E. Porter, Glendale, California. Two roadsters were made.

SERA
F 1960
Sera S.A., Paris. Sports cars with "Panhard" air-cooled engines.

SERENISSIMA
I 1965–1971
Conte Giovanni Volpi di Misurata, Modena; Bologna. Sports cars.
See "ATS."

SERPENTINA
USA 1915
Claudius Mezzacasa, New York, N.Y. 1:2:1 (rhomboid) wheel arrangement, designed by Fuscaldo.
See "Fuscaldo" (I).

SERPOLLET
F 1887–1907
Leon Serpollet (1887–1900). Gardner Serpollet, Paris (1900–1907). Steam cars.

SERPOLLET ITALIANA
I 1906–1908
Serpollet Italiana S.A., Milano. Steam cars.

SERRA
E 1971–1973
Barcelona. "Dodge" (E) based coupe prototype.

SERRIFILE
USA 1921–1922
Serrifile Motor Co., Hollis, N.Y. 5-passenger sedan.

SERTUM
I 1935–1950
Off. Mec. Fausto Alberti, Milano. One car produced.

SERVICE
USA 1911
Service Motor Car Co., Kankakee, Illinois. Highwheelers.

SERVICE
USA 1914
Rochester Motors Co., Rochester, N.Y. Cyclecars. Optional friction or gear drive.

SERVITOR
USA 1907
Barnes Mfg. Co., Sandusky, Ohio. Runabouts. Became "Barnes."

SESSIONS
USA 1904; 1914
Claude Sessions, Waynesville, Illinois. Steam runabout; air-cooled cyclecar.

SEVEN LITTLE BUFFALOS
USA 1908
De Schaum Motor Syndicate, Buffalo, N.Y. 54 highwheelers were built.

SEVERIN
USA 1920–1922
Severin-Mokaw Motors Co. Severin Motor Car Co., Kansas City, Missouri. Metropolitan Motors Corp., Oakland, California. 307 cars were made.

SEXTO-AUTO
USA 1912
Reeves-Sexto-Octo Co., Columbus, Indiana. Six-wheel experimental car. Built by "Reeves."

SEYMOUR-TURNER
GB 1906–1907
See "Turner."

S.F.A.T.
F 1903–1904
Sté. Francaise des Autos Thermo-Pneumatiques, Paris. A conventional engine drove an air compressor which drove the rear wheels through a turbine.

SFINX STANT
F 1933
Three-wheeler.

SFJ
D 1993
SFJ, Hagenbach. Tuning.

S.G.V.
USA 1911–1915
Acme Motor Car Co. (S.G.V. Co.), Reading, Pennsylvania. Succeeded "Acme." Sold in New York City as "American Lancia." Reported sold by receiver September 1915 for $55,000. Touring cars and runabouts.
See "Phianna."

SH
S 1989–1993
SH-Design, Landskrona. Sports car kit.

SHABAZ
IR 1984
Iran National Industrial Manufacturing Co., Teheran. 4 × 4 Jeep-type car.

SHAD-WYCK
USA 1917–1923
Shadburne Brothers Company, Chicago, Illinois. Factory at Elkhart, Indiana. Associated with Combined Motors Corp.
See "Bour-Davis."

SHAEFFER-BUNCE
USA 1902
Shaeffer-Bunce & Co., Lockport, N.Y. Complete vehicles, less engines. Formerly Shaeffer-Bunce & Marvin.
See "S.B.M."

SHAFER
USA 1915
C.B. Shafer, Detroit, Michigan.

SHAFFER STEAMER
USA 1903–1904
Shaffer Boiler & Engine Mfg. Co., Baltimore, Maryland.

SHAIN
USA 1902–1903
See "Rockaway."

SHAMROCK
IRL 1959–1960
Shamrock Motors Ltd., Tralee, Kerry. Fiberglass bodied sports cars. 4 were made.

SHAMROCK
CDN 1904–1914
William Mimna, Wardsville, Ontario.

SHAMROCK
USA 1906
Henry J. Casey, Seattle, Washington. Runabout.

SHANGHAI
PRC 1965–present
Shanghai Motor Factory, Shanghai (1965–1983). Shanghai-Volkswagen Automotive Corp., Anting, Shanghai (1983–present). Own construction, later "Volkswagen" (D) based cars.

SHANNON
USA 1902–1903
Shannon Automobile Co., Owosso, Michigan.

SHARON
USA 1915
Driggs-Seabury Ordnance Corp., Sharon, Pennsylvania. Cyclecars. Introduced as the "Twombly" (1913–1915).

SHARP
USA 1901
Harry Sharp, Omaha, Nebraska. Steam cars.

SHARP
USA 1914–1915
Sharp Engineering & Mfg. Co., Detroit, Michigan. Cyclecars. Formerly "S.E.M."

SHARP-ARROW
USA 1908–1910
The Sharp-Arrow Automobile Co., Trenton, New Jersey. Reorganized February 1910 with $75,000 new capital. Factory moved to East Stroudsburg, Pennsylvania as International Boiler Co. Speedsters.

SHATSWELL
USA 1901–1903
H.K. Shatswell & Co., Dedham, Massachusetts. Steam cars. Mostly steam components and running gear for home assembly.

SHAUM
USA 1905
Shaum Automobile Mfg. Co., Baltimore, Maryland. Typographical error in contemporary journals.
See "Schaum."

SHAVER STEAMER
USA 1895
Joseph Shaver Granite & Marble Co., Milwaukee, Wisconsin. Built for Chicago Times-Herald Race.

SHAW
USA 1900
Shaw Motor Vehicle Co., Boston, Massachusetts. Steam car.

SHAW
USA 1920–1921
Walden L. Shaw Livery Company, Chicago, Illinois. Touring cars.

SHAW
USA 1920–1930
Shaw Manufacturing Co., Galesburg, Kansas. Runabouts.

SHAWMUT
USA 1906–1908
Shawmut Motor Car Co., Stoneham, Massachusetts. Succeeded Phelps Motor Vehicle Co.
See "Phelps."

SHEARER
AUS 1896
Mannum, S.A.

SHEFFIELD-SIMPLEX
GB 1907–1922
Sheffield-Simplex Motor Works Ltd., Sheffield, Yorks. Flexible engines with 2 forward speeds.

SHELBY
USA 1903
Shelby Motor Car Co., Shelby, Ohio. Succeeded Beardsley & Hobbs Mfg. Co. Formerly "Darling."

SHELBY
USA 1962–1970; 1993–present
Shelby-American Inc., Santa Fe Springs, California (1962); Venice, California (1962–1967). Shelby Automotive, Ionia, Michigan (1967–1968). Ford Motor Co., Detroit, Michigan (1968–1970). Shelby Automobiles, Inc., Whittier, California (1986–1989). Carroll Shelby Enterprises, Gardena, California (1993–present). High performance sports cars.

SHELDON
USA 1905
Robert E. Sheldon, Fairbanks, Alaska.

SHELDON
USA 1909
Sheldon Axle Co., Wilkes-Barre, Pennsylvania.

SHELDON
USA 1941
Roy Sheldon, Redmond, Oregon. "Horse car."

SHELL VALLEY MOTORS
USA 1990s
Shell Valley Motors, Platte Center, Nevada. Kit cars.

SHELTER
NL 1958
Van der Goot, Terborg. About 23 three-wheelers were built.

SHENLONG
PRC 1997–present
Shenlong Automobile Corporation, Shiyan, Hubei. "Citroën" (F) license. See "Fukang."

SHEPHARD
F 1900
E.F. Shephard, Levallois-Perret/Seine. 5hp Dore engine.

SHEPMOBILE
USA 1903–1905
Robert C. Shepherd, Los Angeles, California. 7 hp runabout.

SHEPPEE
GB 1912
Sheppee Motor Co., York. Steam car.

SHERET
GB 1924–1925
Arnott & Harrison Ltd., London. A more expensive version of the "New Carden."

SHERIDAN
USA 1920–1921
Sheridan Motor Car Co., Muncie, Indiana. General Motors subsidiary, plant and tools sold to Durant, announced May 1921. Became "Durant 6."

SHERILL & SMITH
USA 1911
Sherill & Smith, Tullahoma, Tennes.
See Highwheelers.

SHERKATE SAHAMI
IR 1959–1977
Sherkate Sahami Ltd., Teheran. "Jeep" (USA) and "Rambler" (USA) license.

SHERMAN
USA c. 1905
William T. Sherman, Cranston, Rhode Island.

SHERWOOD
GB 1988
Sherwood Universal Vehicle, Pinxton, Nottinghamshire. Estate car.

SHIBAURA
J 1954
Minicar.

SHIELS
AUS 1933
Phoenix Motors Pty Ltd., St. Kilda, Victoria. Light sports cars.

SHILLITO
USA 1901
John Shillito Co., Cincinnati, Ohio. Steam car.

SHOEMAKER
USA 1906–1908
Shoemaker Automobile Co., Freeport, Illinois. Moved to Elkhart, Indiana 1908. Reported bankrupt June 1908. and absorbed by St. Joe Motor Car Co. Touring cars.

SHORT
USA 1914
Henry M. Short, Penn Yan, N.Y. Cyclecar.

SHORT-ASHBY
GB 1921–1923
Short Bros. Ltd., Rochester, Kent (1921–1922). Ashby Motors Ltd., Manchester (1922–1923). Light cars.

SHUGERS
USA 1899
Shugers Brothers, Coldwater, Michigan. Gasoline-powered motor carriage.

S.H.W.
D 1924–1925
Schwäbische Hüttenwerke AG, Böblingen. Three experimental cars with front-wheel drive, independent suspension and aluminum body.

SIAC
I 1907–1911
Societa Italiana Auto Cars, Alessandria.
See "Auto Cars."

SIAD
I 1906–1909
Societa Italiana Automobili Darracq.
See "SAID."

SIAL
I
Societa Italiana Automobili Lentz.
See "Lentz."

SIAM
I 1907
Societa Italiana Automobili Marittima, Genova.

SIAM
I 1921–1923
Societa Italiana Automobili Milano, Olivio Pellegati, Milano. 2-litre 6-cylinder OHC engine.

SIATA
I 1926–1970
Societa Italiana Applicazioni Techniche Auto-Aviatore (1926–1949). Societa Italiana Auto Trasformazioni Accessori (1949–1959). Siata-Abarth (Giorgio

Ambrosini & Carlo Abarth) (1959–1961). Siata Auto, Torino (1961–1970). Sports cars.

SIBAT
PI 1975
"Citroën" (F) based open cars.

SIBLEY
GB 1902
John Sibley & Co., Maidstone, Kent.

SIBLEY
USA 1910–1911
Sibley Motor Car Co., Detroit, Michigan. Became "Sibley-Curtiss."

SIBLEY-CURTISS
USA 1911–1912
Sibley-Curtiss Motor Co., Simsbury, Connecticut. Succeeded "Sibley"; Touring cars.

SIBONA-BASSANO
I 1962–1969
Carrozzeria Sibona-Bassano, Torino. Sports cars with "Simca" (F) components.

ŠIBRAVA
CS 1921–1926
Jaroslav Šibrava, továrna automobilních tříkolek, Praha. Three-wheelers of "Walter" design; 4-wheeled cars of own design.

SIC
I 1924–1925
Societa Italiana Cyclecar, Chiavari. Cyclecars.

SICAM
F 1919–1922
SICAM, Pantin/Seine. 496cc cyclecars.

SICRA
I 1972
Sicra Big-buggy, Roma. Dune buggy.

SIDDELEY
GB 1902–1904
Siddeley Autocar Co. Ltd., Coventry, Warwickshire (1902–1903). Vickers, Son and Maxim Ltd., Crayford, Kent (1903–1904). Complicated inter-relationship between "Siddeley," "Deasy," "Wolseley" and "Armstrong." Touring cars.

SIDDELEY-DEASY
GB 1912–1919
Siddeley-Deasy Motor Manufacturing Co. Ltd., Coventry, Warwicks. Derived from the "Deasy" cars.

SIDÉA
F 1912–1924
Sté. Industrielle des Automobiles "Sidéa," Mezieres-Charleville. Sports cars.

SIDEA
I 1914
M. Fabry, Torino.

SIDUS
I 1936
Milano.

SIEFKER
USA 1880
William Siefker, Seymour, Indiana. Steam automobile.

SIEGEL
D 1908–1910
Feodor Siegel, Automobil- und Maschinenfabrik, Schönebeck/Elbe. 2-cylinder 9 hp cars.

SIEGFRIED
D
    See "Reissig."

SIEMENS-SCHUCKERT
D 1906–1910
Siemens-Schuckert GmbH, Automobilwerk Nonnendamm, Berlin. Gasoline and electric cars.

SIENNA
GB 1976–1978
Anthony Stevens Automobiles Ltd., Warwick. Replicars.

SIEVER
USA 1903
Siever Carriage Co., Oneida, N.Y. Experimental gasoline touring car.

SIG
CH 1921; 1928–1929
Schweizerische Industrie-Gesellschaft, Neuhausen. Tandem cyclecars. "Martini" passenger cars assembled 1928–1929. Later electric light delivery vans.

SIGMA
CH 1909–1914
Sté. Industrielle Genevoise de Mécanique et Automobiles, Chene-Bougeries. Medium-sized touring cars.

SIGMA
F 1913–1928
Sté. des Automobiles Sigma, Levallois-Perret/Seine. Ballot engines.

SIGMA
H 1988
Tiszántúli Autojavító Vállalat. City car.

SIGMA
USA 1914
Sigma Motor Car Co., Boston, Massachusetts. Cyclecars.

SIGMA
ZA 1976–?
Sigma Motor Corporation. "Chrysler" (AUS), "Mitsubishi" (J) and "Mazda" (J) under license.

SIGNET
USA 1913–1914
Fenton Engineering Co., Fenton, Michigan. Cyclecar. Known as "Fenton," then "Koppin." Name "Signet" never used.

SILA
I 1960
Societa Industriale Lavorazioni Acciai, Torino. 200 cc 11 hp minicar prototype.

SILENT
USA 1910–1912
Sioux Automobile Co., Milwaukee, Wisconsin.
    See "Silent Sioux." Both names apply to same vehicle.

SILENT
USA 1915
Silent Engine Co., Los Angeles, California.

SILENT KNIGHT
USA 1905–1907
Knight & Kilbourne Co., Chicago, Illinois. Touring cars.

SILENT NORTHERN
USA 1902
Correct name for this vehicle is "Northern."

SILENT SIOUX
USA 1909–1912
Sioux Automobile Mfg. Co., Sioux Falls, North Dakota (1909–1910). Became Sioux Automobile Mfg. Co., Milwaukee, Wisconsin (1910–1912). Former "Fawick Flyer."

SILHOUETTE
GB 1970–1972
Silhouette Cars Ltd., London. Sports cars and kits.

SILVA
I 1906
Milano.

SILVA
I
Società Italiana Licenza Veronese Amilcar.
See "Amilcar Italiana."

SILVA-CORONEL
F 1927–1928
Five cars were built.

SILVANI
I 1921–1924
Silvani Fabbrica Automobili, Milano.
See "SB."

SILVER
USA 1914–1919
C.T. Silver, New York, N.Y. Roadsters.

SILVER HAWK
GB 1920–1921
Silver Hawk Motors Ltd., Cobham, Surrey. Sports cars.

SILVER KNIGHT
USA 1914–1915
C.T. Silver, New York, N.Y. Rebuilt "Willys-Knight."

SILVERTOWN
GB 1905–1910
The Silvertown Co., London. Electric cars.

SILVESTER
USA 1897
Henry Silvester, St. Louis, Missouri.

SIMA
I
Società Italiana Motori Aster.
See "Aster Italiana," "Auto Cars."

SIMA-STANDARD
F 1920–1922
Automobiles Sima-Standard, Courbevoie/Seine. 860cc light cars.

SIMA-VIOLET
F 1924–1929
Sté. Industrielle de Materiel Automobile, Paris; Courbevoie/Seine. 496cc sports cars.

SIMCA
F 1935–1981
Sté. Industrielle de Mécanique et Carrosserie Automobile, Nanterre/Seine (1935–1961). Poissy/Seine-et-Oise (1954–1970). Chrysler France SA, Poissy/Seine-et-Oise (1970–1981). Passenger cars.

SIMI
F c. 1984
S.I.M.I. SA, Saint-Germain Laval. 4 × 4 vehicles.

SIMMERINGER
A 1905–1906
Maschinen- und Waggonbau-Fabriks AG, Wien-Simmering. Passenger cars.

SIMMONDS
USA 1891–1894
Clarence L. Simmonds, Lynn, Massachusetts. Steam car.

SIMMONS
USA 1910
Simmons Motor & Truck Co., Wilmington, Delaware.

SIMMONS
USA c. 1905
H.C. Simmons, North Bennington, Vermont. 6.5 hp automobile.

SIMMS
GB 1901–1908
Simms Manufacturing Co. Ltd., London. Passenger cars.
See "Simms-Welbeck."

SIMMS
USA 1920
Simms Motor Car Co., Atlanta, Georgia. Started in Wilmington, Delaware, reported March 1920. Reported bankrupt October 1920. Touring cars.

SIMMS-WELBECK
GB 1898–1908
See "Simms."

SIMONDS
USA 1893
Clarence L. Simonds, Lynn, Massachusetts. Steam carriage.

SIMPA
F 1984–1988
Simpa SA, Avrille. City cars.

SIMPLEX
NL 1899–1914
NV Maatschappij Simplex, Amsterdam. Not more than 250 cars built.

SIMPLEX
USA 1899–1901
Simplex Motor Vehicle Co., Danvers, Massachusetts. Sream car.
See "Hood."

SIMPLEX
USA 1907–1915
Simplex Automobile Co. Inc., New York, N.Y. (1907–1913). Simplex Motor Car Co., New Brunswick, New Jersey (1913–1919). Succeeded S & M Simplex (Smith & Mabley) 1904–1907. Merged with Crane Motor Co. 1915. Became "Crane-Simplex," model of "Simplex-Crane"; 1,865 cars were made.

SIMPLEX-PERFECTA
GB 1900
Randolph Works, Normanton, Derby. Light cars.

SIMPLIC
GB 1914
Wadden & West, Cobham, Surrey. G.W. Wadden, Weybridge, Surrey. Cyclecars.

SIMPLICIA
USA 1910
Simplicia Automobile Co., New Orleans, Louisiana.

SIMPLICITIES
USA 1907–1910
Simplicities Automobile Co., Middletown, Connecticut.
See "Kitto."

SIMPLICITY
USA 1902
Ira J. Hollensbee, Greensburg, Indiana.

SIMPLICITY
USA 1907–1911
Evansville Automobile Co., Evansville, Indiana. Former "Windsor." Touring cars.

SIMPLICITY SIX
USA 1920–1921
Simplicity Motorss Corp., Seattle, Washington. Touring cars.

SIMPLO
USA 1908–1909
Cook Motor Vehicle Co., St. Louis, Missouri. Highwheelers.

SIMPLUM
A 1920
Simplum-Autobau- und Vertriebsgesellschaft, Wien. Cyclecars.

SIMPSON
GB 1897–1904
John Simpson, Stirling. About 20 steam cars built.

SIMPSON
USA 1906
William G. Simpson, Detroit, Michigan.

SIMS
I 1908–1909
Societa Italiana Merz & Stinchi, Torino.

SIMSON
D 1911–1934
Waffenfabrik Simson & Co., Suhl/Thüringen. Sports and touring cars.

SINCLAIR
GB 1899–1902
E.H. Clift & Co., London. Light car.

SINCLAIR
GB 1983–1987
Sir Clive Sinclair Vehicles Ltd., Electric one-seater three-wheelers.

SINCLAIR-SCOTT
USA 1906–1907
Sinclair-Scott Co., Luke, Maryland. Succeeded "Ariel." Became "Maryland."

SINGER
GB 1905–1970
Singer & Co. Ltd., Coventry, Warwickshire (1905–1936); Birmingham (1927–1936). Singer Motors Ltd., Coventry, Warwickshire (1936–1956); Birmingham (1936–1956); Ryton-on-Dunsmore, Warwickshire (1956–1970). Passenger and sports cars.

SINGER
USA 1914–1918
Singer Motor Co., Long Island City, N.Y.; Mount Vernon, N.Y. Succeeded Palmers & Singer Mfg. Co. Formerly "Palmer-Singer."

SINGLE-CENTER
USA 1906–1908
Single-Center Buggy Co., Evansville, Indiana. Auto-buggy. Became "Traveler."

SINPAR
F 1907–1914
Automobiles Sinpar, Courbevoie/Seine. Voiturette.

SINPAR
F 1964–c. 1974
Sinpar Appareils S.A., Colombes/Seine. 4 × 4 conversion of "Renault."

SINTZ
USA 1902–1904
Sintz Gas Engine Co., Grand Rapids, Michigan. Gasoline motor carriage. Acquired by "Pungs-Finch."

SIPANI
IND 1982–present
Sipani Automobiles Limited, Bangalore. "Reliant" (GB) based cars.

SIPE & SIGLER
USA 1900
Sipe & Sigler Co., Cleveland, Ohio. Electric cars.

SIROCCO
USA 1970
Sirocco Industries, Santa Ana, California. Kit cars with gull wing doors, hard top body on a "Volkswagen" (D) chassis.

SIRRON
GB 1909–1916
Cresswell, Norris & Co. Ltd., London. Sirron Cars Ltd., London; Southall, Middlesex. Conventional shaft-driven cars.

SIR VIVAL
USA 1960
Hollow Boring Co., Worcester, Massachusetts. Safety car prototype.

SIVA
GB 1969–1975
Neville Trickett Design Ltd., Blandford, Dorset (1969–1971). Siva Motor Car Co. Ltd., Aylesbury, Bucks. (1972–1975). Small plastic-bodied sports cars.

SIVA
I 1907
Societa Italiana Vetture Automobili, Milano.
See "Ardita," "Barison," "Chiribiri."

SIVA
I 1967–1970
SIVA Srl, Lecce. Sports cars.

SIVE
I 1899–1903
Societa Italiana Vetture Elettriche Turrinelli & C., Milano.
See "Camona."

SIVIERE
F 1933
Three-wheelers.

SIX & VANCE
USA 1914
Don Six & Claire Vance, Logansport, Indiana. Propeller-powered light car.

SIZAIRE-BERWICK
F/GB 1913–1927
Sté. Nouvelle des Autos Sizaire, Courbevoie, Seine (1913–1927). F.W. Berwick & Co. Ltd., London (1920–1925). 4.5-litre touring cars.

SIZAIRE-FRÈRES
F/B 1923–1931
Sté. Nouvelle des Autos Sizaire, Courbevoie, Seine (1923–1929). Sté. Belge des Automobiles Sizaire, Anvers (1929–1931). Passenger cars.
See "Belga Rise" (B).

SIZAIRE-NAUDIN
F 1905–1921
Ets Sizaire et Naudin. Sté. Nouvelle des Autos Sizaire, Paris. Small sporting voiturettes.

SIZER
USA 1911
Sizer Co., Buffalo, N.Y.

S.J.R.
USA 1915–1916
S.J.R. Motor Co., Boston, Massachusetts. $945 4-seater roadsters.
See "Salvador."

SK
USA 1968
Stevens Boat Co., Gardena, California. Dune buggy.

SKAF
PL 1921
Fabryka Malych Samochodow Skaf, Warszawa. 3 cyclecar prototypes were built.

SKAVRONSKIY
SU 1901–1902
Sankt Peterburg.

SKELTON
USA 1920–1922
Skelton Motors Corp. Travers Motors Co., St. Louis, Missouri. Car introduced December 1919. Built in plant of St. Louis Car Co. 1,355 cars were made.

SKENE
USA 1900–1901
J.W. Skene Cycle & Automobile Co., Lewiston, Maine. Two steam cars built. Later Skene American Automobile Co.

SKEOCH
GB 1921
J.B. Skeoch, Dalbeattie, Kirkcudbright. 8 or 10 cyclecars built.

SKIMABOUT
USA 1908
Palmer & Singer Mfg. Co., New York, N.Y.
See "Palmer & Singer."

SKIRROW
GB 1936–1939
H. Skirrow, London. About 100 cars with tuned 1-litre 80 hp JAP engine were made.

SKLAREK
USA 1905
Clifford Sklarek, Canton, Illinois. One runabout built for inventor's use.

ŠKODA
CS/CZ 1925–present
Akciová společnost dříve Škodovy závody, Plzeň (1925–1930). Akciová společnost pro automobilový prumysl, Mladá Boleslav (1930–1945). Automobilové závody, n.p. (1946–1987). Automobilový koncern Škoda, s.p. (1987–1990). Škoda, automobilová a.s., Mladá Boleslav (1991–present). Passenger cars. Member of the Volkswagen Group from 1991.

ŠKODA HISPANO-SUIZA
CS 1925–1927
Akciová společnost dříve Škodovy závody, Plzeň. Luxury passenger cars built under "Hispano-Suiza" (F) license. 100 cars were built.

SKOPAK
PAK c. 1973
Haroon Industries Ltd., Karachi. "Škoda" (CS) assembled cars.

SKORPION
USA 1952–1954
Wilro Company, Pasadena, California. Fiberglass sports cars.

SKRIVA
F 1922–1924
Automobiles Skriva, Paris. 2.4-litre Sergant engine.

S.K. SIMPLEX
GB 1908–1910
Smeddle & Kennedy Ltd., Newcastle-upon-Tyne. Light two-seater.

SKYLINE
USA 1964
Skyline Inc., Jamaica, N.Y. Sports cars.

SLAMA
USA 1901
Lewis Slama, Humboldt, Nebraska. Steam car.

SLATER
USA c. 1905
C.B. Slater, Waterbury, Connecticut.

SLATTERY
USA 1889
M.M.M. Slattery, Ft. Wayne, Indiana. Electric tricycle.

SLEVOGT
D 1930–1933
Karl Slevogt Kleinwagenbau, Würzburg. Three-wheelers.

S.L.I.M.
F 1920–1929
Sté. Lyonnaise de l'Industrie Mécanique et Autos Pilain, Lyon. Touring cars.

S.L.M.-PESCARA
CH 1899; 1934–1935
Schweizerische Lokomotiv- und Maschinenfabrik, Winterthur. Sports cars.

SLOAN
USA 1900
Ernest V. Sloan, Bridgeport, Connecticut. Gasoline motor carriage.

SLOANE
GB 1907
Sloane Motor Works, London. Light cars.

SLY
USA 1902
Ethan E. Sly, Norwalk, Ohio. Steam car.

S.M.
GB 1904–1905
S.M. Car Syndicate Ltd., London. Steam cars.

SMALL
USA 1910–1911
Small Motor Car Co., Detroit, Michigan.
See "Cavac."

SMART
D 1997–present
Micro Compact Car GmbH, Renningen. Mini cars.

SMB
I 1907–1910
Societa Meccanica Bresciana, Brescia. 3.8- and 4.2-litre cars.

SMELSER
USA 1904
Smelser Automobile Co., Akron, Ohio.

SMIG
I 1906–1907
Societa Meccanica Italo-Ginevrina, Torino.

SMILE
D 1996
Greenpeace e.V., Hamburg. SmILE (Small, Intelligent, Light, Efficient) car with low fuel consumption engine technology.

SMISOR
USA 1899
Smisor Bros., Webster City, Iowa. Two-seater buggy.

SMITH
DK 1907
Odense.

SMITH
USA 1895
O.E. Smith, Hartford, Connecticut.

SMITH
USA 1895
I.D. Smith, Pittsburgh, Pennsylvania.

SMITH
USA 1896–1899
Springfield Cornice Co. (Hinsdale Smith), Springfield, Massachusetts.
See "Meteor." Also called "Smith Spring Motor."

SMITH
USA 1900
Smith Automobile & Machine Co., Los Angeles, California. One car produced.

SMITH
USA 1903–1911
Smith Automobile Co., Topeka, Kansas. Also known as "Veracity" (1899–1904). Became "Great Smith" (1907–1911). 770 cars were made.

SMITH
USA 1910–1915
A.O. Smith Co., Milwaukee, Wisconsin.

SMITH & BIGGS
USA 1900

A.D. Smith & George T. Biggs, St. Paul

SMITH & DIENHART
USA   1901
Edgar F. Smith & Frank Dienhart, Lafayette, Indiana.

SMITH & MABLEY SIMPLEX
USA   1904–1907
Smith & Mabley Co., New York, N.Y.
   See "S & M Simplex."

SMITH FLYER
USA   1916–1919
A.O. Smith Co., Milwaukee, Wisconsin. Patents sold to Briggs & Stratton 1919.
   See "Briggs & Stratton."

SMITH F.W.D. BUGGY
USA   1906
D.W.G. Smith, Lexington Junction, Missouri.

SMITH STEAMER
USA   1902
Smith Co., Topeka, Kansas. Two cars produced.

SMOKE
USA   1959
Argonaut Motor Machine Co., Cleveland, Ohio. Listed at $26,000–$32,000.
   See "Argonaut."

SMRTKA
CS   1924–1926
Bratří Smrtkové, továrna malých automobilu, Praha. Cyclecars.

SMS
D   1993–present
SMS-Motorsport, Cadolzburg. Tuning.

SMYK
PL   1957–1958
Szczecinska Fabryka Motocykli, Szczecin. Small car prototypes.

SMYSER
USA   1902
L.B. Smyser & Co., New York, N.Y.

SMZ
SU   1952–1990
Serpukhovskii Motocikletnii Závod, Serpukhov. Small cars for handicapped.
   See "Oka," "SEAZ."

S.N.
USA   1921
Standard Engineering Co., St. Louis, Missouri.

   See "Standard Steam" (1920), and "Scott-Newcomb."

S.N.A.
CH   1903–1913
Sté. Neuchateloise d'Automobiles, Bourdy, Neuchatel. Passenger cars.

SNAC
F   1941
Usine d'Aviation SNAC, Paris. Rhomboid wheel placement.

SNELL
USA   1900
Frank Snell, Waterville, N.Y. Gasoline runabout.

SNELL
USA   1904–1905
Snell Motor Car & Truck Co., Toledo, Ohio.

SNOBURNER
USA   1914
Pittmans & Dean, Detroit, Michigan.

SNODEAL
USA   1902
Snodeal Mfg. Co., Baltimore, Maryland. Electric car.

SNOECK
B
   See "Bolide."

SNYDER
USA   1900
H.P. Snyder & Co., Little Falls, N.Y. Steam cars.

SNYDER
USA   1908–1909
D.D. Snyder & Co., Danville, Illinois. Runabouts.

SNYDER
USA   1914
Snyder Motor & Mfg. Co., Cleveland, Ohio. Cyclecars.

SOAMES
GB   1903–1904
Langdon-Davies Motor Co. Ltd., London. Chain-driven 11 hp cars.

SOCEMA-GREGOIRE
F   1952
Société de Construction et d'Équipements Mecaniques pour l'Aviation, Paris. Experimental gas turbine cars.

SOCIETA ITALO-SVIZZERA
I   1905
Societa Italo-Svizzera Costruzioni Meccaniche, Bologna.

SOCIETA MILANESE
I   1904
Societa Milanese Industrie Meccaniche, Milano.

SOCIETA ROMANA
I   1899–1903
Societa Romana per l'Esercizio e la Costruzione di Automobili. Elettriche, Roma.

SOCIÉTÉ DES PONTS MOTEURS
F   1913–1914
Sté. des Ponts Moteurs, Paris. Forecars.

SÖDERBLOM
S   1903
Söderbloms Gjuteri & Mekaniska Verkstad, Eskilstuna. 2-cylinder cars.

SOFRAVEL
F   c. 1953
"Coccinelle" minicar.

SÖHNLEIN
D   1873; 1877
Julius Wilhelm Heinrich Söhnlein, Schierstein. Primitive gasoline powered three- and four-wheelers.

SOLAIRE
USA   1981
Solaire Corporation, Santa Ana, California. Convertibles only.

SOLAR KING
USA   1965
International Rectifier Co., El Segundo, California. Experimental electric car.

SOLEC
CH   c. 1989
SOLEC Solar- & Elektromobil AG, Safnern. Electric city cars.

SOLETTA
CH   1956
Ingenieurbureau für Fahrzeugbau, Solothurn. Small car prototype.

SOLIDOR
D   1905–1907
Beaulieu & Krone, Berlin. Gasoline and electric cars.

SOLIGNAC
F   1900–1903
Sté. des Voitures Électriques, Paris. Electric cars.

SOLOCAR
GB 1948–1950
Nelco Electric Co., Surrey. Single-seater electric cars.

SOLOMOBIL
D 1920–1922
E. Moll, Berlin. Kraftwagenfabrik Solomobil GmbH, Berlin. Three-wheelers.

SOLON
S 1991–present
Solon AB, Uddevalla. Electric cars.

SOMEA
B 1921
SA des Automobiles Leroux-Pisart, Bruxelles. Sports cars.
See "Leroux-Pisart."

SOMMER
DK 1982
Ole Sommer, Naerum. Sports cars.

SOMMER
USA 1904–1905
Sommer Motor Co., Detroit, Michigan. "Sommer" touring cars were built late 1904 and 1905. Company built engines at Bucyrus, Ohio into 1915. Also built "Allen" cyclecar in 1916.

SONCIN
F 1900–1902
Emile Ouzou et Cie., Paris. Voiturette.

SONNY BOY
D 1981–1986
Bölter-Bracker Kleinwagen GmbH. Electric and gasoline minicars.

SORIANO-PEDROSO
F 1919–1924
SA des Automobiles Soriano-Pedroso, Biarritz; Neuilly/Seine. Light sports cars.

SORRELL
USA 1956
Sorrell Engineering Co., Inglewood, California.

SOUCIN
F 1899
Three-wheeler.

SOUDAN
USA 1900–1901
Soudan Mfg. Co., Elkhart, Indiana. Few automobiles were built.

SOURIAU
F 1912–1914
A. Souriau et Cie., Montoire/Loire-et-Cher. Three-wheelers.

SOUSEDÍK
CS 1932
Josef Sousedík, Vsetín. Electric car.

SOUTH BEND
USA 1913–1914
South Bend Motor Car Works, South Bend, Indiana. Roadsters and touring cars.

SOUTHEASTERN
USA 1982
Southeastern Replicars, Largo, Florida. "Auburn" and "Cord" replicars.

SOUTHERN
USA 1906–1908
Southern Automobile Mfg. Co., Jacksonville, Florida. Highwheelers.

SOUTHERN
USA 1908–1910
Southern Motor Works, Nashville, Tennessee. Became "Marathon" 1910. Company renamed Marathon Motor Works 1911.

SOUTHERN
USA 1914
Southern Car Mfg. Co. Southern Automobile Co., New Orleans, Louisiana. Cyclecars.

SOUTHERN
USA 1920–1922
Southern Automobile & Equipment Co., Atlanta, Georgia; Memphis, Tennessee.

SOUTHERN CROSS
AUS 1933–1935
Marks Motor Construction Ltd., Sydney, N.S.W. Laminated timber frame.

SOUTHERN ROADCRAFT
GB 1984–1993
Southern Roadcraft Ltd., Brighton, Sussex. Sports cars.
See "SR."

SOUTHERN SIX
AUS 1921–1922
Australian British Motors Ltd., Sydney, N.S.W. 2.4-litre Sage engine.

SOUTHERN SIX
USA 1920
Southern Automobile Mfg. Co., Memphis, Tennessee. 6-cylinder touring cars.

SOUTHERN SIX
USA 1920–1921
Southern Motors Co., Houston, Texas.
See "Ranger."

SOUTHGATE
GB 1974
Southgate Motors Ltd., London. "Bentley" replica.

SOUTHLAND
USA 1910
Southland Motor Car Co., Owensboro, Kentucky. 30 hp cars.

SOVAM
F 1964–1969
SA Automobiles Sovam, Parthenay/Deux-Sevres. Sports cars.

SOVEREIGN
USA 1906–1907
Mathews Motor Car Co., Camden, New Jersey. Also known as "Mathews."

SOVRA
F 1969–1986
Sovra, Corbeilles-en-Gatinais. Dune buggy and sports cars.

SP
GB 1972
Hooe Garage (East Sussex) Ltd., Battle, Sussex. Made to customers' order.

SPA
I 1906–1926
SPA-Societa Piemontese Automobili Ansaldi-Ceirano (1906–1908). SPA-Societa Ligure Piemontese Automobili, Torino (1908–1926). Sports cars. Absorbed by "FIAT" in 1925.

SPACKE
USA 1919
F.W. Spacke Machine & Tool Co., Indianapolis, Indiana. Reported September 1920 receiver had been named.
See "Brook."

S.P.A.G.
F 1927–1928
Automobiles S.P.A.G., Asnieres/Seine. Sports and racing cars.

SPAHR
USA 1895
Otto A. Spahr, Millersburg, Ohio. Runabout.

SPANGLER
USA 1903
E.E. Spangler, Lewistown, Pennsylvania.

SPARKS
USA 1899–1903
Sparks Automobile Co., San Francisco, California.

SPARKS
USA 1903
C.F. Sparks Machine Co., Alton, Illinois. Runabout.

SPARKS
USA 1980–1984
Pacific Motors Corporation, Marina del Rey, California. Replicars.

SPARTAN
GB 1973–1993
Spartan Car Co., Mapperley, Nottinghamshire. "MG" replica. 350 cars built in 1974.

SPARTAN
USA 1910
C.W. Kelsey Mfg. Co., Hartford, Connecticut. Touring car prototype only. Became "Kelsey Motorette."

SPARTAN
USA 1982
Spartan Classic Motors, San Marcos, California. Neoclassic convertibles.

SPARVIERO & MARCADALLI
I 1948
Mini car.

SPATZ
D 1955–1957
Bayerische Autowerke GmbH, Traunreut. 250cc small cars.

SPAULDING
USA 1902–1903
Spaulding Automobile & Motor Co., Buffalo, N.Y. Runabouts. Became "Morlock."

SPAULDING
USA 1910–1916
Spaulding Mfg. Co., Grinnell, Iowa. About 1,480 cars were made.

SPEAR
USA 1902
William H. Spear, Cleveland, Ohio.

SPEAR
USA c. 1905
Arthur E. Spear, Windsor, Vermont. 12 hp automobile.

SPECIAL
USA 1904
Special Motor Vehicle Co., Cincinnati, Ohio.

SPECIAL
USA 1910
Johnson Service Co., Milwaukee, Wisconsin.

SPECIALTY
USA 1898
Specialty Carriage & Motor Vehicle Co., Cincinnati, Ohio. Electric carriage.

SPECIALTY
USA 1990s
Specialty Motor Cars LLC, Fayetteville, Arizona. Kit cars.

SPECTRE
GB 1996–present
Spectre Supersports Ltd., Poole, Dorset. Sports cars.

SPEEDEX
GB 1960
Speedex Castings and Accessories Ltd., Luton, Beds. Sports cars.

SPEEDSPORT
B 1924–1927
Bruxelles. Modified version of the Model T "Ford."

SPEEDSTER
D 1993–1996
Speedster Cabrio KG, Fuldabrück. Convertibles.

SPEEDWAY
USA 1904–1905
Gas Engine & Power Co., Morris Heights, N.Y. Side-entrance tonneau.

SPEEDWAY
USA 1989–1993
Speedway Motors, Inc., Lincoln, Nebraska. Replicars.

SPEEDWAY SPECIAL
USA 1917–1918
Wolverine Motors, Kalamazoo, Michigan.
See "Wolverine."

SPEEDWELL
GB 1900–1907
Speedwell Motor and Engineering Co. Ltd., Reading, Berks. New Speedwell Motor Co. Ltd., London.

SPEEDWELL
USA 1903–1904
Speedwell Automobile Co., Milwaukee, Wisconsin. Formerly Kunz Automobile & Motor Co.

SPEEDWELL
USA 1907–1914
Speedwell Motor Car Co., Dayton, Ohio. Featured Mead rotary valve engine designed by Cyrus E. Mead. Reported bankrupt March 1915. Plant sold to W.M. Pattison Supply Co. Roadsters and touring cars.

SPEEDY
GB 1905
Jackson Brothers & Lord, Salford, Lancs. Three-wheelers.

SPEEDY
GB 1920–1921
Pullinger Engineering Co. Ltd., London. Cyclecars.

SPEIDEL
CH 1914–1922
Paul Speidel, Geneve. Passenger and sports cars.

SPEIRS
USA 1895; 1898
Speirs Mfg. Co., Worcester, Massachusetts. Electric and steam carriages.

SPENCER
USA 1862–1864
C.M. Spencer, South Manchester, Connecticut; Windsor, Connecticut. Steam cars.

SPENCER
USA 1901–1902
Spencer Automatic Screw Machine Co., Hartford, Connecticut. Steam cars. Founded by C.M. Spencer.

SPENCER
USA c. 1905
John E. Spencer, Salem, Massachusetts. 10 hp automobile.

SPENCER
USA 1921–1922
Research Engineering Co., Dayton, Ohio. Air-cooled 42 hp cars.

SPENCER
USA 1923
Earl B. Spencer, Los Angeles, California.

SPENNY
USA 1913–1914
Spenny Motor Car Co., Tucson, Arizona (1913); Holland, Michigan (1914). 4- and 6-cylinder touring cars.

SPERBER
D 1911–1919

Norddeutsche Automobilwerke, Hameln a.d. Weser. Touring cars. 1919 taken over by "Selve."

SPERLING
USA 1921–1923
Associated Motors Corp., Elkhart, Indiana; New York, N.Y. Built for export only. Announced December 1921.

SPERRY
USA 1898–1901
Cleveland Machine Screw Co., Cleveland, Ohio. National Battery Co., Buffalo, N.Y. Electric cars. Sold to American Bicycle Co.
See "Waverley."

SPHINX
D 1920–1925
Sphinx Automobilwerke AG (1920–1925). Georg Kralapp Automobilwerke, Zwickau/Sachsen (1925). Passenger cars.

SPHINX
F 1912–1925
F. Terrier, Courbevoie/Seine (1912–1916). Sphinx Automobiles Établissements Perfecto, Puteaux/Seine (1920–1925). Touring cars.

SPHINX
USA 1914–1915
Sphinx Motor Car Co., York, Pennsylvania. Touring cars. Became Bell Motor Car Co.
See "Bell" (1915–1921).

SPHYNX
CH 1971
Experimental sports car prototype with rhomboid wheel placement.

SPICER
USA 1902
Clarence W. Spicer, Plainfield, New Jersey. One runabout produced while inventor was student at Cornell University.

SPIDER
USA 1914
Detroit Body Co., Detroit, Michigan. One cyclecar prototype.

SPIDOS
F 1921–1925
Cyclecars Spidos, Lyon.

SPIESS
D 1992–?
Spiess-Fahrzeugbau GmbH & Co., Wolfratshausen. 500 hp sports car.
See "R.H.P."

SPIJKER
NL
See "Spyker."

SPIJKSTAAL
NL 1970
Spijkstaal B.V., Spijkenisse. Electric minicar prototype.

SPILLER
USA 1900
Pringst-Spiller Power & Auto Co., Trenton, New Jersey. Spiller Motor Carriage Co., Dorchester, Massachusetts.

SPILLMAN
USA 1900–1901
Herschell-Spillman Co., North Tonawanda, N.Y.
See "Herschell-Spillman."

SPINELL
D 1924–1925
Spinell Motorfahrzeuge GmbH Otto Krell Jr., Berlin. Small sports cars.

SPITZ
A 1902–1907
Arnold Spitz, Wien. 1-, 2- and 4-cylinder cars. Later built by "Raba" (H).

SPLINTER
USA 1982
Splinter Auto Works, Plymouth, Indiana. Replicars.

SPLITT
USA 1909
Louis Splitt, Milwaukee, Wisconsin. One motor buggy was made.

S.P.M.A.
F 1908
Sté. Parisienne de Mécanique Appliqué, Courbevoie/Seine. 10/12 hp light cars.

S.P. MOTORS
GB 1989–1993
S.P. Motors, Barwell, Leics. Replicars.

SPOERER
USA 1908–1914
Carl Spoerer & Sons, Baltimore, Maryland. Touring cars.

SPOKANE
USA 1904–1905
Spokane Motor Co., Spokane, Washington. Steam cars.

SPOOK ELECTRIC
USA 1968
Dynamic Development, Pasadena, California. Electric cars.

SPORTOLET
D 1962
Fahrzeugfabrik Peter Bauer, Koln. Sports car prototype.

SPORTS
GB 1900–1901
Sports Motor Car Co., London. Light cars.

SPRAGUE
USA 1895–1896
H.A. Sprague, Fowlerville, Michigan.

SPRINGER
USA 1903–1905
Springer Motor Vehicle Co., New York, N.Y. Touring cars. Succeeded Kidder Motor Vehicle Co.
See "Kidder."

SPRINGFIELD
USA 1899–1903
Springfield Automobile & Industrial Co., Springfield, Ohio. Gasoline carriages.

SPRINGFIELD
USA 1900–1901
Springfield Motor Vehicle Co., Springfield, Massachusetts. Steam cars.

SPRINGFIELD
USA 1900–1901
Springfield Cornice Works, Springfield, Massachusetts.

SPRINGFIELD
USA 1903–1904
Springfield Automobile Co., Springfield, Ohio. 2-stroke 1.6-litre engine.
See "Bramwell."

SPRINGFIELD
USA 1907
Med-Bow Automobile Co., Springfield, Massachusetts. 5.2-litre 5-seater.

SPRINGFIELD
USA 1908
R. Haas Electric & Mfg. Co., Springfield, Illinois. Electric car.

SPRINGFIELD
USA 1907–1910
Springfield Motor Car Co., Springfield, Massachusetts (1907–1908); Springfield, Illinois (1909–1910). Touring cars.

SPRINGUEL
B 1907–1910
SA des Automobiles Springuel, Liege. Touring and sports cars.

SPRITE
USA 1914
W.S. Frazier & Co., Aurora, Illinois. Cyclecars.

SPURR
USA 1900–1901
Spurr Automobile Co., East Orange, New Jersey. Runabout.

SPUTNIK
SU 1963–c. 1969
Small cars for handicapped drivers.
See "SMZ."

SPU-TRI
USA 1990s
Oklahoma. Three-wheelers.

SPYKER
NL 1900–1925
De Industrieele Maatschappij Trompenburg (1899–1916). Nederlansche Automobiel- en Vielgtuigenfabriek Trompenburg, Amsterdam (1916–1925).

SQUARE DEAL
USA 1910
Auto Parts & Equipment Co., Chicago, Illinois. Highwheelers.
See "Auto Parts."

SQUIER & ROOT
USA 1899
E. Squier & A. J. Root, Virginia City, Nevada. Steam car.

SQUIRE
GB 1934–1936
Squire Car Mfg. Co. Ltd., Henley-on-Thames, Oxfordshire. 1.5-litre sports cars.

SQUIRE SS
USA c. 1971
Auto Sports Importers Inc., Philadelphia, Pennsylvania. "SS" (GB) sports car replicars.

SR
GB
See "Southern Roadcraft."

S.R.C.
E 1922–1925
Stevenson, Ramagosa y Cia., Barcelona. 11 hp assembled cars.

SRIKANDI
RI 1984
Bachana Timur Motors. Three-wheelers.

S.R.K.
USA 1915
S.R.K. Motor Co., Detroit, Michigan. Roadsters.
See "Strouse."

SS
GB 1900
S.S. Motor Car Co., London. Light cars.

S.S.
GB 1931–1945
Swallow Coachbuilding Co. Ltd. (1931–1934). S.S. Cars Ltd., Coventry, Warwickshire (1934–1945). Sports cars.
See "Jaguar."

SSANGYONG
ROK 1988–1998
SsangYong Motor Company, Seoul. 4 × 4 vehicles.

S.S.E.
USA 1914–1917
S.S.E. Automobile Co., Kensington, Pennsylvania. Runabouts.

SSG
PL 1992
Studio Samochodowe Gepard, Warszawa. Replicars.

STABILIA
F 1908–1930
Automobiles Stabilia, Neuilly/Seine (1908–1910). Giraldy et Vrard, Neuilly/Seine; Asnieres/Seine (1911–1920). Vrard et Cie., Asnieres/Seine (1920–1930). Underslung frame.

STABLE
USA 1990s
Stable Autoworks, Richardson, Texas. Sports kit cars.

STACK
GB 1921–1925
G.F. Stack & Co., East Croydon, Surrey. 766cc light cars.

STAE
I 1905–1913
Societa Torinese Automobili Elettriche Krieger, Torino. Electric cars.
See "Krieger Italiana."

STAFFORD
GB 1920–1921
Stafford Associated Engineering Co. Ltd., London. 1.8- and 2.7-litre cars.

STAFFORD
USA 1908–1915
Perry Stafford Motor Car Co., Topeka, Kansas (1908); Kansas City, Kansas (1910–1915). Perry Stafford bought out Paul Mulvance reported October 1908. Touring cars.

STAG
GB 1913–1914
The Stag Co., Sherwood, Nottingham. Cyclecar.

STAGEWAY
USA c. 1968
Stageway Coaches Inc. Stretched limousines.

STAIGER
D 1923–1924
Automobilfabrik Paul Staiger, Stuttgart. Sports cars.

STAINES-SIMPLEX
GB 1906–1911
Staines Motor Co. Ltd., Staines, Middlesex. Assembled cars.

STALLION
D 1986–1993
SMS AG, Schmidt Engineering, Cadolzburg bei Nürnberg. Replicars.

STAMM
USA 1901–1905
Frederick B. Stamm, Los Angeles, California. Three Stamms were built.

STAMMOBILE
USA 1900–1905
Stammobile Mfg. Co., Stamford, Connecticut. Steam carriage.

STANBURY
GB 1903
Stanbury & Co., Liverpool. 12 hp model.

STANDARD
D 1911–1912
Standard Automobilfabrik GmbH, Berlin. Henriod rotary-valve engines.

STANDARD
D 1933–1935
Standard Fahrzeugfabrik GmbH, Ludwigsburg. Small cars designed by Josef Ganz.

STANDARD
GB 1903–1963
Standard Motor Co. Ltd., Coventry, Warwickshire. Touring and sports cars.

STANDARD
I 1906–1912
Fabbrica Automobili Standard, Torino. 14/20 hp cars.
See "FAS."

STANDARD
IND 1960s–1970s
Standard Ltd., Madras. "Triumph" Herald (GB) license.

STANDARD
USA 1899
Standard Motor Carriage Co., Boston, Massachusetts.

STANDARD
USA 1899–1901
Standard Automobile Co., Chicago, Illinois.

STANDARD
USA 1900
Boston Automobile Co., Bar Harbor, Maine. Steam car.

STANDARD
USA 1900–1901
Standard Motor Vehicle Co., Philadelphia, Pennsylvania.

STANDARD
USA 1900–1901
Standard Auto-Vehicle Co., Winchester, Massachusetts. Steam car.

STANDARD
USA 1902
Standard Mfg. Co., Kokomo, Indiana.

STANDARD
USA 1902–1903
Standard Automobile Co., Pittsburgh, Pennsylvania. Formerly Mfg. Co.

STANDARD
USA 1903
Standard Automobile Co., Indianapolis, Indiana.

STANDARD
USA 1904–1905
Standard Motor Construction Co., Jersey City, New Jersey. Succeeded "United States Long Distance" (1901–1903). Became Hewitt Motor Co. Five-seater in wood or in aluminum.

STANDARD
USA 1908–1910
Standard Gas & Electric Power Co., Philadelphia, Pennsylvania.

STANDARD
USA 1909–1910
St. Louis Motor Car Co., St. Louis, Missouri. 7.8-litre 6-cylinder cars.

STANDARD
USA 1913–1915
Standard Automobile Co., Warren, Ohio.

STANDARD
USA 1915–1923
Standard Steel Car Co., Pittsburgh, Pennsylvania; Butler, Pennsylvania. Reorganized as Standard Motor Car Co. 1922. 14,262 cars were made.

STANDARD
USA 1914
Standard Engineering Co., Chicago, Illinois. Cyclecar.

STANDARD
USA 1916
Standard Car Construction Co., Philadelphia, Pennsylvania.

STANDARD ELECTRIC
USA 1911–1915
Standard Electric Car Co. Standard Car Mfg. Co., Jackson, Michigan.

STANDARD G.E.
USA 1909–1910
Standard Gas Electric Power Co., Philadelphia, Pennsylvania. Touring cars and limousines.

STANDARD SIX
USA 1909–1911
St. Louis Car Co., St. Louis, Missouri (1910). 1910 reorganized as Standard Automobile Co. of America, Wabash, Indiana (1910–1911). Formerly "American Mors" (1906–1909).

STANDARD STEAM
USA 1919–1921
Standard Engineering Corp. Standard Steam Corp., St. Louis, Missouri.
See "Scott-Newcomb."

STANDARD STEAMER
USA 1905
Standard Automobile & Vehicle Co., Boston, Massachusetts.

STANDARD TOURIST
USA 1905
Standard Motor Construction Co., Jersey City, New Jersey.
See "Standard" (1904–1905) Both names apply to same vehicle.

STANDISH
USA 1924–1925
Luxor Cab Manufacturing Co., Framingham, Massachusetts. Sedans.

STANFORD
USA 1908
Stanford Automobile & Mfg. Co., Palo Alto, California.

STANGUELLINI
I 1946–1962
Officine Stanguellini Trasformazione Auto Sport e Corsa, Modena. Sports cars.

STANHOPE
GB 1915–1925
Stanhope Motors Ltd. (1915–1922). Bramham Motors Ltd. (1922–1924). Stanhope Bros. Ltd., Leeds, Yorks. (1925). Three-wheelers.

STANHOPE
USA 1904–1906
Twyford Motor Car Co., Brookville, Pennsylvania.

STANLEY
USA 1896–1900
Stanley Bros. Motor Carriage Co., Newton, Massachusetts. Steam cars. Became Automobile Co. of America and Locomobile Co. of America.
See "Mobile" and "Locomobile."

STANLEY
USA 1901–1924
Stanley Motor Carriage Co., Newton, Massachusetts. Steam cars. 1929 reorganized as Steam Vehicle Corp. of America. 1925 moved to Allentown, Pennsylvania. Sold to Stanley Steam Motors Corp., Chicago, Illinois. 10,830 cars were made.

STANLEY
USA c. 1905
George E. Stanley, East Whitman, Massachusetts. 8 hp automobile.

STANLEY
USA 1907–1908
Stanley Automobile Mfg. Co., Mooreland, Indiana. Became Troy Automobile & Buggy Co., Troy, Ohio (1909–1910) Absorbed "Peoples" Automobile Co., Cleveland, Ohio 1908.

STANLEY
USA 1910–1911
Stanley Motor Car Co., Detroit, Michigan. Reported two cars being built December 1910.

STANLEY-WHITNEY
USA 1899
Stanley Machine Co., Lawrence, Massachusetts. Steam cars.
See "McKay" and "Whitney."

STANSBURY
GB 1903
Prototype.

STANTON
USA 1900–1901
Stanton Mfg. Co., Waltham, Massachusetts. Steam cars. Absorbed New England Motor Carriage Co.
See. "Waltham Steamer."

STANTON
USA 1905
Stanton Mfg. Co., Rochelle Park, New Jersey.

STANWOOD
USA 1920–1922
Stanwood Motor Car Co., St. Louis, Missouri. 6-cylinder touring cars.

STAPLES
USA 1899–1900
W.J. Staples, Maryville, Missouri. Gasoline motor buggy.

STAR
I 1904–1921
Societa Torinese Automobili Rapid, Torino.

STAR
USA 1903–1904
Star Automobile Co. (1903). H.S. Moore Co. (1903–1904), Cleveland, Ohio. Runabouts.

STAR
USA 1907–1908
Star Automobile Co., Chicago, Illinois. 1-cylinder 2-stroke 10 hp runabout.

STAR
USA 1908–1909
Model Machine Co., Peru, Indiana. Mier Carriage & Buggy Co., Ligonier, Indiana.
See "Mier" and "Izzer."

STAR
USA 1909
Minneapolis Motorcycle Co., Minneapolis, Minnesota.

STAR
USA 1909–1911
Star Motor Car Co., Indianapolis, Indiana. One car produced.

STAR
USA 1914
Star Cyclecar Co., Los Angeles, California. Cyclecar.

STAR
USA 1916
Star Motor Car Co., Cincinnati, Ohio. Steam car.

STAR
USA 1922–1928
Durant Motors Inc., Elizabeth, New Jersey. 4- and 6-cylinder passenger cars. 358,868 cars were made.

STAR DUST
USA 1953
Grantham Motor Car Co., Los Angeles, California. Used "Ford" chassis and engine.

STARIN
USA 1903–1904
Starin Co., North Tonawanda, N.Y. Runabouts.

STAR LIGHT
USA 1962–1963
Electric car.

STARLING
GB
See "Star."

STARLITE
USA 1959
Kish Industries, Inc., Lansing, Michigan. Electric sports cars.

STARR
USA 1909–1910
Fred W. Starr, Minneapolis, Minnesota. Runabouts.

STAR STARLING, STUART
GB 1898–1902
Star Motor Co. (1898–1902). Star Engineering Co. (1902–1909). Star Cycle Co. (1905–1909). Star Engineering Co. Ltd. (1909–1928). Star Motor Co. Ltd., Wolverhampton, Staffs. (1928–1932). Touring cars.

START
CS 1921–1928
František Petrášek, Továrna automobilu Start, Kukleny. Voiturette.

START
CS 1949
Ivan Nahodil. Rear-engined light car prototype.

STATAX-HANSEN
D 1922–1923
F.J.M. Hansen KG, Köln.

STATES
USA 1914–1915
States Cyclecar Co., Detroit, Michigan. Cyclecars.

STATES
USA 1916–1918
States Motor Car Mfg. Co., Toledo, Ohio; Kalamazoo, Michigan. Touring cars.

STATIC
USA 1923
Static Motor Co., Philadelphia, Pennsylvania. Air-cooled cars.

STATIONETTE
USA 1950–1955
Martin Development Co., Rochelle Park, New Jersey.

STAUNAU
D 1950–1951
Staunau Werk, Hamburg-Harburg. About 80 cars with 400 and 750 cc 2-cycle engines were built.

STAVER
USA 1907–1914
Staver Carriage Co., Chicago, Illinois. Experimental car 1906. Highwheelers 1907–1908. 7,092 cars were made.

STE
I
Societa per la Trazione Elettrica.
See "Frigerio."

STEALEY
USA 1899
A.D. Stealey, San Francisco, California. Experimental four-wheeled carriage.

STEAMOBILE
USA 1900–1902
Steamobile Co. of America, Keene, New Hampshire. Steam cars.
See "Keene Steamer," "Rogers," "Transit Steamer" and "Trinity."

STEAM VEHICLE
USA 1900–1903
Steam Vehicle Co. of America, Reading, Pennsylvania.
See "Reading Steam Carriage."

STEARNS
USA 1896–1911

F.B. Stearns Co., Cleveland, Ohio. Became "Stearns Knight."

STEARNS
USA 1899–1901
E.C. Stearns Co., Syracuse, N.Y. Electric cars. Became Stearns Automobile Co. 1900.

STEARNS-KNIGHT
USA 1912–1929
F.B. Stearns Co., Cleveland, Ohio. Former "Stearns" cars. Absorbed by Willys-Overland Co. 1925. Luxury cars. 43,412 cars were made (Stearns + Stearns Knight).

STEARNS STEAM
USA 1901–1903
Stearns Steam Carriage Co., Syracuse, N.Y.

STEBER
USA c. 1860
Antoine Steber, Utica, N.Y. Steam automobile.

STECO
USA 1914
Stevens Engineering Co., Chicago, Illinois. Cyclecars.

STEEL BALL
USA 1900–1901
Steel Ball Co., Chicago, Illinois. Steam cars.

STEELE
USA 1914
The William Steele Co., Worcester, Massachusetts. Cyclecars.
    See "Morgan."

STEEL SWALLOW
USA 1907–1908
Steel Swallow Automobile Co., Jackson, Michigan. Highwheelers.

STEELY
USA 1910
Steely Auto Engine Co., Detroit, Michigan,

STEGMAIER
USA 1906–1907
Stegmaier Bros., Cumberland, Maryland. Steam cars.

STEIGER
D 1920–1926
Walter Steiger & Co. (1920–1925). Steiger AG, Burgrieden (1925–1926). Passenger and sports cars.

STEINBOCK
USA 1912
Steinbock Engineering Co., Westchester County, N.Y. Touring car prototype.

STEINHART-JENSEN
USA 1908
Steinhart-Jensen Automobile Co., Joliet, Illinois.

STEINMETZ
USA 1901
Jenny-Steinmetz & Co., Philadelphia, Pennsylvania.

STEINMETZ
USA 1922–1923
Steinmetz Electric Motor Car Co., Baltimore, Maryland; Arlington, Maryland. Electric cars.

STEINWAY
USA 1888–1896; 1905–1907
Steinway & Sons, New York, N.Y. "Daimler" (D) derivative.

STEINWINTER
D 1977–1988
Steinwinter Fahrzeuge GmbH, Stuttgart. Dune buggy and city cars.

STELA
F 1941–1944
Vehicules Electriques Stela, Villeurbanne, Lyon. Electric cars.

STELKA
CS 1921–1922
Rudolf Stelsovský, výroba automobilu, Příbram. Příbramská strojírna slévárna, spol s r.o., Příbram. 2-cylinder 1.1-litre small cars. From 1925.
    See "Aspa."

STELLA
CH 1906–1913
Compagnie d'Industrie Électrique et Mécanique, Geneve. Gasoline-electric cars.

STELLA
D 1907
Kraftwagen Gesellschaft Roland, Berlin. Light cars.

STELLA
F 1900–1901
Sté. de Construction Mecaniques Stella, Levallois-Perret/Seine. Light voiturette.

STELLITE
GB 1913–1919
Electric and Ordnance Accessories Co. Ltd., Birmingham. 1.1-litre economy cars.

STEMAT
F 1977
Stemat S.A., Aubin. Jeep-type vehicles.

STEPHENS
GB 1898–1900
R. Stephens, Clevedon, Somerset. Light cars.

STEPHENS
USA 1917–1924
Stephens Motor Branch, Moline Plow Co. Stephens Motor Car Co. Inc., Freeport, Illinois. 1918 Moline Low Co. became subsidiary of Willys-Overland Co. 1920 name changed to Stephens Motor Co., Moline and Freeport, Illinois. First car completed May 8, 1916. 19,146 cars were made.

STERKENBURG
USA 1931
John Tjaarda, Detroit, Michigan. Experimental car.

STERLING
GB 1913
Sterling Engineering & Automobile Co. Ltd., Leeds, Yorks. Cyclecars.

STERLING
USA 1897–1899
Clarence Sterling, Bridgeport, Connecticut.

STERLING
USA 1901
Howell & Meehan Co., Boston, Massachusetts.

STERLING
USA 1909–1911
Elkhart Motor Car Co., Elkhart, Indiana. Touring cars. Became "Elcar."

STERLING
USA 1913–1916
Sterling Motor Car Co., Flint, Michigan; Detroit, Michigan. Became "Scripps-Booth."

STERLING
USA 1914
Sterling Garage, White Plains, N.Y. Cyclecar.

STERLING
USA 1915–1916
Sterling Motor Car Co., Brockton, Massachusetts. Roadsters and touring cars.

STERLING
USA 1914–1923
Sterling Automobile Co., Paterson, New Jersey; Amston, Connecticut; Bridgeport, Connecticut. Consolidated Motor Car Co., New London, Connecticut (1920); New Britain, Connecticut. Touring cars.

STERLING-KNIGHT
USA 1920–1926
Sterling-Knight Motors Co., Cleveland, Ohio (1920–1922); Warren, Ohio (1923–1926). Touring cars. Production: 1924 = 253, 1925 = 121 cars.

STERLING-NEW YORK
USA 1916
Sterling Automobile Mfg. Co., Paterson, New Jersey. Roadsters.

STERLING STEAMER
USA 1900–1902
Sterling Automobile & Engine Co., Sterling, Illinois.
See "Empire" steamer.

STERNAD
USA 1917
A.F. Sternad, Chicago Solder Co., Chicago, Illinois. "Locomotive automobile."

STESROC
GB 1905–1906
Johnson Bros., Knaresborough, Yorks. Steam motor carriages.

STETSON
USA 1907–1911
Stetson Motor Car Co., Dover, Delaware; Pittsfield, Massachusetts. Former "Pittsfield."

STEUDEL
D 1904–1909
Horst Steudel Motorwagenfabrik, Kamenz. Voiturette.

STEVENS
GB 1977–1983
Anthony Stevens Cars Ltd., Warwick. "MG" replicars, sports cars.

STEVENS
USA 1899
Frederick Stevens, Peoria, Illinois.

STEVENS-DURYEA
USA 1902–1927
J. Stevens Arms & Tool Co. The Stevens-Duryea Co. Stevens-Duryea Motors Inc. Stevens-Duryea Inc., Chicopee Falls, Massachusetts. Final years with Rauch & Lang electric, "Raulang" electric cars and taxicabs. About 13,000 cars were made.

STEWART
USA 1895
Richard F. Stewart, Pocantico Hills, N.Y. Gasoline wagon.

STEWART
USA 1901; 1904
Alfred C. Stewart Co., Los Angeles, California. Runabouts; 40 hp racer for Frank A. Garbutt.

STEWART
USA c. 1905
Stewart, Massachusetts. 5 hp car.

STEWART
USA 1915–1916
Stewart Motor Corp., Buffalo, N.Y. 4.7-litre touring cars.

STEWART-COATS
USA 1921–1922
Y.F. Stewart Motor car Mfg. Co., Bowling Green, Ohio (1921); Columbus, Ohio (1922). Steam cars. Succeeded Coats Steam Car Co.
See "Coats Steamer."

STEYR
A 1920–1940; 1953–present
Österreichische Waffenfabriks-Gesellschaft AG (1920–1926). Steyr-Werke AG (1926–1935). Steyr-Daimler-Puch AG, Steyr (1935–1940); Graz (1953–present). Passenger cars.

STICKNEY
USA 1901–1903
Henry R. Stickney, Portland, Maine. Runabout.

STICKNEY
USA 1913–1914
Charles A. Stickney Co., St. Paul, Minnesota. Cyclecars. Reported out of business June 1914.

STIETENCRON-SCHWENKE
D c. 1923
Robert Schwenke, Iwan Freiherr von Stietencron, Berlin. Front-wheel-drive cars.

STIGLER
I 1921–1925
Vetture Elettriche Stigler, Milano. Electric cars.

STILL
CDN 1899–1903
Canadian Motor Syndicate, Toronto, Ontario. Electric cars.

STILSON
USA 1907–1909
Stilson Motor Car Co., Pittsfield, Massachusetts. Touring cars. In receivers' hands January 1911.

STIMULA
F 1905–1914
De la Chapelle Freres et Cie., St. Chamond/Loire. Tricars and voiturettes.

STIMULA
F 1978–c. 1987
Automobiles Stimula, Lyon. Replicars.

STIRLING
GB 1897–1903
J. & C. Stirling (1897–1898). Stirling's Motor Carriages Ltd., Hamilton, Lanarkshire (1898–1902); Granton, Edinburgh (1902–1903). Voiturette.

STIRLING
GB 1956–1959
S.E. Opperman Ltd., Boreham Wood, Herts. Small sports cars.
See "Unicar," "Opperman."

STIRLING
USA 1920–1921
Stirling Motors Inc., Newark, New Jersey. About 6 cars were made.

STOCK
D 1932–1933
W. Stock Fahrzeugbau GmbH, Leipzig. Three-wheelers.

STOCKWELL
USA 1905
M.E. Stockwell, Grand Rapids, Michigan.

STODDARD-DAYTON
USA 1904–1913
Dayton Motor Car Co., Dayton, Ohio. Successor to Stoddard Mfg. Division of U.S. Motor Corp. 1910. Became Maxwell Motor Co. 1914. Touring cars, limousines, roadsters.

STOEWER
D 1899–1939
Gebrüder Stoewer, Fabrik für Motorfahrzeuge (1899–1916). Stoewer-Werke AG vorm. Gebr. Stoewer, Stettin (1916–1939). Passenger cars. "Tatra" (CS) license 1936–1939.

STOKESBURY
USA 1922–1923
Steam Automotive Works, Denver, Colorado. Stokesbury Steam Motors Co., Los Angeles, California. Steam cars.

STOKVIS
NL 1901
W.J. Stokvis, Arnhem. Voiturette.

STOLLE
D 1925–1926
Vorster & Stolle Motoren AG, München. Only 15 touring cars were produced.

STOLZ
USA 1900–1902
The Stolz Cycle Co., Brooklyn, N.Y. W.G. Stolz Automobile & Cycle Works, Groton, N.Y. Gasoline cars built to order.

STOMMEL
USA 1897–1899
Hugh Stommel, Plainfield, New Jersey.

STONE & MAYNARD
USA 1895
Stone & Maynard Co., Avonia, Pennsylvania.

STONEBOW
GB 1901
Payne & Bates, Coventry, Warwickshire. Light cars.

STONELEIGH
GB 1912–1924
Stoneleigh Motors Ltd., Coventry, Warwickshire. V-twin air-cooled engines.

STORCK
USA 1901–1902
Frank C. Storck, Red Bank, New Jersey. Steam cars.

STORERO
I 1912–1919
Fabbrica Automobili Storero, Torino. 4.4- and 5.5-litre cars.
See "Caesar," "Scacchi."

STOREY
GB 1919–1930
Storey Machine Tool Co. Ltd, London; Tonbridge, Kent (1919–1920). Storey Motors (1921–1925). Storey Motors Ltd., London (1925–1930). 8 different models.

STORK-KAR
USA 1919–1921
Stork-Kar Sales Co., New York, N.Y. Four-cylinder touring cars. Factory at Martinsburg, West Virginia.

STORM
E 1924–1925
Jose Boniquet Riera, Barcelona. 6/8 hp light cars.

STORM
USA 1954
Sports Car Development Corp., Detroit, Michigan. Two-passenger sports cars using Dodge V-8 engine in Bertone body.

STORMS
USA 1915
Storms Electric Car Co., Detroit, Michigan. Electric cars.

STORY
NL 1941–1944
N.V. Internationale Automobielmij, Den Haag. Small electric three-wheelers, about 100 built.

STOUT
USA 1914
Stout Engineering Co. Stout Cyclecar Co., Chicago, Illinois. Cyclecars.

STOUT
USA 1946
William B. Stout, Kaiser-Frazer Corp., Detroit, Michigan. Owens-Corning Fiberglass Corp., Newark, Ohio. One fiberglass-bodied car.

STOUT SCARAB
USA 1934–1939
Stout Engineering Laboratories, Detroit, Michigan.
See "Scarab."

STOVER
USA 1909
Stover Motor Car Co., Freeport, Illinois.

STRADA
GB 1974–1975
Sports cars built from October 1974 to January 1975.

STRAKER-SQUIRE
GB 1906–1926
S. Straker & Squire Ltd., Bristol (1906–1918). Straker-Squire Ltd., London (1918–1926). Touring cars.

STRALE
I 1967
Strale, Torino. Sports cars.

STRANAHAN
USA 1906–1908
Stranahan-Eldridge Co., Boston, Massachusetts.

STRAND
USA 1906
C.M. Strand, Hastings, Minnesota. Motor buggy.

STRANG
USA 1902
C.G. Strang, Colorado Springs, Colorado. 20 hp gasoline vehicle.

STRATHCARRON
GB 1999–present
Strathcarron Sportscars, Tebworth. Sports cars.

STRATHMORE
USA 1899–1901
Strathmore Automobile Co., Boston, Massachusetts. Steam and gasoline cars. Former International Auto Co.

STRATO
A 1970
Fa. Custoka, Kranbath. Sports kit cars.

STRATO
CH 1961
A. Petignat-Comment, Porrentruy. Sports car prototype.

STRATTAN
USA 1923
Strattan Motors Corp., Indianapolis, Indiana. Touring cars.

STRATTON
USA 1901
Stratton Motor Cycle Co., New York, N.Y.

STRATTON
USA 1907
Stratton Rotary Engine Co., Fitchburg, Massachusetts. Prototype only.

STRATTON
USA 1909
C.H. Stratton Carriage Co., Muncie, Indiana. Highwheelers.

STRATTON-BLISS
USA 1922
Stratton-Bliss Co., New York, N.Y. Brougham.

STRATTON-PREMIER
USA 1923
Stratton Motors Corp., Indianapolis, Indiana. Absorbed "Monroe." Absorbed by "Premier."

STREAMLINE
USA 1913
Streamline Motor Car Co., Indianapolis, Indiana.

STREAMLINER
USA 1932
Hill Auto Body Metal Works, Cincinnati, Ohio. Streamlined experimental car.

STREATOR
USA 1902
Streator Automobile Mfg. Co. Streator Motor Car Co., Streator, Illinois.

STREET DREAMS
USA 1990s
Street Dreams, Ft. Lauderdale, Florida. Kit cars.

STREETER & SMITH
ZA 1913
Streeter & Smith, Cape Town. Cyclecars.

STREIT
D 1905
K.H. Streit. Three-wheelers.

STRIBLING
USA 1882
Colonel John V. Stribling, Anderson, South Carolina.

STRINGER
USA 1899–1902
J.W. Stringer. Stringer Automobile Co., Marion, Ohio. Steam cars.

STRINGER-WINCO
GB 1921–1932
Stringer & Co., Sheffield, Yorkshire. 1.1-litre light cars.

STROHM
D 1991–present
Automobilbau Strohm KG, Laichingen. Sports cars.

STROMMEN
N 1933–1940
AS Strommen Vaerksted, Strommen. Assembled "Dodge" (USA).

STRONG
USA 1904
Strong Automobile Mfg. Co., Minneapolis, Minnesota.

STRONG & GIBBONS
USA 1895
Strong & Gibbons Co., Chicago, Illinois.

STRONG & ROGERS
USA 1900–1901
Strong & Rogers, Cleveland, Ohio. Electric runabouts.

STROSEK
D 1972–present
Strosek Auto Design GmbH, Mellingen; Utting. Tuning.
See "Vistro" (for Vittorio Strosek).

STROUD
USA 1919
Stroud Motor Mfg. Association, Ltd., San Antonio, Texas. Touring cars.

STROUSE
USA 1915–1916
Strose, Ranney & Knight, Detroit, Michigan. Cyclecars. Name changed to "S.R.K."

STRUSS
USA 1897
Henry Struss, New York, N.Y. 4-cylinder runabout.

STUART
GB
See "Star."

STUART
USA 1961
Stuart Motors, Kalamazoo, Michigan. Electric car. Prototype only.

STUCCHI
I 1902–1906
Stucchi & C., Milano.
See "Prinetti & Stucchi."

STUDEBAKER
USA/CDN 1902–1966
Studebaker Automobile Co. Studebaker Corp., South Bend, Indiana. Studebaker Co. of Canada Ltd., Hamilton, Ontario (1964–1966). Electric cars 1902–1912; gasoline cars 1904–1966. Studebaker Automobile Co. absorbed "Tincher" 1907 and "Garford" 1908. Contracted to sell output of "E.M.F." 1909. "Flanders" 1909–1910. Purchased "E.M.F." 1910. Reorganized as Studebaker Corp. 1911. Absorbed "Pierce-Arrow" 1928. Controlled White Corp. 1928 and Indiana Truck Corp. Released "Pierce-Arrow" 1933 and "White" 1934. Amalgamated with Packard Motor Car Co. into Studebaker-Packard Corp. 1954. Dropped "Packard" from name 1962.

STUDILLAC
USA 1953–1955
Bill Frick Motors, Rockville Centre, N.Y. "Studebaker" hardtops with "Cadillac" V-8 engines.

STURGES
USA 1895
Sturges Electric Motorcycle Co., Chicago, Illinois. Electric cars.
See "Morrison Electric."

STURGIS
USA 1897
Sturgis & Bros., Los Angeles, California. Electric cars.
See "Erie & Sturgis."

STURMEY
GB
See "Lotis."

STURTEVANT
USA 1905–1907
Sturtevant Mills Co., Boston and Hyde Park, Massachusetts. Touring cars. Automatic transmission and air brakes from 1904.

STUTZ
USA 1911–1935
Stutz Auto Parts Co. Ideal Motor Car Co., Indianapolis, Indiana. 1913 name changed to Stutz Motor Car Co.; "of America" added 1916.
See "Blackhawk." 36,249 cars were made.

STUTZ BLACKHAWK
USA 1970–present
Stutz Motor Car Co. of America, New York, N.Y. A $22,500–$110,000 handbuilt two-passenger car.

STUTZMAN
USA 1899
Frank Stutzman, Williamsport, Pennsylvania. Experimental gasoline automobile.

STUTZNÄCKER
D
See "Regent."

STUYVESANT
USA 1911–1912
Stuyvesant Motor Car Co., Cleveland, Ohio. Succeeded Gaeth Motor Car Co.

See "Gaeth." Bought by Grant-Lees 1911. Touring cars.

STYLE AUTO
D c. 1985
Style Auto GmbH, Wegberg. Tuning.

STYLING GARAGE
D 1983–1995
Styling Garage Handelsges. MbH, Hamburg. Tuning.

SUBARU
J 1958–present
Fuji Heavy Industries Ltd., Tokyo. 4 × 4 passenger and sports cars.

SUBURBAN
USA 1911–1912
DeSchaum Motor Car Co., Ecorse and Detroit, Michigan.

SUBURBAN STEAM
USA 1904
Edward S. Clark, Boston, Massachusetts.

SUCCES
B 1952
M. Borgerhout, Anvers. Three-wheelers.

SUCCESS
USA 1906–1909
J.C. Higdon. Success Auto Buggy Mfg. Co., St. Louis, Missouri. Highwheelers.

SUERE
F 1909–1930
J. Suere, Paris. Touring cars.

SUFFIELD & BROWN
GB
See "New Century."

SUHE
D 1985
Suhe Design, Autohaus Fritz Stoll KG, Görwihl. Tuning.

SULAM
BR 1976–present
Sulam Ind. e Com. Ltda., São Paulo. Estate car tuning.

SULLIVAN
USA 1904
Roger S. Sullivan & Co., Detroit, Michigan.

SULLIVAN
USA 1914
A.H. Sullivan, St. Louis, Missouri. Cyclecars.

SULMAN SIMPLEX
AUS 1923
Tom Sulman, Camperdown, N.S.W. Light cars.

SULTAN
USA 1908–1912
Sultan Motor Car Co., Springfield, Massachusetts Touring cars.

SULTANE
F 1903–1910
Lethimonnier et Cie., Paris. Touring cars.

SUMIDA
J 1933–1937
Jidosha Kogyo Co. Ltd., Tokyo. Passenger and light military vehicles. Later "Isuzu."

SUMINOE
J 1954–1955
Suminoe Engineering Works, Ltd., Tokyo. "Flying Feather" small cars.

SUMMERS
D
See "Moll."

SUMMERS & HARDING
GB 1913
Cyclecars.

SUMMIT
AUS 1922–1926
Summit Motors, Sydney, N.S.W. Assembled cars using a Lycoming engine.

SUMMIT
USA 1907–1909
Summit Carriage-Mobile Co., Waterloo, Iowa. Also called "Carriage Mobile." Highwheelers.

SUMNER
USA 1901–1902
Harry Sumner, Cincinnati, Ohio. Gasoline automobiles to custom order.

SUN
D 1906–1908
Sun Motorwagen-Gesellschaft E. Jeannin & Co. KG, Berlin. High quality passenger cars.

SUN
D 1920–1924
Sun Automobil-Kleinkraftwagen Ges. (1920–1923). Sun Motorfahrzeuge Henri Jeannin, Berlin (1924). Small cars.

SUN
USA 1915–1917
Sun Motor Car Co., Buffalo, N.Y. (1915); Elkhart, Indiana (1916–1917). Founded by R. Crawford and R.C. Hoffman, formerly of "Haynes." Plant reported sold to W.L. Hoffman, Omaha, Nebraska for truck mfg. September 1918. Roadsters and touring cars.

SUN
USA 1921–1922
The Automotive Corp., Toledo, Ohio. Air-cooled cars.

SUNBEAM
GB 1899–1937; 1953–1978
John Marston Ltd. (1899–1905). Sunbeam Motor Car Co. Ltd., Wolverhampton, Staffs. (1905–1935). Sunbeam Motors Ltd., London (1936–1937). Sunbeam-Talbot Ltd. (1953–1970). Chrysler UK Ltd., Ryton-on-Dunsmore, Warwickshire (1970–1978). Passenger and sports cars.

SUNBEAM-TALBOT
GB 1938–1954
Sunbeam-Talbot Ltd., London (1938–1945); Ryton-on-Dunsmore, Warwicks. (1946–1954). Sports cars.

SUNCAR
F 1979–1983
SunCar, Annecy. Replicars.

SUNRAY
USA 1990s
Sun Ray Productions, Minneapolis, Minnesota. Kit cars.

SUNRAY
USA 1995
Suntera Electric Chariot Co., Hawaii. Electric three-wheelers. Assembled also in Belgium by the Suntera Europe.

SUNROAD
D 1986
Walz & Kessler, Dusslingen. "MG" (GB) replicars.

SUNSET
USA 1900–1913
Sunset Automobile Co., San Francisco, California (1900–1906). Victor Motor Car Co., San Jose, California (1906–1913). 1900–1904 steam cars. 1904–1906 gasoline cars. Factory burned down during San Francisco earthquake.

SUN VALLEY
USA 1990s

Sun Valley Autotech, Scottsdale, Arizona. Kit cars.

SUNWATT
CH c. 1989
Sunwatt Bio, Chene-Bourg. Electric city cars.

S.U.P.
F 1919–1922
Usines du Paquis, Cons-la-Granville/Ardennes. Sergant 1.8-litre engine.

SUPER
F 1912–1914
Leveque Freres, Asnieres, Seine. Cyclecar.

SUPERIOR
CDN 1910
William English, Petrolia, Ontario. 60 cars were built.

SUPERIOR
D 1905–1906
Superior Fahrrad- und Maschinen-Industrie Hans Hartmann, Eisenach. Voiturette.

SUPERIOR
USA 1901
Superior Gas Engine Works, West Superior, Wisconsin.

SUPERIOR
USA 1902
Superion Motor Carriage Co., Cleveland, Ohio.

SUPERIOR
USA 1909
Superior Fire Department, Superior, Wisconsin. 3 feet long and 18 inches high vehicle.

SUPERIOR
USA 1910
Superion Motor Vehicle Co., Buffalo, N.Y.

SUPERIOR
USA 1914
Crescent Motor Car Co., St. Louis, Missouri.

SUPER KAR
USA 1946
Louis R. Elrad, Cleveland, Ohio. Three-wheelers.

SUPER LAMINÁT
CS 1962
Vývojové středisko družstevního podniku Služba, Česká Třebová. 350cc invalid car prototype.

SUPER MINI
CH 1972
Carrosserie Schwarzenbach AG, Thalwil. "Mini" (GB) shortened version, one-off.

SUPER SPORT
USA 1970
Automotive Design Associates, Inc., Monroe, Connecticut. Fiberglass street buggy, kit cars, with 78½ inch "Volkswagen" chassis.

SUPER STATION WAGON
USA 1954
Henney Motor Co., Freeport, Illinois. 12-passenger wagon.

SUPER-STEAMER
USA 1918–1919
Peterson-Culp Gearless Steam Auto. Mfg. Co., Denver, Colorado. One touring steam car produced.

SUPER-TRAHUIT
F 1947–1949
Lucien Rosengart, Neuilly-sur-Seine. "Mercury" (USA) V8 4-litre engine powered sports cars.
    See "Rosengart."

SUPER TWO
GB 1960–1965
Super Accessories (L.R. Montgomery & Co. Ltd.), Bromley, Kent. Sports cars.

SUPPAN
CH 1972
Dr. Peter Suppan, Lausanne. Rhomboid wheel placement, prototype.

SUPREME
USA 1917–1922
Supreme Motors Corp., Cleveland, Ohio. Company formed in 1918 to build engines (Warren, Ohio).

SURAHAMMAR
S
    See "Vabis."

SURREY
GB 1921–1930
West London Scientific Apparatus Co. Ltd. (1921–1922). Surrey Service Ltd. (1922–1927). Surrey Light Cars, London (1927–1930). Assembled light cars.

SURREY
USA 1959–1960
E.W. Bliss Co., Canton, Ohio. Replica of 1903 "Oldsmobile."

SURRIDGE
GB 1912–1913
Robert Surridge, London. Cyclecars.

SUTTON
AUS 1900–1901
Austral Otis Co., Melbourne, Victoria. 6 hp paraffin engine drove the front wheels by chains.

SUZUKI
J 1961–present
Suzuki Motor Co., Hamamatsu. Passenger and sports cars.

SUZUKI-SANTANA
E 1996–present
Suzuki-Santana Motor S.A., Linares/Jaen. 4 × 4 cars.

S.V.
USA 1924–1927
Steam Vehicle Corp. of America, Allentown, Pennsylvania. 133 steam cars were made.

SVA
I 1949
Societa Valdostana per la Costruzione di Motori, Aosta. Sports cars.

SVAN
I 1906
Venezia.

ŠVEJDA
CS 1931
Jan Švejda, Mladá Boleslav. Water-cooled 6-cylinder open car prototype.

SVELTE
F 1904–1907
SA de Construction Mecaniques de la Loire, St. Étienne/Loire. Engines from 16 hp to 50 hp.

S.V.G.
USA 1910–1911
Reading, Pennsylvania.

S.V.P.
F 1905–1906
Sté. des Voitures Populaires, Paris. Light two-seater.

SWALLOW
GB 1922
Sir J.F. Payne-Gallwey, Brown & Co. Ltd., London. Light cars.

SWALLOW DORETTI
GB 1954–1955
Swallow Coachbuilding Co. Ltd., Walsall, Staff. Sports cars.

SWAN
F 1923
E. Bloch, Neuilly/Seine. 1.2- and 2-litre Altos engines.

SWAN
USA 1903–1904
Swan Electric Co. (W.J. Swan), Middletown, California. Electric cars.

SWANSON
USA 1910
Swanson Brothers, Stromsburg, Nebraska. Juvenile car.

SWARTZ
USA 1920
Reading, Pennsylvania.

SWATCH
CH/D 1990–1993
SMH Schweizerische Gesellschaft für Mikroelektronik und. Uhrenindustrie AG, Biel. Electric cars or gasoline motor powered minicars.

SWEANY
USA 1895
Charles S. Caffrey Co., Camden, New Jersey. One steam car produced.
See "Caffrey."

SWEDLAND
USA c. 1902
E.J. Swedland, Atwater, Minnesota. Two cars were built.

SWENEY
USA 1901
Busby P. Sweney, Marion, Ohio. Friction-drive gasoline runabout.

SWIFT
CDN 1910
Swift Motor Car Co. of Canada Ltd., Chatham, Ontario. One prototype was built.

SWIFT
GB 1900–1931
Swift Motor Co. Ltd (1900–1919). Swift of Coventry Ltd., Coventry, Warwickshire (1919–1931). Cyclecars and light cars.

SWIFT
USA 1899–1900
Swift & Co., St. Joseph, Missouri.

SWIFT
USA 1904
A.T. Swift, Readfield, Maine. 6 hp automobile.

SWIFT
USA 1910
Swift Automobile Co., Wayne, Michigan. 20 and 40 hp cars.

SWIFT
USA 1959
Swift Manufacturing Co., El Cajon, Califonia. ⅝ scale copies of antique cars.

SWINGER
USA 1968
Fibercraft, Inc., Reno, Nevada. Dune buggy.

SWINNERTON
AUS 1907
Leichhardt, N.S.W. Passenger cars.

SWISS BUGGY
CH 1972–1977
René Schmid & Co., Otelfingen. Dune buggy.

SYCAR
GB 1915
Three-wheeler.

SYLPHE
F 1920
Sté. S.E.D.A.S., Bois Colombes/Seine. 6 hp light cars.

SYLVA
GB 1982–1993
Sylva Autokits Ltd., Manby, Louth, Lincolnshire. Sports cars.

SYLVESTER
USA c. 1905
S.A. Sylvester, Newton Centre, Massachusetts. 6 hp automobile.

SYMBOL
GB 1982
Symbol International Group, London. Convertibles.

SYMETRIC
F 1951–1958
Loubiere Freres & Automobile Francois Arbel, Paris. Plastic and wooden coachworks, gas-electric powered.

SYMINGTON
GB 1786
William Symington, Edinburgh. Steam car.

SYNNESTVEDT
USA 1904–1905
Synnestvedt Vehicle Co. Synnestvedt Machine Co., Pittsburgh, Pennsylvania. Electric cars. After 1905 built trucks only.

SYRACUSE
USA 1899–1903
Saul & Van Wagoner Co., Syracuse, N.Y. Electric cars.

SYRENA
PL 1955–1972
Fabryka Samochodow Osobowych, Warszawa. Small cars with 2-cycle engine.

SZARITS
H c. 1903
János Szarits, Szabadka. Primitive car.

SZAWE
D 1920–1922
Szabo & Wechselmann Automobilfabrik, Berlin. Luxury cars with silver radiator and nickel-plated pipes and linkages.

SZL
SU 1952–1955
Serpukhovskii Motocikletnii Závod, Serpukhov. Three-wheeled version of small invalid "SMZ" cars. 19,128 vehicles were made.
See "SMZ."

T

T.
CH 1956
Henning Thorndahl, Thun. Sports coupe prototype.

TAFCO
USA 1982
Tafco Engineering, Bradenton, Florida. Replicars.

TAFT
USA 1901–1902
United States Mobile & Power Co., Worcester, Massachusetts. Ariston Bicycle Co., Westborough, Massachusetts. Steam cars.

TAG
CH 1978
TAG Function Car SA, Geneve. "Cadillac" (USA) Eldorado based 6-wheeled car prototype.

TAGLIABUE
I 1949
Milano. Sports cars with "Fiat" engines.

TAINCLER
USA c. 1905
Taincler & Co., Manchester, Massachusetts. 18/24 hp vehicle.

TAKURI
J 1907–1909
Tokyo Jidosha Seisakusho, Tokyo. 17 cars were made.

TALBO
USA 1994–present
TLC Carrossiers, Inc., Riviera Beach, Florida. "Talbot" Lago (F) replicars.

TALBOT
F
See "Darracq."

TALBOT
GB 1903–1938
Clement-Talbot Ltd., London. Touring cars.

TALBOT
GB 1980–1988
Talbot Motor Company Ltd., Whitley, Coventry. Passenger cars.

TALBOT-DARRACQ
F
See "Darracq."

TALON
GB 1979–1980
GP Concessionaires Ltd., London. Kit cars.

T.A.M.
F 1908–1925
Sté. de Travaux Mecaniques et Automobiles, Courbevoie/Seine. H. Gendron, Boulogne-sur-Seine. Light cars.

TAMA
J 1947–1951
Tokyo Electric Motorcar Co. (1947–1949). Tama Electric Motorcar Co., Tachikawa (1949–1951). Electric cars.

TAMAG
D 1932–1934
Ernst Wilhelm Taschner GmbH, Krefeld. Three-wheelers.

TAMM
D 1922
Tamm-Wagen GmbH, Karlsruhe. Cyclecars.

TAMPLIN
GB 1919–1927
Tamplin Motors, Staines, Middlesex (1912–1923); Cheam, Surrey (1923–1927). Light two-seaters.

T & F
USA 1914
T & F Cycle Car Co., New Salem, Massachusetts. Cyclecars.

TANKETTE
GB 1919–1921
Ronald Trist & Co. Ltd., Watford, Herts. Tankette Ltd., London. Three-wheelers.

TANTOR
LT
See "Baltijas."

TARASCHI
I 1947–1955
Officina Meccanica Taraschi, Teramo. Sports cars.

TARKINGTON
USA 1922–1923
Tarkington Motor Car Co., Rockford, Illinois. 6-cylinder touring cars.

TARPAN
PL 1972–c. 1994
See "FSR."

TARRANT
AUS 1901–1907
Tarrant Automobile & Engineering Co., Melbourne, Victoria. Not more than 20 cars were built.

TAS
YU/BIH 1972–1992
Tvornica automobila Sarajevo, Sarajevo-Vogosca. "Volkswagen" (D) license.

TASCO
USA 1947–1948
The American Sports Car Co., Hartford, Connecticut. One prototype built. Body by Derham, Rosemont, Pennsylvania.

TATA
IND 1994–present
Tata Engineering and Locomotive Co. Ltd., Bombay. Estate cars.

TATE
CDN 1912–1913
Tate Electric Ltd., Windsor, Ontario. Electric cars.

TATIN
F 1899
V. Tatin, Paris. Simple three-wheelers.

TATRA
CS/CZ 1919–1998
Tatra, akc. spol. pro stavbu automobilu a železničních vozu (1919–1945). Tatra, n.p. (1945–1990). Tatra, akc. spol., Kopřivnice (1990–1998). Famous for streamlined air-cooled rear-engined cars.
See "NW."

TAU
I 1924–1926
Pietro Scaglione, Torino. About 100 cars built.

TAUNTON
GB/B 1914–1920
Taunton Manufacturing Co. Ltd., London. Taunton Cars Ltd., Liege. Passenger cars.

TAUNTON
USA 1901–1903
Taunton Automobile Co., Taunton, Massachusetts. Steam cars.

TAUNTON
USA 1904–1905
Taunton Motor Carriage Co., Taunton, Massachusetts. One-cylinder runabout with 68-inch wheel base was the only model built.

TAUNUS
D 1907–1909
Taunus Automobilfabrik GmbH, Frankfurt am Main. 4-cylinder 12 hp cars.

TAURA
I 1924–1926
Three-wheelers.

TAURINIA
I 1902–1908
Societa Taurinia (1902–1907). Fabbrica Automobili Taurinia, Giuseppe Alby, Eugenio Canfari, Francesco Darbesio, Torino (1907–1908).

TAUZIN
F 1899
Tauzin et Cie., Levallois-Perret/Seine. Voiturette.

TAVRIA
SU/UA 1987–present
Avto ZAZ, Zaporozhie. Small cars.
  See "ZAZ."

TAYLOR
GB 1922–1924
Taylor's Motors Ltd., Newcastle upon Tyne. Meadows engine.

TAYLOR
GB 1990s
Stuart Taylor, Ilkeston, Derbyshire. Sports kit cars.

TAYLOR
CDN/USA 1867
Henry Seth Taylor, Stanstead, Quebec; Derby Line, Vermont. Steam cars.

TAYLOR
USA 1895
E.E. Taylor, Fitchburg, Massachusetts.

TAYLOR
USA 1899
George W. Taylor, Long Beach, California. Three-wheelers.

TAYLOR-DUNN
USA 1948–1968
Taylor-Dunn Manufacturing Co., Anaheim, California. Electric cars.

TAYLOR-SWETNAM
GB 1913
Taylor, Swetnam & Co., Coventry, Warwickshire. Light cars.

TAZ
CS/SK 1973–1998
Trnavské automobilové závody, n.p., Trnava. Taxicabs and minibuses.

TB
GB 1919–1923
Thompson Bros. (Bilston) Ltd., Bilston, Staffs. Three-wheelers.

T-BUG
USA 1968
Lincoln Industries, Lincoln, California. Dune buggy.

T.D.C.
GB
  See "Crompton."

TECHART
D 1993–1998
TechArt, Leonberg. Tuning.

TECHNICAL EXPONENTS
GB 1976–?
Technical Exponents Ltd., London. Sports cars.

TECNAUTO
I 1936
One car produced with coachwork by Balbo.

TECO
D 1924–1925
Teco-Werke GmbH, Stettin. 30 hp passenger cars.

TECO
GB 1905
Thornton Engineering Co. Ltd., Bradford, Yorks. Assembled from English and French components.

TEETOR-HARTLEY
USA 1916
Teetor-Hartley Motor Co., Hagerstown, Indiana.

TEFFT
USA c. 1905
John H. Tefft, Hope Valley, Rhode Island. 5 hp automobile.

TEILHOL
F 1972–1992
Teilhol Voiture Electrique, Ambert/Puy-de-Dome. Electric cars.

TEMPELHOF
D
  See "B.M.F."

TEMPERINO
I 1907–1925
Fratelli Maurizio, Giacomo & Carlo Temperino (1907–1919). Vetturette Temperino S.A., Torino (1919–1925). Light cars.

TEMPEST
GB 1989
John Box. Three-wheeler based on the "Reliant" Fox.

TEMPLAR
USA 1917–1924
S.P. Mfg. Co. (1917). Templar Motors Corp. (1918–1924). Templar Motor Car Co. (1924), Cleveland, Ohio. Roadsters and touring cars. 5,519 cars were made.

TEMPLE
USA 1899
Robert Temple, Denver, Colorado. Gasoline car.

TEMPLE
USA 1902–1903
T.W. Temple, McPherson, Kansas. Automobiles to order.

TEMPLE-MARVEL
USA 1907
T.W. Temple, Chicago, Illinois. Marvel Motor Car Co., Detroit, Michigan.

TEMPLETON
USA 1895
John Templeton, Chicago, Illinois.

TEMPLETON-DUBRIE
USA 1910
Templeton-Dubrie Car Co., Detroit, Michigan.

TEMPLE-WESTCOTT
USA 1921–1922
Bealer Body Co., Framingham, Massachusetts.

TEMPO
D 1933–1956
Suhr & Co., Altona. Tempo GmbH, Hamburg. Vidal & Sohn, Hamburg. Vidal & Sohn Tempo-Werk, Hamburg. Three-wheelers.

TEMPO
IND c. 1958–present
Bajaj-Tempo, Poona. Three-wheelers and estate cars.

TENNANT
USA 1915
Tennant Motors Ltd., Chicago, Illinois. Roadsters and touring cars.

TENTING
F 1891–1899
Sté. Nationale de Construction de Moteurs H. Tenting, Boulogne-sur-Seine. Variable-speed friction transmission.

TERMAAT & MONAHAN
USA 1914
Termaat & Monahan Co., Oshkosh, Wisconsin. Cyclecars.
See "Ziebell."

TERRA BUGGY
USA 1968
Terra Knife Inc., Crawfordsville, Indiana. Dune buggy.

TERRAL
D 1987
Sun-Car GmbH, Quickborn. Sports cars.

TERRAPLANE
USA 1932–1938
Hudson Motor Car Co., Detroit, Michigan. Formerly "Essex-Terraplane"; roadsters and touring cars.

TERRA TIGER
USA 1968–c. 1973
Feldmann Engineering & Mfg. Co., Sheboygan Falls, Wisconsin. Six-wheeler. "Jeep"-type off road vehicles.

TERRIER
GB 1959–1961; 1975
L. Terry, London; Thornwood, Essex. Sports cars.

TERROT
F 1912–1914
SA des Établissements Terrot, Dijon/Cote d'Or. Voiturette.

TERWILLIGER
USA 1897; 1902
Terwilliger & Co., Amsterdam, N.Y. Steam cars.
See "Empire Steamer" (1904–1905).

TESINI
I
See "Martes."

TESTE ET MORET
F 1898–1903
Teste et Moret, Lyon-Vaise/Rhone. Light cars.

TEUFELSKÄFER
D 1924–1927
Felix Wankel, Heidelberg. Streamlined three-wheeler prototype.

TEX
USA 1915
Texas Motor car Co., San Antonio, Texas. 35 hp 5-passenger touring cars.

TEXAN
USA 1920–1922
Texas Motor Car Association, Fort Worth and Cleburne, Texas. Touring cars and roadsters. Receiver operated from October 1920.

TEXAS
USA 1920
Texas Truck & Tractor Co., Dallas, Texas.

TEXMOBILE
USA 1920–1921
Little Motor Kar Co., Grand Prairie, Texas.

T.G.E.
J
See "Chiyoda."

T.H.
E
See "Ideal."

THACHER
USA 1902
Thacher Car Wheel Works, Albany, N.Y.

THAMES
GB 1906–1911
Thames Ironworks, Shipbuilding & Engineering Co. Ltd., London. Sports cars.

THANET
GB
See "Whitehead-Thanet."

THAON
CH 1970–1975
Montreux. Electric minicars.

THAYER
USA 1907–1908
Thayer Isham Automobile Co., Marinette, Wisconsin.

THEIN & GOLDBERGER
A 1907
Thein & Goldberger, Wien. Voiturette.

THEIS
D 1923–1924
Karl Theis, Berlin. Three-wheelers.

THEIS
D 1985–1993
Karl Theis GmbH, München. Tuning.

THEYER & ROTHMUND
A 1900
Theyer, Rothmund & Co., Wien. Electric cars called "Excelsior."

THIEM
USA 1901–1904
Thiem & Co., St. Paul, Minnesota. Virtue, Pound & Co., Rushford, Minnesota.

THIES
USA 1908
Frank Thies, Chaffee, North Dakota. 10/12 hp automobile.

THIEULIN
F 1907–1908
Automobiles Thieulin, Besancon/Doubs. Light cars.

THOLOME
F 1920–1922
M. Tholome, St. Ouen/Seine. Cyclecars.

THOMAS
GB 1903
W.F. Thomas, Birmingham. Light cars.

THOMAS
USA 1900
D.W. Thomas, Boston, Massachusetts. Experimental steam car.

THOMAS
USA 1904
Charles C. Thomas, Ann Arbor, Michigan. Runabout.

THOMAS
USA 1903–1918
E.R. Thomas Motor Co., Buffalo, N.Y. Founded 1898. Absorbed Buffalo Auto & Auto-Bi Co. 1902. Established Detroit Branch 1906.
See "Thomas-Detroit." Merged with Columbus Buggy Co. 1914. See "Firestone-Columbus." More than 8,000 cars were made.

THOMAS
USA 1914
Acme Engine Co., Lansing & Saginaw, Michigan. 18 hp small cars.

THOMAS
USA 1939
Charles D. Thomas, Batavia, N.Y. Streamlined coupe.

THOMAS-DETROIT
USA 1906–1908
E.R. Thomas-Detroit Co., Detroit, Michigan. Became Chalmers-Detroit Co.
See "Chalmers-Detroit."

THOMASSINA
I
Thomas Maede, Modena. Sports car prototype.

THOMOND
IRL 1925–1929
J.A. Jones, Dublin. Sports cars.

THOMPSON
USA 1899–1900
Thompson Automobile Co., Camden, New Jersey.

THOMPSON
USA 1901
Andrew C. Thompson, Plainfield, New Jersey. Electric cars.

THOMPSON
USA 1901–1902
Zenas Thompson & Brothers, Portland, Maine. Steam cars.

THOMPSON
USA 1901–1907
Zenas Thompson & Bros. Thompson Automobile Co., Providence, Rhode Island. Steam cars.

THOMPSON
USA 1909
Newton Thompson, Beverly Farms, Massachusetts. Roadster.

THOMPSON-KANTER
USA 1901
William M. Thompson & Harold B. Kanter, Meadville, Pennsylvania. Gasoline runabout.

THOMSON
AUS 1896–1901
Thomson & Co., Melbourne, Victoria. Steam cars.

THOMSON
AUS 1947
See "Wiles-Thomson."

THOMSON
F 1913–1928
Établissements Industrielles Raymond Thomas, Talence/Gironde. Light cars; 6.6-litre Janvier engined tourer.

THOMSON
USA 1900
General Electric Co., Lynn, Massachusetts. Steam car built by Prof. Elihu Thomson.

THOMSON
USA 1900–1903
Thomson Automobile Co., Philadelphia, Pennsylvania. Steam and gasoline vehicles.

THOMSON
USA 1911–1913
Malcolm Thomson, Lynn, Massachusetts. Roadsters with 4- and 2-stroke engines.

THOR
GB 1904–1906
Thor Motor Car Co., London. Light cars.

THOR
GB 1919–1921
Simpson, Taylor Ltd., London. Touring cars.

THOR
USA 1907–1909
Thor Power Tool Co., Aurora, Illinois. Touring cars.

THORN
USA c. 1905
John G. Thorn, Lynn, Massachusetts. 4.5 hp automobile

THORN ET HOGAN
F 1901–1902
Thorn, Hogan et Cie., Puteaux/Seine. Four-seater tonneau.

THORNE TIGER
USA 1944–1945
Thorne Engineering Co., Los Angeles, California. Designed by Art Sparks. Became "Californian" and "Davis."

THORNYCROFT
GB 1903–1913
John I. Thornycroft & Co. Ltd., Basingstoke, Hampshire. Passenger cars.

THOROUGHBRED
USA 1981–1985
Thoroughbred Motorcars, Inc., Redmond, Washington. Replicars.

THREE BOYS' CAR
USA 1908
Leslie Brewer, Freddy Richardson & Willie Dolliver, Bar Harbor, Maine. 4 hp automobile.

THRESHER
USA 1900
Thresher Electric Co., Dayton, Ohio. Electric cars.

THRIFT-T
USA 1947–1955
Tri-Wheel Motor Corp., Springfield, Massachusetts. Three-wheelers. Max. production 50 per month.

THRIGE
DK 1909–1918
Thomas B. Thrige AS, Odense. Ballot and Daimler-Knight engines.

THRUPP & MABERLY
GB 1896
Thrupp & Maberly, London. Electric cars.

TH. SCHNEIDER
F 1910–1931
Automobiles Th. Schneider, Besancon/Doubs; Boulogne-sur-Seine. 4- and 6-cylinder touring cars.

T.H.T.
USA 1910
T.H.T. Motor Co., Detroit, Michigan.

THULIN
S 1920–1928
AB Thulinverken, Landskrona. About 300 passenger cars built.

THUNDER RANCH
USA 1990s
Thunder Ranch, El Cajon, California. Kit cars.

THÜRINGER MOTORWAGENFABRIK
D 1894
Thüringer Motorwagenfabrik A. Schütterer & L. Schneider, Neustadt (Orla). 5 cars were built.

THURLOW
GB 1920–1921
Thurlow & Co., London. Three-wheelers.

THURNER
D 1969–1973
Rudolf Thurner, Karosseriebau & Sportwagen, Bernbeuren. About 100 sports cars were built.

THURSTON
USA 1903
Silas Thurston, Sunbury, Pennsylvania. Belt-driven three-wheeler.

THURY & NUSSBERGER
CH 1877–1878
R. Thury & J. Nussberger, Geneve. Steam three-wheelers.

TIANJIN
PRC 1988–c. 1993
Tianjin Automobile Factory, Hanjiasho, Tianjin. "Daihatsu" (J) license.
   See "Xiali."

TIBICAR
I 1978–1984
Roma. 2-seater three-wheelers.

TICI
GB 1966–1973
TiCi Cars Ltd., Loughborough, Leics; Sutton-in-Ashfield, Notts. 848cc two-seater minicars.

TIC-TAC
F 1920–1924
F. Dumoulin, Puteaux/Seine. Cyclecars.

TIDAHOLM
S 1906–1913
Tidaholm Bruks AB, Tidaholm. Trucks mainly, but about 4 passenger cars were also built.

TIENTSIN
PRC 1959–1980s
Passenger cars and 4 × 4 vehicles.

TIFFANY
USA 1913–1914
Tiffany Electric Car Co., Flint, Michigan. Electric cars.

TIFFANY
USA 1967–1988
Tiffany Motor Cars, Bay Products Corporation, Opa Locka, Florida. Kit cars and replicars.

TIFFANY-BIJOU
USA 1914
E.L. Pelletier, New York, N.Y. Electric cars.

TIGER
USA 1914–1915
Automobile Cyclecar Co. (W.A. DeSchaum), Detroit, Michigan. Cyclecars.

TILBURY
F 1986–present
Martin Automobiles, Olonne-sur-Mer. Replicars.

TILEY
USA 1904–1913
Tiley-Pratt Co., Essex, Connecticut. Experimental car 1904. About 25 cars built.

TILIKUM
USA 1914–1915
Yukon Auto Shop. Tilikum Cyclecar Co., Seattle, Washington. Cyclecars.

TILLI
AUS 1957
Tilli Motor Company, Melbourne. Three-wheeler prototype.

TIME
USA 1916
Time Mfg. Co., Oustburg, Wisconsin.

TIME MACHINE
USA c. 1993
Time Machine Motorcar Comp., Brooksville, Florida. Replicars.

TIMMIS
CDN 1968–1993
Timmis Motor Co. Ltd., Victoria, B.C. Replicas using original parts of the 1930s.

TINCHER
USA 1903–1909
Chicago Coach & Carriage Co., Chicago, Illinois (1903–1906). 1904 became Tincher Motor Car Co. South Bend, Indiana (1907–1909). Absorbed by Studebaker Automobile Co. 1907. Touring cars.

TINGLE
USA 1939
J.G. Tingle, Miami, Florida. Two-wheeled car.

TINKHAM
USA 1898–1899
Denison & Walton. Tinkham Cycle Co., New York, N.Y.; New Haven, Connecticut. Three-wheelers. Built by Denison Motor Carriage Co.
   See "Denison."

TINKHAM
USA 1900–1901
Piper & Tinkham Co., Waltham, Massachusetts. Steam cars.

TIN-LIZZIE
USA 1960–1974
McDonough Power Equipment Co., McDonough, Georgia. ½ scale 1910 "Ford" T replicars.

TINY
CH c. 1989
Selec AG, Neunhof. Electric folding minicars.

TINY
GB 1913–1915
Nanson, Barker & Co. Ltd., Esholt, Yorks. Cyclecar.

TINY
H 1968
Elektromos Kutató Intézet, Budapest. Electric car prototype.

TIPPEN DELTA
GB 1967
Coventry. Three-wheelers.

TIPPMANN
D 1902–1904
Max Tippmann & Co., Dresden.

TISCHER
USA 1914
Tischer-Linton Tri-Car Co., Peoria, Illinois. Three-wheelers.

TITAN
GB 1911
Titan Motor Wheel Co., Coventry, Warwickshire. Three-wheelers.

TITAN
USA 1911–1913
United States Motor Co., Detroit, Michigan. Little taxicabs.

TIVY
USA 1901–1903
Tivy Cycle Mfg. Co., Williamsport, Pennsylvania. Steam cars.

TJAARDA
USA 1935
Briggs Mfg. Co., Detroit, Michigan. Experimental prototype of "Lincoln Zephyr."
   See "Briggs."

T.J.K. SPECIAL
USA 1909
T.J. Kehoe, Ft. Wayne, Indiana.

T.M.
1906

T.M.F
USA 1909
Termott, Monahan & Farney, Oshkosh, Wisconsin. Highwheelers.

TOBEY
USA c. 1905
W.L. Tobey, Winthrop, Massachusetts. 15 hp automobile.

TOBOGGAN
GB 1905–1906
Toboggan Tri-car Co. Ltd., London. Three-wheelers.

TOD
GB 1897
Michael Tod, Scotland. One-off three-wheeler.

TODD
USA 1895
Chicago Fireproof Covering Co., Chicago, Illinois.

TODESCHINI
I 1899
Vetture Lecas Todeschini, Milano.

TOFAS
TR 1966–present
Türkiye Otomobil Fabrikasi Ananim Sirketi, Istanbul. Tofas Oto Ticaret A.S., Levent, Istanbul. "Fiat" (I) license.

TOJEIRO
GB 1952–1962
Tojeiro Automotive Developments Ltd., Royston, Herts. Sports cars.

TOLEDO
USA 1901–1903
American Bicycle Co. Toledo Motor Carriage Co. International Motor Car Co., Toledo, Ohio. Steam and gasoline vehicles. Became Pope Motor Car Co.
  See "Toledo-Toledo," "Hydrocar."

TOLEDO
USA 1909
Apperson-Toledo Motor Co., Toledo, Ohio. Limousines.

TOLEDO
USA 1913–1914
Toledo Autocycle Co. National United Service Co., Detroit, Michigan; Toledo, Ohio. Cyclecars.

TOM
D
  See "Ferbedo."

TOMÁNEK
CS 1938
Automobilka Tománek, Český Těšín. Light car prototype.

TOMASZO
A 1984–1993
Tomaszo Fiberglas Produkte GmbH, Achau. Replicars.

TOMCAR
F 1984
50 cc engine powered minicars.

TOMLINSON
USA 1900
D.W. Tomlinson Jr., Batavia, N.Y.
  See "Cooley."

TOMMASI & RIZZI
I
  See "IENA."

TOMMY
J 1997–present
Tomita Auto Co. Ltd., Kita-ku, Tokyo. Sports cars.

TOMOS
YU 1961–1973
Tovarna Motornih Vozil, Koper. "Citroën" (F) license.
  See "Cimos."

TOM POUCE
F 1920–1924
Blanc et Guillon, Puteaux/Seine (1920–1923). Garage Ernault, Dommartin/Somme (1923–1924). Cyclecars.

TOM THUMB
USA 1910
Detroit Boat Works, Detroit, Michigan.

TONAWANDA
USA 1900–1902
Tonawanda Motor Vehicle Co., Tonawanda, N.Y. Electric cars.

TONE
USA 1913
Tone Car Corp., Indianapolis, Indiana.

TONELLO
I 1921–1923
Automobili Tonello, di Guido Meregalli, Milano.

TONTALA
AUS 1956
Fiberglass coupe kit cars.

TONY HUBER
F 1902–1906
Automobiles Tony Huber, Billancourt/Seine. 8 and 11 hp cars.

TOPLISS
USA 1928
L.G. Topliss, Wisconsin. Roadster.

TOQUET
USA 1905
Toquet Motor Car & Construction Co. Toquet Motor Co., Boston, Massachusetts; Saugatuck, Connecticut. Touring cars.

TORBENSEN
USA 1902–1906
Torbensen Gear Co., Bloomfield, New Jersey. Mostly running gear and delivery cars. Runabouts.

TORINO
RA 1966–c. 1976
Industrias Kaiser Argentina SAIC (1966–1968). IKA-Renault SAIC y F., Cordoba (1968–c. 1976). Cars of foreign design ("Jeep" USA, "Rambler" USA, "Renault" F).

TORNADO
GB 1958–1964
Tornado Cars Ltd., Rickmansworth, Herts. 2- and 4-seater sports cars. About 600 were built.

TORNADO
GB 1984–1993
Tornado Sports Cars, Kidderminster, Worcs. Sports cars.

TORNADO
USA 1990s
Tornado Sports Cards, Meriden, Connecticut. Kit cars.

TORNAX
D 1934–1937
Tornax Fahrzeug- und Apparatebau Wewer & Schmidtmann GmbH, Wuppertal. About 150 cars were built.

TORO
PI 1974–1978
R.V. Alfonso, DMG Inc., Manilla. Sports cars.

TORPEDO
A/CS 1907
Trojan a Nágl, Kolín. 6/7 hp voiturette.

TORPEDO
D 1913
Berliner Automobil-Fabrik "Torpedo," Berlin. Three-wheelers.

TORPEDO
GB 1909
T. Hopper & Co. Ltd., Barton-on-Humber, Lincs. Light 2-cylinder cars.

TORPEDO
I 1989–1993
Torpedo Srl, Bergamo. Electric cars based on "Fiat" Marbella and "Oltcit" (RO).

TORPILLE
B 1920
M.M. Schoofs, Ixelles-Bruxelles. Tandem two-seater three-wheelers.

TORRELARO
E/U 1993–present
Torrelaro Barcelona Grial Art, Barcelona (E). Guitolar Ltda., Montevideo (U). Replicars.
See "Leggatti" (D).

TORRENCE
USA 1903
William W. Torrence, Montrose, Colorado. Runabouts.

TOSCANA
I 1901–1905
Firenze.

TOTAL
USA 1977–1983
Total Performance, Inc., Wallingford, Connecticut. "Ford" (USA) Type A replica.

TOTEM
USA 1921–1922
Davis Car Co., Seattle, Washington. 38 hp light cars.

TOURAINE
USA 1907
Automobile Parts & Equipment Co., Chicago, Illinois.

TOURAINE
USA 1912–1916
Touraine Co., Philadelphia, Pennsylvania. Touring cars and runabouts. Succeeded "Nance."

TOURAND
F 1900–1907
Tourand et Cie., Le Havre/Seine-Inferieure; Suresnes/Seine. 4-cylinder shaft-drive cars.

TOURETTE
GB 1956–1958
Carr Bros (1956). Progress Supreme Co. Ltd., Purley, Surrey (1957–1958). Three-wheelers.

TOUREY
F 1898
Jules Tourey, Paris. 4 hp horizontal 1-cylinder engine.

TOURING
I 1953–1960s
Carrozzeria Superleggera Touring, Milano. Sports cars.

TOURIST
D 1907–1920
"Tourist" Automobil-Werke GmbH, Berlin (1907–1911). Berliner Automobil-Fabrik "Torpedo," Georg Beck & Co., Berlin (1911–1920). Three-wheelers.

TOURIST
USA 1902–1910
Auto Vehicle Co., Los Angeles, California. 2,692 cars were made.

TOWANDA
USA 1902–1904
Towanda Motor Vehicle Co., Towanda, Pennsylvania. Sold without motor. Succeeded Centaur Motor Vehicle Co.

TOWER
USA 1899
C.E. Tower, Syracuse, N.Y. 2-cylinder 4 hp gasoline trap.

TOWNE SHOPPER
USA 1947–1948
International Motor Co., San Diego, California. Air-cooled rear-engined small cars.

TOWNSEND
USA c. 1905
Guy G. Townsend, Winchendon, Massachusetts.

TOYOTA
J 1936–present
Toyota Automatic Loom Work, Kariya City (1936). Toyota Motor Co. Ltd., Toyota City (1937–present). Passenger and sports cars.

TRABANT
DDR 1959–1991
VEB Sachsenring Automobilwerk, Zwickau. Light 2-stroke 500cc and 594cc mass-produced cars.

TRABOLD
USA 1898; 1905
Adam G. Trabold, Johnstown, Pennsylvania. Two cars were built.

TRACFORD
F 1934–1935
Automobiles Tracford, Gennevilliers/Seine. Sports cars based on Model Y "Ford" (GB).

TRACKSON
AUS 1900
Brisbane, Queensland.

TRACTA
F 1926–1934
SA des Automobiles Tracta, Asnieres/Seine. Front-wheel drive.

TRACTION AÉRIENNE
F 1921–1926
Sté. La Traction Aérienne, Neuilly/Seine. Propeller-driven cars.

TRACTOBILE
USA 1990–1902
Pennsylvania Steam Vehicle Co., Carlisle, Pennsylvania. Steam cars. An attachment for horse-drawn vehicles.

TRAEGER
D 1928
A. Traeger, Freiburg. Light cars.

TRAIL BLAZER
USA 1961–1974
Hickey Mfg. Co., Downey, California. Four-wheel drive.

TRAIN
F 1924–1925
Motorcycles et Moteurs Train, Courbevoie/Seine. Cyclecars.

TRANSFORMER
GB 1987–1993
Transformer Cars Ltd., Frant, East Sussex. Sports cars.

TRASCO
D 1985–1994
Trasco Export GmbH, Bremen. Tuning.

TRANSIT STEAMER
USA 1901–1902
Steamobile Co. of America. W.S. Rogers Roller Bearing & Equipment Co., Keene, New Hampshire. Tonneau in front, driver in rear. Convertible to use on rails.
See "Steamobile."

TRASK
USA c. 1905

James H. Trask, Revere, Massachusetts. 3.5 hp automobile.

TRASK-DETROIT
USA 1922–1923
Detroit Steam Motor Corp., Detroit, Michigan. Schlieder Mfg. Co., Detroit, Michigan. Steam cars.
See "Detroit Steam Car."

TRASK-STEAM
USA 1921–1922
Trask-Kennedy Co., Detroit, Michigan. Steam cars.

TRAVELER
USA 1904
Neustadt-Perry Co., St. Louis, Missouri.
See "Neustadt."

TRAVELER
USA 1906–1908
Bellefontaine Automobile Co., Bellefontaine, Ohio. Succeeded Zent Automobile Co.
See "Zent."

TRAVELER
USA 1910–1911
Traveler Automobile Co. Single Center Buggy Co., Evansville, Indiana. Highwheelers.

TRAVELER
USA 1913–1914
Traveler Motor Car Co., Detroit, Michigan. Also called "Traveler-Detroit."

TRAVELER
USA 1924–1925
Taxicab Mfg. Co., New York, N.Y. Taxicabs.

TRAVERSE CITY
USA 1917–1918
Traverse City Motor Car Co., Traverse City, Michigan. Formerly Napoleon Motor Co. November 1916; 6 delivered and 18 under construction.
See "Napoleon."

TRAX
NL c. 1982
Interstate Motor Vehicle Co. Ltd., Delft. 4 × 4 vehicle.

TREBERT
USA 1907–1908
Trebert Auto & Marine Motor Co. Trebert Gas Engine Co., Rochester, N.Y. 4-cylinder 30 hp touring cars.

TREKKA
NZ 1966–1973
Motor Industries (International) Ltd., Otahuhu. "Škoda" (CS) based Jeep-type cars.

TRELBA
F 1933
Three-wheelers.

TRESCOWTHICK
AUS 1903
Angaston, S.A.

TRESER
D 1981–present
Walter Treser GmbH, Automobiltechnik und Design, Ingolstadt. "Audi" tuning. Sports cars of own design from 1987.

TRESKOW
D 1906–1908
Robert Treskow Motorwagenfabrik, Schönbeck bei Berlin. 10hp cars.

TRE SPADE
I 1907
Forno Rivara.
See "Bertoldo."

TREVITHICK
GB 1802
Robert Trevithick, London. Steam car.

TREY
USA c. 1923
Trey Air-Cooled Motors Corp., New York, N.Y.

TRIAD
GB 1973–present
Malvern Autocraft, Malvern, Worcester. Three-wheelers.

TRIANGEL
DK 1918–1927
De Forenede Automobilfabrik A/S, Kobenhavn. Passenger cars. Trucks and buses until 1945.

TRIBELHORN
CH 1902–1920
A.Tribelhorn, Feldbach (1902–1918). Electrische Fahrzeuge AG, Altstetten (1918–1920). Electric three-wheelers.

TRIBET
F 1909–1914
Tribet et Cie., Villeneuve-la-Garenne/Seine. Conventional shaft-driven cars.

TRIBUNE
USA 1913
Tribune Motor Co., Detroit, Michigan. Touring cars.

TRIBUNE
USA 1917
Tribune Engineering Co., Owego, N.Y. Cyclecars.

TRI-CAR
USA 1955
Lycoming Division, Avco Corp., Williamsport, Pennsylvania. Three-wheelers.

TRI-CITY
USA 1899
Tri-City Carriage Co., Davenport, Iowa. Two automobiles were built.

TRICOLET
USA 1904–1906
H. Pokorney Automobile & Gas Engine Co., Indianapolis, Indiana. Three-wheelers. Became "Pokorney."

TRIDENT
GB/F 1919–1920
Three-wheelers.

TRIDENT
GB 1965–1978
Trident Cars Ltd., Woodbridge, Suffolk (1965–1968); Ipswich, Suffolk (1968–1978) 450 sports cars built.

TRIDENT ELECTRIC
USA 1959
Taylor Dunn Mfg. Co., Anaheim, California.

TRIHAWK
USA 1983
Joseph N. Spada, Los Angeles, California. "Citroën" (F) 82 hp engine powered three-wheeler.

TRIKING
GB 1978–present
Triking Cars Ltd., Norwich, Norfolk. "Morgan" three-wheeler replicars.

TRIMAK
E 1959–1972
Madrid; Barcelona. 250cc three-wheelers.

TRIMCO
S 1971
Trimco, Stockholm. Sports coupe kit cars.

TRIMOBILE
GB
See "Avon."

TRI-MOBILE
USA 1938
W.F. Mehl, Kansas City, Missouri. Three-wheeled roadster.

TRI-MOTO
USA 1900–1901
Western Wheel Works (American Bicycle Co.), Chicago, Illinois. Three-wheelers.

TRINITY
USA 1900–1901
Trinity Mfg. Co., Keene, New Hampshire. Steam cars. Became Keene Steamobile Co., then Steamobile. Co. of America.
See "Keene Steamobile."

TRINKS
D 1924–1925
Otto Trinks Maschinenfabrik, Berlin. Three-wheelers.

TRIOMOBIL
D 1907
Otto Spiess, Spandau. Three-wheelers.

TRIONETTE
D 1921–1930
Trionette GmbH, Bremen (1921–1923); Haste bei Osnabrück (1923–1930). Three-wheelers.

TRIOULEYERS
F 1896
Compagnie Générale des Automobiles, Paris. "Benz" (D) derivative.

TRI-PHIBIAN
USA 1935
Constantios H. Vlachos, Washington, D.C. "Land-sea-air car."

TRIPLE
GB 1984–1993
Challenger Cars Ltd., Corby, Northants. Replicars and sports cars.

TRIPLER
USA 1900–1901
Tripler Liquid Air Co., Washington, D.C. Runabout.

TRIPLEX
USA 1954–1955
Kethem's Automotive Corp., Chicago, Illinois. Sports cars.

TRIPPEL
D 1934–1944; 1950–1952
Trippelwerke, Homburg/Saar (1934–1940). Trippelwerke GmbH, Molsheim (1940–1944). Protek-Gesellschaft für Industrie-Entwicklungen mbH, Tutlingen; Stuttgart (1950–1952). Light cars and amphibians.

TRI-RICKSHA
USA 1914–1915
International Tri-Ricksha Co., New York, N.Y.

TRI-STATE
USA 1903
Tri-State Automobile & Supply Co., Memphis, Tennessee,

TRITT
USA 1905
Tritt Electric Co., South Bend, Indiana. Electric cars.

TRIUMPH
D 1933
Triumph-Werke AG, Nürnberg. 3-wheeled coupe.

TRIUMPH
GB 1923–1980
Triumph Cycle Co. Ltd (1923–1929). Triumph Motor Co. Ltd., Coventry, Warwickshire (1930–1980). Passenger and sports cars.

TRIUMPH
USA 1900–1901
Triumph Motor Vehicle Co., Chicago, Illinois. Steam and electric cars.
See "Ellis Electric" 1901.

TRIUMPH
USA 1906–1907
Triumph Motor Car Co., Chicago, Illinois. First car placed on road November 1905. Firm dissolved May 1908.
See "Bendix."

TRIUMPH
USA 1907–1912
Triumph Motor Car Co., Chicago, Illinois. Touring cars and runabouts.

TRIUMPH ITALIA
I 1959
Ruffino SpA. "Triumph" (GB) based sports cars.

TRIVER
E 1957
Construcciones Acoracadas SA. 339 cc 14 hp minicars.

TROJAN
GB 1922–1936; 1961–1965
Leyland Motors Ltd., Kingston-on-Thames, Surrey (1922–1928). Trojan Ltd., Croydon, Surrey (1928–1965). Passenger cars on solid tires until 1929. "Heinkel" (D) license small cars.

TROJAN
USA 1903
Trojan Launch & Automobile Works, Troy, N.Y. Two cars were built.

TROLL
N 1956–1957
Troll Plastik- og Bilindustri, Lunde i Telemark. In limited numbers produced 3-cylinder 2-cycle 700 cc small cars.

TROSSI CATTANEO
I 1934
Milano. Sports car derived from "Isotta Fraschini."

TROSSI MONACO
I 1935
Gaglianico.
See "Monaco Trossi."

TROTT
USA 1917
Trott Automobile Co., Detroit, Michigan.

TROTT & STUBBLEFIELD
USA 1915
Trott & Stubblefield Co., Bloomington, Illinois.

TROUVE
F 1881
Gustave Trouve. Electric three-wheeler.

TROXEL
USA 1902
Troxel Mfg. Co., Eluria, Ohio. Experimental gasoline carriage.

TROY
USA 1905
Troy Carriage Works, Troy, N.Y.

TRUE
USA 1913
Badger Brass Mfg. Co., Kenosha, Wisconsin. Cyclecars.

TRUE BLUE
USA 1910
True Blue Motor Co., Detroit, Michigan. $1,300 gasoline car built as a prototype only.

TRUFFAULT
F 1907–1908
Sté. des Automobiles Truffault, Paris. Belt-driven light cars.

TRUMBULL
USA 1899–1902
Warren Machine Works. Trumbull Mfg. Co., Warren, Ohio.
See "Pendleton."

TRUMBULL
USA 1914–1915
American Cyclecar Co. Trumbull Motor Car Co., Bridgeport, Connecticut. Cyclecars. First three cars shipped May 8, 1914.

TRÜMMER
A 1907
Ferdinand Trümmer, Automobilfabrik, Wien.

TRUNER
GB 1913
Truner & Co., London. Cyclecars.

TST
GB 1920
Three-wheelers.

TSUKUBA
J 1935–1937
Tokyo Jidosha Seizo Co. Ltd., Tokyo. 750cc light cars.

TUAR
F 1913–1925
A. Morin, Thouars/Deux-Sevres. About 800 cars were made.

TUCK
USA 1904
Tuck Petroleum Co., Brooklyn, N.Y. Kerosene runabout.

TUCKER
USA 1900–1908
J.O. Tucker, Santa Clara, California. Fewer than 20 made. 1894 and 1899 also claimed as founding date.

TUCKER
USA 1936
G.S. Tucker, Los Angeles, California. Streamlined three-wheeler.

TUCKER
USA 1947–1948
Tucker Corp., Chicago, Illinois. Purchased Air-Cooled Motors Corp. (Franklin Air-Cooled Engines). Streamlined rear-engined sedan of innovative design; 51 cars produced.

TUDHOPE
CDN 1906–1913
Tudhope Motor Car Co., Orillia, Ontario. 15 models were available.

TULSA
USA 1912–1922
Tulsa Auto & Mfg. Co (1912–1913). Tulsa Four Automobile Co. Tulsa Automobile Corp., Tulsa, Oklahoma (1918–1922). 1,159 cars were made; succeeded Dowagiac Motor Car Co.

TUNISON
USA 1921
Murray C. Tunison, Oakland, California. Speedster.

TURBINE ELECTRIC
USA 1904
Turbine Electric Truck Co., New York, N.Y.

TURBO
CH 1920–1921
Small cars.

TURBO
D 1923–1924
Turbo Motoren AG, Stuttgart. 25- and 32hp cars.

TURCAT-MÉRY
F 1898–1928
Automobile Turcat-Méry SA, Marseilles. Large 10–12-litre cars; later engines from 2.6- to 6.3-litres.

TURGAN-FOY
F 1899–1906
Turgan, Foy et Cie., Levallois-Perret/Seine. Filtz engines.

TURICUM
A/CS 1912
R.A. Smekal, Praha. Probably Swiss cars assembled in Bohemia.

TURICUM
CH 1904–1914
Automobilfabrik Turicum AG, Uster, Zürich. Passenger cars.

TURICUM
I 1912
Automobili Turicum, Torino.

TURIST
SU 1972
A. Bdaion, Tbilisi. Rear-engined Jeep-type one-off.

TURKHEIMER
I
See "OTAV."

TURNER
GB 1906–1907; 1911–1930
Turner's Motor Manufacturing Co. Ltd., Wolverhampton, Staffs. Steam and gasoline cars.

TURNER
GB 1951–1966
Turner Sports Cars Ltd., Wolverhampton, Staffs. About 850 sports cars were made.

TURNER
USA 1899
J.C. Turner, Augusta, Georgia.

TURNER
USA 1900
Richard S. Turner, Marysville, Ohio.

TURNER
USA 1901–1903
Turner Automobile Co., Philadelphia, Pennsylvania.

TURNER
USA 1904
Turner Brass Works, Chicago, Illinois. Three-wheeler.

TURNER
USA c. 1905
Thomas L. Turner, Danbury, Connecticut. 6 hp automobile.

TURNER-MIESSE
GB 1902–1913
Turner's Motor Manufacturing Co. Ltd., Wolverhampton, Staffs. Steam cars.

TURRELL
GB
See "Accles-Turrell."

TURRINNELLI
I
See "SIVE."

T.V.D.
B 1923–1925
Ets Thiriar et Van den Daele, Bruxelles. Passenger cars.

T.V.E.
F 1972–c. 1979
T.V.E. Teilhol Voiture Electrique, Ambert. Electric minicars.

T.V.R.
GB 1954–present
Layton Engineering (1954–1957). Layton Sports Cars Ltd. (1957–1962). Grantura Engineering Ltd. (1962–1963). T.V.R. Cars Ltd. (1964–1965). T.V.R. Engineering Ltd., Blackpool, Lancs. (1965–present). Sports cars.

TWIKE
CH 1995–present
Twike AG, Gelterkinden. Electric three-wheelers.

TWIN CITY
USA 1914
Twin City Motor Car Co., Minneapolis, Minnesota. Cyclecars.

TWOMBLY
USA 1904
Twombly Motor Carriage Co., New York, N.Y. Steam cars.

TWOMBLY
USA 1910
Twombly Motor Car Co. Twombly Motors Co., New York, N.Y. 6.4-litre 40 hp engine.

TWOMBLY
USA 1913–1915
Twombly Car Corp., Nutley, New Jersey. Cyclecars. Experimental car, 1910. Built by Driggs-Seabury. Ordnance Co., Sharon, Pennsylvania. Taxicabs 1915. Cyclecars and light cars.

TWYFORD
USA 1899–1907
Twyford Motor Vehicle Co., Pittsburgh, Pennsylvania (1899–1902). Twyford Motorcar Company, Brookville, Pennsylvania (1904–1907). Four-wheel driveroadsters and tonneau.

TX
GB 1970–1975
Technical Exponents Ltd., Denham, Bucks. Sports cars.

TYNE
GB 1904
W. Galloway & Co. Ltd., Gateshead, Co. Durham. Light cars.

TYSELEY
GB 1912–1913
Tyseley Car Co. Bowden Brake Co., Tyseley, Birmingham. Cyclecars.

T.Z.
E 1956–1966
Talleres Zaragoza, Zaragoza. Light cars.

U

U.
A 1919–1923
U-Wagen Werke Ing. Umann, Wien. Cyclecars.

U.A.
GB 1981–c. 1993
Unique Autocraft Co., Harlow, Essex. Sports car replica.

UAZ
SU/RUS 1956–present
Ulyanovskii Avtomobilnii Zavod, Ulyanovsk. 4 × 4 vehicles.

UFFES
S 1972
Uffes Bil & Motor, Motala. Dune buggy.

UIRAPURU
BR 1967–1974
Sociedad Tecnica de Veiculos SA, São Paulo. Sports cars powered by a 4.3-litre "Chevrolet" (USA) V-8 engine.

ULMANN
D 1903
Edmund Ulmann, Berlin. 12hp cars.

ULTIMA
F 1912–1914
Bournay, Levallois-Perret/Seine. Friction transmission and chain drive.

ULTIMA
GB c. 1996
Ultima Sports Ltd., Hinckley, Leicestershire. Sports cars.

ULTIMOTOR
USA 1915
Frank N. Martindale, Franklin, Indiana.

ULTRA
USA 1912–1914
Ultra Motor Car Co., Amesbury, Massachusetts. 6-cylinder 38 hp cars.

ULTRA
USA 1990s
Ultra Designs, Brockton, Massachusetts. Kit cars.

ULTRAMOBIL
D 1904–1908
Deutsche Ultramobil GmbH, Berlin. "Oldsmobile" (USA) Curved Dash made under license.

ULTRAMOBILE
F 1908
Voitures Ultramobile, Paris. Light cars.

UMAP
F 1958
Plastic bodied coupe with "Citroën" 2 CV engine.

UMM
P 1978–present
Uniao Metalo-Meccanica Lda., Lisboa. 4 × 4 vehicle.

UNDERBERG
F 1899–1909
Underberg et Cie., Nantes/Loire-Inferieure. Voiturette.

UNDERWOOD
USA 1896–1899
Frank M. Underwood, Bucyrus, Ohio. Motor buggy.

UNDERWOOD
USA 1900
Underwood Motor Co., Sandusky, Ohio.

UNIC
F 1904–1939
Sté. des Anciens Ets Georges Richard (1904–1914). SA des Automobiles Unic, Puteaux/Seine (1914–1939). Passenger and sports cars.

UNICAR
GB
See "Opperman."

UNICAR
USA 1974
Unicar, Orange, California. Three-wheelers.

UNICLIP
GB c. 1991–1997
Uniclip Automotive, Byfleet, Surrey. Sports cars and replicars.

UNION
USA 1899
Union Electric Vehicle Co., Portland, Maine. Electric cars.

UNION
USA 1902
Springfield, Massachusetts.

UNION
USA 1902–1905
Union Automobile Co., Union City, Indiana; Anderson, Indiana. Subsidiary of Buckeye Mfg. Co. 1905 reorganized with Lambert Gas & Gasoline Engine Co. in Buckeye Mfg. Co. 325 cars were built.
See "Lambert" (1904–1917).

UNION
USA 1905
Union Automobile Mfg. Co., St. Louis, Missouri. Touring cars.

UNION
USA 1908–1909
Union High Wheel Automobile Co. Union Carriage Co., St. Louis, Missouri. Highwheelers. Became Union Automobile Co.

UNION
USA 1915–1916
Union Car Co., Los Angeles, California.

UNION
USA 1916
Auburn Automobile Co., Auburn, Indiana. Touring cars.

UNION CITY SIX
USA 1916
Union City Automobile Co., Union City, Ohio. Touring cars.

UNION 25
USA 1911–1912
Union Motor Car Co. Union Motor Sales Co., Columbus, Ohio. Roadsters.

UNIPOWER
GB 1966–1970
Universal Power Drives Ltd., Perivale, Middlesex (1966–1968). Unipower Cars, London (1968–1970). Sports cars based upon "Mini" components. About 70 were made.

UNIQUE
GB 1916
The Motor Carrier & Cycle Co., London. Cyclecars.

UNIQUE
USA 1903–1904
Philip Bingman, Detroit, Michigan. Runabout.

UNIQUE
USA 1906
C.B. Hatfield Jr., Cortland, N.Y.
See "Hatfield."

UNIQUE
USA 1997–present
Unique Motorworks, Gadsden, Alabama. Sports kit cars.

UNIQUE AUTOCRAFT
GB 1986–1994
Unique Autocraft Ltd., Templefields, Harlow. Replicars.

UNIS-TAS
YU 1975–1989
UNIS-TAS Tvornica Automobila, Sarajevo. "Volkswagen" (D) assembled.

UNIT
GB 1920–1923
Rotary Unit Co. Ltd., Wooburn, Bucks. Cyclecars.

UNITÁS
H 1928–1931
Unitás Automobil-Ipari és Kereskedelmi R.T., Budapest. Light cars designed by Uher. "Tatra" (CS) Type 57 license. About 500 cars were sold.

UNITED
USA 1900–1901
United Power Vehicle Co., Rutland, Vermont.

UNITED
USA 1904–1905
United Motor & Vehicle Co., Boston, Massachusetts.
See "Ormond." Both names apply to same vehicle.

UNITED
USA 1914
National United Service Co., Detroit, Michigan. Cyclecars.

UNITED
USA 1919–1920
United Engine Co., Greensburg, Indiana. Cars assembled of parts by many suppliers.

UNITED MOTOR
USA 1902–1904
United Motor Corp., Pawtucket, Rhode Island.
See "Cameron."

UNITED POWER
USA 1901
United Power Vehicle Co., New York, N.Y. Steam, gasoline or electric powered cars.

UNITED STATES
USA 1899
United States Automobile Co., Milwaukee, Wisconsin. Gasoline motor carriage.

UNITED STATES
USA 1899–1900
United States Motor Vehicle Co., New York, N.Y. Electric cars. Succeeded Wisconsin Auto & Machinery Co. and Dey-Griswold Co.

UNITED STATES
USA 1900
United States Construction Co., Chicago, Illinois.

UNITED STATES
USA 1900–1901
United States Carriage Co., Runford, Maine. U.S. Motor Carriage Co., Andover, Maine. Steam cars.

UNITED STATES
USA 1909–1915
United States Carriage Co., Columbus, Ohio.

UNITED STATES ELECTRIC
USA 1899–1901
United States Automobile Co., Attleboro, Massachusetts.

UNITO
USA 1909
Unito Motor Buggy Co., Cleveland, Ohio.

UNIVERSAL
GB 1914
See "Turner."

UNIVERSAL
USA 1910
Universal Motor Co., Denver, Colorado; New Castle, Indiana.

UNIVERSAL
USA 1914
Universal Motor Co., Washington, Pennsylvania. Cyclecar.

UNIVERSAL
USA 1917
Universal Service Co., Detroit, Michigan.

UNIVERSITY
USA 1907–1909
University Auto Co., New Haven, Connecticut.
See "Continental."

UNIVERSITY
USA 1910
University Motor Car Co., Detroit, Michigan.
See "Warsity."

UNWIN
USA 1921–1922
Unwin Motor Car Co., New York, N.Y. 22.5 hp automobile.

UPDIKE & BUELY
USA 1899
Milton E. Updike & Levi Buley, Horseheads, N.Y.

UPHAM
USA c. 1905
Willis H. Upham, Leominster, Massachusetts. 9 hp automobile.

UPTON
USA 1902–1903
Upton Machine Co., Beverly, Massachusetts. 1905 became Upton Motor Co., Lebanon, Pennsylvania.
See "Beverly" and "Lebanon." Light runabouts.

UPTON
USA 1903
Upton Pump Co., New Castle, Indiana.

UPTON
USA c. 1905
S. Upton, Somerville, Massachusetts. 3.5 hp automobile.

UPTON
USA 1914
J.L. Upton, Constantine, Michigan; Bristol, Indiana. Light cars.

URANIA
I
Teramo.
See "Taraschi."

URBANINA
I 1964–1968
Urbanina S.p.A., Santa Croce sull Arno (Pisa). Electric and gasoline city cars.

URBANIX
D 1972
Louis Lepoix, FTI Design, Baden-Baden. City car prototype.

URBANUS
D
See "Hagen."

URECAR
GB 1923
Urecar Motor Co., Bournemouth, Hampshire. Light cars.

UREN
GB 1969–1974
Jeff Uren Ltd., Hanwell, London. Sports cars.

URO
E 1998–present
Urovesa, Santiago de Compost. 4 × 4 vehicles, similar to "Hummer" (USA).

URSUS
F 1908
G. Menegault-Basset, Arcueil/Seine. Friction-driven light cars.

URSUS
PL 1921–1925
Fabryka Samochodow Ursus, Czechowice. Passenger cars; later trucks only.

U.S.
USA 1907–1908
United States Motor Co., Upper Sandusky, Ohio. Runabouts.

U.S. LONG DISTANCE
USA 1900–1904
United States Long Distance Automobile Co., Elizabethport, New Jersey. Became Standard Motor Construction Co.
See "Long Distance."

U.S. MARK II
USA 1956
U.S. Fiberglass Co., Norwood, New Jersey. Fiberglass convertibles.

U.S. MOBILE
1901
See "Taft."

UTILE
GB 1904
Utile Motor Mfg. Co. Ltd., Kew Gardens, Surrey. Light cars.

UTILIS
F 1923–1925
Camille Lafarge, Paris. Simple 2-seater belt-driven cyclecars.

UTILIS
USA 1907
Buckeye Foundry Co., Rockdale, Illinois. 12 hp gasoline runabouts.

UTILITAS
D 1920–1921
Utlitas-Gesellschaft Ritzer & Co. mbH, Berlin. Small 1-, 2- and 4-cylinder cars.

UTILITY
USA 1909
Utlity Motor car Co., Ludington, Michigan.

UTILITY
USA 1913
Utility Car Co., New York, N.Y. Three-wheelers.

UTILITY
USA 1918
Utility Car Co., Richmond, Indiana.

UTILITY
USA 1921–1922
Victor W. Pagé Motor Co., Stamford, Connecticut. Cyclecars and light cars.
See "Pagé."

UTOPIAN
GB 1914
Utopian Motor Works, Leicester. Three-wheelers.

ÚTTÖRÖ
H 1954
Janos Schadek, Debrecen. 250 cc minicar prototype.

UVA
GB 1982–1993;
The Unique Vehicle & Accessory, Newbury, Berkshire. TAG Automotive Ltd., Whitchurch, Hamps. Sports cars.

ÚVMV
CS 1970
Ústav pro výzkum motorových vozidel, Praha. Sports coupe based on "Skoda" was built by this research institute.

U-WAGEN • VANDY

U-WAGEN
A 1919–1923. U-Wagen-Werke Ing. Umann, Wien. 2- and 4-cylinder cars.

V 200
I 1953
Mini car prototype.

VABIS
S 1897–1915
Vagnfabrik AB Södertälje, Södertälje. Touring cars.

VACCA
USA 1938
Peter Vacca, Buffalo, N.Y. Streamlined car.

VACCARI
I 1908
Mantova.

VAD
A/CS
Small car prototype.
See "Věchet."

VAGHI
I 1922–1924
Officine di Portovaltravaglia (Ditta Lodovico Boltri di Mezzi, Ganna & C.), Milano. Three-wheelers.

VAGNON ET CANET
F 1898–1900
Vagnon et Canet, Lyon. Cars built to order.

VAGOVA
F 1924–1926
Vereille et Godet, Levallois-Perret/Seine. 745cc 6-cylinder engine.

VAILLANT
F 1922–1924
Cyclecars Vaillant, Lyon.

VAIROGS
SU 1930s
Riga, Latvia. "Ford" (USA) license.

VAJA
CS 1929–1930
Vaja, A. Valeš, Praha. Cyclecars.

VAJA
CS 1938
Ing. J. Mackerle, Plzeň. Sports car prototype.

V.A.L.
GB 1913–1014
V.A.L. Motor Co. Ltd., Birmingham. Cyclecars.

VALE
GB 1932–1936
Vale Engineering Co. Ltd., Maida Vale, London. Low-built sports cars.

VALIANT
USA
See "Plymouth."

VALKYRIE
GB 1900
Springfield Cycle Co. Ltd., Sandiacre, Notts. Voiturette.

VALKYRIE
USA 1967–1973
Fiberfab Division of Velocidad, Inc., Santa Clara, California. Sports cars. Also in kit form.

VALLÉE
F 1895–1901
Sté. des Automobiles Vallée, Le Mans/Sarthe. Sports and racing cars.

VALLEY
USA 1908
Newell O. Allyn, Warren, Ohio. 8 cars were built.

VALMET
FIN c. 1970–present
Valmet Automotive, Uusikaupunki. Convertibles, special bodied cars.

VALT
I 1911–1914
Vetture Automobili Leggere Torino, Torino. Light cars.

VALVELESS; LUCAS VALVELESS
GB 1901–1914
Ralph Lucas, London (1901–1908). Valveless Cars Ltd., Huddersfield, Yorks. (1908–1914). 2-cylinder 2-stroke engines with common combustion chamber.

VAN
USA 1911–1912
Van Motor car Co., Grand Haven, Michigan. Roadsters.

VAN
USA 1911
L.C. Erbes, Waterloo, Iowa.
See "L.C.E."

VANCLEE
B 1972
Vanclee, Roozelare. Dune buggy.

VANDEN PLAS
GB 1960–1980
Vanden Plas (England) 1923 Ltd. (1960–1970). Austin-Morris Division, British Leyland Motor Corporation Ltd., London (1970–1980). Luxury passenger cars.

VANDERBILT
USA 1921
Union Steel Manufacturing Co., Brazil, Indiana.

VANDERGRIFT
USA 1906–1907
Vandergrift Automobile Co., Philadelphia, Pennsylvania. Rhomboid wheel placement. Became "Autocycle."

VANDEWATER
USA 1911
Vandewater & Co., Elizabeth, New Jersey.
See "Correja."

VANDY
GB 1920–1921

Vandys Ltd., London. Assembled cars with U.S. components.

VANELL
USA 1895
Frank Vanell, Vincennes, Indiana. Chicago Times-Herald Race entry. Steam car with rotary motor.

VAN ETTEN
USA 1912–1913
S. Van Etten, Columbus, Ohio.

VAN GINK
NL 1899–1900
Van Gink, Otto Bultman & Co., Amsterdam. Light car.

VANGUARD
USA 1972–1976
Vanguard Vehicles, Inc., Kingston, N.Y. Electric cars.

VAN LANGENDONCK
B 1901–1902
Compagnie Générale d'Automobiles, Bruxelles. "De Dion" (F) or "Buchet" (F) engined cars.

VANNOD
F 1958
Louis Vannod, Neuilly/Seine. Small car with rhomboid wheel placement.

VAN RENSSELAER
USA 1922
Arthur M. Van Rensselaer, New York, N.Y. Electric runabout.

VAN RUNABOUT
USA 1909
H.F. Van Wambeke & Sons, Elgin, Illinois.
See "Van Wambeke."

VAN STONE
USA 1914
Westone Co., Los Angeles, California. Cyclecar prototype; front-wheel drive.
See "Westone" (typo error).

VAN WAGONER
USA 1899
Saul & Van Wagoner Co., Syracuse, N.Y. Steam, electric and gasoline carriages. 1900 became Century Motor Vehicle Co.
See "Syracuse."

VAN WALLEGHEM
B 1902
Van Walleghem et Cie., Bruxelles. Voiturette.

VAN WAMBEKE
USA 1907–1909
H.F. Van Wambeke & Sons, Elgin, Illinois.
See "Van Runabout."

VAN WINKLE
USA 1905
C.W. Van Winkle, San Joaquin, California. Four-wheel-drive touring cars.

VAPOMOBILE
GB 1902–1904
Motor Construction Co. Ltd., Nottingham. Steam cars.

VAR
CH 1924
Gianni Varrone, Hard, Vorarlberg. Light car prototype.

VARLEY-WOODS
GB 1918–1921
High Speed Tool Co. Ltd. (1918–1919). H.S. Motors Ltd., London (1919–1920); Wolverhampton (1919–1920). Assembled cars.

VARSITY
USA 1910
University Motor Co., Detroit, Michigan.

VASESCU
RO/F 1880
Dimitrie Vasescu, Paris. Steam car built by the Romanian student in Paris.

VASKO
E 1997
Gayfa S.L., Sa. Ursula, Tenerife. Sports cars and replicars.

V.A.T.E.
F 1908
Voitures Automobiles de Transmission Electrique, Paris. Light cars using petrol-electric transmissions.

VAUGHAN
USA c. 1905
Vaughan Carriage Co., Lynn, Massachusetts. 5 hp automobile.

VAUGHAN
USA 1909
Whiteside Wheel Co., Indianapolis, Indiana. Highwheeler.

VAUGHAN
USA 1910–1914
Vaughan Motor Car Co., Kingston, N.Y. November 1915 reported sold to Remmington Motor Co. Touring cars.
See "Guy Vaughan."

VAUGHN
USA 1912
Marion E. Vaughn, Indianapolis, Indiana. Runabout.

VAUGHN
USA 1921–1923
American-Southern Motors Corp. Irvine Automobile Co., Greensboro, North Carolina. Designed by Hiram M. Browne.

VAUXHALL
GB 1903–present
Vauxhall Iron Works Ltd., London (1903–1904); Luton, Beds. (1905–1906). Vauxhall and West Hydraulic Engineering Co. Ltd. (1906–1907). Vauxhall Motors Ltd., Luton, Beds. (1907–present). Passenger cars.

VAUZELLE-MOREL
F 1902
Emile Vauzelle, Morel et Cie., Paris. Voiturette.

VAZ
SU/RUS 1970–present
Volzhskii Avtomobilnii Zavod, Togliatti. "Fiat" (I) license.
See "Lada."

VB
D 1924
Richard Vogtle, Berlin. Light cars.

V.C.S.
D 1903–1906
Victor Christian Schilling, Suhl/Thür.
See "Schilling," "Liliput."

V.E. (V.E.C.)
USA 1901–1906
Vehicle Equipment Co., Brooklyn & Long Island City, N.Y. Electric cars.

VĚCHET
A/CS 1911–1913
Vojmír Věchet a spol., Nymburk (1911–1912). Věchet a Flos, Nymburk (1913). 2- and 4-cylinder light cars.
See "VAD" and "Derby" (A/CS).

VECTOR
USA 1979–1997
Vehicle Design Force, Vector Cars Division, Venice, California. Vector Aeromotive Corporation, Wilmington, California. Sports cars.

VÉDRINE
F 1904–1910
S.A. des Voitures Électriques A. Védrine, Neuilly/Seine. Electric cars.

VEE GEE
GB 1913
Vernon Gash & Co., Leeds, Yorks. Cyclecars.

VEERAC
USA 1905
Veerac Motor Car Co., Springfield, Massachusetts. Air-cooled cars.

VEHEL
F 1899–1901
M. et A. Dulac, Paris. 6 and 8 hp cars.

VEHMA
CDN 1986–1994
Vehma International, Inc. Sports car.

V.E.L.
F 1947–1948
Sté. V.E.L., Paris. Two-seater minicars.

VELAM
F 1954–1957
Société Vehicule Leger a Moteur, Suresnes/Seine. "ISO" (I) based minicars. 1,220 cars built in 1955.

VELIE
USA 1909–1928
Velie Motor Vehicle Co. Velie Motors Corp., Moline, Illinois. Touring cars. 74,542 cars were made.

VELOCAR
F
    See "Mochet."

VELOCE
GB 1909
Veloce Ltd., Birmingham. Prototype.

VELOMOBIL
D 1905–1908
Motorfahrzeugfabrik Hermann Dettmann, Berlin. Velomobil-Kraftfahrzeugfabrik, Berlin. Three-wheelers.

VELOREX
CS 1957–1974
Velorex VD, Solnice. Three- and four-wheeled minicars for handicapped drivers.

VELO ROSSA
USA 1991–present
Velo Rossa Engineering, Tempe, Arizona. Kit cars.

VELOTO
F 1976–c. 1983
Bel Motors International, Paris. 50cc citycars.

VELOX
A/CS 1906–1910
Pražská továrna automobilu Velox, Praha. Passenger cars and taxicabs.

VELOX
GB 1902–1904
Velox Motor Co. Ltd., Coventry, Warwickshire. Light cars.

VELTRO
I 1920
Societa Automobili Veltro, Torino.

VEMAG
BR 1962–1968
Vemag S.A., São Paulo. "DKW" (D) license.

VENTURI
F 1984–present
Manufacture de Voitures de Sport, Cholet. Venturi S.A., Coueron. Sports cars.
    See "MVS."

VENTURINA
I 1962
Roma. Antique car replicas.

VERA
USA 1912
Vera Motor Car Co., Providence, Rhode Island. Touring cars.

VERACITY
USA 1899–1904
Dr. L. Anton Smith, Topeka, Kansas. Later Smith Automobile Co.
    See "Smith."

VERGNANO
I 1911–1915
Torino.

VERITAS
D 1948–1953
Veritas GmbH, Messkirch (1948–1949). Veritas Badische Automobilwerke GmbH, Rastatt (1949–1950). Veritas Automobilwerke GmbH, Nürnberg (1950–1953). Sports cars.

VER LINDEN
USA 1922–1923
Edward Ver Linden, Detroit, Michigan.

VERMOREL
F 1908–1930
Établissements V. Vermorel, Villefranche/Rhone. Touring cars.

VERNANDI
F 1928–1929
Naudillon, Garches/Seine-et-Oise. Sports and racing cars.

VERNON
USA 1911
Vernon Motor Car Co., Detroit, Michigan. Touring cars.

VERNON
USA 1918–1921
Vernon Automobile Corp., Mt. Vernon, N.Y. Roadsters.

VEROLD
CS 1992
Verold, Praha. Sports cars.

VERONA
D 1984–1994
Verona Automobile GmbH & Co. KG, Aschaffenburg. Replicars.
    See "E.S.W."

VERONAC
CDN 1981–1989
Veronac Automobile Enterprises Ltd., London, Ontario. Replicars.

VERONESI
I 1951
One car registered.

VERRETT
USA 1895
N.J. Verrett, Pine Bluff, Arkansas. Chicago Times-Herald Race entry.

VERTEX
GB
    See "James & Browne."

VERZA
I
    See "CAR."

VESPA
F 1958–1961
Ateliers de Constructions de Motos et Accessoires, Fourchamboult/Nievre. Small cars.
    See "A.C.M.A."

VESPA
I 1913–1916
Clemento Antonelli, Modena. 1.5-litre light cars.

VESSA
CH 1982
Véhicule Électrique Suisse S.A., Clarens. Electric cars.

VESTA
D 1981–present
VMB Vesta Maschinenbau GmbH & Co. KG, Rheinstetten/Mörsch. Amphibious vehicles.
See "Rhino."

VESTATEC
D c. 1977–1982
Gebrüder Habbich GmbH, Wuppertal. Tuning.

VESUV
D 1900
Alfred Haupfeld, Kassel. Three- and four-wheeler.

VETCOR
GB 1985–1993
Vetcor Enterprises Inc., Dayton, Ohio. Sports cars.

VETTA VENTURA
USA 1964–1965
Vanguard Motors Corp., Dallas, Texas. Identical to "Apollo." Coupe and convertible.

V.H.
GB
See "F.D." and "Vining-Hallett."

V.H.
E 1961
Pedro Vargas Fernandes, Villafranca de los Barros. Three-wheeled minicars.

VIA
GB 1909–1910
Norburys Ltd., Manchester. 6-cylinder tourer.

VIA
H 1921–1922
Villamos Autógyár Részvénytársaság, Budapest. Small electric cars with tandem seating.

VIALL
USA 1913–1919
Viall Motor Car Co., Chicago, Illinois. Mostly trucks, but some passenger cars.

VIBRACTION
F 1997–present
Société Vibraction, Roanne. 4 × 4 vehicles and sports cars.

VICARAGE
GB 1984–present
Vicarage Jaguars Ltd., Four Ashes, Wolverhampton. "Jaguar" replicars.

VICEROY
GB 1915
Viceroy Sidecar Co. Ltd., New Basford, Nottingham. Light cars.

VICI
GB 1906–1907
Vici Motors Ltd., London. Sports car.

VICKERS
USA 1910–1911
Vickers Motor Car Co., Coshocton, Ohio. Roadsters.

VICKSTOW
GB 1913
Vickers, Bristow 7 Co., London. Prototype.

VICTOR
GB 1914–1915
Victor Motors Ltd., Eynsford, Kent (1914–1915). Victor Cars Ltd., London (1915). Cyclecars.

VICTOR
USA 1899–1903
Victor Automobile Co., Bridgeport, Connecticut. A.H. Overman, Chicopee Falls, Massachusetts. Steam car. Became Overman Automobile Co. Absorbed by Locomobile Co. of America, 1902.

VICTOR
USA 1902
Victor Engine & Motor Carriage Co., San Francisco, California.

VICTOR
USA 1906–1909
Victor Automobile Co., Ridgeville, Indiana. Also built "Senator."

VICTOR
USA 1905–1911
Victor Motor Car Mfg. Co. Victor Auto Mfg. Co. Victor Automobile Co., St. Louis, Missouri. Highwheelers.

VICTOR
USA 1913–1917
C.U. Stahl, Philadelphia, Pennsylvania. Victor Motor Car Co., Greenville, South Carolina (1914–1915). Victor Motor Co., Grubbs Landing, Delaware (1916); Jenkintown, Pennsylvania (1916); York, Pennsylvania (1917). Runabouts and touring cars.

VICTOR
USA 1914
Victor Motor Car Co., Philadelphia, Pennsylvania. Cyclecars.

VICTOR
USA 1914
Richmond Cyclecar Mfg. Co., Richmond, Victoria. Cyclecars.

VICTORIA
D 1900–1909; 1957–1958
Victoria Fahrradwerke vorm. Frankenberger & Ottenstein AG, Nürnberg (1900–1909). Victoria-Werke AG, Nürnberg (1957–1958). Voiturettes; Small cars.

VICTORIA
E 1905–1907
SA Automobiles Victoria, Barcelona.

VICTORIA
E 1919–1923
Talleres Franco Espanoles, Madrid. 950cc small cars.

VICTORIA
GB 1906–1907
The Victoria (Peacock) and Autocar Co., Dennistoun, Scotland. "Peugeot" (F) and "Chenard-Walcker" (F) based cars.

VICTORIA
GB 1907
Victoria Motor Works, Godalming, Surrey. Assembled cars.

VICTORIA
USA 1900
Victoria Motor Vehicle Co., Indianapolis, Indiana. Electric cars.

VICTORIA COMBINATION
F
See "Parisienne."

VICTORIAN
CDN c. 1900
Hopewell, Nova Scotia. Only one was built.

VICTORIETTE
USA 1901
Waltham Mfg. Co., Waltham, Massachusetts.

VICTORMOBILE
USA 1900–1901
Victormobile Co., Omaha, Nebraska. Steam cars.

VICTOR PAGE
USA 1921–1924
Victor Pagé Motors Corp., Farmingdale, N.Y (1921–1922); Stamford, Connecticut (1922–1923). Touring cars.
See "Pagé."

VICTORY
USA 1906
See "Sunset."

VICTORY
USA 1920–1921
Victory Motor Car Co., Boston, Massachusetts. Reworked Model T "Ford" using Raja head, special roadster body and cycle fenders.

VICTRESS
USA 1954
Victress Mfg. Co., North Hollywood, California.

VICTRIX
F 1921–1924
Automobiles Victrix, Les Lilas/Seine. 15 hp 4-cylinder cars.

VICTRIX
GB 1902–1904
Victrix Motor Car Works, Kendal, Westmoreland. DeDion engine.

VICTRIX
I 1911–1913
Officine Meccaniche Torinesi (OMT), Torino.
See "OMT."

VIDAL & SOHN
D
See "Tempo."

VIDEX
USA 1903
Videx Automobile & Carriage Co., Marlboro, Massachusetts.
See "Marlboro."

VIGNALE
I 1956–1974; 1986
Carrozzeria Vignale, Grugliasco. Sports cars, mostly based on the "Fiat" components. Coachbuilders since 1946.

VIKING
GB 1914
Viking Motors Ltd., Coventry, Warwickshire. Light car.

VIKING
USA 1907–1908
Viking Company, Boston, Massachusetts. 7-passenger touring car.

VIKING
USA 1929–1930
Olds Motor Works, Lansing, Michigan. Started April 13, 1929. Companion car to "Oldsmobile." 7,224 cars were made.

VIKING
USA 1966
Viking Corp., Miami, Florida.

VILAIN
F 1900–1902
Vilain Freres, Paris. Light two-seater.

VILLAIRE
USA 1906
Louis Villaire, Sanford, Maine.

VILLARD
F 1925–1935
Sté. des Automobiles Villard, Janville/Oise. Cyclecars.

VIM
USA 1914
Touraine Co., Philadelphia, Pennsylvania. Cyclecars.

VINCENT
GB 1984–1993
Dwornik Engineering, Chiseldon, Swindon, Wiltshire. Sports cars.

VINCKE
B 1895–1905
Vincke & Delmer, Malines. SA des Automobiles Nestor Vincke, Malines. Light cars.

VINDEC
D
See "Allright."

VINDELICA
D 1899–1900
Heinle und Wegelin, Oberhausen. Light two-seaters.

VINET
F 1900–1904
Automobiles Vinet, Neuilly/Seine. Voiturette.

VINING-HALLETT
GB
See "F.D." and "V.H."

VINOT
CDN 1912–1913
Vinot Car Company of Canada, Montreal, Quebec.

VINOT-DEGUINGAND
F 1901–1926
Vinot et Deguingand, Puteaux/Seine (1901–1926); Nanterre/Seine (1919–1926). Touring cars.

VINTAGE SPEEDSTERS
USA 1990s
Vintage Speedsters, Hawaiian Gardens, California. Kit cars.

VIOLET-BOGEY
F 1913–1914
Marcel Violet, Paris. Cyclecars.

VIOTTI
I 1921–1964
Carrozzeria Vittorio Viotti, Torino. "Fiat" based sports cars.

VIPEN
GB 1898–1904
East Riding Cycle Co., Hull, Yorks. "Panhard" (F) and "DeDion" (F) lines.

VIQUEOT
USA 1905–1906
Viqueot Co., Long Island City, N.Y. French chassis with American touring coachwork.

VIRATELLE
F 1922–1924
Sté. des Moteurs et Automobiles Viratelle, Lyon. Cyclecar.

VIRGINIA
USA 1923
Virginia Motors Inc., Lynchburg, Virginia.

VIRGINIAN
USA 1911–1912
Richmond Iron Works Corp., Richmond, Virginia. First car reported completed September 1910. Touring cars. Bankruptcy reported April 1912.

VISTRO
D
See "Strosek."

VITREX
F 1974–c. 1982
Jacques Riboud. Three-wheeler minicars.

VITTORIA
I 1914–1915
Giorgio Ambrosini, Torino. 3.2-litre engine.

VIVINUS
B 1899–1912
Ateliers Vivinus SA, Bruxelles. Voiturettes and passenger cars.

VIXEN
USA 1914–1916
Davis Mfg. Co., Milwaukee, Wisconsin. Tandem cyclecars with friction transmission and shaft drive.

VLAH
CS 1948

Vladimír Hadrba, Náměšt. 500 cc minicar prototype.

V.L.A.M.
NL 1907–1908
Verwey & Lugard's Automobiel Maatschappij, Den Haag. Voiturettes.

VM
D 1988–1993
VM Exklusiver Fahrzeugbau GmbH, Bergisch Gladbach. Sports cars.

VNIITE
SU 1964
Vsesoyuznii Nauchno-Ispitatelnii Institut Tekhnicheskoi Estetiki, Moskva. Passenger car prototype.

VOGT
USA c. 1900
Vogt Automobile Co., Newark, New Jersey. Electric car.

VOGTLAND
D 1910–1912
Maschinen- und Automobilfabrik Endesfelder & Weiss, Plauen. 2-, 4- and 6-seaters.

VOGUE
USA 1916–1922
Vogue Motor Car Co., Tiffin, Ohio.
  See "Economy."

VOISIN
F 1919–1939
SA des Aeroplanes G. Voisin, Issy-les-Moulineaux/Seine. Sports and passenger cars. Also some prototypes of cars with rhomboid wheel placement.

VOLANIS
F 1980–c. 1993
Design Volanis, Argenteuil. Advanced designed prototypes.

VOLGA
SU/RUS 1955–present
GAZ, Gorkovskii Avtomobilnii Zavod, Nizhnii Novgorod. Passenger cars.
  See "ZIM" and "GAZ."

VOLK
GB 1895
Volk's Electric Tramway, Brighton, Sussex. Electric cars.

VOLKSROD
GB 1967–c. 1980
Volksrod Ltd., Doncaster, Yorks. Dune buggy.

VOLKSROD
USA 1968
Allied Industries Inc., Lincoln, Nebraska. Dune buggy.

VOLKSWAGEN
D 1936–present
Dr. Ing. h.c. F. Porsche GmbH, Stuttgart (1936–1937). Gesellschaft zur Vorbereitung des Volkswagens, Berlin; Stadt des KdF-Wagens (1937–1938). Volkswagenwerk GmbH, Berlin; Wolfsburg (1938–1960). Volkswagenwerk AG, Wolfsburg (1960–present). Passenger cars.

VOLKSWAGEN
BR 1968–present
Volkswagen do Brasil SA, São Bernardo do Campo. Special Brazilian models are built.

VOLKSWAGEN-PORSCHE
D 1969–1976
VW-Porsche Vertriebsgesellschaft mbH, Ludwigsburg. Sports cars.

VOLOMOBILE
USA 1902
New York Motor Vehicle Co., New York, N.Y. Steam cars.

VOLPE
I 1947–1949
Anonima Lombarda Cabotaggio Aereo, Trento (Milano). Small cars.
  See "ALCA."

VOLPI
I 1901
Volpi & C., Milano.

VOLTA
F 1994–present
Société Européenne des Électromobiles Rochelaises, Perigny. Electric cars.

VOLTA-CAR
USA 1915–1916
Cyco-Electric Car Co., New York, N.Y. Electric cyclecar.

VOLTOR
F 1922–1925
Construction Électriques Voltor, Sainte-Étienne/Loire. Electric cars.

VOLTRA
USA 1962
Voltra, Inc., New York, N.Y. Compact electric cars.

VOLTZ
USA 1912–1913
Voltz Bros., Chicago, Illinois.

VOLUGRAFO
I 1946–1958
Officine Meccaniche Volugrafo, Torino. Mini cars.

VOLVO
S 1927–present
AB Volvo, Göteborg. Passenger cars.

VOMAG
D
  See "Dux."

VOODOO
GB 1971–1973;
Normandale Products, Long Itchington, Warwickshire. Sports cars.

VORAN
D 1926–1928
Voran Automobilbau AG, Berlin. Front-wheel drive.

VORTEX
USA 1990–1996
Dolphin Vehicles, Campbell, California. Three-wheelers.

VOSCHO
D
  See "Voss & Schorn."

VOSS
USA c. 1905
Fred A. Voss, Hartford, Connecticut. 1.75 hp automobile.

VOTEX
D c. 1985
Votex GmbH, Dreieich. Tuning.

VOUSEMOI
F 1904
Two-seaters.

VOX
GB 1912–1915
Lloyd & Plaiser Ltd., London. 750cc light cars.

V 200
I 1953
Microcar, Milano; Lugano. Minicars.

VULCAN
CH 1905
Zürich. Voiturette.

VULCAN
GB 1902–1928
Vulcan Motor Manufacturing and Enginering Co. Ltd. (1902–1906). Vulcan Motor & Engineering Co. Ltd., Southport, Lancs. (1906–1928). Voiturette and touring cars. Trucks to 1953.

VULCAN
USA 1911
Vulcan Motor Car Co., Detroit, Michigan.

VULCAN
USA 1913–1915
Vulcan Motor Car Co., Painesville, Ohio. 4-cylinder 27 hp roadsters. In hands of receiver January 1915.

VULKAN
D 1899–1905
Vulkan Automobilgesellschaft mbH, Berlin. Electric cars.

VULPES
F 1905–1910
Automobiles Vulpes, Paris (1905–1907); Clichy/Seine (1907–1910). Voiturettes and light cars with DeDion and Janus engines.

W.A.C.
USA 1905
Woodburn Automobile Co., Woodburn, Indiana.
See "Woodburn."

WACHMAN
USA 1908
Wachman Auto Mfg. & Supply Co., Detroit, Michigan.

WACO
USA 1915–1917
Western Automobile Co., Seattle, Washington. Touring cars.

WADDINGTON
GB 1903–1904
Waddington & Sons., Middlesbrough, Yorks. Light car.

WADDINGTON
USA 1904
Locke Regulator Co., Salem, Massachusetts.
See "Puritan" steam.

W.A.F.
A 1910–1926
Wiener Automobil-Fabrik GmbH, Wien. Passenger cars.

WAGENHALS
USA 1910–1915
W.G. Wagenhals. Wagenhals Motor Co., St. Louis, Missouri (1910); Detroit, Michigan (1911–1915). Three-wheelers. Also built electric cars 1914–1915.

WAGNER
USA 1900–1901
Wagner Mfg. Co., Rochester, N.Y. Three-wheelers and steam runabouts.

WAHL
USA 1913–1914
Wahl Motor car Co., Detroit, Michigan; Streator, Illinois. Touring cars. Company bought by A.C. Barley in December 1914.

WAINER
I 1959–1960
Milano. Sports cars.

WALCO
GB 1905
W.A. Lloyd's Cycle Fittings Ltd., Birmingham. Three-wheelers.

WALCYCAR
GB
See "Wall." Three-wheelers and cyclecars.

WALDON
USA 1920
Sidney D. Waldon, Detroit, Michigan. Prototype.

WALDRON
USA 1909–1912
Waldron Runabout Mfg. Co., Kankakee, Illinois. Waldron Automobile Mfg. Co., Waldron, Illinois. Highwheelers.

WALKER
USA 1900–1903
John B. Walker, Tarrytown, N.Y. Steam cars.
See Mobile."

WALKER
USA 1900–1902
Marlboro Automobile & Carriage Co., Marlboro, Massachusetts. Steam cars.
See "Marlboro."

WALKER
USA 1905–1906
Walker Motor Car Co., Detroit, Michigan. Runabouts.

WALKER & HUTTON
GB 1902
Walker & Hutton, Scarborough, Yorks.

WALKER SIX
CDN 1910
Walker Motor Company, Walkerville, Ontario.

WALKER SIX
USA 1910
Walker Motor Car Co., Detroit, Michigan. Not same as 1905–1906 company.

WALKER STEAMER
USA 1890; 1901; 1904
Walker Bros., New Albany, Indiana. Steam cars.

WALKINS
USA 1896
Bay State Motive Power Co., Springfield, Massachusetts. Electric runabout.

WALKLEY & CHUDOBA
USA c. 1905
F.H. Walkley & F.F. Chudoba, Hartford, Connecticut. 3 hp automobile.

WALL
GB 1911–1916
A.W. Wall Ltd., Tyseley, Birmingham. Three-wheelers and cyclecars.

WALL
USA 1900–1903
R.C. Wall Mfg. Co., Philadelphia, Pennsylvania. Runabouts.

WALLABUG
USA 1968

Hooker Industries, Ontario, California. Dune buggy.

WALLIS
USA c. 1905
Frank G. Wallis, Providence, Rhode Island.

WALLOF
USA 1902; 1910–1912
E.G. Wallof Machine Works, Minneapolis, Minnesota. Steam runabout; depot cars.

WALMOBIL
D 1919–1920
Walter Loebel Maschinenfabrik, Leipzig. Three-wheelers.

WALSCHE
USA 1899–1900
M.E. Walsche & Sons, Syracuse, N.Y. Electric cars.

WALTER
A/CS 1908–1936
J. Walter a spol., akciová továrna automobilu, Praha. Akciová továrna na automobily a letecké motory J. Walter a spol., Praha. Three-wheelers, touring and sports cars.

WALTER
USA 1902–1909
Walter Car Co., New York, N.Y. American Chocolate Machinery Co., New York, N.Y. (1902–1906). Reorganized January 1, 1906 as Walter Automobile Co., Trenton, New Jersey (1906–1909). 1909 developed "Planche" car. Roebling Planche Co. a subdivision. Became "Mercer." Touring cars.

WALTERS
USA 1899–1900
J.W. Walters, New York, N.Y. "Detachable tractor" with 2-stroke gasoline engine.

WALTERSCHEID
USA 1902–1903
Charles W. Walterscheid & Alexander Glass, Wichita, Kansas. Steam car.

WALTHAM
USA 1905–1908
Waltham Mfg. Co., Waltham, Massachusetts. Became C.H. Metz Co. 1908. Absorbed American Motors Co.

WALTHAM
USA 1922–1923
Waltham Motors Mfg. Inc., Waltham, Massachusetts. Succeeded Metz Co.
See "Metz."

WALTHAM-ORIENT
USA 1905–1908
Waltham Manufacturing Co., Waltham, Massachusetts. Air-cooled car. "Waltham-Orient" succeeded "Orient." Became "Metz."

WALTHAM STEAMER
USA 1898–1902
Waltham Automobile Co. Waltham Motor Carriage Co., Waltham, Massachusetts.

WALTOMOBILE
USA 1902
William Walter, New York, N.Y.
See "Walter."

WALTON
USA 1902–1904
W.L. Walton, Bantry, North Dakota. Runabouts.

WALTON SPECIAL
USA 1917
Wirt M. Walton, New York, N.Y. Roadster.

WALWORTH
USA 1904–1905
A.O. Walworth & Co., Chicago, Illinois. Rear entrance tonneau.

WAMBACH
D 1986
Wambach KG, Hamburg. Sports cars.

WANDERER
D 1911–1939
Wanderer Fahrradwerke vorm. Winkelhofer & Jaenicke AG,. Schönau (1911–1917). Wanderer-Werke AG, Siegmar (1917–1939). Passenger cars.

WARCIA
H 1988
Panonautó, Pécs. "Wartburg" (DDR) with "Dacia" (RO) engine. 58 planned to produce.

WARD
USA 1913–1914
Ward Cyclecar Co., Chicago, Illinois (1913); Milwaukee, Wisconsin (1914). Cyclecars and roadsters.

WARD
USA 1914–1916
Ward Motor Vehicle Co., Bronx, N.Y. (1914); Vernon, N.Y. (1915–1916). Electric cars.

WARD BUTLER
USA 1913
Ward Butler, Chicago, Illinois.

WARD LEONARD
USA 1903
Ward Leonard Electric Co., Bronxville, N.Y. Electric and gasoline cars. Became "Knickerbocker."

WARDWAY
USA 1910–1913
Montgomery Ward & Co., Chicago, Illinois.
See "Modoc."

WARDWELL
USA c. 1905
Parris E. Wardwell, South Norwalk, Connecticut.

WARE
USA 1861; 1867
Elijah Ware, Bayonne, New Jersey. Steam vehicles.

WARE
USA c. 1905
Ware Mfg. Co., Salem, Massachusetts. 4.5 hp automobile.

WARFIELD
GB 1903
Warfield Motor Car Co., Teddington, Middlesex. Steam cars.

WARNE
GB 1913–1915
Pearsall-Warne Ltd., Letchworth, Herts. Cyclecars.

WARNER ELECTRIC
USA 1898
Lewis E. Warner, Northampton, Massachusetts. Electric runabout.

WARNER
USA 1900
Warner Mfg. Co., Dayton, Ohio. Steam carriage.
See "Dayton."

WARNER
USA 1902
Thomas W. Warner, Muncie, Indiana. Touring cars.

WARNER
USA 1903–1906
Muncie Wheel & Jobbing Co., Muncie, Indiana.

WARREN
USA 1900
Edward C. Warren, Providence, Rhode Island.

WARREN
USA 1903
George I. Warren, Paterson, New Jersey.

WARREN
USA 1905
Warren Automobile Co., Warren, Pennsylvania. 44 hp automobile.

WARREN
USA c. 1905
G.E. Warren, Dorchester, Massachusetts. 12 hp automobile.

WARREN
USA 1911–1914
Rands Mfg. Co., Detroit, Michigan. Successor to Warren Motor Car Co. Formerly "Warren-Detroit."

WARREN-DETROIT
USA 1910–1913
Warren-Detroit Motor Car Co., Detroit, Michigan. Became Warren Motor Car Co. 1911.
    See "Warren."

WARREN ELECTRIC
USA 1892
Holtzer Cabot, Brookline, Massachusetts. One car produced for Fiske Warren.

WARREN-LAMBERT
GB 1912–1922
Warren-Lambert Engineering Co. Ltd., London (1912–1914); Richmond, Surrey (1919–1922). Cyclecars and light sports cars.

WARRINGTON
USA 1881
Charles Warrington, West Chester, Pennsylvania. Three-wheeled gas carriage.

WARRIOR
USA 1963
Vanguard Products Inc., Dallas, Texas. Sports cars.

WARSZAWA
PL 1951–1972
Fabryka Samochodow Osobowych, Warszawa. Passenger cars based on "Pobieda" (SU) cars.

WARTBURG
D 1898–1904
Fahrzeugfabrik Eisenach, Eisenach. Voiturettes and light cars.

WARTBURG
DDR 1956–1991
VEB Automobilwerk Eisenach, Eisenach. Passenger cars with 2-cycle motors.

WARWICK
GB 1957–1962
Bernard Rodger Developments Ltd., Colnbrook, Bucks. Sports cars.

WARWICK
USA 1901–1905
Warwick Cycle & Automobile Co., Springfield, Massachusetts. Engines supplied by DeDion-Bouton (F); Stanhope.

WASHBURN
USA 1896–1902
George A. Washburn, Cleveland, Ohio. Electric cars.

WASHINGTON
USA 1901
Washington Auto Vehicle Co., Washington, D.C.

WASHINGTON
USA 1902
George Washington, Chicago, Illinois. Large car with two gasoline engines.

WASHINGTON
USA 1909–1912
Carey A. Davis, Washington, D.C. Carter Motor Car Co., Washington, D.C.; Hyattsville, Maryland. Became Washington Motor Co. Touring cars.

WASHINGTON
USA 1908–1911
Washington Mfg. Co., Washington, Indiana.

WASHINGTON
USA 1909
Washington Motor Vehicle Co., Washington, D.C. Electric cars.
    See "Capitol" Electric.

WASHINGTON
USA 1921–1924
Washington Motor Car Co., Eaton and Middletown, Ohio. Formerly Union Motor Car Corp. Touring cars. 3 steam cars built 1923–1924.

WASHINGTON
USA 1922–1923
Detroit Motor Co. (John A. Barr), Detroit, Michigan.

WASHINGTON SIX
USA 1921
Washington Automobile Co., Cleveland, Ohio.

WASP
GB 1907–1908
Thames Bank Wharf Motor Works, London. 50/60 hp Mutel engine.

WASP
USA 1919–1924
Martin Wasp Corp., Bennington, Vermont. Also referred to as "Martin-Wasp" but correct designation is "Wasp." 4- and 6-cylinder touring cars.

WASSON
USA 1904
Scott Iron Works, Baltimore, Maryland.

WATCH CITY
USA 1900–1904
Watch City Automobile Co., Waltham, Massachusetts. Steam car. Steam racer also built for Louis S. Ross.

WATERLOO
USA 1903–1905
Waterloo Gas Engine Works. Waterloo Motor Works, Waterloo, Iowa. 3-cylinder phaeton built under "Duryea" patents.

WATERMAN & CHAMBERLAIN
USA 1900
Waterman & Chamberlain, Medford, Massachusetts. Gasoline runabout.

WATERS
USA 1900–1903
Gilbert Waters, New Bern, North Carolina. Two cars produced.

WATERS
USA c. 1905
M. Waters, Charlestown, Massachusetts. 4 hp automobile.

WATFORD
GB 1959–1962
Watford Sports Car Ltd., Watford, Herts. Sports kit cars.

WATKINS
USA 1993
Watkins Racing, Tustin, California. Sports cars.

WATLING
GB 1959–1961. Watling Cars, St. Albans, Herts. Fiberglass-bodied sports cars.

WATROUS
USA 1905
Watrous Automobile Co., Elmira, N.Y. A very light two-cylinder air-cooled car with 85-inch wheelbase. Company later built fire engines.

WATSON
USA 1901
Ralph Watson, Calumet, Michigan. Electric car.

WATSON
USA c. 1905
J.H. Watson, Marlboro, Massachusetts. 3.5 hp automobile.

WATSON
USA c. 1905
James H. Watson, Worcester, Massachusetts. 2.75 hp automobile.

WATSON-CONOVER
USA 1906
Watson Machine Co., Paterson, New Jersey.
See "Conover."

WATT
USA 1910
Watt Motor Co., Detroit, Michigan. Touring cars.

WATTEL-MORTIER
F 1921
Paris. 2.6-litre cars.

WAUGH
USA c. 1905
Charles Waugh & Co., Cambridge, Massachusetts. Two vehicles were built.

WAUKESHA
USA 1906–1910
Waukesha Motor Co., Waukesha, Wisconsin. Touring cars.

WAUSAU FLYER
USA 1910
Wausau Iron Works, Wausau, Wisconsin.

WAVERLEY
GB 1901–1904
Scottish Motor Co., Edinburgh. New Rossleigh Motor & Cycle Co. Ltd., Edinburgh. About 10 cars built.

WAVERLEY
GB 1910–1931
Light Cars Ltd (1910–1915). Waverley Cars Ltd., London (1919–1931). Light and touring cars.

WAVERLEY
USA 1899–1903
Indiana Bicycle Co., Indianapolis, Indiana. Electric cars. Became American Bicycle Co. Automobile Dept. 1902; International Motor Car Co. 1902–1903; Pope Motor. Car Co. 1903.

WAVERLEY
USA 1909–1916
Waverley Company, Indianapolis, Indiana. Electric cars. Succeeded "Pope Waverley." 1916 became Waverley Electric Vehicle Co.

WAVERLY
USA 1899
Waverly Bicycle Co., Providence, Rhode Island. Steam vehicle.

WAYMAN & MURPHY
USA 1903–1904
Wayman & Murphy, Chicago, Illinois. Runabouts built from Lindsay-Russell parts.

WAYNE
USA 1895
Wayne Sulkeyette & Road Cart Co., Decatur, Illinois.

WAYNE
USA 1904–1908
Wayne Automobile Co., Detroit, Michigan. Absorbed with Northern Motor Car Co. into "E.M.F." Runabouts and touring cars.

WAYNE
USA 1905–1910
Wayne Works, Richmond, Indiana. Became "Richmond."

WAYNICK
USA 1902
Fletcher Waynick, Reidsville, North Carolina. Runabout.

W.B.C.
USA 1921
Well Built Cab, Greenville, South Carolina. Taxicabs.

W.C.P.
USA 1909–1912
W.C.P. Taxicab Co., New York, N.Y. Taxicabs.

WD
A 1953–1957
Wolfgang Denzel, Wien. Sports cars.
See "Denzel."

WEARWELL
GB 1899–1904
Wearwell Motor Carriage Co., Wolverhampton, Staffs.
See "Wolf."

WEBB
GB 1922–1923
V.P. Webb & Co. Ltd., Stourport, Worcs. 9 hp Alpha engine.

WEBB
USA 1903
Albert C. Webb, St. Louis, Missouri. Steam vehicles.

WEBB-JAY
USA 1908–1910
Webb-Jay Motor Co., Chicago, Illinois. Steam touring cars.

WEBER
CH 1899–1906
J. Weber & Co., Uster, Zürich. Three-wheelers; 1-cylinder 2.5-litre models.

WEBER
USA 1900
Weber Gas & Gasoline Engine Co., Kansas City, Missouri.

WEBER
USA 1925
P.H. Weber Co., Hoopestown, Illinois. Miniature replica of the "Moon."

WEBSTER
USA 1902–1903
Webster Automobile Co., New York, N.Y. 16 hp runabout.

WEEBER
USA 1898–1905
Christian F. Weeber Mfg. Co., Albany, N.Y. Air-cooled roadsters.

WEGE
AUS 1920
Peterborough, S.A.

WEGMANN
D 1925
Waggonfabrik Wegmann & Co., Kassel. Open two-seater with wooden streamlined body.

WEGO
USA 1916
Wego Motor Co., Jackson, Michigan. Touring cars.

WEICHELT
D 1908
H. Weichelt, Automobil- und Motorenfabrik, Leipzig. Voiturette.

WEIDE
D 1925–1933
See "RWN."

WEIDNER
D 1957–1958
Weidner OHG, Schwäbisch-Hall. About 200 sports cars were built.

WEIGEL
GB 1906–1909
Weigel Motors Ltd., London. Large limousine.

WEINEM
CH 1972–1992
Jörg Weinem Automobile, Thalwil; Horgen. Dune buggy and replicars.

WEINERT
USA 1914
R.H. Weinert, Detroit, Michigan. Cyclecars.

WEISE
D 1930–1935
Weise & Co. Motor-Dreirad-Fabrik GmbH, Berlin. Three-wheelers and 4-wheeled cars and vans.

WEISS
D 1902–1905
Maschinenfabrik Otto Weiss & Co. (1902–1904). Automobil- und Motorenfabrik vorm. Otto Weiss, Berlin (1904–1905). "Herald" cars with 8–20 hp engines.

WEISS
H 1924–1930
Weiss Manfred Acél és Fémmüvei Rt., Budapest. 2-cycle light cars, later conventionally designed 4-cylinder cars.
See "WM."

WEKTOR
D 1988–1993
Wektor Automobile, Untergiglbach/Ortenburg. Sports cars.

WELCH
USA 1903–1911
Welch Motor Car Co., Chelsea, Michigan (1903–1904); Pontiac, Michigan (1904–1911). 2-, 4- and 6-cylinder cars.

WELCH & LAWSON
USA 1895
Welch & Lawson, New York, N.Y. Motor road wagon.

WELCH-DETROIT
USA 1910–1911
Welch-Detroit Car Co., Detroit, Michigan. Absorbed by General Motors Corp. Became "Marquette." 4-cylinder 40 hp cars.

WELCH-ESTBERG
USA 1906
Welch-Estberg Co., Milwaukee, Wisconsin.

WELCH-TOURIST
USA 1901–1904
Chelsea Mfg. Co., Chelsea, Michigan. Reported in receiver's hands February 1904. Became "Welch."

WEL-DOER
CDN 1914
Welker-Doerr Co., Berlin, Ontario. Cyclecars.

WELLER
GB 1903
Weller Brothers Ltd., London. 20 hp engine.

WELLINGTON
GB 1900–1901
F.F. Wellington, London. Light cars.

WELLINGTON
USA c. 1905
C.E. Wellington, Keene, New Hampshire. 6 hp automobile.

WELLS
USA 1904–1910; 1914
Jesse O. Wells, Des Moines, Iowa. One steam and five gasoline cars were made.

WELLS-MEEKER
USA 1900
Wells-Meeker Motor Vehicle Co., Columbus, Ohio. Electric car.

WENDAX
D 1937–1940; 1950–1951
Wendax-Fahrzeugbau GmbH, Hamburg. About 80 sports and light cars built in 1950–1951.

WENDLAND
D 1993
Wendland Motorsport, Rangendingen. Tuning.

WENKELMOBIL
D 1904–1907; 1933–1934
Automobilwerke Schneider & Co., Berlin. Three-wheelers.

WENTWORTH
USA 1915
E.E. Wentworth Corp., Springvale, Maine.

WERBELL
GB 1907–1909
William and Edward Raikes-Bell, Dundee. 8 cars built.

WERNER
F 1906–1914
Werner Freres et Cie., Billancourt/Seine. Voiturette.

WESEN
D 1900
Fahrzeugfabrik Wesen GmbH, Wesen bei Lindau. Vis-à-vis cars.

WESNIGK
D 1922–1926
Dipl.-Ing. Erwin Wesnigk, Berlin. Three-wheelers.

WESSON
USA c. 1905
Wesson Brothers, Bridgeport, Connecticut.

WEST
USA 1895
H.B. West, Rochester, N.Y. One steam runabout produced. Used balloon tires.

WESTALL
GB 1922
Sidney C. Westall, London. Cyclecars.

WEST & BURGETT
USA 1899
William S. West and C.E. Burgett, Middlesburg, N.Y.

WEST-ASTER; WEST
GB 1904–1913
E.J. West & Co. Ltd (1904–1913). West Ltd., Coventry, Warwickshire (1906–1908). Tourers.

WESTCAR
GB 1922–1926
Strode Engineering Works, Herne, Kent.

WEST COAST
USA 1979–1993
West Coast Cobra, Sterling Heights, Michigan. Sports cars.

WESTCOASTER
USA 1960
Electric three-wheelers.

WESTCOTT
USA 1909–1925
Westcott Motor Car Co., Richmond, Indiana (1909–1916). New plant in Springfield, Ohio (1916–1925). 4- and 6-cylinder cars. 15,025 cars were made.

WESTERN
USA 1900
Western Motor Truck & Vehicle Co., Chicago, Illinois.

WESTERN
USA 1900
Western Automobile Co., Chicago, Illinois.

WESTERN
USA 1907
Western Motor Car Mfg. Co., Denver, Colorado.

WESTERN
USA 1908
Western Automobile Co., Chicago, Illinois. Kit cars.

WESTERNER
USA 1912
Smith Automobile Co., Topeka, Kansas. Touring car.

WESTERN RESERVE
USA 1921
Western Reserve Automobile Co., Warren, Ohio. 6-cylinder 55 hp touring car prototype.

WESTFALIA
D 1906–1914; 1911–1913
Ramesohl & Schmidt AG, Oelde; Bielefeld. DeDion and Fafnir engines.

WESTFIELD
GB 1982–present
Westfield Sports Cars Ltd., Kingswinford, West Midlands. "Lotus" replicars.

WESTFIELD
USA 1901–1903
Charles J. Moore Mechanical Tire Co., Westfield, Massachusetts. Unassembled gasoline and steam vehicles.

WESTFIELD
USA 1915
Westfield Mfg. Co., Westfield, Massachusetts.

WESTINGHOUSE
F 1904–1912
Sté. des Automobiles Westinghouse, Le Havre. High-quality conventional cars. Built also by "Marta" (H).

WESTINGHOUSE
USA 1905–1907
Westinghouse Electric & Mfg. Co., East Pittsburgh, Pennsylvania. First touring cars built in France. Receivers appointed October 23, 1917, and discharged March 31, 1908.

WESTINGHOUSE ELECTRIC
USA 1901–1902
Westinghouse Electric & Mfg. Co., Pittsburgh, Pennsylvania. Electric cars.

WESTLAKE
GB 1907
Westlake Motor Syndicate Ltd., Maidenhead, Berks. Prototype.

WESTMAN
USA c. 1900
Westman, Minneapolis, Minnesota.

WESTMINSTER
GB 1906–1908
Westminster Motor Works Ltd., London.

WESTON
USA 1899–1903
Grout Bros., Orange, Massachusetts. Steam cars.

WESTON
USA 1901
Frank H. Weston, Passaic, New Jersey. About 50 steam cars were made.

WESTONE
USA 1914
Westone Cycle Car Co., Los Angeles, California. 15 hp cyclecars.

WESTWICK
USA 1901
Westwick Foundry, Galena, Illinois. One car was built.

WESTWOOD
GB 1920–1926
Westwood Motor Co. Ltd. (1920–1924). Westwood-Ince Ltd., Wigan, Lancs. (1924–1926). Dorman and Meadows engines.

WETZIKON
CH 1898
Motorenfabrik Wetzikon AG, Wetzikon. Four-seater cars.

WEYHER
USA 1908–1910
Theodore Weyher, Whitewater, Wisconsin. Three cars were built.

WEYHER ET RICHEMOND
F 1905–1910
Automobiles Weyher et Richemond, Pantin/Seine. Steam and gasoline cars.

WFM
PL 1958
Warszawska Fabryka Motocykli, Warszawa. 148 cc 6 hp minicar prototype.

W.F.S.
USA 1911–1912
W.F.S. Motor Co., Philadelphia, Pennsylvania. 25 and 40 hp touring cars.

W-G
USA 1914
White Manufacturing Co., Waterloo, Iowa; Pottstown, Pennsylvania. Cyclecars.

WHALEY-HENRIETTE
USA 1898–1900
Whaley-Dwyer Co., St. Paul, Minnesota. 3 hp gasoline carriage.

WHARTON
USA 1922–1923
Wharton Motors Co., Kansas City, Missouri; Dallas, Texas. Roadsters. Also listed in Johnstown, Pennsylvania October 1922.

WHEELER
USA 1900–1902
E.O. Wheeler & Son, Marlboro, Massachusetts. Three cars built 1900, 1901 and 1902.

WHERWELL
GB 1920–1921
Thompson & Son, Wherwell, Andover, Hampshire. Cyclecars.

WHIFFLER
USA 1903–1904
Charles Whiffler Automobile Co., Detroit, Michigan. Touring car powered by a 2-cylinder horizontally opposed engine.

WHIPPET
USA 1927–1931
Willys-Overland Co., Toledo, Ohio. About 667,000 cars were made.
  See "Willys," "Overland" and "Jeep."

WHIPPLE
USA 1893
Rufus Whipple, Decoto, California.

WHIPPLE
USA 1899

William N. Whipple, Locke, N.Y. Steam carriage.

WHIPPLE
USA 1902–1903
Whipple Cycle Co., Chicago, Illinois.

WHISPER
DK 1982–1993
Whisper Electric Car A/S, Hadsund. Electric cars.

WHITCOMB
USA 1900
G.A. Whitcomb, Natick, Massachusetts.

WHITE
USA 1899
White Motor Wagon Co., Kingston, N.Y.

WHITE
USA 1900
James White, Baltimore, Maryland.

WHITE
USA 1900–1918
White Sewing Machine Co. White Co., Cleveland, Ohio. 21,134 steam and gasoline cars were made. Continued with trucks to date.

WHITE
USA 1903
White Steam Wagon Co., Indianapolis, Indiana. Steam cars.

WHITE
USA 1906–1912
George White Buggy Co., Rochelle, Illinois.

WHITE
USA 1909
White Motor Car Co., Cleveland, Ohio. Former "French-American." No relation to other Cleveland "White."

WHITE
USA 1914
White Manufacturing Co., Waterloo, Iowa. Cyclecars.

WHITEHEAD
GB 1920–1921
Whitehead Light Cars, Bradford, Yorks. Coventry-Simplex engine.

WHITEHEAD-THANET
GB 1920–1921
Amalgamated Motors Ltd., Ashtead, Surrey. Prototype.

WHITE STANHOPE
USA 1901
Voiturette.

WHITE STAR
USA 1909–1911
White Star Automobile Co., Atlanta, Georgia. Touring cars. Became Atlanta Motor Car Co.

WHITE SWAN
USA 1914
White Swan Cyclecar Co., Marysville, California. Cyclecars.

WHITGIFT
GB 1913
Croydon Central Motor Car Co. Ltd., Croydon, Surrey. Cyclecars.

WHITING
USA 1906–1907
Jackson, Michigan.

WHITING
USA 1909–1912
Whiting Motor Car Co. Flint Wagon Works, Flint, Michigan. Roadsters.

WHITING-GRANT
USA 1911–1912
Whiting Motor Car Co., Flint, Michigan.
See "Grant."

WHITLOCK
GB 1903–1932
Whitlock Automobile Co. Lawton-Goodman Ltd., London. Touring cars.

WHITMORE
USA 1914
Whitmore Co., Dayton, Ohio. Cyclecars.

WHITNEY
USA 1896–1900
Whitney Motor Wagon Co., East Boston, Massachusetts. Steam cars. Licensed by Stanley Mfg. Co.
See "Stanley-Whitney" and "McKay."

WHITNEY
USA 1899–1905
Whitney Mfg. Co., Lewiston, Maine. Steam cars. Moved to Brunswick, Maine 1902.

WHITNEY
USA 1900
E.F. Whitney, Manchester, New Hampshire.

WHITNEY
USA 1902–1903
Whitney Automobile Co., Whitney Point, N.Y.

WHITNEY STEAMER
USA 1899–1900
Stanley Mfg. Co., Boston, Massachusetts. Absorbed Whitney Motor Wagon Co., Boston, Massachusetts. 1898–1899.

WHITWOOD MONOCAR
GB 1934–1936
O.E.C. Ltd., Portsmouth, Hampshire. Tandem two-seater on 2 wheels.

WHITWORTH
GB 1920
See "Hammond."

WHYLAND
USA 1914
Whyland-Nelson Motor Co., Buffalo, N.Y. Cyclecars.

WHYLAND-NELSON
USA 1912–1913
See "Whyland."

WICHITA
USA 1920–1921
Wichita Motor Co., Wichita Falls, Texas.

WICHITA FALLS
USA 1914
Wichita Falls Motor Co., Wichita Falls, Texas.

WICK
USA 1902–1903
Hugh B. Wick & Co., Youngstown, Ohio. Used J.M. Quinby Co. bodies.

WIEMEYER
USA 1900
J.L. Wiemeyer, St. Louis, Missouri. 6 cars built.

WIESMANN
D 1985–present
Wiesmann Auto-Sport GmbH & Co., Dülmen/Merfeld. Sports cars.

WIFFLER
USA 1903–1905
Wiffler Automobile Co., Detroit, Michigan.

WIGAN-BARLOW
GB 1922–1923
Wigan-Barlow Motors Ltd., Coventry, Warwickshire. Cars made in very small numbers.

WIIMA
FIN 1957
Antii Wihuri, Oy Uusi Autokoriteollisuus AB, Helsinki. Two-seater minicar prototype.

WIKOV
CS 1925–1936
Wichterle a Kovářík, akc. spol., Prostějov. Touring and sports cars.

WILBROOK
GB 1913
Brroks & Spencer, Levenshulme, Lancs. Cyclecars.

WILCOX
USA c. 1905
E.B. Wilcox, Meriden, Connecticut. Two cars were produced.

WILCOX
USA 1909–1910
H.E. Wilcox Motor Car Co., Minneapolis, Minnesota. Succeeded "Wolfe." Touring cars. Continued with trucks after 1911.

WILCOX-BACHLE
USA 1905
Church Mfg. Co., Adrian, Michigan. Touring cars.

FILDFIRE
USA 1952
Wodoil Motor Co., Downey, California. Sports car prototype with plastic body and "Willys" engine.

WILDMAN
USA 1902
Alfred F. Wildman, Morrisville, Pennsylvania. Runabout.

WILES-THOMSON
AUS 1947
Wiles Manufacturing Co., Adelaide, S.A. 7 hp 2-stroke engine.

WILFORD
B 1897–1901
Ateliers de Construction Mécanique Ch. Wilford et Fils, Tamise. Primitive rear-engine vehicles.

WILKENS
USA 1895
V.H. Wilkens, Evanston, Illinois.

WILKINS
USA 1877; 1899
Wilkins Automobile Co., San Francisco, California.

WILKINSON
GB 1903–1904; 1912–1913
Wilkinson Sword Co. Ltd., London. Light cars.

WILKINSON
USA 1898; 1925
John Wilkinson Automobile Co., Syracuse, N.Y. Experimental gasoline cars.

WILKINSON
USA 1904
Two-passenger runabout.

WILLAM
F 1968–1979
Lambretta S.A.F.D., Paris. Willam, Levallois/Seine. Minicars.

WILLARD
USA 1903–1905
Jacob Hoffman Wagon Co., Cleveland, Ohio. Electric cars.

WILLARD
USA 1905
H.L. Willard, Rutland, Vermont. Steam car.

WILLIAMS
USA 1901–1902
J.J. Williams, Montpellier, Vermont. Two cars were made.

WILLIAMS
USA 1905
D.T. Williams Valvee Co., Cincinnati, Ohio. W.L. Casaday Manufacturing Co., South Bend, Indiana. Air-cooled cars.

WILLIAMS
USA 1906
Williams Motor Carriage Co., Akron, Ohio.

WILLIAMS
USA 1907–1908
Williams Motor Carriage Co. Williams Electric Vehicle Co., Cleveland, Ohio. Electric cars. Succeeded "Blakeslee."
See "De Mars."

WILLIAMS
USA 1914
W.A. Williams, Lima, Ohio.

WILLIAMS
USA 1916
Charles H. Williams, Chicago, Illinois. Cyclecar.

WILLIAMS
USA 1957–1968
The Williams Engine Co., Ambler, Pennsylvania. Steam prototypes.

WILLIAMS
USA 1982–1993
Williams Motor Works Corp., Gardena, California. Stretched limousines.

WILLIAMSON
GB 1913–1916
Williamson Motor Co. Ltd., Coventry, Warwickshire. Three-wheelers.

WILLIAMSPORT
USA 1907
Williamsport Enginering Co., Williamsport, Pennsylvania. Became Imperial Motor Car Co.
See "Imperial."

WILLIS
GB 1913
Finchley Place Garage, London. Cyclecars.

WILLIS
USA 1900
George E. Willis, Auburn, Maine. Steam car.

WILLIS
USA 1927–1928
Willis Motor Corporation, Maywood, Illinois. America's first and only straight-nine cylinder car (in blocks of three).

WILLMENT
GB 1957–1958
Willments Speed Shop, Twickenham, Middlesex. Sports cars.

WILLMENT
GB 1971
John Willment (Mitcham) Ltd., Mitcham, Surrey. Sports cars and tuning.

WILLOUGHBY
USA 1901–1902
Willoughby-Owen Electric Co., Utica, N.Y. Electric cars.

WILLS-LEE
USA 1920–1921
C.H. Wills & J.R. Lee, Detroit, Michigan.

WILLS SAINTE CLAIRE
USA 1921–1926
C.H. Wills & Co., Marryville, Michigan. 1923 reorganized as Wills Sainte Claire Motor Co. Inc. Touring cars.

WILLYS
BR 1958–1967
Willys-Overland do Brasil SA, São Paulo. "Willys-Jeep" (USA) and "Renault" (F) license.

WILLYS
USA 1916–1942; 1952–1963
Willys-Overland Inc., Toledo, Ohio (1916–1918; 1930–1942). Became Kaiser-Jeep Corp. Called "Aero-Willys" 1952–1954. Touring cars.

WILLYS-KNIGHT
CDN 1932
Willys-Overland Sales Co. Ltd., Toronto, Ontario.

WILLYS-KNIGHT
USA 1914–1933
Willys-Overland Co., Toledo, Ohio. Succeeded "Edwards-Knight" and "Garford-Knight."

WILLY'S NOVA
D 1984
Peter Müller-Buchhof, München. 4 × 4 vehicle.

WILMOT
USA 1907
Wilmot Motor & Cycle Mfg. Co., Camden, New Jersey.

WILSON
GB 1922–1923
W. Wilson, Loughborough, Leics. Prototype.

WILSON
GB 1935–1936
Partridge, Wilson & Co. Ltd., Leicester. Electric cars.

WILSON
USA 1902–1905
Wilson Automobile Mfg. Co., Wilson, N.Y. Became "La Salle-Niagara."

WILSON
USA 1906
Wilson Brothers Automobile Co., Minneapolis, Minnesota. Steam car.

WILSON & PEEBLES
USA 1906
Wilson & Peebles, San Jose, California. Custom-made tonneau.

WILSON ELECTRIC
USA 1895
D.H. Wilson, Chicago, Illinois.

WILSON-PILCHER
GB 1901–1907
Wilson & Pilcher, London (1901–1903). Sir W.G. Armstrong, Whitworth & Co. Ltd., Newcastle upon Tyne (1904–1907).

WILTON
GB 1912–1924
Wilton Cycle & Motor Co. Ltd (1912–1914). Wilton Cars Ltd., London (1914–1924). 4-cylinder light cars.

WIMILLE
F
See "J.P. Wimille."

WIMMER
A 1904–1906
Otto Wimmer, Ruhrstorf an der Rott. Light cars, sold also under name "Central-Auto."

WINCHESTER
GB 1970–1975
Passenger and hire cars. About 50 cars built in 1974.

WINCHESTER
USA 1909
Winchester Repeating Arms Co., New Haven, Connecticut.

WINCO
GB 1913–1914
Stringer & Co., Sheffield, Yorks. Light cars.

WINDER
USA 1904
John E. Winder, Cincinnati, Ohio. Steam car.

WINDHOFF
D 1908–1914
Gebr. Windhoff Motoren- und Fahrzeugfabrik GmbH, Rheine/Westf. 4- and 6-cylinder touring cars.

WINDSOR
CDN 1910–1911
Dominion Motors Ltd., Walkerville, Ontario.

WINDSOR
GB 1924–1927
Jas. Bartle & Co. Ltd., London. Cars with very high standard of construction.

WINDSOR
USA 1906
Windsor Automobile Corp., Chicago, Illinois; Evansville, Indiana. Became "Simplicity."

WINDSOR
USA 1929–1930
Windsor Corp., St. Louis, Missouri. Subsidiary of Moon Motor Car Co.
See "Moon," "Diana" and "Hol-Tan."

WINDSOR
USA 1922–1923
Detroit Steam Motors Corp., Detroit, Michigan. Steam car prototypes for Canadian market only.
See "Detroit Steam Car" and "Trask."

WINDSOR WHITE PRINCE
USA
See "Moon."

WINFIELD
USA 1922
Winfield Barnes Co., Philadelphia, Pennsylvania. 1922 model of "Adelphia."

WING
USA 1896
L.J. Wing & Co., New York, N.Y. Gasoline wagon.

WING
USA c. 1905
Chauncey Wing, Greenfield, Massachusetts. 10 hp automobile.

WING
USA 1922
Wing Motors Corp., Binghamton, N.Y. Runabout.

WINGFIELD
GB 1909–1920
Wingfield Motor Co., London. Well built cars with motors ranging from 1.4 to 7.5 litres.

WING MIDGET
USA 1922
Chauncey Wing's Sons, Greenfield, Massachusetts. Wing Motors Corp., Binghamton, N.Y.

WINIGER
CH 1985
Carrosserie Winiger, Frauenfeld. Stretched cars.

WINNER
USA 1899–1901
Elgin Automobile Co., Elgin, Illinois. Runabout.

WINNER
USA 1907–1909

Winner Motor Buggy Co., St. Louis, Missouri. Motor buggy.

WINNIPEG
CDN 1920–1923
Winnipeg Motor Cars Ltd., Winnipeg, Manitoba.

WINONA
USA 1901–1903
New Winona Mfg. Co., Winona, Minnesota. Gasoline automobiles.

WINONAH
USA 1912
Bay City, Michigan.

WINSLOW
USA 1900
Winslow Motor Carriage Co., Doylestown, Pennsylvania.

WINSON
GB 1920
Messrs. J. Winn, Rochdale, Lancs. Cyclecars.

WINTER
GB
See "W.W."

WINTHER
USA 1921–1923
The Winther Motor Co., Kenosha, Wisconsin. 6-cylinder 60 hp touring cars. Company primarily built trucks.

WINTON
USA 1896–1924
Winton Motor Carriage Co. Winton Motor Car Co. Winton Co., Cleveland, Ohio. Touring cars. 1896 experimental car. Reorganized as Winton Engine Co. (engines only). 28,492 cars were made.

WISCO
USA 1910
Wisconsin Motor Co., Janesville, Wisconsin. Touring cars.

WISCONSIN
USA 1899
Wisconsin Automobile & Machinery Co., Milwaukee, Wisconsin. Steam cars.

WISCONSIN
USA 1914
Wisconsin Cyclecar Co., Milwaukee, Wisconsin. Cyclecars.

WISNER
USA 1900–1903
C.H. Wisner, Flint, Michigan.

WISNER
USA 1907
Charles Wisner, Grand Forks, North Dakota. 12 hp automobile.

WISWELL
USA c. 1905
W.E. Wiswell, Lynn, Massachusetts. 4 hp automobile.

WITHERN
USA c. 1905
Withern Mfg. Co., Boston, Massachusets. 16/20 hp automobile.

WITHERS
GB 1906–1915
Withers Motors Ltd., London. Large touring cars.

WITHERS
USA 1908
Charles Withers, Garden City, Kansas.

WITKAR
NL 1974
Witkar, Amsterdam. Electric car prototype.

WITTEKIND
D 1922–1925
Wittekind Automobile GmbH, Berlin. Small cars.

WITTMAN
USA 1900
Wittman Automobile Co., Lincoln, Nebraska. Tonneau.

WIZARD
USA 1914
Wizard Motor Co., Indianapolis, Indiana. Cyclecars.

WIZARD JUNIOR
USA 1920–1921
Wizard Automobile Co., Inc., Charlotte, North Carolina. Very few 2-cylinder 15 hp cars built. Receiver reported named February 1921. Assets reported sold April 1922.

WM
H
See "Weiss Manfred."

W.M.
PL 1927–1928
Inz. Wladyslaw Mrajski, Warszawa. Flat-twin 4-stroke air-cooled engined prototypes.

WMC
GB 1990–present
Webster Motor Company, Brainshfield, Hampshire. Three-wheelers based on the "Reliant" Bug.

WMW
D
See "Siegel."

WOHL MAG
H 1914
Taxicabs for England and Turkey, built by "MAG."

WOLF
D
See "Kleine Wolf."

WOLF
GB
See "Wearwell."

WOLFE
USA c. 1905
Joseph L. Wolfe, Stamford, Connecticut.

WOLFE
USA 1907–1909
H.E. Wilcox Motor Car Co., Minneapolis, Minnesota. Touring cars. Became "Wilcox" April 1909.

WOLO
D 1922–1923
Wolo-Fahrzeugwerk, Berlin.

WOLSELEY
GB 1899–1906; 1911–1975
Wolseley Sheep Shearing Machine Co. Ltd. (1899–1901). Wolseley Tool and Motor Car Co. Ltd. (1901–1914). Wolseley Motors Ltd., Birmingham (1914–1948); Cowley, Oxford (1949–1970). Austin-Morris Division, British Leyland Motor Corp. Ltd., Cowley, Oxford (1970–1975). Touring and sports cars. Complicated inter-relationship between "Wolseley," "Deasy," "Siddeley" and "Armstrong."

WOLSELEY ITALIANA
I 1907–1909
Wolseley Italiana S.A. (Wolsit), Legnano.

WOLSELEY-SIDDELEY
GB 1904–1910
Wolseley Tool & Motor Car Co. Ltd., Birmingham. Four-cylinder touring cars.

WOLSIT
I 1907

Legnano. "Wolseley" (GB) assembled in Italy.

WOLVERINE
USA 1896
Wolverine Motor Works, Grand Rapids, Michigan.

WOLVERINE
USA 1904–1905
Reid Mfg. Co., Detroit, Michigan. 1905 became Wolverine Automobile and Commercial Vehicle Co., Dundee, Michigan. 1906 became Maumee Motor Car Works.

WOLVERINE
USA 1905–1906
Wolverine Automobile & Commercial Vehicle Co., Dundee, Michigan. Became Maumee Motor Car Works, Detroit, Michigan.

WOLVERINE
USA 1910
Wolverine Motor Car Co., Mt. Clemens, Michigan. Absorbed by Alpena Motor Car Co.
See "Alpena."

WOLVERINE
USA 1916–1917
Jackson Automobile Co., Jackson, Michigan.

WOLVERINE
USA 1916–1920
Wolverine Automobile Co., Toledo, Ohio. 1918 name changed to Wolverine Motors Inc., Kalamazoo, Michigan, again in 1919 to Wolverine Motor Car Co.

WOLVERINE
USA 1917
Wolverine Motor Co., Battle Creek, Michigan.

WOLVERINE
USA 1917
Wolverine Car & Tractor Co., Wayne, Michigan.

WOLVERINE
USA 1927–1928
Reo Motor Car Co., Lansing, Michigan. 6-cylinder touring cars.

WOLVERINE-DETROIT
USA 1912–1913
Pratt-Carter-Sigsbee Co., Detroit, Michigan.

WONDER
USA 1909
Wonder Mfg. Co., Syracuse, N.Y.

WONDER
USA 1909
Wonder Motor Car Co., Kansas Sity, Missouri.
See "Kansas City Wonder."

WONDER
USA 1917
Wonder Truck Co., Chicago, Illinois. Touring cars.

WOOD
USA 1902–1903
J.C. Wood Vapor Vehicle Co., Brooklyn, N.Y. Steam cars.

WOODALL
GB c. 1985
Woodall Nicholson, Eagle Works, Well Lane, Halifax. Stretched limousines.

WOODBURN
USA 1905–1912
Woodburn Auto Co., Woodburn, Indiana. Runabouts.

WOOD ELECTRIC
USA 1902
F.R. Wood & Son, New York, N.Y.

WOODILL
USA 1952–1958
Woodill Fiberglass Body Corp., Tustin, California. Two models: Wildfire sports car, Brushfire one-cylinder juvenile car. 15 cars were made.

WOODLAND
USA 1909
Woodland Motor Car Co., Cleveland, Ohio. 4 cars were built.

WOODLAND
USA 1913
Frank O. Woodland, Worcester, Massachusetts. Cyclecars.

WOOD-LOCO
USA 1901–1902; WOOD 1903
Wood-Loco Vehicle Co., Cohoes, N.Y. (1901–1902); Brooklyn, N.Y. (1903). Steam cars.

WOOD & MEAGHER
USA 1896
Wood & Meagher, Richmond, Virginia. Gasoline-propelled vehicles.

WOOD & PICKETT
GB c. 1971–1984
Wood & Pickett Limited, Ruislip, Middlesex. "Mini" based luxury cars.

WOODROW
GB 1913–1915
Woodrow & Co. Ltd., Stockport, Cheshire. Cyclecars.

WOODRUFF
USA 1902–1904
Woodruff Motor Carriage Co. Woodruff Automobile Co., Cleveland & Akron, Ohio. One- and three-cylinder runabouts.

WOODS
USA 1899–1918
Woods Motor Vehicle Co., Chicago, Illinois. Electric cars. 1916 dual power cars, gasoline and electric. 13,583 cars of all types were made.

WOODS
USA 1900–1901
Clinton E. Woods. Woods-Waring Co., Chicago, Illinois. Electric cars.
See "Clinton E. Woods."

WOODS
USA 1901
Woods Motor Co., New York, N.Y. Electric cars.

WOODS
USA 1905–1907
Woods Motor Vehicle Co., Chicago, Illinois.

WOODS ELECTRIC
USA 1898
Fischer Equipment Co., Chicago, Illinois.

WOODSMOBILE
USA 1908
Walter A. Woods, Milwaukee, Wisconsin. Runabouts.

WOODS MOBILETTE
USA 1913–1916
International Cyclecar & Accessories Co. Woods Mobilette Mfg. Co., Harvey, Illinois. Cyclecars.

WOOD STEAMER
USA 1886
J. Elmer Wood, Beverly, Massachusetts. A steam tricycle with single front wheel.

WOODWORTH
USA c. 1905
George N. Woodworth, Broadbrook, Connecticut. 5 hp automobile.

WOOLER
GB 1920–1921
Wooler Enginering Co. Ltd., Alperton, Middlesex. 2 cyclecars were made.

WOOLVERTON
USA 1895
G.C. Woolverton, Buffalo, N.Y.

WOONSOCKET
USA 1907–1908
The Woonsocket Co., Woonsocket, Rhode Island.

WORCESTER
USA c. 1905
Frank Worcester, Waltham, Massachusetts. 4 hp automobile.

WORLD
USA 1905
Arnold Schwinn & Co., Chicago, Illinois.
  See "Schwinn."

WORLDMOBILE
USA 1927–1928
Servise-Relay Motors Corp., Lima, Ohio. Six-passenger sedan. 7 cars produced.

WORTH
USA 1902
J.M. Worth Gas Engine Mfg. Co., Chicago, Illinois. Gasoline touring.

WORTH
USA 1907–1910
Worth Motor Car Co., Evansville, Indiana. Highwheelers. Moved to Kankakee, Illinois 1908. Reported October 1910 creditors pressed bankruptcy. S.R. Hunter, vice-president, disappeared with car and machinery.

WORTHINGTON
USA 1903–1906
Worthington Automobile Co., New York, N.Y. Absorbed Berg Automobile Co.
  See "Berg" and "Meteor."

WORTHINGTON
USA 1957
Worthington Motor Co., Stroudsburg, Pennsylvania. Three-wheelers.

WORTHINGTON-BOLLÉE
USA 1903–1906
Worthington Automobile Co., New York, N.Y.
  See "Worthington."

WORTHINGTON RUNABOUT
GB 1909–1912
Worthington Bros., Hythe, Kent. Prototype.

WORTHLEY
USA 1897–1898
C.A. Worthley, Boston, Massachusetts. Steam car. Reportedly first car to use air brakes.

WOTTRING
USA 1907
Wottring & Son Automobile Works, Prospect, Ohio. Made to order vehicles only.
  See "Prospect."

WRC
USA 1906–1909
WRC Auto Works, El Reno, Oklahoma.
  See "Pioneer."

WREISNER
USA 1901–1904
Nels & Peter Wreisner, Dassel, Minnesota. One-cylinder vehicle started 1901, completed 1904.

WRIGHT
CDN 1929
Benjamin Wright, Montreal, Quebec. "Flexible axle car."

WRIGHT
USA 1900
Frederick C. Wright & Co., Springfield, Massachusetts.

WRIGHT
USA 1904
Fred & Ralph Wright, Dayton, Ohio.

WRIGHT
USA 1910–1911
Wright Motor Co., New Cumberland, Pennsylvania. Touring cars.

WRIGHT
USA 1912–1913
C.E. Wright & Co., Norfolk, Virginia.

WRIGHT
USA 1920
Fred Wright, Buffalo, N.Y.

WRIGLEY
GB 1913
Wrigley & Co. Ltd., Birmingham. Cyclecars.

W.S.C.
GB 1914
Wholesale Supply Co., Aberdeen. Cyclecars.

WSK
PL 1956–1960
Wytwornia Sprzetu Komunikacyjnego, Swidnik. Small cars "Mikrus" and "Meduza."

WUHAN
PRC 1970s–present
Wuhan No. 2 Motor Vehicle Factory, Wuhan, Hu-Bei. 4 × 4 vehicles.

WUNDERLICH
D 1902
Motorenfabrik Carl Wunderlich, Berlin. Voiturette.

WURTENBERG
USA c. 1905
Charles Wurtenberg, Naugatuck, Connecticut.

W.W.
GB 1912–1913
Winter & Co., London. Light cars.

WYCKOFF
USA 1904
L.J. Wyckoff, Newark, New Jersey. Steam carriage.

WYETH
USA 1912–1913
Wyeth Motor Car Co., Waltham, Massachusetts. Runabouts.

WYKOFF
USA 1912
Company name, not name of vehicle. Company was Wykoff, Church & Partridge, "Guy Vaughan" manufacturer.

WYLIE ELECTRIC
USA 1894
W.W. Wylie, Ottawa, Illinois.

WYMAN
USA 1901
W.A. Wyman, Scottsburg, Indiana. One touring car was made.

WYNER
A 1903–1905
Michael A. Wyner, Wien. Voiturettes.

WYNES
GB 1991–1993
N.G. Wynes Glass Fibre, McCoy Cars, Fakenham, Norfolk. Sports car.

WYSS
CH
  See "Berna."

WYVERN
GB 1913–1914
Wyvern Light Car Co. Ltd., Twickenham, Middlesex. Light cars.

XANDER
USA 1901–1902
Xander Machine & Supply Co., Reading, Pennsylvania. Gasoline and steam vehicles built to order.

XENIA
USA 1914
Hawkins Cyclecar Co., Xenia, Ohio. Cyclecars.

XENON
D 1988
Fachhochschule für Gestaltung, Pforzheim. Sports car prototype.

XIALI
PRC 1989–present
Tianjin Small Vehicle Factory, Yangliuquing, Tianjin. "Daihatsu" (J) license.
See "Tianjin."

XIAN-JIN
PRC 1963–1974 ?
H'Sin-Chin Mechanical Works, Chunking, Sechuan. Passenger cars.

XILLION
USA 1989–1993
Xillion Inc., Miami, Florida. Sports car replica.

X-RAY SPECIAL
USA 1955
X-Ray Incorporated, Highland Park, Michigan.

XTC
USA 1987–1993
XTC Co., Fort Lauderdale, Florida. Sports car kit.

XTRA
GB 1922–1924
Xtra Cars Ltd., Chertsey, Surrey. Three-wheelers.

YAK
GB 1969–1970. Grantura Plastics Ltd., Blackpool, Lancs. Light 4 × 4 vehicles.

YAKOVLEV & FREZE
SU 1896
Zavod E.A. Yakovlev, Sankt Peterburg. Very simple car with 2 hp rear engine.

YALE
USA 1900
Denison Electric Engineering Co., New Haven, Connecticut.

YALE
USA 1902–1905
Kirk Manufacturing Co., Toledo, Ohio. First cars delivered June 1902. 1903 became Consolidated Mfg. Co. Touring cars.

YALE
USA 1916–1918
Saginaw Motor Car Co., Saginaw, Michigan. Roadsters and touring cars.

YALE FLYER
USA 1913
Cameron Mfg. Co., West Haven, Connecticut. Prototype only.

YALTA
SU/B
Scaldia-Volga S.A., Bruxelles. "Zaporozhets" (SU) with "Renault" (F) R8 engine.
See "Zaporozhets."

YAMAHA
J/GB 1992
Yamaha Motor Co., Shizuoka-Ken. Ypsilon Technology Ltd., Rooksley, Milton-Keynes. 400 hp sports cars.

YAMATA
J 1916
Osaka. Three-wheeler.

YANASE
J 1964
Sports car on "Volkswagen" components.

YANK
USA 1950
Custom Auto Works, San Diego, California. Sports cars.

YANKEE
USA 1910
Yankee Motor Car Co., Chicago, Illinois. Highwheelers.

YANKEE
USA 1914
Yankee Cyclecar Co., Chicago, Illinois. Cyclecars.

YANKEE CLIPPER
USA 1953–1954
Strassberger Motor Co., Menlo Park, California. Cars used V-8 "Ford" engine.

YARIAN
USA 1925
Yarian Motors Corp., Syracuse, N.Y. 6-cylinder sedans.

YARLOTT
USA 1919–1920
Yarlott Bros. Motor & Car Co., Ft. Wayne, Indiana. Prototype.

YAXA
CH 1912–1914
Charles Baehni et Cie., Geneve. About 100 cars were made.

Y.E.C.
GB 1907–1908
Yorkshire Engine Co., Sheffield, Yorks. 50 cars of the "Mercedes" (D) design were made.

YELLOW
USA 1915–1930
Yellow Taxicab Mfg. Co., Chicago, Illinois (1915–1928); Pontiac, Michigan (1928–1930). Taxicabs.

YENKO
USA 1965–1971
Yenko Sportscars, Inc., Cannonsburg, Pennsylvania. "Chevrolet" Corvair Corsa coupe modified versions.

YEU TYAN
RC 1979–present
Yeu Tyan Machinery Manufacturing Co. Ltd., Taipei, Taiwan. "Peugeot" (F) and "Daihatsu" (J) license.

YLN
RC 1953–1993
Yue Loong Motor Co. Ltd., Taipei, Taiwan. "Jeep" (RA) and "Datsun/Nissan" (J) license.
See "Yue Loong," and "Yulon" from 1993.

YORK
D 1922
York Motoren AG, Plauen/Vogtland. Light cars.

YORK
USA 1903–1909
York Automobile Co., York, Pennsylvania. Became York Motor Car Co. Name changed to "Pullman." Became Pullman Motor Car Co.

YORK-PULLMAN
USA 1906–1907
York Motor Car Co., York, Pennsylvania.

YUE LOONG
RC
See "YLN," "Yulon."

YULON
RC 1993–present
New name for the "YLN."

YUGO
YU 1988–1993
Zavodi Crvena Zastava, Kragujevac.
See "Zastava."

YUKON
USA 1914
Yukon Automobile Co., Seattle, Washington. Cyclecars.

YUNQUE
PRC 1995–present
Guizhou Aero Space Industry Corp., Anshun, Guizhou. "Subaru" (J) license.

Z.
CS 1923–1939
Československá zbrojovka, akc. spol., Brno. Passenger and sports cars with 2-cycle engines.

Z
I 1914–1915
Zambon & C., Torino.
See "Zambon."

ZACHOW & BESSERDICH
USA 1909–1910
Otto Zachow & William A. Besserdich, Clintonville, Wisconsin. Four wheel drive. Became "Beaver" F.W.D. Also called "Z & B."

ZAGATO
I 1947–present
Carrozzeria Zagato, Terrazzano di Rho, Arese (Milano). Primarily a coachbuilder (since 1919). Seven cars registered 1952 for road use. Sports cars on "Lancia," "Fiat" and "Bristol" (GB) chassis mainly.

ZAKSPEED
D 1979–present
Zakspeed Engineering GmbH & Co. KG, Niederzissen. Tuning.

ZAMBON
I 1914–1915
Automobili Z. & C., Torino.

ZANDER
D 1985–present
Zander Exclusiv Tuning, Darmstadt. Tuning.

ZANELLA
I 1967–1970
Zanella SpA, Parma. Sports cars. Coachbuilders since 1943.

ZANZARA
I 1970
Milano Sports car on Fiat 500 base.

ZAPOROZHETS
SU/UA 1960–present
Zaporozheskii Avtomobilnii Zavod "Kommunar," Zaporozhie. Small rear-engined cars.
See "ZAZ."

ZASCHKA
D 1929
Obering. Engelbert Zaschka, Berlin. Folding three-wheelers.

ZASTAVA
YU 1954–1994
Zavodi Crvena Zastava, Kragujevac.
See "Yugo."

ZASTROW
D 1976–present
Zastrow Car Sport GmbH, Kranenburg. Tuning.

ZATO
D 1998–present
Zato GmbH, Niederbreitbach. Sports cars.

ZAZ
SU/UA 1958–present
Zaporozheskii Avtomobilnii Zavod, Zaporozhe. Small cars.
See "Zaporozhets."

ZEBRA
USA 1996–present
Zebra Motors Co., Alameda, California. Electric cars.

ZEDA
CS 1948
Josef Zelenda, Praha. 350cc small car prototype.

ZEDDECO
F 1905–1906
Electric cars.

ZÉDEL
F/CH 1906–1923
Sté. Francaise des Automobiles Zédel, Ponarlier/Doubs (F) (1906–1923). Fabrique de Moteurs et Machines Zédel, St. Aubin, Neuchatel (CH). (1907–1908). Touring cars.

ZEDER
USA 1922
Zeder Motor Co. Allyng-Zeder Motors Co. Cleveland Tractor Co., Cleveland, Ohio.
See "Rollin."

ZEIGLER
AUS 1898
Allansford, Victoria.

ZEILLER ET FOURNIER
F 1920–1924
Automobiles Zeiller et Fournier, Levallois-Perret/Seine. Ballot 1.1-litre engine.

ZENA
I 1906–1908
Fabbrica Automobili Zena, Genova. Wide range of types with SV engines.

ZENDER
D 1969–present
Zender GmbH, Mülheim-Klärlich. Tuning.

ZENDIK
GB 1913–1914
Zendik Cars Ltd., Kingston-on-Thames, Surrey. Cyclecars.

ZENETTE
GB 1907
8 hp three-wheelers.

ZENIA
F 1913–1924
Automobiles Zenia, Paris. 3-litre engine.

ZENITH
F 1910
Fourcalquier. 1-cylinder car with friction drive.

ZENT
USA 1901–1902
S.W. Zent & Co., Marion, Ohio.

ZENT
USA 1904–1906
Zent Automobile Mfg. Co., Bellafontaine, Ohio. Name changed to Bellafontaine Automobile Co. 1907.

ZENTMOBILE
USA 1903
Schuyler W. Zent, Evansville, Indiana. Touring cars.

ZENTRALMOBIL
D 1907–1908
Zentralmobil D. Nolding. Voiturette.

ZEPHYR
GB 1919–1920
James, Talbot and Davidson Ltd., Lowestoft, Suffolk. 2-litre 12 hp cars.

ZETA
AUS 1964–1966
Lightburn & Co. Ltd., Camden, S.A. Small cars.

ZETA
I 1914–1915
F. lli Zambelli, Piacenza. 4-cylinder 1.1- and 1.7-litre engines.

ZETGELETTE
D 1922–1924
Zimmer & Gehlich, Zetge-Fahrzeugwerke GmbH, Görlitz-Moys. Three-wheelers.

ZÉVACO
F 1923–1925
SA des Voiturettes Cyclecars, Eaubonne/Seine-et-Oise. Cyclecars.

ZHIGULI
SU
See "VAZ."

ZIEBELL
USA 1914
A.C. Ziebell, Oshkosh, Wisconsin. Cyclecars.

ZIL
SU/RUS 1958–present
Zavod Imieni Likhacheva, Moscow. Luxury limousines.
See "ZIS."

ZIM
F 1922–1924
Automobiles Zimmermann, Epernay/Marne. 344cc cyclecars.

ZIM
SU 1950–1957
Zavod Imieni Molotova, Gorky. Luxury sedan.

ZIM
USA c. 1914
Jules A. Zimmerlin, San Francisco, California. Cyclecars.

ZIMMER
USA 1980–1992
Zimmer Motor Car Corporation, Pompano Beach, Florida. Replicars.

ZIMMERMAN
USA 1901
Charles Zimmerman, St. Louis, Missouri. Gasoline automobile.

ZIMMERMAN
USA 1908–1915
Zimmerman Mfg. Co., Auburn, Indiana. Highwheelers. Also built "De Soto" 1913–1916.

ZIMMERMANN
A 1904
Steiermärkische Automobilwerke Theodor Zimmermann, Marburg.

ZIMMERMANN
D
See "Biene."

ZIP
USA 1913–1914
H.A. Huebotter. Zip Cyclecar Co., Davenport, Iowa. Cyclecars.

ZIP
USA 1914
B.T. Wagner, Columbus, Texas. Air-cooled 16 hp cyclecar.

ZIS
SU 1936–1958
Zavody Imieni Stalina, Moscow. Luxury limousines and convertibles for the Soviet government purposes.
See "ZIL."

ZLATKO
HR 1995
Zlatko Vukusič, Split. "Cosmopolit" sports car prototype.

ZO
I 1936
Giuseppe Zo, Asti.

ZOE
J 1982–1984
Mitsuoka Motors. Three-wheelers.

ZSCHOCKE
D 1906
E. Zschocke. Three-wheelers.

ZUCCHI
I 1911–1915
Zucchi & C., Brescia.

ZÜNDAPP
D 1931; 1956–1958
Zündapp-Werke GmbH, Nürnberg; München. Small cars.

ZUNDER
RA 1960–1963
Industrias del Transporte Automotor srl, Rio Cuarto. Rear-engined sedan using a 1.5 litre air-cooled Porsche engine. About 200 were made.

ZÜST
I 1903–1917
Ing. Roberto Züst, Fabbrica Italiana di Automobili SA, Milano. (1903–1912). Brixia-Züst SA, Brescia (1906–1911). Fabbrica Automobili Züst, Brescia (1912–1917). Touring cars.

ZWALUW
NL 1899
C. van Rosendaal, Nijmegen. One built.

ZWICKAU
DDR 1955–1959
VEB Automobilwerk Zwickau, Zwickau. Successor of the "IFA" F8. Fiberglass bodied cars with 2-cycle engine. About 25,000 were made. Succeeded by "Trabant" P50.

ZZIPPER
USA 1988
Sebring Auto-Cycle Co., Sebring, Florida. Electric three-wheelers.

Bibliography

General Automotive Histories

Alternative Cars 79: The Complete Guide to Motoring Individuality. Special Car Consultants, Brighton, Sussex, 1979.

Ash, David. *Automobile Almanac 1974.* Automobile Almanac Ltd., Nyack, N.Y., 1974.

Burgess-Wise, David. *The Illustrated Encyclopedia of Automobiles.* New Burlington Book, London, 1979.

Car Stora Billexikon. Nordbok, Göteborg, 1988-1989.

Caunter, C.F. *The Light Car: A Technical History.* H.M.S.O. & Science Museum, London, 1970.

Dale, Rodney. *Early Cars.* The British Library, London, 1994.

Eckermann, Erik. *Von Dampfwagen zum Auto: Die Motorisierung des Verkehrs.* Rowohlt-Verlag, Hamburg, 1981.

de la Rive Box, Rob. *Groot Auto Boek.* Unieboek, Bussum, 1977.

Encyklopédia automobilov: Značky, modely, technické údaje. Gemini, Bratislava, 1994.

Fersen, Olaf von (Ed.). *Ein Jahrhundert Automobiltechnik: Personenwagen.* VDI Verlag, Düsseldorf, 1986.

Georgano, G.N. (Ed.). *The Complete Encyclopedia of Motorcars 1885 to the Present.* Ebury Press, London, 1973.

_____. *Die schönsten Autos der 70er und 80er Jahre.* Motorbuch Verlag, Stuttgart, 1990.

_____. *Die schönsten Autos 1886–1930.* Motorbuch Verlag, Stuttgart, 1990.

_____. *A Source Book of Classic Cars.* Ward Lock Ltd., London, 1977.

_____. *A Source Book of Veteran Cars.* Ward Lock Ltd., London, 1974.

_____. *A Source Book of Vintage and Post-Vintage Cars.* Ward Lock Ltd., London, n.d.

Gloor, Roger. *Nachkriegswagen—Personenautos von 1945 bis 1960.* Hallwag-Verlag, Bern 1981.

_____. *Personenwagen der 60er Jahre.* Hallwag, Bern, 1984.

Harding, Anthony (Ed.). *The Guinness Book of Car Facts & Feats.* Guinness Superlatives Ltd., London, 1980.

Heinz, Vilém, and Václav Klement. *Z dějin automobilu.* V. Klement, Mladá Boleslav, 1931.

Krebs, Rudolf. *Fünf Jahrtausende Radfahrzeuge: Über 100 Jahre Automobil.* Springer-Verlag, Berlin, 1994.

Linz, Harald. *Automobil-Markenzeichen: Geschichte und Bedeutung.* Battenberg Verlag, Augsburg, 1995.

_____, and Halwart Schrader. *Die grosse Automobil-Enzyklopädie.* BLV Verlagsgesellschaft, München, 1986.

Lustig, Alois, Jaroslav Jezdinský. *Od dřevěného kola k automobilu.* Karel Synek, Praha, 1938.

Macbeth, Graham. *Vel'ký obrazový atlas automobilu: Sto rokov automobilu.* Mladé letá, Bratislava, 1987.

Mende, Hans-Ulrich von, and Matthias Dietz. *Kleinwagen—Small Cars—Petites Voitures.* Benedikt Taschen Verlag, Köln, 1994.

Robson, Graham. *A-Z of Cars of the 1970s.* Bay View Books, Bideford, 1989.

Schrader, Halwart. *Automobil-Faszination.* BLV Verlagsgesellschaft, München, 1982.

Schrader, Halwart. *Seltene Automobile.* Weltbild Verlag, Augsburg, 1991.

_____. *Grosse Automobile.* Weltbild Verlag, Augsburg, 1991.

Sedgwick, Michael. *The Motor Car 1946–56.* B.T. Batsford Ltd., London, 1979.

_____. *Passenger Cars 1924–1942.* Blanford Press, London, 1975.

_____. *Die schönsten Autos der 30er und 40er Jahre.* Motorbuch Verlag, Stuttgart, 1990.

_____. *Die schönsten Autos der 50er und 60er Jahre.* Motorbuch Verlag, Stuttgart, 1990.

_____, and Mark Gillies. *A-Z of Cars of the 1930s.* Bay View Books, Bideford, 1989.

_____, and _____. *A-Z of Cars 1945–1970.* Bay View Books, Bideford, 1989.

Simons, Rainer. *Geschichte der Automobile mit Frontantrieb.* Schrader Automobil-Bücher, München, 1981.

Stein, Ralph, and W.M. Schnitzler. *Legendäre Automobile.* Weltbild Verlag, Augsburg, 1991.

Zeichner, Walter. *Kleinwagen International: Mobile, Kleinwagen und Fahrmaschinen von 1945 bis heute.* Motorbuch Verlag, Stuttgart, 1999.

Annual Publications

Auto-Jahr. Edita SA, Lausanne, several yearbooks.

Auto-Modelle; Auto Katalog. Vereinigte Motor-Verlage GmbH, Stuttgart, 1968–1999.

Katalog der Automobil Revue. Hallwag Verlag, Bern, several yearbooks.

Motor-Jahr: Eine internationale Revue. Transpress-Verlag, Berlin, 1958–1988.

Quattroruote Dizzionario delle Auto. Editoriale Domus, Milano, several yearbooks.

Tutte le Auto dell Mondo. Editoriale Domus, Milano, several yearbooks.

World Motor Vehicle Data. Motor Vehicle Manufacturers Association, Detroit, several yearbooks.

World Cars. L' Editrice dell' Automobile, Milano, several yearbooks.

Nationally Oriented Books

NORTH AMERICA

Automobiles of America. Wayne State University Press, Detroit, Michigan, 1970.

Brigham, Grace. *The Serial Number Book for U.S. Cars 1900–1975.* Motorbooks International, Osceola, Wisconsin, 1994.

Burness, Tad. *Automobile in Amerika 1920–1980.* Schrader-Verlag, Suderburg, 1990.

Durnford, Hugh. *Cars of Canada.* McClelland & Stewart, Toronto, 1973.

The Editors of Old Cars Publications. *The Standard Catalog of American Cars 1946–1975.* Krause Publications, Iola, Wisconsin, 1982.

Encyclopedia of American Cars from 1930. Publications International, Lincolnwood, Illinois, 1993.

Kimes, Beverly Rae, and Henry Austin Clark, Jr. *The Standard Catalog of American Cars 1805–1942.* Krause Publications, Iola, Wisconsin, 1989.

Scott-Bailey, L. *The American Car Since 1775.* Automobile Quarterly Publications, Princeton, N.J., 1971.

AUSTRIA

Seper, Hans, Helmut Krackowizer and Alois Brusatti. *Österreichische Kraftfahrzeuge von Anbeginn bis heue.* Verlag Welsermühl, Wels, 1982.

BELGIUM

Kupelian, Yvette, Jacques Kupelian and Jacques Sirtaine. *Histoire de l'Automobile Belge.* Paul Legrain, Bruxelles, 1979.

CZECHOSLOVAKIA

Kuba, Adolf. *Automobil v srdci Evropy.* Nadas, Praha, 1986.

———. *Atlas našich automobilu*, 1. 1815–1913; 2. 1914–1928; 3. 1929–1936; (Milan, Spremo). 4. 1937–1963 (Nadas, Praha), 1988–1991.

Stechmiler, Rudolf, Otakar Peukert and Dagmar Loučková. *Nase automobily včera.* Mladá fronta, Praha, 1957.

Šuman-Hreblay, Marián. *Pramene k dejinám výroby cestných motorových vozidiel na území Československa v rokoch 1815–1965.* (Bibliography). Autoantikvariát, Liptovský Mikuláš, 1991.

FRANCE

Bellu, Rene. *Les voitures francaises des annees 50.* Jean-Pierre Delville, Paris, 1983.

GERMANY

Fersen, Hans-Heinrich von. *Autos in Deutschland 1885–1920.* Motorbuch Verlag, Stuttgart, 1976.

Gränz, Paul and Peter Kirchberg. *Ahnen unserer Autos.* Transpress Verlag, Berlin, 1980.

Hack, Joachim. *Deutsche Sportwagen.* HEEL-Verlag, Königswinter, 1993.

Metternich, Michael Graf Wolff. *100 Jahre auf 3 Rädern: Deutsche Dreispur-Fahrzeuge im Wandel der Zeiten.* Neue Kunst Verlag, München, 1994.

Oswald, Werner. *Deutsche Autos 1920–1945.* Motorbuch Verlag, Stuttgart, 1977.

Oswald, Werner. *Deutsche Autos 1945–1975.* Motorbuch Verlag, Stuttgart, 1987.

Seherr-Thoss, H.C. Graf von. *Die Deutsche Automobilindustrie.* Deutsche Verlags-Anstalt, Stuttgart, 1974.

GREAT BRITAIN

Buyers' Guide to the Motor Industry of Great Britain. S.M.M.T., London, several yearbooks.

Culshaw, David, and Peter Horrobin. *The Complete Catalogue of British Cars.* W. Morrow & Co., New York, 1974.

Georgano, G. Nick (Ed.). *Britain's Motor Industry: The First Hundred Years.* G.T. Foulis & Co., Sparkford, Somerset, 1995.

Hack, Joachim. *Englische Sportwagen.* HEEL-Verlag, Königswinter, 1993.

Oliver, George. *Motor Trials and Tribulations: A History of Scottish Motor Vehicle Manufacture.* Glasgow Museums, Edinburgh, 1993.

HUNGARY

Horváth, Árpád. *A gépkocsi regénye.* Zrínyi Katonai Kiadó, Budapest, 1972.

ITALY

Amtmann, Georg, and Halwart Schrader. *Italienische Sportwagen.* 2 vols. Verlagsgesellschaft, München, 1987.

Costantino, Augusto. *Le Piccole Grandi Marche Automobilistiche Italiane.* Istituto Geografico de Agostini, Novara, 1983.

de Boer, John. *The Registry of Italian Oddities.* Riopress, Pittsburg, California, 1990.

THE NETHERLANDS

Wallast, M. *Historisch overzicht van de Nederlandse Automobielindustrie.* Uitgeverij Omniboek, Den Haag, 1979.

SOVIET UNION

Gogolev, L.D. *Evolucia avtomobilya.* Tekhnika, Kiev, 1983.

Kratkii avtomobilnii spravochnik. Transport, Moskva, 1975.

SWITZERLAND

Günther, Dieter, Rob de la Rive Box and Max Stoop. *Schweizer Automobile: Personenwagen und Sonderkarosserien von 1945 bis heute.* Autovision, Hamburg, 1992.

Schmid, Ernest. *Automobiles suisses des origines a nos jours.* Edition du Chateau de Grandson, Grandson, 1967.

Periodicals

ADAC Motorwelt (D), *AMCAR Magazine* (N), *Allgemeine Automobil-Zeitung* (A, D), *Austro-Classic* (A), *Auto* (CH, CS, D), *Auto & Moto Veterán* (CS, SK), *Autocar* (GB), *Auto-Classic* (H), *Auto Italiana* (I), *Autojournal* (CS, F), *Autoklub* (CS), *Automobil* (CS), *Automobil- und Motorrad Chronik* (D), *Automobile* (F), *Automobile Engineer* (GB), *Automobile International* (USA), *Automobile-Quarterly* (USA), *Automobil-Industrie* (D), *Automobil Revue* (CH), *Automobiltechnische Zeitschrift* (D), *Automotive Industries* (USA), *Automotive News* (USA), *Auto-moto* (CS), *Autó Motor* (H), *Auto, Motor und Sport* (D), *Avtomobilnaya Promyshlennost* (SU), *Classic American* (GB), *Classic and Sportscar* (GB), *Classic Car Mart* (GB), *Czechoslovak Motor Review* (CS), *Horseless Age* (USA), *Illustrierter Motorsport* (DDR), *Mobilisti* (FIN), *Motor* (CS, D, GB, PL, USA), *Moto Revija* (YU), *Motoristická současnost* (CS), *Motor-Klassik* (D), *Motorwagen* (D), *Motoryzacja* (PL), *Old Cars Weekly* (USA), *Oldtimer-Markt* (D), *Oldtimer-Praxis* (D), *Popular Mechanics* (USA), *Retroviseur* (F), *SAH Journal* (USA), *Stop auto-moto-revue* (CS), *Svět motoru* (CS), *Veteran & Vintage Magazine* (GB), *Za rulem* (SU), *Za volantem* (CS).